Encyclopedia of
Modern
Separatist
Movements

Encyclopedia of
Modern Separatist Movements

Christopher Hewitt
and Tom Cheetham

ABC-CLIO

Santa Barbara, California
Denver, Colorado
Oxford, England

Library of Congress Cataloging-in-Publication Data

Hewitt, Christopher.
    Encyclopedia of modern separatist movements / Christopher Hewitt and Tom Cheetham.
        p.   cm.
    Includes bibliographical references and index.
    ISBN 1-57607-007-7
        1. Intergroup relations—Encyclopedias. 2. Cultural relations—Encyclopedias. 3. Ethnic relations—Encyclopedias. 4. Social problems—Encyclopedias. I. Title: Modern separatist movements. II. Cheetham, Tom. III. Title.
    HM716.H48   2000
    305.8'003—dc21   00-024975

05 04 03 02 01 00   10 9 8 7 6 5 4 3 2 1

ABC-CLIO, Inc.
130 Cremona Drive, P.O. Box 1911
Santa Barbara, California 93116-1911

This book is printed on acid-free paper ⊚ .
Manufactured in the United States of America

Encyclopedia of Modern Separatist Movements, 11

Contents

Contents

Contents

Ethnic Separatist Movements

From Kosovo to Kashmir, from Northern Ireland to Nigeria, most conflicts in the world today are ethnic conflicts over territory. This encyclopedia covers *ethnic separatism* and related topics. Members of an ethnic group share a common culture and can be distinguished from members of other groups by some social characteristic such as race, language, and religion. They typically feel solidarity with other members of their group and a sense of common identity (a "we–they" feeling). This feeling of distinctiveness leads to social contacts, especially close relationships like marriage, being concentrated within the group. Ethnic identities may be nested within one another; for example, a Shetland Islander may also feel Scottish, and many Scots still feel British. Ethnic groups may be assimilated by other ethnic groups or merge to form a new group. Hundreds of years ago, Angles, Saxons, Jutes, Celts, Danes, and Normans fused together to become the English. Ethnic identities may result from contacts between societies, or they may be created by outsiders. In Africa, for instance, the Shirazis of Zanzibar are the result of intermarriage between Persian traders and local Africans. Colonial rulers in Africa, for the purpose of administrative convenience, often made tribal divisions more rigid or even introduced new ones. During the period when Uganda was a British colony, several new ethnic groups emerged, and they modeled themselves on traditional tribes (Lewis 1983).

These social and cultural identities are often linked with political and territorial identities. Separatist movements make territorial claims, arguing that a particular territory or region should separate from the state of which it is a part and create for itself a new political identity. The movement may seek full independence or some degree of regional autonomy, devolution, or home rule. We consider movements that do not seek full independence as separatist, because the conceptual distinction between autonomy and independence is best looked upon as a continuum. Furthermore, several movements have historically

Introduction

shifted their goals from autonomy to independence or vice versa. In the case of Quebec, a demand for increased federalism turned over time into a demand for independence. The Sri Lankan Tamils and the southern Sudanese are both examples of moderate autonomist movements turning into savage national liberation struggles.

Separatist movements overlap, empirically and conceptually, with unification and reunification movements. In several cases, separatist movements want to separate from one state and unite with another. For example, Irish nationalists in Northern Ireland want to separate from the United Kingdom and unite with the Irish Republic. This encyclopedia, therefore, covers unification movements as well as separatist movements. Unification movements are also known as "irredentist" movements. The term *irredentism* comes from the late nineteenth-century when Italian patriots referred to those regions still under foreign rule as *Italia irredenta*—"unredeemed Italy."

Irredentist movements are based on claims of both ethnic kinship and history. In the 1930s, Hitler claimed that the Sudetenland, which was part of Czechoslovakia, should belong to Germany because it was inhabited by ethnic Germans. The Germans justified the *Anschluss* (a "joining together") of Austria and Germany on the same grounds: the Austrians were ethnic Germans and therefore should be part of a greater Germany. Claims for territory can also be made by a state on the grounds that some city or place had been, or should have been, an integral part of the national heritage. Greek politics were dominated for decades by "the great dream," a movement seeking "the renewal of the Byzantine Empire, and, of course, the *sine qua non* of their aspirations was the appropriation of Constantinople. They had to have Constantinople just as the Italians had to have Rome and the Jews Jerusalem. The grounds were not ethnic or linguistic, but their historical and religious significance" (Ben-Israel 1991).

The following cases are included in this encyclopedia: (1) cases in which there is a separatist movement within a particular territory, (2) cases in which there is an irredentist movement that seeks to unite/reunite members of an ethnic group living in different countries, and (3) cases in which a territory is claimed by a state on the grounds of history or ethnicity. *Anticolonial* movements are excluded on the grounds that colonies are regarded as distinct entities in international law and because colonial subjects do not possess the same citizenship rights as the inhabitants of the colonial power. Sometimes states claim that they do not have any colonies and that all the inhabitants of their territories share a common citizenship. If indeed this common citizenship results in equal political rights for all the people wherever they live, and freedom of movement between the different territories, then it is not considered to be a colonial relationship. On these grounds, Puerto Rico is not a colony of the United States, nor are Martinique and Guadeloupe colonies of France. On the other hand, Angola, Mozambique, and Guinea-Bissau were colonies of Portugal, despite the fact that Portugal claimed they were "overseas provinces" and an integral part of the Portuguese nation. The Portuguese asserted that there was no color bar in their territories and that under their system, any Africans who spoke Portuguese and had divested themselves of tribal customs could become *assimilados* and have the same rights enjoyed by the white settlers. Less than 1 percent of

Africans ever achieved this status (Chilcote 1967).

The Extent of Ethnic Separatism

If ethnicity and political citizenship coincided completely, there would be no ethnic separatism. Everybody would live in "their" state in a world of homogeneous nation-states. In fact, very few states approximate this nationalist ideal. In a pioneering study, Foster (1980) identified 20 "minority nations" in Western Europe alone, and according to Gunnar Nielson, in 1981 only 45 out of 168 sovereign states could be classified as "single nation group states" (Tiryakin and Rogowski 1985). Snyder (1982) identifies 66 "mini-nationalisms." In a comprehensive survey, *Minorities at Risk*, Gurr (1993) lists 70 "separatist" minorities. This encyclopedia contains information on almost 300 cases of ethnic separatism and irredentism that have occurred since 1945.

Since the end of World War II, separatist movements have emerged on almost every continent and in almost every region. The cases can be broken down into three main clusters in terms of when and where they occurred. After the end of the war, Britain, France, Portugal, the Netherlands, and other colonial powers lost their empires. Sometimes the colonies had to fight for their independence; in other cases the imperial powers—with varying degrees of reluctance—granted them their independence. The potential for separatism and irredentism in postcolonial Africa and Asia was obvious, as most of the new states on those continents were artificial creations with arbitrary frontiers that divided ethnic groups and traditional political entities.

Whereas ethnic separatism in the Third World was anticipated by scholars and policymakers, its occurrence in Western societies took most experts by surprise because it was thought that Western societies had successfully assimilated their ethnic minorities. The process of nation-building carried out over the centuries meant that "Cornishmen, Scots and Welsh had become thoroughly British . . . Alsatians, Bretons, and Corsicans had become

French" (Connor 1977). Indeed, conventional scholarship saw Western Europeans abandoning nationalism as an anachronism in the modern world and creating a new united European community. However, in the 1950s and 1960s, ethnic separatism reemerged as a powerful force throughout Western Europe and North America.

After the end of Communist rule in Eastern Europe and the Soviet Union in the late 1980s, long-suppressed aspirations for national and ethnic autonomy became manifest. In newly democratic Czechoslovakia, the Czech and Slovak republics voted to separate, and Yugoslavia disintegrated in an orgy of civil wars and "ethnic cleansing." Slovenia, Croatia, and Macedonia declared independence, and in Bosnia, old hatreds between Serbs, Croats, and Muslims resulted in a partition. In 1999 approximately one million refugees fled Kosovo, creating an international crisis and provoking NATO air strikes against the Serbs. In the Soviet Union, the Baltic republics of Estonia, Latvia, and Lithuania, where national feelings combined with anticommunism, were the first to secede from the USSR. Ethnic separatism erupted into civil war in the former Soviet republics of Azerbaijan, Georgia, and Moldova, and in the newly constituted Russian Federation, which includes more than 100 ethnic groups, demands for more autonomy and for a redrawing of local boundaries pose a chronic threat to political stability. In Chechnya, the demand for national autonomy has led to chronic warfare with Russia.

In Latin America, despite important cultural and racial differences among the populations of most countries within the region, ethnic separatist movements are conspicuously absent. Peru, for example, is often described as a dual society, divided between the "Indian" highlands and the predominantly white and mestizo coastal region, which differ in terms of culture, economic development, and social welfare. Yet social conflict in Peru, even between whites and Indians, has never taken a separatist form in modern times. Instead, the historic resentment of poor Indians toward the largely white economic and political elite has

been channeled into leftist movements like Sendero Luminosa. Bernard Segal argues that this is because the divisions between Indians, mestizos, and whites are amorphous and shifting, with individuals moving from one status to the other (Hall, ed. 1979). The presence of strong multiracial national ideologies in Brazil and Mexico ("the mestizo nation") has discouraged the emergence or expression of ethnic separatism in those two countries. However, the revolt by the Miskito Indians in Nicaragua and the insurrection in the southern Mexican state of Chiapas are, perhaps, signs of a change in the ethnic relations between indigenous peoples and the ruling whites and mestizos.

Causes and Outcomes of Ethnic Separatism

Separatist movements are a result of many factors, some unique to the history and conditions of a given region, but all are driven by the belief that a particular ethnic group is suffering some injustice—economic, political, or cultural. Separatist movements begin with a grievance, but writers attempting to explain their emergence emphasize different grievances. One group of theorists sees the root cause as being regional economic disparities and the ethnic inequality that results. Michael Hechter's model of "internal colonialism" and Tom Nairn's "uneven development theory" both use a modified version of Marxism to analyze the emergence of ethnoregional movements in Western nation-states. Hechter (1975) emphasizes the core-periphery relationship between ethnic groups as the primary factor in determining their relative degree of economic development. The dominant political position of the core ethnic group allows it to exploit the peripheral ethnic groups in a manner analogous to what goes on between metropolitan powers and their colonies. This cultural division of labor provokes a reaction from the peripheral group, which takes the form of an ethnoregionalist movement, often with a separatist ideology. Hechter's study of the British economic system explains the rise of Scottish, Welsh, and Irish nationalism in this fashion. Nairn's argument (1977) is very similar in that he considers the uneven economic growth associated with imperialism, which creates different economic roles for different regions within the British Isles. This economic differentiation, coinciding with regional cultural cleavages, results in the growth of nationalism in those regions.

Other writers emphasize the interaction between modernization and regional ethnic cultures. Ernest Gellner (1964) argues that in multiethnic societies, modernization and the concomitant growth of a mass education system and government bureaucracy lead to one language (and one cultural tradition) becoming dominant. The regional intelligentsia are sometimes assimilated, but more often they become frustrated by this cultural barrier. The populations with their disdained regional cultures can then turn to separatist movements, which are created and led by the regional intelligentsia. Anthony Smith (1995), like Gellner, proposes that the rise of a centralized system of administration and a class of secular intellectuals makes up the first stage in the development of ethnic nationalism. Educated professionals, unable to win a place for themselves in metropolitan society, become alienated and lead a revival in ethnic culture and history.

The "new ethnicists," such as Walker Connor (1977), emphasize that ethnic identities, based on race, language, and religion, are likely to persist despite economic and political changes. In contrast to early theories of nation-building, which anticipated that modernization and concomitant increases in urbanization, literacy, and communication would lead to a decline in ethnic and regional loyalties, the new ethnicists argue that modernization will have the opposite effect. Connor argues that by bringing isolated groups into contact with one another, modernization increases their sense of cultural distinctiveness. Furthermore, the growth of both education and communication has an effect as they make people aware of other self-determination movements.

In postcolonial plural societies, the centralization of state power, the political dominance of one ethnic group, and the penetration of central government authority into outlying areas set the stage for communal and regional competition. As a result of their study of Ghana and Lebanon, David and Audrey Smock (1975) claim that the centralization of political power leads the citizen to "feel almost naked before the anonymous and distant government and to crave some form of identity in which to clothe himself." The civil war in the Sudan began because the black southerners, who under British colonial rule had been administered separately from the north, resented domination by Arab northerners when the Sudan became independent in 1956. In particular, as non-Muslims the black southerners were angered by the imposition of Islamic law.

Michael Keating (1988) suggests that a "rational choice" model may explain the emergence of ethnoregionalism. Although socialist parties and trade unions have tended to favor a centralized government, economic interests do not necessarily unite the workers of a state. "Territorial politics [is] a perfectly rational way for citizens to frame their demands on the economic and political systems.... Material interests may be seen in territorial as well as class terms." In the case of Scotland, the Labour Party, which promised economic subsidies from London, was outflanked by the Scottish National Party, which, with the help of North Sea oil, was able to promise both home rule and wealth. "SNP voting can thus be seen as a rational response to . . . the changing geography of wealth in the form of a call for the restructuring of the territorial power system." Similarly, ethnic separatist rebellions in Katanga and Tatarstan were motivated in part by the desire to control the rich natural resources of those regions. Donald Horowitz (1991) argues that "whether a group is integrationist or secessionist depends, in large measure, on its assessment of its prospects in the undivided state." In the case of Nigeria, the Ibo, who had migrated all over the country in their search for economic opportunity, were the most prominent proponents of national unity, but when violence drove them back to their home region, "then and only then did the Ibo become secessionist."

International politics are an important factor in explaining ethnic separatism. Neighboring states have political, economic, and strategic interests in what happens and may intervene to encourage or discourage separatist movements. Ethnic conflicts tempt external parties to intervene, and secessionists themselves often try to provoke such external involvement. Abeysinghe Navaratna-Bandara (1995) examines the role played by "big neighbors" in four cases—East Pakistan, Cyprus, Papua New Guinea, and Sri Lanka—and concludes that the "external dimension of the secession conflict management is of more significance than the internal dimension." Involvement by outside powers, who provided military aid to different factions, exacerbated the ethnic conflict in Lebanon, a conflict that led to the breakdown of central government control and the emergence of autonomous ethnic enclaves.

The success of any separatist movement is contingent upon the unity, leadership, and resources of the ethnic group and on the ability of the state to defuse ethnic discontent or to suppress the separatist movement. Democracies pledged to cultural pluralism frequently grant concessions of territorial or cultural autonomy to minorities that have suffered past injustices. Canadian treaties signed with Native American groups in recent years illustrate such an accommodation. In contrast, authoritarian regimes rarely tolerate such insubordination on the part of their minorities and respond to ethnic demands with repression. China has permitted no significant autonomy for the Uighurs, Mongols, or Tibetans, nor did Serbia offer concessions to the Albanians of Kosovo. In such instances the outcome is often chronic civil strife or (as in the cases of Bosnia and Kosovo) international intervention. When the state is too weak to contain the separatist threat, an ethnic region such as Chechnya or Eritrea may gain independence.

Coverage and Organization of the Encyclopedia

A separatist movement is considered to exist whenever there is violence in pursuit of separatist goals or whenever a separatist political party contests elections. Irredentist territorial claims by governments are included if they have resulted in military confrontations or have played a role in domestic politics. If the evidence is ambiguous, we have erred on the side of inclusiveness in order to ensure comprehensive coverage. This encyclopedia therefore contains a handful of cases—Aztlan, the Republic of New Africa, and the independent Republic of Texas—in which the separatist movements are or were no more than fringe groups. The amount of space devoted to each case reflects both its importance and the information available. Thus, Northern Ireland receives greater coverage than Sardinia because separatism has been a far stronger force in the former than in the latter.

Most entries concern disputed territories, geographical areas where there is a conflict as to what the political status should be (e.g., Biafra, Corsica, Kashmir, Quebec). When ethnic separatism spills over into several areas, there are entries for the ethnic group itself (e.g., Kurds, Basques, Tuaregs). Countries with numerous separatist movements (such as France, India, and Russia) are given their own entry, as are countries like Afghanistan and Lebanon where ethnic separatism has led to a de facto partition. In addition, there are separate entries for over 100 of the more important separatist leaders, political parties, and organizations. For the most important cases of ethnic separatism, we include a general entry, an entry for each separatist party and organization, and entries for significant events, issues, and individuals. If a separatist movement has been short-lived and is politically inconsequential, then all the information is presented in a single entry. This work also contains entries on related topics, such as "ethnic cleansing," and on international bodies that play a major role in ethnoregional issues.

Regional Maps

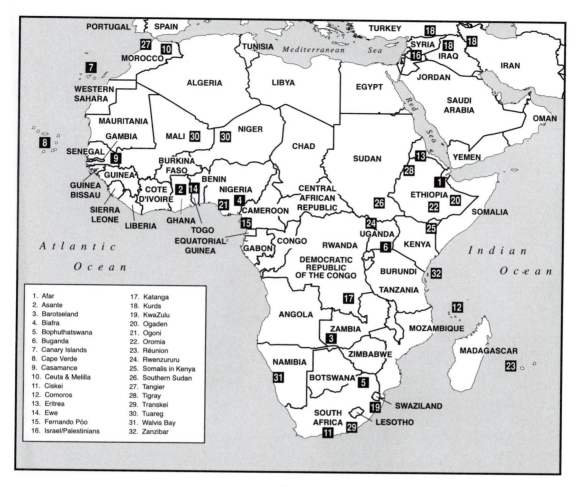

PORTUGAL SPAIN
TURKEY
MOROCCO
27 10
TUNISIA Mediterranean Sea
SYRIA 18
18 18
7 IRAQ
16
WESTERN
SAHARA IRAN
ALGERIA LIBYA JORDAN
EGYPT
SAUDI
ARABIA
MAURITANIA OMAN
GAMBIA MALI 30 30 NIGER
SENEGAL CHAD SUDAN 13 YEMEN
8
9 BURKINA 28
GUINEA FASO ETHIOPIA 20
GUINEA BENIN 1
BISSAU COTE 2 14 CENTRAL SOMALIA
D'IVOIRE NIGERIA AFRICAN 26 22
SIERRA 21 4 REPUBLIC
LEONE GHANA CAMEROON 25
LIBERIA TOGO 15 24
EQUATORIAL CONGO UGANDA
GUINEA GABON RWANDA 6 KENYA
Atlantic
DEMOCRATIC
Ocean REPUBLIC BURUNDI 32 Indian
OF THE CONGO
TANZANIA Ocean

1. Afar   17. Katanga
2. Asante   18. Kurds   17
3. Barotseland   19. KwaZulu   ANGOLA
4. Biafra   20. Ogaden   ZAMBIA   12
5. Bophuthatswana 21. Ogoni   3   MOZAMBIQUE
6. Buganda   22. Oromia   MADAGASCAR
7. Canary Islands 23. Réunion   ZIMBABWE
8. Cape Verde   24. Rwenzururu   NAMIBIA
9. Casamance   25. Somalis in Kenya   23
10. Ceuta & Melilla 26. Southern Sudan 31 BOTSWANA 5
11. Ciskei   27. Tangier
12. Comoros   28. Tigray   19 SWAZILAND
13. Eritrea   29. Transkei   SOUTH
14. Ewe   30. Tuareg   AFRICA 29 LESOTHO
15. Fernando Póo 31. Walvis Bay   11
16. Israel/Palestinians 32. Zanzibar

Africa

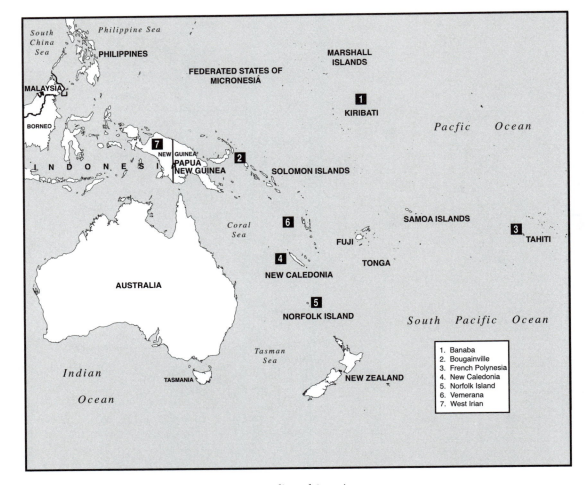

Australia and Oceania

1. Alsace
2. Andalusia
3. Basques
4. Bavaria
5. Brittany
6. Catalonia
7. Cornwall
8. Corsica
9. Faeroes
10. Friesland
11. Friuli
12. Galicia
13. Gibraltar
14. Istria
15. Jura
16. Kosovo
17. Malta
18. Montenegro
19. Northern Ireland
20. Occitania
21. Padania
22. Saami
23. Saar
24. Sardinia
25. Scotland
26. Shetlands
27. Sicily
28. South Tirol
29. Valle d'Aosta
30. Wales

Europe

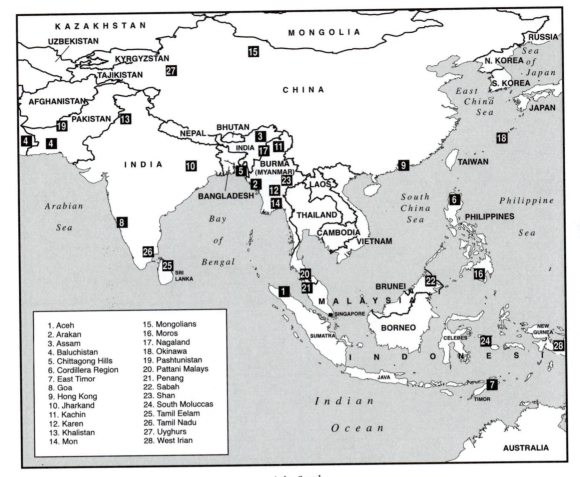

Asia, South

NORWAY

SWEDEN

RUSSIA

LATVIA

FINLAND

LITHUANIA

ESTONIA

BELARUS

MOLDOVA

UKRAINE

EUROPE

Black Sea

TURKEY

GEORGIA

ARMENIA

IRAQ

AZERBAIJAN

IRAN

OMAN

Arabian Sea

Arctic Ocean

UNITED STATES

Bering Strait

Bering Sea

RUSSIA

Sea of Okhotsk

JAPAN

Caspian Sea

Aral Sea

KAZAKHSTAN

TURKMENISTAN

UZBEKISTAN

Lake Balkhash

KYRGYZSTAN

TAJIKISTAN

AFGHANISTAN

PAKISTAN

INDIA

NEPAL

BANGLADESH

BHUTAN

ASSAM

MYANMAR

Bay of Bengal

Lake Baikal

MONGOLIA

CHINA

NORTH KOREA

SOUTH KOREA

1. Abkhazia
2. Adygea
3. Bashkortostan
4. Buryatia
5. Chechnya
6. Chuvashia
7. Dagestan
8. Donbas
9. Ingushetia
10. Kabardino-Balkaria
11. Kalmykia
12. Karachai-Cherkessia
13. Karelia
14. Komi
15. Mari El
16. Mordovia
17. South Ossetia
18. Southern Kurils
19. Tatarstan
20. Tuva
21. Udmurtia

Russia

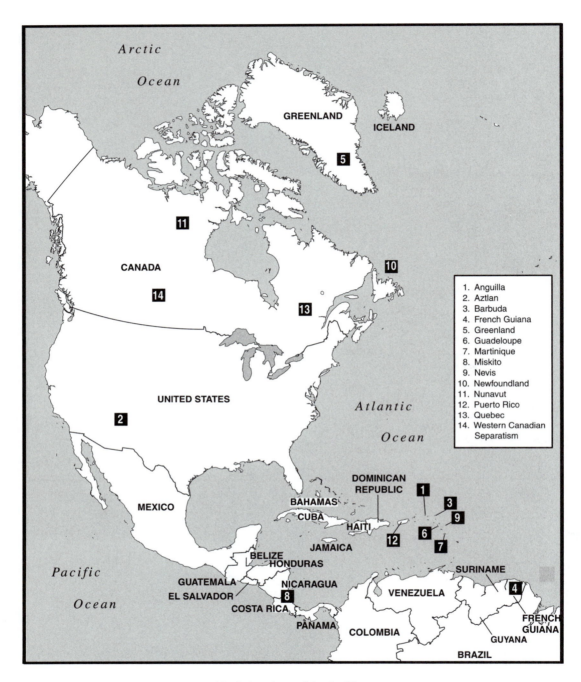

1. Anguilla
2. Aztlan
3. Barbuda
4. French Guiana
5. Greenland
6. Guadeloupe
7. Martinique
8. Miskito
9. Nevis
10. Newfoundland
11. Nunavut
12. Puerto Rico
13. Quebec
14. Western Canadian Separatism

North America and the Caribbean

Encyclopedia of
Modern
Separatist
Movements

Abkhazia

Abkhazia is a breakaway autonomous republic of Georgia located in the northwest of Georgia on the Black Sea. Abkhazians speak a Caucasian language distinct from Georgian. Religiously, Abkhazians are equally divided between Sunni Muslims and Orthodox Christians. Prior to the recent conflict with Georgia, Abkhazia had a population of more than 500,000 with the Abkhazians forming a minority of about 20 percent. After the conflict, some 200,000 Georgians, Russians, and other non-Abkhazians fled the region.

Abkhazia was first established as a kingdom in the eighth century A.D. In the thirteenth century, it was invaded by Mongols, and by the sixteenth century, it had come under control of the Ottoman Empire. In the early nineteenth century, it was absorbed by the Russian Empire. In 1921, Abkhazia became an autonomous Soviet socialist republic (SSR) but was ceded to the Georgian SSR in 1930. Georgia then attempted to force the Abkhazians to assimilate into Georgian culture. In 1978, Abkhazia appealed to Soviet Union authorities to allow Abkhazia to secede from Georgia and join with other Abkhazians in the Russian Republic. The request was denied.

In 1992, after Georgia had declared independence from the Soviet Union, Abkhazians revolted and declared themselves independent. In the ensuing war, Abkhazian forces prevailed and drove the Georgian army from the capital of Sukhumi. In an election not recognized by Georgia or Russia, Vladislav Arzinba was declared president of the Abkhaz Republic. The Commonwealth of Independent States dispatched troops to the region and threatened economic sanctions. To date, Abkhazia has refused to relinquish its sovereignty.

See also Georgia.
Reference Suny, Ronald Grigor. *Making of the Georgian Nation* (1994).

Abrene

A district surrounding the town of Abrene on the border between Latvia and the Russian Federa-

tion, Abrene was part of the independent Republic of Latvia from 1920 to 1940, annexed by the Soviet Union in 1940, and ceded to the Russian Soviet Socialist Republic in 1944. At that time, ethnic Russians made up about 86 percent of the population and Latvians 13 percent. After the collapse of the Soviet Union, Latvia regained its independence in 1991, and in January 1992, Latvia issued a decree rejecting the annexation of Abrene by Russia and calling for compensation. The Russian Federation, however, argues that this would violate the treaty of 1991 between Latvia and Russia in which both parties agreed to accept the current borders.

See also Russian Federation.
Reference Forsberg, Tuomas. *Contested Territory: Border Disputes at the Edge of the Former Soviet Empire* (1995).

Aceh

Aceh, in North Sumatra, was an independent state until 1870 when it was conquered by the Dutch. The 3 million Acehnese have a strong sense of identity, based on their distinctive language as well as a long history as an independent sultanate and center of Islamic scholarship. After Indonesia became independent in 1949, the province was the center of a rebellion by Darul Islam, a movement that sought to transform Indonesia into an Islamic state. In response to the rebellion, the central government granted Aceh

Young Acehnese women in traditional dress pose with assault rifles at a Free Aceh Movement camp in Pidie, Aceh Province, in November 1999. (AP Photo/Hamza)

the status of a special region in 1959, with control over religion, culture, and education. A council of religious scholars *(majelis ulama)* issues pronouncements and maintains the dominance of Islamic principles in all aspects of Acehnese social life. Currently, the strongly Muslim population resents what it sees as a lack of respect for its traditional religious practices and the exploitation of the region's rich mineral resources by Jakarta.

Although the Free Aceh Movement (Gerakan Aceh Merdeka) has been waging a guerrilla war since 1976, it has been unable to establish a liberated zone. Unlike the earlier Darul Islam rebellion, the current revolt is overtly separatist. With the end of former president Suharto's repressive rule in 1998, separatist activity increased. Guerrillas killed several Indonesian soldiers, and the military responded harshly. In May 1999, troops opened fire on a crowd of Acehnese demonstrators, killing seventeen.

In November 1999, Abdurraham Wahid, the newly elected president of Indonesia, held talks with the Free Aceh Movement. Afterward Wahid announced that he was willing to allow an independence referendum in the rebellious province, but a few days later he said that in the referendum, the Acehnese would only be allowed to choose between greater autonomy and the status quo.

See also Indonesia.
Reference Christie, Clive J. *A Modern History of Southeast Asia* (1996).

Adams, Gerry (1948–)

Leader of Sinn Fein, the political wing of the Provisional Irish Republican Army (IRA), Gerry Adams was born in West Belfast on October 6, 1948, the eldest of thirteen children. His parents were both from strongly republican families. His father had been in the IRA, and as a child he

Gerry Adams, Sinn Fein president, before the start of Sinn Fein's annual conference, Dublin, Ireland, May 8, 1999. (Reuters/Ferran Paredes/Archive Photos)

learned Irish Gaelic and played Irish sports. In 1964, after a meeting held at the local Gaelic Athletic Association Club (whose members were not allowed to play British games like cricket), Adams joined Sinn Fein. He is believed to have been on the IRA Army Council during the late 1970s and to have reorganized the organization into hard-to-penetrate cells. Adams stressed the need for a combined military and political strategy, and under his leadership, Sinn Fein took the radical step of running in British elections. This policy was justified in an October 1981 speech at the party convention: "Who here really believes we can win the war through the ballot box? But will anyone here object if, with a ballot paper in one hand, and an armalite in the other, we take power in Ireland?" In the 1983 British general elections, Sinn Fein took 13.4 percent of the Northern Irish vote, and Adams himself won in the West Belfast constituency. However, since republicans do not

recognize British rule, he refused to take his seat in the Westminster parliament. Adams played an important role in the negotiations that led to the current peace agreement, and in the June 1998 elections for the new Northern Irish Assembly, Sinn Fein won 18 of the 108 seats.

When interned by the British authorities in the early 1970s, Adams wrote an account of his experiences, *Cage Eleven* (1990), and he has also written two other highly praised books, *Falls Memories* (1982) and *The Street and Other Stories* (1992).

See also Irish Republican Army; Northern Ireland; Northern Irish Peace Agreement.
References Keena, Colm. *A Biography of Gerry Adams* (1990); O'Clery, Conor. *Phrases Make History Here* (1986).

Adjarian Autonomous Republic
See Adzharia

Adygea

Adygea, a republic in the Russian Federation, is completely surrounded by Krasnodar territory. It has a population of 450,000, of which 70 percent is Russian (including Cossacks) and 20 percent is Adygean. Descended from the Circassians, early inhabitants of the region, the Adygeans, like the neighboring Kabardinians and Cherkessians, speak a Caucasian language and are Sunni Muslims. The three ethnic groups, along with Abkhazian and Shapsug organizations, have formed the Muslim Confederation of the Peoples of the Caucasus (CPC).

Adygea was conquered by the Mongols in the thirteenth century. In the sixteenth century, Adygea became part of the Russian Empire. After the Russian Revolution, Adygea was set up as an autonomous district of the Soviet Union in 1922. Its current borders were established by a 1936 territorial reorganization. In 1991, Adygea was elevated to the status of an autonomous republic, and when the Soviet Union collapsed, Adygea became a republic within the Russian Federation.

In 1995, following pressure from Adygean nationalists, the Russian Federation approved a new constitution for the Adygean Republic. In addition to redrawing electoral districts in favor of Adygeans, the constitution also stipulates that the president of the republic must speak Adygean as well as Russian. This provision effectively eliminates Russian citizens from candidacy because few Russians speak Adygean. Aslan Djanov, an Adygean, has been president since 1991.

Greater Adygea sentiment has also been on the rise, with some groups calling for the unification of the Adygean-Abkhazian peoples within their historical territories. The Abkhazians, who speak a related Caucasian language, are found in both Dagestan and the breakaway Georgian republic of Abkhazia. Another nationalist proposal asks that some 150,000 Adygeans be repatriated from Turkey, Syria, Iraq, and Jordan.

Ethnic conflict in the republic has arisen because of Cossack claims on Adygean territory.

As in other areas of Russia, Cossacks have formed self-governing units and are pressing for autonomy.

See also Abkhazia; Cossacks; Russian Federation.
References Nupi. *Adygey* (1998); Smith, Sebastian. *Allah's Mountains* (1998).

Adzharia

Adzharia (the Adjarian Autonomous Republic) is a breakaway republic located in the southwest of Georgia with a population of 400,000. It is located on the Black Sea, and its capital is Batumi. Adzharia was under Turkish control from the seventeenth century until 1878 when it was annexed by Russia. In 1922, it became an autonomous republic of the Soviet Union, attached to Georgia. When the Soviet Union collapsed in 1991, Georgia declared independence. Because of revolts in South Ossetia and Abkhazia, Georgia has never clarified the constitutional status of Adzharia in the new Georgian state. Adzharia, fearing the loss of its administrative freedom, declared itself sovereign. Its status has not been resolved.

Adzharia is named for the Adzhars, Georgians who converted to Islam under Turkish rule. However, the secession movement is not based on ethnic or religious grounds. The territory is ruled by Aslan Arbindze, a hard-line ex-Communist who claims descent from a Turkish pasha. Arbindze, a supporter of the ousted Georgian president Eviad Gamsokhurdia, is able to maintain his power in part because he has the support of the citizens of Adzharia. Additionally, Russian troops stationed in Adzharia have buttressed Arbindze's government and Adzharia's claim to sovereignty. Georgian commentators claim that Moscow wishes to use Adzharia, South Ossetia, and Abkhazia as leverage against the Georgian government of Edvard Shevardnadze.

See also Georgia.
Reference Suny, Ronald Grigor. *Making of the Georgian Nation* (1994).

Afar

The Afar people, also known as the Danakil, live in eastern Ethiopia, Djibouti, and Eritrea. They speak a Cushitic language and are split among several small chieftaincies. Most of the Afar are nomadic pastoralists. The Afar Liberation Front (ALF), formed in 1975 under the leadership of Sultan Ahmed Ali Mirah and his son, carried out a series of guerrilla attacks against the Dergue, the Ethiopian Marxist regime. The ALF was opposed by the Afar National Liberation Front, a radical Marxist faction that gave "critical support" to the Dergue program and defended the region of Assab against the Eritreans in return for a promise of autonomy. However, it was not until the overthrow of the Dergue that an Afar region was set up.

The 1992 territorial reorganization made the Afar region bordering Djibouti and Eritrea one of nine autonomous states with the theoretical right to secede from Ethiopia. Within Eritrea, the Afar Revolutionary Democratic Union Front has been fighting since 1991 to liberate Assab, and talks with the Eritrean government have resulted in a promise of an Afar regional state.

See also Eritrea; Ethiopia.
Reference Lewis, I. M. *Nationalism and Self Determination in the Horn of Africa* (1983).

Afghanistan

Overrun by neighboring empires since antiquity, the borders of modern Afghanistan were not established until the nineteenth century when the Afghans and British agreed on the Durand Line, which now separates Afghanistan from Pakistan. The border, however, is artificial in that it arbitrarily divides the Pashtun, the dominant Afghan ethnic group, between the two nations. Prior to the Soviet invasion of Afghanistan in 1979, Afghan political leaders frequently called for the reunification of Pashtunistan, and even during the struggle against the Soviets, the Afghan Millat Party continued to advocate a united Pashtunistan, but this was the exception. Since the anti-Communist resistance grew to rely on Pakistan for sanctuary and military supplies, irredentist claims were muted.

Although a state by the beginning of the twentieth century, Afghanistan has never coalesced as a nation. For much of recent Afghan history a de facto separatism has prevailed. The country still consists of a multitude of ethnic groups divided by clan, language, and regional loyalties. Even though 99 percent of the population is Muslim, there is a split between the Shi'ites, who comprise 15 percent, and the Sunni majority. Within both sects there are cleavages based on doctrinal orientations and views concerning the roles of religion and the state. Among religious Muslims, one can find secularists, traditionalists, and radicals, and each has a different Muslim country model: secularists point to Turkey and post-Soviet Uzbekistan; traditionalists, to Pakistan and Saudi Arabia; and radicals look to Iran. In this largely preindustrial culture, in which tribal pride and honor are valued, feuds are the common way of addressing wrongs, and revenge is seen as a religious duty. Consequently, intergroup conflict has become the behavioral norm among the Afghanis. Between 1979—the beginning of Soviet occupation—and 1993—when the Taliban began to gain power—no central government, if one could be agreed on at all, was able to offset the centrifugal forces ravaging the country.

Afghanistan was slowly drawn into the Cold War after 1973 when the last monarch Zahir Shah was overthrown and outside powers began to contend for influence within the Afghanistan government. Although poor in resources, Afghanistan is an important East-West transportation corridor, and for varied economic, political, ethnic, and religious reasons, Russia, the United States, Pakistan, Iran, Saudi Arabia, and more recently the former Soviet republics of Uzbekistan and Tajikistan have all tried to shape Afghanistan's destiny. To date, the outsiders seem to have done more to destabilize than to strengthen the country. Their support of particular factions has intensified the conflict; their supplying the factions with modern

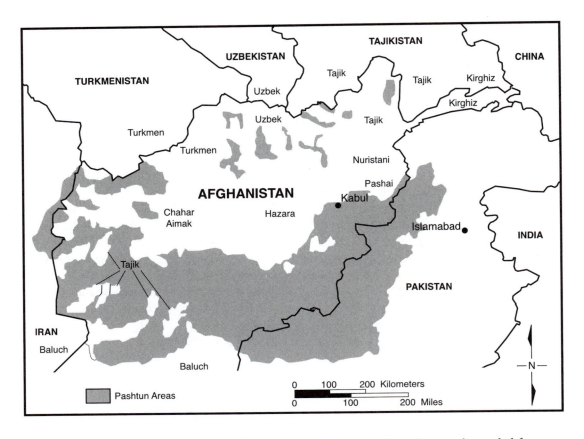

TAJIKISTAN

UZBEKISTAN

CHINA

TURKMENISTAN

Tajik

Tajik

Kirghiz

Uzbek

Kirghiz

Turkmen

Uzbek

Tajik

Turkmen

Nuristani

Pashai

AFGHANISTAN

Kabul

Chahar
Aimak

Hazara

Islamabad

INDIA

Tajik

PAKISTAN

IRAN

Baluch

Baluch

0   100   200 Kilometers

0   100   200 Miles

—N—

Pashtun Areas

armament has made the conflict deadlier and more destructive than ever before.

Because of war, refugee flight, and unreliable demographic data, it is difficult to discuss Afghanistan's population statistics with any degree of precision. One estimate places the country's population at 20 million with an additional 3 million in refugee camps in Iran and Pakistan. Pashtuns, who make up the most numerous group, nearly 40 percent of the population, are divided into two confederations: the Durrani, found in the south and west, and the Ghilzai, in the east toward the Pakistan border. Although both speak Pashtu, an Indo-Iranian language, the two groups can be distinguished by their dialects. They have also competed politically, with the Durrani dominating the monarchy and ruling elite and the Ghilzai coming into prominence as leaders with the Communist coup of 1979. Both groups have sought to dominate smaller Pashtun tribes as well as the non-Pashtun minorities.

Pashtuns believe they are descended from an Old Testament tribe that became mujahidin under Muhammad. Pashtuns are Sunni Muslims, and Pashtuns headed all Afghan governments in the twentieth century until 1992, except for a few brief months in 1929.

Dari, sometimes called Afghan Farsi, another Indo-Iranian language, is the second major language of the country and is often spoken as a second language among western Pashtuns. Dari is the primary language of the Tajik and Hazzara minorities. Although both Pashtu and Dari are recognized as official languages by the Afghanistan government, non-Pashtuns have generally resisted learning Pashtu.

The second major Afghan ethnic group is composed of the Tajiks, who make up 20–25 percent of the population. They speak Dari (also called Tajiki), which is the language spoken across the border in Tajikistan. The Tajiks are Sunni Muslims. Although they have served in administrative positions in government, they have largely been excluded from the military and political elite. Tajiks are located in the northeastern part of the country adjacent to Tajikistan. The secular government of Tajikistan blames militant Islamist groups in Afghanistan for destabilizing Tajikistan, and to stop the free movement of people and ideas across the border, Russia and Tajikistan have posted 20,000 troops there.

The Hazzara, an impoverished ethnic group residing in the isolation of the central mountain region, may constitute 9–10 percent of the population. The Hazzara, like the Tajiks, are Dari speakers. Unlike the Tajiks, they are Shi'ite Muslims. Racially, the Hazzara may be descended from Mongolian tribes, and their physical appearance distinguishes them from other Afghans. Historically, they have been discriminated against by Pashtuns both for their race and for their religion. During the civil war, the Hazzara developed closer ties to Shi'ite Iran to the west. From July 1997 to May 1998, the Pashtun Taliban, which controlled the territory surrounding the Hazzara, shut off the movement of supplies into and out of the region in an attempt to starve the Hazzara into submission and to prevent them from aiding the militias of the anti-Taliban Northern Alliance.

The last major ethnic group is made up of the Uzbeks, who live along the border with Uzbekistan. The Uzbeks, who may account for 10 percent of the population, are Sunni Muslims and speak a Turkic language. In alliance with neighboring Turkmen, who are 200,000 strong and like the Uzbeks are Sunni Muslims and Turkic speakers, the Uzbeks under General Abdul Dostum have created a formidable militia and political organization, the National Islamic Movement, which receives support from Uzbekistan and Russia. Dostum's secularly headed movement makes him much more acceptable ideologically to Russia and Uzbekistan, which fear the spread of Islamic revivalism of the type that led to civil war in Tajikistan. Dostum's service in the Communist army also strengthens his credentials

with the largely former Communist governments of Uzbekistan and Russia.

Among the more than twenty other ethnic groups in Afghanistan, the largest are the Nuristani, the Aimak, and the Baluchis. None of these peoples have played a significant role in the recent war. Of more importance has been the Ismaili religious sect, which draws members from several ethnic groups. The Ismailis are primarily Dari speakers and represent the Seveners branch of Shi'ism. Numbering 250,000 in Afghanistan and with ties to fellow believers in neighboring countries, the Ismailis, who are led by the Agha Khan, play an active role in Afghanistan politics. They tend to support the Tajik elements of the Northern Alliance.

The Communist coup of 1978 marked the beginning of the civil war. It triggered the formation of anti-Communist armed militias (mujahidin) and began the long holy war (jihad). In multiethnic Afghanistan, mujahidin formed around, not just religious and political ideologies, but ethnicity as well. Each militia usually recognized religious leaders whose interpretations of sacred law were to be taken as prescriptions for an ideal postwar Afghanistan. Following the Soviet withdrawal from Afghanistan that began in 1989 under the Gorbachev administration, an Afghan interim government was established. Its second president—the office was to rotate among resistance leaders—was Burhanudin Rabbani, a Tajik. However, Rabbani was unacceptable to five of the ten principal mujahidin groups, and war broke out among the factions. This effectively ended the power of the central government. The chief rival to Rabbani and his militia general Ahmad Shah Masood was the radical Pashtun warlord General Gulbuddin Hekmatyar. The two militias engaged in a battle for Kabul that nearly leveled the city. Although Hekmatyar later joined with Rabbani and was named prime minister, his army ultimately was defeated by the Taliban in 1996, and his militia disintegrated.

As the civil war continued and banditry became more prevalent, a new mujahidin that emerged on the scene in 1994, the Taliban ("students"), grew in strength. A Pakistan-trained and -supported Pashtun militia, the Taliban swept up from the south and by 1994 had succeeded in capturing the capital, Kabul, and had declared that it ruled Afghanistan. The radical Sunni Taliban imposed strict Islamic law upon all the areas it controlled and disarmed the fractious militias in the territory it controlled.

Remaining undefeated, although holding less than a third of the country's territory, several militias regrouped to form the Northern Alliance. Uniting former bitter rivals—Rabbani's Tajiks, Dostum's Uzbeks, Shi'ite militias from the Hazzara region, and some disgruntled Pashtun forces—the alliance held tenaciously to its positions into 1998. In the summer of 1998, Taliban forces launched a major drive in the north and succeeded in capturing the key city of Mazar-i-Sharif as well as substantial territory. Before its military drive stalled, the Taliban appeared to be on the verge of defeating the armies of the Northern Alliance.

Today, Afghanistan is divided into two camps: the Pashtun Sunni led by the Taliban and all non-Pashtun Sunni and all Shi'ites who are supporting the Northern Alliance. The Taliban claims that the Northern Alliance plans to drive all Pashtuns from the territories they control. The Northern Alliance denies this and has said it would support a Pashtun as the prime minister of a unified Afghanistan.

In May 1998, the Taliban agreed to meet with the Northern Alliance to set up a religious council (ulema) to govern Afghanistan. The Taliban's refusal to compromise any of its strict religious and social principles makes finding a compromise difficult with the more pluralistic coalition of ethnic and religious minorities that make up the Northern Alliance. Calls to join parts of northern Afghanistan to greater Uzbekistan or greater Tajikistan have also been voiced more frequently since the Taliban conquest.

See also Mujahidin; Pashtunistan; Taliban.
References Dupree, Louis. *Afghanistan* (1997); Magnus, Ralph, and Eden Naby. *Afghanistan* (1998); Maley, William, ed. *Fundamentalism Reborn: Afghanistan and the Taliban* (1998); Rubin, Barnett. *The Fragmentation of Afghanistan* (1995).

Afrikaners

The Afrikaners are descended from Dutch settlers who came to South Africa after 1652. Even though they were the politically dominant group in South Africa, the Afrikaners formed a demographic minority in the country as a whole and were a local majority in only a few small areas. The apartheid system was an attempt to maintain political control by defining the black majority as citizens of ten tribal homelands. However, even in the remaining area, whites were still only a minority of the population. In the early 1980s, as it became clear that apartheid was doomed, a number of radical partition plans were suggested. The South African Bureau of Racial Affairs proposed that the black homelands be expanded, giving them 40 percent of South Africa. The Afrikaner Resistance Movement argued for a "Boerestaat" that would restore the Boer republics of the nineteenth century. The Maasdorp Plan advocated a division of South Africa into the two states of Capeland and Capricornia. It is significant that the Boerestaat and Capeland would have been in completely different areas. The Boerestaat would have had a black majority population, and Capeland would have been 48.5 percent "colored" (mixed race) and only 27.4 percent white. Also, a majority of whites would have lived in Capricornia.

During the 1994 election, the Freedom Front, led by Constand Viljoen, called for the establishment of a Volkstaat, or Afrikaner homeland. The party received an estimated 14 percent of the white vote nationally, but even where its support was highest it never exceeded 6 percent of the total vote. The concept of a Volkstaat is therefore unrealistic because it lacks demographic viability. A subsequent attempt to set up an exclusively white enclave (Oranje) in a rural district of the Orange Free State also failed for lack of support.

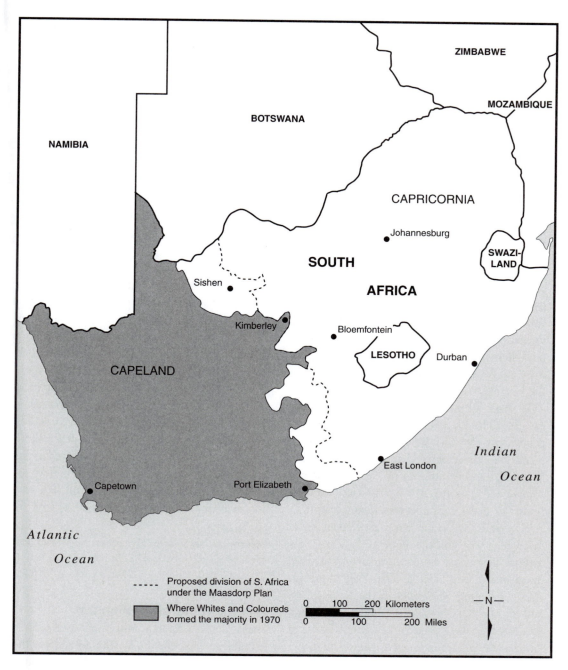

Proposed division of S. Africa
under the Maasdorp Plan

Where Whites and Coloureds
formed the majority in 1970

0   100   200 Kilometers
0   100   200 Miles

— N —

See also Apartheid; Black Homelands.
Reference Lemon, Anthony. *Apartheid in Transition* (1987).

Albizu, Pedro (1893–1965)

Pedro Albizu Campos, the Puerto Rican nationalist leader, was born in 1893 the illegitimate son of a white merchant and a black servant woman. His intellectual brilliance was recognized by the local masonic lodge, which awarded him a scholarship to study in the United States. He received degrees from Harvard College and Harvard Law School and served as an officer in the U.S. armed forces during World War I. However, his experience of racial prejudice during this period apparently transformed him from being a firm admirer of American democracy into a nationalist imbued with a hatred of the United States.

Returning to Puerto Rico at the age of twenty-eight, he became increasingly radical and in 1924 joined the recently founded Nationalist Party. At the funeral of four young Nationalists who had been killed by the police, Albizu accused the American Chief of Police, E. Francis Riggs, of responsibility for their deaths and swore "that assassination will not go unpunished in Puerto Rico." When Riggs was shot by two members of the Nationalist Party on February 23, 1936, Albizu and seven other members of the party were charged with sedition. The first trial ended in a hung jury, with the seven Puerto Rican jurors voting to acquit and the five American jurors voting to convict Albizu. A second trial, with a jury of ten Americans and two Puerto Ricans, resulted in the Nationalists being sentenced to ten years in the federal penitentiary in Atlanta, Georgia.

In 1943, Albizu was released from prison because of ill health and remained under house arrest in New York City. He refused to report to his probation officer since that would involve acknowledging U.S. authority. In 1947, his sentence completed, he returned to Puerto Rico and continued to make fiery speeches denouncing U.S. rule. In 1950, the Nationalists organized an uprising, which was quickly suppressed. Albizu was arrested, tried, and sentenced to forty-four years in prison, where he died in 1965. Even in prison, Albizu remained the leader of the Nationalists, and on March 1, 1954, acting under his orders, four Nationalists opened fire in the U.S. House of Representatives, wounding five congressmen.

See also Puerto Rico.
Reference Fernandez, Ronald. *Prisoners of Colonialism* (1994).

Alsace

Annexed by France in 1648, the German-speaking region of Alsace was ceded to Germany in 1871 after the Franco-Prussian War and then regained by France in 1918. In the period between the two world wars, a strong autonomist movement flourished. The strongly religious Alsatians distrusted the anticlerical policies of the French government and resented the fact that French was the language of administration, despite the fact that most of the population spoke only German. Currently, however, the region is peaceful, and there is little autonomist agitation. In part this is because France has become more tolerant of regional and cultural differences, with German being allowed as the language of instruction in elementary schools.

The border location of Alsace has become an advantage in a united Europe, and Strasbourg was chosen as the site for both the Council of Europe and the European Parliament. The language issue still arouses some concern, and there are demands for an increase in bilingual education, the promotion of Alsatian culture, and the study of local history. However, autonomist political groups have little support. The Movement of Alsace-Lorraine, founded in 1969, called for "a free Alsace-Lorraine within a European federation," but its founder was accused of neo-Nazi sympathies and convicted of inciting racial hatred. An autonomist candidate running in the 1978 national election won only 4 percent of the vote.

See also France.
Reference Gras, Solange. "Regionalism and Autonomy in Alsace since 1918" (1982).

American Indian Movement

The American Indian Movement (AIM) was founded in Minneapolis in 1968 to address the issue of police brutality against Native Americans. AIM also established health, legal, and educational programs as well as lobbying for better housing for Indians. The movement became involved in several extralegal actions. In 1969, AIM members joined the United Indians of All Tribes in the occupation of Alcatraz. In 1971, AIM seized abandoned military property in Minnesota, par-

Leaders of the American Indian Movement; Dennis Banks is on the left, Russell Means in the center. (Agence France Presse/Archive Photos)

ticipated in the takeover of the Washington, D. C., headquarters of the Bureau of Indian Affairs, and assisted the Ojibwa tribe of Wisconsin in taking over a dam that was flooding reservation land. In 1973, AIM leaders Dennis Banks and Russell Means joined Lakota Sioux in occupying Wounded Knee, South Dakota, the historic site of a U.S. Army massacre of an Indian community in 1890. The Wounded Knee siege lasted seventy days; two Native Americans were killed. Although charges were filed against the occupiers and a trial was held, no convictions were obtained, for a federal judge dismissed the charges because of government misconduct.

In 1975, AIM joined with Oglala Sioux in a confrontation with police on a South Dakota reservation. Two policemen died, and AIM mem-

ber Leonard Peltier was subsequently sentenced to life imprisonment on a charge of murder, a verdict still protested by Indian activists.

AIM's goals and grievances were spelled out in a 1972 manifesto, "The Trail of Broken Treaties." The document assumes tribes are sovereign nations and calls for the right of individual tribes to deal with the federal government on an equal basis. It argues for the abolition of all state jurisdiction over native nations. In addition, the manifesto seeks compensation for past treaty violations and the restoration of 110 million acres of land taken by the federal government.

By 1979, the AIM national organization had dissolved, although local AIM chapters continued to function and sponsored educational and legal activities. In the 1990s, an organization called the

American Indian Movement Grand Governing Council claimed to be the successor to the former AIM national organization and to represent Indian interests at the federal level.

See also Lakota Nation; Native Americans of the United States.
References Smith, Paul, and Robert Warrior. *Like a Hurricane: The Indian Movement from Alcatraz to Wounded Knee* (1996); Weyler, Rex. *Blood of the Land: The Government and Corporate War against the American Indian Movement* (1982).

Andalusia

Andalusia is one of the poorest regions of Spain, with high unemployment and consequent out-migration. The agricultural sector is dominated by large estates and large numbers of landless laborers. The first Andalusian regionalist movement, the Congreso Andalucista de Ronda, which was founded by Blas Infante, adopted a flag and an anthem in 1918, and called for regional autonomy. The movement persisted through the second republic but disappeared during the Franco years. Paralleling similar trends in the Basque region and Catalonia, a strong sense of Andalusian identity emerged prior to the first democratic elections in 1977, and in December of that year more than 1 million people took to the streets to demonstrate for Andalusian autonomy.

The Partido Socialista de Andalucia (PSA) participated in the 1979 elections and received 10 percent of the vote. However, the drive for autonomy was opposed by both the Union del Centro Democratico (UCD) government in Madrid and by the local branch of that party. The UCD called on its supporters to abstain in the autonomy referendum and tried to block coverage of the campaign by the state-owned media. Although a clear majority of those voting were in favor, the vote in one province fell below 50 percent so the initiative failed on a technicality. However, the controversy led to new legislation concerning the process of obtaining autonomy, and by 1983, autonomous governments had been set up in all the Spanish regions.

See also Spain.
Reference Keating, Michael. *State and Regional Nationalism: Territorial Politics and the European State* (1988).

Anglo-Irish Agreement

The growing Northern Irish crisis led to meetings between Margaret Thatcher, the British prime minister, and Charles Haughey, the Irish prime minister, in 1980. On November 15, 1985, the Anglo-Irish agreement was signed between the two countries. The two governments affirmed that any change in the status of Northern Ireland would come about only with the consent of the majority of the people of Northern Ireland; recognized that currently, the majority wanted no change in the status of Northern Ireland; and declared that if in the future, a majority clearly wished for and formally consented to the establishment of a united Ireland, the two governments would introduce legislation to bring about that wish. The agreement also gave the Irish Republic a consultative role in setting policy and established an intergovernmental council that would consider (i) political matters, (ii) security and related matters, (iii) legal matters, including the administration of justice, and (iv) the promotion of cross-border cooperation.

The agreement was greeted with bitter hostility from the unionists, who saw it as a first step to forcing them into a united Ireland rather than remaining as part of the United Kingdom. Massive demonstrations followed, and in 1986 all the unionist members of parliament resigned their seats in the British House of Commons in protest against the agreement. Irish nationalists, on the other hand, objected to the majority consent principle, which they saw as giving the unionists a veto on any constitutional changes.

See also Northern Ireland.
Reference Arthur, Paul. *Government and Politics of Northern Ireland* (1984).

Anglo-Saxonism

Anglo-Saxonism, the belief in the superior qualities of the English "race," was linked to the growth of the British Empire. In the nineteenth century, the idea that Britain's economic and political supremacy was explained by the racial qualities of the country's people was propounded by several writers, including Thomas Macauley, James Froude, Edward Freeman, Charles Dilke, and Thomas Carlyle. Carlyle wrote, "Our little isle is grown too narrow for us, but the world is wide enough." In *Greater Britain* (1868), Charles Dilke described the British dominions of Australia, Canada, and New Zealand; pointed to the English origins of American institutions; and stated, "Through America, England is speaking to the world." Politicians such as Joseph Chamberlain (1836–1914) advocated imperial preference, whereby the British Empire would be integrated through trade tariffs. Cecil Rhodes, the diamond magnate and founder of Rhodesia, established the Rhodes scholarships for students from the British dominions, Germany, and the United States to study at Oxford University in an attempt to link together the elites of those countries.

In the United States, many Americans also emphasized the cultural and racial links between themselves and the English. John Fiske believed that the descendants of the Anglo-Saxons would eventually form a majority of the world's population and that such institutions as federalism owed their origins to them. Josiah Strong, in *Our Country: Its Possible Future and its Present Crisis* (1885), saw the Anglo-Saxons as the most vital force in history: "This powerful race will move down upon Mexico, down upon Central and South America out upon the islands of the sea, over upon Africa and beyond." Such beliefs were influential in providing a rationale for the opposition to immigration from southern and eastern Europe. Madison Grant's *The Passing of the Great Race, or The Racial Basis of European History* (1916) and Lothrop Stoddard's *Rising Tide of Color against White World Supremacy* (1920) argued that the new immigrants would dilute the

country's Anglo-Germanic stock and destroy American greatness. Their books were influential in creating the climate that led, in 1926, to restrictive immigration laws that favored immigrants from northwestern Europe. These national-origin quotas were scrapped when the 1965 Immigration Act was passed.

Since the end of World War II, the links between the English-speaking countries have weakened considerably. Immigration has reduced the proportion of the populations of Australia, Canada, and New Zealand that is of English descent, and imperial preference was abandoned when Britain joined the European Common Market.

See also League of Empire Loyalists.
Reference Snyder, Louis L. *Macro-Nationalisms: A History of the Pan-Movements* (1984).

Angola

A Portuguese colony until 1975, guerrilla warfare to liberate the country of Angola began in the early 1960s. Three separate insurgent groups were active: the Popular Movement for the Liberation of Angola (MPLA), the National Front for the Liberation of Angola (FNLA), and the National Union for the Total Independence of Angola (UNITA). Each group was based on one of the major ethnic groups in Angola. The MPLA was supported by the Mbundu, the FNLA by the Bakongo, and UNITA by the Ovimbundu. Originally, the FNLA was called the Union of the People of North Angola (UPNA) and stood for the separation of the Bakongo lands from Angola and their reunification with the Bakongo of Zaire.

A coalition among the three groups was organized by the Portuguese, but it fell apart when the MPLA seized control of Luanda, the capital city. This was followed by a civil war among the three groups. The MPLA, supported by military aid from the Soviet Union and thousands of Cuban troops, was victorious, and the Organization of African Unity recognized the MPLA as the legitimate government in February 1976. UNITA, backed by South Africa and the United States, continued to struggle against the Marxist government, and the result was a de facto separation of Angola into two zones. UNITA dominated the Ovimbundu areas, and the rest of the country was controlled by the governing MPLA.

Several attempts at a negotiated settlement have failed. In 1992, national elections resulted in a victory for the MPLA and were promptly denounced as fraudulent by Jonas Savimbi, the UNITA leader (UNITA won 70 seats out of 220, all in the Ovimbundu region). In 1994, a peace agreement was reached whereby UNITA would share power at the national and provincial levels. Within days of the signing of the agreement, renewed fighting broke out with accusations of bad faith on both sides.

In addition to the conflict between UNITA and the MPLA, there is also a separatist movement in the oil-rich Cabinda enclave. The region accounts for two-thirds of the country's oil production but receives little back from the national government. The Cabinda separatists were originally split between several groups, but in 1963 they became united as the Front for the Liberation of the Enclave of Cabinda (FLEC). The separatists have received support from Zaire and the Congo and have allied themselves with UNITA.

Reference Martin, Phyllis. *Historical Dictionary of Angola* (1980).

Anguilla

After the breakup of the Federation of the West Indies in 1962, the separatist impulse continued to result in the emergence of smaller units. The three islands of St. Kitts, Nevis, and Anguilla were grouped together for administrative purposes by Britain, but first Anguilla and later Nevis broke away. The Anguillans agitated to secede from the union throughout the 1960s, and two plebiscites showed that overwhelming majorities favored a separate state. In the second of the plebiscites, held on February 6, 1969, voters favored separation by a margin of 1,739 to 4. The day after the

plebiscite, Anguilla declared itself independent and expelled the local police back to St. Kitts. Fearing that the island would fall under the influence of international criminal syndicates, the British sent in troops and police and regained control. In 1976, Anguilla was formally declared to be a British dependency with its own legislative assembly.

See also Federation of the West Indies; Nevis.
Reference Alexander, Robert J. *Political Parties of the Americas* (1982).

Apartheid

Apartheid, the name given to the South African system of racial segregation, is a word in the Afrikaans language meaning "apartness." "Petty apartheid" attempted to minimize social contacts between whites and nonwhites by providing separate (and unequal) facilities for such things as toilets, park benches, buses, railway station platforms, post office counters, and beaches. In addition, the Group Areas Act required that whites, blacks, coloureds (people of mixed race), and Indians live in different neighborhoods and attend separate schools. In this sense, the system was similar to the segregation practiced in the American South until the 1960s.

"Grand apartheid" involved an attempt to divide the country into a white South Africa and a number of black "homelands," which would eventually become independent states. In theory, blacks were citizens of these homelands. Hence, they were required to carry pass books when living and working outside their homelands and were regarded as temporary sojourners in South Africa. For decades, the Nationalist government tried to realize the grand design of apartheid, transferring millions of blacks from white areas and building factories and new towns in the homelands.

The plan ultimately failed because of several factors. First, the land allocated to the homelands was insufficient, consisting of only 13 percent of the total area of South Africa while blacks

A sign in Smithtown warning nonwhites that they are prohibited from using the beaches. (Archive Photos)

constituted about three-quarters of the population. Second, the black population was growing faster than the white population, and the growth of the economy and consequent demand for black workers meant that blacks made up an increasing proportion of the urban populations in white South Africa. Many residents of black townships, such as Soweto, were second- or even third-generation and had never lived in their homelands. Third, there were no large areas where whites constituted a majority. The problem of what to do with the mixed-race "coloureds," who were in the majority in the western part of

the Cape Province, was never solved. Fourth, the obvious injustice of the system prevented any but a handful of blacks from accepting apartheid. Black resistance increased and, in combination with international pressure, led to negotiations between the African National Congress and the Nationalist government. In 1992, the South African president, F. W. de Klerk, apologized for apartheid saying, "For too long we clung to a dream of separate nation-states when it was already clear that it could not succeed."

See also Black Homelands.
References Lapping, Brian. *Apartheid: A History* (1987); South African Institute of Race Relations. *Race Relations Survey* (1993).

Arabistan

Arabistan is the name given by Arab separatists to the Iranian province of Khuzestan (also known as Ahvaz). The Arab population numbers 530,000, and they constitute a minority within the province. In the 1960s, Iraq encouraged Arab separatist forces in this oil-rich region but withdrew its support after coming to a diplomatic agreement with Iran in 1975. The Popular Front for the Liberation of Ahvaz and the Revolutionary Movement for the Liberation of Arabistan engaged in intermittent attacks against Iranian army units. After the fall of the shah and the rise of Khomeini's Islamic republic, Iraq again called on the Arabs of Khuzestan to "liberate Arabistan" from Persian rule, but by and large, they remained loyal to Khomeini.

Arabs

The original homeland of the Arabs was the Arabian peninsula. After Muhammed (570–632) founded the Islamic religion, it served to unify the previously warring tribes and led to their rapid political and territorial expansion. By 800, Arab armies had conquered North Africa and established their language and religion from the Persian Gulf to the Atlantic coast of North Africa. The caliphs of Damascus were dominant over the eastern part of the Arab world until 900, when local dynasties achieved virtual independence. Historically, this represented the high point of Arab political unity, and most Arab lands fell under the rule of the Ottoman Turks in the 1500s.

The ideology of Pan-Arabism—that there existed an Arab nation that should be united politically—emerged in the decade before World War I. Pan-Arab intellectuals emphasized the cultural links between the Arab peoples based on a common language and the Islamic religion, but despite its popular and intellectual appeal, the movement has been ineffectual.

In 1945, the Arab League was established to strengthen links between the Arab states. The original members included Algeria, Egypt, Iraq, Jordan, Kuwait, Lebanon, Libya, Morocco, Saudi Arabia, Sudan, Syria, Tunisia, and Yemen. When the state of Israel was established in 1948, the Arab League declared war. However, hostility to Israel produced only temporary unity, and dissension among the different Arab regimes has been apparent. Gamal Abdel Nasser, prime minister and president of Egypt from 1954 to 1970, put himself forward as the leader of the Arab masses against "Western imperialism and Zionist aggression." In 1958, he formed the United Arab Republic with Syria, but it lasted only until 1961 when Syria withdrew.

A rival vision of Arab unity based on socialism was promulgated by the Ba'ath Party founded by Michel Aflaq. The Ba'ath achieved power in Syria and Iraq and in October 1963, proposed to unite the two countries, but before this could be done, the Ba'athists were overthrown in Iraq. A proposed union between Egypt and Libya, announced in August 1972, also came to nothing. Ideological differences between monarchies and revolutionary socialist regimes, and sectarian antipathies between Sunni and Shi'ites, have proved more influential than Pan-Arab sentiments.

References Antonius, George. *The Arab Awakening: The Story of the Arab National Movement* (1969); Nusseibeh, Hazem. *The Idea of Pan-Arabism* (1956).

Arafat, Yasir (1929–)

The first president of the Palestinian Authority (PA), the government of the self-ruled areas of the West Bank and the Gaza Strip, Yasir Arafat was born in Cairo on August 24, 1929. Much of his childhood was spent in Jerusalem. He received a degree in civil engineering from Cairo University in 1956.

Active in Palestinian causes at the outbreak of the Arab-Israeli war of 1948, Arafat was to become the president of the union of Palestinian students in 1952. After fighting on the Egyptian side in the 1956 war against Israel, he founded Fatah, the Palestinian militia in 1957. Fatah engaged in guerrilla actions against Israel and fought in the 1967 Arab-Israeli war. In 1968, Fatah distinguished itself in a battle against Israeli troops in the refugee camp of Al Jarameh in Jordan. In 1969, Fatah and other Palestinian militias took control of the Palestine Liberation Organization (PLO), which Arafat had helped to establish. In 1969, Arafat became chairman of the PLO in a defeat for the pro-Arabist faction, which had been in control. Arafat's philosophy was that Palestinians and not other Arab states should lead the Palestinian movement. Under Arafat as commander in chief of the united Palestinian Revolutionary Forces, the PLO guerrillas conducted operations against Israel from bases in Jordan and Lebanon.

In 1988, Arafat recognized Israel's right to exist and declared the PLO to be the government in exile of Palestine. In 1993, he signed the Oslo peace accord with Israel, which led to the withdrawal of Israeli troops from portions of the West Bank and the Gaza Strip and created the Palestinian Authority. Arafat also renounced the use of violence by the PLO to achieve statehood. In 1994, he was awarded the Nobel Peace Prize. In the first elections in the self-governing regions of Palestine, held in 1996, Arafat was elected president of the new government. The Wye River accords, which he signed with the Israeli prime minister, Benjamin Netanyahu, in 1998, led to further Israeli withdrawals from the Gaza Strip and the West Bank.

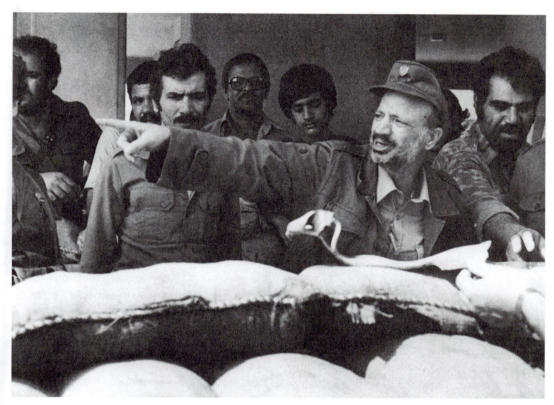

PLO chairman Yasir Arafat gives orders to soldiers during a battle with the Israeli army in Beirut, 1982. (Corbis/Bettmann)

Arafat's domestic critics include Palestinian organizations like Hamas, which refuse to accept the peace agreements, and others who argue that Arafat runs the PLO and the PA dictatorially.

See also Fatah; Palestine Liberation Organization; Palestinians.
Reference Wallach, Janet, and John Wallach. *Arafat: In the Eye of the Beholder* (1997).

Arakan

The Arakan region of Burma (also known as Myanmar) has a long tradition of independence, having been under Burmese rule only from 1784 to 1825. The population of the region is divided between the Muslim Rohingya and the Buddhist Rakhine, groups that are bitterly hostile to one another. Fearing dominance by the Buddhist Burman majority, in 1946 the North Arakan Muslim League called for the Muslim-majority areas to be included in East Pakistan (later Bangladesh). Immediately following Burmese independence in 1948, the mujahidin rebels set up an Islamic republic in northern Arakan while the Buddhists, organized into the Arakan Independence League, also demanded independence. Both revolts were crushed, and in 1962, the state of Rakhine was established. A military zone covering the Muslim border regions was set up in 1961, and the Burmese army has launched numerous sweeps in order to capture and deport illegal immigrants from Bangladesh. The undiscriminating brutality of the military against the Muslim population has resulted in a de facto process of ethnic cleansing.

See also Burma.
Reference Christie, Clive J. *A Modern History of Southeast Asia* (1996).

Armenia

In 1990, Armenia had a population of 3.4 million. Armenians had migrated to their current homeland by the seventh century B.C., and although often controlled by stronger neighboring empires, Armenia managed to attain a degree of autonomy as a state several times. In the first century B.C. under King Tigranes I, greater Armenia extended from Georgia in the north to Mesopotamia in the south and bordered on the Black, Caspian, and Mediterranean Seas. In 69 B.C., Armenia became part of the Roman Empire, and in A.D. 304, it became the first Christian state. Its people still belong predominantly to the Armenian Orthodox Church. From the fifth century until the nineteenth century, greater Armenia was subjected to Byzantine, Persian, Arab, Turk, and Mongol control. In the sixteenth century, Persians and Ottoman Turks divided the Armenian lands, and Persian Armenia was seized by Russia in 1828. In 1915 the Ottoman Empire expelled Armenians from Anatolia, and an estimated 600,000 to 1 million deaths resulted from the forced migration. This ended any significant Armenian presence in the western regions of historic greater Armenia. Following this, Armenian terrorist groups began to carry out reprisals against Turkish diplomats and officials throughout the world.

In 1918, with the Russian Empire disintegrating, Armenia, led by the Armenian Revolutionary Federation (ARF), declared its independence. The Bolshevik forces succeeded in regaining control over the area, and in 1922, Armenia was incorporated, along with Georgia and Azerbaijan, into the Transcaucasian Federated Soviet Republic. In 1936, Armenia became a separate Soviet socialist republic. After Mikhail Gorbachev ascended to power in the USSR in 1985 and began loosening Moscow's central control, an independence movement spread quickly throughout Armenia.

In 1991, Armenians voted to secede from the Soviet Union, and the country subsequently joined the Commonwealth of Independent States. Its elected president, Ter-Petrosyan of the Armenian National Movement (APM), was forced to resign on February 8, 1998. He was replaced by former prime minister and Armenian nationalist Robert Kocharian. In a subsequent presidential election in that same year, Kocharian was victorious. Kocharian, a former president of the breakaway Azerbaijan region of Nagorno-Karabakh, pledged never to return the region to Azerbaijan control.

Nagorno-Karabakh, an ethnic Armenian enclave within Azerbaijan, had revolted against Azeri rule in 1988. With the backing of the ARF and the Armenian military, Nagorno-Karabakh came under Armenian control in 1988–1989. In the subsequent Azeri-Armenian war, which lasted until a 1994 cease-fire, Armenia seized an additional 20 percent of Azerbaijan land, including a corridor linking Nagorno-Karabakh to Armenia. Although the Russian-sponsored cease-fire is still in effect, the territorial dispute between the two ex-Soviet republics remains unresolved. The new Armenian government has also demanded reparations from Turkey for the 1915 massacre.

See also Armenian Secret Army for the Liberation of Armenia; Azerbaijan; Justice Commandos of the Armenian Genocide; Nagorno-Karabakh; Union of Soviet Socialist Republics.
Reference Masih, Joseph, and Robert Kirkorian. *Armenia* (1999).

Armenian Georgians

Numbering about 400,000, Armenians constitute about 8 percent of Georgia's population. In the four districts of South Georgia where they are in the majority, Armenians have pressed the Georgian government for the creation of an Armenian autonomous region. Led by Yervan Sherenian, the Armenian nationalist organization Djavakhk has drafted a separate constitution for the region. The organization is also opposed to close ties between Georgia and Turkey.

See also Armenia; Georgia.
Reference Radio Free Europe. *Newsline*, September 16, 1998.

Armenian Revolutionary Army
See Justice Commandos of the Armenian Genocide

Armenian Secret Army for the Liberation of Armenia

The Armenian Secret Army for the Liberation of Armenia (ASALA) began its campaign on January 20, 1975, with the bombing of the Beirut office of the World Council of Churches. Terrorism is justified by ASALA and other Armenian terrorist groups as a response to the deaths of 1 million Armenians living in the Ottoman Empire during World War I. In 1973, an Armenian-American killed two Turkish diplomats in revenge for the murder of his family in 1915, and this act served as a catalyst for the emergence of both ASALA and the Justice Commandos of the Armenian Genocide (JCAG).

A leftist group formed by Hagop Hagopian and closely linked to the Palestine Liberation Organization (PLO), which operated as a virtual state within Lebanon, ASALA modeled itself organizationally and tactically upon the Popular Front for the Liberation of Palestine faction. ASALA saw the Soviet Union as an ally and denounced the United States, Britain, and West Germany. The group's goal was to annex the historically Armenian districts of eastern Turkey to Soviet Armenia, and it attacked not only Turkish targets but also countries that aid Turkey militarily or economically. Turkish diplomats and their families were attacked in Lebanon, Greece, France, and Italy. In 1981, ASALA terrorists seized the Turkish consulate in Paris; in 1982, they bombed Ankara airport in Turkey; and in 1983, they bombed Orly airport in Paris.

Following the Orly bombing, ASALA split into two factions, with the more moderate anti-Hagopian faction rejecting the use of indiscriminate terrorism against innocent civilians and non-Turkish targets. Feuding between the two factions resulted in several deaths and a decline in the number of terrorist attacks overall. The Armenian diaspora in the United States, France, and Lebanon gave significant support to the Armenian militants. For example, over $250,000 was raised to defend Hampig Sassounian, who was convicted of the 1982 murder of the Turkish consul in Los Angeles. There is also evidence that ASALA received training and weapons from the Soviet Union and the PLO.

See also Armenia; Justice Commandos of the Armenian Genocide.
References Gunter, Michael. *Pursuing the Just Cause of Their People: A Study of Contemporary Armenian Terrorism* (1986); Hyland, Francis P. *Armenian Terrorism: The Past, the Present, the Future* (1991).

Ashanti

The National Liberation Movement (NLM) called for self-determination for the Ashanti (or Asante) region of Ghana and rejected Kwame Nkrumah's plan for a unitary state. The Ashanti confederation, led by their king, the Asantehene, and linked by the sacred Golden Stool, which represented their dead ancestors, had a history dating back to the 1600s. The first meeting of the NLM, in September 1954, was attended by a crowd of over 40,000 who swore an oath on the Golden Stool and chanted Ashanti war cries as the movement's flag was displayed. The design of the flag showed a cocoa tree and a porcupine, symbolizing the source of Ashanti wealth and the warlike spirit of the Ashanti. Because of its use of such traditional symbols, the NLM is regarded by many historians as representing a reactionary tribalism. However, the NLM was able to forge a coalition between the main social groups in Ashanti.

The founders of the NLM were journalists, teachers, clerks, and traders, and many had earlier been members of Nkrumah's Convention People's Party (CPP). They led the opposition when the CPP government fixed the price of cocoa at a third of what it was getting on world markets, thus gaining support from the cocoa farmers. By defending their traditional role against Nkrumah, the movement forged an alliance with the chiefs and the Asantehene, who gave them legitimation as well as financial support.

There was chronic violence in Ashanti between NLM and CPP supporters, and fearing for his life, Nkrumah did not visit the region until 1957. An angry crowd even stoned the British governor's car when he visited the Asantehene in 1955. In the elections of 1956, the NLM won a majority of the Ashanti seats. Although the NLM won a degree of autonomy for Ashanti and constitutional recognition of the position of the Asantahene, this was a temporary victory, and Nkrumah quickly transformed Ghana into a one-party state.

See also Ghana.
References Allman, Jean Marie. "The Young Men and the Porcupine: Class, Nationalism, and Asante's Struggle for Self-determination, 1954–57" (1990); Morrison, Minion. *Ethnicity and Political Integration: The Case of Ashanti, Ghana* (1982).

Assam

Assam, which lies in the northeastern region of India, is joined to the rest of the country by only a narrow corridor of land and was originally inhabited by hill tribes, including the Nagas, Mizos, Bodo, and Meitei who are ethnically distinct from the rest of the Indian population. Immigration into the region from West Bengal and Bangladesh created tensions between the indigenous population and the settlers and led to the growth of insurgent separatist movements. The most important insurgent groups include the United Liberation Front of Assam (ULFA); the Mizo National Front; the National Socialist Council of Nagaland; the People's Liberation Army of Manipur, which attempted to unite the Meitei tribe living in Manipur and Burma into an independent state; the Tripura National Front; and the All-Bodo Students Union.

An insurrection by the Mizos that began in 1966 was precipitated by the state government's mishandling of famine relief. The Mizo National Famine Front, formed to organize tribal discontent over the issue, became the Mizo National Front and called for the creation of an independent "Mizoram." The Mizos were regrouped into new settlements, and this regrouping together with a massive Indian troop presence effectively pacified the area. In 1971, the Indian government attempted to satisfy the demand of the different hill tribes for greater autonomy by an administrative reorganization of the region. In addition to Nagaland, which had been set up in 1963, three new states were created (Meghalaya, Manipur, and Tripura), and two other areas (Mizoram and Arunachal Pradesh) were designated union territories. All these new states and territories were designed so that their populations were largely composed of tribal peoples.

The issue of how many immigrants would be eligible to vote in the 1983 state elections led to widespread violence. The central government attempted to resolve the conflict by negotiations, and the Assam accord of August 1985 declared that persons who entered the state illegally before March 1971 would be allowed to remain but were disenfranchised for ten years while those who entered after that date would be expelled. In the elections held after the accord, the Assam People's Assembly won a majority in the state legislature but was unable to implement the provisions of the accord and lost support to the more militant ULFA. A 1993 agreement with the Bodo insurgents established the Bodoland Autonomous Council, which granted the Bodo some degree of administrative autonomy.

Violence intensified in the late 1980s, with ULFA militants operating what was virtually a parallel government, which levied "taxes" on the tea plantations. This breakdown of law and order led to the imposition of "president's rule" from November 1990 until June 1991. During this period the army carried out Operation Bajrang and Operation Rhino and arrested over 7,000 suspected terrorists. By 1995, more than 300,000 people were living in refugee camps, and over 5,000 had been killed by the army or the insurgents.

See also India; Nagaland.
Reference George, Sudhir. "The Bodo Movement in Assam" (1994).

Australian Aborigines

The indigenous inhabitants of Australia, the aborigines, number about a quarter of a million, are racially distinct from other human populations, and are believed to have entered Australia some 40,000 years ago. They lived in small nomadic groups of hunter-gatherers and had a stone-age technology. Britain began to colonize Australia in 1788, and as the number of settlers increased, the aborigines were driven off most of their lands. The Tasmanian aborigines were exterminated, and on the mainland only a fraction survived. By the end of World War II, the number of full-blooded aborigines was around 40,000, most of them desperately poor. They were not granted citizenship until 1962 and not counted in the census until 1967.

The issue of aboriginal land rights has been a major grievance. It was originally held under the doctrine of *terra nullius* that Australia prior to British settlement was "waste and substantially unoccupied." Hence, there was no native title. A federal commission, headed by Justice Woodward, recommended that aborigines be allowed to claim their traditional lands, which would then be granted to them as inalienable freehold (i.e., the land could not be sold or taken over by the state). In 1976, legislation was passed to that effect under the Aboriginal Land Rights Act, which applied only to the federal territory of Northern Australia. Elsewhere aboriginal land rights were regarded as a state issue, but by the end of the 1980s, all states (except Western Australia) had passed similar legislation. This was partly in response to direct action taken by aboriginal groups. For example, following demonstrations, the South Australian state government declared that an aboriginal reserve belonged to the Pitjantjatjara tribe and

A demonstration in Brisbane for Australian Aboriginal land rights during the 1982 Commonwealth Games. (Corbis/Sean Sexton Collection)

vested title in "those persons who in Aboriginal law and tradition have rights in it."

In 1992, the Australian High Court, in the Mabo decision, decided that native title survived even after Britain acquired sovereignty over Australia. This was followed by federal legislation in 1993 setting up a National Native Title Tribunal to adjudicate aboriginal claims. Subsequently, in 1998, a federal judge ruled that the Miriuwung tribe held native title to large sections of Western Australia and Northern Territory. The government responded by passing the Native Title Amendments Act, also in 1998, which restricted aboriginal land rights. In response to demands for greater self-determination, the Australian government replaced the Department of Aboriginal Affairs with sixty regional councils.

These measures did not satisfy many of the aborigines. Militants belonging to the Aboriginal Provisional Government call for aboriginal sovereignty over all crown lands, which would mean that any persons living within this territory would have to obey traditional laws and customs. The group designed an aboriginal flag and set up an aboriginal embassy (a tent) on the lawns of Parliament House on Australia Day, 1972. Other activists argue that individual tribes constitute domestic dependent nations and that each is entitled to self-determination.

See also Indigenous Peoples.
References Brennan, Frank. *One Land, One Nation* (1995); Coombs, H. C. *Aboriginal Autonomy* (1994); Tonkinson, Robert, and Michael Howard. *Going It Alone? Prospects for Aboriginal Autonomy* (1990).

Azerbaijan

Azerbaijan, a land of 7.6 million people, was once part of the ancient Persian Empire. In the eleventh and twelfth centuries, Azerbaijan came under the control of the Seljuk Turks and adopted the Azeri language, a Turkic dialect. In the sixteenth century, Azeris were converted to Shi'ite Islam and gradually fell under Persian control once more. As a consequence of this history, modern Azerbaijanis are linguistically related to

Turkey but in cultural and religious matters are more closely tied to Iran. Following the Russian-Persian wars in the early nineteenth century, most of contemporary Azerbaijan became part of the Russian Empire. Nearly 90 percent of the population is Azeri; 2 percent of the population is Armenian, and 2 percent Russian. However, nearly twice as many Azeri speakers reside in Iran as in Azerbaijan. Although the Iranian Azeris speak a South Azeri dialect, which is grammatically distinct from the North Azeri spoken in Azerbaijan, in recent years organizations in both countries have pushed for the unification of all Azeris into one state. The United Azerbaijan Union, an opposition political party, wants Iranian Azerbaijan united with the Azerbaijan Republic so that South Azerbaijans can be liberated from "cultural and linguistic oppression." The pro-government Fatherland party proposes a confederation of North and South Azerbaijan as a first step to unification. Both parties emphasize pan-Turkism in their ideology.

The first Azerbaijan state came into being in 1918 following the collapse of the Russian Empire. In a brief alliance with Turkish army forces in 1919, Azeris engaged in a massacre of Armenian Christians living in Azerbaijan. In 1920, the Red Army occupied the country, and in 1922 Azerbaijan was incorporated into the Soviet Union, along with Armenia and Georgia, as part of the Transcaucasian Federated Soviet Republic. In 1936, Azerbaijan became a Soviet socialist republic.

In 1988, Armenians, who constituted 80 percent of the population of the province of Nagorno-Karabakh, revolted against Azerbaijan rule. With the help of Armenia's military, the secessionists secured control over the province as well seizing about 20 percent of Azerbaijan territory adjoining Nagorno-Karabakh. The Azeris retaliated by persecuting the Armenians who still lived within Azerbaijan. As a consequence of the war, many Armenians fled the country, leaving the republic far more ethnically homogeneous. Ten years after the Armenian revolt, no diplomatic solution to the Nagorno-Karabakh dispute had been achieved. It is estimated that 130,000 Armenians continue to live in the province.

In 1990, the Soviet Union intervened on the Armenian side in the Azeri-Armenian war. This generated anti-Russian sentiments that translated into a call for independence from the Soviet Union, and in 1991, Azerbaijan seceded from the USSR. Initially, Azerbaijan refused to join the Commonwealth of Independent States, joining only after Grigori Alievev became president in 1993.

Internally, the Lezgin and Talysh minorities have agitated for secession from the Azerbaijan state. The Lezgins, who speak a Caucasian language and are Sunni Muslims, wish to be reunited with the Lezgins living in the Russian Republic of Dagestan. The Persian-language-speaking Talysh want to create a state with the Talysh of Iran.

See also Armenia; Iranian Azerbaijan; Lezgins; Nagorno-Karabakh; Talysh; Union of Soviet Socialist Republics.
Reference Swietochowski, Tadeus. *Russia and Azerbaijan* (1995).

Azores

A group of islands in the North Atlantic, the Azores were discovered and settled by the Portuguese in the 1400s. After the left-wing Portuguese revolution of 1974, strong separatist sentiments emerged, particularly on the island of Terceira, where it was feared that the government might close the U.S. military base there. The Liberation Front of the Azores attacked Communist and Socialist Party offices on the islands and forced the withdrawal of the governors and military commanders sent from Portugal. Claiming that it was in favor of democracy and afraid of Communist influences in Lisbon, the front called for independence.

The Portuguese constitution of 1976 granted the Azores and Madeira regional assemblies. An autonomy statute, which became law on July 25, 1980, was accepted with reservations by Jose de Almeida, the leader of the Liberation Front. Separatist sentiments also exist on Madeira, and the

Madeira Archipelago Liberation Front calls for independence from Portugal and a federation with the Azores.

References Gallagher, Tom. "Portugal's Atlantic Territories: The Separatist Challenge" (1979); Guill, James. *A History of the Azores* (1993).

Aztlan

Aztlan, the land of the Aztecs, is claimed by Mexican-American activists as a separate nation. In the 1848 Treaty of Guadalupe Hidalgo, Mexico ceded large tracts of territory to the United States. Although the treaty guaranteed the land and property of the Mexicans living in these areas, the guarantees were not respected.

In the early 1960s, a series of confrontations occurred as descendants of the Mexican settlers demanded the return of their ancestral lands. This agitation culminated in an armed raid on a county courthouse in New Mexico, which was followed by a massive manhunt and trial. Two years

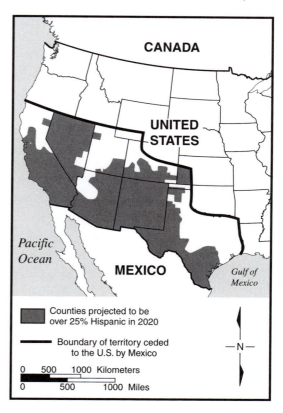

later, at a 1969 Chicano Youth Liberation Conference held in Denver and attended by more than 1,500 Chicano militants, the demand was made that most of southwestern United States become the independent country of "Aztlan." The conference document defined Aztlan to include most of the territory lost to Mexico through the Treaty of Guadalupe Hidalgo in 1848 and before (Colorado, New Mexico, California, Arizona, and parts of Texas). Activists such as Rodolfo Acuna refuse to recognize the treaty and refer to the ceded territory as "occupied America." The Aztlan concept has been adopted by a number of Chicano organizations, including the Alianza Federal de Pueblas Libres and the Movimiento Estudiantil Chicano de Aztlan.

See also Chicano Movement.

References Anaya, Rudolfo A., and Francisco A. Lomeli. *Aztlan: Essays on the Chicano Homeland* (1989); Barrera, Mario. *Beyond Aztlan: Ethnic Autonomy in Comparative Perspective* (1988); Garcia, Ignacio. *Chicanismo: The Forging of a Militant Ethos* (1997).

Baluchistan

Baluchistan is the largest and poorest of Pakistan's four provinces. Most Baluchis live outside the province, and the Azad Baluchistan movement seeks a greater Baluchistan, which would include large areas of southeastern Iran. In 1955, the tribal rulers were pressured into giving up their powers to the Pakistan government. Economic development of the area did little to benefit the local population, and in the 1960s, Marxist groups began to organize the population. An abortive rebellion by the khan of Kalat, the most important tribal ruler, was the pretext for a declaration of martial law by the president in October 1958. This was followed by a military takeover by General Ayub Khan.

An insurgency organized by the Popular Front of Armed Resistance Against National Oppression and Exploitation in Baluchistan began in May 1973 and was put down by the Pakistani army only after heavy fighting. At its peak in late 1974, nearly 55,000 Baluchi insurgents were involved in the insurrection. The Pakistani army suffered 3,300 casualties and the Baluchis 5,300. In 1979, the National Awami Party, the largest provincial party, called for increased autonomy for Baluchistan, and in the same year there was fighting in Iranian Baluchistan when rebels tried to assert their independence from the Teheran government.

See also Afghanistan; Baluchistan Liberation Front; Pakistan.
References Harrison, Selig. "Nightmare in Baluchistan" (1978); Sayeed, Khalid. *Politics in Pakistan* (1980).

Baluchistan Liberation Front

In southeastern Iran, the Baluchistan Liberation Front (BLF) made intermittent attacks on Iranian forces. Set up by Baluchi exiles in 1964, the BLF was first supported by Iraq, but after an agreement between the shah and Saddam Hussein in which Iraq agreed to withdraw its support of the BLF if the shah stopped aiding the Iraqi Kurds, the campaign petered out. After the shah was over-

thrown in 1979, violence broke out anew under the leadership of Rahim Zardkoui, but Khomeini's revolutionary guards crushed the rebellion and killed Zardkoui. The Khomeini regime also provided economic aid to the region in an attempt to reduce support for the separatists.

See also Baluchistan.

Banaba

Banaba is an island in the Pacific nation of Kiribati (formerly the Gilbert and Ellice Islands). In 1980, one year after Kiribati became independent, the Banabans called for independence, but after an agreement was reached concerning revenue sharing and other financial matters, the island agreed to remain part of Kiribati.

Bangladesh

Today's Bangladesh was previously known as East Pakistan. Pakistan, created as a result of the partition of India into Hindu and Muslim areas in 1947, was a geographical oddity as it consisted of two parts that were separated by 1,000 miles of Indian territory. According to one popular joke, the only things holding West Pakistan and East Pakistan together were the Muslim religion, a fear of India, and Pakistan International Airlines. West Pakistan was an arid region dependent upon irrigation and inhabited by light-skinned Punjabis, Pathans, and Baluchis whereas East Pakistan was a low-lying region that was subject to severe floods and inhabited by dark-skinned Bengalis. Although East Pakistan contained 56 percent of Pakistan's total population, West Pakistan was the dominant partner and exploited the eastern region economically. East Pakistan's jute exports were sold to West Pakistan at artificially low prices, and East Pakistan became a captive market for West Pakistan's manufactured goods. Government expenditures disproportionately benefited West Pakistan. The result was that the per capita income difference between the two regions increased significantly, and by the late 1960s was 60 percent lower in East Pakistan. In addition, East Pakistan had cultural and political grievances. Urdu was declared to be the official language of the whole country, and Bengali was not granted official status until the mid-1950s. The East Pakistanis were grossly underrepresented in the military and the civil service, and during the rule of General Mohammad Ayub Khan, East Pakistanis rarely played a role in national politics.

The Awami League, which emerged as the main party in East Pakistan, put forward demands for increased autonomy on several occasions. In 1966, the leader of the party, Sheikh Mujibur Rahman, called for a loose federal system with each region having its own armed forces and currency. When Ayub resigned in early 1970, his successor, General Agha Yahya Khan, promised elections in which seats would be allocated on the basis of population, thereby ensuring that East Pakistani voters would determine the outcome. In West Pakistan the Pakistan People's Party, led by Zulfiqar Ali Bhutto, won a majority of the seats while the Awami League won all but two seats in East Pakistan, giving it a majority in the National Assembly. Negotiations among Rahman, Bhutto, and Yahya over autonomy for East Pakistan began, but during the talks large numbers of West Pakistani troops were moved into East Pakistan. When the talks broke down at the end of March 1971 and troops were unleashed on the Bengalis, as many as 3 million were killed, and 8 million were driven into India.

The Awami League set up a government in exile and declared that "Pakistan is now dead and buried under a mountain of corpses.... independent Bangladesh is a reality sustained by the indestructible will and courage of 75 million Bengalis who are daily nurturing the roots of this new nationhood with their blood." A guerrilla force, the Mukti Bahini, was organized but had little success against the well-equipped Pakistani army. India allowed Bangladesh to set up a government in exile in Calcutta and provided the Mukti Bahini with sanctuary and weapons. The mass exodus of Bengalis fleeing the conflict created a tremendous financial burden for India, which spent an estimated $500 million to feed over 10 million refugees. This, in addition to the strategic advantage to be gained by the dismemberment of its arch rival, led India to declare war on Pakistan on December 4, 1971. The Pakistani army in Bangladesh surrendered two weeks later, and a new state was born.

See also Pakistan.
References Choudhury, G. *The Last Days of United Pakistan* (1974); Heraclides, Alexis. *The Self-Determination of Minorities in International Politics* (1991).

Barbuda

The Caribbean island of Barbuda (population 1,200) achieved independence from Britain in 1981 along with the larger island of Antigua. However, Barbudans feel they have been neglected by the Antiguan legislature as little has been spent on roads, schools, or health services on their island. Two separatist parties, the Barbuda People's Movement (BPM) and the Barbuda Independence Movement, have campaigned for independence from Antigua. In March 1989, the BPM won control of the local council, and Thomas Frank, the party leader, was elected to the Barbudan seat in the House of Representatives.

Barotseland

Formerly the British colony of Northern Rhodesia, Zambia became independent in 1964. Barotseland is the most western province of Zambia, bordering Angola and the Caprivi Strip, and is inhabited by the Lozi. The Lozi kingdom was established in the late 1700s, when the Lozi people invaded and conquered the local tribes. Since that date, there has been considerable intermarriage, but the Lozi continued to dominate a wide territory throughout the time of an agreement between Litunga (King) Lewanika and the British South Africa Company. The 1890 treaty, under which the kingdom became a protectorate, granted the company mineral rights but pledged that there would be no interference with "the King's power and authority over any of his own subjects." The Lozi were divided into a large royal family, an aristocracy, and the commoners, all of whom felt themselves superior to members of the vassal tribes. The company ruled through the traditional Lozi ruling class and gave it a share of the hut tax, the main source of revenue. The imposition of the hut tax transformed Barotseland into a source of labor for the mines of southern Africa, as this was the only way that the peasants could earn the money to pay the tax.

After World War II, Barotseland remained an economic backwater with half the able-bodied males working outside the province. The proposal to create a federal union between Northern and Southern Rhodesia and Nyasaland was met with hostility by Africans in Northern Rhodesia. The ruling litunga, Mwanawina, demanded that Barotseland be detached from Northern Rhodesia and recognized as a separate protectorate. However, after guarantees that the status and power of the royal family would be maintained and that there would be recognition of Barotseland's "special position," he accepted federation.

The growth of an African nationalist movement, spearheaded by Kenneth Kaunda and the United National Independence Party (UNIP), led to political polarization in Barotseland between the traditionalists and UNIP militants. UNIP meetings were broken up, and UNIP members arrested or deported. In 1960, Mwanawina flew to London to demand secession from Northern Rhodesia, but the British government refused to allow this. When territorial elections were held in Northern Rhodesia in 1962, the Lozi aristocracy backed the Sicaba (National) Party, which pledged to free Barotseland from UNIP rule and to separate from Northern Rhodesia. However, the Sicaba candidates went down to a humiliating defeat, and in the 1963 elections to the Katengo, the Barotseland national council, UNIP won all twenty-five seats and 84 percent of the vote. This decline in his support led the litunga to sign the Barotseland Agreement of 1964, whereby he accepted that Barotseland was an integral part of Zambia.

After independence, there was growing conflict between UNIP, whose motto was, One Zambia, One Nation, and Lozi separatists. Tensions were heightened by fears that Barotseland separatism would be exploited by South Africa, since Zambia played a major role as a base for the African liberation movements that were attempting to overthrow the white minority regimes in Rhodesia and South Africa. Matters came to a head in June 1965 when the government announced plans to reduce the litunga's traditional powers. The Katengo declared that the Lozi would "resist to the death" any encroachment on their rights, and this provoked the government to abolish the council and replace it with five district councils. Under a separate act, the litunga lost virtually all his powers, including control of the Barotseland Treasury.

Amid renewed rumors of secession, many Lozi politicians withdrew from the UNIP in anger. Lozi alienation was increased by Kaunda's decision to cancel the agreement between Zambia and South Africa whereby large numbers of local men were recruited to work in South Africa's mines. In the 1968 general elections, UNIP was soundly defeated in Barotseland, with the opposition African National Congress (ANC) winning eight of the eleven constituencies in the province and 61 percent of the vote. Many of the winning ANC candidates were known secession-ists. Kaunda responded by terminating the Barot-seland Agreement and the province's special sta-tus. The litunga's powers to redistribute land were removed, and Barotseland was renamed Western Province.

References Caplan, Gerald L. *The Elites of Barotseland 1878–1969* (1970); Pettman, Jan. *Zambia: Security and Conflict* (1974).

Bashkortostan

Bashkortostan, a republic of the Russian Federa-tion, is named after the Bashkirs, but Bashkirs account for only 25 percent of the republic's pop-ulation of 4 million. Russians, found principally in urban areas, account for 40 percent of the pop-ulation, and Tatars account for 30 percent. In ad-dition to the 1 million Bashkirs residing in Bashkortostan, another 600,000 live in neighbor-ing Russian areas.

Bashkirs are Sunni Muslims and speak a Tur-kic language closely related to Tatar. However, throughout history, relations between Bashkirs and Tatars have been strained with Bashkirs fear-ing absorption into the more powerful Tatar na-tion. During the Russian Revolution, the Bashkirs refused to associate with Tatars in a joint Tatar-Bashkir republic. In 1919, Bashkortostan became the first autonomous republic of the newly formed Soviet Union. Previously, the Bashkirs had been absorbed into the Russian Empire in the eighteenth century, and the capital of Bashkor-tostan, Ufa, had been established by Russians as early as 1574. In 1991, with the disintegration of the Soviet Union, Bashkortostan became a repub-lic of the Russian Federation.

The presence of three large ethnic groups within Bashkortostan has generated several na-tional movements. The Bashkir People's Center (BPC) calls for greater sovereignty. It also declares that Bashkortostan belongs exclusively to the Bashkirs. It would grant Bashkirs a monopoly on the political institutions of the country as well as

giving Bashkirs preferential treatment in terms of property rights. Under one proposal, Bashkirs would have priority in the distribution of formerly nationalized land. The sixth congress of the BPC argued for the creation of a shadow government of Bashkirs. The BPC also opposes the establishment of any semiautonomous Tatar districts.

The Tatar Civic Center (TCC), in response to the BPC, has called for the establishment of an autonomous Tatar district in the Ufa region. Tatars in the northeastern region of Bashkor-tostan have called for that area to be joined with Tatarstan. The Ufa Historico-Patriotic Assembly, set up in 1990, represents Russian interests in the republic. Essentially, the assembly calls for the elimination of ethnic sovereignties within the Russian Federation and for a single and indivisi-ble Russia within its historical boundaries.

See also Russian Federation.
Reference Mastyugina, Tatiana, and Lev Perelkin. *An Ethnic History of Russia* (1996).

Basques

The Basques speak a language unrelated to any other in the world, and because of this and their distinctive genetic characteristics, it has been suggested that they are the direct descendants of the first Europeans, the prehistoric Cro-Magnons. The Basque homeland straddles the western Pyrenees with about 200,000 Basques living in France and the rest living in Spain. The Basque region of Spain is composed of four provinces: Alava, Guipuzcoa, Vizcaya, and Navarra. With a population of just under 3 million, about 60 per-cent are ethnic Basques, and the rest are immi-grants from other parts of Spain. The two groups tend to live in separate neighborhoods, to belong to separate unions and political parties, and to re-gard one another with mutual suspicion. Ethnic Basques are more likely to be middle-class or skilled workers than the immigrant Spaniards, and one study found that the average Basque in-come was 10 percent higher. The Basque lan-guage, Euskera, is a key component of Basque ethnicity, although only about a third of the Basques can speak it fluently.

The last independent Basque state was the Kingdom of Navarra, which lasted until 1035. Thereafter the Basque area south of the Pyrenees gradually came under the control of the Spanish crown. However, each of the Basque provinces retained a high degree of autonomy and its own laws *(fueros)*. In the nineteenth century, when a centralized state began to emerge, Guipuzcoa and Vizcaya became the most industrialized region of Spain.

Basque nationalism dates from the latter part of the nineteenth century when the Basque Nationalist Party (PNV) was founded by Sabino de Arana. The nationalist movement struggled to revive the Basque language, which it believed was central to Basque identity. The PNV was strongly Catholic, drew its initial support from the petty bourgeoisie, and favored a nonviolent parliamentary strategy. The PNV remained the main vehicle of Basque nationalism throughout the Second Republic and the Spanish Civil War. During the civil war, the PNV sided with the republic, and in return, Guipuzcoa and Vizcaya were granted autonomy. The autonomous government had a brief existence from October 1936 until June 1937 when Francisco Franco's forces overran the territory. All expressions of Basque nationalism were savagely repressed during the Franco era, and it became illegal to speak Euskera or to display the Basque flag. In the 1950s, younger and more radical Basques became increasingly dissatisfied with the PNV leadership and formed Euskadi ta Askatasuna (ETA), which launched a guerrilla campaign in 1968.

After Franco's death in 1975, Spain made a swift transition to a constitutional democracy, with the first democratic elections taking place in 1977 and a new constitution being promulgated in 1978. The constitution contained provisions for the creation of regional governments, and an autonomy statute for the Basque region was quickly drafted and approved by the Basque voters. Navarra, which is distinct in several ways from the other three provinces, was not included in the Basque region.

The first elections for an autonomous Basque government were held in March 1980.

See also Enbata; Euzkadi ta Askatasuna; Partido Nacionalista Vasco.
References Clark, Robert P. *The Basque Insurgents* (1984); Conversi, Daniel. *The Basques, the Catalans, and Spain* (1997).

Bavaria

Germany was only united into a Prussian-dominated empire in 1871, and the component states *(Länder)* have a strong sense of their own historic and regional identities. This is especially so in the case of Bavaria, the largest and most important of the southern German states. In 1918, after the abdication of the last Bavarian king, Ludwig III, Georg Heim founded the Bavarian Peoples Party (BVP). The BVP was strongly anti-Prussian, and for a while flirted with the idea of an independent Bavaria or a federation of the southern German states (including Austria). Throughout the interwar years, the BVP advocated a highly decentralized Germany in which Bavaria would have considerable autonomy.

At the end of World War II, many of the leaders of the BVP were active in the Christian Social Union (CSU), which became the dominant party in Bavaria. Regional sentiments were strong in Bavaria, and in 1949 the Bavarian legislature was the only one of the eleven *Länder* to vote against the new constitution, on the grounds that it gave too much power to the central government. Indeed, a faction split from the CSU to form the Bavarian Party (BP), which favored the dissolution of Germany, the restoration of the Bavarian monarchy, and the formation of a European confederation. In the local elections of 1948, the BP received 8.9 percent of the Bavarian vote, and in the federal elections of 1949, it got 20.9 percent compared to 29.2 percent for the CSU. Eventually, however, the CSU beat back the challenge of the more radically separatist BP by advocating a moderate federalist alternative.

Reference Dorondo, D. R. *Bavaria and German Federalism* (1992).

Befreiungs Ausschuss Sudtirol

The Befreiungs Ausschuss Sudtirol, or the Liberation Committee for the South Tirol, waged a terrorist campaign in the region from 1957 until 1969. The number of attacks increased dramatically in the early 1960s as did their severity. Over 200 incidents were reported, with half of them occurring in 1961–1963. Although the majority of the attacks consisted of bombings of property, beginning in 1961 the Italian national police became the main target, and at least 32 carabinieri were killed and 558 wounded.

The committee was based in Austria, and most of the people who were tried for and convicted of terrorist offenses were Austrian, although the campaign was supported by many South Tirolese. Italian officials charged that the terrorism was directed by neo-Nazi Austrian and German groups and that the goal was the reunion of the South Tirol with Austria rather than local autonomy. After the granting of increased autonomy for the South Tirol in 1969, the terrorist campaign petered out, with the last two explosions taking place in October of that year. There was a resurgence of terrorism in the 1980s with a few explosions claimed by Ein Tirol (which literally means "One Tirol").

See also South Tirol.
Reference Katzenstein, Peter J. "Ethnic Political Conflict in South Tyrol" (1977).

Begin, Menachem (1913–1992)

Born in Brest-Litovsk in Russia in 1913, Menachem Begin became active in Betar, a Zionist youth organization. In 1942, residing in Palestine, Begin joined Irgun, a right-wing, anti-British guerrilla organization that advocated an independent Jewish state. Under Begin's control, Irgun blew up the British headquarters in Jerusalem and hanged two British soldiers. After Israeli independence in 1948, Irgun became Herut, a conservative political party with Begin as its head. In 1977, Begin became prime minister of Israel following the electoral victory of the Likud bloc. He is remembered for signing, in 1979, the first Israeli peace treaty with an Arab nation, Egypt. In 1982, Begin ordered the invasion of southern Lebanon, thereby involving Israel in the Lebanese civil war and engaging Palestine Liberation Organization (PLO) militias in combat. In 1983, citing ill health, Begin resigned as prime minister and retired from public life.

See also Irgun; Israel; Lebanon.
Reference Seidman, Hillel, and Mordecai Schreiber. *Menachem Begin: His Life and Legacy* (1990).

Belarus

Belarus (Byelorussia) is a country of 10.5 million people. It borders Russia, Ukraine, Poland, Lithuania, and Latvia. More than 80 percent of the population is Belarusian, but Russian is the first language of 90 percent of the population. Minorities include 500,000 Russians, 300,000 Poles, 250,000 Ukrainians, and 140,000 Jews. Tatars, Lithuanians, and Germans make up the remainder of the population. Belarusian, like Ukrainian and Russian, is an eastern Slavic language, and although distinct, the three languages are mutually comprehensible.

The Belarusian region was part of Kievan Rus and later came under Lithuanian and then Polish rule. In 1596, Polish authorities forced the Belarusian Orthodox churches to unite with Rome, thus forming the Uniate Church. By 1795, Belarus had been incorporated into the Russian Empire. A period of Russification began, and the Orthodox Church was reestablished. Use of the term *Belarusian* was officially proscribed.

The nineteenth century saw a revival of Belarusian nationalism. Following the disintegration of the Russian Empire in 1917, Belarus proclaimed its independence. However, it was not strong enough to withstand the military strength of its neighbors, and by 1921, Belarus had been partitioned by Russia and Poland. In 1922, The Belarusian Soviet Socialist Republic was established in the Russian zone. In the early years, local Communists in Belarus played a major role in the state's governance. In the 1930s, Stalin launched another Russification program, and many Belarusian Communists were purged. The German-Soviet Non-Aggression Treaty of 1937 restored the Polish-held Belarusian lands to the USSR.

After 1985 when Mikhail Gorbachev's glasnost (openness) policies took root in Russia, Belarusian nationalist and human rights groups became more active in Belarus. After Chernobyl and the publication of papers implicating Stalin in the deaths of more than 200,000 Belarusians, a nationalist group, the Belarusian Popular Front (BPF) called for independence from the USSR. In 1990, the Belarus parliament restored Belarusian as the state language. Following an abortive 1991 coup against Gorbachev, the BPF, in alliance with disaffected Communists in parliament, voted for Belarusian independence. The first president of the new republic was the former Communist Stanislav Shushkevic.

Since 1994 and the election of Aleksandr Lukashenko, another Communist, as president, Belarus has moved closer to Russia. For example, Russian was reestablished as an official state language. Belarus has also promoted an integration of the Russian and Belarusian economies through the Commonwealth of Independent States, and Lukashenko has even talked about fusing Belarus with Russia.

The BPF has led mass demonstrations against both Russification and the increasingly autocratic style of government Lukashenko has imposed on Belarus. However, Lukashenko has consolidated his power to such a degree that there are few legitimate means of opposing his policies. It should be noted that the Belarusian population is not, on the whole, anti-Russian and that BPF's nationalist platform may represent only a minority opinion in Belarus.

See also Union of Soviet Socialist Republics.
References Fedor, Helen, ed. *Belarus and Moldova: Country Studies* (1996); Marples, David R. *Belarus: A Denationalized Nation* (1999).

Belgium

The population of Belgium is divided by language into two groups of nearly equal size. The northern region of Flanders is Dutch speaking while the southern region of Wallonia is French speaking. (There is also a small German-speaking minority in the eastern part of the province of Liege). The French speakers constitute about 44 percent and the Dutch speakers about 55 percent of the population, and these proportions have remained remarkably constant since Belgium became independent from the Netherlands in 1839. The reason for this stable linguistic balance is to be found in two countervailing social processes, which over time canceled one another out.

Although Flanders had a higher birthrate than Wallonia, French was the language of the elite, and a number of Flemings became first bilingual and eventually French speaking. Initially, the official language of Belgium was French, and it was not until 1898 that Dutch (also known as Flemish) was recognized as the second official language. Around the turn of the century, Flemish activists pressed for Flanders to become unilingual and for the University of Ghent to become a Dutch-language institution. World War I exacerbated tensions between Flemings and Walloons, since a number of Flemings collaborated with the occupying Germans. The Allied victory was followed by a purge of Flemish activists, and any talk of federalism was regarded as treasonable. This, in turn, provoked the rise of a Flemish nationalist movement, which called for Belgium to become a federal state divided along linguistic lines.

In the 1930s, legislation was enacted that divided the country into three parts: two unilingual zones and the bilingual capital city of Brussels. In the aftermath of World War II, several issues divided French and Dutch speakers, the most important of which was the language situation in Brussels and its suburbs. According to the prewar agreement, the linguistic status of the suburbs was to be determined by the decennial census. However, owing to the assimilation of upwardly

Language Regions

- Dutch
- French
- Bilingual
- German

mobile Flemings into the French group, the capital and its growing suburbs were predominantly French speaking—85 percent according to some estimates made in the 1960s. Flemish nationalists threatened a boycott of the census and called for a freezing of the linguistic boundaries and increased autonomy for Flanders. The population of the Walloons continued to decline, and they feared that Wallonia, already in economic decline, would be denied financial aid by the Flemish majority.

Surprisingly, despite the historic importance of regional and language issues, the party system at the beginning of the 1960s was still based on a cleavage between Catholics, socialists, and liberals. This situation began to change in the mid-1960s when the vote going to the linguistic-regional parties increased. The Flemish party, the Volksunie, received 11.1 percent of the national vote in the 1971 elections while the two francophone parties, the Walloon Rally and the Democratic Front of Francophones, obtained 11.3 percent on a joint list. Since that date, the Francophone party vote has declined, and the Flemish party vote has remained constant.

The increased politicization of the regional and linguistic issues was resolved temporarily by a constitutional amendment in 1971, which established separate cultural councils for Dutch and French speakers composed of the members of their respective language groups in parliament. The councils had the power to legislate over cultural matters, education, international cultural exchanges, the language used in administration, and labor relations. A similar council was to be set up for the small German minority, but this and a proposal for three regional legislatures remained in limbo because the political parties were unable to agree on the details.

Subsequently, after lengthy negotiations between the major parties and another constitutional amendment in 1980, an even more comprehensive package of regionalization was enacted. The cultural councils, renamed community councils, were provided with an executive to carry out their administrative functions, and a similar set of institutions was created for Flanders and Wallonia. The Flemings combined their regional and community councils, but the French speakers kept them separate. The representatives from Brussels could sit on either the Dutch or the French councils, but they were not allowed to vote on regional issues. As a result of all these constitutional changes, contemporary Belgium might be described as a society in which its two ethnic components have mutually separated from one another although they still retain a nominal identity as a nation within the international system.

See also Volksunie; Walloon Rally.
References Fitzmaurice, John. *Politics of Belgium: A Unique Federalism* (1996); Hooghe, Liesbet. *A Leap in the Dark: Nationalist Conflict and Federal Reform in Belgium* (1991); Irving, Ronald. *The Flemings and Walloons of Belgium* (1980).

Belize

The coastal strip of the Caribbean that is known today as Belize, formerly British Honduras, was occupied by British pirates and log-cutters from the 1600s onward, despite Spanish attempts to drive them away. When neighboring Guatemala became independent in 1839, it reasserted the Spanish colonial territorial claims. In an 1859 treaty, Guatemala recognized British sovereignty over the colony, and Britain promised to build a road from the Guatemalan capital to the coast. Since the road was never built, the Guatemalans considered the treaty null and void. The issue of the Guatemalan claim was still unresolved when Belize became independent in 1981, so the British maintained a small garrison to defend the new country.

Things appeared promising when the first civilian government in Guatemala since World War II negotiated a settlement with the Belizean premier, George Price, in 1991. According to that agreement, Guatemala recognized Belizean independence, and the two countries announced that a joint economic development zone would be established along the border between the two. However, the agreement led to a military coup against the Guatemalan president, Jorge Serrano, and a defeat for George Price's People's United Party (PUP) in Belizean elections.

From its formation in 1949, PUP had advocated closer relations with Guatemala, and its party colors of blue and white were the same as those of the Guatemalan flag. The party's unexpected defeat was attributed to Belizean resentment over the large influx of refugees and landhungry Central American peasants. The population, which just prior to independence was 52 percent "creole" (black and English speaking) and 22 percent mestizo, had become predominantly mestizo by the 1991 census. The United Democratic Party criticized Price for making too many concessions in the negotiations and for allowing Hispanic immigration. The Guatemalan claim thus is a factor that leads to political polarization along ethnic lines.

References Wallace, Elizabeth M. *The British Caribbean: From the Decline of Colonialism to the End of Federation* (1977); Zammit, J. Ann. *The Belize Issue* (1978).

Ben-Gurion, David (1886–1973)

An immigrant from Poland, David Ben-Gurion was the most important figure in the Jewish movement that led to the creation of the state of Israel. Ben-Gurion first arrived in Palestine in 1906 and subsequently established the Zionist socialist party. Although expelled by the Ottoman Empire for his nationalist activism, Ben-Gurion returned to the Middle East with the British forces during World War I. In 1920, he founded Histradut, the confederation of workers that would become, in effect, a Jewish shadow government. In 1930, Ben-Gurion became head of Mapai, the social democratic party, and in 1935, he was elected chairman of the Jewish Agency, the world Zionist organization. From 1939 on, Ben-Gurion led the Zionist fight for Israeli independence, engaging British forces for control over Palestine. Following independence in 1948, Ben-Gurion became Israel's first prime minister and led the country almost continuously until his resignation in 1963.

See also Israel.
Reference Zweig, Ronald, ed. *David Ben-Gurion: Politics and Leadership in Israel* (1991).

Bhutan

A Himalayan kingdom situated between India and Tibet, Bhutan is the only state in the world in which Buddhism is the established religion. The majority of the population is culturally and racially akin to the Tibetans, but the southern part of the country is inhabited by ethnic Nepalese. The latter minority is increasing owing to immigration; officially estimated at 28 percent, the Nepalese may make up as much as 40 percent of the population. Fearing that they would become a minority in their own country, the Bhutanese adopted a "one nation, one people" policy in the 1980s and encouraged the use of the Dzongkha language and the wearing of the national costume. This resulted in widespread unrest in the Nepalese areas, and when violence between government troops and supporters of the

Biafran soldiers charge into the bush after having stripped opponents killed in a fire fight, 1968. (Express Newspapers/H007/Archive Photos)

illegal Bhutan Peoples Party (BPP) claimed hundreds of lives, the government accused the BPP of "antinational activities." Strict immigration controls were imposed because it was feared that if the Nepalese became a majority, Bhutan would be absorbed by India, as had occurred with the neighboring state of Sikkim.

A 1949 Treaty of Friendship between India and Bhutan recognized Bhutan's independence, but the royal government agreed to accept India's guidance on foreign policy. The threat from China led to a close alignment with India with respect to defense policy. Not only did Bhutan receive an annual subsidy of 500,000 rupees and other economic aid but an Indian adviser was posted to Bhutan from 1963 to 1965. Since 1971, when Bhutan joined the United Nations, there have been calls for the revision of the 1949 treaty on the grounds that it limits Bhutanese sovereignty.

See also Sikkim.
Reference Rose, Leo E. *The Politics of Bhutan* (1977).

Biafra

Biafra was the name given to the short-lived separatist nation that existed in southeastern Nigeria from 1967 until 1970. Established as the eastern state in the new Nigerian Federal Republic in 1960, the territory that was to become Biafra was predominantly populated by the Ibo, an ethnic group of about 17 million, roughly 17 percent of the total population of Nigeria. The Ibo are one of the three dominant ethnic groups in Nigeria, but their cultural traditions, local organizational structures, and history differ considerably from those of the other two major groups, the Hausa-Fulani and the Yoruba. In religion, the Ibo are largely Catholic; the Yoruba, Muslim or Anglican;

and the Hausa-Fulani, predominantly Muslim. The Ibo language is distinct from the languages spoken by the other two groups. The Ibo culture stresses individual achievement, personal advancement, and political participation. Education is highly valued, and Ibos made use of it to advance in the Nigerian federal civil service. They were also successful as small businessmen, and many migrated into cities in other parts of the country. Ibos were resented by other ethnic groups both for their competitiveness and for their successes.

Following chaotic elections in 1964 and 1965, a military coup in January 1966 established Major General Johnson Aguiyi-Ironsi, an Ibo, as head of state. Ironsi wanted to establish a unitary federal state, but his proposal that many administrative functions be taken away from the regional governments aroused fears in the north that the more highly educated Ibos would soon dominate the federal government. In July 1966, northern army officers engineered a coup, assassinated Ironsi, and replaced him with a northern general, Yakubu Gowon. Gowon decided to split the Ibo eastern region into three states. The two new states would have non-Ibo majorities, and they would cut off the remaining Ibo state from the oil fields in the old eastern region and from seaports.

In October 1966, a popular rampage against Ibos and their businesses in northern cities left thousands dead and drove nearly a million Ibos back into their eastern homeland. Although attempts to reach an accommodation between Ibos and the federal government were undertaken, the effort failed. On May 30, 1967, the Ibo, under the leadership of General Odumegwu Ojukwu, declared the secession of the former Ibo region from Nigeria. The new country was named Biafra, after the bay known as the Bight of Biafra.

The federal government refused to recognize the breakaway state, and in July 1967, the federal army, with superior numbers and weaponry, began efforts to retake the region. In hostilities that lasted until January 1970, the federal forces were victorious. Ojukwu fled the country, and on January 15, the remaining Biafran forces surrendered. Estimates of deaths from all causes in the conflict range as high as 2 million. Although the nation of Biafra ceased to exist, the federal government of Nigeria undertook a massive reconstruction of the Biafran economy, and Ibos were encouraged to participate in national life.

See also Nigeria; Ojukwu, Odumegwu.
Reference Ekwe-Ekwe, Herbert. *The Biafra War* (1990).

Black Homelands

Black homelands was the name given to those areas of South Africa that, under the apartheid system of racial segregation, were defined as the legal place of residence for the black population. According to the South African government, the blacks, who made up about three-quarters of the South African population, were divided into several nations, each with its own homeland. The homelands, which were originally called native reserves and then Bantustans, occupied about 13 percent of the total area of the Republic of South Africa. The ten homelands were largely rural, with few natural resources. Located in the eastern half of the country, they consisted of scattered strips of territory and were desperately overcrowded. The three most important were KwaZulu, Transkei, and Bophuthatswana.

Under the Bantu Homelands Citizenship Act of 1970, blacks, regardless of how long their families had lived in "white" South Africa, were considered citizens, not of the republic, but of whatever homeland their ethnic group had been allocated. Thus, Zulu were citizens of KwaZulu, Xhosa citizens were citizens of either Ciskei or Transkei, Tswana were citizens of Bophuthatswana, and so on. This policy was often implemented in an arbitrary fashion, so that Lebowa was supposedly the homeland for two groups, the Pedi and the North Ndebele, while Gazankulu was inhabited by both the Tsonga and the Shangaan.

Even in the early 1970s, most blacks lived out-

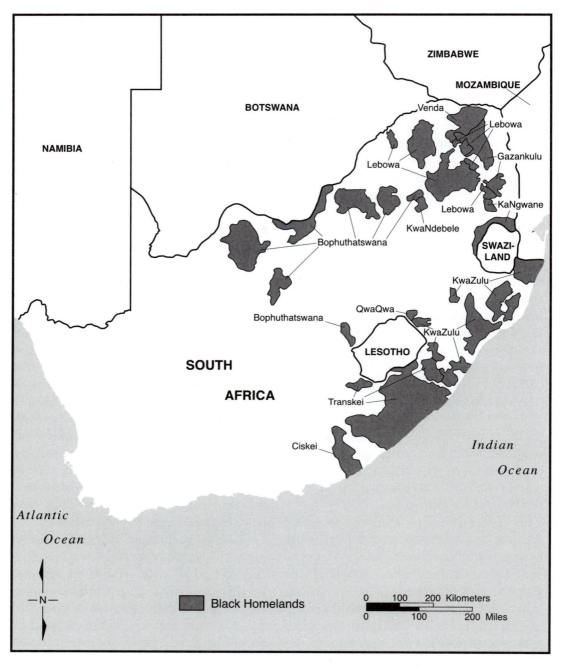

side their designated homelands, with the proportion varying from 33 percent for the Venda to 98 percent for the South Sotho. Despite an increase in the size of the homelands in 1975 and determined efforts to remove blacks from "white areas" and resettle them, 52 percent of the blacks lived outside the homelands in 1992. The failure of the government's policies reflected both the demand for black labor in the South African economy and the lack of economic opportunities in the homelands. In practice, the homelands remained impoverished labor reserves, with most of the able-bodied men working in the mines and towns of South Africa.

The homelands were granted a degree of self-government, and the ultimate goal was for them all to become independent. However, most of the revenue for the governments of the homelands came from the republic, and many of their senior officials were whites, seconded from the South African civil service. The homelands never achieved legitimacy in the eyes of either South African blacks or the international community. The four homelands that became independent by agreement with the South African government (Ciskei, Transkei, Bophuthatswana, and Venda) were never recognized diplomatically by any other country. After negotiations between the African National Congress and the South African government led to a 1994 agreement on a new democratic constitution, the homelands were reintegrated into South Africa.

See also Apartheid; Bophuthatswana; Ciskei; Gazankulu; KwaNdebele; KwaZulu; Lebowa; QwaQwa; South Africa; Transkei; Venda.
References Butler, Jeffrey, Robert Rotberg, and John Adams. *The Black Homelands of South Africa* (1977); Carter, Gwendolyn, Thomas Karis, and Newell M. Stultz. *South Africa's Transkei: The Politics of Domestic Colonialism* (1967); Hill, Christopher. *Bantustans: The Fragmentation of South Africa* (1964); Horrell, Muriel. *The African Homelands of South Africa* (1973).

Black Separatism in the United States

Black Americans in the United States have, for the most part, sought full citizenship rights and integration into society. However, a minority has sometimes embraced a separatist or black nationalist ideology. In the 1920s, Marcus Garvey's Negro Improvement Association called on blacks to emigrate back to Africa. Subsequently, the Nation of Islam, popularly called the Black Muslims, became the main bearer of black nationalist sentiments, and many African Americans who joined the movement found its racial separatism appealing.

After World War II, the preconditions for black separatism were fostered by the massive migration of rural southern blacks to New York City, Chicago, Detroit, Los Angeles, and other large cities. Concentrated in racially segregated neighborhoods, urban blacks developed a distinctive culture and a sense of common identity. Kenneth Kusmer argues that black nationalism appealed to many because they were, for the first time, living in a social environment that resembled (on a small scale) an all-black nation. Those favoring a "separate negro nation" increased from 4 percent in 1963 to 21 percent in 1969.

Black nationalism took several forms. The leader of the Nation of Islam, Elijah Muhammed, wavered between the emigration option and the demand that a black state be set up in the American South. In a speech given in New York City, he demanded that whites hand over "three or four or more states" for the establishment of a sovereign black nation and provide financial assistance to it for twenty-five years. The similarities between black separatist and white racist ideologies led to a meeting between Malcolm X and the Ku Klux Klan, at which a nonaggression pact was negotiated. Elijah Muhammad also corresponded with George Lincoln Rockwell, the leader of the American Nazi Party, and a contingent of uniformed Nazis attended a Nation of Islam convention in February 1962.

Another black separatist group, the Republic of New Africa (RNA), founded in March 1968, called for an independent black nation to be carved out of the states of Alabama, Georgia, Louisiana, South Carolina, and Mississippi. In 1971, 150 members of the group purchased twenty acres of farmland in Mississippi and declared it the capital of the Republic of New Africa. RNA members were involved in a series of shootouts with police and FBI agents.

Maulana Karenga, another black separatist, argued that black liberation required a cultural revolution, and he advocated that American blacks learn Swahili, change their "slave names" to African names, and adopt other aspects of African culture. He created the holiday of Kwanzaa, a week-long celebration of black heritage. Karenga's organization, US, soon became involved in a deadly rivalry with the Black Panthers, who were led by Huey Newton and Eldridge Cleaver. The Black Panthers were opposed to cultural nationalism, seeing it as a reactionary diversion from the need to create a revolutionary consciousness among blacks. The two groups also disagreed over who the main enemy was and who they should make alliances with. Karenga argued for a united front of all black groups against white racism while the Black Panthers were willing to ally with white radicals to overthrow capitalism. Hostilities between the Black Panthers and the government led to several deaths.

Several attempts were made to unite the different black political groups, the most successful being the Congress of African People held in Atlanta in 1970, which attracted 3,000 participants. Those attending included civil rights leaders like Whitney Young of the National Urban League and Ralph Abernathy of the Southern Christian Leadership Conference as well as representatives of the Nation of Islam and the RNA. The influence of the black nationalist ideology was seen in the slogan on the conference banners, It's Nation Time! The congress represented the high point of black nationalism in the United States, and the influence of that ideology declined subsequently. However, the black nationalist ideology inspired political mobilization and led to the election of black mayors in many cities, the creation of Afrocentric schools, and black studies programs. The African Liberation Support Committee played a major role in supporting African anticolonial struggles and the anti-apartheid movement in South Africa.

See also Pan-Africanism.
References Clegg, Claude. *An Original Man: The Life and Times of Elijah Muhammed* (1997); Hall, Raymond L. *Black Separatism in the United States* (1978); Kusmer, Kenneth. *A Ghetto Takes Shape* (1978); Woodard, Komozi. *A Nation within a Nation* (1999).

Bophuthatswana

The homeland for the Tswana people of South Africa, Bophuthatswana was set up in 1971 and became independent in 1977 under Lucas Mangope. Originally consisting of nineteen separate pieces of land scattered throughout the northern Transvaal and Cape provinces in South Africa, these were consolidated into ten and the area increased by 254,000 hectares in 1973. Mangope himself had proposed that a much larger amount of land, totaling several million hectares, be transferred to Bophuthatswana. The first election of 1972 pitted Mangope's Bophuthatswana National Party against the Unity Party of Tidimane Pilane. Backed by the rural electors, Mangope won twenty of the twenty-four seats and two-thirds of the vote. However, only about half those eligible voted, and in urban areas less than one in ten. As in other homelands, a majority (65 percent) of Bophuthatswana's citizens lived outside its borders. Furthermore, almost a third of the population was not ethnic Tswana.

Although he took part in the first summit of eight homeland leaders convened in 1973, which concluded with calls for a black federation, Mangope expressed a preference for links with Botswana. Botswana, like Bophuthatswana, is predominantly inhabited by ethnic Tswana and had been independent since 1966. In November 1975, a meeting of Tswana chiefs and headmen called for independence, and this was followed by supportive resolutions passed by the Bophuthatswana National Party and the legislative assembly. After independence, Mangope's rule became increasingly authoritarian, and his opponents were imprisoned and intimidated. Economically, Bophuthatswana had several assets including a $1 billion mining industry and a booming tourist trade. Ironically, the main attractions of the country's Sun City tourist complex were gambling and interracial sex, both forbidden in South Africa.

During negotiations between the South African government and the African National Congress (ANC) about the constitution for a postapartheid state, Mangope took a hard-line position and called for Bophuthatswana to remain independent. However, the evidence suggests that his regime lacked popular support. According to a 1991 survey commissioned by the South African government, less than half the population supported Mangope, and in the homeland's last election in 1985, the turnout was less than 1 percent. An attempted military coup in 1988 was thwarted only by the intervention of the South African army.

In March 1994, first Bophuthatswana's civil servants and then the police went on strike, students took over the university, and looters rampaged unchecked through Mmabatho, the capital. Mangope then appealed for assistance to the Volksfront, a militia force organized by right-wing whites. The ill-disciplined militia drove through the streets of Mmabatho yelling racial abuse and shooting at the local blacks. Their behavior so outraged Bophuthatswana's army that the soldiers mutinied and joined the rebellion against Mangope. The militia withdrew in disarray, and television cameras broadcast the execution of three wounded whites by the Bophuthatswana police. The failure of the intervention meant that the threat of military resistance by white extremists was over. Mangope was forced to resign, and Bophuthatswana was reincorporated into South Africa. In the first multiracial elections held in April 1994, it was estimated that 83 percent of the Tswana voted for the ANC.

See also Black Homelands; Mangope, Lucas.
Reference Sparks, Allister. *Tomorrow Is Another Country: The Inside Story of South Africa's Road to Change* (1995).

Bosnia and Herzegovina

Bosnia and Herzegovina were settled by southern Slavs in the seventh century. Although both Serbs and Croats claim the land as theirs, it is unclear which group, if either, made up the original Slav settlers. From the twelfth century to the fourteenth, an independent Bosnian kingdom existed, and it was populated by Catholic and Orthodox believers as well as a substantial number of Bogomils, an ascetic Christian sect later con-

demned for heresy because of its rejection of much of the Old Testament. Following the Turkish conquest in 1463, large numbers of Bosnians converted to Islam, partly because only Muslims were permitted to own land. Muslims then dominated the feudal agrarian system until large-scale land reforms were undertaken in the twentieth century.

In 1875 the Christian peasantry, backed by Serbia, revolted. To prevent Serbian domination of Bosnia, the Austro-Hungarian monarchy assumed administrative control over the area in 1878, although Bosnia remained nominally under Turkish suzerainty. In 1918, following the defeat of the Austro-Hungarian and Ottoman Empires, Bosnia-Herzegovina was annexed to Serbia and became part of the Kingdom of Serbs, Croats, and Slovenes, later known as Yugoslavia. In World War II, as an ally of Germany and Italy, Croatia was awarded Bosnia and Herzegovina. Following the war, Bosnia and Herzegovina became one of the six republics of the Communist Yugoslav federation. In 1991, as the Yugoslav state disintegrated, Bosnia feared Serbia's power and declared independence. This action triggered a Serb, Croat, and Muslim civil war in the republic.

In marked contrast to Serbia, Slovenia, and Croatia, the Bosnian republic of Yugoslavia was a multiethnic state—40 percent Serb, 38 percent Muslim, and 22 percent Croat. Its president, Alija Izetbegovic, elected in 1990, stood for an autonomous, multireligious, and democratic Bosnia, and his views prevailed in a 1992 referendum that declared Bosnia independent. However, an analysis of voting in the election reveals a pronounced and persistent split along ethnic lines, with Muslims and Croats generally favoring independence, because of their fears of Serb domination, and Serbs opposing it.

The Bosnian declaration of independence led Bosnian Serbs to declare their territories an independent state, the Republic of Srpska, under the leadership of Radovan Karadzic. By 1994, aided by the truncated Yugoslav state in Belgrade, Serbian military forces under General Ratko Mladic had taken control of over 70 percent of the territory of Bosnia-Herzegovina. Despite appeals from the Bosnian government, UN intervention in the conflict was ineffective in slowing Serbian advances or in preventing the slaughter, imprisonment, or expulsion of non-Serbs from the territories controlled by Karadzic supporters. The strategy of "ethnic cleansing" pursued by the Serbs may have resulted in the expulsion of up to 700,000 Muslims from areas under their control. With encouragement from Zagreb, Bosnian Croats seized control of territory inhabited by Croats and engaged in military battles with Muslims, declaring Croatian areas of Bosnia to be the new state of Herzeg-Bosnia.

As a result of international pressure, Bosnian Muslims and Croats ceased overt hostilities and formed a Bosnian-Croat federation, which, along with the Serbian Republic of Srpska, would constitute the new Bosnian state. The Dayton peace accord, signed in 1995 by the presidents of Bosnia, Croatia, and Serbia, awarded the Bosnian-Croat federation 51 percent of the territory of Bosnia; Serbs received 49 percent. A central government with a parliament and a collective presidency was established with the top vote getter serving as chairman of the presidency. In subsequent elections, the three major nationalist parties prevailed in their own areas of control. Alija Izetbegovic of the Muslim Party of Democratic Action (SDA) received the most votes—over 700,000—followed by Momcilo Krajisnic of the Serbian Democratic Party (SDS) and, in third place, Kresimir Zubak of the Croatian Democratic Union (HDZ). The Muslim SDA also won the largest number of seats, nineteen, in the forty-two-member Bosnian parliament.

The presence of 30,000 NATO troops has to date maintained an uneasy peace in the region. However, there has been no meaningful reconciliation among the three parties to the conflict, and Bosnia continues to function as three separate substates divided by their historical antagonisms, their religions, and their social and civic institutions. Efforts to resettle refugees have been disappointing in every area of the country.

See also Croatia; Dayton Peace Accord; Ethnic Cleansing; Greater Serbia; Herzeg-Bosnia; Izetbegovic, Aliya; Milosevic, Slobodan; North Atlantic Treaty Organization; Organization for Security and Cooperation in Europe; Srpska; Tudjman, Franjo; Yugoslavia.

References Friedman, Francine. *The Bosnian Muslims: Denial of a Nation* (1996); Malcolm, Noel. *Bosnia: A Short History* (1996); Sells, Michael Anthony. *The Bridge Betrayed: Religion and Genocide in Bosnia* (1996).

Bougainville

Bougainville Island is culturally and geographically a part of the Solomon Islands but is politically part of Papua New Guinea. Bougainville declared independence as the Republic of the North Solomons in September 1974, three weeks before Papua New Guinea became independent. The rebels set up their own administration and in January 1976, fearing an attack, dug up the airstrips. The conflict was temporarily resolved by granting Bougainville autonomy within a provincial structure. The secessionist movement was partly inspired by a desire to control the island's rich Panguna copper mine, which provides 40 percent of the value of Papua New Guinea's exports.

The influx of immigrants to work in the mines caused tensions between the black Bougainvilleans and the Papuans, who are referred to as "redskins." Violence broke out again in 1989, and the Bougainville Revolutionary Army forced the withdrawal of police and army units from the island. The central government blockaded the island, and the deadlock between the two sides lasted despite several rounds of talks. A 1995 agreement set up a provincial legislature for Bougainville and granted amnesty to the rebel leaders, but fighting resumed again in 1996. In 1998, a permanent cease-fire agreement was signed between the Bougainville Revolutionary Army and the government of Papua New Guinea, ending a conflict that has claimed almost 20,000 lives. The rebels declared themselves to be the Bougainville Interim Government/ Bougainville Revolutionary Army (BIG/BRA), but it is unclear if they are in control of the whole island.

Papua New Guinea, which was administered by Australia until 1975, still receives considerable economic aid and military assistance from that country. Australia was opposed to the secession, although the legislature of the Solomon Islands has called for the "reunion" of the island with the North Solomons.

Reference May, J. R., and Matthew Spriggs, eds. *The Bougainville Crisis* (1990).

Brittany

Brittany has been a province of France since 1532, and of the four million people living in the peninsular region, about ten percent still speak Breton, a Celtic language related to Welsh. Until very recent times, schoolchildren using the Breton language were punished and humiliated. Teachers would hang an old shoe, referred to as "the symbole," around the neck of any pupil who was overheard speaking in Breton. Signs posted in school playgrounds warned that it was illegal to spit or to speak in Breton. In the late-nineteenth and early-twentieth centuries, a Breton separatist movement grew up among writers and other intellectuals, and the Union Regionaliste Bretonne was set up in 1898 to revive and develop Breton culture. Most of those active in the movement were strongly Catholic and royalist in their politics. During the German occupation of France, a number of Breton separatists were collaborators, and some even formed a military unit within the German army. After the liberation, the French government banned many Breton organizations and imprisoned or executed several hundred separatists. Tainted by its wartime history, Breton nationalism remained a marginal force until the late 1950s when falling agricultural prices provoked widespread and violent demonstrations by angry Breton farmers.

In 1957, Yann Fouere, a veteran nationalist leader who had been cleared of charges of wartime collaboration, launched the Mouvement pour l'Organization de la Bretagne (MOB) to study the socioeconomic problems of the region and to pressure the French government into implementing a development plan. MOB declared itself to be a nonpartisan movement, and the movement included all shades of opinion from extreme right to extreme left. MOB put forward a colonialist interpretation of Brittany's situation, arguing that Paris treated the region as a source of cheap labor, stripped it of its natural resources, and deliberately retarded its economic development. In the 1958 parliamentary elections, candidates running on a Breton regionalist platform won 23 percent of the vote in their districts. The following month, MOB candidates were elected to three municipal councils. However, despite these early successes, the movement suffered from increasingly bitter ideological divisions, and in 1962, the left-wing broke away to form the Union Democratique Bretonne.

During the 1960s, there was a revival of Breton culture, which served to foster an increasing sense of Celtic identity, particularly among the young. Concerts by Breton folksingers such as

Gilles Servat were like mass political rallies, with the audience enthusiastically applauding songs about French oppression and Breton resistance. During the same period, there was also a campaign for the increased use of Breton in the schools led by the journal *Ar Falz* and the emergence of the Front de Libération de la Bretagne, a terrorist organization. In 1975, the French government announced that it would begin subsidizing the teaching of the Breton language in state schools. Currently 10,000 adults are enrolled in evening classes in Breton, and there are 5,000 pupils in the 34 schools where instruction is in the Breton language.

See also Front de Libération de la Bretagne; Union Democratique Bretonne.
Reference Reece, Jack E. *The Bretons against France* (1977).

Buganda

Buganda was one of four "treaty kingdoms" in the British colony of Uganda in East Africa until they were abolished in 1966. The other three kingdoms were Toro, Bunyoro, and Ankole. Beginning in the 1500s, the Baganda people evolved a highly advanced state under a ruling monarch, the kabaka. The famous explorer Henry Stanley described Kabaka Mutesa I as "a powerful emperor, with great influence over his neighbours." In 1893, the British negotiated a treaty with Mutesa under which Buganda became a protectorate, and British power was gradually extended to the three other kingdoms and to the northern tribes.

Buganda was the nucleus of the British colony, and Kampala, the capital of Buganda, became the commercial center of the whole of Uganda. The British adopted a policy of indirect rule, whereby Britain administered Buganda (and the other parts of Uganda) through the established system of indigenous government. Thus, the kabaka was recognized as the legal head of state, and the kingdom was divided into twenty counties, each one under a chief selected by the kabaka. A legislature, the Lukiiko, consisting of representatives of the feudal nobility from each county, had extensive powers. The Baganda were the largest tribe in Uganda, numbering nearly 1.5 million (about 17 percent of the total population) at the time of independence in 1962. Its members regarded themselves as superior to the other tribes, and this cultural chauvinism created resentment among other Ugandans. When the kabaka was deported by the British in 1953 for his opposition to Britain's proposal that Uganda should be included in an East African Federation with Kenya and Tanganyika, there was widespread indignation. The kabaka was restored to his position in 1955, with his prestige and popularity enhanced.

When it became clear that Britain was preparing to grant Uganda independence, the Bagandan traditionalists became apprehensive. What would be the position of the kabaka in an independent Uganda, and what would be the relationship between Buganda and the central government? They boycotted the legislative elections held in 1958, and although nationally almost 80 percent of the electorate voted, in Buganda the proportion was only 4 percent. In December, the Lukiiko sent a memorandum to London calling for the termination of Buganda's agreement with Britain. The memorandum emphasized Buganda's special position and argued that most of the government's tax revenue "comes from Buganda. . . . while Buganda receives back a mere pittance of what it subscribes." It went on to imply that Ankole, Toro, and Bunyoro were dependencies of Buganda, but this arrogant claim antagonized the three other kingdoms and further isolated Buganda politically. During the constitutional negotiations with Britain, the Lukiiko demanded Buganda's own army, courts, and legislature. Finally, on December 31, 1960, the Lukiiko declared Buganda independent, although the declaration had no practical effect.

In the Ugandan elections of 1961, the Democratic Party (DP) achieved a narrow victory by winning forty-three seats, and the Uganda Peoples Congress (UPC) won thirty-five. However, despite winning a bare plurality of the total vote, the DP victory was based on the fact that it won twenty-one seats in Buganda. That total did not reflect any significant support within Buganda for the party but was a result of the election boycott by the traditionalists. In one constituency, for example, the DP polled only seventy-two votes and won with a majority of eleven. Following the elections, a constitutional commission, headed by Lord Munster, proposed a quasi-federal system with Buganda having the right to legislate on matters involving the kabaka and traditional custom. The other three kingdoms received somewhat less autonomy. A dispute between Buganda and Bunyoro over "the lost counties" was to be resolved by a postindependence referendum.

The UPC, led by Milton Obote, and the Baganda traditionalists then entered into a tactical alliance. The Lukiiko abandoned its secessionist stance and organized a new political party to represent Buganda—the Kabaka Yekka (literally, "the king alone"). The UPC and the Kabaka Yekka together won a majority in the April 1962 elections and formed a coalition government, with Milton Obote becoming the first prime minister of an independent Uganda. In October 1962, when Uganda became independent, the kabaka, Sir Edward Mutesa II, became the country's first president. Over the next few years, Obote consolidated his power, and in February 1966, he suspended the constitution and assumed absolute power. The kabaka was dismissed as president, and the Lukiiko passed a secession resolution calling on the central government to quit Buganda. Unrest in Buganda increased with insurgents blocking roads and attacking police posts. This precipitated the Battle of Mengo in May 1966, when the kabaka's palace was assaulted by the Ugandan army and hundreds lost their lives in the attack. The kabaka escaped and went into exile in England. Subsequently, the Kingdom of Buganda was abolished, as were the other three treaty kingdoms of Ankole, Bunyoro, and Toro.

See also Kabaka Yekka; Lost Counties of Bunyoro.
References Ibingira, Grace Stuart. *The Forging of an*

African Nation (1973); Mutibwa, Phares. *Uganda since Independence* (1992).

Burma

Physically and culturally, Burma (also known as Myanmar) is divided into two regions. The central lowlands and Irrawaddy delta are inhabited by the Burmans, the dominant ethnic group, who make up about 60 percent of the population, and the surrounding plateau and mountain region is the home of a diverse collection of more than a hundred ethnic minorities. The most important of these are the Karen (10 percent), the Shan (8 percent), the Mon (8 percent), the Arakanese (4 percent), the Kachin (3 percent), and the Chin (2

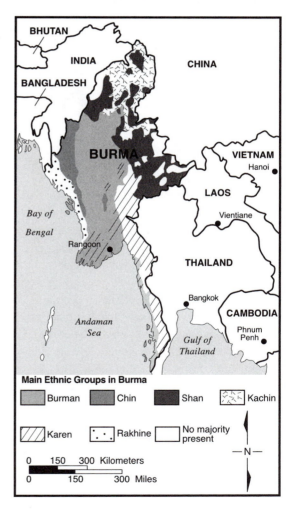

Main Ethnic Groups in Burma

Karen fighters parade at a camp in western Burma (Myanmar). Karen rebels have been resisting the central government since the country's independence in 1948. (AP/Sakchai Lalit)

percent). The Burmans, Mon, and Shan are Buddhists; the Karen, Kachin, and Chin are predominantly Christian; and many of the Arakanese are Muslims. Since independence from Britain in 1948, Burma has been plagued by persistent dissension and chronic insurgencies arising from the separatist movements of the hill peoples.

The Burmese kings were able, for brief periods, to extend their control over most of the territory that now makes up modern Burma, receiving tribute from the Shan, Chin, and other peoples. While Burma was a British colony, the ethnic minorities were administered separately from the rest of the country, which exacerbated the division between them and the majority Burmans. Under the 1937 constitution, "ministerial Burma" was divided from the border areas, which were themselves divided into part-one areas

under the direct control of the governor and part-two areas under the legislature.

Aung San, who led Burma to independence, argued that nationalism should be based on a sense of oneness and that a nation was "a conglomeration of races and religions that should develop a nationalism that is common with the welfare of one and all." After a series of meetings at Panglong between the British and Aung San, a quasi-federal structure was proposed for what was to become the Union of Burma. Under the Panglong agreement, a Kachin state, a Shan state, and a Kayah state were created, and a Chin special division was established. However, the Karen demand for a separate Karen state was denied, and the Karen therefore boycotted the Constituent Assembly elections. During the first few years of independence, the country was torn apart by insurgencies mounted by two Communist factions, the Karen and a group seeking to set up an independent Islamic state in northern Arakan. At one point in 1949, most of the countryside was in the hands of one or the other insurgent group.

After a military coup, negotiations between the new government and the various Communist and ethnic insurgents began in June 1963 but broke down later in the year without any peace agreement being concluded. In 1964, the military government issued a declaration on "the question of the union nationalities," which warned that divisive movements would not be tolerated, and embarked on a policy of Burmanization. Burmese was declared the only language for education and government business while Buddhist missions to the hill peoples were organized by the Ministry of Religious Affairs. The government replaced the federal-style administrative structure with a more centralized system, dividing the country into seven states (corresponding in a sense to the areas occupied by the seven most important minorities) and seven divisions (mostly inhabited by ethnic Burmans). There is, however, a considerable degree of geographical mixing of the groups, so the ethnic populations in each state rarely match the name of the state. Thus, there are large numbers of Burmans and Karen in the Mon state and large numbers of Kachin in the Shan state.

The unwillingness of the Burman-dominated government to recognize the rights of the minority peoples has produced chronic warfare between the Burmese army and the ethnic insurgents, with at least twenty-seven rebel groups being active as of 1992. However, the involvement of many of these groups in the opium trade makes it difficult to distinguish them from mere bandits and warlords. In recent years, the military dictatorship has been successful in reducing ethnic insurgencies. Cease-fire agreements were negotiated with the Kachin and other groups, incorporating the guerrillas into the national militia and tolerating the guerrillas involvement in smuggling activities. Government troops captured the main base of the Karen National Union in 1992.

See also Arakan; Kachin; Karen; Mon; Shan.
References Cady, John. *A History of Modern Burma* (1960); Fredholm, Michael. *Burma: Ethnicity and Insurgency* (1993); Smith, Martin. *Burma Insurgency and the Politics of Ethnicity* (1991).

Buryatia

Buryatia, a republic within the Russian Federation, is located in southern Siberia to the north of Mongolia. Out of a population of 1 million, only one-third are Buryats; the remainder are mostly Russian and other Slavs.

The Buryats are related by language and history to the Mongols. In the seventeenth century, traditionally shamanistic Buryats were converted to Buddhism. In 1727, czarist Russia annexed Buryatia and encouraged Russians to settle in the region. In 1923, now under Soviet control, Buryatia became the Buryat-Mongol Autonomous Region. Buryat's status was raised to that of an autonomous republic in 1958. With the breakup of the USSR in 1991, Buryatia became a constituent republic of the Russian Federation.

The nationalist Buryat Mongolian People's Party and a cultural organization, the Buryat Cultural Heritage Association, have been instrumental in securing changes in the Buryatia constitution. The Buryat language is now taught in the public schools. A knowledge of both Russian and Buryatian is a prerequisite for high government offices, a measure unpopular among ethnic Russians.

The rise of Buryat nationalism is linked to the revival of the traditional Lamaist Buddhist religion. The Buddhists, however, have split into two rival factions, and they battle each other on the streets. With Russians forming a majority of the voters and a pro-Russian Buryat president, Leonid Potapov, separatist agitation in Buryatia remains muted.

See also Russian Federation.
Reference Wixman, Ronald. *The Peoples of the USSR: An Ethnographic Handbook* (1984).

Buthelezi, Mangosuthu (1928–)

Mangosuthu Buthelezi is a political leader of the Zulu of South Africa. Born in 1928, Buthelezi is of royal lineage and was brought up in the household of his uncle, the paramount chief of the Zulu. While a student at Fort Hare University, he became a member of the African National Congress (ANC) and was expelled for his political activities. After receiving a degree in history from the University of Natal, he succeeded his father as a tribal chief of the Buthelezi clan in 1953. Buthelezi led the resistance to South African attempts, under the Bantu Authorities Act, to set up a system of local government in the Zulu region. Finally, deciding that further resistance was useless, he was elected chief councillor and later chief minister of KwaZulu, the Zulu homeland. Buthelezi used his position as head of KwaZulu to

denounce the injustices of the apartheid system. The *Washington Post* declared in an editorial on March 23, 1975, that Buthelezi had "trapped white South Africa in its own bantustan logic" since the government could not remove him without destroying the legitimacy of its homeland policy. He demanded the right to pay state visits to foreign countries and made English the language of instruction in the KwaZulu schools.

As a more militant mood grew among young blacks, Buthelezi found himself increasingly at odds with the ANC. Buthelezi objected to the destruction and violence of the radicals and their calls for foreign businesses to pull out of South Africa, arguing that this would only hurt the black community. Finally in 1980, the ANC broke off relations with him, accusing Buthelezi of betraying the struggle against the apartheid

Children next to an Inkatha Freedom Party campaign poster during a rally in Thokoza township, May 13, 1999. Hundreds of supporters turned out to see party leader Mangosuthu Buthelezi. (Reuters/Juda Ngwenya/Archive Photos)

regime. There were repeated clashes between those who supported the ANC and Inkatha, the organization Buthelezi created to mobilize his traditional Zulu supporters.

When negotiations began between the ANC and the South African government in 1991, Buthelezi was a reluctant participant and agreed to participate in the first all-race elections only days before they were due to be held. In the 1994 elections, Inkatha won a narrow victory in KwaZulu-Natal. Buthelezi continues to demand more autonomy for the Zulu.

See also Black Homelands.
References Butler, Jeffrey, Robert Rotberg, and John Adams. *The Black Homelands of South Africa* (1977); Reed, D. "South Africa's Champion of Nonviolence" (1983).

Cameroon

The German colony of Kamerun (now Cameroon) became a League of Nations mandate after World War I and was divided between Britain and France. France received most of the territory while Britain acquired two noncontiguous strips along the Nigerian border. The first call for reunification of the Cameroons came in 1948, from the Cameroons Federal Union, which had been set up by Dr. Emmanuel Endeley in the British Southern Cameroons.

The British administered the territory as though it were an integral part of the eastern region of Nigeria. However, the inhabitants of the Southern Cameroons resented the immigration of Nigerian Ibos into their land and what they saw as neglect by both Nigeria and the government of the eastern region. Endeley, who was the son of a Bakweri chief, saw the unification issue as a way of attracting UN attention and also of pressuring the British into concessions over Bakweri land claims. In 1949, Endeley organized a conference of political groups from both the British and the French Cameroons, at which he charged that the British Cameroons had been "shockingly neglected" and demanded that they be transferred to French trusteeship. In the French Cameroons, calls for reunification came from the Douala and Bamileke, who straddled the border between the two Cameroons. This demand was taken up by the Um Nyobe, the leader of the Union des Populations du Cameroun (UPC) and by the French Cameroons Welfare Union.

It appears, however, that Endeley was primarily interested in using the unification issue as a tactic for gaining greater autonomy within Nigeria. At the Nigerian constitutional talks held in London in 1953, he argued for a separate Cameroons region with its own legislature. After his Kamerun National Congress (KNC) party had captured all six Cameroon seats in the next Nigerian federal elections, a Southern Cameroons Assembly was set up in 1954, and the KNC won twelve of the thirteen elective seats. The growth of anti-Nigerian feeling within the region

resulted in declining support for the KNC. Endeley's party won a slim majority in the 1957 assembly elections but lost to the strongly pro-unification Kamerun National Democratic Party (KNDP) in 1959.

The United Nations, which had responsibility for overseeing the trusteeship, called for plebiscites to be held separately in both the Northern and the Southern Cameroons. The plebiscites, which were held in February 1961, showed a clear majority (70.7 percent) of those voting in the south favoring unification with the Cameroun Republic and an equally clear majority (60.0 percent) in the north favoring integration with Nigeria. After negotiations between the Cameroon Republic, which had become independent in January 1960, and the Southern Cameroons, the two united to become the Federal Republic of Cameroun on October 1, 1961. Up until 1972, the country remained a loose federation, with the president being from the French-speaking eastern part and the vice-president from the English-speaking western region. In 1972, Cameroun became a unitary one-party state when the two main political parties merged to form the Union Nationale Camerounaise.

There have been signs of tension between the two regions. The anglophone Cameroon Action Movement (founded in 1980) advocates a return to the federal government system, and the Southern

Cameroon National Congress (SCNC) is avowedly secessionist. The discovery of oil in the western part of the country has been an additional factor in encouraging separatist sentiments. In August 1995, the SCNC petitioned the United Nations, calling for independence for the western region, and in March 1997, SCNC guerrillas attacked a police post in the town of Bamenda.

References Gardinier, David. *Cameroon: United Nations Challenge to French Policy* (1963); LeVine, Victor T. *The Cameroons: From Mandate to Independence* (1964).

Canary Islands

A group of Atlantic islands, the Canary Islands lie sixty-five miles off the northern coast of Africa. The original inhabitants, the Guanche, were killed or absorbed by Spanish colonists in the early 1400s. The islands are part of Spain and include the provinces of Las Palmas and Tenerife. Although Castilian in language and culture, the islanders perceive their region to be neglected by the central government. In a 1979 survey, 51 percent thought that the Canaries were treated unfairly compared to other parts of Spain. However, the survey found that only 4 percent wanted independence while a majority favored a limited degree of autonomy. Regionalist parties obtained 6.8 percent of the vote in the Spanish national elections of 1977 and 14.5 percent in 1979, with the pro-independence Union del Pueblo Canario winning one seat in 1979. The pro-autonomy Independent Grouping of the Canaries received 60,000 votes in the 1986 elections and won one seat. The Canarian Coalition won a plurality of seats in the 1994 regional elections while the pro-independence Canarian Nationalist Party won four seats.

In 1961, the Movement for the Self-Determination and Independence of the Canary Archipelago (MPAIAC) was set up by Antonio Cubillo, with its headquarters in Algiers. The MPAIAC called on Spain to negotiate the independence of the Canaries, and in 1976, announced a campaign of armed struggle. Over eighty bombings took place in 1977, most intended to disrupt the island's tourist industry. Several fatalities have resulted from the MPAIAC's activities: a terrorist was shot dead by a soldier while planting a bomb, a student was killed during an MPAIAC demonstration, and a policeman died from injuries he received while defusing a bomb. When MPAIAC terrorists bombed Las Palmas airport, two jets were diverted to Tenerife, where they collided killing 582 passengers. In 1978, an attempt was made to assassinate Cubillo in Algiers, allegedly by agents of the Spanish secret service. The MPAIAC has carried out no actions since 1980.

Reference Gunther, Richard, Giacomo Sani, and Goldie Shabad. *Spain after Franco* (1986).

Cape Verde

A group of islands lying 400 miles off the west coast of Africa, Cape Verde was a Portuguese colony until 1975. Most of the population is mestizo, of mixed Portuguese and African descent. The main independence movement, the African Party for the Independence of Guinea and Cape Verde (PAIGC), called for the union of Cape Verde and Guinea-Bissau, but the Democratic Union of Cape Verde rejected the idea. Although both countries were ruled by the PAIGC, the issue of unification between the two Portuguese ex-colonies remained in limbo until 1980 when a coup in Guinea-Bissau overthrew the government of Luis Cabral. The coup was apparently motivated by black resentment against the mestizo-dominated government (Cabral was a mestizo, as were the only two cabinet ministers to be killed during the coup).

Following the coup, the Cape Verdean Assembly voted to amend the constitution to remove all references to eventual union with Guinea-Bissau. The Cape Verdean branch of the PAIGC changed its name to the African Party for the Independence of Cape Verde (PAICV). Although diplomatic ties between the two countries were resumed in 1982, any political union between them seems unlikely. In the first multiparty elections held in early 1991, the PAICV was soundly defeated by the Movement for Democracy.

Reference Davidson, Basil. *No Fist Is Big Enough to Hide the Sky: The Liberation of Guine and Cape Verde* (1981).

Casamance

The Casamance region of southern Senegal is inhabited by the Diola (or Jola), who differ from the rest of the population with regard to language. Also unlike the majority of the Senegalese, the Diola are not Muslims. The Casamance region, which is isolated from the rest of Senegal by the Gambia, was historically neglected, both under French colonial rule and after Senegal became independent in 1960. Several movements for independence emerged in the early 1960s, but the first serious clashes between separatists and the Senegalese army occurred in 1982 in the town of Ziguinchor. Violence broke out again in 1987 and 1990, and over 1,000 people were killed.

Talks between the separatist Casamance Movement of Democratic Forces, led by Augustin Senghor, and the Senegalese government took place in 1991 and 1996 but were unsuccessful in resolving the conflict. Guinea-Bissau was accused of supporting the separatists, and Senegalese aircraft have bombed suspected Casamance bases in that country. The government set up regional councils throughout Senegal with powers over education and development policy, but this had little effect on the rebellion. In 1997, heavy fighting was reported with over 400 dead. The rebels were accused of laying personnel mines, which led to large numbers of civilian casualties, and it was reported that the Senegalese army used torture and summary execution against suspected separatists.

Reference Phillips, Lucy Colvin. *Historical Dictionary of Senegal* (1981).

Catalonia

Despite a long history of resistance, Catalonia has been ruled as part of Spain since 1714 and is one of the most prosperous and industrialized regions of that country. Massive immigration of workers from the rest of Spain changed the ethnic-linguistic mix of the area, and non-Catalan speakers now constitute a majority in the capital city of Barcelona and about half the total population. During the Spanish Civil War, Catalonia sided with the republic, and under Franco's dictatorship its autonomy was revoked and its culture repressed. No books or newspapers could be printed in Catalan, and the use of the language was forbidden in schools and colleges. People were even fined for speaking Catalan in public; all official business had to be transacted in Castilian. The names of towns, rivers, and mountains were changed to conform to the Castilian spelling.

When the first democratic elections after the death of Franco were held in 1977, the parties in favor of regional autonomy swept the board, and in a 1979 referendum, 89 percent voted in favor of restoring the Generalitat, the traditional regional government. In elections to the new legislature, the moderate nationalist Convergencio i Unio (CiU) took 43 of the 135 seats while the Catalan Socialist Party came in second with 33 seats. In later elections, the CiU consolidated its dominant political position. A 1984 poll taken in Barcelona found a strong sense of Catalan national identity, with 27 percent of the respondents saying they felt "only Catalan" and 16 percent saying they felt "more Catalan than Spanish." Nineteen percent wanted an independent Catalan state. Catalan nationalism appeals to all classes and to both native born and immigrants. A handful of terrorist bombings have been carried out by a group calling itself Terra Lluire (Free Land), but for the most part, Catalan separatism has been nonviolent.

See also Spain.
References Conversi, Daniel. *The Basques, the Catalans, and Spain* (1997); Moxon-Brown, Edward. *Political Change in Spain* (1989).

Césaire, Aimé (1913–)

A writer and politician in Martinique, Aimé Césaire, along with Leopold Senghor, was one of the major figures in "négritude," a literary movement that stressed racial consciousness in opposition to the prevailing assimilationist philosophy. According to Césaire, négritude is "the affirmation that one is black and proud of it . . . that there is a solidarity between all blacks." His first book, *Return to My Native Land* (1939), is a rejection of the white world with its slavery and racism, and his later works, *The Tragedy of King Christophe* (1963) and *A Season in the Congo* (1967), deal with the formation of independent black nations. Négritude as a philosophy was challenged in the 1970s by an alternative theory of "creolite," which argues that West Indian culture is a blend of diverse elements.

As deputy to the French National Assembly and mayor of Fort-de-France, Césaire dominated Martinican politics from 1945 until he retired in 1993. In 1958, he broke with the Communist Party and created the Parti Progressiste Martiniquais (PPM). The PPM stood for autonomy but wished to retain Martinique as part of France. A socialist victory in the French presidential elections of 1981 was followed by a policy of decentralization, whereupon Césaire declared a moratorium on further discussion of the political status of Martinique. During this period, the PPM served as the conduit for aid from France, thereby not only consolidating its local power base but also preventing social unrest. It appears that the dominant role of the PPM in the island's politics ended even before Césaire's retirement. In the regional elections of 1992, the party polled only 15.8 percent of the vote.

See also Martinique.
Reference Burton, Richard D., ed. *French and West Indian* (1995).

Ceuta and Melilla

Two Spanish enclaves on the coast of Morocco, Ceuta and Melilla have a combined population of 130,000, of which one-third are Muslims. The Ceuta Liberation Movement and the Moroccan Patriotic Front, which call for the integration of the cities with Morocco, carried out several bombings and other acts of terrorism in the late 1970s and early 1980s. It is difficult to know how much support exists for a Moroccan takeover among the Muslims, and Spanish newspapers claim that the terrorism is largely carried out by Moroccan secret police. In November 1986, the Muslims went on strike demanding that they be given Spanish nationality. The status of Ceuta and Melilla was raised from "presidios" (garrison towns) to autonomous regions in 1994.

Chad

A landlocked state in Africa, Chad was a French colony until 1960. The northern part of the country is part of the Saharan desert and is inhabited by Muslim nomads, including the Fulani and Toubou peoples, while the more fertile southern part is inhabited by black agriculturalists. At the time of independence, the southerners were more educated and dominated the government. Under the rule of François Tombalbaye, Chad became a one-party state in 1962. Northern Muslims were treated harshly, and the Muslim sultans lost their traditional authority. In their place, government officials, who usually come from the southern Sara tribe, enforced government measures with a heavy hand and with a contemptuous disregard for Muslim traditions. Even the wearing of turbans was prohibited. The army, also recruited from the south, was notorious for its brutality and behaved like an occupying army in Muslim areas.

In 1965, a revolt broke out in central Chad after Muslims protesting against the imposition of new taxes were fired upon by soldiers. The revolt, led by the National Liberation Front of Chad (FROLINAT), spread throughout the Muslim regions, and in 1968, Tombalbaye was forced to appeal to France for military assistance. French troops succeeded in putting down the rebellion temporarily, but France also pressured Tombalbaye into restoring the authority of the Muslim chieftains and making other reforms. Although Tombalbaye was overthrown and killed in a coup d'état in 1975, the new ruler, General Felix Malloum, was faced with renewed insurgency in the north. The northern Muslims were, however, divided into several rival factions, and in 1976, the Forces Armées du Nord (FAN) split into two groups because of a bitter rivalry between Hissene Habre and Goukouni Oueddei.

In 1973, Colonel Muammar al-Gadhafi of Libya invaded the Aazou strip on the borders of Chad and Libya and began supplying weapons to Goukouni's forces. As a result of this Libyan support, Goukouni was able to take control of most of the northern provinces, and in 1978, in alliance with another Muslim rebel group, he began a drive toward the capital of N'Djamena. French troops were again called in and successfully stopped the rebel advance. After the defeat of Goukouni, Malloum and Habre temporarily formed an alliance, but it broke down in February 1979. After a fierce battle, Habre's forces routed the southerners and occupied N'Djamena. During the fighting, both sides massacred thousands of civilians belonging to the other side.

Libyan army units were sent in to support Goukouni in 1980 and 1983, and after French troops intervened to block the Libyan advance, the country was essentially partitioned into a southern zone controlled by Habre and the French and a northern zone controlled by Goukouni and the Libyans. However, Goukouni's troops rebelled against their Libyan allies in 1986 and united with Habre's army in early 1987 to drive the Libyans out of Chad.

References Maier, Karl. *Into the House of the Ancestors: Inside the New Africa* (1998); Thompson, Virginia, and Richard Adloff. *Conflict in Chad* (1982).

Chameria

The Chams are Albanian Muslims who lived in the northwestern Greece in the province of Chameria, which is now known officially by the Greek name, Threspotia. At the end of World War II, more than 150,000 Chams were forcibly expelled into Albania on the grounds they had collaborated with Fascist Italy. The Cham Society, organized and supported by the international organization the Unrepresented Nations and Peoples Organization (UNPO), has pressed the Greek government to repatriate the Chams and allow them to return to their lands. The Greek government has not responded to the demand.

See also Greater Albania.
Reference Vickers, Miranda, and James Pettifer. *Albania: From Anarchy to Balkan Identity* (1997).

Chechnya

Chechens, who are estimated to number 1 million, are native to the Caucasus region. They are Sunni Muslims and speak a Caucasian language similar to Ingush. The Chechens adopted the Latin alphabet in the 1920s but, under Stalin, replaced it with Cyrillic in 1938. After their dispute with the Russians began in 1991, the Chechens officially reverted to the Latin alphabet.

Chechnya has a stormy history. Mongols, Persians, Ottomans, Russians, and Georgians all fought to control the Chechens between the fifteenth and the nineteenth centuries. In the eighteenth century, Sheik Mansur resisted the invaders until his capture by the Russians in 1791. Under Imam Shamil, the Chechens resisted the Russians from the 1830s until 1859 when Shamil was captured by the Russians. Chechnya was then absorbed into the Russian Empire. During the Russian Civil War (1918–1920), Chechens again revolted. In 1920, Chechnya was brought under Soviet control and became an autonomous Soviet socialist republic. In 1936, Chechnya and Ingushetia were constituted as an autonomous republic within the Russian Soviet Socialist Republic. Following World War II, Stalin, accusing the Chechens and the Ingush of collaborating with the Nazis, abolished the republic and exiled many Chechens to central Asia and Siberia. In 1957, Nikita Khrushchev reestablished the Chechen-Ingush Republic and allowed the exiles to return.

As the Soviet Union was disintegrating, the National Chechen Congress voted to move toward

Hundreds of refugees make their way out of the Chechen capital Grozny, August 20, 1996, after a Russian military leader threatened aerial and artillery bombardment of separatist forces. (Reuters/Vladimir Svartsevich/Archive Photos)

sovereignty in November 1990. In 1991, former Soviet general Dzhokar Dudayev ousted the ruling Communist government; in October 1991, he was elected president of the republic and declared Chechnya independent of Russia. Russia refused to acknowledge this. In 1992, Chechnya and Tatarstan both rejected a revised Russian treaty redefining the status of the two republics within the Russian state. In 1994, the Russians attempted a coup d'état headed by the Chechen opposition leader Jomar Avurkhanov, who declared his provisional council the new ruling body of the nation. The council never achieved legitimacy. In December 1994, Russia invaded and, in February 1995, succeeded in capturing the nearly de-

stroyed capital of Grozny. It is estimated that more than 20,000 died in this campaign. The Russians then appointed ex-Soviet official Doku Zavgayev as the head of Chechnya.

Dudayev and the Chechen military fought on from strongholds in the mountainous countryside, and the Chechens also carried out a series of raids and kidnappings on Dagestan and Russian territory. Attempts to arrange a cease-fire were unsuccessful, and the fighting continued. In April 1996, Dudayev was killed in battle. A May 1996 cease-fire, arranged by Boris Yeltsin and Zelimkhan Yandarbiyev, acting Chechen president, was never successfully implemented. In August 1996, Chechen forces, under General Aslan

Maskhadov, retook Grozny. Later that month, a peace agreement reached by former Soviet general Aleksandr Lebed and Chechen leaders finally brought an end to the fighting. The agreement called for a withdrawal of Russian troops and for Russia's provision of economic assistance to help rebuild war-ravaged Chechnya. In return, Chechnya agreed not to press publicly for independence until completion of further negotiations scheduled for 2001.

After the agreement, Russian troops withdrew from Chechnya, but little economic assistance was provided by Moscow. The Chechen general Aslan Maskhadov was elected president in January 1997. In January 1998, Maskhadov vowed he would never permit Chechnya to become a dependency of Russia, nor would he accept the status of Chechnya as a freely associated member of the Russian Federation. In the summer of 1999, Islamic radicals from Chechnya invaded the neighboring republic of Dagestan, and a series of bombings in Moscow were blamed on Chechen terrorists. In response Russian troops launched a second invasion of Chechnya in October 1999. The invasion, which resulted in large numbers of civilian casualties and a flood of refugees out of Chechnya, was condemned by President Bill Clinton and other western leaders.

See also Dudayev, Dzhokhar; Ingushetia; Russian Federation.
References Dunlop, John B. *Russia Confronts Chechnya: Roots of a Separatist Conflict* (1998); Gall, Carlotta, and Thomas De Waal. *Chechnya: Calamity in the Caucasus* (1998); Lieven, Anatol. *Chechnya: Tombstone of Russian Power* (1998).

Chicano Movement

The term *Chicano movement* refers to several Mexican-American organizations whose goals include raising cultural consciousness, improving the economic conditions of Mexican Americans, and achieving political power through the ballot box. Underlying these conventional ethnic activities is a separatist theme that reached its peak of support in the late 1960s but remains a

Cesar Chavez, leader of the United Farm Workers Union, speaks in a demonstration at the Labor Board headquarters in Sacramento, September 15, 1975. (Archive Photos)

recurrent, though minority, position for several contemporary Mexican-American groups.

Chicano, derived from the word Mexicano, refers to people of Mexican-American descent living in the United States. Mexicans are predominantly a Spanish-speaking Roman Catholic mestizo ethnic group whose members trace their biological and cultural heritages to both Spanish and Native American roots. Emphasis on the Aztec origins of Mexican society on the part of Chicano groups—the Aztecs were conquered by Spain in 1521—provides an anti-European bias to much radical Chicano writing.

Chicanos frequently refer to themselves as La Raza ("the race"), thereby designating Mexican Americans as biologically distinct from white

Americans. Chicano activists also base their separatist claims on the fact that much of the American Southwest, originally Spanish territory, was seized from Mexico following the Mexican-American War (1846–1848). They reject the Treaty of Guadalupe Hidalgo, which awarded the land to the United States, and refer to the lost territories as Aztlan, land of the Aztecs, asserting, without supporting evidence, that this area was the original homeland of the Aztecs. Radical separatists like Rodolfo "Corky" Gonzales have called for the creation of an independent state of Aztlan, which would include California, Arizona, New Mexico, Texas, Nevada, Utah, and Colorado. In 1969, at the Chicano Liberation Conference, a separatist manifesto, "Spiritual Plan of Aztlan," was adopted, and the document still remains influential.

The Chicano movement in the United States emerged in the 1960s. As part of the broader civil rights movement, it involved union organizing, student activism, and political mobilization. Beginning in 1965, Cesar Chavez led the largely Mexican United Farm Workers Union in a series of strikes and boycotts. In 1966, Rodolfo Gonzales established the Crusade for Justice in Denver. A cultural and political movement, the crusade rejected white America, denounced assimilation, and advocated Chicano power. It proclaimed Emiliano Zapata and Pancho Villa, early-twentieth-century Mexican revolutionaries, as its heroes. In Texas, La Raza Unida Party, founded in 1969, organized Mexican-American voters and succeeded in winning several local government and school board elections. Before it faded from prominence in the 1970s, La Raza Unida played an important role in Texas state politics.

In 1969, the Movimiento Estudiantil Chicano de Aztlan (MECHA), or Chicano Student Movement of Aztlan, became active on several college and high school campuses. Unlike other Chicano political groups, MECHA continues to thrive. It succeeded in establishing Chicano studies programs and departments in colleges and universities throughout the country, and it organized mass protests in support of bilingual education, the acceptance of Spanish as a second language of the country, and immigration rights.

The most militant Chicano group is the Brown Berets. Inspired by the Black Panthers, the Brown Berets adopted a militaristic stance, which resulted in several confrontations with police. In support of its nationalist position, the Brown Berets organized school boycotts, rallies, and sit-ins. Largely inactive between 1972 and 1992, the Brown Berets have reconstituted their chapters in recent years and taken an active role in promoting causes related to the concept of a nation of Aztlan.

Since the early 1970s, calls for a separate Aztlan have diminished. Large-scale legal and illegal Mexican migration to the United States brought about an increased emphasis on realizing Chicano goals through electoral processes. Rather than an independent state, Chicano leaders now advocate that the United States become a bicultural society with Spanish being recognized as a second language. Groups like MECHA have organized voting drives to prevent the passage of antibilingual education and English-only laws. Although Mexico's lower standard of living and its suspect political system have precluded support for formal reunification with the mother country, Mexico's support of Chicano and immigrant causes remains strong. Recent Mexican legislation granting Mexican Americans dual citizenship further strengthened the ties between Mexicans on both sides of the border.

See also Aztlan.
Reference Garcia, Ignacio. *Chicanismo: The Forging of a Militant Ethos* (1997).

China's Nationality Policy

Although the overwhelming majority (93 percent) of China's population is ethnic Chinese, most of its territory is inhabited by non-Chinese ethnic groups. The Chinese Republic, which was set up after the revolution of 1911, inherited the territories of the former Manchu Empire, and

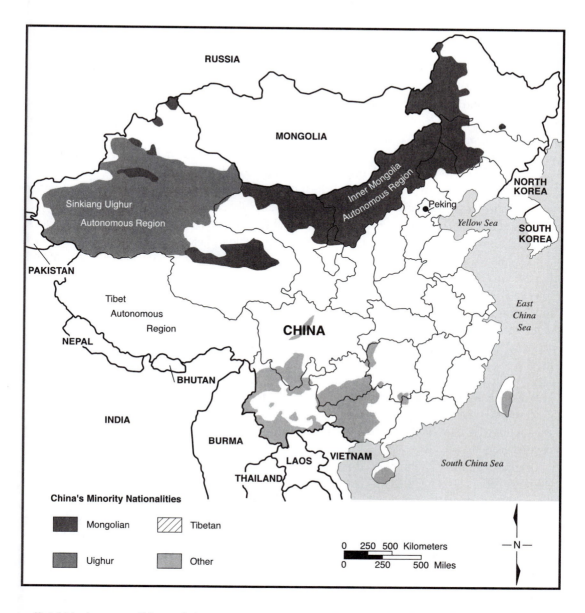

RUSSIA

MONGOLIA

Inner Mongolia Autonomous Region

NORTH KOREA

Peking

Yellow Sea

SOUTH KOREA

Sinkiang Uighur Autonomous Region

PAKISTAN

Tibet Autonomous Region

CHINA

East China Sea

NEPAL

BHUTAN

INDIA

BURMA

LAOS

VIETNAM

South China Sea

THAILAND

China's Minority Nationalities

Mongolian | Tibetan

Uighur | Other

0 250 500 Kilometers
0 250 500 Miles

—N—

official ideology saw China as being composed of five "races," "clans," or "nationalities." In addition to the ethnic Chinese (or Han), these were the Manchu, Mongols, Tatars, and Tibetans, and the five-stripe design of the national flag symbolized the union of these groups within the Chinese Republic. In keeping with the traditional Chinese worldview, it was assumed that the non-Han minorities would ultimately become assimilated into the superior Chinese civilization. In his book *China's Destiny,* Chiang Kai-shek argued that

China "was able by virtue of its great and enduring civilization to blend the neighboring clans into the nation. . . . [The Chinese nation] accepted and absorbed their civilizations while at the same time imparting to them the civilization of China. This has been the outstanding characteristic of the survival and expansion of our Chinese nation."

The Chinese Communists not only accepted these assumptions but were also influenced by Marxist-Leninist theories about nationalism.

Marxism saw class conflict as the driving force of human history, and nationalism could be either a progressive or a reactionary force depending upon the historical stage that had been reached in a given country. Marx assumed that as the working class became truly class conscious, "proletarian internationalism" would grow in strength. Lenin's theory of imperialism served to explain why this had not occurred. Imperialism represented the final stage of capitalism, in which the developed capitalist nations exploited their colonies. Thus, the struggle against colonialism was a necessary stage in the socialist revolution, and anticolonial nationalism was therefore a progressive force. Lenin regarded the right to secede as a key aspect of the alliance between socialism and "progressive" nationalism. Since socialist states were by definition not exploitive, minority nationalities would not exercise this right but instead freely choose to remain united with the larger polity. The fact that several nationalities within the new Soviet state opted for independence showed that they were not truly progressive—otherwise they would not have chosen to separate from the socialist state.

Originally, Chinese Communist Party (CCP) policy on nationalities followed Marxist-Leninist theory and declared that Mongolia, Tibet, and East Turkistan were to be self-governing republics with the right to secede from China. However, after coming to power, the CCP argued that a federal system was impractical for China since none of China's minorities inhabited contiguous territories and all regions contained large numbers of individuals belonging to other ethnic groups. In reality, security considerations were a major factor, for the Chinese feared that many of the frontier nationalities would declare themselves independent if allowed to do so. Furthermore, the frontier regions were rich in natural resources, and their sparsely populated territories could be colonized by Chinese settlers.

The CCP therefore adopted a system whereby national minority areas were granted autonomy at various levels—county, district, or provincial—depending upon local conditions. Although this system allowed for the exercise of autonomy by scattered minorities, the policy also prevented large minorities from controlling a unified territorial entity. Hence, the Uyghurs, the majority nationality of Xinjiang (Sinkiang), were divided into several districts, and only a minority of Tibetans were included in the Tibet Autonomous Region.

China officially recognizes fifty-five minority nationalities numbering about 70 million people, the most important being the 6 million Uyghurs, 4.3 million Manchus, 3.8 million Tibetans, and 3.4 million Mongols who inhabit the sensitive frontier regions. According to the 1982 census, there are also 13.4 million Zhuang, 7.2 million Hui, 5.5 million Yi, and 5 million Miao scattered throughout the southwestern provinces of Yunnan and Guizhou and the Guangxi Zhuangzu Autonomous Region.

See also Mongolians; Tibet; Uyghurs.
References Dreyer, June. *China's Forty Millions: Minority Nationalities and National Integration in the People's Republic of China* (1976); Smith, Warren W. *Tibetan Nation: A History of Tibetan Nationalism and Sino-Tibetan Relations* (1996).

Chittagong Hill Tracts

Bangladesh is one of the most ethnically homogeneous nations in the world as 98 percent of its population is made up of Bengali-speaking Muslims. However, the Chittagong Hill Tracts are inhabited by tribal peoples of Mongoloid appearance who speak Tibeto-Burman languages. A guerrilla insurgency by the Shanti Bahini (Peace Force) has been going on since 1975. The rebels, who are drawn from the Chakma tribe, are seeking an autonomous status for the region, the expulsion of Bengali settlers from their lands, and the restoration of tribal rights they enjoyed under British rule. A 1986 Amnesty International report accused the Bangladeshi army of engaging in reprisals, torture, and brutality against local civilians. It is estimated that at least 1,400 members of the security forces and 7,000 civilians have been killed in the conflict. In December 1997, the rebels and the government signed an accord giving the tribes greater control over the resource-rich southeastern hills but not the autonomous status they sought.

See also Bangladesh.

muted any calls on the part of the leadership for outright independence, and no major demonstrations have occurred.

See also Russian Federation.

Reference Kolga, Margus, et al., eds. *Red Book of the Peoples of the Russian Empire* (1993); Mastyugina, Tatiana, and Lev Perelkin, *An Ethnic History of Russia* (1996).

Chuvashia

Chuvashia is a republic of the Russian Federation. The Chuvash are a Turkic-speaking people and are predominantly Orthodox in religion. Their language incorporates some Finno-Ugric elements, which makes it distinct from other Turkic languages spoken in the Russian Federation. Conquered by the Mongols in the thirteenth century, Chuvashia was incorporated into the Russian Empire in 1551. It became an autonomous province in 1920, and in 1925, it was elevated to the status of an autonomous republic of the USSR. Following the collapse of the Soviet Union in 1991, Chuvashia became a republic of the newly independent Russian Federation.

Within the Chuvash Republic, the Chuvash number about 1 million out of a population of 1.5 million. Another 850,000 Chuvash live in other republics of Russia, making it one of the federation's largest ethnic groups. As the USSR was disintegrating, calls for the creation of a greater Chuvashia were aired in the press. Alarmed by a more nationalist Chuvashia, Russians in the Alatyr and Poleisye districts talked of seceding from Chuvashia.

Two nationalist groups are active in Chuvashia—the Chuvash Party of National Rebirth (CPNR) and the Chuvash Sociocultural Center. The CPNR favors incorporating Chuvash-populated areas outside the Chuvash Republic. It also advocates greater sovereignty for Chuvashia and points to Tatarstan's success in signing a separate treaty with Russia granting it greater autonomy internally and more control over its economy and natural resources. However, Chuvashia's dependence on economic subsidies from Moscow has

Ciskei

One of the ten black homelands of South Africa, Ciskei reveals the arbitrary manner in which the apartheid policy of "separate development" was carried out. In theory, blacks were supposed to be citizens of one of the several black nations that had existed before the arrival of the whites. Bophuthatswana, for example, was the homeland of the Tswana, and KwaZulu the homeland of the Zulu. There was, however, no distinctive Ciskeian language, and the population spoke Xhosa, like the inhabitants of the Transkei homeland. The Ciskei homeland is separated from the Transkei by a narrow strip of white-owned land and had a resident population of about 650,000 in 1980. Another 1.4 million Ciskeians "citizens" lived outside the borders of the homeland. Many of the leaders of the anti-apartheid movement, including Nelson Mandela and Steve Biko, were from the area, which has a long tradition of resistance to white domination.

The population of Ciskei is divided into two hostile groups, the Rharhabe and the Mfengu. The Rharhabe are the original Xhosa-speaking inhabitants while the Mfengu arrived as refugees fleeing from the Zulu in the early 1800s. The Mfengu (sometimes called the Fingo) fought on the side of the whites in the colonial wars, and because they were educated by Christian missionaries, they held most of the best jobs. The 1973 elections were won by the Ciskei National Independence Party of Lennox Sebe, who openly attributed his victory over the previous chief minister to tribalism: "We belong to different tribes. [He] is a Fingo and I am a Rharhabe. My tribe is bigger than his." In a December 1980 referendum, 98.7 percent of those voting were in favor of independence for the Ciskei (just under 60 percent of the registered electors voted in the referendum). After the vote Sebe announced that independence would mean the "rebirth of a nation" but that Ciskeians would retain the right to live and work in South Africa.

Lennox Sebe, along with his half-brother Charles, dominated Ciskeian politics until 1990. Their rule was marked by widespread corruption and increasing repression. Sebe attempted to create a Ciskeian identity through newly invented traditions. A national shrine was built on a sacred hill, with an 18,000-seat arena where official ceremonies were held. The existence of the Ciskei was challenged by Kaiser Matanzima, the president of the Transkei, who called for the two states to be joined together to form a single Xhosa homeland. In 1987, relations between the Ciskei and the Transkei were so bad that an armed attack against President Sebe's palace was blamed on Transkeian mercenaries. Following this attack, the South African government pressured the two homeland leaders into signing an agreement that they would not plan, incite, or carry out acts of aggression against each other. Even more threatening was the growth of popular opposition to the Ciskeian authorities, which was revealed by school and bus boycotts, riots, and an attack on President Sebe's motorcade. In 1990, Sebe was overthrown by a coup led by Brigadier Joshua Gqozo, who held power until the Ciskei was reincorporated into South Africa along with the other black homelands in 1994.

See also Black Homelands; Transkei.
References Charton, Nancy, ed. *Ciskei: Economics and Politics of Dependence in a South African Homeland* (1980); Peires, Jeffrey. "Ethnicity and Pseudo-Ethnicity in the Ciskei" (1995).

The Commonwealth

With forty-nine member countries containing almost one-quarter of the world's population, the Commonwealth (formerly the British Commonwealth of Nations) is one of the largest and most diverse of the international blocs. Consisting of the United Kingdom and most of its former colonies, its size and extent are a reflection of the historic importance of the British Empire. Of Britain's ex-colonies only Burma chose not to join the Commonwealth, although Ireland, South Africa, and Pakistan later withdrew from the organization. English is still the language of law, commerce, and government for most of the Commonwealth's members, and the bloc is held together by historical, cultural, and economic ties but has little organizational cohesion. The British monarch is recognized as the symbolic head of the association, and periodic conferences provide an opportunity for an exchange of views between heads of state and other government officials. However, these meetings often reveal deep divisions between members, and acrimonious confrontations have occurred over such issues as apartheid.

A distinction is often made between the "Old Commonwealth" countries—Canada, Australia, and New Zealand—which were settled by people from the British Isles, and the "New Commonwealth" countries, whose populations are largely of non-British origin. The former are all constitutional monarchies while the others are republics. The ties of common heritage between Britain and Australia, Canada, and New Zealand have weakened in recent years as their populations have become more diverse. Within Australia, for example, there is a growing sentiment in favor of becoming a republic. Britain's entry into the European Economic Community (now the European Union) reduced the importance of the Commonwealth as a trading bloc, and the Commonwealth Immigration Act of 1962 restricted the free flow of immigration into Britain from the Commonwealth countries.

See also Anglo-Saxonism; League of Empire Loyalists.
Reference Ball, Margaret. *The Open Commonwealth* (1971).

Commonwealth of Independent States

The Commonwealth of Independent States (CIS) is an association of Russia and eleven former Soviet republics. It was created in 1991 by Russia, Ukraine, and Belarus to replace the Union of Soviet Socialist Republics (USSR). Subsequently, Armenia, Azerbaijan, Georgia, Kyrghzstan, Moldova, Tajikistan, Turkmenistan, and Uzbekistan have become members of CIS. The former Soviet republics of Estonia, Latvia, and Lithuania declined membership.

Although envisaged as a means of coordinating economic, diplomatic, and military policies and fulfilling international treaties signed by the defunct Soviet Union, particularly those regarding nuclear disarmament, the CIS has achieved few of its stated goals. Squabbling among member nations and resistance to Russian domination have resulted in an ineffective international organization. By 1993, the hope of maintaining the Russian ruble as a universal currency had been largely abandoned.

The one area in which CIS has had limited success is in its interventions in former Soviet republics in which there is civil and ethnic strife. CIS forces have been dispatched to Georgia—to Abkhazia, Adzharia, and South Ossetia—to Azerbaijan for the Nagorno-Karabakh war of secession, to Russia to mediate the Ingushetia–North Ossetia conflict, to Moldova, and to Tajikistan. CIS troops have also been employed as border guards along the southern borders of the former Soviet Union, working to interdict the supply of illegal arms and drugs and prevent the entry of hostile forces, usually Islamic fundamentalist guerrillas, into the border nations. At best, CIS military missions have succeeded in maintaining uneasy truces in states undergoing civil and ethnic strife. As CIS military missions are to a great extent dominated by the Russian Federation, they have been criticized by Azerbaijan, Georgia, and Moldova as pursuing Russian interests rather than the interests of the nations in question.

See also Union of Soviet Socialist Republics.

References Brzezinski, Zbigniew, and Paige Sullivan, eds. *Russia and the Commonwealth of Independent States* (1997); Khazanov, Anatoly. *After the USSR: Ethnicity, Nationalism, and Politics in the Commonwealth of Independent States* (1995); Mozaffari, Mendi, ed. *Security Politics in the Commonwealth of Independent States* (1997).

Comoros

An archipelago in the Indian Ocean inhabited by a population of mixed Arab and African ancestry, the Comoros were a French colony from 1841 until 1975 when they became independent. The majority of the population of one of the Comoros, Mayotte, did not want to become independent and remained a French dependency, despite the objection of the UN General Assembly. On August 3, 1997, Anjouan, one of the three main islands, declared itself independent of the Comoros and expressed a wish to reunite with France. After an abortive attempt at crushing the rebellion, in which about forty Comoran soldiers lost their lives, the Comoran government withdrew its troops. In a referendum held two months later, 99.88 percent of the Anjouans voted in favor of secession, but the Comoros government refused to accept the breakaway and claimed that the rebellion was backed by foreign powers. France declared its support for the political integrity of the Comoros but called for a more equitable distribution of foreign aid among the three islands.

Confederation of the Caucasian Peoples

Established in 1989, the Confederation of the Caucasian Peoples (CCP) is made up of representatives from the Russian Federation republics of Adygea, Chechnya, Dagestan, Ingushetia, Kabardino-Balkaria, Karachai-Cherkessia, and North Ossetia (Alania), as well as minority groups in the Caucasus. The confederation was originally conceived of as a stepping-stone toward the creation of an independent Caucasian state. It took as its model the Caucasian Mountain Republic

(1920–1921), which had been suppressed by the Red Army. In recent years the CCP has become more involved with mediating Caucasian disputes such as the Chechen-Russian and the Abkhazian-Georgian wars. Internally, conflicts within countries of the CCP—such as Karachai-Cherkessia—and between them—for instance, Ingushetia–North Ossetia—have weakened the unity of the confederation. The confederation is chaired by Yosup Soslambekov, the former prime minister of Chechnya.

See also Adygea; Chechnya; Dagestan; Kabardino-Balkaria; Karachay-Cherkessia; Russian Federation.
Reference Smith, Sebastian. *Allah's Mountains* (1998).

Congo
See Zaire

Cordillera Autonomy Movement

The Cordillera mountain region of Luzon in the Philippines is home to a number of tribal groups such as the Ifugao, Bontoc, and Kalinga. These groups resisted Spanish colonial rule, but during the U.S. occupation of the Philippines, the Public Lands Act of 1905 stripped the Cordillera tribes of any legal rights to their traditional lands. Under the authoritarian regime of Ferdinand Marcos (1972–1985), a series of presidential decrees allowed extensive logging and mining within the Cordillera region. Large hydroelectric dams were constructed, flooding dozens of villages, which led to massive resistance and the emergence of a Cordillera autonomy movement.

With the overthrow of the Marcos regime, the newly elected president, Corazon Aquino, attempted to respond to the grievances of the Cordillera peoples. The Chico River Dam project was canceled, and logging concessions were revoked. A Cordillera Administrative Region was established, and legislation was passed granting autonomy to the region. However, when the autonomy measure was put to a referendum in January 1990, it was rejected by a five-to-one margin, with only one of the five Cordillera provinces voting in favor of the proposal. The autonomy measure was rejected because it was seen as being too restricted. A revised version of the autonomy bill, with a provision for the recognition of ancestral land rights, is currently being considered by a regional consultative committee.

Reference Eder, James. *On the Road to Extinction* (1982).

Corsica

The Mediterranean island of Corsica enjoyed a brief period of independence in the middle of the eighteenth century when Pascal Paoli led a rebellion against Genoese rule. In 1769, French troops put down the revolt, and the island was ceded to France by Genoa. Since that date, Corsica has been governed as an integral part of France, but Corsicans have always been ambivalent about their relationship with that country. On the one hand, poor communications with mainland France and the Italian dialect spoken on the island have created a distinctive identity, yet Corsicans (such as Napoleon) have played a notable role in French history.

The first autonomous movement, the Parti Corse Autonomiste, was founded in 1927, but opposition to French rule was insignificant until the 1960s. Corsican grievances were primarily economic and involved complaints of unemployment, pollution, high transportation costs, and population decline. Corsican anger increased because agricultural development schemes were seen as primarily benefiting non-Corsicans, in particular the French settlers who were repatriated to the island after Algeria became independent in 1962. Cultural and linguistic issues emerged in the 1970s, with demands for a Corsican university, more local language broadcasts, and the teaching of Corsican in schools. The Scola Corsa encouraged Corsicans to rediscover their culture and traditions.

The major autonomist groups include the Azzione per Rinascita Corsa, which focused on publicizing regional economic grievances; its successor organization, the Union du Peuple Corse (UPC); and the militant Front de Libération Nationale de la Corse (FLNC). Although autonomists have occasionally run in local and national elections, their candidates have done poorly, getting only 3.4 percent of the vote in the 1973 legislative elections and 7.3 percent in 1978. Perhaps as a result, separatist violence increased steadily after 1973, and since that date several hundred explosions in Corsica and on the French mainland have been attributed to pro-independence groups.

In response to separatist agitation and violence, France took measures to improve the Corsican economy and made several concessions to regional aspirations. Financial aid was increased, sea and air links were improved, and transportation fares were reduced. A regional council was set up in 1972, and in 1982, the political status of the island was elevated to that of a "territorial collectivity" with a directly elected assembly and increased administrative powers. The moderate nationalist UPC participated in the first elections, but the FLNC called for a boycott and declared a resumption of its bombing campaign. In the August 1982 elections, the abstention rate was only 31.5 percent, and the pro-autonomy lists got 15.1 percent of the vote and nine of the sixty-one seats. In February 1998, Claude Erignac, the most senior French government official on Corsica, was assassinated by separatist gunmen. His murder led to protest marches throughout the island.

See also Front de Libération Nationale de la Corse.
Reference Ramsey, Robert. *The Corsican Time Bomb* (1983).

Cossacks

The Cossacks, whose name means "free people," number about 3 million today. They are found largely in southern Russia and Siberia although a substantial number live in northern and northeastern Kazakhstan. The Cossacks were originally Russian and Ukrainian peasants who fled serfdom in Poland, Russia, and Lithuania at the end of the fifteenth century. A large Cossack community, the Zaporozhian Cossacks, established an independent state around 1650 on the west bank of the Dnieper River in what is now part of Ukraine. By the end of the seventeenth century, there were at least eleven Cossack communities, and the Don and Kuban River valleys were the home of significant populations.

By that time, the Cossacks, who were then ethnically mixed and even included Muslims in their ranks, had agreed to provide military service to the Russian Empire in return for grants of land and the right to govern their own communities free of all feudal obligations. The Cossacks, in effect, had become a military caste. In the ensuing centuries, the Cossacks became a Russian-speaking, staunchly Orthodox people. However, Cossack communities developed apart from mainstream Russian society. Their villages were autonomous, governed by a village council, and presided over by a headman or ataman. Land was held in common. The culture stressed military values and skills and the character traits associated with them. Each community had its own militia and its own flag.

The Cossacks' first military obligations were to guard Russian borders against incursions by Turkish and Tatar raiders. As Russia became more expansionist in the seventeenth and eighteenth centuries, Cossacks established advance outposts for the empire, and they played an important role in colonizing the Caucasus and settling Siberia. Although threats to Cossack autonomy quickly led to revolts against the Russian government, on the whole, prior to World War I, the Cossacks were faithful in battling the czar's enemies, both internal and external. They were also vigilant in defending the Orthodox Church against nonbelievers, particularly Muslims.

During the Russian Civil War (1918–1920), a majority of the Cossacks fought on one side, that of the Whites, and when the Reds consolidated their power over Russia, Cossack autonomy was severely curtailed. Cossack military units were abolished, the authority of the ataman was subsumed under that held by the local party secretary, and community land was collectivized and effectively controlled by the local Communist officials.

The end of communism and the disintegration of the Soviet Union in the early 1990s brought about a revival of the Cossack communities. Village councils and the post of ataman were revived, and Cossack militias were reconstituted. A Russian national council of Cossack leaders was formed and began to negotiate with the Russian government. The Cossacks asked to be recognized as an official ethnic group and to again provide military service to the state. Faced with a disintegrating Russian army and increased smuggling and ethnic strife along its southern borders, the Yeltsin government granted both requests and also promised the Cossacks land for military service. Cossack units were first put in place in the Caucasus and along the border with Georgia.

Ideologically, most Cossacks remain committed to the idea of a greater Russia and the Orthodox Church. Many Cossacks volunteered to serve with Serbian forces in Bosnia in their battle against the Muslims, and Cossacks also joined Russians and Ukrainians in Transdniester in opposing the Romanian-based government of Moldova. In Kazakhstan, Cossacks have demonstrated against the government of the newly independent state, calling for northern Kazakhstan to be made part of Russia.

Many Cossack communities have at times demanded their own republic in the Russian Federation or else that their communities be detached from the non-Russian republics in which they were placed. Cossacks came into conflict with the Muslim government of Chechnya, when they demanded that the traditionally Cossack regions of Naursky and Shelkovsky be annexed to Russia. The Kizlar region of the largely Muslim Dagestan republic, the historic home of the Terek Cossacks, had been part of the Russian Stavropol administrative district until 1957 when it was transferred to Dagestan. In recent years, an influx of mountain Avars and Darghins have migrated into the Cossack lowlands, and the Cossacks of the region have asked that their communities be returned to the Stavropol district. In the Karachai-Cherkessian Republic, Cossacks in the Batalashinsk, Zelenchuk, and Urup regions have also demanded either sovereignty or a return to Russian jurisdiction. In North Ossetia, the Cossack communities of Mosdok and Prigorodny have asked to be separated from North Ossetia and incorporated into the Stavropol district.

See also Dagestan; Karachai-Cherkessia; Kazakhstan; Russian Federation; Russians in the Former Soviet Republics; South Ossetia; Ukraine.
Reference Cresson, William. *Cossacks: Their History and Country* (1981).

Crimea

A peninsula in the northern part of the Black Sea, Crimea was conquered by Tatars who established a khanate there in 1475. In 1783, it was annexed to the Russian Empire by Catherine the Great. Heavily populated by Tatars, a Turkic people, the Crimea was designated an autonomous Soviet socialist republic in 1921. The region was overrun by German forces during World War II, and the important Soviet naval base at Sevastopol was captured in 1942. In 1945, after the Red Army had regained control of the peninsula, Stalin accused the Tatars of having collaborated with the Nazis and ordered them expelled to Soviet republics in central Asia. The autonomous republic status was revoked, and Crimea was attached to the Russian Republic.

Mining, manufacturing, and military operations as well as a developing tourist industry brought a large Russian population to the area in the postwar period. In 1954, to celebrate the three hundredth anniversary of Russian-Ukrainian association, Nikita Khrushchev gave Crimea to the Ukrainian Soviet Republic. In 1991, Ukraine restored the autonomous republic status to Crimea.

When Ukraine declared itself independent of the Soviet Union, Crimean Russians, who controlled the republic's parliament, launched an independence movement. Kiev acted decisively in 1994 to circumscribe Crimean government actions and to revoke much of the autonomy of the region. As the power of the Soviet Union waned in the late 1980s, Crimean Tatars began returning to the area from their places of exile, and they, too, began to agitate for citizenship rights and compensation for their forfeited assets.

See also Crimean Russians; Crimean Tatars; Russians in the Former Soviet Republics; Ukraine.
Reference Drohobycky, Maria, ed. *Crimea: Dynamics, Challenges, and Prospects* (1996).

Crimean Russians

Seventy percent of Crimea's 2,700,000 inhabitants are Russians. In the tightly integrated and Russian-dominated Soviet Union, Nikita Khrushchev's transfer of the Crimea from Russian to Ukrainian jurisdiction in 1954 had few negative consequences for Crimean Russians because they had no fears about maintaining their Russian cultural, linguistic, and educational institutions. This situation changed in 1989. For the Ukrainian Soviet Republic, glasnost provided an opportunity to make Ukrainian the national language. In 1991, following an abortive coup in Moscow, Ukraine declared itself independent, and the Crimean Russians became a minority in a non-Russian state. Even though Ukraine restored the autonomous republic status Crimea had enjoyed from 1921 to 1945, a movement for independence gathered momentum among the Russian population.

In 1992, the parliament of the Russian Republic passed a resolution restoring Crimea to Russia. Ukraine's independence, it was argued, nullified the 1954 action. Although the Ukrainian parliament immediately rejected the resolution, it gave further impetus to Russian separatists in Simferopol. Spearheaded by the Republican Movement of Crimea and in control of the local parliament, Crimean Russians adopted a constitutional amendment affirming Crimea's right to secede from Ukraine. In 1994, the legislature elected a president of the Crimean Republic, the Russian separatist Yuri Meshkov, and further measures were approved that weakened Crimea's ties to Ukraine. Ukraine reacted strongly. It abolished the new office of president and nullified the Crimean Republic constitution and much assembly legislation it deemed illegal under the Ukrainian constitution. By 1995, Ukraine had assumed direct rule over much of Crimean affairs.

The situation in Crimea has been made more complicated by the involvement of politicians in the Russian Federation. Russian nationalists in Moscow like Aleksandr Rutskoi and, more recently, Moscow's mayor Yuri Luzkhov, have encouraged Crimean separatism in order to further their own political ambitions. Ukrainian-Russian relations since 1991 have also been strained over the division of the Soviet Black Sea fleet and whether the important Soviet naval base at Sevastopol and the city itself should be Russian or Ukrainian. By 1997, these issues appeared to be resolved, thus eliminating a source of Russian-Ukrainian hostility.

In Crimea, popular enthusiasm for separation appears to have waned since 1995. The Ukrainian government has legalized the use of Russian as an official language of the region, and Russian nationalists suffered great losses in parliamentary elections in Crimea. Yevhen Suprunyuk, a pro-Kiev centrist, is now parliamentary chairman, replacing Sergei Tsekov, who was an outspoken opponent of the Ukrainian government.

Russian nationalism, though much less powerful than in previous years, remains active in Crimea. A new organization, the Congress of Russian People, chaired by Sergei Shuvalnikov, set up a shadow parliament to oversee the interests of Russian citizens in Crimea. It is also appealing to the Russian Republic for financial assistance for Crimean compatriots. It is unlikely that Russian dissatisfaction with the situation in Crimea will lessen unless there is a significant improvement in the standard of living under Ukrainian rule. The downgrading of the military and defense industries, the collapse of the Soviet-sponsored tourist industry, the growth of organized crime, and the influx of 300,000 destitute Tatars are all factors sustaining an atmosphere of discontent in Crimea.

See also Crimea; Crimean Tatars; Russians in the Former Soviet Republics; Ukraine.
Reference Drohobycky, Maria, ed. *Crimea: Dynamics, Challenges, and Prospects* (1996).

Crimean Tatars

The Tatars, a Turkic-speaking and Sunni Muslim people, arrived in Crimea as allies of the Mongols. They established a khanate there in 1475, and it became a vassal of the Ottoman Turks in 1485. After several military incursions by Russian troops, Catherine the Great was able to annex Crimea to the Russian Empire in 1783. After the Russian Revolution, the Crimea was organized as an autonomous Soviet socialist republic. German troops overran the region in 1941–1942, and when Soviet troops recaptured the Crimea in 1945, Stalin accused the Tatars of collaborating with Hitler. Consequently, some 200,000 people were expelled to Soviet central Asia—primarily to Uzbekistan but also in significant numbers to Tajikistan, Turkmenistan, and Kazakhstan.

With the collapse of the USSR in the late 1980s, Tatars began returning to Crimea, and by 1995, some 200,000–300,000 had returned. Many remained homeless and without employment. Led by Mustafa Djemilev, the Tatars organized a majlis, or shadow government, to handle social and political matters of importance to the ethnic community. Tatars have been pressing the Ukraine and Crimea parliament for a restoration of their rights and properties seized under Stalin and staged demonstrations in Moscow prior to the breakup of the Soviet Union. In Crimea, there were hunger strikes and sit-ins, and in 1995, in a violent clash between Tatars and Russians, four persons were killed. During the 1991–1995 period, when Russian nationalists were in the ascendancy in the Crimean government, Tatars gained few concessions. In 1995, after the Ukrainian government had reasserted control over Crimean affairs and pro-Russian national-

ists had lost control over the Crimean parliament, Tatars received 10 percent of the seats in the parliament. This was equal to their proportion in the total population, but radical Tatar spokespersons, claiming the Crimea had been stolen from them, demanded one-third of the parliamentary seats.

The decline of local Russian sentiment for Crimean independence has assuaged Tatar disaffection with the Crimean government. The newly elected chairman of the Crimean parliament, Yevhen Suprunyuk, is a moderate centrist interested in accommodating Tatars. Even though the Organization for Security and Cooperation in Europe has tried to find international assistance to relieve the destitution of many Crimean Tatars, the continuing economic decline of the region, accompanied by further immigration of exiled Tatars into a new nation that has few funds to allocate to appease disaffected groups, creates uncertainty as to the future.

See also Crimea; Crimean Russians; Ukraine.
References Allworth, Edward. *The Tatars of the Crimea: Return to the Homeland* (1998); Fisher, Alan. *Crimean Tatars* (1978); Sheehy, Ann, and Bondan Nahaylo. *The Crimean Tatars, Volga Germans, and Meskhetians* (1980).

Croatia

Croats, a southern Slavic people, settled in present-day Croatia in the fifth through the seventh centuries. The Croats were Christianized in the ninth century. In the tenth century, a Croatian kingdom was established and reached its greatest heights under Tomislav the Great, the first king. Hungarian and Austrian influence and control prevailed for most of the subsequent period until the collapse of the Austro-Hungarian monarchy in 1918. Croatia then entered an independent federation known as the Kingdom of Serbs, Croats, and Slovenes. In 1929, the kingdom became known as Yugoslavia.

Although Serbs and Croats speak the same language, Croats use the Roman alphabet, and Serbs use the Cyrillic. The two alphabets reflect the differing cultural and historical orientations of the two peoples. Croats, influenced by Austro-

Hungary, are Roman Catholic and Western European in orientation while the Serbs are Eastern Orthodox and heavily influenced by the Byzantine, Turkish, and Russian cultures. These differences were underscored during World War II when the Croat Ustasha dictatorship, the German-installed regime in Croatia, embarked on a murderous campaign against Serbs, Jews, and partisans. Following World War II, Croatia became part of the Yugoslav Communist state.

As had been the case when Yugoslavia was a kingdom, Croats chafed under the power wielded by Serbia in the central government. During a period of liberalization from 1969 to 1971, Croatian nationalist sentiments were frequently expressed, and these tendencies were strengthened by the support of Croatian émigré groups in Europe and the United States. In 1971, the central government in Belgrade, fearing a threat to national unity, launched a crackdown and purged and imprisoned Croat politicians and intellectuals, including Franjo Tudjman, who became president of the Croatian republic in 1990.

Aggravating Croatian antipathy toward the federal state was the belief that Croatia was being unfairly taxed to subsidize the poorer republics of the nation. In 1990, with the weakening of Communist rule in Eastern Europe and the ascension to power in Belgrade of the Serb nationalist, Slobodan Milosevic, the Croatian Democratic Union (HDZ), founded and led by Franjo Tudjman, won 75 percent of the vote in the Croatian elections. Tudjman assumed the presidency, and the newly elected parliament drew up a new constitution. In 1991, Croatia, along with Slovenia, Macedonia, and Bosnia and Herzogovina declared independence from Yugoslavia, touching off a war between Croatia and the rump Yugoslav state, which now consisted of only Serbia and Montenegro. In 1992, the new Croatian state was recognized by the European Community and the United States.

Within Croatia, Serbs composed 15 percent of the population and were concentrated in Slavonia and Krajina. After Croatia declared its independence, Croatian Serbs feared a resurgence of anti-Serbian measures, such as those carried out under the Ustasha dictatorship during World War II, so, with the aid of the Serb-dominated Yugoslavian army, Serbs in Krajina and Slavonia seceded from Croatia and established Serbian autonomous regions (SARs) throughout those areas. The ensuing fighting between Serbs and Croats soon spread from Croatia proper into Bosnia. Although initially forced to yield considerable territory to the Serbs, in 1995, the Croatian army reconquered the bulk of the captured territories in Krajina and western Slavonia, forcing Croatian Serbs to flee into Bosnia and Serbia proper. In the same year, the Dayton peace accord, which brought a cease-fire to Croatia and Bosnia, introduced NATO peacekeeping troops into the remaining Serb-held areas of eastern Slavonia. Under the Dayton treaty, eastern Slavonia was repatriated to Croatia in January 1998. By then, most of the original Serb inhabitants had fled. Few have returned.

Although Croatia has complied with the Dayton peace accord, it has done so only under duress. Some analysts argue that Tudjman ultimately wanted to annex the Croatian populated areas of Bosnia to Croatia proper. However, Croatia's desire to join the European Union acted as a restraint on Tudjman's ambitions in Bosnia.

See also Bosnia and Herzegovina; Dayton Peace Accord; Ethnic Cleansing; Herzeg-Bosnia; Krajina; Slavonia; Srpska; Tudjman, Franjo; Yugoslavia.
References Suljak, N. Dinko. *Croatia's Struggle for Independence* (1977); Tanner, Marcus. *Croatia: A Nation Forged in War* (1997).

Cyprus

An island in the eastern Mediterranean, Cyprus has been ruled at various times by the Byzantine Empire, the Crusaders, the Venetians, the Ottoman Turks, and the British. In 1878, the Ottoman Turks agreed to let Britain administer the island while retaining legal sovereignty. In 1914, when World War II broke out and Turkey allied with Germany, Britain annexed the island outright. The majority of the population spoke Greek and belonged to the Greek Orthodox Church, but almost a fifth were Turkish-speaking Muslims. The two communities were socially segregated, went to separate schools, and lived in separate neighborhoods, with each community patronizing its own shops and cafes. The Turkish population was dispersed throughout the island, and there was no administrative district in which they constituted a majority.

Since the early days of British rule, the Greek Cypriots aspired to reach *enosis* (political union with Greece), and their sense of Greek identity was encouraged by the schools where Greek history and literature was taught. The church was also a powerful force in maintaining enosist sentiments, and religion and ethnicity were regarded as virtually synonymous. During the centuries of Ottoman rule, the archbishop had been the secular as well as the spiritual leader of the Greek Cypriot community. Turkish Cypriots were bitterly opposed to the prospect of Cyprus being united with Greece, and as Greek agitation increased, the Turks raised the counterdemand of *taksim* ("partition") should Britain withdraw. The Turks were noticeably poorer, with a per capita income 20 percent lower than that of the Greeks.

In 1931, poor economic conditions and enosist agitation led to a revolt during which Government House was burned to the ground. The British responded by deporting two bishops, alleged leaders of the revolt, and by suspending the constitution. After World War II, the enosis issue emerged again. Delegations were sent to London, petitions were presented to visiting dignitaries, and in 1950, in a church-sponsored plebiscite, 96 percent of the Greek Cypriots declared themselves in favor of enosis. British proposals for a new constitution were rejected with the slogan, Enosis and Nothing but Enosis. In 1952, Archbishop Makarios III began a campaign to gain international support for enosis and visited London, Athens, Washington, D.C., and New York City. The Greek government raised the Cyprus issue at the United Nations in 1954 and called for a plebiscite.

In 1955, a guerrilla campaign was launched by the group Ethnike Organosis Kyprion Agoniston (EOKA). Although the British were unable to suppress the insurgency, EOKA did not achieve its goal of enosis. Instead, under the Zurich agreement of 1959 between Britain, Greece, and Turkey, Cyprus became independent with a constitution that gave the Turkish minority veto powers, extensive autonomy, and disproportionate representation in the legislature and civil service. Britain, Greece, and Turkey agreed "to prohibit, so far as it concerns them, any activity aimed at promoting, directly or indirectly, either union of Cyprus with any other State or partition of the Island." The three countries were given the right to intervene should the terms of the agreement be violated. In addition, the British retained control of two military bases, which meant an area of ninety-nine square miles. Archbishop Makarios was elected head of state, and his administration attempted to modify key aspects of the constitution, which quickly proved unworkable.

The Greeks objected to separate municipal governments for each community, the reserving of 30 percent of government jobs for the Turks, and the veto powers enjoyed by the Turkish vice-president. Both sides smuggled in weapons, and in 1963 fighting broke out between Greek Cypriots and Turkish Cypriots. The United Nations sent in troops to supervise a cease-fire between the two sides, but the political stalemate remained unresolved despite several rounds of negotiations.

In 1974, supporters of enosis, backed by the ruling Greek military regime, staged a coup and overthrew Makarios. This provoked the Turkish government to invade, and their forces overran the northern part of Cyprus, turning some 200,000 Greek Cypriots into refugees. The Turkish zone, occupying 37 percent of the island, was declared to be the Turkish Federated State of Cyprus, with Rauf Denktash as its president. In 1983, this became the independent Turkish Republic of Northern Cyprus. The entity is not recognized diplomatically by any state except Turkey, and it has languished economically in contrast to the Greek sector. The Cyprus question remains unresolved with the Greeks demanding a reduction in the territory controlled by the Turks and a strong federal government while the Turks are adamant in their desire for a bizonal system in which they would enjoy virtual independence.

See also Ethnike Organosis Kyprion Agoniston; Grivas, George; Makarios, Archbishop.
References Crawshaw, Nancy. *The Cyprus Revolt* (1978); Markides, Kyriacos. *The Rise and Fall of the Cyprus Republic* (1977).

Czech Republic

Settled by Slavic tribes in the fifth and sixth centuries A.D., the inhabitants of Bohemia and Moravia—the major territories of the Czech Republic—were Christianized in the ninth and tenth centuries. From the tenth century until the end of World War I, the Bohemians and Moravians were effectively under the control of the great European empires beginning with the Holy Roman Empire in 950 and ending with the Austro-Hungarian Empire. Although periodically Czech principalities achieved a significant degree of autonomy, the Germanic influence of the Hapsburgs greatly influenced Czech cultural, social, and artistic life. Nevertheless, the idea of a Czech nation was never extinguished. Czech nationalism was heightened in the nineteenth century under the leadership of Frantisek Palacky

(1798–1876) and later of Thomas Masaryk (1850–1937), both of whom advocated an independent democratic Czech state.

In 1918, following the demise of the Austro-Hungarian Empire, the Republic of Czechoslovakia was declared. The new state united Bohemia, Moravia, and Slovakia, a territory inhabited by Slovaks, a western Slavic people like the Czechs. Although speaking a mutually comprehensible language, Czechs and Slovaks shared different histories and traditions. While Czechs had historically been associated with Vienna, the Slovaks had been dominated by Budapest and the Hungarian monarchy. Whereas the Czechs had developed a prosperous commercial economy and a cosmopolitan culture, the Slovaks had remained an isolated agrarian society.

Never satisfied with what it perceived as its subordinate role in the Republic of Czechoslovakia either before or after World War II, Slovakia, after the fall of communism in 1989, began to press for independence. After negotiations in the summer of 1992 between the two leading parties of the federation, the Czech Civic Forum and the Slovak Movement for a Democratic Slovakia, a decision was made to dissolve the union. On January 1, 1993, the Czech Republic came into being.

See also Slovakia.
References Leff, Carol. *Czech and Slovak Republics* (1996); Stein, Eric. *Czecho/Slovakia: Ethnic Conflict, Constitutional Fissure, Negotiated Breakup* (1997).

Dagestan

Dagestan, a republic of the Russian Federation, lies in the northeastern Caucasus, and its location on the Caspian Sea makes it a vital transportation corridor between the Russian Republic and the oil fields to the south. Dagestan has a population of about 2 million and is the most multiethnic of all the republics of the Russian Federation—more than thirty ethnic groups reside in Dagestan. Some groups, such as the Nogays, Lezgins, Abkhazians, and Chechens, are found in both Dagestan and adjoining republics and frequently agitate to be reunited with their own territories. Dagestan's proximity to such hot spots as Chechnya, Abkhazia, and Ingushetia tends to exacerbate tensions within the republic. Additionally, there has been an influx of formerly exiled groups who have returned to the republic to claim their former lands, which are now held by others.

The Avars are the largest ethnic group, making up 32 percent of the population and, along with the Darghins, are Caucasian language speakers and Sunni Muslims. Russians, the only non-Muslim community, constitute only 9 percent of the population. In recent years, Islamist movements like the Islamic Democratic Party of Dagestan and the Islamic Revival Party have become increasingly active. After skirmishes between traditional Muslim groups and the Wahabis, a rapidly growing fundamentalist Muslim sect, the government outlawed the Wahabis.

An ongoing cleavage exists in Dagestan between the mountain peoples and the plains dwellers. The Kumyks, a Turkic-speaking lowland people represented by Tenglik, the Kumyk People's movement, complain that the Avar-dominated government has favored the mountain groups (Avars, Darghins, and Lakhs) in the distribution of land and control of natural resources. The Kumyks have called for the creation of separate national republics within the country and have engaged in strikes and demonstrations in support of their demands. In 1997, the election of an Avar as mayor of a town formerly governed by Kumyks resulted in a riot.

The Caucasian-language-speaking Lezgins, led by Sadval, and the Lezgin National Council, are divided between Azerbaijan and Dagestan, and they advocate a unitary Lezgin state to be incorporated into Russia. The Turkic Nogays call for the establishment of an autonomous Nogay district; Chechens want the reincorporation into Chechnya of Khasavyurt, historically a Chechen territory.

In August 1999, Chechen militants under Shamil Basayev captured several villages in the Botlik and Tsunadinsky regions. Their goal was the creation of an Islamic republic uniting Chechnya and Dagestan. The incursions were denounced by the Dagestan government and received little public support. Russian Federation troops subsequently entered the conflict, driving the rebels back into Chechnya.

See also Lezgins; Nogays; Russian Federation.
References Chenciner, Robert. *Daghestan: Tradition and Survival* (1997);Wesselink, Egbert. *The Russian Federation: Dagestan* (1995).

Dayton Peace Accord

Engineered by Richard Holbrooke, U.S. assistant secretary of state, the Dayton peace accord provided the basis for a cease-fire in Bosnia. Ratified by the presidents of Serbia, Croatia, and Bosnia in November 1995, the accord granted 51 percent of Bosnia's territory to the Muslim-Croat federation and 49 percent to the Bosnian Serb Republic of Srpska. In addition, a national parliament and a three-person collective presidency were established. Local parliaments in both the federation and the republic were also authorized. Monitored free elections were to be held, and refugees who had been uprooted by the war were to be allowed to return to their homes. In practice, there has been widespread intimidation of refugees attempting to return to areas now held by another ethnic group. Since the signing of the accord, NATO troops have acted as monitors and peacekeepers.

See also Bosnia and Herzegovina; Croatia; Greater Serbia; Izetbegovic, Alija; Krajina; Milosevic, Slobodan; Srpska; Tudjman, Franjo; Yugoslavia.
Reference Holbrooke, Richard. *To End a War* (1998).

Democratic Front for the Liberation of Palestine

The Democratic Front for the Liberation of Palestine (DFLP) is a secular Palestinian Marxist organization that calls for the creation of a socialist Palestinian state. It was formed in 1969, and its leader is Naif Hawatmeh. It receives funding from Libya and Syria and claims a membership of 20,000. Originally aligned with the Popular Front for the Liberation of Palestine (PFLP), it has broken its alliance with that group. A member of the Palestine Liberation Organization (PLO) from the beginning, the DFLP instigated a number of terrorist actions in the 1980s. Dissatisfied with the 1993 agreements between the PLO and Israel, the DFLP boycotted the 1996 elections for the new Palestinian legislature. At its 1998 convention, the party called for an international solution to the Palestine question. In 1999, after prodding by Syrian President Hafez Assad, Naif Hawatmeh reconciled with PLO leader Yasir Arafat. The DFLP now supports the peace agreements with Israel and has resumed its activities within the PLO.

See also Palestine Liberation Organization; Palestinians.
Reference Farsoun, Samih. *Palestine and the Palestinians* (1997).

Djibouti

The French Territory of the Afars and the Issas became the independent Republic of Djibouti in June 1977. Prior to 1958, the area was known as French Somaliland. Consisting of the port of Djibouti and 9,000 square miles of desert, the territory was claimed by both Ethiopia and Somalia. Djibouti's population is divided between the Issas, who are Somalis, and the Afars, with most estimates putting the Issas in the majority. Independence was delayed because of the political rivalry between the Issas, who wished to be united into a greater Somalia, and the Afars, who were opposed to that idea. Violence on the part of the Front for the Liberation of the Somali Coast led to the organization's being banned by the French. In referendums held in 1958 and 1967, the population voted to remain linked with France, but in a May 1977 referendum, 98.9 percent voted for independence.

The newly independent government was headed by President Hassan Gouled Aptidon, an Issa; the prime minister was an Afar; and the cabinet was carefully balanced between Issas and Afars. In an attempt to defuse tensions between the two groups, the president emphasized "the Arab identity" of Djibouti, and Arabic was made the official language. Djibouti's attempt to balance the opposing forces of Somali and Ethiopian nationalism is threatened by outbreaks of violence by both Afar and Somali guerrillas and by an influx of refugees following the conflict between Ethiopia and Somalia over the Ogaden in 1977–1978.

See also Afar; Ethiopia; Ogaden; Somalia; Somalis.
Reference Morrison, Donald G. *Black Africa: A Comparative Handbook* (1989).

Donbas Russians

The Donbas region of eastern Ukraine comprises the provinces of Donetske and Luhanske. Although Ukrainian speakers outnumber Russian speakers 51 percent to 42 percent, only 32 percent of all residents claim Ukrainian as their mother tongue. The Donbas region is home to major coal-mining operations, and strikes have been common since Ukrainian independence.

Under the USSR, Donbas miners enjoyed a privileged economic status. The industry was closely integrated with the Russian economy, receiving up to 70 percent of its supplies and parts from there, and much of its coal output was sold in the Soviet Union. Ukrainian independence broke many of these connections. Furthermore, the lack of funds at its disposal caused the Ukrainian government to fail to pay miners' wages. Finally, in order to qualify for International Monetary Fund loans, Ukraine set in motion a plan to shut down many of the now economically unprofitable and technologically backward mining operations. All of these factors increased miner hostility to Kiev and caused simple economic strikes for back wages to blossom into more all-encompassing political movements.

A major demand of Donbas Russians has been for a realignment of the region's economy with that of Russia and the Commonwealth of Independent States. More radical demands call for regional autonomy for Donbas within a Ukrainian federation, complete independence for the region, and even reunification with Russia. The Donbas leader of the Ukrainian Communist Party, Giorgiv Biko, has called for the restoration of the former Soviet Union.

The government in Kiev has responded to these challenges by agreeing to permit Russian to be one of the two official languages of the region. It has flatly rejected the idea of Donbas autonomy and a federal Ukrainian state. The election of Leonid Kuchma as Ukrainian president in 1994 was seen as a positive gain for the region by both pro-Russian and left-wing political parties. Kuchma's efforts to build new economic ties with Boris Yeltsin's Russia met with approval in the region, and by 1997, calls for independence in Donbas had receded although the coal industry was still wracked by strikes.

Another factor facilitating a more practical resolution of problems in Donbas is that there is no great antagonism between Russian and Ukrainian citizens living there. The major conflict in Ukraine is between a cosmopolitan, nationalist western Ukraine and a more ethnically mixed, pro-Russian eastern Ukraine. The failure of the central government to implement successful economic reforms only heightens that antagonism.

See also Russians in the Former Soviet Republics; Ukraine.
References Kuromiya, Hiroaki. *Freedom and Terror in the Donbas* (1998); Magocsi, Paul. *History of Ukraine* (1996).

Dudayev, Dzhokhar (1944–1996)

The first president of the breakaway Chechen nation, Dzhokhar Dudayev, was born in Chechnya but spent many of his earlier years in exile with his family in Kazakhstan. He later embarked on a military career in the Soviet air force, serving from 1966 through 1990. At the age of thirty-six, he was promoted to the rank of major general, the first Chechen to attain that rank. A member of the Communist Party, at the time of his resignation, he was commanding a military base in Estonia.

Returning to Chechnya in 1990, as the Soviet Union was disintegrating, Dudayev became actively involved with the ultranationalist faction of the National Chechen Congress. In September 1991, he led an armed coup that ousted the Communist government of Doku Zavgayev, and in October of the same year, he received 75 percent of the vote to become Chechnya's first post-Communist president. In early November 1991, he signed a decree declaring Chechnya independent.

Boris Yeltsin, now president of the Russian Federation, the republic to which Chechnya had been attached under the Soviet constitution, refused to acknowledge Chechen independence. On November 8, Yeltsin ordered troops dispatched to Grozny to restore order, but Dudayev's national guard was able to thwart the invasion at the airport. That led to a prolonged confrontation between Dudayev and Russia, which finally resulted in a massive Russian invasion of Chechnya in 1994 and a war that lasted until 1996, when Russian troops withdrew. Toward the end of the war, in April 1996, Dudayev was killed by a Russian rocket attack. He was succeeded by the Chechen vice-president, Zelimkhan Yandarbiyev.

As president, Dudayev was noted for his ultra-nationalistic rhetoric and abrasive negotiating style, often publicly insulting Russia. Although his leadership resulted in Chechnya's retaining its autonomy, Dudayev did little to improve living conditions in the republic. Under his rule, most civic institutions collapsed, and criminal activity flourished. In 1993, Dudayev dissolved parliament after efforts were undertaken to oust him from the presidency. Although a Muslim, in the early years of his rule he opposed the creation of an Islamic state in Chechnya. As the war with Russia intensified, he espoused more radical Islamist ideas, including the adoption of the sharia, or Islamic law. Despite his efforts to position himself as the leader of the Caucasus Muslims, Dudayev was never able to generate significant support for his military cause among the other neighboring Muslim republics.

See also Chechnya.
References Lieven, Anatol. *Chechnya* (1998); Smith, Sebastian. *Allah's Mountains* (1998).

East African Federation

On June 5, 1963, the governments of Tanganyika, Kenya, Uganda, and Zanzibar announced their intention to create an East African Federation, an idea that appeared to have every chance of success. The colonial divisions between the four territories were recognized as arbitrary, corresponding to no natural geographic boundaries, and the legacy of British colonial rule meant that the legal and administrative procedures of the four countries were very similar. The British had set up not only a customs and currency union but also a central legislative assembly. Social contacts among the political elites of the four countries were close, since many of them had been educated at Makerere College, the sole institution of higher education in the region. (In 1963, of the forty-nine cabinet members in Kenya, Uganda, and Tanganyika, twenty were Makerere graduates). The nationalist movements had cooperated closely in their common anticolonial struggles through the Pan African Freedom Movement for East and Central Africa (PAFMECA), and in 1961, PAFMECA had unanimously passed a resolution in favor of federation.

However, when negotiations began, it quickly became clear that the parties had very different ideas about the kind of federation they desired. Should each of the constituent territories have equal representation in the upper legislative chamber, as Uganda and Zanzibar wanted? Would each retain its seat in the United Nations? There were also rivalries between Jomo Kenyatta of Kenya and Julius Nyerere of Tanganyika over who would be the political leader of the new federation. Lacking any real popular support among the African masses, by the end of 1964, the idea of a federation had been rejected by Uganda and Kenya, and only President Nyerere of Tanganyika still declared himself in favor of it.

See also Pan-Africanism.

References Franck, Thomas M., ed. *Why Federations Fail* (1968); Hughes, Anthony. *East Africa: The Search for Unity* (1963).

East Timor

The eastern half of the island of Timor in the East Indies was a Portuguese colony from 1566 until 1975 when it declared itself independent. In 1974, when the armed forces movement came to power in Portugal, three political factions were in existence in East Timor. The Uniao Democratica Timorense (UDT) advocated association with Portugal, the Associacao Popular Democratica Timorense wanted integration with Indonesia, and the Revolutionary Front for an Independent East Timor (FRETILIN) called for complete independence. An attempt by the UDT to seize power led to a brief civil war, which ended with victory on the part of FRETILIN. The new government declared independence, set up agricultural cooperatives, and commenced a mass literacy campaign. In early December 1975, the Indonesian army overran East Timor and declared the region to be Indonesia's twenty-seventh province. Two reasons for the Indonesian invasion have been suggested: fear that an independent East Timor would encourage separatist movements in other parts of Indonesia and fear that under the left-wing FRETILIN government, the island would become a Communist outpost.

The invasion and subsequent harsh treatment of the East Timorese resulted in the death of at least 15 percent of the population (some accounts claim that as many as half the population per-

East Timorese women in an emotional protest outside the Indonesian consulate in Hong Kong, urging the Indonesian government to stop the violence in East Timor by the pro-Jakarta militia, September 1999. (Corbis/ Reuters Newsmedia Inc.)

ished). Indonesian rule was marked by massacres, widespread torture, and the destruction of crops leading to famine. Guerrilla resistance by the East Timorese continued, and after the downfall of President Suharto in 1998, talks began between Indonesia and Portugal as to the future of East Timor—Portugal was recognized by the United Nations as the legal ruler of East Timor. In an agreement signed in May 1999, Indonesia promised to allow a UN-supervised plebiscite to be held in August 1999. If the Timorese rejected increased autonomy, Indonesia agreed to grant independence to the territory. On August 30, a large majority of the East Timorese voted for independence, but the vote was followed by wide-spread violence from pro-Indonesian militias. In response the United Nations sent an international force to restore peace in the region.

References Suter, Keith. *East Timor and West Irian* (1982); Taylor, John. *Indonesia's Forgotten War: The Hidden History of East Timor* (1991).

Egypt's Claim to the Sudan

In 1899, the Sudan theoretically became an Anglo-Egyptian condominium, and Egypt formally appointed its governor general. In practice, the Sudan was ruled as though it were a British colony. Sudanese nationalists were divided as to whether the Sudan should become independent or be united with Egypt. The Umma Party supported independence; the National Unionist Party (NUP) wanted unification. When Britain set up a legislative assembly in 1948, Egypt protested, and the elections were boycotted by the NUP. Egypt's King Farouk then declared himself king of the Sudan. However, after the Egyptian revolution of 1952, which overthrew the monarchy, London and Cairo signed an Anglo-Egyptian accord in which it was agreed that the Sudanese would decide their future status in a 1956 plebiscite. Although the pro-unification NUP won the elections of 1953, the party's leader, Ismail al Azhari, realized that public opinion had shifted in favor of independence. On January 1, 1956, Sudan became independent.

See also Sudan.
Reference Woodward, Peter. *Sudan, 1898–1989: The Unstable State* (1990).

Enbata

Enbata is a French Basque organization founded in 1963; its name means "freedom wind." The group's main activity is to provide support for Basque refugees from Spain, although it also publishes a newspaper. Enbata candidates received about 2 percent of the vote in the 1968 French elections. There are about 200,000 French Basques (although only 80,000 speak Basque) concentrated in the French department of Pyrénées-Atlantiques.

See also Basques.

English Speaking Union

The English Speaking Union (ESU) was founded in Britain in 1918 by Evelyn Wrench. The first edition of its magazine argued that world peace and progress depended on the unity of the English-speaking democracies and pledged to promote "good understanding between the peoples of the USA and the British Commonwealth." The article went on to hope that the ESU would link "the sheep farmer in Australia with the New York businessman and the gold miner in South Africa with the fruit grower in California." In 1920, the ESU was established in the United States with the ex-ambassador to Britain being one of the founding members.

The current goals of the organization are far removed from its early Pan Anglo-Saxonism. In 1975, the definition of "English-speaking" was expanded to include those for whom English was a second language. The purpose of the contemporary ESU is the promotion of international understanding through the widening use of English, as it is believed that the English language offers a means of shared communication between peoples of different races and cultures in the emerging global village.

See also Anglo-Saxonism.

Eritrea

The Eritrean separatist struggle against Ethiopian rule lasted four decades before Eritrea became independent in 1993. Eritrea was an Italian colony from 1889 until 1941 and under British administration from 1941 until 1952. Then, since the four victorious Allies were unable to decide what should happen to Eritrea, the question was referred to the United Nations. After investigating the matter, the UN General Assembly decided that Eritrea should form an "autonomous unit federated with Ethiopia under the sovereignty of the Ethiopian Crown." The federation, with a separate executive and legislature for Eritrea, was probably acceptable to the majority of Eritreans at that time.

The Eritreans were divided into two main communities of approximately equal size, the Tigrinya-speaking Christians of the highlands and the Muslims who inhabited the lowlands. The Tigrinya were not only similar culturally to the Amhara of Ethiopia but far more developed economically than the Muslim pastoralists. The Unionist Party, which favored union with Ethiopia, was predominantly Christian while the Muslims generally favored independence. However, two lowland groups, the Afar and the Kunari, were opposed to independence, in part because the separatist movement was dominated initially by their traditional enemies, the Beni Amir.

In less than a decade, Emperor Haile Selassie whittled away at Eritrean autonomy and the freedoms enjoyed by the Eritrean people until, in 1962, the federation was dissolved and Eritrea became the fourteenth province of Ethiopia. The head of the Eritrean executive and the speaker of the assembly were both dismissed. Political parties, trades unions, and newspapers were banned. Amharic was declared to be the official language of Eritrea, replacing Tigrinya and Arabic. The Eritrean flag was abolished, the Eritrean constitution suspended, and all opposition crushed. The Eritreans soon discovered that they were economically worse off than under either the Italians or the British. Predictably, this all led to the growth of armed resistance.

The Eritrean Liberation Front (ELF) began guerrilla warfare in 1961, and after the Eritrean People's Liberation Front (EPLF) split from the ELF, it began its own campaign in 1970. Generally speaking, the ELF was supported by the Muslims, and the EPLF was supported by the Christians. The EPLF was more radical than the ELF and carried out a popular land reform program in the areas under its control. Its ability to organize food distribution and to provide education and medical services won it increasing support even in the Muslim lowlands. Fighting between the two movements occurred in 1972–1974 and again in 1981–1982, when the EPLF defeated the ELF.

After 1982, the ELF fragmented, with some of its members joining the EPLF and others going into exile. The ELF sought support from the Arab world; established offices in Egypt, Syria, and Iraq; and called for Muslim solidarity against the "infidel" Haile Selassie and his Zionist allies. Later, after the overthrow of Haile Selassie by a group of radical Marxist officers, the EPLF played down its revolutionary rhetoric and appealed to Saudi Arabia and other conservative Arab states. Significant amounts of military aid flowed to the rebels from Syria, Libya, and Saudi Arabia. The Sudan played a Machiavellian game, first allowing the Eritreans to use its territory as a base, then using that fact to pressure Ethiopia into withdrawing its support from the southern Sudanese rebels. The Organization of African Unity was reluctant to become involved in the dispute, both because of its principle that the territorial integrity of African states should be accepted and because the site of the organization's headquarters was in the Ethiopian city of Addis Ababa.

Even though Haile Selassie was overthrown by the army in 1974, the military regime of Mengistu Haile Mariam maintained Haile Selassie's policy of attempting to crush the Eritreans by force. Mengistu announced that his goal was to "affirm Ethiopia's historic unity and to safeguard her outlet to the sea and to defend her very existence." By the mid-1970s, the ELF and EPLF between them had gained control over virtually all the rural areas and most of the towns, but the situation was reversed after 1978 when the Soviet Union provided the Ethiopians with massive military support. A military stalemate lasted for several years, with the EPLF defending a small liberated zone around the town of Nafca against repeated Ethiopian offensives. In 1984, the EPLF went on the offensive and defeated the Ethiopian forces in May 1991, subsequently occupying Asmara, the Eritrean capital, and setting up a provisional government. Mengistu's Ethiopian regime was itself subsequently overthrown by the Ethiopian People's Revolutionary Democratic Front, which was allied with the EPLF. In a referendum held in April 1993, 99.8 percent of the Eritreans voted for independence.

After Eritrean independence, relations with Ethiopia deteriorated. In 1997, Eritrea introduced its own currency, and in 1999, heavy fighting broke out between the two countries in the Badme region with several thousand fatalities on each side. The 600-mile border had never been demarcated, and both countries claimed the area.

See also Afar; Eritrean Liberation Front; Eritrean People's Liberation Front; Ethiopia.

Frontline fighters of the Eritrean Peoples' Liberation Front in Eritrea, October 1986. (Corbis/Caroline Penn)

References Legum, Colin, and James Fairbrace. *Eritrea and Tigray* (1983); Pool, David. *Eritrea: Towards Unity in Diversity* (1997); Woodward, Peter, ed. *Conflict and Peace in the Horn of Africa* (1994).

Eritrean Liberation Front

The Eritrean Liberation Front (ELF), the first guerrilla group to take up arms against the Ethiopians, was formed in Cairo by a group of Eritrean exiles. Its first leaders were Idris Muhammed Adam, former speaker of the Eritrean Assembly; Ibrahim Sultan, the secretary of the Muslim League; and Woldab Wolde Mariam, a trade union leader. The ELF campaign was supported by the Beni Amir, a warrior Muslim clan. As the insurgency spread, four autonomous, tribally based military commands were organized, which meant that the ELF reflected and heightened the regional and religious divisions within Eritrea. Dissidents within the ELF argued for "unity of forces" and against the emphasis on the Muslim character of the liberation move-

ment. When the ELF expanded its operations into the Christian highlands, tensions between the leadership and the predominantly Christian dissidents led to factional violence and the emergence of the Eritrean People's Liberation Front. The latter became the main liberation movement, and after fierce fighting between the two groups in 1981 and 1982, the ELF was driven out of Eritrea.

See also Eritrea; Eritrean People's Liberation Front; Ethiopia.
Reference Pool, David. "Eritrean Nationalism" (1983).

Eritrean People's Liberation Front

Formed as a splinter group from the Eritrean Liberation Front (ELF), the original membership of the Eritrean People's Liberation Front (EPLF) was largely Christian, but the group took a strong stand against religious sectarianism. One of the group's early pamphlets charged the ELF with defining the struggle as an Islamic one rather than as a struggle for the liberation of the Eritrean people as a whole.

As a Marxist movement, the EPLF followed a strategy of land reform and political education. In liberated areas, literacy classes, medical assistance, and political education were used to mobilize the population while the EPLF fighters themselves received six months of intensive political propaganda along with their military training. Even in the Ethiopian-occupied towns, the EPLF established an infrastructure of supporters. To break down Christian-Muslim distinctions, songs and dances from all regions were blended together in an attempt to create a common Eritrean culture. Female emancipation was emphasized, and 13 percent of the front-line fighters were women. When famine hit the region in 1983–1985, the EPLF insisted that international relief should be distributed through its organization. The resulting ability to deliver emergency supplies of food to the peasants further increased popular support for the EPLF.

See also Eritrea; Eritrean Liberation Front; Ethiopia.
Reference Pool, David. "Eritrean Nationalism" (1983).

Estonia

An ancient Baltic people, Estonians speak a Finno-Ugric language. By the thirteenth century, they were under the control of the Teutonic knights, and in 1645, Estonia became part of the Swedish kingdom. In 1721, the heavily Protestant country was absorbed into the Russian Empire, and in the nineteenth century, a Russification policy was forced upon Estonia. During the revolutionary upheavals of 1905 in Russia, the Estonian National Liberal Party Congress demanded autonomy for the country. The party was subsequently suppressed by Russian authorities. Following the Russian Revolution of 1917, Estonian nationalism gained strength, and in 1918, Estonia declared itself an independent republic, although it was not until 1920 that the country was free of Russian troops and able to conduct its own affairs. It then adopted a democratic constitution and was admitted the League of Nations.

In 1940, following the signing of the Soviet-German Nonaggression Pact, Estonia was again occupied by Russian troops and forced to become a Soviet socialist republic. Briefly under German control during World War II, Estonia underwent a draconian transformation after Soviet troops recaptured the country. Massive Russian immigration, forced collectivization, and large-scale deportations occurred swiftly, and the Communist elite was mostly non-Estonian.

When liberalization began sweeping the Soviet Union in the 1980s, an umbrella organization, the Popular Front, advocated Estonian sovereignty. In open elections in 1990, supporters of independence gained control in parliament, and in August 1991, following a coup attempt against Mikhail Gorbachev, Estonia formally declared its independence.

As a consequence of Soviet rule, Estonia's population of 1.5 million is nearly 30 percent Russian. Estonia, like Latvia, has adopted chauvinistic citizenship laws that largely bar postwar immigrants, mainly Russian, from becoming Estonian nationals. Although permitted to vote in local elections, noncitizens may not participate in voting for national offices, and to become a citizen, non-Estonians must pass a rigorous examination in Estonian language and history. In 1997, only 8,000 people were granted citizenship, and only 10 percent of Russians between the ages of eighteen and twenty-nine have been granted citizenship, although two out of three of this age group would like to become citizens. Sixty percent of all Russian Estonians have taken out Russian citizenship because they felt it was too difficult to meet the Estonian standards. It is estimated that some 100,000 Russians have no citizenship and possess no internationally recognized passports. In contrast to older Russians, many of them pensioners, younger Russian Estonians consider Estonia to be their country.

Estonia's rapid economic growth and rising standard of living compared to the standard of living in Russia make few Russians desirous of leaving Estonia. The Russian government, the Organization for Security and Cooperation in Europe, and international human rights watchdogs have all protested the lack of citizenship possibilities for many Russian Estonians. The Estonian government is attempting to revise the language and history examinations, but it will not waive them. It has introduced measures to teach more Estonian classes for those wishing to take the exams and for all Russian-speaking children. The government also proposes to grant automatic citizenship to all children born in Estonia.

See also Narva and Petserimaa; Russians in the Former Soviet Republics; Union of Soviet Socialist Republics.
References Smith, Graham, ed. *The Baltic States: The National Self-Determination of Estonia, Latvia, and Lithuania* (1994); Taagepara, Rein. *Estonia: Return to Independence* (1993).

Ethiopia

The ancient Kingdom of Ethiopia is situated to the west of the Red Sea and borders the Sudan, Somaliland, and Kenya. The ruling dynasty claimed to be descended from the son of King Solomon and the queen of Sheba, and this Solomonic lineage was the basis of its political legitimacy. The kingdom of Aksum, forerunner of the Ethiopian kingdom, was converted to Coptic Christianity in the fourth century, and the church has traditionally played a major role in Ethiopian society.

The historic core of the Ethiopian state lies in the highland provinces of Gojjam, Begemeder, and Shoa, which are inhabited by the Amhara. A Muslim invasion in 1529 overran most of Ethiopia, and imperial power was not restored until the beginning of the reign of Emperor Tewodros II in 1855. Under Menelik II (1889–1913), the borders of Ethiopia were extended to their current position. Ethiopia is unique among African states in that it was never a European colony. Indeed, after defeating the Italians at the Battle of Adowa in 1896, Ethiopia itself became an imperial power when Menelik II conquered the low-

land areas inhabited by the Somali, Afar, and Oromo peoples. No census has ever been taken, but most estimates suggest that the Amhara-Tigray speakers constitute a third of the population, the Oromo about 40 percent, and the Somalis and Afar 6 percent each.

These statistics may be misleading because Amhara ethnicity is different from that in most African societies. Most African groups are based on the idea that all members of a group are related by blood to one another through descent from a common mythological ancestor. The Amhara, however, recognize both patrilineal and matrilineal descent. Furthermore, since the name of an Ethiopian male consists of his personal name followed by his father's personal name, it is impossible to identify the ethnic origins of a person beyond that of his father. Thus, the leader of the military government, or Dergue, Mengistu Haile Mariam, is Mengistu the son of Haile Mariam, but little is known of his ethnicity. An Orthodox Christian with an Amharic name who speaks Amhara would be accepted by other Amhara. Ethnic identities are consequently fluid, and there is much assimilation. The Emperor Haile Selassie himself had two Oromo grandparents, one Gurage grandmother, and only one Amhara grandmother, his father's mother, yet he was regarded by all as an Amhara.

The Italians invaded Ethiopia in 1935, and Haile Selassie did not regain his throne until 1941. In 1952, Eritrea, which had been an Italian colony, was federated with Ethiopia. Despite some attempts at modernization, the country remained basically feudal in character. Haile Selassie ruled autocratically, and the nobility dominated local and provincial government. Few peasants owned their own land, and it has been estimated that most paid at least half of their crop as rent as well as being liable for tithes and unpaid labor duties.

An army revolt in February 1974 led to the overthrow of the dynasty. The military rulers, known as the Dergue, although radical Marxists, were determined to maintain the integrity of the

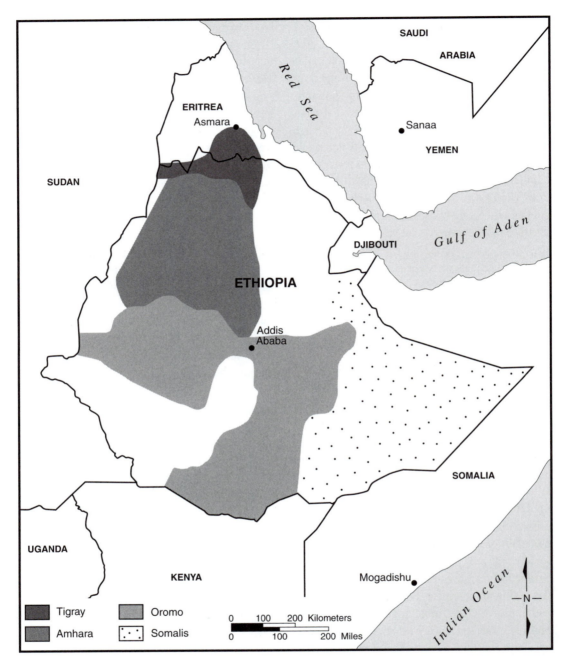

Tigray
Amhara
Oromo
Somalis
0 100 200 Kilometers
0 100 200 Miles

state and Amhara dominance, despite the existence of at least five separatist movements. In addition to Eritrea, these movements included the Somalis, the Oromo, the Afar, and the Tigray. The movements gradually expanded their activities, and by 1990, they controlled most of Ethiopia. Peace talks organized by the United States were held in May 1991, but when the leader of the Dergue, Mengistu Haile Mariam, fled the country, the Ethiopian government collapsed. The rebels, organized as the Ethiopian People's Revolutionary Democratic Front, marched into Addis Ababa and set up a transitional government in which the various separatist movements were represented. The constitution, ratified in December 1994, provided for a federal system and the division of the country into nine states: Tigray, Afar, Amara, Oromia, Somali, Benshangui, Gambela, Harer, and one comprising the southern peoples. Each state was given considerable autonomy and the right to secede.

See also Afar; Eritrea; Ogaden; Oromia; Somalis; Tigray.
References Gilkes, Patrick. *The Dying Lion: Feudalism and Modernization in Ethiopia* (1975); Legum, Colin. *Ethiopia: The Fall of Haile Selassie's Empire* (1975).

Ethnic Cleansing

The strategy of removing members of targeted ethnic groups from a territory to secure that territory for another ethnic group is known as "ethnic cleansing," and it was employed to greater and lesser degrees by Serbians, Croatians, and Bosnian Muslims in the Yugoslavian civil war from 1991 to 1995. Tactics used by Serbians against Muslims in Bosnia and documented by the United Nations included administrative sanctions (loss of jobs and housing), intimidation (threats to life), destruction of property (burning of mosques and shelling of Muslim neighborhoods), forced expulsion, imprisonment (concentration camps), violence against persons (rape, torture, and execution), and mass extermination. In overrunning the town of Srebrenica, Serbian forces are alleged to have executed some 8,000 Muslim civilians.

The policy is associated with former president Radovan Karadzic of the Republic of Srpska and General Ratko Mladic, head of Serb military forces. Croatian troops in Bosnia also engaged in "cleansing" practices—at Mostar, for example—to remove Muslims from villages and towns with Croat populations. In 1998 and early 1999, Serbian forces engaged in an "ethnic cleansing" of the Albanians of Kosovo. Although numerous indictments for war crimes have been issued by the United Nations, arrests have been few.

See also Bosnia and Herzegovina; Croatia; Greater Serbia; Karadzic, Radovan; Kosovo.
References Bell, Andrew. *Ethnic Cleansing* (1996); Rieff,

David. *Slaughterhouse: Bosnia and the Failure of the West* (1996).

Ethnike Organosis Kyprion Agoniston

Two terrorist groups on Cyprus have used the name Ethnike Organosis Kyprion Agoniston (EOKA, National Organization of Cypriot Fighters). The first was founded by George Grivas, and it fought against the British during 1955–1959. At the start of that revolt, there were fewer than 50 EOKA guerrillas, but eventually they numbered almost 300 in addition to another 750 organized into auxiliary village militia groups. These guerrillas were young, and half of those brought to trial for terrorist offenses were under twenty years old. Grivas noted that "among young people one finds audacity, a love of taking risks," and he deliberately recruited such "passionate youths." Although women were used as couriers, he refused to allow them to play a combat role. Grivas and some other leaders were from comfortable middle-class backgrounds, but most of the rank-and-file were peasants, craftsmen, or laborers.

It is generally agreed by most commentators that enosis (political union with Greece) was supported by the overwhelming majority of Greek Cypriots, but a number were opposed to EOKA. Bitter antagonism developed between Grivas, an extreme right-wing nationalist, and the Cypriot Communist Party. However, demonstrations in favor of enosis and EOKA were frequent and well-supported. Sympathizers could be found in the police force, the civil service, and among workers on British bases. Churches and monasteries were used to store arms and ammunition and served as terrorist hideouts. Orthodox clergy even smuggled explosives into Cyprus. Some EOKA weapons came from Greek army stores and were carried to Cyprus on ships of the Royal Hellenic Navy.

This EOKA campaign involved sabotage against military installations, throwing grenades at British patrols, ambushes, and assassinations.

Although the primary target of the guerrillas was the British military, the number of Greek Cypriots executed as informers (142) almost equaled the number of British military fatalities (158). Several British civilians were deliberately murdered, including two British women who were shot in the back while shopping with their children. EOKA's killing of Turkish policemen heightened tensions and led to the emergence of Turkish counterterrorism. The British responded with heavy-handed repression: mass arrests, curfews, and collective punishments. Villages in which terrorism took place were fined.

After the signing of the Zurich agreement of 1959, Grivas left Cyprus for Athens and later denounced Archbishop Makarios for betraying the cause of enosis. In 1971, Grivas returned to Cyprus and set up a second organization, EOKA B, which continued the struggle for enosis, this time against Makarios. The EOKA B militants were largely drawn from the ranks of the national guard, who were trained by Greek officers. These militants differed from the members of the former EOKA in that they were older and usually came from rural backgrounds.

See also Cyprus; Grivas, George; Makarios, Archbishop.
References Grivas, George. *Memoirs of General Grivas* (1965); Markides, Kyriacos. *The Rise and Fall of the Cyprus Republic* (1977).

Etzel
See Irgun

European Union
The idea of a united Europe has a long history, but the modern movement dates from the period following World War II and the setting up of the European Coal and Steel Community (ECSC) in 1952. The original six members were Germany, France, Italy, Belgium, the Netherlands, and Luxembourg. Jean Monnet, the first president of the ECSC, argued that "their prosperity and social development are impossible unless the states of Europe form themselves into a federation or Eu-

ropean entity which will make of it a common economic unit." The ECSC was the forerunner of the European Economic Community (also known as the Common Market), which was formed in 1957. By 1968, all tariffs and quotas on industrial goods had been abolished among the community members.

The membership of the group, which was renamed the European Union, was expanded when Britain, the Republic of Ireland, and Denmark joined in 1973. Later Austria, Greece, Portugal, Spain, Sweden, and Finland also became members. The first elections to a European Parliament were held in 1979. A European monetary union began on January 1, 1999, and a common currency is planned to go into circulation by the year 2002. Paradoxically, the economic union of the countries of Western Europe has also allowed many previously ignored ethnoregional identities to emerge, since the issue of their economic viability is no longer so relevant.

Reference Snyder, Louis L. *Macro-Nationalisms* (1984).

Euzkadi ta Askatasuna
Euzkadi ta Askatasuna (ETA—the name means "homeland and freedom" in Basque) is a Basque terrorist organization that was founded in 1959 by dissident members of the Basque Nationalist Party's youth group. In the next decade, the group split into several factions divided by issues of ideology and strategy. The key issues involved the significance of class versus language and whether armed struggle or political agitation would be more effective. By the end of 1974, two organizations had emerged, ETA politico-militar and ETA militar. The former was Marxist-Leninist in ideology and favored a combined strategy of mass organization and armed struggle while the latter defined the conflict as one of national liberation and advocated a purely military strategy. ETA militar grew more rapidly and has been responsible for the great majority of attacks. In 1976, the ETA politico-militar decided to form a socialist party and to abandon armed struggle.

The membership of ETA is divided into three categories: *liberados, legales,* and *apoyos.* The first category is composed of members who work for the organization full-time, are paid a small salary, and carry out the actual attacks. They are divided into small cells, or *comandos,* of three to five persons each. The *legales,* who continue to hold a regular jobs, gather intelligence, and act as couriers. The *apoyos* supply shelter and other kinds of support to the active members. The total membership of ETA may have reached 700 in 1979, but then it declined.

The ETA campaign began in 1968 with the assassination of an unpopular police commissioner, Meliton Manzanas, outside his home. The original strategy of ETA was to provoke the Spanish authorities into adopting repressive policies that would, in turn, radicalize the Basque public and produce a mass uprising. Sporadic attacks occurred during the final years of the Franco regime, the most dramatic of which was the killing of the Spanish prime minister, Carrero Blanco, in 1973. An ETA unit tunneled under the street outside the church that Blanco attended each day and set off a massive explosion as his car passed over the spot. ETA attacks increased after the death of Franco and reached a peak during the transition to democracy, although they have declined since the granting of autonomy to the Basque region in 1980.

Over 800 people have been killed by the ETA, two-thirds of the victims being soldiers and police, especially members of the hated Guardia Civil. ETA also targets political figures and government officials, and at least four provincial governors and seven mayors have been murdered. Although a few bombs have exploded in public places such as cafes, railway stations, and airports, such attacks have been rare, with only a handful of civilians killed or wounded. More than sixty people, most of them wealthy businessmen, have been kidnapped and held for ransom. Not only do the kidnappings raise money directly, but they frighten other people into paying a sizable annual "revolutionary tax" to the ETA.

Popular support for the terrorist organization in the Basque provinces is considerable, although it appears to have declined somewhat in recent years. The number who favor independence reached 32 percent in 1979 but declined after the granting of autonomy to 12 percent in the early 1980s. In 1978, an opinion poll found that almost half had a positive image of ETA members as "patriots" or "idealists," although by 1989, less than a quarter thought so and the proportion who saw them as "crazy" or "common criminals" had increased. About a sixth of the population votes for Herri Batasuna, the political wing of ETA, although the party has begun losing election support, with its representation in the regional assembly falling from fourteen in 1986 to eleven in 1994. In 1998, after Herri Batasuna was banned, its successor, Euskal Heritarrok, won fourteen seats.

ETA's ultimate goal is an independent socialist Euzkadi, which would include Navarra and the French Basque provinces. Their negotiating demands, which are known as "the KAS alternative," call for recognition of the Basque right to secede, the withdrawal of all national security forces and the Guardia Civil, the integration of Navarra into Euzkadi, and an amnesty for all Basque political prisoners. ETA announced a truce in early 1989, and negotiations between the Spanish government and ETA took place in Algeria. Although the negotiations failed to produce a peace agreement, ETA violence declined, and another cease-fire was declared in September 1998. Although the Spanish government has made no new concessions to the ETA, the cease-fire is still in effect.

See also Basques; Partido Nacionalista Vasco.
References Clark, Robert P. *The Basque Insurgents* (1984); Sullivan, John. *ETA and Basque Nationalism* (1988).

Ewe

The Ewe people, numbering about 1 million, live along the West African coast in Ghana and Togo. As the most educated group within Togoland, the Ewe dominated the civil service during both the

German and the French colonial periods. Several movements have called for the reunification of the Ewe under one administration. These include the All Ewe Conference (AEC) set up in the Gold Coast in 1946, which campaigned for all the Ewe to be under British administration, and the Comité de l'Unité Togolaise (CUT), which was founded in French Togoland in 1941. The AEC, led by Daniel Chapman, became defunct in 1949, and CUT was regarded with suspicion by the French administration, which saw it as a pro-British secessionist movement. Consequently, the French favored the Parti Togolais du Progrès, which held power during the 1952–1958 period. However, CUT, led by Sylvanus Olympio, won the UN-supervised elections of 1958.

Olympio was the first president of Togo after the country became independent in April 1960. Relations between Ghana and Togo became tense after Olympio called for the Ewe districts of Ghana to be reunited with Togo. Ghana closed the border between the two countries, and there were clashes between Ghanaian and Togolese troops. Although making up only 44 percent of the population, the Ewe dominated the Togo government under Olympio, and his successor, Nicholas Grunitsky, and it was not until the overthrow of Grunitsky by Etienne Eyadema in 1967 that they lost their majority status in the cabinet.

See also Ghana; Togoland.
Reference Decalo, Samuel. *Historical Dictionary of Togo* (1976).

Faeroe Islands

A group of islands in the North Atlantic with a population of about 45,000, the Faeroes are heavily dependent upon the fishing industry. Part of the Danish kingdom, they were occupied by British forces during World War II. After the war, the islands declared themselves independent. The king of Denmark then dissolved the local council, negotiations followed, and by an act of the Danish parliament, the island became self-governing in 1948. Denmark retains control of foreign relations, the Faeroese are Danish citizens, and both Danish and Faeroese (related to Old Norse) can be used in official business.

Reference Lapidoth, Ruth. *Autonomy: Flexible Solutions to Ethnic Conflict* (1997).

Falkland Islands/Islas Malvinas

The Falkland Islands/Islas Malvinas, located 300 miles off the Argentine coast, consist of two large islands, East and West Falkland, and several smaller islands. The first recorded landing was by a British ship in January 1690, and its captain named them after Viscount Falkland, the treasurer of the Royal Navy at the time. French sailors from St. Malo, who visited the islands in the 1700s, called them "les Isles Malouines," from which is derived their Spanish name, Islas Malvinas. In 1764, the French established a settlement on East Falkland, and the following year the British established one on a small island off West Falkland. In 1767, the French relinquished their claims to Spain, and in 1770, the Spaniards drove off the British settlers.

After a small Spanish garrison was withdrawn in 1811, the islands remained uninhabited until 1820 when Argentina, newly independent of Spain, established a settlement. Following a fishing dispute, the USS *Lexington* destroyed the settlement in 1831 and deported the Argentine settlers. Two years later, the British reoccupied the islands, which were thereafter administered as a British colony. The British settlers introduced

sheep, which became the mainstay of the islands' economy. By 1972, the population of the islands numbered just under 2,000, almost all of British descent.

Although Argentina has disputed Britain's possession of the islands since 1833, it did not actively press its claim until after World War II. The president of Argentina, Juan Perón, not only revived his country's claim to the Falklands but also extended it to include the South Georgia, South Sandwich, and South Shetland Islands as well as a large sector of Antarctica. (Pregnant women were encouraged to go to Antarctica to have their babies in order to strengthen the Argentine claim.) The military junta, which succeeded Perón in 1957, formally declared the Falklands and other South Atlantic islands to be part of Argentina.

The Argentine public strongly supported such claims, and when a group of students hijacked a plane in 1966, landed on the Falklands, and proclaimed Argentine sovereignty over the islands, massive demonstrations took place throughout the country. Several rounds of negotiations between Britain and Argentina failed to result in a settlement. When General Leopoldo Galtieri, commander in chief of the army, became president in December 1981, he decided to invade, and in April 1982, Argentine forces quickly overwhelmed the tiny British garrison. However, the

British Army vehicles in Port Stanley, the Falkland Islands, August 13, 1982. (Corbis/Bettmann)

British, contrary to Argentine expectations, mounted a counterattack and sent a naval task force to regain the islands. The conflict, in which 255 British soldiers and an estimated 800 Argentines were killed, led to the downfall of the junta and a sweeping electoral victory in the subsequent British elections for Margaret Thatcher. Speaking to the House of Commons, Prime Minister Thatcher rejected further negotiations over the status of the Falklands saying: "Our men did not risk their lives for a UN trusteeship. They risked their lives for the British way of life, to defend British sovereignty. I do not intend to negotiate on the sovereignty of the islands in any way. . . . Those islands belong to us."

References Calvert, Peter. *The Falklands Crisis* (1982); Dabat, Alejandro. *Argentina, the Malvinas and the End of Military Rule* (1984); Femenia, Nora. *National Identity in Times of Crisis: The Scripts of the Falklands-Malvinas War* (1996).

Fatah

Fatah is a political and military organization founded in the 1950s by Yasir Arafat. It is secular rather than Islamic in ideology and includes student, worker, and civic organizations. Regionally organized in the Gaza Strip, the West Bank, and other Arab states where Palestinians live, Fatah is governed by a central committee headed by Arafat. Fatah's goal is the creation of a democratic Palestine with Jerusalem as its capital.

At its inception, Fatah refused to accept the legitimacy of the state of Israel, arguing that Israeli territory was part of Palestine. In the 1960s, Fatah engaged Israeli forces in several operations and participated in the Six Day War of 1967. Fatah also approved the use of terror against Israeli citizens to help achieve its ends. An extremist faction of Fatah, Black September, was accused of killing twelve Israeli athletes at the 1972 Olympic Games in Munich, Germany.

In 1964, Fatah joined the new umbrella organization, the Palestine Liberation Organization (PLO). Fatah became the most dominant faction in the PLO, giving it a militarist orientation and loosening its dependence on the Arab states for leadership. In 1969, Yasir Arafat was elected president of the PLO.

With the signing of the Israeli-PLO peace accords of 1993, Fatah renounced violence as a tactic. Functioning as a political party, Fatah's slate of candidates in the 1996 elections for the newly created Palestinian Legislative Council took sixty-five of eighty-eight seats. In the same elections, Yasir Arafat was elected president of the Palestinian Authority (PA), the executive branch of the new government. Officials of the PA and its security forces under Arafat have been drawn mainly from Fatah ranks. Despite its dominance of the PA, Fatah organizations, including militia units, continue to function independently.

See also Arafat, Yasir; Palestine Liberation Organization; Palestinians.
References Nassar, Jamal Raji. *The Palestine Liberation Organization: From Armed Struggle to the Declaration of Independence* (1991); Robinson, Glenn. *Building a Palestinian State* (1997).

Federation of Rhodesia and Nyasaland

Of the many attempts at federation in Africa, the Federation of Rhodesia and Nyasaland lasted the longest. Created in 1953, the federation was intended to foster "partnership" between the white minority and the black majority in the three British colonies of Southern Rhodesia, Northern Rhodesia, and Nyasaland (now Zimbabwe, Zambia, and Malawi, repectively). The federation was favored by the whites and opposed by the blacks. African opposition was based on the fear that federation would allow the white minority in Southern Rhodesia to extend its domination to the other territories. (Roy Welensky, the leader of the white settlers of Northern Rhodesia, is supposed to have said that the partnership between the two races would be like the partnership between horse and rider.) African political leaders

boycotted the constitutional negotiations and continued to resist the federation until it was dissolved in 1963. The constitution was complicated with four different requirements for voting in the three territories and the federal elections, and only a handful of Africans registered to vote in the federal elections.

Although federation led to an economic boom in Southern Rhodesia and a reduction in racial discrimination in all three territories, these facts had little effect on African attitudes. Unrest in Northern Rhodesia led to the declaration of a state of emergency in 1959 during which sixty Africans were killed. After the British government extended the territorial franchise in Nyasaland and Northern Rhodesia, the next elections were won by the antifederation Malawi Congress Party in Nyasaland and the United National Independence Party in Northern Rhodesia. In Southern Rhodesia, the largely white electorate gave the Rhodesian Front a majority over the United Federal Party. The next year, on March 29, 1963, the British government formally recognized that the federation was doomed and negotiated the division of its financial assets and liabilities among the three territories.

Reference Spiro, Herbert. "The Federation of Rhodesia and Nyasaland" (1968).

Federation of the West Indies

The Federation of the West Indies (1958–1962), which grouped together most of the British Caribbean territories, fell apart after Jamaica withdrew from it. In 1947, at a Montego Bay conference, representatives of the various islands agreed in principle to set up a federal union. After a series of constitutional conferences and commissions, the West Indian Constitution of 1957 was published. Port-of-Spain on Trinidad was selected as the federal capital over objections from Barbados and Jamaica. The constitution left most of the power in the hands of the component territories, and the central government had no major source of revenue. The authority of the

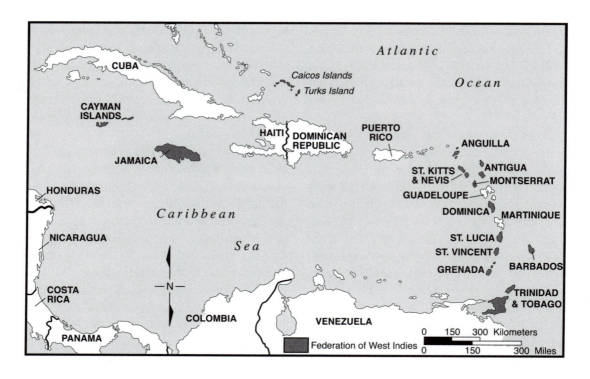

central government was further weakened by the London Conference of 1961, at which, as a result of Jamaican pressure, federal powers of taxation were restricted.

After the London Conference, Jamaican Premier Michael Manley announced that a referendum would be held to approve Jamaica's continued membership. His People's National Party supported federation while the opposition Jamaica Labour Party argued that federation would be more costly than independence. With only 60 percent of the electorate voting, 55 percent were against remaining in the federation. Although some hoped that a smaller federation led by Trinidad could be established, Dr. Eric Williams, the leader of Trinidad, took the position that the secession of Jamaica meant the abandonment of the whole scheme. As he put it, "One from ten leaves none."

Several factors contributed to the breakup of the federation. The weak federal structure reflected the diversity of interests and cultures among the different islands. One West Indian politician described it as "the most improbable

historical venture that one can imagine." The islands were widely separated, Jamaica and Trinidad being 1,250 miles apart, and communications among them were poor. Most West Indians had never visited any of the other islands, and even their leaders had little contact with one another. The disparities in population and living standards were substantial.

Jamaica had over half the total population; Montserrat had only 0.5 percent. To prevent domination by Jamaica and Trinidad, the two islands were given considerably fewer seats in the legislature than they were entitled to on the basis of their populations. Jamaica wanted a loose confederation while Trinidad advocated a strong central government. Trinidad, the most prosperous of the territories, was worried that freedom of movement would result in large-scale immigration from the poorer islands. Jamaica was afraid that its industrial sector would suffer competition from low-cost producers on other islands and was reluctant to accept free trade within the federation. The constitutional provision that prevented members of local legislatures from being elected to the federation's parliament made many politicians reluctant to seek federal office.

References Franck, Thomas M. *Why Federations Fail* (1968); Wallace, Elizabeth M. *The British Caribbean: From the Decline of Colonialism to the End of Federation* (1977).

Fernando Póo

The island of Fernando Póo (now Bioko) is situated in the Gulf of Guinea a hundred miles from the African mainland. Until 1968, Fernando Póo and Río Muni (now Mbini) formed the Spanish colony of Equatorial Guinea. Most of the island's population consisted of Nigerian contract laborers and their descendants. In 1960, out of a population of about 64,000, 40,000 were Nigerian while the indigenous Bubi numbered only 12,000. As a result of the bad treatment of the Nigerian workers, there was considerable pressure on the newly independent government of Nigeria to annex the island. Nigerian newspapers and politicians called on Spain to hand over the island because of its geographical proximity and the fact that ethnic Nigerians formed a majority. However, fearing that a military takeover would encourage territorial claims against Nigeria, the government resisted the pressure.

When the Spanish colony became independent, both parties on the island were against union with the mainland territory of Río Muni, and in a 1968 UN referendum, the islanders voted 7,150 to 5,340 for an independent Fernando Póo. However, their wishes were ignored, and the island remains united with the mainland.

Reference Akinyemi, Bolaji. "Nigeria and Fernando Poo: The Politics of Irridentism" (1970).

France

The French Revolution of 1789 abolished the ancient provinces and replaced them with departments, and a constant theme of French politics since that date has been the conflict between "Jacobin" centralism and the conservative provinces.

One aspect of this struggle was the attempt by the central government to stamp out the use of local languages in the educational system and elsewhere. One French revolutionary called for "a sacred competition to banish from all parts of France those jargons which are the remains of feudalism and the monuments of slavery." The rationale for this policy was that regional languages and cultures represented a danger to the survival and integrity of the French state.

Indeed, almost half of the territory of France consists of regions with linguistic minorities, which share in varying degrees a sense of cultural uniqueness. These include Alsace-Lorraine, Brittany, Corsica, the French Basque country, French Catalonia, Occitania, and Westhoek-Flanders. There was a dramatic increase in ethnic activism in the late 1960s, especially after 1968, with about two-thirds of the ethnic organizations being founded after that date. The increase is probably attributable to the effects of the French withdrawal from Algeria in 1962, which demonstrated that France was not really "one and indivisible" and raised questions about the basis of French identity. The near-revolution of May 1968 not only revealed the vulnerability of the French state but also encouraged a rejection of the inhumane and technocratic centralism of French society.

In 1969, President Charles de Gaulle proposed a number of constitutional changes that would have resulted in considerably more power being exercised at the regional level. The twenty-one existing economic regions would be raised to the status of "territorial collectivities of the republic" with the "task of contributing to the economic, social, and cultural development of the national territory." A regional council would be set up in each region comprising (a) all the National Assembly deputies representing constituencies within the region, (b) territorial councillors elected by the departmental and municipal councils of the region, and (c) councillors representing the economic, social, and cultural spheres to be chosen by trade unions, employers associations, organizations representing family interests, and so on. The regions would have limited powers of taxation transferred to them, the right to be consulted on regional aspects of the national economic plan, and responsibility for debating and approving the regional budget.

A national referendum on the reform proposals was narrowly defeated, and de Gaulle resigned. In 1974, regional councils with very limited powers and functions were set up. However, the dissolution of four autonomist movements in the same year was widely interpreted as a sign that the French government intended to discourage any trend toward meaningful regional autonomy. After a Socialist government took office in 1997, a more tolerant policy allowed the teaching of Alsatian, Basque, Breton, and other regional languages in the nation's schools.

See also Alsace; Brittany; Corsica; Enbata; Front de Libération de la Bretagne; Front de Libération Nationale de la Corse; Guadeloupe; Martinique; Occitania; Saar.
Reference William R. Beer. "The Social Class of Ethnic Activists in Contemporary France" (1977).

French Guiana

French Guiana, located on the northern coast of South America, became an overseas department of France in 1946. Its inhabitants are French citizens, and they have a legal status identical to that of citizens in France. The population was officially estimated to be 97,300 in 1990, but it may be much higher because of the large number of illegal immigrants from neighboring Brazil and Surinam. The largest group is made up of the black and mixed-race "creoles" (72 percent), and there are small minorities of Amerindians, whites, and Asians. The country's economy is heavily dependent on France, with almost two-thirds of the employed population working as civil servants or at the missile-launching site at Kourou. Consequently, support for independence is low, with the Guyanese Movement for Decolonization receiving less than 3.5 percent of the vote in the 1973 election. The Guianese Socialist Party, which advocates

autonomy, won a majority of seats in the Regional Council elections of 1994.

Reference Alexander, Robert J. *Political Parties of the Americas* (1982).

French Language Charter

Throughout Canada's history, the language issue has posed a seemingly insolvable problem. The British North America Act (1867) guaranteed Quebec that French would be the official language of that province's legislature and courts and recognized English as the province's other language. French speakers feared, however, that as a linguistic minority within North America, they would be drowned in a sea of English speakers. These fears were strengthened by the facts that English was the language of business and commerce in Montreal and that almost all immigrants into the province learned English rather than French.

The federal prime minister, Pierre Trudeau, attempted to make Canada a bilingual country. The federal parliament passed the 1969 Official Languages Act, which implemented the official use of both languages in all federal institutions. This act was followed in 1974 by regulations requiring bilingual packaging and labeling throughout Canada. Within Quebec, however, the French still felt threatened and attempted to impose French unilingualism. Act 22 required that immigrant children be educated in French, and in 1977, the newly elected Parti Québécois passed Act 101, the French Language Charter.

That act ordained that wherever a child came from—even another Canadian province—it had to be educated in French unless one of its parents had attended an English-language school in Quebec. The act ordered that any business with more than fifty employees must conduct all internal business in French, declared all bilingual signs illegal, and established a commission to rename any towns or geographical features having English names. The rule banning English signs was enforced by self-appointed vigilantes who photographed them and then lodged an official complaint. The ban on English signs was appealed to the Canadian Supreme Court, which ruled in 1988 that commercial signs did not have to be in French only but that Quebec was entitled to require the predominant display of French. In a compromise that pleased neither side, a new law, Act 178, legalized bilingual signs inside but not outside commercial buildings and specified that the French letters must be bigger than the English letters, the French must be on top, and if the colors of the letters were different, the French should be in the "stronger" color.

The unilingualism policy led to large-scale emigration of English speakers from Quebec and to tensions between Quebec and the other provinces, However, it has increased the use of French within Quebec, so that currently, over 90 percent of students are educated in French-language schools.

See also Parti Québécois; Quebec.
References Richler, Mordecai. *Oh Canada! Oh Quebec!* (1992); Sancton, Andrew. *Governing the Island of Montreal: Language Differences and Metropolitan Politics* (1985).

French Polynesia

An overseas territory of France, French Polynesia consists of 120 islands in the South Pacific and had a population of 238,000 as of 1998. Native Polynesians form the majority of the population (78 percent), and French and Chinese make up the remainder. The territory has an assembly that legislates on local affairs and sends one senator and two deputies to the French National Assembly. A pro-independence party, the Liberation Front of Polynesia, won ten of the forty-one territorial assembly seats in 1996, and the party's leader received 42 percent of the vote when he ran for the French National Assembly in 1997. This electoral success was attributed to local resentment of French nuclear testing in the area. However, advocates of the territory's remaining linked to France won both National Assembly seats and a majority in the territorial assembly.

The Liberation Front has called for French Polynesia to be reinstated on the decolonization agenda of the United Nations.

French West Africa

Some supporters of Pan-Africanism argue that the best way to achieve a united Africa is to begin with regional federations, and French West Africa is an example of such a federation. Unlike the British colonial policy of indirect rule (i.e., maintaining traditional rulers and indigenous cultures), the French favored direct rule and assimilation, creating "black Frenchmen" out of the educated Africans. The French colonies were treated merely as administrative divisions, with colonial service officers often being transferred between the different territories. Trade and migration further unified them. Laborers migrated from the Upper Volta (now Burkina Faso) to the Ivory Coast, and Dahomeyans could be found staffing government offices in every colony. Most important, higher education either in France or at the University of Dakar brought together African students from throughout the whole area. Just before World War II, the French set up a West African federation with its capital in Dakar.

After the war ended, the political evolution of French West Africa was rapid. In 1956, the territories were granted self-government, each with its own assembly. In 1958, the new French constitution offered the territories the choice of becoming a department of France, retaining a quasi-federal relationship with France within the French Community, or becoming independent. Guinea alone voted for independence; all the other states chose membership in the community.

Several factors served to integrate the members of the French Community in Africa. The French-speaking African states functioned as a customs union and were all members of the franc zone. These arrangements benefited them by providing a protected metropolitan market for their tropical products as well as compensating for their foreign-exchange deficits. However, the political links between these states gradually weakened with the growth of nationalism. Although in 1958 Senegal, the Sudan, Dahomey, and Upper Volta initially agreed to form a federation, this idea soon fell apart. Another abortive attempt, to create a Mali federation consisting of Senegal and the Sudan, also failed. Senegal withdrew in August 1960, after less than three months, leaving Sudan with the new name of Mali.

Cooperation agreements between France and its ex-colonies on such matters as defense, communications, and other matters means that relations between the French-speaking African states have remained close. French has remained the common language of the elites, and the number of French experts and teachers even increased after independence. Diplomatically, most of the French-speaking states were aligned with the Brazzaville group, a moderate pro-Western bloc established in 1960. The rival Casablanca group, which adopted a more revolutionary stance, included Ghana, Guinea, Libya, Mali, Morocco, and the United Arab Republic.

See also Pan-Africanism.
Reference Julienne, Roland. "The Experience of Integration in French-Speaking Africa" (1967).

Friesland

The Frisians, numbering about 600,000 persons, inhabit the two northernmost provinces of the Netherlands, known as Friesland. Their language is closely related to English, and most Frisians speak Frisian rather than Dutch in their daily life. A strong sense of Frisian identity persists based not only on language but also on the geographical isolation of the region from the rest of the Netherlands. Around the turn of the century, a movement to preserve the Frisian language developed, and one of its leaders, E. B. Folkertsma, founded a Friesland Free group that called for a federal system in which Friesland would have a high degree of autonomy. In 1951, after a local judge had refused to allow a defendant the right to use Frisian in court, there were mass protest

demonstrations. Subsequently, legislation was enacted to allow the use of Frisian in courts and elementary schools, and two counties have adopted a policy of unilingual Frisian road signs. In 1962, the Fryske Nasjonale Partij was set up to obtain regional self-government and an increased use of the Frisian language, but the party receives only a handful of votes.

Reference Mahmood, Cynthia Keppley. *Frisian and Free* (1989).

Friuli

Friulian is a Rhaeto-Romance language similar to Ladin and Romansh. The Friulians, who number about 600,000, live in the Italian region of Friuli–Venezia Giulia, which borders Austria and Slovenia. The Friuli movement advocates increased autonomy for Friuli, its own university, and the teaching of Friulian in the schools. The party has never won more than two or three seats in the regional council, and it received only 4.5 percent of the vote in 1978.

See also Italy.

Front de Libération de la Bretagne

An openly terrorist group, the Front de Libération de la Bretagne (FLB, Breton Liberation Front) has carried out sporadic bombing attacks since 1966. The initial attacks were a response to the arrest and trial of three Bretons for desecrating French flags, but in a later communiqué, the FLB declared itself to be a national liberation movement struggling to free the Bretons from colonial oppression. The first network was broken up by the police in 1969, but subsequent waves of terrorism occurred throughout the 1970s by other groups using the same name. A left-wing faction, the FLB-LNS, split off from the main organization in 1973 and declared that its goals were "national and socialist liberation."

Generally, the targets of the bombers were government offices, utilities, and the summer homes of wealthy non-Bretons. Their most spectacular attack was the bombing of the Palace of Versailles in June 1978 as a "protest against the humiliation of Breton culture." By the early 1980s, most of the known FLB activists were in prison, and the level of violence was minimal. Those arrested came from diverse occupational backgrounds and included factory workers, farmers, students, businessmen, and priests. Two-thirds were under thirty. There was widespread sympathy for those arrested, and a 1969 poll reported that 25 percent of the Breton population felt solidarity with them.

See also Brittany.
Reference Reece, Jack E. *The Bretons against France* (1977).

Front de Libération du Quebec

The Front de Libération du Quebec (FLQ) is the name used by a series of Quebec separatist groups that engaged in intermittent terrorism from 1963 to 1972. A theorist of the province's revolutionary separatists, Pierre Vallieres, has stated that "there was never an FLQ organization as such, but rather a collection of groups or cells with little or no contact between them." The first wave of terrorism took place in 1963, and it ended with the arrest of the eight members of the cell founded by a Belgian immigrant, George Schoeters. The second wave, which lasted from late 1963 until early 1964, was led by Gabriel Hudon, a younger brother of one of the members of the original cell. The third wave of violence was carried out by "l'armee revolutionnaire du Quebec," which was led by a Hungarian, Francois Schirm. The fourth wave, from 1965 to 1967, was marked by socialist rhetoric and inspired by the writings of Charles Gagnon and Pierre Vallieres.

A lull in the violence lasted until late 1968, when the final and most dramatic outbreak of FLQ terrorism began with a series of bombings. The high point came in October 1970 with the kidnapping (by two separate cells) of James Cross, the British trade commissioner, and Pierre Laporte, the Quebec minister of labor. On Octo-

ber 17, after the proclamation of the War Measures Act by the Canadian government, Laporte was murdered by his captors. In December 1970, the kidnappers of Cross released him in exchange for safe conduct to Cuba. In addition to the murder of Laporte, FLQ terrorism resulted in seven deaths, a score of robberies, and over a hundred bombings.

Two factors brought about the end of FLQ terrorism. The murder of Laporte (who was strangled with his own crucifix) led to a backlash against the group, and the growth of the Parti Québécois demonstrated that the struggle for independence could take place through democratic means and did not require acts of terrorism.

See also Parti Québécois; Quebec; Vallieres, Pierre.
Reference Morf, Gustav. *Terror in Quebec: Case Studies of the FLQ* (1970).

Front de Libération Nationale de la Corse

The Corsican terrorist group Front de Libération Nationale de la Corse (FLNC) was organized by former members of the Front Paysan Corse de Libération in May 1976 after that group was banned by the French government. The FLNC declared itself to be fighting for the "destruction of all instruments of French colonialism, the setting up of a people's democracy, the confiscation of all large colonial properties, land reform, and the right to self-determination." Although separatist terrorism had begun in 1964, the level of violence increased dramatically in the mid-1970s with the emergence of the FLNC.

From 1971 to 1982, over 3,000 terrorist incidents were reported on the island; about half of them were claimed by the FLNC. The targets included power lines, government offices, police stations, and military bases. Attacks were also carried out against the property of French "colonialists" on the island. Separatist violence provoked counterviolence by pro-French extremists. In January 1980, separatists captured and held hostage three pro-French militants, and this incident escalated into a

A protest march in San Juan, Puerto Rico, August 29, 1999, demanding that President Clinton pardon sixteen imprisoned FALN members. (AP Photo/Ricardo Figueroa)

shootout that left three dead and five injured. In April 1981, the front announced that it would halt its campaign until after the French presidential elections, but the truce broke down in February 1982 and the attacks resumed. In 1983, the French government appointed a new police chief with special antiterrorist powers, and the arrest of scores of suspected terrorists produced a significant reduction in the level of violence.

The FLNC violence has been condemned by the moderate autonomist party, the Union du Peuple Corse (UPC), and the FLNC in turn has denounced the UPC's willingness to accept the island's status as "treason." By the late 1980s, the FLNC had split into more than a dozen factions, some of which had become heavily engaged in extortion, counterfeiting, and other criminal activities. The FLNC claimed responsibility for two separate attacks on police stations in October 1996 and a wave of bombings on the island in February 1997.

See also Corsica.
Reference Ramsey, Robert. *The Corsican Time Bomb* (1983).

Fuerzas Armadas de Liberacion Nacional

Fuerzas Armadas de Liberacion Nacional (FALN) is a Puerto Rican terrorist group that has claimed responsibility for over 150 bombing incidents, six deaths, and over $3.5 million in property damage since 1973. Whereas Los Macheteros, another Puerto Rican terrorist group, has been active mostly within Puerto Rico, the FALN has carried out its attacks within the United States. Its targets have included corporations with economic interests in Puerto Rico, banks, and other symbols of American colonialism.

On a few occasions it has deliberately bombed civilian targets in retaliation for what it saw as mistreatment of, or violence against, Puerto

Rican *independistas*. For example, the bombing of the Fraunces Tavern in New York's financial district in January 1975, in which five people were killed, took place two weeks after the bombing of an *independista* rally in Puerto Rico. The FALN communiqué left at the site stated that the bombing was "in retaliation for the CIA-ordered bombing that murdered two innocent young workers who supported Puerto Rican independence. We warned the North American government that to terrorize and kill our people would mean retaliation by us."

In 1984, the FBI labeled the FALN as the most dangerous terrorist group in the United States but was not able to make an arrest until July 1978 when, after an explosion in a bomb factory, William Morales was captured and sentenced to eighty-nine years in prison. Morales, who lost an eye and several fingers in the explosion, subsequently escaped from the hospital by lowering himself from a window using ten feet of elastic bandage. The FALN has links to the Puerto Rican Socialist Party and is allegedly supported by Cuba. In late 1999, despite a Justice Department report that declared that Puerto Rican separatist groups posed an "ongoing threat" to national security, President Clinton offered clemency to sixteen imprisoned FALN members in what was widely regarded as an attempt to help his wife win the Puerto Rican vote in the upcoming New York Senate race.

See also Macheteros; Puerto Rico.
Reference Fernandez, Ronald. *Prisoners of Colonialism* (1994).

Gagauzia

The Gagauz, who number about 120,000, are located in Moldova on the Ukrainian border. They speak a Turkic language and are Orthodox in religion. An ethnically cohesive group, the Gagauz attempted to secede from Russian control in 1906, but the revolt was crushed. After World War II, a minority in a predominantly Romanian-speaking country, the Moldavia Soviet Socialist Republic, the Gagauz pressed for the right to use the Gagauz language, and in 1986, they were finally permitted to use Gagauz in limited radio and television broadcasts. In 1989, when Romanian-speaking nationalists were in power, Romanian was declared the only official language. Fearful that Moldova might unite with Romania, several thousand Gagauz held a protest rally.

In August 1990, the Gagauz movement, Gagauz Khalk, a separatist organization, declared the secession of Gagauz from Moldova and petitioned Moscow to become a socialist republic of the Soviet Union. The movement set an October date for Gagauz elections. Moldova reacted by rejecting the secession demand and sending troops and volunteers into the region to prevent the elections. Three Gagauz died in clashes, and Soviet troops were dispatched to restore order. In 1991, following the disintegration of the USSR, Moldova declared its independence, and Gagauzia and the heavily Russian Transdniester region, fearing Romanian nationalism, continued to press for autonomy.

In July 1994, the Moldovan parliament granted Gagauzia autonomy within the Moldovan Republic. The Gagauz were permitted to establish a parliament and executive and to have their own budget. They were also granted the right to secede if Moldova ever merged with Romania. In June 1995, a former Communist, Georgy Tabunshik, became Gagauzia's first president. In August 1995, Moldova granted an amnesty to Gagauz movement activists, and the movement's troops then disbanded.

See also Moldova.
Reference Fedor, Helen, ed. *Belarus and Moldova: Country Studies* (1996).

Galicia

Galicia is an economically backward region in northwestern Spain, and many young people have been forced to emigrate to other parts of Spain in search of work. The regional language, similar to Portuguese, is regarded with disdain by other Spaniards. During the Franco era, posters urged Galicians, Don't be a country bumpkin, speak Spanish! In the 1960s, two separatist movements emerged: a revolutionary socialist group, the Union do Povo Galego (Union of the Galician People—UPG), and the more moderate Partido Socialista Galego (Galician Socialist Party). The goal of the UPG was independence from Spain, and the party engaged in an abortive attempt at an armed struggle in 1975, which was foiled by police action.

Divisions among the regionalist parties prevented them from electing any representatives in 1977, but when a referendum was held in December 1980, 71 percent endorsed the proposed regional autonomy statute. The statute was supported by almost all the major Galician political parties. In the 1985 elections for the seventy-one-seat regional parliament, the conservative Popular Alliance won the most votes and seats while the separatist Galician Nationalist Bloc obtained a mere 3.2 percent of the votes and only one seat. However, the separatist party has steadily improved its position, and in 1993 it elected thirteen deputies.

See also Spain.
Reference Moxon-Brown, Edward. *Political Change in Spain* (1989).

Gambia

The Gambia became independent from Britain in 1965. Consisting of a thin sliver of territory along the banks of the Gambia River, this West African country is completely surrounded by Senegal. Indeed, for a brief period from 1765 to 1783, the two were united as the British colony of Senegambia. Given its artificial boundaries and the fact that its ethnic composition (Mandingo, Wolof, and Fulani) is so similar to that of Senegal, there is a movement to establish a federal union between the two countries.

Reference Robson, Peter. "The Problem of Senegambia" (1965).

Gazankulu

One of the black homelands of South Africa, Gazankulu was designated as the homeland for both the Shangaan and Tsonga, and its legislature was mostly composed of tribal chiefs. Self-governing since 1973, Gazankulu has had only one chief minister, Hudson Ntsanwisi. He took part in the 1973 summit meeting of homeland leaders, where he said that blacks "must de-emphasize all things that separate us and rather emphasize those things which unite us." He rejected independence for Gazankulu but was opposed to international sanctions against South Africa because of the suffering such sanctions would cause to the black population. During negotiations over a new constitution for South Africa, which began in December 1991, Ntsanwisi advocated a system of government in which power would be decentralized as much as possible. Gazankulu, as all the homelands were, was reincorporated into South Africa in 1994.

See also Black Homelands.

Georgia

The Republic of Georgia has a population of more than 5 million. Georgians, who are Orthodox Christians and speak Kartvelian, a southern Caucasian language, compose nearly 70 percent of the population. Armenians, Russians, and Azeris each constitute about 7 percent. However, two smaller groups, the Abkhazians, with a population of 100,000, and the Ossetes, who number about 150,000, are the ethnic groups most reluctant to be ruled by Georgia. The Abkhazians, who reside in the northwest of Georgia, speak Abkhaz, a Caucasian language distinct from Georgian. They also include a significant number of Muslims in their population. The Ossetes, found in the north-central region, speak a Persian dialect although they are predominantly Orthodox in religion. They call themselves the Alans and seek to rejoin a larger population of Alans found in North Ossetia, an autonomous republic of the Russian Federation.

Georgia first appeared as a kingdom in the fourth century B.C. and was Christianized in the fourth century A.D. Byzantines, Persians, Arabs, and Turks contended for power over Georgian territory from the third century to the thirteenth. In the eleventh and twelfth centuries, another transient Georgian state emerged, and at one time it stretched from Azerbaijan to Circassia. In the thirteenth century, Mongols subjugated the land. Beginning in the late-fifteenth century, Persians and Ottomans fought to control Georgia, and they were replaced by the Russians who, by 1801, had absorbed the country into the Russian Empire.

In 1918, following the collapse of the empire, Georgia declared its independence, but in 1921, the Red Army invaded and installed a Communist government. In 1922, Georgia, along with Armenia and Azerbaijan, formed the Transcaucasian Federated Soviet Republic. In 1924, an anti-Communist revolt in Georgia was put down, and in 1936, Georgia was raised to the status of a Soviet socialist republic.

In the late 1980s, as Georgia moved toward independence from the USSR, two of its ethnic regions, South Ossetia and Abkhazia, effectively seceded and today remain outside the control of the Georgian capital of Tbilisi. A cease-fire arranged by Russia and the stationing of Russian troops between the combatants has stopped the shooting, but no diplomatic resolution to the disputes has been effected. The Adzharia region continues to insist on the semiautonomous status granted it during the Soviet era.

The Georgian parliament declared its independence from the Soviet Union in 1992. An atmosphere of violence, clan conflict, and criminal activity has prevented the government of Edvard Shevardnadze from dealing with the ethnic problems of the new republic.

See also Abkhazia; Adzharia; South Ossetia.
Reference Suny, Ronald Grigor. *Making of the Georgian Nation* (1994).

German Reunification

The dissolution of the German Democratic Republic (DDR) and its incorporation into the Federal Republic of Germany in October 1990 marked the end of forty-five years of separation of the German people. Reunification, which came about when East Germany was absorbed by the Federal Republic, resulted in the restoration of pre-Nazi Germany's borders, except for the territory ceded to Poland after World War II.

The DDR, or East Germany, was created in 1949 from the Soviet-occupied sector. Bordering Poland and Czechoslovakia, it included the former provinces of Brandenburg, Mecklenburg, Thuringia, Saxony, and Saxony-Anhalt, and East Berlin was its capital. In 1986, the DDR's population was 18.6 million.

The political and economic systems of the DDR were patterned after the model of communism developed in the Soviet Union under Stalin. The country's economy was centrally planned and based on heavy industry centered in large enterprises. Private business was effectively prohibited. For most of its existence, the DDR was led by two Communist Party leaders, Walter Ul-

bricht and Erich Honecker. Political life was dominated by the Socialist Unity Party, the name given the Communist Party. Although more affluent than other nations of the Soviet bloc, East Germany's standard of living was inferior to that of the burgeoning capitalist Federal Republic of Germany, or West Germany. The 1950s saw a great number of defections from the DDR to the West, and the government responded by making it extremely difficult to flee the country. The construction of the Berlin Wall in 1961 represented the culmination of the government's measures to eliminate the emigration of its citizens.

With the hold of the Soviet Union over Eastern Europe weakening as a consequence of Mikhail Gorbachev's liberalization measures, the DDR opened its borders in November 1989 and held its first free elections in December. The East Germans elected a parliament committed to reunification.

Unification did not bring about a synthesis between two different social systems, but the replacement of socialism by capitalism. Despite the infusion of great amounts of aid into the eastern region by the federal government, East Germans paid a high price for unification. The heavily subsidized social benefits that had been provided by the socialist state in the form of housing, vacation benefits, health care, and higher education were severely curtailed. Guaranteed lifetime employment came to an end. Inefficient and environmentally hazardous industries were closed, which resulted in massive unemployment. Lacking either adequate professional training or small business skills, many East Germans found they had no place in the new economy and were unlikely to find one. Unemployment in 1998 was nearly 20 percent in what had been East Germany, compared with about 11 percent in the former West Germany.

Disaffection in the eastern part of Germany took several forms. Among older East Germans, or "Ossies," nostalgia cults developed celebrating the lifestyle of the DDR. Many young people were attracted to skinhead and neo-Nazi gangs, which terrorized non-German immigrants. Among the

Celebrations for German reunification at the Brandenburg Gate in Berlin, October 1990. (Reuters/Wolfgang Rattay/Archive Photos)

electorate at large, support grew for both the ultra-right-wing party, the National Democratic Party, and the Party of Democratic Socialism, the successor to the old Communist Party. However, it was the strong support of the East German voters that helped elect Gerhard Schroeder, the Social Democrat, chancellor in the 1998 elections. Helmut Kohl, the Christian Democratic political leader who was most responsible for bringing about unification, was convincingly rejected by the East German electorate.

Although there is no sign of a significant separatist movement developing in the eastern part of Germany, alienation remains high. Germans still define themselves as either Ossies or "Wessies," though in the East this tendency is diminishing among younger people. In the West, the heavy costs of unification combined with high unemployment have decreased sympathy for East Germans.

See also Oder-Neisse Line.
References Larres, Klaus, ed. *Germany since Reunification* (1998); Maier, Charles. *Dissolution: The Crisis of Communism and the End of East Germany* (1997).

Ghana

Previously the British colony of the Gold Coast, Ghana became independent in 1957. The colony had been divided into four regions: the Gold Coast itself, Ashanti, Trans-Volta-Togo, and the Northern Territories. After World War II, a new constitution was introduced, and it provided for a legislative council in which the majority of the members were elected. The first political party, the United Gold Coast Convention (UGCC), was formed in 1947 under the leadership of J. B. Danquah and Kwame Nkrumah. Two years later, Nkrumah split from the UGCC and set up the Convention People's Party (CPP). That party agitated for a rapid transition to self-government, and when elections were held in 1951, it won almost all the elected seats and Nkrumah became "the leader of government business," a position similar to that of prime minister.

Nkrumah and the CPP were opposed by traditional tribal leaders who feared the growth of central power. In the 1954 elections, the CPP won 71 of the 104 seats, but the Northern People's Party (NPP) won a majority in the north while the Togoland Congress wanted a separate legislature in its region. More threatening was the emergence of a regional party in Ashanti, a party backed by the Ashanti king and the paramount chiefs, just after the elections. The National Liberation Movement (NLM) advocated a federal form of government and criticized the dictatorial tendencies of the CPP. Nkrumah had attempted to reduce the authority of the Ashanti nobility, and Ashanti hostility was further increased by the fact that the CPP government had fixed the price of cocoa at a level well below world prices. Fighting between CPP and NLM supporters resulted in several deaths. The British government then declared that another election must be held before independence, and in that election, held in July 1956, the CPP won an overall majority with 72 seats. However, the party lost to the NLM in Ashanti and to the NPP in the North.

In the Togoland Trust Territory, a UN plebiscite was held in May 1956 to determine whether the territory would join Ghana. The vote was 58 percent in favor and 42 percent opposed. Voting largely followed ethnic lines, with the Ewe voting against integration and the non-Ewe in favor. In the southern, predominantly Ewe-inhabited section, there was a slim majority against integration. The issue reemerged in 1975–1979, with demands that the Ewe areas should be joined to the neighboring country of Togo.

After independence, Nkrumah moved to crush any separatist tendencies. The regional assemblies were abolished, and the Avoidance of Discrimination Act prohibited regional, religious, or tribal parties. Several opposition political leaders were deported or imprisoned. By 1961, Ghana was virtually a one-party state whose slogan was, The CPP is the government, and the government is the CPP.

See also Ashanti; Ewe; Togoland.
References Apter, David. *The Gold Coast in Transition* (1955); Kimble, David. *A Political History of Ghana* (1963).

Ghorkhaland

The Darjeeling district of West Bengal is inhabited by the Gurkhas, a Nepali-speaking group also found in Sikkim and Nepal. The Ghorkhaland National Liberation Front demanded that the area become a separate state and organized a violent campaign during which over 200 people were killed. After two years of fighting (1986–1988), the government of West Bengal established the Darjeeling Ghorkha Hill Council, which has control over the district's economic development and educational policy.

Gibraltar

Situated at the tip of southern Spain, Gibraltar had been conquered from the Moors by the Spanish in 1462 and in 1704 was captured by the British, who have occupied it since that date. An important naval base, Gibraltar was crucial to Britain's control of the Mediterranean route to India. The 1713 Treaty of Utrecht is interpreted by the British as giving them full sovereignty over the tiny peninsula (2.5 square miles), but Spain claims that the treaty merely ceded control of Gibraltar to Britain, not sovereignty. Spain imposed restrictions on cross-border traffic in 1954 and closed the border completely in 1966.

In 1963, Spain raised the issue of Gibraltar's status at the United Nations, and after hearing from both sides, the decolonization committee called for a negotiated solution in keeping with the provisions of UN Resolution 1514. (Since Resolution 1514 refers to the territorial integrity of countries, the United Nations was thereby implicitly supporting the Spanish claim.) In negotiations between the two countries held in 1966, Spain offered to allow Britain to retain its military base and promised a high degree of local autonomy for the local population. When the talks broke down, Britain held a referendum to determine the wishes of the Gibraltarians, and in September 1967, they voted to remain associated with Britain by 12,138 to 44. In 1969, the Integration with Britain Party, led by Major Robert Peliza, won control of Gibraltar's elected legislative council. Several rounds of talks have been held between the Britain and Spain, but no agreement has been reached, owing primarily to the opposition of the local population to Spanish rule. However, relations have improved, and the border was reopened in 1985.

Reference Hills, George. *Rock of Contention* (1974).

Goa

The Portuguese territories in India included Goa, Daman, and the island of Diu and totaled about 1,500 square miles. In 1954, the population of 638,000 was approximately 40 percent Christian and 60 percent Hindu. Goa possessed not only one of the best harbors on the Indian subcontinent but also rich iron and manganese mines, producing 4.7 million tons of iron ore annually. Goa presented Jawaharlal Nehru, the prime minister of newly independent India, with a dilemma. The Portuguese presence eroded Nehru's claim to leadership of the anticolonial bloc of states, yet any attempt to use force would lay him open to the charge of hypocrisy. Nehru was constantly urging other powers to settle their disputes peacefully and offering to mediate armed conflicts such as the one in Korea. In 1953, he announced that respect for territorial integrity, nonaggression, noninterference in internal affairs, and peaceful coexistence were the basis for India's relations with other nations.

The Portuguese declared that Goa was an integral part of Portugal, an overseas province, not a colony. Nehru regarded this claim as ridiculous. Goa's mother country, he said, "is as much India as mine. Goa is outside British India but it is within geographical India as a whole. And there is very little, if anything, in common between the Portuguese and the Indians of Goa." Nehru first attempted to resolve the Goan issue through negotiation, a method that had worked successfully with the French, who had surrendered their colonial possessions (Pondicherry and three smaller enclaves) in 1956. However, the

Portuguese rejected talks, and the Indian government subsequently broke off diplomatic relations with Portugal.

Demonstrations in favor of uniting Goa with India began in 1954, and two small enclaves of Portuguese territory were occupied by the demonstrators. India's Praja Socialist Party called for a mass march into Goa; the Portuguese responded by giving its soldiers shoot-to-kill orders. As tensions mounted, Nehru declared that the march must be composed solely of Goanese, but only forty-seven people turned out, suggesting that Goanese support was not substantial. However throughout India, thousands demonstrated against Portuguese rule. In 1955, when marchers crossed the border, police fired on them, killing 20 and wounding over 200. In response, a mob attacked Portuguese consulates in Bombay and other cities. Although the issue of Goa was never brought before the United Nations, India waged a campaign against Portuguese colonialism, and in December 1960, the General Assembly of the United Nations declared Goa a dependent territory and called on Portugal to grant independence to all its colonies.

Indian public opinion grew increasingly impatient with Nehru's moderation, and Congress politicians demanded action. Finally, at midnight on December 17, 1961, 30,000 Indian soldiers attacked a Portuguese force of less than 3,500. The defenders put up only token resistance, and only 39 (on both sides) were killed in the fighting. The United States and other Western countries condemned the invasion. In his history of the Kennedy presidency, *A Thousand Days,* Arthur Schlesinger comments that "the contrast between Nehru's incessant sanctimony on the subject of aggression of nonaggression and his brisk exercise of *Machtpolitik* was too comic not to cause comment. It was a little like catching the preacher in the hen house, and . . . it was almost too much not to expect the targets of Nehru's past sermons not to respond in kind." However, the invasion was enthusiastically approved within India and by the Afro-Asian bloc of states.

Goa became a union territory, and its inhabitants, while displaying little enthusiasm with regard to their incorporation, expressed no opposition to the ending of 450 years of Portuguese rule. In the first elections held after the Indian takeover, the United Goan Party, representing the Catholic minority, won twelve of the thirty seats while a Hindu Party, which called for Goa to be merged with the surrounding state of Maharashtra, won fourteen.

See also India
Reference Gaitonde, P. D. *The Liberation of Goa* (1987). Rubinoff, Arthur. *India's Use of Force in Goa* (1971).

Greater Albania

The greater Albania movement calls for the incorporation of the Albanian populated areas of Albania, Montenegro, Macedonia, Serbia, and the Serbian province of Kosovo into one Albanian state. Although Albanians in all these countries share a common culture, they have never been unified into an independent state. The movement was particularly strong in Kosovo where Serbs governed ruthlessly over a population that was 90 percent Albanian. Unlike the Albanians in Enver Hoxha's Communist Albania, the Albanian citizens of Tito's more open Yugoslavia were able to develop a cultural and social infrastructure that was far more advanced than that permitted by the government in Albania. Consequently, the impetus for a greater Albania emanates more from Kosovo, than from Albania itself. However, the idea is receiving increasing support in Albania proper and has been supported by members of the Albanian parliament. The insurrection that broke out in Kosovo in 1996 was backed by Albanians throughout Eastern Europe and increased the appeal of the greater Albania idea.

The Albanians are descendants of Illyrian and Thracian tribes, and they speak an Indo-European language that is quite distinct from the Slavic languages of their neighbors. In the third century, an independent Albanian kingdom existed for a brief time, but the Albanians then came under Byzantine rule and were converted to Christianity. In the fifteenth century, the Albanian lands were conquered by the Ottoman Turks. During the period of their rule, the population was converted to Islam, and Albania remains overwhelmingly Muslim to this day.

In 1912, Albania declared itself independent. The new state was internationally recognized in 1920 but included within its borders only half of the regional Albanian population. Albania's highly homogeneous population numbers about 3 million today. Significant numbers of unassimilated and disaffected Albanians can be found in Macedonia, Montenegro, and Serbia, all predominantly Orthodox and Slavic states. The largest numbers of Albanians are found in Kosovo, nearly 2 million, and Macedonia, about 600,000. Both states have seen growing demands for more freedom for Albanians. In Kosovo, a civil war between Serbs and Albanians ended in June 1999 when NATO forced the Serbian forces to withdraw from the province.

Regardless of Kosovo's future status, any attempt to create a greater Albania would meet with strong objections not only from Montenegro, Macedonia, and Serbia but also from the European Union and the United States, which, in principle, are opposed to the realignment of national borders in Europe. The political anarchy and turmoil that has reigned in Albania itself, following the disastrous financial collapse of the 1990s, has also rendered impractical, for the foreseeable future, any active role by the Albanian government in spearheading such a movement.

See also Chameria; Kosovo; Kosovo Liberation Army; Macedonia; Montenegro; Yugoslavia.
References Jacques, Edwin E. *The Albanians: An Ethnic History from Prehistoric Times to the Present* (1995); Vickers, Miranda, and James Pettifer. *Albania: From Anarchy to Balkan Identity* (1997).

Greater Serbia

The idea of a greater Serbia, advocated since the late 1980s, implied the creation of a monoethnic, contiguous state that would include Serbia proper and all predominantly Serbian areas outside its boundaries—primarily Slavonia and Krajina in Croatia and the Serb regions of Bosnia and Herzegovina, Macedonia, and Montenegro. Greater Serbia would also include the territory of Kosovo, which no longer has a Serbian majority but does have historical significance for Serbian nationalists. Serb nationalists also claim such strategically important places as a Dalmatian naval base (now part of Croatia).

With the disintegration of Communist Yugoslavia, the aspiration for a greater Serbia was originally associated with Slobodan Milosevic, president of Yugoslavia—a state that now includes Serbia and Montenegro. However, since signing the Dayton peace accord in 1995, Milosevic has been denounced as a traitor to the greater Serbian cause. The most outspoken advocate of a greater Serbia is now Vojislav Seselji, head of the Serbian Radical Party. Seselji finished second in the 1997 election for the presidency of the Serbian Republic, and had he been elected, Seselji had vowed to renounce the Dayton peace accord and resume the war in Bosnia and Croatia. Seselji and his followers remain powerful in the Serbian parliament and are currently part of the Milosevic government. The withdrawal of Serbian troops from Kosovo in 1999 following NATO air strikes makes it unlikely that the dream of a greater Serbia can be realized in the near future.

See also Bosnia and Herzegovina; Dayton Peace Accord; Krajina; Milosevic, Slobodan; Yugoslavia.
Reference Judah, Tim. *History, Myth, and the Destruction of Yugoslavia* (1997).

Greenland

Greenland was a colony of Denmark until 1953 when it became an integral part of the Danish kingdom. Greenland has a population of 55,000, with 80 percent being native Inuit and 20 percent Danish. After Denmark entered the European Economic Community in 1973, tensions developed between the island and the rest of Denmark because of fears on the part of Greenlanders that Denmark's membership would lead to the depletion of Greenland's fishing resources. A joint commission was set up, and on its recommendation, Greenland was granted home rule by an act of the Danish parliament in 1978.

In a referendum on the agreement held in Greenland in January 1979, 70.1 percent voted in favor, and 25.8 percent voted against, with the division apparently running along ethnic lines. In the first election to the Greenland parliament, the Inuit Ataqatigiit (Eskimo movement), whose program called for complete independence and the restriction of the franchise to those persons with at least one Eskimo parent, received less than 2 percent of the vote. Currently, there is virtually no support in Greenland for complete indepen-

dence, mainly because the island is heavily dependent upon Danish subsidies of over $400 million annually.

Reference Lapidoth, Ruth. *Autonomy: Flexible Solutions to Ethnic Conflict* (1997).

Grivas, George (1898–1974)

The leader of Ethnike Organosis Kyprion Agoniston (EOKA), the Greek Cypriot nationalist movement, George Grivas was born in the small village of Trikomo in 1898, the second son of a prosperous merchant. Grivas describes how in his village school "the glories of Greek history always took first place." Later, while at secondary school, which was "staffed by teachers from Greece who brought fresh fervor to our nationalism," he decided to become a soldier. In 1916, Grivas went to

George Grivas, Cypriot nationalist guerilla hero, broadcasts from Nicosia to the fighting Greek and Turkish Cypriots, urging them to settle their grievances peacefully, June 1964. (Archive Photos)

the Royal Hellenic Military Academy in Athens and eventually became a lieutenant colonel in the Greek army. During World War II, he set up a right-wing paramilitary group, Xhi, that fought first the Germans and later the Communists during the Greek civil war.

A Cypriot liberation committee made up of Cypriot émigrés and conservative Greek politicians chose Grivas to lead the struggle for enosis (political union with Greece). During the EOKA campaign of 1955–1959, Grivas, by using a system of couriers, exercised an extraordinary degree of personal control over the organization. He selected many of the targets, decided which Greek Cypriots would be executed as traitors, and even disbursed the petty cash. Several times, Grivas narrowly escaped capture by the British forces, thus increasing his legendary status.

When Cyprus became independent after the Zurich agreement of 1959, Grivas went into exile in Greece. Feeling that Archbishop Makarios had betrayed the cause of enosis, Grivas became the archbishop's bitter opponent. When fighting broke out between Greek and Turkish Cypriots, Grivas returned to Cyprus, and in 1964, the Greek government appointed him head of the Cypriot National Guard. He subsequently formed an anti-Makarios group, EOKA B, and went underground. He died in January 1974.

See also Cyprus; Ethnike Organosis Kyprion Agoniston; Makarios, Archbishop.

References Grivas, George. *Memoirs of General Grivas* (1965); Marquises, Kyriacos. *The Rise and Fall of the Cyprus Republic* (1977).

Guadeloupe

The Caribbean island of Guadeloupe was a French colony from 1635 until 1946 when it became an overseas French department. In 1968, members of the Group of National Organizations of Guadeloupe (GONG) received suspended sentences for advocating independence. Some ex-members later set up a pro-independence party, the Popular Union for the Liberation of Guadeloupe (UPLG). Although there has been little electoral support for independence, separatist violence has been widespread on the island. The Armed Liberation Group (GLA) called for the end of "French colonialism" and carried out several terrorist attacks in 1980, including the shooting of a white city councillor and the attempted bombing of an Air France plane. In January 1981, the GLA bombed a department store in the center of Paris. Since 1983, the Caribbean Revolutionary Army (ARC), successor to the GLA, has set off more than fifty bombs on the island, causing one fatality and wounding twenty-five. The leader of the ARC, Luc Reinette, wanted for the bombing of the local prefecture, became a hero after evading an islandwide manhunt.

Guadeloupe differs from Martinique, the other French Caribbean department, in several ways, which may explain why it has experienced a much greater degree of violence. The local whites are less powerful, with most of the agricultural land being in the hands of French companies, so, unlike in the patriarchal plantation society of Martinique, labor relations have historically been marked by bitter conflicts. The island has a much smaller mulatto population, which has been suggested as a reason why assimilationist sentiments are much weaker on Guadeloupe. Instead, Guadeloupean nationalists have emphasized the black and African aspects of the island's population and culture. The creole language has been seen as "the umbilical cord binding us to Africa," and the UPLG has promoted the African-derived style of drumming as a symbol of opposition to French culture. Since the dominant force in local politics is the Communist Party, which asserts the significance of class, Guadeloupean nationalists mobilize their supporters on the basis of race.

See also Martinique.

Reference Burton, Richard D., ed. *French and West Indian* (1995).

Guatemala
See Maya of Guatemala

Guyana

Guyana, which lies on the mainland of South America, was previously the colony of British Guiana. The population is divided between East Indians (51 percent) and blacks (42 percent), and there are small minorities of Amerindians, Chinese, and whites. The ill-defined border between Venezuela and British Guiana was submitted to arbitration in 1899, and Britain was then awarded the area between the Orinoco and Essequibo Rivers. The issue of the border was reopened in the early 1960s, but the Venezuelan claim was still unresolved when Guyana became independent in 1966.

Venezuela claims all the land west of the Essequibo River, about a third of Guyana's territory. Several minor skirmishes between Venezuelan and Guyanese forces took place in October 1966, February 1970, and July 1982. In January 1969, a rebellion in the Rupununi region began with an attack on a police post, but, the revolt by local ranchers and Amerindians was quickly suppressed by Guyanese soldiers and police. The Guyanese government accused the Venezuelans of organizing and training the rebels, and after the insurgents fled into Venezuela, they were given land and jobs.

Reference Braveboy-Wagner, Jaqueline A. *The Venezuelan-Guyana Border Dispute* (1984).

Haganah

Haganah, or "defense" in Hebrew, was the Zionist military organization under the control of Mapai, the social democratic party of Palestine, and Histradut, the socialist trade union. Beginning in 1920, Haganah functioned as an underground militia in British Mandate Palestine. In the 1930s, after a large-scale Arab uprising, Haganah evolved from a purely defensive organization into an activist militia and began initiating actions against hostile Arab forces. In 1941, the organization established Palmach, a permanent professional commando force. Following World War II, Haganah turned to terrorist tactics to open Palestine for Jewish immigration from Europe and to force the British to yield control over Palestine to the Jews. Following the establishment of the state of Israel in 1948, Haganah became the foundation for the new Israeli Defense Forces.

See also Israel.
Reference Sachar, Howard. *History of Israel* (1996).

Hamas

Hamas, which means "bravery" in Arabic, is a militant Palestinian organization that advocates the use of force to achieve an Islamic Palestinian state. It evolved from the Muslim Brotherhood, a fundamentalist group that is active throughout the Middle East. Hamas, like the Muslim Brotherhood, wants to create a society governed by Sharia, the Islamic law. Although adhering to the Sunni branch of Islam, Hamas takes postrevolutionary Iran as a model for a future Palestinian state. It is thought that Saudi Arabia, Syria, and Iran all help fund Hamas's activities.

Hamas, under its leader Sheik Ammed Yassin, was first established in Israel in the 1980s and offered a religious alternative to the secular Palestine Liberation Organization (PLO). Hamas was active in the Intifada (uprising) that swept the West Bank and Gaza Strip after 1987. During that period, Hamas carried out several actions against the Israeli occupation forces, and its support grew.

Hamas runs schools and medical clinics and sponsors religious activities. In contrast to the PLO, Hamas has a reputation for honesty and efficiency. Its social activities are funded by donations raised in Palestine and throughout the world.

Clandestine activities of Hamas include the punishment of Palestinian collaborators with Israel and terrorism against Israeli citizens and soldiers. Hamas claimed credit for a suicide bombing of a Jerusalem bus on February 26, 1996, in which seventeen civilians and nine Israeli soldiers were killed. Israel claims Hamas has been involved in numerous other terrorist incidents. Hamas is considered the second most powerful Palestinian nationalist group—only Fatah is more powerful.

Although Hamas cooperates with the PLO in matters it agrees with, it is independent of the PLO and the Palestinian Authority (PA), the government of post-1996 Palestine. Hamas denounced the 1993 peace accord as a sellout and refuses to recognize the state of Israel.

Israel has attempted to eliminate Hamas. It imprisoned Sheik Yassin from 1989 through 1997 and has jailed and assassinated many other leading members. In 1989, it expelled 400 suspected Hamas activists to Lebanon. The 1993 PLO-Israeli peace accord brought no end to Hamas terrorist actions, and Israel has made it a condition for further concessions that the PA bring Hamas

Palestinian boy waving a Hamas flag at a rally in the Gaza Strip refugee camp of Jabalia against the Israeli-Palestine Wye River accords, November 1998. (Corbis/AFP)

under control in its own territory. The Wye River accords of 1998 call for the arrest by Palestinian authorities of thirty named terrorists, many of them involved with Hamas. Muhammed Deif, leader of the Hamas militia in Gaza, has been targeted for arrest, and Yasir Arafat placed Sheik Yassin under house arrest and ordered the roundup of suspected terrorists. Because of the popular support for Hamas, attempts by the PA to suppress the organization have proved ineffective. Qassam, the Hamas military brigade, has threatened to turn its guns on Palestinian security forces. In August 1999, the government of Jordan, under King Abdullah, moved to curtail Hamas activity in that state in order to encourage the Israeli-Palestinian peace negotiations. Four Hamas officials were expelled and Hamas offices were ordered closed.

See also Islamic Jihad; Israel; Palestinians.
Reference Farsoun, Samih. *Palestine and the Palestinians* (1997).

Hawaii

A joint resolution of the U.S. Congress, signed by President Clinton on November 23, 1993, apologized to native Hawaiians for the overthrow of the Kingdom of Hawaii by U.S. Marines in 1893. Hawaii was annexed by the United States in 1898 and became a state in 1959. Because of heavy immigration and intermarriage, pure-blooded Hawaiians make up less than 1 percent of the island's population today, although those who claim some Hawaiian ancestry number about 200,000, or 19 percent of the population. Native Hawaiians are disproportionately poor and suffer from a variety of social problems.

Hawaiian activism gained momentum in 1976 when, after a long protest campaign, the U.S. Navy agreed to stop bombing practice on a remote island. Two years later, during a constitutional convention, the Office of Hawaiian Affairs was established to administer funds derived from the sale of Hawaiian crown lands. The revenue, amounting to millions of dollars each year, is supposed to provide native Hawaiians with education and housing. In 1987, a sovereignty movement, Ka Lahui Hawai'i, was established, and even though membership is restricted to persons of Hawaiian ancestry, it now claims over 18,000 members. The movement calls for the return of land to the native Hawaiians and the encouragement of the Hawaiian language. In 1979, a number of attacks were carried out against U.S. military personnel by a group called Hawaii for the Hawaiians. In August 1996, in a ballot sponsored by the state government and restricted to persons of Hawaiian descent, 73 percent voted in favor of sovereignty.

Reference Trask, Haunani-Kay. *From a Native Daughter: Colonialism and Sovereignty in Hawaii* (1993).

Herzeg-Bosnia

After Bosnia declared its independence from the federal republic of Yugoslavia in 1992, Serbian areas of Bosnia revolted and established the Serbian autonomous republics (SARs). Croats, who constitute 22 percent of Bosnia, followed suit and declared the Croatian region of western and central Bosnia to be an independent nation, the Republic of Herzeg-Bosnia. With its capital in Mostar, Herzeg-Bosnia was led by Mate Bobar.

In May 1993, Croats and Muslims began fighting a ten-month war for control of central Bosnia, and both sides were accused of carrying out atrocities. In September 1994, the Washington Agreement, signed by Croatian and Muslim leaders, ended the war, and a Muslim-Croat federation, the Federation of Bosnia and Herzegovina, was created. The Dayton peace accord of 1995 established a new Bosnian state, which consists of the federation and the consolidated Serbian republics known as the Republic of Srpska.

Although part of the new Bosnian state, Herzeg-Bosnia continues to function as a Croatian ministate in all but name. Ante Jelavic, the Croatian representative to the tri-ethnic collective presidency of Bosnia, is a member of the nationalist Croatian Democratic Union, a party that favors separatism and was led by the Croatian president, Franjo Tudjman.

See also Bosnia and Herzegovina; Croatia; Dayton Peace Accord; Tudjman, Franjo.
Reference Rogel, Carole. *The Breakup of Yugoslavia and the War in Bosnia* (1998).

Hezbollah

Hezbollah (or Hizbollah), "the party of God," is a Lebanese Shi'ite political party, civic and social welfare organization, and militia. Sheik Muhammad Fadallah is the clerical head of the movement. Its population centers are in Beirut, the Bekka Valley, and southern Lebanon. Supported by Syria and Iran, Hezbollah has two goals: the establishment of an Islamic republic in Lebanon and the destruction of the state of Israel.

Hezbollah emerged during the Lebanese civil war (1975–1989) and gained supporters from Amal Shi'ite members lead by Nabih Berri. In the 1990s, Hezbollah launched numerous attacks against Israeli forces in southern Lebanon and settlements in northern Israel. The organization is believed to have organized the deadly attack on the U.S. Marine barracks in Beirut in 1983, and during the Lebanese civil war, Hezbollah carried out several kidnappings.

Under the Taif agreements, which ended the civil war, Hezbollah is the only sectarian militia that has not been disarmed, and it continues to exert military pressure on Israeli forces in southern Lebanon. Hezbollah's growing popularity is aided by its nonmilitary activities. It has established schools, hospitals, libraries, newspapers, and radio stations and has also undertaken public works projects. In the 1992 elections, eight of its members won parliamentary seats. With Shi'ites now the most populous sect in Lebanon and Hezbollah continuing to increase its membership, other religious groups worry that some day Hezbollah may attain sufficient strength to impose Sharia, or Islamic law, on the country.

See also Lebanon.
Reference Picard, Elizabeth. *Lebanon: A Shattered Country* (1996).

Hong Kong

Hong Kong, a small island off the Chinese mainland, became a British possession after the Opium War of 1842, and in 1860 the adjacent Kowloon peninsula was also ceded to Britain in perpetuity. In 1898, the colony was further enlarged by the addition of the New Territories, which were leased to Britain for ninety-nine years. The People's Republic of China regarded the treaties as invalid because they were imposed on China, and it maintained its sovereignty over Hong Kong and other lost territories, such as Macau. With the reversion of the New Territories to China, the British recognized that Hong Kong would become unviable. At the same time, China did not want to disrupt the economy of Hong Kong, as China derived almost 40 percent of its foreign exchange earnings from there.

A joint declaration of September 1984 between Britain and China agreed that all of Hong Kong would be restored to China on July 1, 1997. Although China would be in charge of foreign policy and defense, the Hong Kong Special Region would enjoy considerable autonomy and have its own executive, judiciary, and legal systems. Hong Kong would remain a free port with its own customs, and the legislature would be "constituted by elections." The last point has been contentious, and a democracy movement has emerged in Hong Kong, arguing that only a strong local legislature would provide meaningful safeguards for the city's 6 million inhabitants. This "one country, two systems" formula is considered by some to be a prototype for a resolution of the Taiwan issue.

Two years after the transition to Chinese sovereignty, the press remained uncensored, demonstrations were still held, and for the most part, the central government had not interfered in Hong Kong's internal affairs. However, a decision by China to overturn a decision by Hong Kong's highest court did raise fears that the autonomy of Hong Kong's legal system might be threatened. At issue was whether children of Hong Kong residents had the right to live in the territory. Hong Kong's court said they did, but the Chinese legislature argued that the decision would lead to a mass influx of mainland immigrants.

See also Macau; Taiwan.
Reference Cayrol, Pierre. *Hong Kong in the Mouth of the Dragon* (1998).

Hume, John (1937–)

John Hume, the leader of the Social Democratic and Labour Party (SDLP, the moderate nationalist party of Northern Ireland) since 1979, was born in 1937 in Londonderry. He became active in the civil rights movement, which protested against religious discrimination and in favor of local government reforms. In Londonderry, for instance, a city in which Catholics made up 62 percent of the voters, the ward boundaries were gerrymandered so that Catholics elected only eight of the twenty local councillors. In the 1969 elections for Northern Ireland's parliament, Hume defeated the sitting Nationalist member of parliament for the Foyle constituency, and the following year, he helped found the SDLP.

In 1979, Hume became leader of the party and in the same year was elected to the European Parliament. Since 1983, Hume has been the United Kingdom member of parliament for Foyle. Hume is the most important spokesperson for moderate Irish nationalism and has played an important part in persuading Irish-American politicians to play a constructive role in resolving the conflict in Northern Ireland. In 1998, he received the Nobel Peace Prize along with David Trimble, the leader of the main Protestant party.

See also Northern Ireland; Social Democratic and Labour Party.
Reference White, Barry. *John Hume: Statesman of the Troubles* (1984).

Hungarians

The Hungarian people speak Magyar, a Finno-Ugric language. Originally from western Siberia, the ancestors of the Hungarians migrated to the present location between the fifth and ninth centuries and subjugated the Slavs and Huns who were living there. The Kingdom of Hungary was established in the tenth century and consolidated as a Christian state under King Stephen in the eleventh century. In the seventeenth and eighteenth centuries, Hungary came under Hapsburg control, and throughout the nineteenth and early twentieth centuries, it was part of the Austro-Hungarian Empire.

In 1918, Hungary became a republic; in 1920, the Treaty of Trianon reduced the size and population of Hungary by about two-thirds. Although the majority of Hungarians today live in Hungary, the forced breakup of the Hungarian nation after World War I created significant Hungarian minorities in Romania, Croatia, Serbia, Slovakia, and Ukraine. Demands for more autonomy or independence have arisen in the Voivodina Province of Serbia, in Transylvania in Romania, and in the Hungarian-populated region of southern Slovakia. Since the downfall of communism, Hungarians in each of these countries have organized ethnic political parties. Currently, the main issues concern cultural autonomy for the Hungarian minorities, the right to maintain or establish Hungarian-language schools and universities, and the level of government funding for such programs.

Sentiment for creating a greater Hungary is widespread, both in Hungary itself and in the Hungarian diaspora in Eastern Europe. It is particularly prevalent in Transylvania, which many Hungarians perceive as legitimately belonging to Hungary. The Hungarian government in Budapest, which wishes to achieve full membership in both the European Union and NATO, has disavowed any irredentist goals and officially recognizes current international boundaries. However, the Hungarian government has been outspoken in pushing for more rights and privileges for Hungarian communities outside Hungary proper. Slovakia and Romania, on several occasions, have accused the Hungarian government of meddling in their internal affairs.

See also Romania; Slovakia; Transylvania; Voivodina.
Reference Hoensch, Jorg, and Kim Traynor. *A History of Modern Hungary (1867–1994)* (1996).

Hutt River Province

The Hutt River Province is a self-declared principality in Western Australia set up by an eccentric wheat farmer. Leonard Casley, who styles himself Prince Leonard, "seceded" from Western Australia after a dispute over wheat quotas, and the principality issues its own currency, stamps, and passports. Becoming a citizen costs about $150, and 20,000 people have availed themselves of the opportunity. Hutt River has been recognized diplomatically only by Macao, and the Western Australian government describes Prince Leonard as ruling a fairytale kingdom that exists only as a figment of his imagination.

Reference Chipperfield, Mark. "Safe Haven for Aussie Royalists" (1999).

India

With an electorate numbering 590 million, India is often called the world's largest democracy. India's ancient civilization dates back to the Harappan culture, which flourished during the third millennium B.C. In the second millennium, the Aryans invaded from the northwest, and the caste system, the basic principle of Indian social organization, has its origins in the Aryan conquest of the dark-skinned Dravidians. The four basic castes are called *varnas* ("colors"). A series of other conquerors followed the same path, including Arab invaders, who brought the Islamic religion in the eighth century, and the Moguls, who united most of the subcontinent in the seventeenth century. Portuguese traders arrived in 1498, and they were followed by traders from other European nations. The British East India Company emerged as the dominant force, and India was ruled by Britain until independence in 1947.

The Indian National Congress led the drive for independence and dominated Indian politics until the early 1990s. The political dynasty of Jawaharlal Nehru, his daughter Indira Gandhi, and her son Rajiv Gandhi served as prime ministers except for a brief period from 1977 to 1980. The dominance of the Congress Party has been challenged in recent years by the rise of both regionalist and Hindu nationalist parties.

India is divided by caste, language, and religion. Thirty-three languages are spoken by more than 1 million persons, and 112 "mother tongues" were tabulated in the 1981 census. Although the Congress Party had endorsed the idea of redrawing administrative boundaries along linguistic lines in 1920, Nehru initially resisted demands that a Telugu-speaking state be carved out of northern Madras. However, after the leader of the movement fasted to death, Nehru bowed to popular feelings, and the Telugu-speaking state of Andhra Pradesh was established in 1953. Subsequently, a states reorganization commission was established to study the linguistic issue, and state boundaries were redrawn in 1956 to coincide

with the distribution of regional languages. Although the majority of Indians (82 percent) follow the Hindu religion, 12 percent are Muslims, and there are smaller minorities of Christians, Sikhs, Jains, and Buddhists.

Regional identities based on linguistic and religious factors have led to the growth of separatist movements seeking either greater autonomy or outright independence. In the southern state of Tamil Nadu, a secessionist movement calling for an independent state of Dravidasthan emerged in the 1950s, and in 1967, parties advocating Tamil nationalism won control of the state government. Violent struggles by separatist groups in the Punjab, Kashmir, and tribal areas of Assam have created serious security problems and exacted a heavy death toll. However, even in those regions, the advantages of remaining part of India are still greater than those of independence, and the Indian armed forces have shown themselves capable of controlling any insurgency. The Terrorist and Disruptive Activities (Prevention) Act of 1987 provides for the punishment of certain broadly defined activities, including the peaceful expression of any opinion that questions the territorial integrity of India or that supports any secessionist claim.

Both Jawaharlal Nehru and his daughter Indira Gandhi feared and distrusted regional and ethnic movements, but in recent years, the central

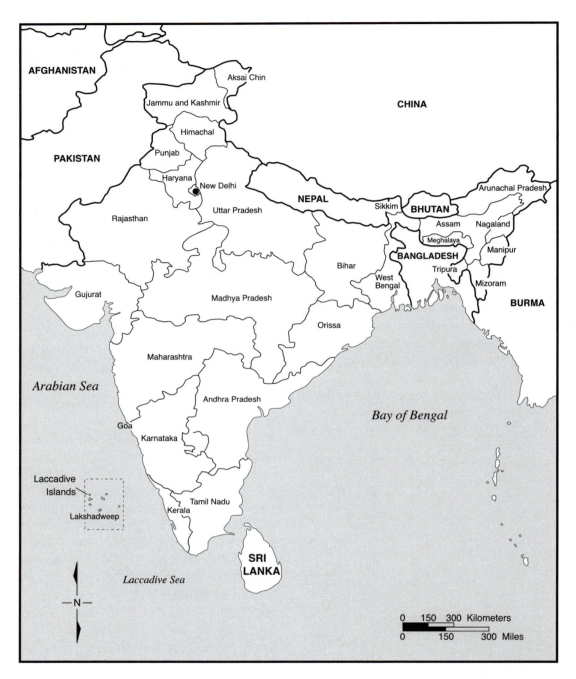

government has been more willing to respond to regional demands. This change reflects not only a general tendency to decentralize state powers on the grounds of greater efficiency but also a recognition of the costs of repression. Although recognition of linguistic and ethnic divisions was originally believed to be "antinational," the granting of autonomy may be a way of maintaining national unity in a society as diverse as India.

See also Assam; Ghorkhaland; Goa; Jammu and Kashmir; Jharkand; Khalistan; Nagaland; Tamil Nadu; Telangana.

References Brass, Paul. *Politics of India since Independence* (1992); Chadda, Maya. *Ethnicity, Security, and Separatism in India* (1997).

Indigenous Peoples

Several international organizations and conferences have affirmed the right of indigenous peoples to self-determination. In 1993, the declaration of the UN Working Group on Indigenous Populations stated that "indigenous peoples have the right of self-determination. By virtue of that right they freely determine their political status and freely pursue their economic, social, and cultural development." Similar statements can be found in the International Covenant on Civil and Political Rights, the Covenant of the Unrepresented Nations and Peoples Organization, the Kari-Oca declaration, and the Indigenous Peoples Earth Charter.

In practice, most states are reluctant to accept and implement such principles. However, several nations have recognized the rights of indigenous peoples in their constitutions or adopted constitutional amendments that provide them certain protections. The Inuit (Eskimo) of Canada were granted a degree of self-government under constitutional amendments of 1983 and 1992. The revised Brazilian constitution of 1988 recognized the right of the Indians to the "exclusive enjoyment of those lands they have traditionally occupied" and provided for their demarcation and protection. Australia enacted the Northern Territory Aboriginal Land Rights Act, which recognizes the title of the aboriginal people to the lands they occupy and guarantees them royalties on any development projects.

See also Australian Aborigines; Maori; Mapuche; Maya of Guatemala; Moskitia; Native Americans of Canada; Native Americans of the United States; Nunavut.
References Dyck, Noel. *Indigenous Peoples and the Nation State* (1985); van der Vliet, Leo, ed. *Voices of the Earth: Indigenous Peoples, New Partners, and the Right to Self-Determination* (1994).

Indonesia

The Dutch conquest of the East Indies (which became Indonesia after independence), begun in the 1600s, was not completed until the 1800s. The Japanese invaded the Dutch East Indies in 1941 and were welcomed by many as liberators. Indonesian nationalists, led by Sukarno, declared independence on August 17, 1945, but the Dutch made a futile attempt to regain control before finally recognizing the new state on December 27, 1949.

The Republic of Indonesia is an artificial creation, and there is little in common between the densely populated island of Java, where two-thirds of the total population live, and the outer islands save their common history as a Dutch colony. Prior to independence, Indonesian nationalists disagreed as to what the country's boundaries should be, with some calling for it to include Malaysia but not New Guinea. The new nation's extraordinary diversity in language, race, and culture partially explains the fact that twenty-one regional revolts occurred within twenty years after independence. (At least 250 mutually incomprehensible languages are spoken, and the official language, Bahasa Indonesian, is used by only 12 percent of the population.)

The Dutch proposal that a federal system be set up was accepted by the Indonesian nationalists in the Linggadjati agreement of 1946, but this federal system was replaced by a unitary constitution in 1950. The Dutch encouraged separatist aspirations, and colonial Dutch troops played a major role in the separatist insurgency in the southern Moluccas. By the mid-1950s, most of the separatist movements had been suppressed by the Indonesian army, but in two territories taken over by Indonesia—West Irian (Irian Jaya)—and East Timor—separatist guerrillas activity continued. In the North Sumatra province of Aceh, the Free Aceh Movement (Gerakan Aceh Merdeka) has been waging a guerrilla war since the 1970s. In August 1999, East Timor voted for independence from Indonesia, and this in turn encouraged separatists in Aceh, who demanded that they too should be allowed an independence referendum. However, many analysts believe that if Aceh is allowed to secede, this will lead to increased separatist activity in other restive provinces and the eventual disintegration of Indonesia.

See also Aceh; East Timor; South Moluccas; West Irian.
References Drake, Christine. *National Integration in Indonesia* (1989); Kahin, Audrey R., ed. *Regional Dynamics of the Indonesian Revolution* (1985).

Ingushetia

The residents of Ingushetia, the Ingush, are a predominantly Sunni Muslim people who speak a Caucasian language similar to Chechen. The language is currently written in Cyrillic. The Ingush were mountain people until the sixteenth century when they began settling the surrounding plains. In 1810, the Ingush became Russian subjects, and they accepted Russian rule more easily than some of their Caucasian neighbors, who resisted Russian encroachment with arms.

In 1920, Soviet forces took control of Ingushetia, and in 1924, the Ingush Autonomous District was created. In 1936, the Chechen-Ingush Autonomous Republic was established within the Union of Soviet Socialist Republics. After World War II, accusing the Ingush of collaborating with the Nazis, Joseph Stalin abolished the republic and dispersed the Ingush to central Asia and Siberia. Nikita Khrushchev reestablished the Chechen-Ingush Republic in 1957 but assigned the traditional Ingush district of Prigorodny to North Ossetia (now Alania). The Ingush demanded the return of the territory but were ignored by Moscow.

In 1990, as Chechens moved to declare sovereignty, Russia encouraged the Ingush to separate from the Chechen-Ingush Republic. In 1991, Ingushetia, with a population of only 300,000, became the smallest autonomous republic of the post-Communist Russian Federation.

In 1992, hostilities broke out between Ingushetia and North Ossetia over Prigorodny, which Ingushetia still claimed. North Ossetian forces prevailed, and some 40,000 Ingush were expelled from North Ossetia. Russian intervention brought about a cease-fire, and after prolonged negotiations, an accord was reached between the two warring Russian republics. As of 1998, some 13,000 Ingush refugees had been able to return to their homes in North Ossetia.

See also Russian Federation.
References Kasaev, Alan. "Ossetia-Ingushetia" (1996); Nichols, Joanna. *Ingush* (1997).

Intifada

The Intifada refers to an unplanned sustained uprising of Palestinians in the Gaza Strip and the West Bank against Israeli occupation forces. It began on December 8, 1987, following a motor vehicle accident in which an Israeli military truck killed four Palestinians from the town of Jabalya in Gaza. The subsequent funeral generated a massive protest to which the Israeli forces responded with tear gas and live ammunition. Hatem al-Sisi was killed and later proclaimed a martyr for the Palestinian cause. Further demonstrations followed, spreading into the West Bank. The Palestinians used primitive means to resist the well-armed Israeli forces—stones, slingshots, burning debris and makeshift barricades—and often young children were involved. The uprising continued until 1991.

Although the Intifada arose spontaneously, the Palestine Liberation Organization (PLO), Hamas, and the Islamic Jihad became involved in the movement as it progressed. Israel was ultimately able to contain the movement, but at a high cost economically and militarily. Furthermore, the Intifada increased world support for the Palestinians and their demands for their own state. Ultimately, the Intifada may have goaded both Israel and the PLO into reaching the accommodations spelled out in the 1993 Oslo peace accord, which granted Palestinians a measure of self-government.

See also Israel; Palestinians.
References Farsoun, Samih. *Palestine and the Palestinians* (1997); Hadawi, Sami. *Bitter Harvest: A Modern History of Palestine* (1991).

Iranian Azerbaijan

The Azerbaijanis inhabit northwestern Iran and the Republic of Azerbaijan (formerly the Soviet

Socialist Republic of Azerbaijan).They speak a Turkic language and follow the Shi'ite form of Islam. The Azerbaijanis living in Iran number almost 8 million, about 7 percent of the Iranian population. Although occupied at various times by the Ottoman Turks, the Azerbaijanis were for the most part under Persian rule until, following a series of military defeats, the northern part of Azerbaijan was ceded to Russia by Persia in 1828.

British and Soviet troops invaded Iran in August 1941 in order to overthrow Reza Shah Pahlavi, who was suspected of pro-German sympathies. During his rule, government policy had emphasized the supremacy of the Persian-speaking majority and suppressed ethnic minority cultures. This policy was supported by the intellectual elite. The magazine *Iranshahr* called for "the Turkish tongue to be torn out by the roots" and argued that "achieving national unity means that the Persian tongue must be established throughout the whole country, that regional differences in clothing, customs and suchlike must disappear. . . . Kurds, Lors, Quasqa'is, Arabs, Turks, Turkmens, etc., shall not differ from one another by wearing different clothes or speaking a different language." Books and newspapers could only be published in Persian, the official national language. The teaching of other languages was forbidden, and even Arabic, the language of the Koran, was eliminated from the primary school curriculum. A government agency was set up to purify the Persian language by eliminating Arabic and other foreign words.

During the same period, ethnic minorities were uprooted from their traditional homelands and resettled in other areas. Thousands of Kurds were transferred to Mazandaran and Khorasan, and Azerbaijanis were driven into Kurdistan. Administrative boundaries were redrawn so that Azerbaijan, which had previously been governed as a single province, was divided into two with East Azerbaijan including parts of Kurdistan. Reza Shah's industrialization policy favored his home province of Mazandaran and neglected Azerbaijani cities.

When Soviet troops invaded and occupied Azerbaijan, they encountered no serious resistance. During the Soviet occupation, several Azerbaijan groups were organized, the first Azerbaijani-language newspaper was published, and peasant revolts broke out throughout the region. In September 1945, the recently founded Democrat Party of Azerbaijan set up a National Government of Azerbaijan, and its forces rapidly took control of most of the major cities in the region. The Soviet army helped the rebels not only by supplying them with weapons but also by intercepting Iranian troops who had been sent to put down the rebellion. The Democrat Party, led by Mir Ja'far Pishevari, did not seek full independence but rather autonomy within Iran. The party declared Azerbaijani the official language of the province, demanded increased representation in the central legislature, and advocated universal suffrage, the prohibition of child labor, and the confiscation of lands owned by absentee landlords. The republic lasted until December 1946, when it was crushed by the Iranian army.

See also Azerbaijan; Pishevari, Mir Ja'far.
Reference Atabaki, Touraj. *Azerbaijan: Ethnicity and Autonomy in Twentieth-Century Iran* (1993).

Iranian Kurds

About 6 million Kurds live in northwestern Iran. During World War II, British and Soviet troops invaded Iran and forced Reza Shah Pahlavi, who was thought to be pro-German, to abdicate in favor of his son Mohammad Reza Pahlavi. Between the territories occupied by the two Allied armies lay a narrow buffer of land centered on the city of Mahabad. With encouragement from the Soviet Union, Kurdish rebels led by Qazi Mohammad and his two brothers proclaimed the Republic of Mahabad in 1946. The rebels sought autonomy within Iran and Kurdish language rights rather than independence. The republic lasted for a year before Iranian troops overthrew it and executed the Qazi brothers. (The American ambassador sought an audience with the new shah, who promised that he would not have them shot. He kept his word and had them hanged instead.)

Kurdish separatist activity resumed in 1960 when the Kurdish Democratic Party (KPDI) began a guerrilla insurgency. However, Mustafa Barzani, the Iraqi Kurdish leader who was receiving aid from the shah in his struggle against Iraq, withdrew his support from the KDPI, even going so far as to hand over some Iranian Kurdish rebels to the shah. The insurgency was finally crushed by the Iranian army in 1968. After the 1979 Islamic revolution, the Kurds again demanded autonomy, but the Khomeini regime refused, fearing that if it made concessions to the Kurds, other Iranian minorities would make similar demands.

See also Kurdistan.
References Eagleton, W. J. R. *The Kurdish Republic of 1945* (1963); Meisalas, Susan. *Kurdistan: In the Shadow of History* (1998).

Iraqi Kurds

The dissolution of the Ottoman Empire after World War I led to the creation of several new states, among them Iraq. An artificial entity, Iraq is made up of three groups of people: Shi'ite Arabs, Sunni Arabs, and Kurds. Although Shi'ites constitute a majority, and the Kurds as much as 25 percent of the population, the Sunni Arab minority has always been dominant politically.

The Kurds revolted against Iraq in the 1920s and again in the 1940s. The latter uprising was led by Mustafa Barzani and ended when Barzani and his followers retreated across the border into the Soviet Union. Barzani returned in 1958, after a coup had overthrown the monarchy. The new republican constitution recognized Iraq as a binational state and guaranteed the national rights of the Kurds. However, when the Kurds were unable to negotiate autonomy for their region, conflict broke out again, resulting in more than 60,000 casualties before a cease-fire agreement was concluded in 1970.

The fifteen-point agreement recognized Iraq as a binational country. Kurdish would be the official language, along with Arabic, in Kurdish majority areas and also the language of instruction in the schools. Wherever possible, government officials in Kurdish areas would be Kurdish speakers. Public offices would be divided in an equitable ratio between Arabs and Kurds. Kurds would be represented on the Revolutionary Command Council (Iraq's governing body), and they would have the right to set up their own organizations. The Kurdish people would share in the legislature in proportion to their numbers, and one of the vice-presidents would be a Kurd. Most important, an autonomous Kurdish region with its own legislature would be set up within four years.

However, because of disagreements concerning the extent of the autonomous region, a new round of fighting broke out in 1974. (The Iraqi government used the 1957 census to determine the boundaries, thereby excluding almost half the Kurdish majority areas, in particular the Kirkuk oil fields, from the autonomous region.) Arms were supplied to the Kurdish forces by the shah of Iran and by Israel, but after a diplomatic agreement between Iran and Iraq in March 1975, Iran cut off military aid to the Kurds. The Kurdish resistance collapsed in a matter of weeks, and Barzani and thousands of refugees fled into Iran.

The war devastated the area, and thousands of Kurdish guerrillas and civilians were massacred by the victorious Iraqi army—there were allegations that poison gas had been used against some villages. Over 100,000 Kurds were relocated to government-controlled "strategic hamlets." Another revolt occurred in the late 1980s, and it, too, was suppressed with great brutality. Over 4,000 villages were destroyed, 100,000 people were killed, and a UN inquiry concluded that mustard, cyanide, and nerve gases were used against the civilian population.

After Saddam Hussein's defeat in the Persian Gulf War in 1991, the Iraqi Kurds (and the Shi'ites in the south) rose up in revolt, but both revolts were brutally put down by the remnants of the Iraqi army. The United States, Britain, and France thereupon declared the area north of the thirty-sixth parallel a no-fly zone for the Iraqi air force.

This policy enabled the Kurds to liberate most of their ancestral homelands, and the two rival Kurdish groups, the Kurdistan Democratic Party (KDP) and the Patriotic Union of Kurdistan (PUK), set up a joint administration in the city of Arbil (or Erbil).

The region had been economically devastated by decades of warfare, and the population was dependent upon foreign aid, without which the Kurds would have starved. The two groups began to struggle for control over the lucrative border trade, and the PUK drove the KDP out of Arbil in 1994. All attempts to resolve the differences between the two groups were futile, and the KDP entered into an alliance with Saddam Hussein. In August 1996, the KDP militia, backed by Iraqi troops and tanks, forced the PUK into the mountains. Although the PUK regained most of its lost territory, the willingness of the KDP to ally itself with the president of Iraq, the archenemy of the Kurdish people, showed the strength of factionalism among the Kurds.

See also Kurdistan; Kurdistan Democratic Party.
References Barkey, Henri J. "Kurdish Geopolitics" (1997); McDowall, David. *A Modern History of the Kurds* (1996).

Irgun

Irgun Zvai Leumi (or Etzel), the national military organization, was a Jewish militia group founded in Palestine in 1931 by Avraham Tehomi. Originally a splinter group of Haganah, the military wing of the Jewish Agency, Etzel functioned as a right-wing nationalist group. Led first by David Raziel and Avraham Stern, and from 1944 until its disbandment at independence in 1948 by Menachem Begin, Irgun waged a war for independence against British forces in Palestine and assisted in bringing illegal immigrants into the country. In 1946, Irgun blew up the King David Hotel in Jerusalem, headquarters of several British operations. Ninety-one people died. Irgun also raided Arab territories. Following the creation of the state of Israel in 1948, Irgun disbanded its military forces and evolved into Herut, a right-wing political party.

See also Begin, Menachem; Haganah; Israel.
Reference Sachar, Howard. *History of Israel* (1996).

Irish Republican Army

One of the oldest terrorist groups in the world, the Irish Republican Army (IRA) can be traced back organizationally and ideologically to the nineteenth century. During the struggle for Irish independence, the IRA was the main element of the rebel forces. When the Anglo-Irish Treaty of 1921 was signed partitioning the island, a civil war broke out between protreaty and anti-treaty forces. The anti-treaty forces were militarily defeated but survived in the form of the IRA.

The embodiment of the most intransigent form of Irish nationalism, the goal of the IRA was to end partition and create a thirty-two-county Irish republic, not only driving out the British forces "occupying" Northern Ireland but also toppling the treacherous twenty-six-county government in Dublin. Intermittent terrorist attacks were made against both English and Northern Irish targets in every decade after partition. In 1956, the IRA launched Operation Harvest, a series of cross-border attacks against police and military targets. After the campaign petered out in 1962, a debate broke out within the IRA about what to do next. The new left-wing leadership opted for a political rather than a military strategy, and the IRA got rid of its weapons and emphasized social issues in an attempt to unite Protestant and Catholic workers. Consequently, the IRA played an important role in the civil rights movement that became active in Northern Ireland in the mid-1960s.

However, the civil rights marches and demonstrations provoked an angry backlash from Protestants, who believed them to be IRA-inspired. When riots broke out in 1968 and Protestant mobs attacked Catholic areas, the IRA was unable to protect the Catholics. This led to a split within the IRA between the Officials and the Provisionals. The faction supporting the leadership, the Officials, was made up of Marxists who emphasized class rather than communal identity while the Provisionals were traditional nationalists who were hostile to the Protestants and favored a military strategy. The Provisional IRA has been responsible for the great majority of violent incidents. The Official IRA carried out some attacks, but in May 1972, it declared a truce and transformed itself into a political party, Republican Clubs. Frustrated militants broke away from the Officials in December 1974 to form the Irish National Liberation Army, which promptly launched its own terrorist campaign.

In the past the IRA was quasi-military with brigades, companies, and a clearly defined hierarchy. The brigades were territorially organized with one in each of the main Catholic population centers. Companies were composed of local "volunteers" who operated in their home districts. This organizational structure was extremely vulnerable to penetration and sometime around 1977 was replaced by a cell structure. The IRA may have numbered 2,000 in 1972, but current estimates place its strength at about 200. Those convicted of terrorist offenses have been overwhelmingly male, young (about three-quarters of them under twenty-five), and largely working class in terms of occupation.

The degree of support for the IRA has fluctuated over time, but surveys show that almost half the Catholics in Northern Ireland consider the IRA as "basically patriots and idealists." This support depends on a number of factors. Many Catholics share the IRA's goal of a united Ireland, and IRA violence is legitimated by the "rebel" tradition in Irish history. In the closely knit Catholic areas, IRA volunteers are protected and sheltered because they are known to the local population as neighbors, friends, and relatives. Furthermore, the IRA serves as a defense force against "loyalist" (Protestant) terrorism and in the absence of a police presence maintains law and order within Catholic areas.

The IRA campaign has been the longest and most deadly urban guerrilla insurgency in post–World War II Western history. According to official statistics, over 15,000 explosions and almost 20,000 shooting incidents took place in Northern Ireland between 1969 and 1994, most of them attributed to the IRA. Of the more than 3,200 people killed as a result of the conflict, at least 1,926 were killed by one of the three IRA groups. The basic strategy of the IRA is to raise the costs to Britain of remaining in Northern Ireland. By killing British soldiers, the IRA hopes to generate public pressure for withdrawal, and British soldiers have been the primary targets of IRA attacks. Bombing offices, shops, and restaurants serves the same purpose, since the British government pays compensation to property owners. The IRA has rarely targeted Protestant civilians, but large numbers have been killed or maimed as a result of explosions.

In December 1993, the British and Irish prime ministers in a joint declaration offered the IRA's political wing a place in negotiations concerning the future of Northern Ireland if the organization would renounce violence. The following year, U.S. President Clinton granted a visa to Gerry Adams, the head of Provisional Sinn Fein, in an attempt to help the process along. This action, along with concessions by the British and Irish governments, persuaded the IRA that there were benefits to be gained in stopping its campaign and taking its chances at the negotiating table. The IRA declared a cease-fire on August 31, 1994, but the British government demanded that the IRA turn in its weapons before being allowed to join the negotiations. The IRA thought this demand was a prevarication and ended the truce by detonating a bomb in London on February 9, 1996. However, the truce was renewed on July 19, 1997, and Provisional Sinn Fein entered the peace talks.

See also Adams, Gerry; Northern Ireland; Northern Irish Peace Agreement.

References Coogan, Tim Pat. *The IRA* (1972); Cronin, Sean. *Irish Nationalism: A History of Its Roots and Ideology* (1980); Taylor, Peter. *Behind the Mask: The IRA and Sinn Fein* (1997); Toolis, Kevin. *Rebel Hearts: Journeys within the IRA's Soul* (1996).

Irredentism

Irredentism (the word comes from the Italian word *irredenta*—"unredeemed") was first used in the nineteenth century in connection with Italy's desire to annex Italian-speaking regions under Austrian rule to the new Italian state. The term now has a wider meaning and refers to any attempt to unite ethnically or historically linked territories under common political rule.

Two subtypes can be identified. First, there is the attempted incorporation of adjacent territories and people into an existing state. Historically, there is Hitler's claim to the Sudetenland, and contemporary instances include Somalia's attempt to incorporate the Somalis living in Ethiopia and Pakistan's claim to Muslim Kashmir. Second, a people divided among several states may seek to be united in a single new state. An obvious example of this subtype is the Kurds, who now live as minorities in Iraq, Iran, and Turkey.

The ethnic rationale and the historical claim may not always coincide—for instance, Serbia's claim to Kosovo on historical grounds is not supported by the ethnic criterion since over 80 percent of the people in the province are Albanian. Similarly, Argentina's historical claim to the Falklands is opposed by the British government because of the wishes of the local population.

Reference Chazan, Naomi, ed. *Irredentism and International Politics* (1991).

Islamic Jihad

Like Hamas, the Islamic Jihad (Holy War) is a fundamentalist Sunni Palestinian guerrilla group. Its goal is to create an Islamic republic in Palestine that would include the territory now occupied by the state of Israel. Such a state, like early postrevolutionary Iran, would be ruled by a council of religious leaders. Islamic Jihad grew out of the Muslim Brotherhood in the 1980s in the Gaza Strip. The movement was influenced by Ayatollah Khomeini and the Iranian revolution, and Iran is one of its chief financial supporters. Islamic Jihad is most active in Gaza and southern Lebanon, where it is aligned with Hezbollah, the Lebanese Shi'ite militia and political party.

Although the group's membership in the occupied territories is small compared to Hamas, another Palestinian fundamentalist organization, Islamic Jihad has carried out numerous terrorist actions. A bombing in Bet Lid in January 1995, for which it claimed responsibility, killed nineteen Israeli soldiers. Following the Israeli-PLO signing of the Wye River accords in November 1998, Islamic Jihad, which is not a member of the Palestine Liberation Organization (PLO), orchestrated a suicide bombing in Jerusalem that injured twenty-four people and caused some members of the Israeli government to balk at pressing forward with the next stages of the treaty. Islamic Jihad refuses to recognize the existence of Israel and denounces the peace accords as a betrayal of the Palestinian cause.

Islamic Jihad was founded by Fathi Shakaki, who was born in the Gaza Strip in 1951 and studied medicine in Egypt. Linked to the assassination of President Anwar Sadat in Egypt in 1981, Shakaki was expelled to Gaza where he began to put together the organization. Shakaki was murdered in Malta in 1995, allegedly by Israeli agents. He was succeeded by Ramadan Shalah, a Florida resident for several years, who moved the organizational headquarters to Damascus in 1996.

See also Hamas; Israel; Palestinians.
Reference Farsoun, Samih. *Palestine and the Palestinians* (1997).

Israel

The state of Israel was established in 1948 as a national homeland for the Jewish people. It occupies some of the land once held by the Kingdom of Israel (circa 1020–922 B.C.). Most Jews were expelled by the Romans following a revolt in A.D. 135, but over the centuries, Jewish tradition kept alive the Jews' desire to return to their ancestral homeland. Zionism, a nineteenth-century ideology that arose

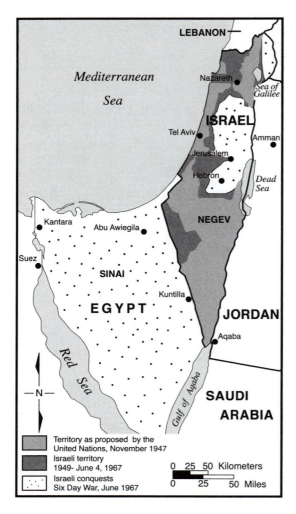

Territory as proposed by the United Nations, November 1947

Israeli territory 1949- June 4, 1967

Israeli conquests Six Day War, June 1967

0   25   50 Kilometers

0   25   50 Miles

Israel was overrun by Assyria in 722 B.C., and in 586 B.C., Babylon conquered Judah and deported most of the population. A later Persian conquest permitted the return of some Jews to Palestine. Ruled in turn by Alexander the Great, the Ptolemies, and the Seleucid dynasty, Jews managed to set up an independent state for a brief period before being conquered by Rome. After a revolt in A.D. 135, the Jews were driven from Jerusalem. Many were killed or sold into slavery, and the Jews were reduced to a small percentage of the population of Palestine.

In 1880, Palestine, then ruled by the Ottomans, was inhabited by a predominantly Arabic-speaking Muslim population. Jews numbered about 25,000, roughly 5 percent of the total. Discrimination against Jews in Russia and Eastern Europe in the late-nineteenth century led to the first significant wave of new immigration to Palestine. The writings of the Austro-Hungarian Theodore Herzl provided a secular and intellectual rationale for Jews to move to there, as Herzl advocated the creation of a Jewish state in Palestine as the only practical way for European Jews to escape discrimination and persecution. In 1897, Herzl helped found the World Zionist Organization (WZO), which called for Palestinian land to be allocated for the creation of a Jewish state. The WZO adopted a plan for colonizing Palestine, established organizations to aid new settlers there, and secured funding from Jewish sources throughout the world. Although secular in nature, Zionism encouraged the immigration of Jews whose motives for returning to Palestine were purely religious and who were, in some cases, hostile to the idea of creating a secular Jewish state.

By 1914, the Jewish population of Palestine had grown to 85,000, and in 1917, the British foreign secretary, Arthur Balfour, issued a memorandum approving the idea of a Jewish homeland in Palestine. In 1922, the League of Nations approved what had become known as the Balfour Declaration when it established the British Mandate in Palestine.

among Eastern European Jews, called for the creation of a Jewish state, and Zionist organizations encouraged emigration to Palestine.

Palestine (named after the Philistines) is located on the eastern Mediterranean shore and is bordered by Lebanon, Syria, Jordan, and Egypt. Since ancient times, the land has been a battleground for outside empires who prized its location as a link between Europe and Asia. Ruled by Egypt in the fourteenth century B.C., the area was invaded and settled by the Hebrews circa 1200 B.C. Under first Saul and then David, an Israelite kingdom with Jerusalem as its capital was established. Following the death of David's son, Solomon, the kingdom split into Israel in the north and Judah in the south.

Israeli soldiers pray at the Wailing Wall in Old Jerusalem at the end of the Six Day War, June 1967. (Corbis/ Bettmann)

Under British rule, more than 240,000 Jewish immigrants arrived in Palestine prior to World War II. In 1929, the Jewish Agency was established. It functioned as a semiautonomous government in the Jewish community, overseeing civic and military organizations and making major policy decisions. Arab Palestinians, fearful of the growing Jewish presence in what they considered their land and angry that the victorious democracies had reneged on promises to create an independent Palestinian state, engaged in anti-Jewish and anti-British protests. These culminated, in the 1936–1939 period, in a full-blown insurrection, with Arabs demanding a moratorium on Jewish immigration and land purchases. The British attempted to mediate the

Arab-Jewish conflict but with no success. A British proposal for the creation of a Palestinian state that included both Jews and Arabs was rejected by the Zionists.

During and following World War II, Jewish migration continued despite British attempts to control it. Jewish terrorist activities against the British government and in support of increased Jewish immigration and the creation of a Jewish state intensified after 1945, and in 1947, the British government, tiring of trying to find a workable solution to the area's conflicts, referred the Palestine issue to the United Nations for resolution. In November 1947, the UN General Assembly approved the partition of Palestine into Jewish and Arab sectors. Jerusalem was to be an international city in view of its historic and religious importance to Jews, Muslims, and Christians. Even though Jews constituted only 30 percent of the population, they were granted 55 percent of the territory. Leaders of the Arab League, an alliance of neighboring Arab states, refused to recognize the new arrangement, but on May 14, 1948, the state of Israel came into being.

Palestinians living in the new Jewish state revolted, and to support them, the neighboring Arab states declared war on Israel. Israeli military forces crushed the local uprisings and defeated the Arab armies. By its victory in the conflict, Israel increased its share of territory to 76 percent of historic Palestine. An estimated 800,000 Palestinians fled their homes in the Jewish-controlled areas, which left a Jewish majority in Israel. A large hostile Palestinian exile community was also created, and its descendants still believe their homeland was expropriated from them unjustly.

Following the cessation of overt hostilities, Israel continued to strengthen the new state. It passed the Law of Return, which made Israeli citizenship possible for all Jews throughout the world. By 1951, an additional 600,000 people had migrated to Israel. The Arab nations continued to refuse to recognize the state of Israel, and Arab-Israeli wars were fought in 1956, 1967, and 1973 with Israel continuing to prevail. Victory in the 1967 war brought further territory under Israeli control, necessitating the creation of occupied zones in the Gaza Strip and the West Bank. East Jerusalem and the Golan Heights, formerly controlled by Syria, were annexed outright. An undivided Jerusalem was declared the capital of Israel. UN Resolution 242, passed in 1967, called on Israel to withdraw from the occupied lands in return for a pledge of peace from its adversaries and a recognition of the right of the state of Israel to exist. Although the resolution produced no immediate results from either Israel or the Arab states, ultimately it was to prove a foundation for later accommodations among Israel, some Arab states, and the Palestine Liberation Organization (PLO).

In 1979, Egypt recognized Israel. For its part, Israel returned occupied Egyptian territory and also pledged to allow a self-governing administration to be established in the Gaza Strip and the West Bank. In 1988, the Palestinian National Council, headed by Yasir Arafat, recognized Israel with the expectation that Israel would withdraw from areas of occupied Palestine. This "land for peace" formula came to fruition in 1993 when Israel and the PLO signed a treaty calling for the establishment of limited self-rule in specific occupied areas. Israel also promised to withdraw from Jericho and other occupied territories. However, military bases and Jewish settlements were excluded from Palestinian control as were strategic highways connecting them. Palestinians were not to control international borders, but they were allowed to establish civil governments and their own security forces. Discussions of the future status of Jerusalem and the possibility of an independent state of Palestine were postponed. Continuing negotiations, including the Wye River accords signed in 1998, represent attempts to consolidate earlier agreements concerning Israel's turning over of occupied territories in the West Bank and Gaza.

A smooth transition seems unlikely, however. Strong opposition to returning territory to a Palestinian government exists in the Knesset, the Israeli parliament. Conservative religious groups argue that the occupied territories are part of Eretz Israel, the biblical Israeli kingdom. The existence of functioning Jewish settlements in the occupied areas puts further pressure on the Israeli government to guarantee their safety. But, in order to do so, Israel would have to limit Palestinian sovereignty, which would undermine Arafat's shaky legitimacy. Although Arafat has pledged the PLO and its dominant faction, Fatah, to nonviolence, he does not speak for the rejectionist groups Hamas and Islamic Jihad, which have strong popular support in the occupied territories for continuing a terrorist war against the state of Israel. Israel wonders whether the Palestinian Authority, the government of the liberated territories, will be able to control anti-Israeli terrorists operating in its jurisdiction.

After more than fifty years of existence, the state of Israel has proved its durability. With a population of 5.5 million, which includes 1 million Arabs and more than 700,000 recent immigrants from states of the former Soviet Union, the internal stability of the Jewish homeland seems secure. However, the festering resentments found among the nearly 7 million Palestinians in Israel, in the West Bank and Gaza, and in neighboring states will continue to challenge Israel as well as provide ardent recruits for terrorist activities. Anti-Israeli guerrilla actions are likely to continue to receive funding from sympathetic nations such as Syria, Iraq, Iran, and Libya.

In July 1999, the newly elected Israeli prime minister, Ehud Barak, assured Arafat that he intended to withdraw Israeli troops from much of the West Bank and implement the Wye River accords. Barak also began peace talks with Syria about the Golan Heights.

See also Begin, Menachem; Ben-Gurion, David; Fatah; Haganah; Hamas; Irgun; Islamic Jihad; Palestine Liberation Organization; Palestinian Authority; Palestinians; Stern Gang.
References Bickerton, Ian J., and Carla L. Klausner. *A Concise History of the Arab-Israeli Conflict* (1998); Cohen, Michael J. *Palestine to Israel: From Mandate to Independence* (1989); Ra'anan, Uri. *The Frontiers of a Nation* (1976); Sachar, Howard. *History of Israel* (1996).

Istria

Although heavily populated by Slavs, the Istrian peninsula was under Austrian and Venetian rule for 500 years until 1918 when it became part of Italy. In 1945, when the peninsula was awarded to Yugoslavia, there was an exodus of 300,000 Italians from the region. In 1991, following the disintegration of Yugoslavia, Istria was divided between the newly independent states of Slovenia and Croatia.

Two Italian-dominated movements are seeking changes in Istria. The Italian-Istrian Community in Exile functions as a pressure group in Italy, and it demands that the Italian government take measures to effect the return of Istria to Italian sovereignty or failing that, to ensure compensation to Italian families and property holders who fled Istria after the Yugoslavian takeover. Within Istria, the remaining 30,000 Italians have pressed their demands for Italian minority rights, particularly in the widening of biculturalism in public affairs and education.

A broader, more ethnically inclusive movement in the Croatian sector of the Istrian Peninsula has also become active. This has been spearheaded by the Istrian Democratic Party (IDP), which in 1993 polled 70 percent of the votes in Istria. The IDP has called for increased regional autonomy for Istria, but the Croatian government, partly fearing the loss of significant income from tourism, has called the movement a threat to national unity.

See also Croatia; Trieste.
Reference Tanner, Marcus. *Croatia: A Nation Forged in War* (1997).

Italy

For both historical and geographical reasons, Italy is a country of great regional diversity and strong local identities. The national language is known as standard Italian, but most Italians speak regional dialects that differ from one another in vocabulary and pronunciation and are often mutually unintelligible. Some dialects (such as that spoken in Sardinia) are so distinctive that they are often considered to be separate languages. In addition, there are a quarter of a million German speakers in the province of Bolzano (in German, Bozen), 600,000 speakers of Friuli in Friuli–Venezia Giulia, and a substantial population of French speakers in the Valle d'Aosta.

In 1970, a system of regional decision making was created. In addition to fifteen ordinary regions, five "special regions" (Friuli–Venezia Giulia, Sardinia, Sicily, Trentino–Alto Adige, and Valle d'Aosta) were granted extensive autonomous powers. These five areas were regarded as having distinctive cultural, social,

or linguistic characteristics. The existence of these special regions was recognized soon after World War II as a result of separatist sentiments in Sicily and international pressures in the South Tirol and Valle d'Aosta. Because of a dispute with Yugoslavia over the status of Trieste and the Slovene minority, the internationally recognized border was not determined until 1954, and it took until 1962 before the Christian Democratic government succeeded in passing the required legislation to set up a regional government in Friuli–Venezia Giulia.

See also Friuli; Istria; Padania; Sardinia; Sicily; South Tirol; Trieste; Valle d'Aosta.

Izetbegovic, Alija (1925–)

Alija Izetbegovic, a Muslim, was elected president of Bosnia and Herzegovina in 1990 and again in 1995. An attorney and a construction executive, Izetbegovic was jailed by the Tito government for

Bosnian President Alija Izetbegovic waves to the crowd during a military parade, December 10, 1995. (Reuters/Peter Andrews/Archive Photos)

pro-Islamic activism and for advocating a Western-style parliamentary democracy. As founder and head of the Party of Democratic Action, Izetbegovic has tried to keep the multiethnic Bosnian state intact since independence from Yugoslavia in 1992. The ensuing Bosnian civil war led to the loss of major Muslim population centers to Croat and Serb armies. Izetbegovic remains head of state in the reconstituted Bosnia and Herzegovina, which the Dayton peace accord effectively divided into three ethnic zones. Although the Muslim-Croat federation is charged with creating an integrated armed forces, progress has been slow, and schools and neighborhoods remain segregated by religion. Suffering from poor health, Izetbegovic has announced he will not seek reelection when his term expires in 2000.

See also Bosnia and Herzegovina; Dayton Peace Accord.
Reference Malcolm, Noel. *Bosnia: A Short History* (1996).

Jammu and Kashmir

The Indian Independence Act of 1947 transferred sovereignty from the British crown to the governments of India and Pakistan. However, the British also had treaty relations with 528 nominally independent principalities outside British India, and it was necessary for their status to be determined. In most cases, they were persuaded to become part of the Indian Union in return for recognition of their rulers' privileges. There were two important exceptions: Hyderabad and Jammu and Kashmir.

The first, a large and wealthy princely state, had a predominantly Hindu population and was surrounded by Indian territory. Its Muslim ruler, the nizam, sought to maintain the state's independence and appealed to the UN Security Council in August 1948, whereupon India invaded and Hyderabad was forced to join India.

In Jammu and Kashmir, the situation was reversed. The vast majority of the state's population was Muslim, but the ruling maharajah was a Hindu, and he refused to join either India or Pakistan. Although the British governor general, Viscount Mountbatten, urged the maharajah to join Pakistan, the maharajah procrastinated. When irregular Pakistani troops invaded, the maharajah fled to India and appealed for assistance. Indian troops were sent in, and after some fighting a cease-fire was signed in January 1949, leaving India in control of about two-thirds of the territory. A UN-supervised plebiscite was supposed to determine the wishes of the Kashmiris, but it was never held.

Jawaharlal Nehru, who was himself from a Kashmiri family, desperately wanted Kashmir to join India, and during one emotional outburst, he declared that Kashmir was more important to him than anything else. Kashmir was also symbolically important to Nehru and the Congress Party because as the only Muslim-majority state, Kashmir validated India's claim to be a secular multireligious society. In 1952, Nehru and Sheikh Abdullah, the leader of the dominant political movement in Kashmir, the National Conference, signed an

agreement. In return for renouncing its claim to independence, Kashmir was granted a special status under Article 370 of the Indian constitution. India was to control defense, foreign affairs, and communications, but otherwise Kashmir would enjoy a high degree of internal autonomy. The agreement was ratified by the Constituent Assembly of Jammu and Kashmir, and regarding this vote as an adequate expression of the popular will, India refused to hold the promised plebiscite.

However, popular resentment against Indian rule encouraged Sheikh Abdullah to argue that Kashmir had never fully consented to union with India and that India had eroded Kashmir's autonomy. The sheikh, popularly known as the Lion of Kashmir, was placed under arrest in 1953 and remained in detention until 1972. After lengthy negotiations, he signed an agreement with Indira Gandhi on November 13, 1974, was released from house arrest, and returned to Kashmir to become its chief minister in March 1975. The National Conference remained the dominant political force in the state, even after the death of the sheikh in 1982.

In 1983, his son Farooq Abdullah was elected chief minister, but by supporting a group of defectors from the National Conference, the local Congress Party was able to bring down his government. In 1987, the Congress Party switched its support back to Farooq, but these political maneuvers discredited Farooq and alienated Kashmiri opinion. Islamic fundamentalism had been growing stronger throughout the period, and the Congress–National Conference alliance was opposed by the newly formed Muslim United Front. The alliance won the election amid claims of widespread electoral fraud. Increasing violence climaxed in December 1989 when massive demonstrations by Muslim militants in Srinagar, the capital city, led to the declaration of "president's rule." By the early 1990s, a full-scale insurgency was raging.

The insurgents fall into two groups: those fighting for an independent Kashmir and those fighting to join Kashmir to Pakistan. Although more than 100 organizations are involved, the main ones are the Jammu and Kashmir Liberation Front, which seeks independence, and the Hezb ul Mujahideen, which favors union with Pakistan. The former originally had the most widespread support, but Muslim fundamentalism, stimulated by the Islamic revolution in Iran, is growing stronger.

The dispute over Kashmir has led to warfare between India and Pakistan on two occasions—in 1947 and again in 1965, when armed infiltrators from Pakistan crossed the cease-fire line, which provoked a full-scale confrontation between the two countries. The most recent crisis began in May 1999 when armed rebels seized strategic mountain strongholds on the Indian side of the cease-fire line. India charged that the intruders were really Pakistani soldiers, and there are fears that the incursion might precipitate a full-scale war between the two countries.

Precise casualty figures are not available, but at least 10,000 people have been killed in Kashmir since 1989. The Indian army conducts house-to-house searches and has been accused of brutality and torture, but under the Armed Forces (Jammu and Kashmir) Special Powers Act, members of the armed forces cannot be prosecuted for actions committed in good faith.

See also India.
References Chadda, Maya. *Ethnicity, Security, and Separatism in India* (1997); Kadian, Rajesh. *The Kashmir Triangle* (1993); Thomas, Raju, ed. *Perspectives on Kashmir* (1992).

Jharkand

Jharkand is a forested region of eastern India inhabited by tribal peoples, many of whom have been converted to Christianity. Rich in mineral resources, the area was targeted for industrialization after independence, but the local people complained that immigrants from outside the region got most of the new jobs. The Jharkand Party won most of the tribal vote in the first national elections and asked that a Jharkand state be established, but the States Reorganization Commission rejected the proposal because the region did not have a common language. The party remained the largest opposition party in the state of Bihar throughout the 1950s but gradually declined in strength. In 1995, Bihar established a Provisional Jharkand Area Autonomous Council.

See also India.
Reference Heitzman, James, and Robert L. Worden, eds. *India: A Country Study* (1996).

Jinnah, Mohammad Ali (1876–1948)

The founder of Pakistan, Mohammad Ali Jinnah (1876–1948) was the son of a rich merchant and studied law in England. He became interested in politics while in London and joined the Indian National Congress, and later the Muslim League, in the hope of uniting the Hindu and Muslim communities. Partly as a result of Jinnah's efforts, in the 1916 Lucknow Pact, the two organizations pledged to work together toward representative government for India. However, when Mahatma Gandhi called for passive resistance and massive demonstrations, Jinnah argued that such an approach was contrary to the rule of law. At the 1920 Congress Party conference, Jinnah was shouted down by the delegates and then angrily resigned from the organization. He went into self-imposed exile in England until 1934, when he returned to lead the Muslim League. When Pakistan became independent in 1947, Jinnah was appointed governor general, but he was in ill health and died a few months later.

Although the leader of a movement to establish a state based on and defined by the Islamic religion, Jinnah was himself not particularly devout, and in his dress and lifestyle, he resembled an upper-class Englishman. As head of state he appealed to the Muslim majority to accept the minority Hindus and Christians as their fellow countrymen.

See also Pakistan.
Reference Ziring, Lawrence. *Pakistan in the Twentieth Century* (1997).

Jura

Swiss history is remarkably free of linguistic conflicts, even though Switzerland contains four language groups (German, French, Italian, and Romansh) within its borders. One glaring exception to this general ethnic harmony is the conflict within the Jura region, which resulted in the establishment of a new canton in 1979. In 1815, at the Congress of Vienna, the Jura region, predominantly French-speaking and Catholic, was annexed by the Swiss canton of Bern, which was German-speaking and Protestant. During the nineteenth century, separatist movements arose four times in the Jura, usually provoked by religious issues, and in 1947, a separatist organization, the Rassemblement Jurassien (RJ), was formed.

The RJ argued that as a minority within the canton, the French culture was oppressed by the German majority, and it called for a separate French canton to be formed. In a 1959 plebiscite, the separatist option was narrowly defeated, with the three French-speaking Catholic districts voting in favor while the German Catholic and French Protestant districts were opposed. The RJ refused to accept the results of the plebiscite and organized a series of demonstrations and disturbances. The organization's youth group disrupted a session of the federal parliament and occupied the Swiss embassies in Paris and Brussels. A handful of terrorist incidents occurred in 1962, 1965, and 1966 in which a bank, military barracks, railway lines, and buildings belonging to

antiseparatists were blown up. Finally, a new plebiscite, in which each district was allowed to vote separately, was held in 1974. The pattern was the same as in 1959, and the three French Catholic districts voted to become a new canton while the others remained part of Bern.

Reference Mayer, Kurt. "The Jura Conflict" (1980).

Justice Commandos of the Armenian Genocide

Also known as the Armenian Revolutionary Army, the Justice Commandos of the Armenian Genocide (JCAG) are believed to be the militant wing of the Dashnaks, the leading Armenian nationalist group in the 1890s and early 1900s. The Dashnaks formed the government of the Armenian Republic of 1918–1920 and considered themselves a government in exile. Their original goal was an independent, non-Communist Armenia. The Dashnaks are now a parliamentary party in independent Armenia.

The JCAG emerged in 1975 and carried out several attacks against Turkish diplomats, including the murder of the Turkish consul general in Los Angeles in 1982. In another incident, five Armenian terrorists attempted to seize the Turkish embassy in Lisbon, but the attack was a fiasco in which all five terrorists were killed along with a Turkish security guard. In 1982, the JCAG split into two factions, and violence between the two groups as well as between the JCAG and the Armenian Secret Army for the Liberation of Armenia (ASALA, a pro-Soviet Armenian terrorist group) has claimed several lives. In November 1999, the JCAG was rumored to be involved in an attack on the Armenian parliament in which Prime Minister Vazgen Sarkissian was killed.

See also Armenia; Armenian Secret Army for the Liberation of Armenia.
References Gunter, Michael. *Pursuing the Just Cause of Their People: A Study of Contemporary Armenian Terrorism* (1986); Hyland, Francis P. *Armenian Terrorism: The Past, the Present, the Future* (1991).

Kabaka Yekka

Literally "the king alone," the Kabaka Yekka was a movement that stood for the solidarity of the Baganda people of Uganda and their ruler, the kabaka. The movement was formed in June 1961 following several days of demonstrations against the recently elected government of Benedicto Kiwanuka. Kiwanuka, although Bagandan himself, was considered an enemy because he had ignored the kabaka's call for an election boycott (as a result of the boycott, less than 3 percent of the Baganda had voted in the election). The Kabaka Yekka spread rapidly throughout Buganda and became a mass movement in defense not only of Bagandan separatism but also of the traditional status quo. Within Buganda, there was a growing division between the progressives who wanted to reform Buganda's parliament, the Lukiiko, to allow direct elections and the traditionalists who wanted to preserve the authority of the kabaka and the chiefs.

The Kabaka Yekka was founded by Sepiraya Masembe, a wealthy landowner whose family had served the kabaka for generations. The other founders included not only landowners like Masembe but also a more radical group of political activists. They were all either Anglicans or Muslims and opposed to the predominantly Catholic Democratic Party led by Kiwanuka. The movement's strength lay in its appeal to the intense patriotism and royalism of the Baganda. One election pamphlet asked voters whether they were willing for anyone to have authority over "his highness the kabaka of Buganda." In the 1962 elections, Kabaka Yekka won decisively with over 90 percent of the vote in Buganda.

See also Buganda.

References Apter, David. *The Political Kingdom in Uganda* (1961); Hancock, I. R. "Patriotism and Neo-traditionalism in Buganda: The Kabaka Yekka Movement, 1961–1962" (1970).

Kabardino-Balkaria

Kabardino-Balkaria, a republic in the Russian Federation, is located in the Caucasus and is bor-

dered by Georgia, North Ossetia, and Karachai-Cherkessia. It has a population of 800,000. Kabardians, who are related to Cherkessians and Adygeans and speak a Caucasian language, constitute 48 percent of the population; Russians make up 32 percent; and the Balkars, who speak a Turkic language, 10 percent. Similar to the situation in Karachay-Cherkessia, the two ethnic groups for whom the republic was named do not share a common language. However, both are Sunni Muslims.

In 1557, the Kabardian rulers asked Ivan the Terrible for Russian protection. Since then, despite local revolts, the area and its peoples have been under Russian domination. In 1922, Kabardino-Balkaria became an autonomous region of the USSR. In 1936, it was elevated to the status of an autonomous republic. In 1944, Joseph Stalin exiled the Balkars to central Asia for collaborating with the Nazis; they were repatriated in 1957 under Nikita Khrushchev. In 1991, after the collapse of the Soviet Union, Kabardino-Balkaria joined the Russian Federation as a republic.

In November 1991, a congress of Balkarians proclaimed a Balkar republic within the Russian Federation, laying claim to all land and property held in March 1944 when Stalin exiled them. Because property issues had not been dealt with under communism, the congress also petitioned the Kabardino-Balkaria Supreme Soviet to suspend privatization measures so their claims could be presented. A referendum held among the Balkars in December of the same year found Balkars voting 95 percent in favor of a separate Balkar republic. In July 1992, the National Council of the Balkarian People petitioned the president of the Russian Federation, Boris Yeltsin, asking for independence. Another vote, in 1996, reaffirmed the Balkars desire to separate.

Similar nationalist sentiments can be found among the Caucasian-speaking Kabardians. A 1992 congress of the Kabardian people proclaimed the formation of a Kabardian republic within the Russian Federation. The proclamation asserted that all other nationalities would be treated equally in the new state. At the same congress, a Cossack representative called for the separation of the Maisky and Prokhladnaya districts from the proposed Kabardian republic.

As in the Karachai-Cherkessia Republic, the leaders of Kabardino-Balkaria, supported by Moscow, resisted measures to break up the state. Widespread demonstrations called for the ouster of the Kabardinian-Balkar leadership, largely holdovers from Soviet days. The opposition leader, A. N. Shubanov, was arrested. While pledging increased economic aid to the region, Russian authorities have taken no steps to meet the separatists' demands or to bring about changes in the political elite.

See also Cossacks; Karchay-Cherkessia; Russian Federation.
References NUPI. *Kabardino-Balkariya* (1998); Smith, Sebastian. *Allah's Mountains* (1998).

Kachin

The Kachin are a tribal group in northern Burma (also known as Myanmar). Although a minor rebellion among the Kachin broke out in 1949, the Kachin Independence Organization (KIO) was not formed until 1961. The establishment of Buddhism as the official state religion of Burma in 1961 was resented by the Kachin, a predominantly Christian group, as was the ceding of three Kachin villages to China in a boundary agreement between China and Burma in 1960. The

Kachin Independence Army (KIA), the military wing of the KIO, contained many veterans of the British armed forces and adopted British military customs, such as the use of bagpipes. After heavy fighting during the 1966–1971 period, the Burmese army was forced to withdraw from the Kachin region. In the 1980s, the KIA received arms from China and extended the area under its control. By 1992, the KIA was the largest rebel group in Burma with an estimated 10,000 troops.

See also Burma.
Reference Fredholm, Michael. *Burma: Ethnicity and Insurgency* (1993).

Kalimantan Utara

In December 1962, there was an abortive revolt in Brunei, led by A. M. Azahari, that sought to establish the state of Kalimantan Utara, comprising Sarawak, Brunei, and Sabah. The revolt was backed by Indonesia, which provided training and supplies to the rebels. Sukarno, the leader of Indonesia, had ambitions to create a greater Indonesia and was opposed therefore to the creation of Malaysia. Within hours of the declaration of the new federation on September 16, 1963, Indonesian guerrillas attacked across the border and Indonesian infiltrators engaged in terrorism and sabotage on the Malay peninsula. This policy of "confrontation" was intended to provoke a popular uprising, but instead it strengthened support for Malaysia in northern Borneo. British and Malaysian forces easily defeated the Indonesian invaders, and after Sukarno was overthrown by the military in 1966, hostilities between Malaysia and Indonesia were formally ended late that year.

See also Indonesia; Malaysia; Sabah.
References Armstrong, Hamilton Fish. "The Troubled Birth of Malaysia" (1963); Hindley, Donald. "Indonesia's Confrontation with Malaysia: A Search for Motives" (1964).

Kalmykia

Kalmykia, a republic of the Russian Federation, borders the Caspian Sea in the south and Dagestan in the southwest. Kalmykia has a population of 320,000, with Russians constituting 38 percent of the total and Kalmyks 45 percent. Kalmyks are descended from the Mongols and speak an Altaic language. Although many Kalmyks had become members of the Russian Orthodox Church by the twentieth century, Buddhism is still widely practiced.

The Kalmyk khanate first sought Russian protection in 1608, and by the late-eighteenth century, the Kalmyks had been incorporated into the Russian Empire. Following the Russian Revolution, Kalmykia became an autonomous district of the Soviet Union. In 1935, the district was elevated to the status of an autonomous republic. During World War II, Joseph Stalin accused the Kalmyks of collaborating with the Nazis and deported them to central Asia and Siberia. The republic was abolished and not reestablished until 1958, during the Khrushchev administration. In 1992, it became the Kalmykia-Khalmg-Tangch Republic within the Russian Federation. Kalmyk nationalists have pressed the federal government for the return of former Kalmyk territories that are now part of the Astrakhan region and Dagestan.

See also Russian Federation.
References Kolga, Margus, et al., eds. *Red Book of the Peoples of the Russian Empire* (1993); Mastyugina, Tatiana, and Lev Perelkin. *An Ethnic History of Russia* (1996).

KaNgwane
See Swazi

Karachai-Cherkessia
The Karachai-Cherkessia Republic of the Russian Federation is located in western Caucasia north of Georgia. Of a population of 435,000, Russians compose 40 percent, Karachais 30 percent, and Cherkessians 10 percent. The Karachais speak a Turkic language; the Cherkessians, a Caucasian language. Thus, the two ethnic groups for which the republic is named do not speak related languages. They are, however, both predominantly Sunni Muslim.

The two groups were absorbed by the Russian

Empire in the nineteenth century. In 1922, after the Russian Civil War, the Karachai-Cherkess Autonomous District was created. In 1926, the district was divided in two. In 1943, the Karachai district was abolished after Stalin accused the Karachais of collaborating with the Nazis and deported them to central Asia. In 1957, the Karachais returned from exile, and the Karachai-Cherkess Autonomous District was reinstated. In 1991, Karachai-Cherkessia became a republic in the newly formed Russian Federation.

The principal source of ethnic instability in the republic is dissatisfaction on the part of the Karachais with their status in the multiethnic republic. Spearheaded by Dzamagat, a radical Karachai organization, in October 1989 a Karachai Congress called for the creation of an autonomous republic. This call was reaffirmed at the Karachai Congress of People's Deputies in November 1990. The congress also declared its right to secede from the Russian Federation. However, a referendum of all citizens of the republic held in 1992 affirmed the unity of the republic. Russians in the republic generally approved unity while the Karachais voted against it.

The Cherkessians have also expressed a desire for their own republic. In October 1991, a Cherkessian congress voted for the formation of a Cherkessian republic. Another popular notion among the Cherkessians is the creation of a greater Adygea that would unite Cherkessians, Adygeans, Kabardinians, and Shapsugs. Adygh-Hassa and Adyglar are two active Cherkessian organizations.

In addition, Cossacks in the Karachai-Cherkessia Republic have also demanded separation from the largely Muslim republic. The Congress of Upper Kuban Cossacks voted against inclusion in the Karachai-Cherkessia Republic in July 1990 and called for autonomy for the Zelenchuk, Batalpashinsk, and Urup districts.

These separatist tendencies have been held in check by the republic's political leadership, former Communist Party officials, who share Moscow's distaste for dividing administrative territories into ethnic fiefdoms. The situation remains unstable as the major ethnic minorities are dissatisfied with the status quo.

See also Cossacks; Russian Federation.
References NUPI. *Karachay-Cherkessia* (1998); Smith, Sebastian. *Allah's Mountains* (1998).

Karadzic, Radovan (1945–)

The former president of the Republic of Srpska and head of the Serbian Democratic Party, Radovan Karadzic, was forced to relinquish both posts after being indicted in 1995 for war crimes by the UN International Criminal Tribunal. Karadzic is believed to be residing in Pale, a city in eastern Srpska and a stronghold of the Serbian militia. He has never been arrested or tried for his "ethnic cleansing" activities. Although deprived of his official posts, Karadzic exerts great influence in Serbian Bosnia and continues to symbolize the Serbian desire for a completely independent state in Bosnia that ultimately will be rejoined to Serbia proper. Karadzic's chief rival in

Bosnian Serb leader Radovan Karadzic speaking with former U.S. President Jimmy Carter, June 1995. (Reuters/Archive Photos)

the post–Dayton peace accord Srpska was his successor as president, Biljana Plavsic. Although born in Montenegro, Karadzic moved to Sarajevo in his teens where he studied medicine and psychiatry. A member of Bosnia's writer's union, Karadzic has published both poetry and children's books.

See also Bosnia and Herzegovina; Srpska.
Reference Rieff, David. *Slaughterhouse: Bosnia and the Failure of the West* (1996).

Karelia

Karelia is the region ceded by Finland to the Soviet Union during World War II. The Soviet Union first demanded that Finland cede the Karelian isthmus and the naval base of Porkkala to Russia, and when this was refused, Soviet forces attacked Finland in November 1939. As a result of this "winter war" and the subsequent "continuation war" of 1941, Finland lost more than 10 percent of its territory, including not only Karelia but also some small islands in the Gulf of Finland and two strips of territory along the country's northern borders. The Finnish inhabitants of these regions, over 400,000 people, were forced out and replaced with Russians.

The Karelian émigrés organized themselves into a Karelian Association, the main goal of which was the return of Karelia to Finland. Porkkala was handed back to Finland in 1955, but when the Finns attempted to negotiate for the return of Karelia, they were rebuffed. The issue reemerged in the early 1990s, with polls showing that a third of the Finns favor the return of Karelia. However, many worry about the costs of reunification and the difficulties of assimilating the Russians living in the region. All Russians politicians reject the idea of revising the border.

Reference Forsberg, Tuomas. *Contested Territory: Border Disputes at the Edge of the Former Soviet Empire* (1995).

Karen

One of the minority peoples of Burma (also known as Myanmar), the Karen have been engaged in an insurgency against the Burmese government since 1949. Historically, relations between the Karen and the dominant Burmans were marked by hostility. Under British rule, the Karen served as soldiers in the colonial army, and large numbers were converted to Christianity by Baptist missionaries. Mission school education created a sense of unity among the Karen and gave them a modern pro-Western orientation. During World War II, many of the Karen were brutally treated by the Japanese and the Burma Independence Army, a Burmese nationalist group allied with the Japanese invaders.

After the war, the Karen sought to become independent, but according to the Panglong agreement, the Karen and other minorities were included in the newly independent Union of Burma. The Karen National Union (KNU) then proposed that a Karen state be set up in the coastal region, and when this idea was rejected, the Karen boycotted the Constituent Assembly elections. Increasing communal violence between Burmans and Karen, as well as the impasse over a Karen state, led the KNU to take up arms in 1949. Although the Karen were initially successful in seizing large areas of the Irrawaddy delta, the Burmese army eventually pushed the rebels back into a narrow stretch of territory along the border with Thailand. In 1952, the Burmese government created a new Karen state, which roughly coincided with the territory controlled by the KNU at the time. The Karen National Liberation Army, the military arm of the KNU, was estimated to have at least 4,000 men in 1992.

See also Burma.
Reference Fredholm, Michael. *Burma: Ethnicity and Insurgency* (1993).

Kashmir
See Jammu and Kashmir

Katanga

Katanga (now Shaba) was the southeastern province of the Belgian Congo. The Belgian Congo became independent on June 30, 1960, as the Democratic Republic of the Congo. Eleven days later, Katanga declared its independence from the Congo. Katanga is geographically distinct from the rest of the Congo. Most of of the country consists of dense tropical forest, but the Katangan plateau is largely savanna. The Katangan economy was dominated by the Union Minière du Haut-Katanga, a large copper-mining conglomerate that accounted for 20 percent of the Congo's gross national product and approximately half of its tax revenues. In addition to copper, Katanga has important reserves of cobalt, iron, tin, and uranium.

The three largest indigenous ethnic groups in Katanga are the Lunda, the Bayeke, and the Baluba, although by 1960 more than a third of the population consisted of immigrants from the neighboring province of Kasai. The immigrants dominated the urban centers and employment in the mining industry, and in the 1957 municipal elections, immigrants won control of all four African local government districts in Elisabethville, the provincial capital (now Lubumbashi). The rivalry between "the strangers" and "the authentic Katangans" led to the emergence of Conakat, a political party formed from several Katangan ethnic associations.

Conakat called for the repatriation of the immigrants and a federal Congo. The party was supported financially by the white settler community, which saw it as a moderate alternative to the more radical nationalists led by Patrice Lumumba. Originally, Conakat included Balubakat, representing the Baluba ethnic group, but Balubakat broke away from Conakat in 1959. In the May 1960 elections, Conakat won eight of the sixteen Katangan seats in the national legislature and twenty-five of the sixty seats in the provincial assembly. Balubakat and its allies won seven seats in the national legislature and twenty-three provincial assembly seats.

In the period before independence, the leader of Conakat, Moise Tshombe, attempted to alter the constitution in order to obtain more autonomy for Katanga. However, he and other federalists were outmaneuvered by Lumumba, who favored a unitary state. No party obtained a majority in the National Assembly elections, but Lumumba's Congolese National Movement won the largest number with 33 seats out of a total of 137. Lumumba became prime minister, and almost immediately there was a mutiny by the Congolese military, the Force Publique. This resulted in a breakdown of law and order and widespread attacks on whites. (According to the Belgians, 251 women were raped, and 15 civilians were killed during the two-week-long mutiny.) The Belgians sent in troops, who quickly restored order. Tshombe declared Katanga independent on July 11, and the Katangan Assembly unanimously approved the secession (the Balubakat representatives had withdrawn earlier).

The new state was immediately confronted with several problems. The Baluba established a Baluba Republic of North Katanga, and although Katanga's forces were able to recapture the main towns, much of the region remained under rebel control. Despite initial sympathy on the part of some Western governments, and an ambitious lobbying campaign, Katanga was unable to secure full diplomatic recognition from any country.

However, Katanga did receive support from several countries. After Belgian troops had been withdrawn, Belgian officers were seconded to train the Katangan forces. France provided weapons and aircraft, and French mercenaries served in Katanga. The white minority governments of South Africa and Rhodesia (now Zimbabwe) provided supplies and maintained trade and transport links, despite a United Nations call for an embargo on Katanga's copper exports. The Republic of the Congo-Brazzaville, a former French colony, invited Tshombe to a conference of moderate French-speaking African states and gave him diplomatic support. Katanga was financially dependent upon the revenues it received from the Union Miniere du Haut-Katanga, which made up 80 percent of the country's budget. Although it is difficult to determine to what extent Union Minière's support was freely given rather

than forced, it was undoubtably a crucial factor in Katanga's secession.

The main threat to Katanga came from the United Nations. On July 14, 1960 (three days after Katanga's declaration of independence), the UN Security Council called on Belgium to withdraw its troops and authorized the formation of a UN force that would intervene. A later resolution called on all nations to refrain from any action that might "undermine the territorial integrity and political independence of the Republic of the Congo," thus implicitly rejecting the legitimacy of the secessionist regime. However, the political situation in the Congo became more favorable to Katanga with the overthrow of Lumumba in September of 1960.

The new regime, headed by Joseph Kasavubu and Joseph Mobutu, adopted a conciliatory policy toward Katanga, and in March 1961, at a conference in Antananarivo, Madagascar, Kasavubu, Tshombe, and other Congolese leaders agreed to a loose federal structure for the Congo. However, at a second conference held in April at Coquilhatville, Kasavubu renounced the agreement and had Tshombe arrested and detained for two months. Tshombe was released after he agreed that Katangan representatives would attend the National Assembly, but—not surprisingly—he failed to keep his promise.

In August 1961, the UN special representative in Katanga, Conor Cruise O'Brien, delivered an ultimatum to Tshombe. He must go and negotiate with the central government. When Tshombe refused, UN troops seized the center of Elisabethville and attempted to arrest and deport the white mercenaries and advisers employed by Katanga. Heavy fighting broke out, and after a series of cease-fires, Tshombe, in December, recognized the "indivisible unity" of the Congo and President Kasavubu as its chief of state. However, the Katangan assembly refused to accept or implement this declaration, and a further series of abortive discussions took place between the Congolese central government and the Katangese in early 1962. In January 1963, UN forces launched an attack against the Katangese forces, and on January 14, 1963, the Katangan government declared that its secession was ended.

See also Tshombe, Moise; Zaire.
References Gerard-Libois, Jules. *Katanga Secession* (1966); Hempstone, Smith. *Rebels, Mercenaries, and Dividends: The Katanga Story* (1962); O'Brien, Conor Cruise. *To Katanga and Back: A UN Case History* (1962).

Kazakhstan

The Kazakhs, a nomadic people formed from Mongol and Turkish tribes, are related to the Uzbeks, are largely Sunni Muslims, and speak a Turkish language. In the fifteenth and sixteenth centuries, the Kazakhs created a nomadic empire, which has been called the first Kazakh state, and it ruled vast areas of the steppes. Subsequent wars with Mongol tribes led to the disintegration of the unified empire. During this same period, in order to guard against Kazakh raiders, Russia established Cossack outposts along its southern border. The early-nineteenth century saw significant Russian expansion into Kazakh territory, and by 1866, all of modern Kazakhstan was under Russian domination.

Following the Bolshevik victory in 1920, the Kazakh territory was designated an autonomous Soviet republic. In 1936, it was raised to the legal status of a full Soviet republic. Although there had been no agitation for separation from the Soviet Union, when the Soviet Union collapsed in 1991, Kazakhstan declared its independence.

In 1970, Kazakhs made up only 32 percent of the republic's population, for beginning with the establishment of the Cossack outposts, Russians have migrated to Kazakhstan in great numbers. In the pre-Soviet period, Russian peasants were drawn to the farmable lands of the northern plains, and Nikita Khrushchev's "virgin lands policy" of 1953 led to a further influx of Russian farmers to Kazakhstan. The concentration of Soviet military and defense establishments in Kazakhstan provided a further source of employment for urban Russians. By 1970, Russians actually outnumbered Kazakhs in the republic,

but independence brought about a sharp reversal in the demographic situation. The collapse of the Soviet military-industrial complex combined with an unwillingness on the part of many Russians to remain citizens of a relatively poor Muslim state that emphasizes the Kazakh language has led to a massive out-migration of Russians from Kazakhstan, and the trend shows no sign of abating. At present, Kazakhs are the largest ethnic group in the nation with 43 percent of the 17 million population. Russians now account for 36 percent.

The government of President Nursultan Nazarbayev, although increasingly autocratic, has taken care to treat Russians sensitively, and Russian is recognized as the second language of the state. At the same time, the Nazarbayev government has advocated strengthening Kazakh social and cultural institutions while resisting any attempts to make Kazakhstan an Islamic state.

The greatest opposition to government policy has come from a small group of Islamic fundamentalists who want to purge Kazakhstan of all nonbelievers and from the oldest Russian inhabitants, the Cossacks. Since independence, the Kazakh Cossacks, like their Russian counterparts, have been reviving their traditional organizational structures, including armed militias. Cossack leaders, who are fiercely dedicated to the Russian Orthodox Church and the Russian Empire, have demanded that Russia annex the Kazakh Cossack territory, and demonstrations and clashes with the police have occurred. The Kazakh government has responded by trying to suppress the separatist sentiments. It has engaged in a series of "preventive arrests" of Cossack activists and tried to disband Cossack militias. Although official Kazakh-Russian relations remain cordial, the Russian Duma has called on Kazakhstan to stop the persecution of the Russian Cossack population.

See also Cossacks; Russians in the Former Soviet Republics; Union of Soviet Socialist Republics.
References Olcott, Martha Brill. *Kazakhstan: A Faint-Hearted Democracy* (1999); Rumer, Boris. *Central Asia in Transition: Dilemmas of Political and Economic Development* (1996).

Kenya

The East African country of Kenya became independent from Britain on June 1, 1964. The two parties that had emerged prior to independence were the Kenya African National Union (KANU) and the Kenya African Democratic Union (KADU). KANU, led by Jomo Kenyatta, represented the three largest tribes—the Kikuyu, Luo, and Kamba—while KADU was essentially a defensive coalition of the smaller tribes. KADU favored a considerable degree of regional autonomy, and in the independence constitution, seven regional assemblies were established. Since most of the regions (later renamed provinces) were ethnically homogeneous, there was an obvious potential for the growth of separatist movements. In elections held in May 1963, KANU won seventy seats to KADU's thirty-two; smaller parties and independents won ten. However, KANU won control of only three regional assemblies, as did KADU (no elections were held in the North-Eastern region because of unrest among the local Somali population).

Once in power, Kenyatta's government amended the constitution and abolished the regional assemblies in November 1964, despite heated opposition from KADU. This action was followed by a merger between KADU and KANU, so that Kenya became a de facto one-party state. By selecting cabinets that include representatives of most of the main ethnic groups, Kenyatta and his successor, Daniel Arap Moi, have reduced the dangers of tribal conflict. With the important exception of the insurgency in the North-Eastern region by Somalis wishing to secede from Kenya and unite with Somalia, Kenya has been successful in avoiding ethnic separatism.

See also Somalis in Kenya.
Reference Gertzel, Cherry. *The Politics of Independent Kenya, 1963–8* (1970).

Khalistan

Khalistan is the name given by Sikh separatists to the state that they seek to establish after winning independence from India. The Punjab is the homeland of the Sikhs, a community of about 16 million. The Sikh religion, founded in the sixteenth century, combines elements of Hinduism and Islam and emphasizes the breaking down of caste barriers. The Sikhs recognize ten gurus, or spiritual leaders, the first being Nanak Dev and the last Gobind Singh, under whom the Sikhs were transformed into a militant brotherhood dedicated to the defense of their religion. Gobind Singh also created the Khalsa, a Sikh brotherhood with a distinctive lifestyle and an initiation ceremony. In the nineteenth century, under Ranjit Singh, the Sikhs emerged as a powerful military force and controlled a large empire stretching from the Himalayas to the Arabian Sea.

After Britain annexed the Punjab in 1849, the Sikhs became the backbone of the Indian forces and were encouraged to manifest their separate identity. For example, Sikh recruits to the army were required to observe the symbols of their religion, such as uncut hair. A Sikh revivalist movement, the Akali Dal, gained control of the Sikh shrines and temples in the 1920s and purged them of what it considered to be corrupt practices.

When India became independent in 1947, the areas where Muslims constituted a majority were partitioned to create the independent Islamic state of Pakistan. The partition was a disaster for the Sikhs, who were dispersed throughout the Punjab. West Punjab became part of Pakistan, and widespread violence against the Sikhs there led many of them to flee to East Punjab. After a lengthy campaign of civil disobedience, led by the Akali Dal, Indian Punjab was divided in 1966 into two new states: Haryana, with a Hindu and Hindi-speaking majority, and Punjab, with a 60 percent Punjabi-speaking Sikh majority. However, this action did not resolve the conflict between the Sikhs and the central government, which was dominated by the Congress Party.

In 1973, the Akali Dal adopted the Anandpur Sahib Resolution, which argued that "the Sikhs of India are a historically recognized political nation ever since the inauguration of the order of the Khalsa in the concluding years of the seventeenth century" and that "the brute majority of India" had imposed on the Sikhs constitutional arrangements that denied their political identity. The resolution went on to call for greater political autonomy for the Punjab, the transfer of the city of Chandigarh to the Punjab along with other Punjabi-speaking districts, and a larger share of the irrigation waters flowing through the state. However, despite repeated efforts by moderate Sikh politicians, the central government failed to respond to these demands. At the same time, a fundamentalist movement led by Jarnail Singh Bhindranwale emerged, which called on Sikhs to return to a pure version of their faith and abandon such secular practices as smoking, drinking, and cutting their hair.

In the early 1980s, the Akali Dal organized a mass civil disobedience campaign while the followers of Bhindranwale carried out terrorist attacks against moderate Sikhs, government officials, and ordinary Hindus. The Indian prime minister, Indira Gandhi, responded by dismissing the state government and assuming direct rule over Punjab in 1983. In June 1984, in a highly controversial move, the Indian army stormed the Golden Temple in Amritsar, which had been fortified and occupied by Bhindranwale and his followers. This invasion of their most sacred shrine outraged the Sikhs and compelled even moderate Sikh political leaders to condemn the action and adopt a more nationalist stance against the central government. A few months later, in November 1984, Gandhi was assassinated by Sikh members of her bodyguard. Her death touched off bloody rioting in Delhi, in which over 3,000 Sikhs were killed, and completed the mutual alienation between the Sikhs and the Indian government.

After Rajiv Gandhi, Indira Gandhi's son, succeeded her as prime minister, he opened negotiations with the Akali Dal leadership. The Gandhi-Longowal accord, signed between the two sides in July 1985, conceded several of the demands contained in the Anandpur Sahib Resolution and also lifted the state of emergency in effect in Punjab. However, Harchand Singh Longowal, the Akali Dal leader, was assassinated by Sikh extremists, the central government failed to implement the agreement, and most of the Akali Dal members of the Punjab legislature withdrew support from Longowal's successor.

The political crisis deepened throughout 1986, with more Sikhs calling for an independent Khalistan, and the number of killings increased significantly. According to official figures, there were 640 deaths in that year, and between May 1987 and July 1990, over 4,000 people were killed in terrorist attacks, including some 500 members of the security forces. In addition, 1,860 armed Sikhs were reportedly killed by the security forces (unofficial estimates of the casualties are much higher). In May 1987, Punjab was again placed under direct rule from New Delhi, and this lasted until February 1992, following elections for the state assembly. The elections were boycotted by most of the Sikh parties, and the disputed issues between the Sikhs and the central government remain unresolved. However, the level of violence has decreased significantly since early 1994.

See also India.

References Chadda, Maya. *Ethnicity, Security, and Separatism in India* (1997); Kapur, Rajiv. *Sikh Separatism* (1986); Mahmood, Cynthia Keppley. *Fighting for Faith and Nation* (1996).

Komi

One of the larger republics of the Russian Federation in terms of area, Komi has a population exceeding 1.25 million. Ukrainians make up 8 percent of the population and Russians 58 percent. The Komi, who constitute 23 percent of the people, speak a Finno-Ugric language with several dialects. After the fourteenth century, when Komi came under Russian control, many of the Komi converted to the Russian Orthodox religion. In 1921, a Komi autonomous district was established in the Soviet Union, and in 1936, it was elevated to the status of an autonomous republic. In 1991, with the breakup of the Soviet Union,

Komi became one of the twenty-one republics of the Russian Federation.

At the First Congress of the Komi People, held in 1991, a resolution was passed calling for Komi to become, along with Russian, an official language of the republic. A more radical group, the Biarmiya Party, calls for a confederation with other Finno-Ugric peoples (for example, Udmurts, Finns, and Estonians), and Biarmiya would grant Komi citizenship only to those who can speak Komi. Russians and other nationalities who do not know the Komi language would be treated as foreign workers.

See also Russian Federation.
References Kolga, Margus, et al., eds. *Red Book of the Peoples of the Russian Empire* (1993); Mastyugina, Tatiana, and Lev Perelkin. *An Ethnic History of Russia* (1996).

Korean Reunification

Korea is one of the most ethnically homogeneous nations in the world, with a common language and culture that transcend its regional differences and political divisions. The Korean language is very different from both Chinese and Japanese and has its own distinctive alphabet. Japanese rule, which began in 1910, was repressive and marked by unsuccessful attempts at assimilating the Koreans. Economic development occurred but brought little benefit to the population. At the end of World War II, Korea was divided into two zones along the line of the thirty-eighth parallel. North Korea was occupied by the Russians; South Korea, by the Americans. When negotiations to reunite the country broke down, the division was formalized in 1948.

The Russians established a Communist regime under Kim Il Sung, and the Americans set up the Republic of Korea under the autocratic Syngman Rhee. In June 1950, the North Koreans invaded South Korea to begin the Korean War, which ended with an armistice in July 1953. Heavy fighting between the UN forces and the North Koreans (later joined by Communist Chinese troops) devastated the peninsula and claimed 3–4 million casualties. U.S. troops remained in South Korea to protect the country from the threat of another invasion from the North.

The division of Korea was initially regarded as a temporary expedient, and reunification remained a goal of both the North and South Korean governments. The Republic of Korea (ROK) took the position that it was the only legal government, and at a Geneva conference in 1954 called for free elections to be held under UN supervision in both North and South Korea. North Korea rejected this proposal and called for the withdrawal of U.S.troops from South Korea. The Communists anticipated that rising living standards in the North would encourage a revolution in the South, and when a student uprising led to the overthrow of Syngman Rhee, the Communists broadcast appeals to the South Korean people to drive out "the U.S. imperialist aggressors." National unification was the central theme of the 1960 elections in the South, with all parties advocating UN-supervised elections throughout Korea. The main difference between the parties was that the leftists wanted increased social and cultural relations between the two Koreas while John Chang, the newly elected premier, rejected any such contacts.

During the next few years, North Korea several times proposed a federation between the two parts of Korea with each maintaining its own political system. In South Korea, a military coup ousted Chang in 1961, but in 1963, civilian government was nominally restored under President Park Chung Hee. Park held that the ROK was the only legitimate government of Korea and embarked on an ambitious program of economic development, hoping that a prosperous South would be able to defend itself against military attacks from the North. In the early 1970s, the normalization of relations between China and the United States pushed the two Koreas into holding bilateral discussions. President Park proposed that if the North would desist from military provocations, the South would remove "step by step, the artificial barriers existing" between the two states.

South Korean Vice Minister for Reunification Yang Yong-shik (right) greets his North Korean counterpart, Park Young-soo, before they sat down for talks in Beijing, June 22, 1999. (Reuters/Natalie Behring/Archive Photos)

In 1972–1973, under the aegis of the Red Cross, there was a series of talks about uniting families. In July 1972, after secret negotiations between the head of the Korean Central Intelligence Agency and Kim Il Sung, a joint communiqué was issued. It called for peaceful unification of the two Koreas, and both sides agreed not to slander or defame the other and to take measures to avoid provocative military incidents. However, the optimism created by the communiqué was destroyed by the discovery that during the negotiations, the North Koreans had built three tunnels under the cease-fire line so as to be able to invade the South. In a four-point proposal of June 1973, South Korea suggested that social and cultural exchanges should be facilitated in order to encourage mutual trust and understanding. Park also proposed that both states be ad-

mitted simultaneously to the United Nations, but North Korea rejected this as implying the existence of two Koreas.

In the 1980s, further rounds of negotiations took place, but little was achieved. Indeed during this period, the North Koreans twice attempted to assassinate the South Korean president, and in October 1983, an explosion (for which North Korea was held responsible) killed four cabinet members during a state visit to Burma. However, the discussions did establish a tradition of dialogue and created contacts between the two Koreas. Trade and other forms of economic cooperation also gradually increased. In 1990, an important breakthrough occurred with the beginning of a series of prime ministerial talks. These eventually resulted in a landmark agreement signed at the end of 1991, pledging both sides to a policy of nonaggression and cooperation. In June 1999, there was a confrontation between North and South Korean warships in a dispute over territorial waters, indicating that relations remain tense and that reunification is unlikely in the near future.

References Clough, Ralph. *Embattled Korea: The Rivalry for International Support* (1987); Kihl, Young Whan. *Politics and Policies in Divided Korea: Regimes in Contest* (1984); Srivastava, M. P. *The Korean Conflict: Search for Unification* (1982).

Kosovo

Kosovo is the southern province of Serbia and is bordered on the west by Albania. The Serbs consider the region their original homeland in the Balkans, and many churches and monasteries that are sacred to the Serbian Orthodox Church are located in Kosovo. The province also includes the site of the Battle of Kosovo Polije, in which the Serbs were defeated by the Ottoman Turks in 1389. The anniversary of the battle is still celebrated as a Serbian national holiday. After the Ottoman Turks forced the Serbs from the area in the Middle Ages, it was settled by ethnic Albanians. Owing to a very high birthrate, the proportion of Albanians has increased steadily since World War II. Whereas Albanians made up 67 percent of the population in 1961, they constituted nearly 90 percent of Kosovo's 2 million people in 1998. (The Serbs declined from about 27 percent to 10 percent during the same period.)

In 1913, Kosovo was divided between Serbia and Montenegro, and after World War I, it became part of Yugoslavia. In 1970, President Tito declared Kosovo a semiautonomous region of the Yugoslavian federation, partly to check Serb power in the federation. In 1989, after several years of Albanian protests demanding independence, Serbian President Slobodan Milosevic revoked Kosovo's autonomous status. Since then, the province has been ruled as a near police state by Serbian authorities.

After Serbia dissolved the government of Kosovo, Ibrahim Rugova and the Democratic League of Kosovo declared the province independent. In 1992, after unofficial elections, Rugova was elected president of the republic, receiving more than 75 percent of the vote. The shadow government also has an elected parliament and runs health and educational organizations funded by voluntary contributions. A pacifist, Rugova has eschewed violence as a means of reaching full independence, but his lack of progress in gaining concessions from Yugoslavia in the 1990s led to the emergence of more militant forces. The Parliamentary Party, chaired by Adem Demaci, advocated open disruptions and confrontations to focus world attention on Albanian discontent. In December 1997, Albanian students staged a mass protest rally to demand an autonomous Albanian language university in the province's capital, Pristina. However, the most significant development has been the birth and rapid growth of the Kosovo Liberation Army (KLA).

The KLA, an underground army organized into a multitude of local militias, has grown in prominence since its founding in 1992. By 1996, the KLA, with its call for armed resistance against the Serbs, was challenging Rugova for the leadership of the Kosovo Albanians. At the failed Rambouillet peace conference in February 1999, Western diplomats seated KLA representatives at the negotiating table with Rugova. Shortly after the conference, the KLA named Hashim Thaci its prime minister designate for Kosovo, in effect bypassing Rugova's shadow government. To date, Rugova has refused to form a coalition with the KLA but the situation remains fluid. Militarily, the KLA enjoyed some success in early 1998, but its lightly armed fighters proved no match for the armored Yugoslavian army divisions that were sent to the province.

Through 1998, repeated attempts by Western diplomats to improve the situation of Kosovo Albanians were rebuffed by Milosevic. He argued that Yugoslavia was a sovereign state and that the problem in Kosovo was an internal matter. In October 1998, NATO threatened air attacks if Yugoslavia refused to make concessions in Kosovo.

A fireball explodes in a building that Belgrade's civil defense authorities identify as the Interior Ministry in downtown Belgrade, April 3, 1999. (Reuters/EMIL VAS/Archive Photos)

In February 1999, Serbia rejected the installation of NATO peacekeepers into Kosovo, and Serbian forces launched attacks on KLA bases. At the same time, in a well-organized campaign of "ethnic cleansing," a million Albanians were driven out of Kosovo. In late March 1999, NATO began an aerial bombardment of Yugoslavia, and on June 9, after nearly three months of air attacks and the threat of a ground invasion, Milosevic agreed to a full military withdrawal from Kosovo. As Serbian troops evacuated the province, NATO and Russian forces, operating under a UN Security Council mandate, set up zones of occupation in Kosovo. Evidence of atrocities by the Yugoslav army and Serb paramilitaries includes mass graves and torture chambers, at least 10,000 Albanian men of military age were killed, and young women and girls were systematically raped.

Now a de facto NATO and UN protectorate, the immediate task in Kosovo is resettling nearly 1 million refugees and rebuilding the economic infrastructure. At the same time, the occupation forces must prevent violence between Albanians and the Serb minority remaining in the province. An estimated 71,000 of the 200,000 Serbs have fled, some after intimidation by the Albanians. The future of Kosovo as a political entity and its ties, if any, to Yugoslavia remain unclear. How Albanians in Kosovo will govern themselves and which politicians will lead them is also uncertain. Some Kosovo Albanians call for independence while others favor the creation of a greater Albania. At the moment, neither of these alternatives is acceptable to the United States and its European allies, who are committed to maintaining current European boundaries. A possible compromise once pursued by U.S. and European diplomats proposed that Kosovo become, along with Serbia and Montenegro, the third republic of federal Yugoslavia. However, after recent events, this proposal is probably unacceptable to most residents of Kosovo.

See also Greater Albania; Kosovo Liberation Army; Rugova, Ibrahim; Yugoslavia.
References Campbell, Greg. *The Road to Kosovo: A Balkan Diary* (1999); Ignatieff, Michael. "Balkan Physics: Behind the Lines of Europe's Worst Conflict since 1945" (1999); Malcolm, Noel, *Kosovo: A Short History* (1998); Vickers, Miranda. *Between Serb and Albanian: A History of Kosovo* (1998).

Kosovo Liberation Army

The Kosovo Liberation Army (KLA), or Ushtria Clirimtare E Kosoves, had its origins among disaffected Albanian youth in Kosovo and Macedonia. Organized in 1992, the KLA advocates the use of armed force to achieve independence for Kosovo. Some of its members also support the creation of a greater Albania, which would include Kosovo, Albania proper, and Albanian-populated areas of Macedonia, Montenegro, and Serbia. The absence of any discussion of Kosovo in the 1995 Dayton peace accord, as well as the KLA's conviction that the Kosovo shadow president Ibrahim Rugova's nonviolent course was ineffective, prompted the organization to step up its guerrilla actions against Serbian rule.

In 1995, KLA units began engaging in attacks on Serbian police and barracks as well as punishing Albanian collaborators. Serbia declared the KLA a terrorist organization. The KLA expanded its guerrilla operations until February 1998 when Serbia began responding with the full weight of its army and armed paramilitary and police units. The lightly armed KLA, which may have had upward of 5,000 soldiers in the field, was no match for the Serbian forces that drove them from their village home bases. Many KLA soldiers fled with hundreds of thousands of Kosovo refugees to secure camps in Albania and Macedonia where the KLA stepped up its recruitment and training operations. After Serbia capitulated

to the NATO air war in June 1999, KLA units began to redeploy in Kosovo.

The organizational structure of the KLA is unclear. One reason is that the KLA has had to operate clandestinely in an occupied territory and chooses to keep its operations secret. Additionally, many village units arose spontaneously in response to local conditions and were not centrally coordinated. Finally, the KLA contains several factions that sometimes issue contradictory statements. Jacob Krasniqi is recognized as a prominent spokesperson for the KLA, as was shadow parliamentarian Adem Demaci before he abandoned that role after a dispute with KLA leaders. The KLA was represented at the failed Rambouillet peace conference in February 1999. At that time, the twenty-nine-year-old military commander Hashim Thaci emerged as the leader of the KLA. A month later, he was declared prime minister designate of the Kosovo Republic. The KLA has also proposed the creation of a new governing council, which would undermine Rugova's shadow government, but Rugova has rebuffed KLA overtures to form a coalition.

Serbian detractors claim the KLA is ruled by Islamic extremists supported by Iran, Libya, and Saudi Arabia. KLA ranks, they say, are filled with volunteers and mercenaries from other Islamic countries. Others claim the KLA is dominated by hard-line Marxists formerly supported by the Communist Albanian dictator Enver Hoxha. It is also reported that much funding for the KLA derives from criminal activities, particularly the drug trade. Politically, whether the KLA is committed to a democratic Kosovo or will cooperate with Rugovo's Democratic League of Kosovo remains unclear.

On June 20, 1999, the KLA agreed to NATO demands that it disarm and that KLA soldiers no longer wear their uniforms in public. At the same time, other KLA leaders stated that the KLA will continue operating military bases in northern Albania.

See also Kosovo; Rugova, Ibrahim.
References Malcolm, Noel. *Kosovo: A Short History*

(1998); *Political Declarations of the Kosovo Liberation Army* (1998).

Krajina

Krajina, a heavily Serb-populated region of central Croatia, was overrun by Serbian military forces in the 1991–1992 war between Croatia and the rump state of Yugoslavia. It declared itself the Serbian Republic of Krajina and expressed its intentions to unite with Serbia proper. In 1995, Croatian troops recaptured the region, which forced thousands of ethnic Serbs to flee into Bosnia and Yugoslavia.

See also Croatia.
Reference Tanner, Marcus. *Croatia: A Nation Forged in War* (1997).

Krasnodar

Krasnodar is an administrative district in the southwestern part of the Russian Federation and borders on the Black Sea. Russians constitute the majority of the population of over 5 million. The Shapsugs, an Adygean ethnic group that forms a Caucasian language-speaking Sunni Muslim community, have called for the creation of a

Shapsug autonomous region in the Tuapse area. Another proposal would create an autonomous region composed of a larger Caucasian-Muslim grouping of Shapsugs, Adygeans, and Cherkessians. Cossacks are demanding an autonomous region along the Kuban River, and Armenian, Greek, and German ethnic groups have also pressed for self-rule. The Russian administrators of the territory have resisted any attempt to compromise the integrity of Krasnodar.

See also Cossacks; Russian Federation.
Reference Mastyugina, Tatiana, and Lev Perelkin. *An Ethnic History of Russia* (1996).

Kurdistan

The Kurds live in the mountain region known as Kurdistan that stretches along the borders of Iraq, Iran, and Turkey. Kurdistan includes the oil fields around Kirkuk and is rich in other mineral resources. The Kurds speak an Indo-European language related to Persian and are estimated to number well over 20 million, which makes them the largest ethnic group in the world without its own state. About 12 million Kurds live in Turkey, 6 million in Iran, and 4.5 million in Iraq, with perhaps another million in Syria. A majority belong

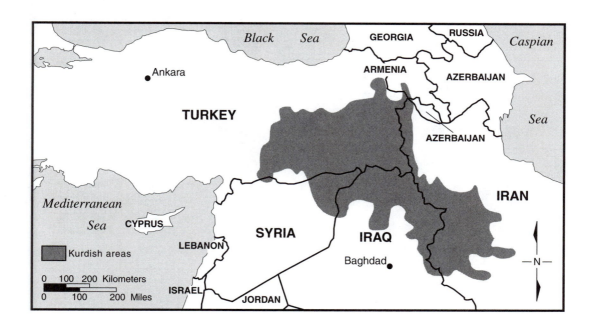

Kurdish rebels fighting for an independent state for Kurds in northern Iraq stand on the ruins of a building, January 1963. (Corbis/Bettmann)

to the Sunni sect of Islam, although a minority are Shi'ites. The Kurds are divided into often hostile tribes and clans and remain strongly loyal to their sheikhs. Cohesion amongst these subgroups is further weakened by the existence of two major dialects, Sorani and Kurmanji, each with considerable local variation.

Under a 1639 treaty, the Kurds agreed to guard the borders of the Ottoman Empire against the Persians, and fifteen families were granted hereditary titles. During the 1800s, imperial rivalries among Ottoman Turkey, Russia, and Persia led to constant warfare throughout the region, which often involved Kurdish tribes fighting on different sides. The first significant Kurdish revolt against Ottoman rule took place in 1806, and in 1880, Sheikh Ubaydallah led a rebellion that enjoyed wide support in both Ottoman- and Persian-ruled Kurdistan.

After the defeat of the Ottoman Empire in World War II, the Kurds submitted a memorandum to the Paris peace conference calling for self-determination in accordance with Woodrow Wilson's fourteen points. The 1920 Treaty of Sevres, between Turkey and the Allied powers, promised that an autonomous Kurdish administration would be set up "in those regions where the Kurdish element is preponderant lying east of the Euphrates, to the south of the still-to-be-established Armenian frontier and to the north of the frontier between Turkey, Syria and Mesopotamia" and that independence would be granted "if after one year has elapsed since the implementation of the present treaty, the Kurdish population of the [designated] areas calls on the Council of the League of Nations and demonstrates that a majority of the population in these areas wishes to become independent of Turkey."

After Kemal Ataturk's victories in Anatolia, however, he refused to recognize the treaty, and in 1923, a new agreement, the Treaty of Lausanne, recognized Turkish sovereignty over northern Kurdistan, while the rest of the Kurdish territories were divided between Iran and Iraq. Since that date, the clash between Kurdish nationalist aspirations and the three governments has resulted in chronic conflict, revolts, and repression. In the years following the Persian Gulf War of 1990–1991, the Kurdish struggle has received increasing attention, and the issue has become a significant factor in Middle East politics.

See also Iranian Kurds; Iraqi Kurds; Kurdistan Democratic Party; Turkish Kurds.
References Chaliand, Gerard. *People without a Country* (1980); McDowall, David. *The Kurds* (1985).

Kurdistan Democratic Party

One of the two main Kurdish groups in Iraq, the Kurdistan Democratic Party (KDP) was founded in 1946 by Mustafa Barzani, the legendary Kurdish leader. Although theoretically under the collective leadership of a revolutionary command council, in practice, Barzani ran the KDP in an autocratic and arbitrary fashion. The party originally claimed to be Marxist-Leninist but became increasingly pro-Western as it sought aid from the United States and the shah of Iran. Barzani died in exile in the United States, and was succeeded as leader of the KDP by his son, Massoud, in 1979.

The Patriotic Union of Kurdistan (PUK), led by Jalal Talabani, split from the KDP in 1964. The two groups differ in ideology, with the KDP being willing to accept some form of autonomy within Iraq while the PUK is more nationalist. The PUK draws its support from the urban population and the southern Sorani speakers; the KDP, from the more traditional tribal sectors of Kurdish society, especially among those speaking the northern Kurmanji dialect.

See also Iraqi Kurds; Kurdistan.

Kurds

See Iranian Kurds; Iraqi Kurds; Turkish Kurds

Kuwait

An oil-rich state on the Persian Gulf, Kuwait was under the suzerainty of the Ottoman Empire until

1914 when it became a British protectorate. Kuwait achieved independence in 1961, and at that time, Iraq claimed the area on the grounds that it had been part of the province of Basra when the area was ruled by the Ottomans. However, in 1963, the Ba'athist government of Iraq recognized Kuwait's independence, although the border between the two countries remained undefined.

During the war between Iran and Iraq (1980–1988), Kuwait supported Iraq with loans totaling more than $10 billion. When the war ended, tensions mounted as Iraq demanded that the loans be written off and called for territorial concessions. When negotiations collapsed, Iraq invaded Kuwait on August 1, 1990. The Kuwaiti ruling family fled to Saudi Arabia, and Iraq annexed Kuwait. In response, the UN Security Council declared that Iraq must withdraw, and on January 16, 1991, one day after the deadline for that withdrawal, Allied forces, led by the United States, attacked. Superior military technology resulted in a complete rout of the Iraqi forces and the destruction of much of the country's military and industrial infrastructure. The Iraqi occupation of Kuwait was marked by widespread looting, and brutality. Although some Kuwaiti residents supported the Iraqi invasion, many defied the occupation forces and engaged in various forms of passive resistance.

KwaNdebele

The last of the black homelands to be established in South Africa, KwaNdebele was supposed to become the home of the Ndebele people, who were scattered throughout the Transvaal and numbered about 500,000. Less than 300 square miles in area, KwaNdebele was patched together from a few white farms and parts of what had previously been Bophuthatswana and Lebowa. The inhabitants were largely people who had been displaced—sometimes forcibly relocated—from other areas of the country. In 1980, the population was officially estimated at 166,000, but unofficial estimates ranged up to half a million. Only

about half of the residents were Ndebele. In reality, KwaNdebele was a gigantic rural slum, where unemployed blacks from South Africa's cities were dumped.

A legislative assembly, consisting of forty-six nominated members, was set up in 1979, and self-governing status was granted in 1981. The chief minister, Simon Skosana, declared in 1982 that KwaNdebele would seek to become independent in 1986. The regime was remarkably corrupt—for instance, all liquor licenses were held by government ministers. In 1985, the Moutse district of Lebowa, although predominantly populated by North Sotho people, was transferred to KwaNdebele. Resistance by the inhabitants led to attacks by government supporters, the Mbokhoto. By 1986, civil unrest had escalated throughout KwaNdebele and had claimed over 2,000 lives as opponents of independence clashed with Mbhokoto vigilantes. The minister of the interior and leader of the Mbokhoto, Piet Ntuli, was killed when his car was blown up in July 1986. A few days later, the KwaNdebele legislative assembly voted against independence. Along with the other homelands, KwaNdebele was reincorporated into South Africa in 1994.

See also Black Homelands.
Reference Murray, Colin. "Displaced Urbanization: South Africa's Rural Sums" (1995).

KwaZulu

KwaZulu is the Zulu homeland in the province of Natal and the scene of the most militant black separatist movement within the Republic of South Africa. The Zulu nation arose in the early 1800s when Shaka (1787–1828) transformed the Zulu into a powerful military machine. His kingdom extended from Mozambique in the north to the Transkei in the south, and the *mfecane* (as the Zulu conquests are called in the Zulu language) sent thousands of refugees fleeing in terror from the Zulu warriors. The Zulu state was highly centralized and had a standing army of over 40,000. Shaka absorbed the conquered peoples into the

Zulu nation, creating a Zulu consciousness that still exists. After Shaka's murder by his half brother, Dingane, the power of the Zulu empire waned. Defeated by the Afrikaners at the Battle of Blood River in 1838, and later by the British in 1879, Zululand became part of the British colony of Natal in 1887. The 8 million Zulu are the largest black group in South Africa, and they retain a strong sense of ethnic solidarity and pride. Most Zulu continue to feel a sense of loyalty to the Zulu royal family and to their tribal chiefs.

The Zulu initially resisted the devolution proposals of the South African government and only accepted the creation of a Zululand Territorial Authority with reluctance. Mangosuthu Buthelezi, the leader of the dissidents, eventually decided that resistance was futile and that blacks had more to gain from working within the system. Elected chief executive officer in 1970, Buthelezi promptly called on South Africa to give the Zulu more land and resources. In 1972, a constitution for KwaZulu was promulgated, with a nominated and indirectly elected assembly.

Political divisions in KwaZulu initially revolved around the political role of chiefs, especially the paramount chief or *ingonyama*. Although the South African government attempted to strengthen the traditional rulers, Buthelezi emerged dominant and the *ingonyama*, Goodwill Zwelithini, agreed not to become involved in politics. The most serious threat to Buthelezi's position came from Irving Dladla, who became the spokesman for Zulu workers outside KwaZulu. Rivalries between the two simmered for several months until Dladla was dismissed from the KwaZulu cabinet in August 1974. In 1975, Buthelezi created Inkatha, a "cultural and liberation movement" open to all Zulu. Only members of Inkatha were eligible for election to the KwaZulu Assembly, and the organization's president was designated the chief minister.

Buthelezi rejected repeated offers of independence for KwaZulu since that would have stripped the 4 million Zulu living outside KwaZulu of their South African citizenship. Instead, he used his position as leader of KwaZulu to articulate the grievances of the black majority and to criticize the apartheid system. This made Buthelezi a popular and respected leader among blacks throughout South Africa. In 1973, when he toured the black townships around Johannesburg, he was warmly welcomed by large crowds. Buthelezi was somewhat inconsistent in his proposals for political change. Speaking to the South African Institute of Race Relations in 1974, he advocated a federal South Africa with autonomous black and white states. He then demanded that KwaZulu be enlarged and given the port city of Richards Bay as an outlet to the sea. Independence, he argued, could only come about after land consolidation had provided KwaZulu with a viable economic infrastructure. However, by 1976, Buthelezi was calling for majority rule and an end to the apartheid policy of separate development.

Relations between Buthelezi and the African National Congress (ANC) were originally amicable but soured when young blacks began to denounce Buthelezi as a collaborator. Clashes between ANC and Inkatha supporters broke out in the early 1980s and intensified after 1987. In both KwaZulu itself and the black townships around Johannesburg a deadly cycle of violence claimed thousands of lives. Communities belonging to one side were attacked by the other, and hit squads assassinated individuals identified with their opponents. The massacre of men, women, and children was common, and thousands of refugees were forced to flee from their homes. It is generally accepted that the South African police were in collusion with the Inkatha, standing by while it attacked ANC villages and even taking part in some attacks. In addition, 200 Inkatha members were trained by the South African army, supplied with weapons, and deployed against ANC supporters.

Negotiations over a new constitution between the South African government, the ANC, and seventeen other political groups began in 1991. These negotiations, called the Convention for a Democratic South Africa (CODESA), were boycotted by

Buthelezi although Inkatha delegates attended. In June 1990, the Inkatha was renamed the Inkatha Freedom Party and attempted to develop a national constituency. This led to further black-on-black violence, culminating in a massacre of thirty-eight people in Boipatong township by Inkatha supporters. The ANC thereupon demanded that Inkatha members be disarmed and forbidden to carry spears and shields. Although CODESA negotiations broke down temporarily, this crisis led to greater cooperation between the ANC and the South African government. Buthelezi, sensing that he was being marginalized, withdrew from the negotiations and began to talk of civil war if his demands were not met. He insisted that the Zulu had the right to self-determination and that KwaZulu-Natal should become a virtually sovereign state with its own president, courts, and army.

A state of emergency was declared in Natal, and only a week before national elections were due to be held in 1994, Buthelezi agreed to participate. The elections resulted in an overwhelming victory for the ANC, which received 62.6 percent of the national vote compared to 20.4 percent for the National Party and 10.4 percent for the Inkatha. However, Inkatha won a narrow majority (50.3 percent) in KwaZulu-Natal itself, as well as being awarded three cabinet posts in the new national coalition government. In early 1995, the Inkatha delegates walked out of the national assembly after repeated clashes between President Nelson Mandela and Buthelezi over the issue of greater autonomy for KwaZulu-Natal. At the present time, the possibility of Zulu separatism is still a real threat in postapartheid South Africa. However, in the 1995 elections, Inkatha's share of the provincial assembly vote in KwaZulu-Natal declined to 42 percent while the ANC's share rose to 39 percent.

See also Black Homelands; Buthelezi, Mangosuthu; Postapartheid South Africa; South Africa.
References Butler, Jeffrey, Robert Rotberg, and John Adams. *The Black Homelands of South Africa* (1977);
Morris, D. *The Washing of the Spears: The Rise and Fall of the Great Zulu Nation* (1985); Sparks, Allister. *Tomorrow Is Another Country: The Inside Story of South Africa's Road to Change* (1995).

Kyrgyzstan

Kyrgyzstan, a central Asian republic, has a population of 4.4 million, of which ethnic Kyrgyz make up 52 percent and Uzbeks another 13 percent. Both Kyrgyz and Uzbeks speak Turkic languages and are Sunni Muslims. Russians, who are predominantly urban, composed about 22 percent of the population at independence in 1991 but have been returning to Russia in great numbers as the Kyrgyz language replaces Russian in the educational and political institutions.

The Kyrgyz people migrated into the region from central Siberia in the early seventeenth century and later came under Mongol rule. They did not convert to Islam until the nineteenth century, and consequently, the roots of Islam in Kyrgyzstan are much weaker than in other neighboring former Soviet central Asian republics. By 1876, Russia had defeated the Mongol khanate, and Kyrgyzstan was incorporated into the Russian Empire as part of the province of Turkistan.

In 1916, a Kyrgyz revolt was suppressed by Russia. In 1924, now controlled by the Bolshevik government, Kyrgyz became an autonomous district of the Russian Soviet Republic. In 1926, Kyrgyzstan's status was raised to that of an autonomous Soviet republic. In 1936, it became a full union republic, the Kyrgyz Soviet Socialist Republic. Following the dissolution of the USSR in 1991, Kyrgyzstan declared its independence. The government of President Askar Akayev has followed a reformist path, introducing extensive market reforms within a democratic framework. Ethnic relations remain cordial within the nation.

See also Union of Soviet Socialist Republics.
References Filonyk, Alexander. "Kyrgyzstan" (1994); Rumer, Boris. *Central Asia in Transition: Dilemmas of Political and Economic Development* (1996).

Lakota Nation

The Lakota Nation, a confederation comprising the Lakota, Nakota, and Dakota tribes and also known as the Great Sioux Nation, claims 100,000 members and occupies some 72,000 square miles, largely in Minnesota, Montana, Nebraska, Wyoming, North Dakota, and South Dakota. Beginning in 1815, the Sioux made treaties of friendship with the United States, but continued encroachment by white settlers on Sioux lands led to conflict. In 1868, after a war between the Sioux under Chief Red Cloud and the U.S. Army, the Laramie Treaty granted the Sioux the right to the Black Hills of South Dakota. However, white settlers and gold prospectors continued to intrude on Sioux land, and led by Chief Sitting Bull, the Sioux killed more than 300 army troops under the command of General George A. Custer in the Battle of Little Big Horn in 1876. In 1877, the U. S. government forced the Sioux to transfer the Black Hills to white settlers, and Sioux territory was partitioned into a number of small reservations. In 1890, after protracted conflict with the Sioux, the U.S. Army massacred hundreds of Sioux men, women, and children at Wounded Knee, South Dakota, and this event ended formal Sioux armed resistance.

During the civil rights movement of the 1960s, the Sioux were one of the most outspoken of the tribes, reasserting their sovereignty and publicizing their grievances against the federal government. They were also instrumental in helping establish the American Indian Movement (AIM). In 1973, armed Sioux and AIM activists seized the town of Wounded Knee and occupied it for seventy days. The siege ended when the federal government agreed to review a list of grievances.

On another front, the Sioux instituted a series of legal suits against the federal government. In 1979, the U.S. Court of Claims ruled that the government had violated the 1868 Laramie Treaty and awarded the tribe $10 million. In 1989, the Sioux were awarded a further $40 million for land taken illegally by non-Sioux in the Black Hills re-

gion. To receive the funds, however, the Sioux would have to renounce their claims to the disputed land. They have refused to do so, and the money remains in a trust fund. In 1991, an activist group, the Lakota Confederacy of the Black Hills, declared the Sioux Nation sovereign over lands taken in violation of the 1815 and 1868 treaties. In 1994, the Lakota Nation became a member of the Unrepresented Nations and Peoples Organization, which has its headquarters in the Hague. In 1998, responding to congressional attacks on tribal sovereignty, Sioux tribes formed the Great Plains Indian Nations Council, an advocacy group seeking to restore the sovereignty promised in the Laramie Treaty.

See also American Indian Movement; Native Americans of the United States.
Reference Welch, James, and Paul Stekler. *Killing Custer: The Battle of Big Horn and the Fate of the Plains Indians* (1994).

Lapps
See Saami

Latvia

Latvia is bordered by Estonia on the north, Lithuania and Belarus to the south, and Russia to the east. Latvians, also called Letts, are a Baltic people who speak a Finno-Ugric language and

The statue of Lenin in the Latvian capital, Riga, lies on its back after having been dismantled in August 1991. (Reuters/Archive Photos)

are predominantly Lutheran. From the thirteenth century until the eighteenth, they were ruled by Germans, Swedes, and Lithuanians. At the end of the eighteenth century, they became part of the Russian Empire. As Latvian peasants gained more freedom toward the end of the nineteenth century, they were drawn to nationalist causes. In 1918, in the aftermath of World War I, a Latvian assembly declared the country independent. However, it was not until 1920, when German and Russian troops were expelled from the country's territories, that a Latvian republic was realized.

The republic existed only until 1940 when it was overrun by Soviet troops and forced to become the fifteenth Soviet socialist republic. Briefly occupied by German troops during World War II, Latvia returned to the Soviet sphere in

1944. The postwar years brought socialization of the means of production along the lines of the Soviet model; Russification of the educational, cultural, and political systems; and a large immigration of Russian nationals to fill positions in industry and government. Armed resistance to communism lasted into the 1950s.

It is estimated that from annexation to the USSR in 1940 until 1990, the percentage of Latvians in the population declined from 75 percent to about 52 percent. In 1991, Russians were estimated to make up 34 percent of the 2,650,000 inhabitants of the country. Ukrainians, Lithuanians, Belarusians, and Poles made up the remainder of the population.

In 1988, when Mikhail Gorbachev's glasnost (openness) policies were sweeping Russia, a national organization, the Latvian Popular Front, began calling for Latvian independence. In 1991, following an abortive coup against Gorbachev, the Latvian parliament, in which significant numbers of Latvian Popular Front members now held seats, declared its independence from the Soviet Union and reinstated the 1922 constitution. In September 1991, Latvia was admitted to the United Nations.

Since independence, Latvia's greatest internal problem has been the Russian question. In no other former Soviet republic has such anti-Russian sentiment arisen in a society in which Russians constitute such a large segment of the total population. Ethnic Latvian movements like the Father and Freedom Party, headed by Maris Grinblats, have called for a constitutional ban on ever granting citizenship to any post–World War II immigrants, primarily meaning Russians. Only ethnic Latvians and pre-1940 residents of Latvia and their descendants were granted citizenship at independence, so almost no Russians were eligible to vote in the 1993 elections. Only in 1994, under strong Russian and European Union (EU) pressure, was a citizenship law promulgated, and even it required applicants to pass a demanding Latvian language and history test. Furthermore, the law restricted by age those eligible to apply for citizenship each year. Not until 2003 would all noncitizens be eligible to apply. Concurrent with its citizenship policies, the Latvian government began to convert the formerly dual Latvian-Russian school system to exclusively Latvian language institutions.

The Russian minority, effectively denied citizenship, has appealed to international bodies and to Moscow to ameliorate their condition. One Russian described Latvia as an apartheid state. Those Latvian Russians still holding Russian citizenship expressed their dissatisfaction with the Latvian situation by casting their votes in the 1996 Russian presidential elections overwhelmingly for Gennady Zyuganov, the Communist candidate who has called for the reestablishment of the Soviet Union. The Yeltsin government continued to criticize the Latvian government for its

discrimination against Russians, and it was particularly incensed when Latvia proposed to apply for NATO membership. In April 1998, more than 1,000 Russian Latvians demonstrated against the government in Riga. The protest was broken up by Latvian police, and the Russian government retaliated by halting shipments of oil through Latvia and threatened to boycott Latvian agricultural products.

Under increasing pressure from the EU, which Latvia hopes to join, and the United States, the Latvian government has begun drafting measures to liberalize citizenship requirements. Under one proposal, quotas would gradually be phased out, and all children born in Latvia could become citizens at the age of sixteen if they can pass a Latvian history and language exam, an examination that has been revised to make it less difficult to secure a passing score. Additionally, children born after 1991 would be granted Latvian citizenship automatically. Even though the new measures would still leave many Russians stateless, particularly adults and retired persons who do not know Latvian, it appears, for the time being, to meet the demands of the EU nations. In July 1998, the High Commissioner on National Minorities of the Organization for Security and Cooperation in Europe, Max van der Stoel, expressed satisfaction with the new constitutional amendments.

See also Abrene; Russians in the Former Soviet Republics; Union of Soviet Socialist Republics.
References Dreifelds, Juris. *Latvia in Transition* (1996); Smith, Graham, ed. *The Baltic States: The National Self-Determination of Estonia, Latvia, and Lithuania* (1994).

League of Empire Loyalists

The League of Empire Loyalists was a British group opposed to the dissolution of the British Empire. Founded in 1954 by Arthur K. Chesterton (a cousin of the famous writer, G. K. Chesterton), the league was also opposed to the United Nations, NATO, and the European Common Market, seeing them as "monster plots to rob Britain of her independence and strength." Hostility to West Indian immigration into Britain was a major theme of their publications. The league's activities included heckling and disrupting official functions, often with considerable ingenuity. Once, dressed as bishops, some members invaded the Lambeth Conference (the assembly of the Anglican communion) to denounce the Church of England's support for Archbishop Makarios of Cyprus. The league occasionally contested elections, but its best showing was in 1957 when its candidate got fewer than 2,000 votes in a by-election.

For a while, the league functioned as a right-wing pressure group and had significant support within the Conservative Party. Many of its members were drawn from the upper class and included an earl, a field marshal, a general, and other high-ranking military men. However, after Loyalist demonstrators disrupted the league's conference in 1958, the Conservative Party denounced the group, and membership declined.

Reference Thayer, George. *The British Political Fringe* (1965).

League of the South

The League of the South is a fast-growing organization in the United States with chapters in all of the states of the ex-Confederacy and a membership of over 6,000. The league wants to secede from the United States, and in its "New Dixie Manifesto" claims that "America is only a geographical expression." According to its founder, Michael Hill, the league affirms the values of "white Anglo-Celtic Southern culture." Although critics accuse the group of racism and nostalgia for the old segregated South, Hill is a professor at Stillman College, a predominantly black school in Tuscaloosa, Alabama.

Reference Roberts, Diane. "The American South and the Rise of the New Right" (1997).

Lebanon

Modern Lebanon has always been divided along religious lines, and the breakdown of central government authority during the civil war that began in 1975 resulted in the de facto partition of the country into several autonomous enclaves, each controlled by different religious factions. Located on the Mediterranean Sea and bordered by Syria and Israel, Lebanon has an estimated population of 3.5 million, of which up to 400,000 are Palestinian refugees without Lebanese citizenship. The first wave of Palestinians, some 140,000, arrived in 1948 when the state of Israel was established. Subsequent Arab-Israeli wars, along with Palestinian expulsions from Jordan in 1970 and Kuwait in 1991 following the Gulf War, account for the growth of the Palestinian population within Lebanon.

The history of Lebanon prior to World War I is one of conquests, from the Assyrians in the ninth century B.C. to the Ottomans who controlled Lebanon from the sixteenth century into the twentieth. By 1920, when Lebanon passed into French hands, several religious communities coexisted in the land. According to a 1922 census, Christians accounted for 53 percent of the population and Muslims for most of the remainder. However, neither Christians nor Muslims were monolithic. The largest Christian sect, the Maronites (Roman Catholic but Eastern rite), composed 60 percent of the Christians, followed by Greek Orthodox at 26 percent and Greek Catholics at 14 percent. Muslims were divided into Sunni, 42 percent; Shi'ites, 34 percent; and Druze, 14 percent. Although the Maronites and Druze had established territorial communities, the Sunni and Shi'ites were more dispersed.

The structure of the Lebanese government, which emerged under the French in 1926 and continued when the country became independent in 1943, was based upon the religious communities. Under the constitution, the president was always to be a Maronite; the prime minister, a Sunni; and the speaker of parliament, a Shi'ite. Christians were allotted six parliamentary seats for every five granted Muslims. In effect, the government was significantly weighted in favor of the Christians. Because of its institutionalization of

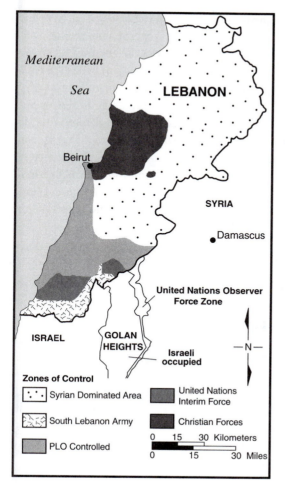

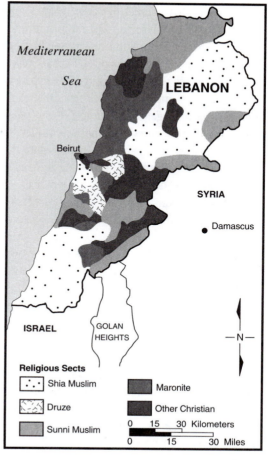

religious sects into the structure of government, Lebanon has been described as a confessional democracy. With the exception of the civil conflict that broke out in 1958 when the Maronite president, Camille Chamoun, attempted to extend his stay in office, the 1926 constitutional arrangements held until 1975 when civil war erupted. It was estimated, however, that by the end of World War II, Muslims constituted a majority of the Lebanese population. The protracted conflict came about because of the new majority Muslim demands for greater political power, strains introduced by the large influx of Palestinians and their militias, and reverberations from the Arab-Israeli struggle in the Middle East.

The civil war, which lasted from 1975 to 1990 and resulted in widespread destruction, was more than a Muslim-Christian conflict. At its height, it involved fighting among Christian and Muslim sects, shifting alliances, ethnic and political militias, and a powerless central government. Israeli and Syrian incursions further complicated the internal situation, and Palestinian militias battled for territory. French and U.S. intervention proved ineffective, and troops from those countries were withdrawn after 1983.

During the strife, several sectarian enclaves emerged, each with its own government, militias, media, and social service organizations. By 1988, these included the Maronite stronghold north of Beirut, the Druze territory south of Beirut, and the Amal-Hezbollah Shi'ite communities in the southern part of the country. Beirut itself was segregated into a Christian east and a Muslim west, and armed conflict between militias and warlords within each sector was not uncommon. In east Beirut, the Christian militias of Michael Aoun and Bashir Gemayel engaged in deadly conflict. Until peace was arranged in 1990, Lebanon consisted of a number of de facto separatist communities based largely on religion. The only pacified areas of the country were those controlled by the Syrian army of occupation. In the south, the Israelis, allied with the South Lebanese Army, a Christian militia, dominated the border areas.

It should be pointed out that none of the semi-autonomous communities disavowed the idea of Lebanon. They wanted, not to separate from Lebanon, but to rule it according to their own sectarian beliefs. Bashir Gemayel, the Maronite leader of the Kataib Party, envisaged a return to a Christian-dominated Lebanon, but the Iranian-supported Shi'ite Hezbollah Party hoped for an Islamic Lebanon governed, as Iran was, by Sharia, or Islamic law.

Under the Taif Agreement of 1989, worked out in Taif, Saudi Arabia, the Second Republic of Lebanon was established. Like the previous constitution, the Taif Agreement provides for a tripartite sharing of power with a Maronite president, Sunni premier, and Shi'ite speaker of parliament. However, major policy decisions now require the concurrence of all three. Parliamentary seats are now divided fifty-fifty between Christians and Muslims even though Muslims are thought to now account for 70 percent of the population. Despite the long civil war, Lebanon has chosen to retain its confessional democracy, although recent election results show a growth in support for program-oriented political parties rather than purely communitarian slates.

The disarming of the militias has ended the open warfare of the previous period. Rebuilding is taking place only slowly, both as a result of the massive destruction wrought by the war and as a result of the drying up of investment from the currently less affluent oil-producing Arab countries. The Syrian government continues its occupation, though it professes no interest in annex-ing the region to create a greater Syria. Nevertheless, the Lebanese government cannot make major decisions without the approval of the Syrian leaders in Damascus. Having been expelled to North Africa in 1982 after an Israeli invasion of Lebanon, Palestinian militias no longer operate on Lebanese soil. But in the south, armed militias of the Shi'ite Hezbollah, financed by Iran, continue their attacks against Israel, which often results in deadly retaliation from the Israeli military. The South Lebanese Army continues to hold sway over much of the buffer zone between Israel and UN peacekeeping troops.

See also Hezbollah; Palestine Liberation Organization.
Reference Picard, Elizabeth. *Lebanon: A Shattered Country* (1996).

Lebowa

The South African homeland of Lebowa, which became self-governing in 1972, was intended to be the homeland for two black ethnic groups, the Pedi and the northern Ndebele. Comprising almost 8,600 square miles made up of twelve scattered territories, almost half of Lebowa's legal citizens lived outside the homeland's borders. Ruled by Dr. Cedric Phatudi from 1973 until 1987, Lebowa resisted South Africa's pressure to become "independent." After 1986, Phatudi's government faced increasing political unrest and responded with brutal repression. Several anti-apartheid activists died while in police custody, including the regional president of the United Democratic Front and a journalist belonging to the Azanian People's Organization. In June 1992, a boundary dispute between Lebowa and the neighboring homeland of Gazankulu almost led to a military confrontation. Nelson Ramodike, who succeeded Phatudi as chief minister, welcomed the reincorporation of Lebowa into South Africa in 1994 but called for a regional structure of administration that would bring the government closer to the people.

See also Black Homelands; South Africa.

Levesque, René (1922–1987)

Founder of the Parti Québécois and premier of Quebec from 1976 to 1985, René Levesque was the catalyst in the movement for independence and widely regarded as its most important leader. Born in the Gaspé region of Canada, he grew up in a bilingual community, and his earliest memories were of discrimination against French speakers. The son of a lawyer, he was educated in Catholic schools where he was exposed to nationalist ideas. In an article written for the school newspaper, he praised "the enlightened patriots who watch over and defend our interests, for on their labours depends the future of our race in America." After dropping out of law school, he became a highly successful broadcaster. His program *Point de Mire* established him as Quebec's most outspoken and popular television personality. With a group of young intellectuals, he attempted to reshape the provincial Liberal Party into a progressive alternative to the governing Union Nationale. When the Liberals won the 1960 election, he became a cabinet minister and, with the slogan *Maîtres chez nous* ("masters in our own house"), persuaded the party to take over the hydroelectric power companies.

Levesque championed the cause of Quebec sovereignty with increasing fervor, and in 1967, he was expelled from the Liberal Party over the issue. He then formed the Parti Québécois by joining together two existing nationalist movements. After two defeats, he led the party to power in 1976. The most controversial measure of his administration was the law declaring French the only official language within the province and making English-language signs illegal. However, the sovereignty proposal that the Parti Québécois sponsored was decisively defeated in a 1980 referendum. Levesque resigned as party leader in June 1985 and died of a heart attack on November 1, 1987.

See also French Language Charter; Parti Québécois; Quebec.

References Dupont, Pierre. *How Levesque Won* (1977); Saywell, John. *The Rise of the Parti Québécois 1967–76* (1977).

Lewis, Saunders (1893–1985)

The founder and president of the Welsh Nationalist Party from 1926 to 1939, Saunders Lewis emphasized the cultural and historic roots of Welsh national identity and himself wrote a history of Welsh literature. A romantic who looked back to an idealized, organic medieval society, he became a Catholic convert and advocated a society of small property holders without either capitalists or a "rootless proletariat." In 1936, Lewis and two other party officials set fire to some huts on a Royal Air Force base and then turned themselves in to the authorities in a symbolic protest against British rule. Their subsequent trial and imprisonment—after refusing to give their evidence in English—made them martyrs to the Welsh nationalist movement. Lewis was fired from his university position and retired from public life until a radio lecture he gave ("The Fate of the Language") inspired the formation of the Welsh Language Society in 1962.

See also Wales; Welsh Language Society.

Lezgins

Lezgins are a Sunni Muslim people with a population of 290,000 in Dagestan in the Russian Federation and 190,000 in northern Azerbaijan. Lezgins claim that their Azerbaijan population is much larger because Lezgins frequently register with the government as Azeris to avoid discrimination. They speak Lezghi, a Caucasian language. The Lezgins in Azerbaijan resent living in a Shi'ite country among a Turkic-speaking majority and have demanded to be linked with their compatriots in Dagestan. They claim that the Azerbaijan government actively oppresses Lezgin citizens.

The Lezgin national council was formed in 1993 to push for independence from Azerbaijan at a time when Azerbaijan was bogged down in a war with Armenia over Nagorno-Karabakh. A second Lezgin organization, Sadval, has established paramilitary units and called for the use of force to achieve independence. Sadval was accused of carrying out a bombing in September 1994 in the Baku subway that killed fourteen people. Azerbaijan has banned both groups. In Dagestan, a new political party, Alpan, was established in 1995, and it has called for the unification of Lezgins in both Russia and Azerbaijan in a new state, Lezgistan. Russian troops now patrol the Georgia-Dagestan border, and little progress has been made on Lezgin demands.

See also Azerbaijan; Dagestan; Russian Federation.
Reference Wesselink, Egbert. *The Russian Federation: Dagestan* (1995).

Liberation Tigers of Tamil Eelam

The Liberation Tigers of Tamil Eelam (LTTE) is a Tamil separatist organization in Sri Lanka. The LTTE, also known as the Tamil Tigers, was formed in the early 1970s. The organization began its campaign after an unprovoked attack by police on a crowd of Tamils outside the World Tamil Research Conference, which was being held in Jaffna. The Tigers assassinated the progovernment mayor of Jaffna in reprisal for the police attack and then went underground. The LTTE is led by Velupillai Prabhakaran and A. S. Balasingham, and it seeks an independent state, Tamil Eelam. The guerrillas have received considerable political support and supplies from their fellow Tamils in the Indian state of Tamil Nadu, where they have established training camps. Some financial aid has also come from expatriate Tamils in Europe and North America.

The LTTE was the largest of the more than thirty Tamil guerrilla groups that were active in the 1980s; other important groups included the Eelam People's Revolutionary Liberation Front, the Tamil Eelam Liberation Organization, and the People's Liberation Organization of Tamil Eelam. Most claimed to be Marxist, and the splits and alliances among the different groups can be explained in part by ideological factors and in part by caste. The LTTE members were largely drawn from low-caste urban backgrounds while the People's Liberation Organization of Tamil Eelam recruits were from a high-caste rural group. After

A Tamil guerrilla stands guard in an area controlled by the Liberation Tigers of Tamil Eelam, January 1996. (Reuters/Anuruddha Lokuhapuarachchi/ Archive Photos)

destroying their rivals in a series of attacks in 1986 and 1987, the LTTE emerged as the dominant force in the Tamil separatist movement.

The campaign of the Tamil separatists initially involved sporadic attacks on police, soldiers, and moderate Tamil politicians, but in July 1983, an LTTE ambush took the lives of thirteen Sinhalese soldiers. This event precipitated anti-Tamil riots throughout the island, which increased support for the LTTE among the Tamils, and isolated terrorism was replaced by a full-fledged insurgency. A 1985 massacre of Sinhalese civilians in the city of Anuradhapura left 146 dead, and a 1987 bomb in a Colombo bus station killed 110. In 1984, the Eelam People's Revolutionary Liberation Front kidnapped an American couple who were working on a USAID project. However, this action led to a crackdown by the Indian government on the front's bases in Tamil Nadu, and the hostages were released unharmed after five days.

By early 1986, the LTTE was in effective control of the Jaffna peninsula, but a major offensive by the Sinhalese army put the guerrillas on the defensive. This provoked Indian intervention, and when the LTTE guerrillas refused to hand over their weapons, fighting broke out between the LTTE and the Indian army. Despite repeated military setbacks, the LTTE remains a force to be reckoned with, and in October 1999 it overran a string of government garrisons in the northeast.

See also Tamil Eelam.

Reference Gunasekara, S. L. *Tigers, Moderates, and Pandora's Package* (1996).

Lithuania

Lithuanians are an ancient Baltic people who speak a Finno-Ugric language related to Latvian and are predominantly Roman Catholic. The territory of Lithuania is bordered by Latvia to the north, Russia to the east, and Belarus to the south.

In 1251, King Mindaugus consolidated the Lithuanian tribes into a federation. Within a century, a Lithuanian empire had been created that extended from the Baltic to the Black Sea and included both Belarus and the Ukraine. In 1386, the kingdoms of Poland and Lithuania were merged, and in the eighteenth century, much of Lithuania was absorbed into the more powerful Russian Empire. The nineteenth century witnessed several Lithuanian nationalist uprisings, but they were all unsuccessful. After the collapse of the Russian Empire in World War I, Lithuania declared itself an independent nation and adopted a democratic constitution. An unsettled political period ended when Soviet troops occupied Lithuania in 1940. In the same year, the country became a Soviet socialist republic. Occupied by German forces during World War II, Lithuania was recaptured by Soviet forces in 1944. A period of armed resistance to the reinstalled Communist government lasted until the early 1950s, and the Soviet government responded by deporting some 300,000 Lithuanians to forced labor camps. The Catholic Church was persecuted, and the country experienced an influx of Russian and Polish immigrants beginning in the 1950s.

In the Mikhail Gorbachev years, Lithuanian nationalism revived, and in 1990, the Lithuanian parliament, led by the Sajudis, the Lithuanian Movement for Reconstruction, declared independence. Lithuania's independence was recognized by the Soviet Union in 1991.

Unlike Latvia and Estonia, Lithuania has a small Russian minority—about 10 percent of a population of some 2.7 million. All Russians have been granted citizenship, in contrast to Latvia and Estonia where nonnational ethnics, principally Russians, have been denied citizenship. In 1997, Lithuania signed a border treaty with Russia, the only one of the three Baltic states to do so thus far.

See also Russians in the Former Soviet Republics; Union of Soviet Socialist Republics.

References Kagda, Sakina. *Lithuania* (1997); Krickus, Richard J. *Showdown: The Lithuanian Rebellion and the Breakup of the Soviet Empire* (1997).

Lost Counties of Bunyoro

The area referred to as the lost counties of Bunyoro is in Uganda. It is occupied by Banyoro tribesmen and was part of Buganda until 1965. When the British entered Uganda in the 1890s, they allied themselves with Buganda against Bunyoro. As a reward, the two counties of Buyaga and Bugangaizi were annexed to Buganda. Bunyoro agitated for the return of the counties, and a constitutional commission proposed that there should be a referendum after independence to decide their status. Although the Buganda government resettled thousands of Bagandan ex-servicemen in the area, the referendum held in 1964 showed overwhelming support for the return of the counties to Bunyoro. The result humiliated Buganda and led to the withdrawal of the Bagandan nationalist party, the Kabaka Yekka, from the government coalition. This bitter territorial dispute between the two regions revealed the intensity of ethnic identities and the weakness of any sense of national feeling in Uganda.

See also Buganda.

Macau

Macau was the first European settlement in East Asia and the longest continuously occupied colony in the world. Established by the Portuguese in 1557, Macau was a major trading center for more than a century, but its influence was eventually eclipsed by Hong Kong. At the end of World War II, Macau was a "small, charming anachronism, renowned mainly for its gambling and vice." The population of almost half a million includes 10,000 Eurasians, and the Portuguese culture is deeply entrenched. Macau, like Hong Kong, is a lost territory of China, and nationalist sentiment requires the reunification of both with China. During the Cultural Revolution (1966–1976), mass demonstrations led the Portuguese to accept de facto Chinese control over the city, and in 1972, the government of the People's Republic of China declared Macau to be "Chinese territory under temporary Portuguese administration." Macau was reunited with China on December 20, 1999, but is to retain a high degree of autonomy.

References Porter, Jonathan. "Macau 1999" (1997); Shipp, Steve. *Macau, China: A Political History of the Portuguese Colony's Transition to Chinese Rule* (1997).

Macedonia

Modern Macedonia is a republic with a population of 2 million and consists of the northern areas of the pre-Christian-era kingdom of Macedonia. The southern lands of ancient Macedonia are now part of Greece, and some of the northeastern territory is now part of Bulgaria.

Slavs settled modern Macedonia in the sixth and seventh centuries A.D. From the seventh through the fourteenth centuries, Macedonian Slavs were under the loose control of the Byzantine Empire and, at times, the expansionist but short-lived Bulgarian and Serbian kingdoms. The Macedonians were Christianized by the ninth century. By the fourteenth century, Macedonia had become part of the Ottoman Empire and remained under Turkish rule until the twentieth

century. Although conversions to Islam were widespread, they did not occur on the same scale as in some other areas. Consequently, Macedonia remains predominantly Christian today but has a significant 30–35 percent Muslim minority population. As in Bosnia, the Christian-Muslim split is an important factor in the social landscape.

Following an Ottoman defeat in the Balkan Wars of 1912–1913, Macedonia was annexed to Serbia in 1913. During World War I, Macedonia was claimed and occupied by Bulgaria, an ally of the Central Powers. In 1918, Macedonia was reattached to Serbia and became part of the Kingdom of the Serbs, Croats, and Slovenes, later renamed Yugoslavia. After World War II, Macedonia, which had strong Communist support among the peasantry and supplied many volunteers to Josip Broz Tito's armed forces, became one of the six republics of Communist Yugoslavia.

Historically, the Macedonian language has served to integrate the people and to antagonize the country's larger Serbian neighbor. Although part of the Slavic language family and written using the Cyrillic alphabet, Macedonian has more in common with Bulgarian than with Serbo-Croatian. Prior to the establishment of the socialist Yugoslav federation, Serbia, which was extremely powerful in the first Yugoslavia, attempted to forcibly assimilate Macedonians by suppressing the Macedonian culture and language, referring to the Macedonian language as an inferior "southern Serbian" dialect. By making Macedonia a republic in the Yugoslav federation, Tito was able to satisfy Macedonian nationalist aspirations. The move also reduced fears in the other republics that Serbia would dominate the second Yugoslavia as it had formerly. As a symbol of Macedonia's autonomy from Serbia, the governing party of Yugoslavia, the League of Communists, allowed Macedonia to install its own national patriarch at Ohrid in 1967, thus freeing the Macedonian Orthodox Church from Serbian control.

The first organized independence movement in Macedonia, the Internal Macedonian Revolutionary Organization (IMRO), emerged at the close of the nineteenth century and led an unsuccessful uprising against Ottoman rule in 1903. In socialist Yugoslavia, with its republic status guaranteed and its strong Communist tradition, Macedonia displayed little overt sentiment for separating from Yugoslavia. However, when secessionist movements began to strengthen in Slovenia and Croatia, Macedonia was again confronted with the prospect of finding itself once again in a Yugoslavian state dominated by Serbia. That and the Macedonian Communist Party's relinquishing of its monopoly of power paved the way for pro-independence proposals to be enacted by the legislature, and in 1991, Macedonia declared itself a sovereign nation.

Since independence, Macedonia has been governed by a coalition led by the former Communist Party, now renamed the Social Democratic Alliance of Macedonians (SDSM). However, the stability provided by President Kiro Gligorov masks a social climate polarized by hostile relations between Orthodox Macedonians and Albanians who may now constitute a third of the total population. Albanians claim their standard of living and rights have deteriorated since the end of communism in Macedonia, and despite concessions from the Gligorov government and representation in parliament by the Party for Democratic Prosperity of Albanians (PDPA), Albanians have engaged in numerous street protests. Com-

plaining about discrimination in education, Albanians have established their own university in their stronghold city of Tetovo. The government has declared the university illegal. Younger Albanians, some migrants from neighboring Kosovo, have been espousing the greater Albania cause, calling for the unification of all Eastern European Albanians into one state. In 1997, Albanians were involved in several protests and demonstrations against the government.

In reaction to the growing Albanian stridency, an ultranationalist party has gained adherents among Macedonian Christians. The Internal Macedonian Revolutionary Organization (VMRO), modeled after the late-nineteenth-century radical nationalist party, IMRO, captured a third of the vote in a recent election. VMRO seeks an ethnically pure Macedonia linked to Bulgaria. It also encourages, somewhat unrealistically, the retaking of Macedonian lands that are now part of Greece. Further compounding the ethnic situation in Macedonia is the fact that some Macedonian Christians claim to be Serbians, which provides greater Serbia nationalists in Belgrade with a justification for advocating the incorporation of Macedonian territory into an expanded Serbian state.

When war broke out in Croatia and Bosnia in 1991 and 1992 and given the continuing tense situation in neighboring Kosovo, concern was expressed in international quarters that the conflict might spread to Macedonia, possibly adding Greece and Bulgaria to the list of Balkan combatants. To forestall that possibility, in 1993, a 1,000-member UN force, largely American, was dispatched to Macedonia.

In 1998, Serbian forces launched an offensive against ethnic Albanians in neighboring Kosovo. In March 1999, NATO responded with air strikes against Yugoslav army units in Kosovo. Hundreds of thousands of Kosovars fled into Macedonia, which further strained ethnic relations in that country. Pro-Serb Macedonians held rallies in support of Yugoslavia's President Slobodan Milosevic while Macedonian Albanians supplied the Kosovo Liberation Army with recruits and supplies. The imposition of a UN-NATO protectorate in Kosovo in June 1999 encouraged many refugees to return to Kosovo. Currently, the presence of NATO forces in Macedonia precludes overt conflict between Albanians and Slavs, but the situation remains precarious.

See also Greater Albania; Kosovo; Macedonian Question; Yugoslavia.
References Georgieva, Valentina, and Sasha Konechni. *Historical Dictionary of the Republic of Macedonia* (1998); Shea, John. *Macedonia and Greece: The Struggle to Define a New Balkan Nation* (1997).

Macedonian Question

Who are the Macedonians who inhabit the former Yugoslav Republic of Macedonia? Historically, the land has at times been ruled by Greeks, Turks, Serbians, and Bulgarians, and all but the Turks currently lay claim to the land or the people or both. The Greeks argue that the territory now inhabited by the Slavic Macedonians is part of historic Greece because it belonged to the kingdom of Macedonia in the third century B.C. In this sense, Greece's position is similar to Israel's claim to its state territory in the Middle East; that is, in biblical times, the land belonged to the ancient Israelite tribes and the Jewish people are simply reclaiming what is rightfully theirs. In both cases, the land in question houses sacred historic sites: Solomon's Temple in Jerusalem and the Byzantine monastery at Ohrid to mention but two. However, much as Greece would like to regain control over historic sites and possibly more territory, it is clear that, unlike Israel, which has a large settled population to back up its historic claims, there are almost no Greeks living in Slavic Macedonia. Perhaps for this reason, the thrust of Greek foreign policy since Macedonia seceded from Yugoslavia is, not to press for a return of the land itself, but to forbid its inhabitants from calling themselves Macedonians.

True Macedonians, says Athens, speak Greek. Greece also expresses concern that a country that calls itself Macedonia might seek to regain more of the ancient kingdom. Although the Macedonian government denies having any territorial ambitions, there are Slavic Macedonians (not to mention Serb and Bulgarian nationalists) who envisage the Greek Aegean port of Thessalonika as part of an ideal future state. To show its displeasure at the new republic's name, Greece imposed an economic embargo (since lifted) on Macedonia and forced it to seek admission to the United Nations as the Former Yugoslav Republic of Macedonia. The name issue has not yet been resolved, and as Balkan history shows, very little ever gets resolved quickly or permanently.

Linguistically, defining Macedonian identity is an equally contentious Balkan exercise in futility. Macedonian, a southern Slavic language most closely resembling Bulgarian, has also been defined by Serbs as a "southern Serbian" dialect. As far as the Greeks and the Bulgarians are concerned, Macedonians are speaking Bulgarian. In September 1997, the Bulgarian foreign minister, Nadezhda Mikhailova, announced that residents of Skopje, the capital of the Republic of Macedonia, were not Macedonians but Bulgarians. Officially, Bulgaria recognizes Madedonian independence and statehood but refuses to admit that a Macedonian nation exists. Bulgarian irredentists, particularly in Pirin Bulgaria, territory that was also part of ancient Macedonia, have called for the annexation of Macedonia to the Bulgarian state. Compounding the language matter is that a significant number of Macedonian speakers in the northern part of the country define themselves as Serbian, and their dialect of Macedonian (one of three acknowledged dialects) has been heavily influenced by Serbo-Croatian.

See also Macedonia.
References Poulton, Hugh. *Who Are the Macedonians?* (1995); Shea, John. *Macedonia and Greece: The Struggle to Define a New Balkan Nation* (1997).

Macheteros

Los Macheteros ("the machete wielders") is a Puerto Rican terrorist group that has been active since 1978. The group follows a strategy of armed propaganda whereby it attempts to raise the consciousness of the Puerto Rican people by engaging in attacks that have propaganda value. Therefore, their communiqués typically justify their actions as retaliation for a specific injustice by the Americans. For example, when Los Macheteros fired on a naval bus in December 1979, killing two U.S. sailors, the group described the action as retaliation for the death of Angel Rodriguez, who it claimed had been murdered while in a federal prison (he had been imprisoned for trespassing on the U.S. naval base at Vieques).

Other notable incidents claimed by Los Macheteros include the kidnapping/murder of two police officers in August 1978; the destruction of nine national guard planes, with estimated damages of $50 million, in January 1981; and the murder of a sailor in May 1982. Although most incidents have occurred in Puerto Rico, in September 1983, Los Macheteros robbed a Wells Fargo depot in New Haven, Connecticut, of $7.1 million. This was the second-largest politically motivated robbery in the United States, and although nineteen people were indicted for the robbery, the money was never recovered. Los Macheteros may have as many as 300 members, and according to one survey, although 51 percent of Puerto Ricans thought the group consisted of "terrorists whose goals and actions were unacceptable," 3 percent considered them "patriots whose goals justify their means."

See also Fuerzas Armadas de Liberacion Nacional; Puerto Rico.
Reference Fernandez, Ronald. *Los Macheteros* (1987).

Archbishop Makarios, president of the Republic of Cyprus, March 1964. (Popperfoto/Archive Photos)

Makarios, Archbishop (1913–1977)

Archbishop Makarios, the Greek Cypriot leader, was born in 1913 to a peasant family as Michael Mouskos and entered the monastery of Kykkos when he was thirteen. The abbot, impressed by his intelligence, sponsored his education, and he studied theology and law at Athens University. When he was ordained a priest in 1946, he took the name of Makarios, "the blessed one." He then attended Boston University until he returned to Cyprus to become Bishop of Kitium in 1948. In 1950, he was elected Archbishop of Cyprus and vowed to continue the struggle for enosis (political union with Greece).

When the guerrilla struggle by the Ethnike Organosis Kyprion Agoniston (EOKA) began in 1955, Makarios became its political leader and spokesman. As a result, the British authorities exiled him to the Seychelles in 1956. When Cyprus gained its independence in 1959 under the Zurich agreement, Makarios returned from exile and became president in 1960. Ethnic hostilities between Greek and Turkish Cypriots led to a constitutional stalemate, and after Makarios proposed to amend the constitution, ethnic violence broke out. In foreign affairs, Makarios adopted a policy of nonalignment, but over time became increasingly hostile to NATO and allied with the Communist bloc.

In 1967, the Greek military seized power in Athens, and relations between Makarios and the military rulers of Greece became increasingly strained, with Makarios accusing the junta of plotting his assassination. Makarios was re-elected president of Cyprus in 1968 and again in 1973. In July 1974, a coup by supporters of enosis, backed by the Greek military, overthrew Makarios. Makarios fled, the Turks invaded, and the island was partitioned de facto into a northern Turkish sector and a Greek-Cypriot sector. These events led to the fall of the military junta in Greece, and Makarios returned to Cyprus on December 7, 1974. Negotiations in early 1977 between Makarios and the Turkish Cypriot leader, Rauf Denktash, failed to resolve the Cyprus dispute. Makarios suffered a minor heart attack in April and died on August 3, 1977, after a second attack.

See also Cyprus; Ethnike Organosis Kyprion Agoniston; Grivas, George.

References Mayes, Stanley. *Cyprus and Makarios* (1960); Vanezis, P. *Makarios: Faith and Power* (1971).

Malaysia

At the end of World War II, the British possessions on the Malay peninsula were divided into the three Straits Settlements of Singapore, Penang, and Melaka, which were administered as colonies, and nine Malay states, which were protectorates. In addition, Sarawak, Brunei, and North Borneo on the northern coast of Borneo were under British rule. Malays and other indigenous groups were outnumbered by descendants of immigrant Chinese and Indians. The total population of these areas in 1957 was just under 9 million, of which 41.4 percent were Chinese and 11.8 percent were Indians and "others." The Malays and native Borneans were a minority (47 percent) in their own land. The Chinese, and to a lesser extent the Indians, dominated the commercial sector as well as the rubber plantations and tin mining while the Malays were for the most part subsistence farmers. The Chinese were largely urbanized; the Malays and indigenous

Borneans lived in rural areas. In Singapore and the other Straits Settlements, the Chinese formed the majority. The political consequences of this ethnic demography largely explain the process of nation-building in Malaysia and the strength of the separatist sentiments.

The British first proposed a Malayan union in which equal citizenship rights would be granted to all "who regarded Malaya as their true home and the object of their loyalty." However, Singapore with its largely Chinese population was excluded because its inclusion would have made the Malays a definite minority. The proposed union was opposed by the Malays, who were organized into the United Malays National Organization (UMNO), and was replaced by a new Malaya Federation, which became independent in 1957. The constitution of the new nation emphasized the concept of Malaya as *tanah Melayu* ("land of the Malays"), the role of the Malay sultans was retained, citizenship requirements were made more stringent for non-Malays, Islam became the official religion and Malay the official language.

The constitution was the result of an agreement between the elites of the three main ethnic communities. The agreement resulted in an electoral coalition between the three main communally based parties: the UMNO, the Malayan Chinese Association (MCA), and the Malayan Indian Congress (MIC). The coalition, organized as the Alliance Party, won fifty-one of the fifty-two seats in the legislative elections of 1955 and 79.6 percent of the vote. Although challenged by ultranationalist Malays, and by Chinese wanting a more egalitarian system, the Alliance Party also won the elections of 1959, but with a decreased share of the vote.

In 1960, after talks between Lee Kuan Yew, chief minister of Singapore, and Tengku Abdul Rahman, the Malayan prime minister, it was proposed that the federation be enlarged to include Singapore, Sarawak, Brunei, and North Borneo. The political logic behind the proposal was that the Singapore Chinese would be counterbalanced by the addition of the Malays and the other indigenous tribes of Borneo, which would mean that the Malays would retain their demographic and political dominance. Although there was uncertainty regarding the degree of support for federation in Sarawak and North Borneo, and the sultan of oil-rich Brunei decided against joining, the Federation of Malaysia was proclaimed in 1963.

Malaysia faced a number of external and internal threats to its political stability. Indonesia adopted a policy of confrontation toward the new federation, and the Philippines revived their claim to Sabah. The most serious crisis resulted from Lee Kuan Yew's advocacy of a "Malaysian Malaysia." This idea was considered such a threat to the delicate ethnic and political balance within the country that Singapore was forced to withdraw from the Federation of Malaysia in 1965.

See also Kalimantan Utara; Penang Secessionist Movement; Sabah; Singapore.

References Christie, Clive J. *A Modern History of Southeast Asia* (1996); Crouch, Harold. *Government and Society in Malaysia* (1996); Milne, R. S., and K. J. Ratnam. *Malaysia: New States in a New Nation* (1974).

Malta

Malta, along with the smaller islands of Gozo and Comino, is located in the Mediterranean Sea sixty miles south of Sicily. The population of over 300,000 speaks a distinctive language that is related to Arabic, although Italian was the official language of the courts and schools until 1932. The Maltese are devout Catholics and according to tradition, were converted to Christianity by St. Paul when he was shipwrecked on the island. Ruled in turn by Arabs, Normans, and the Knights of St. John, the islands became a British colony in 1802. The island was an important British naval base, and a large proportion of the population worked in the dockyards and related industries.

Malta enjoyed a substantial degree of self-government, and before World War II, politics was dominated by the struggle between the Nationalist and Constitutionalist Parties. The Nationalist Party advocated close links with Italy and was supported by the church while the Constitutionalists were pro-British and took an anticlerical stance. In the 1930 elections, a pastoral letter warned Catholics that they could not vote for the Constitutionalists without committing a grave sin. After 1945, the Maltese Labour Party was formed with a broad popular base among the dockworkers, and it also took an anticlerical position.

During World War II, Malta was under constant attack from the Italian air force, and the siege strengthened the sense of imperial loyalty felt by the Maltese and weakened pro-Italian sentiments. In 1955, the Maltese Labour Party came to power, and its leader, Dom Mintoff, put forward proposals for the integration of Malta with the United Kingdom under which Malta would elect three representatives to the British Parliament. The party had advocated integration since the 1950 election and in the 1955 election, campaigning on this program, won twenty-three seats to the Nationalists' seventeen. The idea received cautious acceptance by the British Parliament, and an all-party conference report declared that it was for the Maltese people to demonstrate their wishes in the matter.

In a referendum held in February 1956, 74 percent voted in favor and 22 percent against. (Opponents argued, however, that the pro-integration vote was less than half the total electorate, since 41 percent of those eligible had not voted.) During the referendum campaign, the Labour Party had argued that the standard of living would improve, with the average weekly wage increasing from about twenty dollars to thirty-six. The Catholic Church had called for a guarantee that nothing would be done to diminish or detract from the prerogatives of the church, "in particular as regards the marriage laws relating to family life and education." This guarantee clause became a major issue in the campaign and is generally regarded as explaining the high number of abstentions.

Since the referendum results were somewhat ambiguous, the United Kingdom government announced that it wanted a further election before approving the integration plan. Mintoff, on the other hand, called for immediate financial aid. The discussions between the two governments became increasingly acrimonious, and the integration proposals were abandoned. The Nationalists won the next two Maltese elections, and in a 1964 referendum, the Maltese voted to become independent by a narrow margin (52 percent to 43 percent). As a proportion of the total electorate, the independence vote was only 40 percent. Ironically, this was lower than the number who had favored integration in the 1956 referendum. Although other small British dependencies, such as Gibraltar, have called for integration, the British government never repeated the offer of representation at Westminster to any other territory.

See also Gibraltar.
Reference Austin, Dennis. *Malta and the End of Empire* (1971).

Mangope, Lucas (1923–)

Leader of the black homeland of Bophuthatswana. Lucas Mangope was born in the Transvaal Province of South Africa in 1923 the son of a Tswana chief. Educated at an Anglican boarding school and at a teacher's training college, he then worked in the Department of Native Affairs, the South African government agency dealing with the black population. After several years as a teacher, he became active in Tswana tribal affairs and became the first chief minister of Bophuthatswana in 1972.

Fluent in Afrikaans, he had good social relations with Afrikaner politicians and journalists. At first sympathetic to the predicament of the white minority, Mangope became increasingly critical of the South African government in the early 1970s. Although he justified cooperation with the apartheid regime as a means of gaining concessions for the black population, Mangope noted that whenever "Pretoria fails to fulfill the promises implicit in separate development it undermines the position of homeland leaders committed to the policy." Very conscious of the fact that the Tswana were a minority among black South Africans, Mangope declared, "I have been entrusted with the task of serving the Tswana people, and therefore to do what is in the best interest of Bophuthatswana and nothing else."

After Bophuthatswana became independent in 1977 (an independence recognized by no country except South Africa), Mangope's rule became increasingly autocratic. Widely regarded as selling out to the white minority, Mangope was overthrown by a popular uprising in March 1994, and Bophuthatswana was reincorporated into South Africa.

See also Bophuthatswana.
Reference Butler, Jeffrey, Robert Rotberg, and John Adams, *The Black Homelands of South Africa* (1977).

Maori

The Maori are a Polynesian people who migrated to New Zealand sometime between 1200 and 1400. British settlement began in the early 1800s, and in 1840, the Maori chiefs signed the Treaty of Waitangi with the British. In return for ceding sovereignty to the British crown, the Maori were guaranteed full rights as British subjects, and the treaty is regarded by New Zealanders as the constitutional blueprint of their society. The Maori Representation Act of 1867 allocated four parliamentary seats to the Maori, and Maori may vote (or run for election) in either a Maori district or one of the ninety-seven general districts.

As the number of settlers increased, conflicts between them and the Maori led to land wars in the 1860s. By the turn of the century, disease had reduced the Maori population to under 50,000, and it was anticipated that they would soon disappear as a people. In fact, their numbers have increased since then, and they currently make up about 13 percent of a population of about 3 million. They are relatively disadvantaged in a socioeconomic sense, with a median income that is only 83 percent of the income of non-Maori and an unemployment rate that is almost double. Over 80 percent are urbanized.

A Maori demonstrator, part of a protest against the 1995 Waitangi Day celebrations at Waitangi Treaty House that forced cancellation of the event. (Corbis/Paul A. Sonders)

The Maori began to protest their situation in the 1970s. In 1975, Maori activists organized a land march to call for the return of their traditional lands and access to natural resources as guaranteed by the Treaty of Waitangi. There was also concern that by the late 1970s, few young urban Maori were fluent in their native language. Beginning in 1982, the Kohanga Reo movement set up centers to promote the Maori culture and language, and by 1990, almost half of Maori preschoolers were enrolled in the program. In 1990, tribal leaders established a Maori Congress to provide a national forum for Maori issues.

The New Zealand government responded to Maori demands by adopting policies that promoted community-based development using traditional tribal structures, and government departments were reorganized in an attempt to be sensitive to Maori cultural values. Also, the Waitangi tribunal was set up to examine Maori land claims and disputes over natural resources dating back to 1840.

References Fleras, Augie, and Jean L. Elliott. *The Nations Within* (1992); Sharp, Andrew. *Justice and the Maori: Maori Claims in New Zealand Political Argument in the 1980s* (1990).

Mapuche

The Mapuche people are the third-largest indigenous population in South America. They are found in the southern half of Chile and Argentina and speak a language called Mapugundun. An estimated 1.5 million live in Chile (10 percent of Chile's total population), and 200,000 live in Argentina.

In 1614, the Spanish signed the Treaty of Quillin, which recognized the sovereignty of the Mapuche and their claim to 24 million acres of land. When Argentina and Chile became independent in 1810, they abrogated the treaty, seized Mapuche land, and annexed the tribal territory. Resistance by the Mapuche in the late-nineteenth century was ended by the occupation of Mapuche territory by the Argentine and Chilean armies. Many Mapuche were killed in the fighting.

Mapuche grievances in the twentieth century center on their demand for their ancestral lands. Land disputes escalated into armed conflicts into the 1990s, and many Mapuche activists were imprisoned. A protest against the construction of the Ralco hydroelectric dam on Mapuche land led to the detention of several families, and the Mapuche have filed claims of police brutality on several occasions. Activist groups like Consejo de Todas las Tierras (Council of All the Earth) have occupied land they claim is Mapuche.

Beyond specific land claims, the Mapuche are pushing for an autonomous status for their society. Currently, the Chilean constitution does not recognize the Mapuche as a separate nationality. Nor is Mapugundun recognized as an official language and therefore is not taught in the public school system. In 1997, the European Parliament passed a resolution calling on the Argentine government to respect the rights of indigenous peoples. In March 1999, the Mapuche presented a list of grievances to that parliament.

Several organizations representing the Mapuche are coordinated by the Mapuche Interregional Council. Since 1993, the Mapuche have been a member of the Unrepresented Nations and Peoples Organization (UNPO) in the Hague.

See also Unrepresented Nations and Peoples Organization
Reference Faron, Louis. *Mapuche Indians of Chile* (1986).

Mari El

Mari El, a republic within the Russian Federation, is bordered by the Volga River on the south, the republic of Chuvashia to the west, and Tatarstan to the south. Mari El has a population of 765,000, of which 47 percent is Russian, which means Russians are the largest ethnic group. Tatars are the third-largest group with 6 percent of the population. The Mari, a largely rural people, are divided into Mountain and Meadow Mari and account for 43 percent of the people. An additional 350,000 Mari—nearly as many as reside in the republic—live in other areas of the federation. They speak a Finno-Ugric language with Russian and Turkic influences. Most Mari speak

Russian and belong to the Russian Orthodox Church. In 1920, Mari El became an autonomous district within the Soviet Union; in 1991, it became a republic within the Russian Federation.

Mari Ushen (Union of the Mari People), founded in 1990, promotes the Mari language and culture. Oshmari Chimari (White Mari Are True Believers), led by the writer A. Uzikan, calls for a revival of the ancient pagan religion of the people. A more nationalist movement, Kugeze Mlande (Land of Our Fathers), formed in 1990, calls for the separation of Mari El from Russia and strict laws against non-Mari immigrants.

See also Russian Federation.
References Kolga, Margus, et al., eds. *Red Book of the Peoples of the Russian Empire* (1993); Mastyugina, Tatiana, and Lev Perelkin. *An Ethnic History of Russia* (1996).

Martinique

One of five overseas departments *(departements d'outre mer)* of France, Martinique is a Caribbean island with a population that is largely of African descent. A French possession since 1635, the social divisions on the island reflect its history as a plantation society. The large landowners are white, most professionals are light-skinned mulattoes, and blacks make up the lower classes. A policy of assimilation culminated in 1946 when Martinique became an integral part of France, and its inhabitants were granted the same political and legal status as other French citizens.

Originally, the policy of "departmentalism" was supported by all political groups including the Communist Party, which dominated island politics after World War II. Indeed, it was opposed only by the white minority, which feared it would lose its dominant position in society. However, since the 1960s there has been an increase in pro-autonomy and separatist sentiments. In 1958, Aimé Césaire split from the Communist Party and formed the Parti Progressiste Martiniquais (PPM, Martinican Progressive Party), which stands for a recognition of the distinctive characteristics of Martinique society and an in-

creased degree of self-government. The Communist Party of Martinique (its slogan is, To live, work, and decide for ourselves in our own country) similarly favors autonomy rather than independence.

Pro-independence groups include the Socialist Revolution Group, which advocates a united Antillean republic; Workers Fight; the Martinique Independence Movement; and the Martinique Patriots. Until recently, parties advocating independence have done poorly in the legislative elections, receiving between 2 and 3 percent of the total vote, but there are indications that pro-separatist attitudes may be on the increase. In the 1992 elections for the regional council, the Martinique Independence Movement, under its charismatic leader Alfred Marie-Jeanne, got 16 percent of the vote.

The low level of support can be explained by two factors. First, as a result of generations of assimilationist educational policy, many Martinicans think of themselves as black Frenchmen. Indeed, in a 1964 speech, Charles de Gaulle cried out, *"Mon Dieu, mon Dieu, comme vous êtes français!"* ("my God, my God, how French you are!"). Not until the 1930s, did "négritude" emerge as a literary movement—tracing the roots of West Indian identity and culture to Africa, not France. Second, the provision of social services and the expansion of civil service jobs has given Martinique a much higher standard of living than its neighbors. Just before the 1981 presidential elections, a flood of checks for family allowances, agricultural subsidies, and hurricane relief served to remind voters of the benefits of French citizenship.

Contemporary grievances include a high rate of unemployment (32 percent in 1990) and the fact that many high-level government jobs are held by metropolitan French rather than locals. In 1959, racial tensions erupted in rioting, but significantly, the riots were directed against metropolitans rather than local whites. Cars containing whites were stopped, and if they spoke creole (thus showing that they were native-born residents), they were left unharmed while whites who could not speak creole were assaulted. Clashes between striking workers and French gendarmes have resulted in several deaths and have generated anti-French feelings. In the 1960s, members of the Anticolonialist Organization of Martinican Youth were tried for "acts against the unity of the national territory." In 1983–1984, the Caribbean Revolutionary Army bombed the U.S. consulate, a television station, a courthouse, a shopping center, and a police post.

See also Césaire, Aimé.
References Burton, Richard D., ed., *French and West Indian* (1995); Miles, William S. *Elections and Ethnicity in French Martinique* (1986).

Matanzima, Kaiser (1915–)

Kaiser Matanzima was the head of the black homeland of Transkei in South Africa for many years. The Transkei became self-governing in 1963 and independent in 1976. In the early 1960s, Matanzima was the target of several assassination attempts by guerrillas belonging to the Pan-African Congress (PAC) because of his willingness to participate in the new Bantu Authorities system of local government for the black population. As a Xhosa nationalist, Matanzima did not object to the division of South Africa along ethnic lines, and he initially linked independence for the Transkei to a transfer of several "white" areas to the new state. His Transkei National Independence Party (TNIP), advocating a policy of separate development, won only fifteen of the elected seats in the first elections to the Transkei legislative assembly compared to the twenty-nine seats won by the anti-apartheid Democratic Party. However, the support of the nonelected chiefs resulted in a victory for Matanzima, and in subsequent elections, a combination of patronage and repression gave the TNIP a majority of the elected seats.

Although widely denounced as collaborating with the apartheid regime, Matanzima used the autonomy granted Transkei to make changes that were contrary to the policies favored by the South African government. One of his first acts was to replace the hated Bantu education policy, whereby black children had been instructed in their tribal languages, with English-language instruction. Bars, restaurants, hotels, and other facilities were desegregated. White traders and officials were replaced by blacks, and in less than two decades after independence, the number of black officials had grown from 2,000 to 20,000. The Xhosa Development Corporation (later the Transkei Development Corporation) took over white businesses and made loans to black businesses. Corruption was widespread, and Kaiser Matanzima and his brother, George, ended up with a financial stake in many enterprises, including hotels and farms.

Popular resistance to Matanzima increased after 1980, with sporadic terrorism by African National Congress and PAC guerrillas as well as widespread disturbances in schools and colleges. In 1980, Matanzima's daughter and the son of the minister of justice were expelled from college for dissident political activities.

In 1985, Matanzima retired and was succeeded by his brother; in September 1987, George Matanzima was deposed by a military coup. After the coup it was claimed that the Matanzima brothers had embezzled almost $25 million from public funds.

See also Black Homelands; Transkei.
References Carter, Gwendolyn, Thomas Karis, and Newell M. Stultz. *South Africa's Transkei: The Politics of Domestic Colonialism* (1967); Southall, Roger. *South Africa's Transkei: The Political Economy of an "Independent" Bantustan* (1983).

Mauritania

Named for the Moors, an Arabic-speaking people of mixed Berber and Arab stock, Mauritania is situated on the northwestern coast of Africa. The population of over 1 million is divided between the Moors (over 80 percent) who inhabit the arid north and the black minorities who live in the Senegal River valley in the south. Historically, the blacks were slaves, and there is considerable mistrust and ill feeling between the two groups. Blacks regard the Moors as lazy, and the Moors consider themselves racially superior. This ethnic division was initially reflected in a political cleavage between those who advocated a greater Morocco and those who wanted Mauritania to be part of a black sub-Saharan federation.

Beginning in 1956, northern Mauritania was under attack by the Armée de Libération, which aimed at reconstituting a greater Morocco "from Tangier to the shores of the Senegal River." The Front National de Libération Mauritanien was set up in Morocco by Horma Ould Babana as the political wing of the insurgents, but joint action by the French and Spanish crushed the forces of the Armée de Libération in early 1958.

After gaining independence in 1960, the first president, Moktar Ould Daddah, attempted to create a government of national unity by including representatives of all political positions. His first cabinet included both the leading advocate of Moroccan irredentism and the leader of the Bloc Democratique du Gorgol, a black party opposed to any link with Morocco. He refused to consider political or economic federation with any state. When pro-Moroccan extremists caused disorders in the capital city of Nouakchott in 1962, the president purged the administration of suspected sympathizers, and several "terrorists" were executed. In 1966, when new regulations made Arabic the official language of instruction, protests by the black minority escalated into riots in which six persons were killed and scores were wounded. Ould Daddah forbade any discussion of "racial" problems, and several black leaders were arrested for creating discord between the two groups.

In 1970, the Organization of African Unity helped to arrange an agreement between Morocco and Mauritania whereby Morocco gave up its territorial claims to Mauritania. Subsequently, in late 1975, the two countries annexed the former Spanish Sahara (now Western Sahara).

See also Western Sahara.
References Gerteiny, Alfred G. *Mauritania* (1967); Watson, J. H. "Mauritania: Problems and Prospects" (1963).

Maya of Guatemala

The Maya are an indigenous people with twenty-one ethnic and linguistic communities. Because of the disruption caused by the Guatemalan civil war (1960–1996) and the remoteness of many of the Mayan mountain settlements, Guatemalan census figures are only estimates. It is believed that the Maya in Guatemala constitute between 45 percent and 65 percent of the total population of about 12 million. Further compounding the census problem is that the government does not officially recognize any nationality but Guatemalan. Also, assimilation by urban Maya into the developing economy lowers the number of citizens who identify themselves as Mayan. Although a growing number of Maya, particularly in urban areas, speak Spanish, a preponderance of rural Maya speak only their native dialect. Periodically, the Guatemalan government has attempted to suppress the native culture and force the adoption of Spanish, which remains the only official language, throughout the country.

The widespread poverty found among the rural Maya along with the political, economic, and military dominance of European and mestizo elites led many Mayan peasants to support leftist guerrillas in their struggle against the government. Although the rebel military bands that united to form the Guatemalan National Unity in order to negotiate a peace settlement had primarily a leftist political and economic agenda, their goals also included demands for increasing the rights of the Mayan people. The peace settlement, signed in December 1996, called for a national plebiscite on more than fifty constitutional amendments, many of them aimed at raising the security and status of the Maya. The amendments would have restricted the army's role as an internal police force; formally redefined Guatemala as a multiethnic, multicultural, and multilingual society; and granted official status to the Mayan languages. On May 17, 1999, all the amendments were voted on and went down to defeat. Only 18.5 percent of registered voters participated in the balloting, and the low turnout and low support for the measures among Mayan voters was ascribed to a lack of voter information in the native languages, apathy and fatalism caused by war fatigue and poverty, and weak political organization among the Maya.

The Maya are represented by many groups whose views are channeled through an umbrella organization, the Coalition of Mayan People's Organizations. Attempts have been made in recent years to increase contacts between the Guatemalan Maya and the Zapatistas, the Mayan guerrilla army in Chiapas, Mexico.

See also Zapatista National Liberation Army
Reference Carmack, Roger, ed. *Harvest of Violence: The Maya Indians and the Guatemalan Crisis* (1992).

Mebyon Kernow

Mebyon Kernow (literally, "sons of Cornwall") is a political party advocating Cornish independence. The people of Cornwall, a county in southwestern England, originally spoke a Celtic language similar to those spoken in Brittany and Wales, but the Cornish language became extinct in the nineteenth century. Throughout the medieval period, Cornwall remained distinct from the rest of England and several times rebelled against rule from London. Mebyon Kernow has contested most British parliamentary elections since 1970, and in the 1997 elections, the party ran candidates for five of the six Cornish seats and received between 0.4 and 1.1 percent of the vote. The party achieved its greatest success in 1979 when it obtained 5.9 percent of the vote in the Cornwall and Plymouth constituency in elections for the European Parliament.

Despite the lack of electoral support for Mebyon Kernow, there are indications that a sense of Cornish identity is growing. A telephone poll taken by the *Western Morning News* in June 1996 found that a majority of the people surveyed favored "home rule." In 1997, the newly founded Cornish Solidarity Movement organized a protest march from Cornwall to London to protest the county's high unemployment and to lobby for increased economic aid from the European Economic Community. Many Cornish people also resent the incorporation of their county into a newly created Southwestern Region. Cornish Solidarity has carried out several symbolic protests such as "closing the border" between Cornwall and Devon by blocking the Tamar Bridge between the two counties.

Reference Anthony, Andrew. "Passport to Padstow" (1999).

Meech Lake Accord

The Meech Lake accord of 1987 was an attempt to keep Quebec from separating from the rest of Canada. Originally, Canada's constitution and the supreme law of the land was the British North America Act of 1867. This meant that any proposed changes to the Canadian constitution had to be formally submitted to the British Parliament. Prior to the Quebec sovereignty referendum of 1980, Pierre Trudeau, the Canadian prime minister, promised Quebec voters that there would be a "renewed federalism," which was widely understood to mean increased powers for Quebec. In October 1980, three months after the referendum, he announced plans to repatriate the constitution—that is, write a new document that would be entirely Canadian. However, under the new 1982 constitution, Quebec lost its traditional right to veto any amendments to the constitution, and the Charter of Rights was seen as an infringement of provincial authority. Quebec therefore rejected the constitution, the only province to do so.

In an attempt to resolve Quebec's objections, lengthy negotiations between the provincial premiers and the newly elected prime minister, Brian Mulroney, resulted in the Meech Lake accord. According to this accord, Quebec was recognized as a "distinct society," guaranteed disproportionate representation on the Supreme Court and in the Senate, and given the right to opt out of certain national programs. However, opposition began to build against the agreement, and after the provinces of Newfoundland and Manitoba failed to ratify it, the accord died. Even though a new agreement, the Charlestown accord, was approved in 1990, the constitutional debates revealed the deep gulf between Quebec's aspirations and those of English Canada.

See also Quebec; Western Canadian Separatism.
Reference Fournier, Paul. *A Meech Lake Post-Mortem* (1991).

Meskhetian Georgians

The Meskhetians are Georgian Muslims expelled by Joseph Stalin from the Republic of Georgia in 1944 because of their alleged pro-Turkish sympathies. Some 200,000 were resettled in central Asia. In 1956, Nikita Khrushchev admitted Stalin's errors and permitted exiled groups such as the Chechens, Ingush, and Balkhars to return to their homelands. The Meskhetians, however, were reclassified as Turkish and not permitted to return to Georgia. Many resettled in Azerbaijan and, after being driven out of Uzbekistan, in the Krasnodar region of the Russian Federation. Russian officials there have resented their presence and refused to give them residence permits.

Salvation, a Meskhetian activist group, has pushed for repatriation to Georgia. In the late 1980s, Salvation allied itself with the party of Georgian president Zviad Gamsakhurdia that was later ousted. Gamsakhurdia's rival and now president, Edvard Shevardnadze, has been reluctant to approve any large-scale resettlement of Meskhetians. In addition to being embroiled in secessionist struggles in Abkhazia and South Ossetia, the Georgian government also fears creating a Turkish separatist movement within its own borders. Followers of late president Gamsakhurdia also continue to launch terrorist attacks against Shevardnadze. Armenians and Georgians, now settled on former Meskhetian land, are also adamantly opposed to their return. Salvation has appealed to the Organization for Security and Cooperation in Europe and to Turkey for assistance with its cause.

See also Georgia.
References Fuller, Liz. *Georgian Meskhetians Remain Homeless* (1998); Sheehy, Ann, and Bohdan Nahaylo. *The Crimean Tatars, Volga Germans, and Meskhetians* (1980).

Milosevic, Slobodan (1941–)

Slobodan Milosevic, the president of the Federal Republic of Yugoslavia, was born on August 20, 1941, in Pozarevac, Serbia. His father was an Orthodox priest and his mother a schoolteacher and Communist activist. Milosevic received a law degree from the University of Belgrade in 1964 and then worked in industry and banking. He was the president of Tehnogas, a large industrial complex in Belgrade and went on to become director of Beobanka, one of Yugoslavia's largest banks.

A former leader of the Communist Party, Milosevic helped found the Serbian Socialist Party in 1987 and remains the president of that party. In 1990, in the first post-Communist elections, Milosevic was elected president of Serbia. He was reelected in 1992. Constitutionally prohibited from running for a third term, Milosevic announced his candidacy for president of Yugoslavia. In July 1997, he was elected to that office by the two houses of parliament of the federal republic.

Long considered the instigator of the use of military force in Bosnia and Croatia to create a greater Serbia, Milosevic is also credited with suppressing the majority Albanian population of Kosovo. Milosevic undoubtedly helped bankroll the Balkan wars and permitted the use of the Yugoslavian armed forces and their arsenals in combat in Bosnia and Croatia. Only after a UN economic embargo imposed on Serbia and Montenegro in 1992 led to great hardship did Milosevic withdraw from aiding the Serbian combatants in Bosnia. In order to have the embargo lifted, Milosevic signed the Dayton peace accord in 1995, which brought about a cease-fire in Bosnia and ended Serbia's immediate hopes of annexing Bosnian territory.

In signing the Dayton peace accord, Milosevic forfeited his leadership of the greater Serbian cause. Biljana Plavsic, president of Bosnian Serbia,

Slobodan Milosevic outside the Yugoslav Parliament in Belgrade after being sworn in as president, July 23, 1997. (Reuters/Petar Kunjundzic/Archive Photos)

called his actions a sellout of the Serbian people. In Serbia itself, Milosevic's party, the Serbian Socialist Party, has been strongly challenged by the ultranationalist Vojislav Seselji and his Serbian Radical Party. Seselji would abrogate the Dayton peace accord and continue with the goal of establishing a greater Serbia.

Milosevic's power is also eroding in the Yugoslav co-republic of Montenegro. In the 1997 presidential elections the pro-Milosevic candidate, incumbent president Momir Bulatovic, was defeated by Milo Djukanovic, who had called for greater independence for Montenegro. In 1998, to retaliate against Montenegro, Milosevic engineered Bulatovic's installation as prime minister of the federation, replacing Djukanovic's ally, the Montenegrin Radoje Kontic. Montenegro refused to recognize the action.

In 1998, a full-scale insurrection broke out in Kosovo. Milosevic refused to grant any concessions to the Albanians. His refusal led to an uprising by the Albanians, spearheaded by the Kosovo Liberation Army. After negotiations with NATO broke down, Milosevic unleashed the Yugoslav army on the Kosovars, killing thousands and driving nearly a million refugees into neighboring Albania and Macedonia. In June 1999, following three months of NATO bombing, Milosevic withdrew his troops from Kosovo. In the same month, he was indicted as an international war criminal.

Although he remains in control of the army, police, and media, Milosevic's popularity has dwindled in the face of the great destruction wrought by NATO bombs. The patriarch of the Serbian Orthodox Church has called for Milosevic's resignation, and there have been mass rallies against his leadership. Nevertheless, the domestic political opposition remains fragmented, and Milosevic has shown a remarkable ability to survive similar setbacks in the past.

See also Bosnia and Herzegovina; Dayton Peace Accord; Greater Albania; Greater Serbia; Kosovo; Plavsic, Biljana; Srpska; Yugoslavia.

Moldova

Moldova (or Moldavia), once part of the Moldavian kingdom of Stephen the Great (1457–1504), includes much of historic Bessarabia. The region came under Ottoman control in the sixteenth century, eastern Moldova became part of Russia in 1791, and all of Bessarabia was joined to Russia in 1812. The remaining western lands remained in Turkish hands, passing into Romanian control by 1878, and Romania seized eastern Moldova in 1918. In 1924, the USSR established the Moldovan Autonomous Soviet Socialist Republic on Ukrainian land with Tiraspol as its capital. In 1940, Romania was forced to cede Bessarabia to the USSR. After border readjustments with Ukraine, the Moldovan Soviet Socialist Republic, which now included Bessarabia, was established. During World War II, Romania recaptured the area but lost it to the Soviets in 1944. The present boundary between Romania and Moldova was ratified in 1947.

With communism collapsing in Eastern Europe, Moldova called for increased autonomy from the USSR. In 1991, it declared its independence. Moldova's population of 4.5 million is 65 percent Romanian, 13 percent Ukrainian, and 13 percent Russian. The remainder of the population is Gagauz (Christian Turks), Bulgarian, or gypsy.

Following independence, a movement advocating reunification with Romania was led by the Moldovan Popular Front. However, a 1994 referendum approved a new constitution that called for Moldova to remain an independent state. Parliamentary elections gave a majority to President Mircea Snegur's anti-unification Agrarian Democratic Party, but in the 1996 presidential election, Snegur was defeated by former Agrarian Party

parliamentary chairman, Petru Lucinski. Since taking office, Lucinski, a former Communist Party official, has sought closer ties with Russia and vowed to maintain Moldovan independence.

In 1992, the heavily Russian and Ukrainian population of the Transdniester region of Moldova rebelled against the Moldovan state, fearing that Moldova would unite with Romania to the detriment of the Moldovan Slavic population. Civil war broke out. Russian troops under General Aleksandr Lebed entered the territory and enforced a cease-fire. Negotiations conducted by Russia, Ukraine, and Moldova, later joined by the Organization for Security and Cooperation in Europe, resulted in a plan to grant significant freedom to Transdniester while maintaining the integrity of the Moldovan state.

Another source of ethnic strain in the new Moldovan state arose when the Gagauz, a Turkish minority living in southern Moldova, demanded autonomy. By late 1994, a compromise between the Gagauz and the Moldovan government had been reached that granted the Gagauz an autonomous status within the Moldovan state.

See also Gagauzia; Romania; Russians in Former Soviet Republics; Transdniester.
References Bruchis, Michael. *The Republic of Moldavia* (1996); Judah, Tim. *History, Myth, and the Destruction of Yugoslavia* (1997).

Mon

The first inhabitants of lower Burma (also known as Myanmar), the Mon, were conquered by the Burmans in 1057, and thousands of skilled captives were taken back to the Burmans' capital. Over the centuries, there was a high amount of intermarriage between the Burmans and the Mon, and many Mon have assimilated to the Burman culture. However, the fact that the Burmese word for the Mon is *talaing,* which literally means "bastard," may indicate that relations have not always been completely harmonious.

Along with the Karen, the Mon People's Front (MPF) rose up in 1949 seeking independence, but the insurgency was quickly contained, and in

1958, the MPF laid down its arms in return for a promise that an autonomous Mon state would be established. However, after the military seized power in 1962, General Ne Win declared that since the Mon and the Burmans had intermarried so much there was no need for a separate Mon state. Armed struggle was therefore resumed in 1963, and currently, the Mon National Liberation Army, with an estimated 3,000 combatants, controls a small liberated zone on the Thailand border.

See also Burma.
Reference Fredholm, Michael. *Burma: Ethnicity and Insurgency* (1993).

Mongolians

Mongolians speak an Altaic language and are generally Buddhist. Part of an extensive empire forged by Genghis Khan in the twelfth and thirteenth centuries, Mongols today are widely dispersed throughout central Asia. The Russian Federation republics of Kalmykia and Buryatia together have a Mongol population exceeding 600,000, and the second-largest Mongol community is found in the Republic of Mongolia. That republic, also referred to as Outer Mongolia, is located between China and the Russian Federation and has a population of about 2 million. Inner Mongolia, the Inner Mongolian Autonomous Region of China (or Nei Monggol), is home to 4.5 million Mongolians.

From the sixteenth century until the twentieth, much of Inner and Outer Mongolia was under the control of the Manchu dynasty of China. Following the Chinese revolution of 1911, Outer Mongolia gained a degree of autonomy but gradually fell under Russian domination. In 1924, it was declared a people's republic and, until 1991, remained closely tied to the Soviet Union. Inner Mongolia remained under Chinese control, and when the Communists took over the government in 1949, Inner Mongolia became an autonomous region of the People's Republic of China. The Chinese government recognized the independence of the Republic of Mongolia, and in return, the latter accepted Inner Mongolia as an integral part of China. What this has meant is that, throughout much of recent history, the Republic of Mongolia has taken no official actions encouraging Mongolian unification.

In the twentieth century, there have been several movements calling for the unification of the two Mongolias. In 1911, a conference held in Ulan Bator called for the joining of the two territories. Another conference of Mongolian nationalists, held in Gegin in 1945, called for unification and also issued a Declaration of Inner Mongolian Liberation. This and other independence statements were rejected by both the Soviet Union and the Republic of Mongolia.

From 1949 on, the Chinese Communist government has pursued a policy of Sinicizing Inner Mongolia, in part by encouraging the migration of ethnic Chinese into the area. By 1998, nearly 80 percent of the population was Chinese. In 1957, under Prime Minister Zhou Enlai, the Chinese began restricting the use of Mongolian in the public schools, and the Cultural Revolution (1966–1976) led to widespread persecution of Mongolian nationalists and religious leaders. Temples were closed and desecrated, and the Inner Mongolian People's Revolutionary Party was brutally suppressed. In 1981, students conducted a series of demonstrations and strikes, but these were ineffective in changing China's policies. In 1990, Han became the mandatory language of primary and secondary schools, and during 1991–1995, several human rights activists were imprisoned. In 1996, Liu Mingyu, the Communist Party secretary of Inner Mongolia, denounced "ethnic splitists" in the region and accused them of being linked to hostile Western forces. Sporadic resistance to China's policy continues in Inner Mongolia while expatriate organizations based in the United States and Western Europe agitate for minority rights in China. The Southern Mongolian Freedom Foundation demands the unification of the two Mongolias.

See also Buryatia; China's Nationality Policy; Kalmykia; Russian Federation.

References Bulag, Uradyn. *Nationalism and Hybridity in Mongolia* (1998); Lai, David. *Land of Genghis Khan: The Rise and Fall of Nation-States in China's Northern Frontier* (1995).

Montagnards

French Indochina, which included what is now Vietnam, Laos, and Cambodia, was divided into two distinct regions. The densely populated lowlands are occupied by the Vietnamese, Laotians, and Khmer while the mountain ranges running from north to south are inhabited by tribal groups, which the French referred to as "Montagnards." The most important of these are the Hmong, Rhade, Bahner, Cham, and Hre, and together they make up about 10 percent of the population of Vietnam. Although divided into over forty groups speaking more than a dozen languages, French policies, such as recruiting the Montagnards into special units of the colonial army, gradually produced a common sense of identity among them. This was reinforced by Vietnamese encroachment on their traditional lands.

After World War II, the French attempted to reassert control over Vietnam and to defeat the Communist Viet-Minh forces. In order to do this, the French exploited ethnic and regional divisions within Vietnam and, as part of this strategy, set up a special region comprising the five Montagnard provinces in 1946. In 1950, this became the Southern Montagnard Region, with a statute that guaranteed the special status of the Montagnards and protected their languages, traditions, and customary laws. The French also created a number of Montagnard special force units, led by French officers, to fight the Viet-Minh.

After the Geneva accords of 1954, the French withdrew, and Vietnam was divided into the (Communist) Democratic Republic of Vietnam in the north and South Vietnam. The South Vietnamese regime, under Ngo Dinh Diem, abolished the autonomous Southern Montagnard Region, encouraged Vietnamese settlement in the central highlands, and tried to eradicate local cultures and languages. The Montagnards naturally ob-

jected to these policies and formed an organization, Bajaraka, that called for autonomy for the central highlands. Diem responded by imprisoning the Bajaraka leadership.

The U.S. military—like the French before it—organized Montagnard troops into special guerrilla units to fight the Communists. Some of these Montagnard troops rebelled against the South Vietnamese in September 1964, seizing control of four military bases and killing at least seventy South Vietnamese soldiers. The rebels then fled to Cambodia, which had played a major role in organizing the rebellion. An organization calling itself the Unified Front for the Struggle of Oppressed Races (FULRO) claimed that the South Vietnamese government was engaged in genocide against the ethnic minorities, the Montagnards, Cham, and Khmer. FULRO later called for the return of the Mekong delta region to the Khmer and central Vietnam to the Montagnards and the Cham. In actuality, the rebel leaders had more limited demands, essentially a return to the semiautonomous status they had enjoyed in the early 1950s.

As the Vietnamese conflict continued, the central highlands became the site of fierce fighting between the North Vietnamese and the Americans, and this fighting devastated Montagnard society. After the defeat of South Vietnam in 1976, the victorious North Vietnamese reneged on their earlier promises to respect ethnic minority rights, and throughout the 1980s, there were reports of clashes between Communist troops and FULRO guerrillas.

References Christie, Clive J. *A Modern History of Southeast Asia* (1996); Evans, Grant, and Kevin Rowley. *Red Brotherhood at War: Indochina since the Fall of Saigon* (1984).

Montenegro

Settled by Slavs in the seventh century, the people of Montenegro are closely related to Serbians, being Orthodox Christians, speaking the Serbian dialect of Serbo-Croatian, and using the Cyrillic alphabet. Serbian nationalists like Slobodan

Milosevic are adamant that Montenegrins are Serbians. However, Montenegro's history, though often intertwined with that of Serbia, has run a distinctive course and has its own revered cultural figures and political heroes. Traditionally deferential to the post-Tito Serbian dominance of Yugoslavia, Montenegro since 1992 has grown disenchanted with its role in the third Yugoslavia. The 1997 election of the centralization-minded Slobodan Milosevic as president of Yugoslavia only fueled popular sentiment for an independent Montenegro.

Although nominally under either Turkish or Serbian control for much of the period from the seventh through the nineteenth centuries, Montenegrins, because they inhabited a mountainous terrain and were governed by strong local feudal relations, were able to maintain a high degree of autonomy from outside powers. In 1878, the Congress of Vienna recognized the independence of Montenegro. Following World War I and the introduction of Serbian troops into Montenegro, King Nicholas I (1910–1918) was overthrown. Montenegro was then annexed to Serbia and absorbed into the Kingdom of Serbs, Croats, and Slovenes, which was renamed Yugoslavia in 1929. During World War II, Montenegro, with its impoverished peasant society, gave significant support to Josip Broz Tito's partisans, and when the postwar Communist Yugoslavian federation was created, Montenegro was recognized as one of the six constituent republics. In 1991, after the disintegration of socialist Yugoslavia, Montenegro, still governed by Titoists, chose to remain with Serbia in the third Yugoslavia.

When the 1991 conflict broke out over the secession of Slovenia, Croatia, and Bosnia from the socialist Yugoslavian state, Montenegro actively supported attacks on Croatia and Bosnia and participated in the "ethnic cleansing" of Muslims and Croats in Bosnia and within its own borders. The Montenegrin government has also dealt harshly with Albanian separatists living in Montenegro.

UN sanctions imposed on the third Yugoslavia, because of its involvement in the Bosnian war, eventually led to severe economic hardships in Montenegro and a growing resentment toward Serbia. In an assertion of Montenegrin autonomy, a Montenegrin Orthodox Church was reestablished, separating believers from the control of the Serbian patriarch. Serbia denounced the move as a provocation. Politically, by 1993 a new political party, the Liberal Alliance, was calling for Montenegrin independence and gaining support against the pro-Serb Democratic Party of Socialists, the successor to the Montenegrin League of Communists. The Democratic Party of Socialists itself soon split along pro-Serbian and nationalist lines.

The Montenegrin president, Momir Bulatovic, was accused of being subservient to Slobodan Milosevic, the new Yugoslav president, and in the 1997 Montenegrin presidential elections, Bulatovic was opposed by the independence-leaning, Western-oriented prime minister, Milo Djukanovic, who argued that Bulatovic's government had hindered Montenegro's reentry into the international economic community and had impeded democratic reforms. In the election held in November, Djukanovic defeated Bulatovic.

Even though Montenegro had been controlled by the pro-Serb president Bulatovic, as prime minister, Djukanovic had successfully undertaken several foreign policy moves to assert Montenegro's autonomy as an independent republic in the rump Yugoslav state. In retaliation, Milosevic nationalized the Yugoslavian army, incorporating Montenegrin units into a Yugoslav army controlled by Serbian officers. Milosevic's election as president of Yugoslavia and statements that he intended to revise the constitution—which currently gives Montenegrins great power in the upper house—further fed separatist inclinations in Montenegro.

In 1998, in an attempt to assert his dominance in the federation, Milosevic engineered the election of Momir Bulatovic as prime minister of the Yugoslavian state—Djukanovic's ally, fellow Montenegrin Radoje Kontic, was voted out of office. Montenegro has refused to accept the change.

Djukanovic, although denying that he seeks to detach Montenegro from Yugoslavia, continues to seek economic and political ties with Western Europe without deferring to Belgrade. When Milosevic took military action against Kosovo in 1998, Djukanovic refused to allow Montenegrin soldiers to serve in combat with the Yugoslav army.

During NATO's air strikes against Yugoslavia in March 1999, military targets in Montenegro were bombed. This caused an upsurge in pro-Milosevic sentiment and undermined, at least in the short run, the popularity of the Djukanovic government. Although NATO warned Milosevic not to attempt to oust the Montenegrin government, rumors of possible coups were widespread.

In the long run, Montenegro's relatively small size—it has only 6 percent of the Yugoslav population—and the fact that it controls Serbia's only outlet to the sea, make it highly improbable that Serbia would allow Montenegro to peacefully depart the federation, at least as long as Milosevic controls Yugoslavia.

See also Greater Serbia; Milosevic, Slobodan; Yugoslavia.
Reference Boehm, Christopher. *Montenegrin Social Organization and Values* (1983).

Mordovian Republic

The Mordovian Republic lies in the west-central part of the Russian Federation on the Volga River. Of a population of 962,000, Russians account for 60 percent; Tatars, 5 percent; and Mordovians, 32 percent. Mordovians are made up of two groups, the Erzyan and the Mokshan. Each speaks a distinct Finno-Ugric dialect, and they are largely Russian Orthodox. Mordovians are the third-largest Finno-Ugric group in the world. Although 300,000 Mordovians live within the republic, another 800,000 live in other regions of the Russian Federation.

Mordovia (or Modvinia) was established as a national area *(okrug)* of the USSR in 1928. In 1930, it became an autonomous district, and in 1934, it achieved the status of an autonomous re-public. Following the collapse of the Soviet Union in 1991, Mordovia was granted republic status within the Russian Federation.

Mastorova (Mother Earth Society), has demanded that the president of the republic speak a Mordovian language. The society meets periodically in an all-Russian Congress of Mordovian People, and the Congress is seeking recognition from the federal government as a legitimate legislative body. Mordovian activists are divided between adherents of "one Mordovia" and Erzyan and Mokshan separatists. Mastorava has received its strongest support from students at Mordovian State University where several independence rallies have occurred.

See also Russian Federation.
References Kolga, Margus, et al., eds. *Red Book of the Peoples of the Russian Empire* (1993); Mastyugina, Tatiana, and Lev Perelkin. *An Ethnic History of Russia* (1996).

Moro National Liberation Front

The Moro National Liberation Front (MNLF) was the most important organization involved in the Moro insurgency of 1972–1996 in the southern Philippines. It was led by Nur Misuari, a political scientist at the University of Manila; Hashim Salamat, a Muslim cleric; and Abul Alonto, a local politician. The three leaders were from the largest Muslim ethnic groups: the Tausug, Maguindanao, and Maranao. Several factions split from the MNLF after 1977, the most important being the Bangsa Moro Liberation Organization and the Moro Islamic Liberation Front. (The splits were largely explained by traditional tribal rivalries, with each faction being supported by one of the main tribes.)

The MNLF proclaimed that its ideology was Islamic socialist and carefully avoided any links with the Communist guerrillas of the New People's Army. The MNLF argued that between the Moros "and the Christian Filipino people there is an irreconcilable contradiction which no human contrivance can permanently resolve. The only solution is our separation into two distinct and separate political entities." The negotiating position of the MNLF changed over time. Its original demand was an independent homeland of twenty-one provinces, but in the Tripoli Agreement of 1976 between the MNLF and the Philippine government, it accepted an autonomous Moro state within the Philippines that included only thirteen provinces. However, even in those thirteen provinces, Muslims formed a majority in only five, and in the area as a whole, Christians outnumbered Muslims three to two.

See also Moros.

References George, T. J. S. *Revolt in Mindanao* (1980); McKenna, Thomas M. *Muslim Rulers and Rebels* (1998).

Moros

The Spanish conquest of the Philippines in the sixteenth century was strenuously resisted by the Muslims who were spreading throughout the Sulu archipelago and Mindanao at the same time. The sultan of Sulu only recognized Spanish sovereignty in 1876, and the defiant resistance of the Muslims led to their being labeled Moros (or Moors) by the Spaniards. When the United States took over the islands in 1898, it, in turn, had to send several military expeditions to subdue the Moros, and the region was not pacified until 1914.

The Moros constitute between 5 and 6 percent of the total population of the Philippines, and even in the southern region they are a minority in all but a few provinces. The Moros are divided into at least ten linguistic subgroups, with the most important being the Maranao, the Maguindanao, and the Tausug. The cultural distinctions between the Moros and the Christian majority, for whom Catholicism is an integral part of the Filipino identity, set the two peoples apart.

The Moros enjoyed a de facto autonomy until the late 1960s, with traditional Muslim leaders representing the community in the national legislature and being in charge of local administration. However, under the increasingly authoritarian rule of Ferdinand Marcos, this uneasy political equilibrium began to break down. At the same time, an Islamic resurgence was taking place among the Moros, with teachers from Arab countries playing an increased role in Muslim education. A large number of intellectuals went to al-Azhar, the famous Islamic university in Cairo, and returned to create a new and outspoken Muslim elite. More important, the Moros were threatened by a massive immigration of Christian Filipinos into the region.

Land disputes between settlers and Moros escalated in the early 1970s, and Christian-Muslim feuds led to a general breakdown of law and order and over 1,000 killed. In September 1972, martial law was declared in the region, precipitating a separatist insurgency led by the Moro National Liberation Front. The insurgents received large supplies of weapons from the nearby Malaysian state of Sabah, whose leader was a devout Muslim with family ties to the Moros. Libya not only furnished the Moros with arms and financial aid but was also the MNLF's main diplomatic supporter, calling upon Islamic countries to sever diplomatic and trade ties with the Philippines.

The guerrilla forces reached a maximum strength of 30,000–50,000 in 1975 before declining. An estimated 50,000 people were killed in the fighting, but the level of violence began to wane in 1976, and a cease-fire was declared in December. However, the autonomy promised to the Moros never materialized, and fighting resumed in 1977. Over the next few years, tribal rivalries among the Moros further weakened the rebels. President Corazon Aquino attempted to resolve the conflict through negotiations that lasted from 1986 to 1987, but the talks deadlocked over the details of the autonomy plan. In September 1996, President Fidel Ramos and Nur Misuari, the leader of the MNLF, signed a final peace accord ending the twenty-four-year-long insurgency. Under the terms of the accord, Misuari became governor of the four-province region of Muslim Mindanao and head of the Southern Philippines Council for Peace and Development with jurisdiction over thirteen provinces.

See also Moro National Liberation Front; Sabah.

References George, T. J. S. *Revolt in Mindanao* (1980); Heraclides, Alexis. *The Self-Determination of Minorities in International Politics* (1991); McKenna, Thomas M. *Muslim Rulers and Rebels* (1998).

Moskitia

Moskitia is the homeland of the Miskito Indians of Nicaragua. The struggle for autonomy by the indigenous population is rooted in the cultural and racial differences between the Spanish-speaking mestizo majority and the English-speaking Indians of the Caribbean coast. In the seventeenth century, the British formed an alliance with the Miskitos against the Spaniards, and a British protectorate was established over the region. In the nineteenth century, Britain recognized Nicaragua's sovereignty, but the treaty also acknowledged the Miskitos' right to self-government.

After the Sandinista revolution of 1979, conflicts soon developed between the Marxist Sandinistas and the Miskitos. In part, the problem resulted from cultural insensitivity on the part of the Sandinistas; for example, a literacy campaign was originally conducted in Spanish, and it was not until after protests had been made that English and Miskito were used instead. More serious was the dispute over indigenous land rights. Misurasata, the organization representing the Indians, asserted that "the right of indigenous nations over the territory of their community is preferential to the territorial rights of states" and went on to claim most of the Atlantic coast region. The Sandinistas held that the state had the exclusive right to determine land ownership and rejected any unique status for indigenous groups.

In February 1981, the Sandinistas arrested the entire leadership of Misurasata. Thousands of Miskitos fled to Honduras and, under the leadership of Steadman Fagoth, formed a guerrilla group, Misura. That group allied itself with the CIA-backed contras, who were waging a war against the Sandinistas in Nicaragua, who responded by relocating large numbers of Miskitos to government camps. In 1984, the Sandinistas and Misurasata began negotiations, with Misurasata calling for an autonomous territory of Yapti Tasba, which would be virtually independent.

In 1987, an autonomy statute for the region was approved by the Nicaraguan legislature, and two autonomous regions, North Atlantic and South Atlantic, were created, each having an elected regional council with administrative powers and the ability to raise taxes. The northern region, centered on Puerto Cabezas, is the home of the Miskitos while the southern region, centered on Bluefields, is home to the creoles, a mixture of blacks and Indians. However, Spanish-speaking mestizos constitute a majority of the population in both areas. Communal ownership of land is recognized, and Miskito and English are official languages, along with Spanish, within the autonomous regions.

References Hannum, Hurst. *Autonomy, Sovereignty, and Self-Determination* (1990); Latin American Studies Association. *Peace and Autonomy on the Atlantic Coast of Nicaragua* (1986).

Mujahidin

Mujahidin means fighters of a jihad, a holy war in defense of Islam. The mujahidin include not only soldiers but all the faithful who support and give aid to the struggle—students, intellectuals, religious leaders, and noncombatants such as peasants and the elderly. A narrower use of the term refers specifically to armed bands who employ force in order to achieve their political-religious goals.

Mujahidin can be traced back to the time of Muhammad, and since the end of World War II, self-proclaimed mujahidin have made dramatic appearances in Palestine, Lebanon, Bosnia, Iran, Kashmir, Algeria, Chechnya, and Afghanistan as well as other Islamic areas. Other than a dedication to Islam, the causes and visions that motivate the mujahidin are as varied as the theological and sectarian divisions in Islam itself. Mujahidin may fight against secular governments, as in Tajikistan; outside forces occupying what is perceived to be Muslim territory, as in Palestine; or as in Afghanistan and Lebanon, against other mujahidin who are defined as heretical. Often a mujahidin's base of support is drawn from particular ethnic groups, which can lead, as in Afghanistan, to civil war between mujahidin from different communities. In Afghanistan, Tajik, Hazzara, and Pashtun mujahidin fought each other so fiercely the country was left in ruins after the Soviet occupiers had been driven from the country.

Each band usually recognizes the authority of a particular religious leader—an ayatollah or mullah—whose interpretation of sacred law is taken as a prescription for organizing an ideal Muslim state. In Afghanistan, for example, Mullah Muhammed Rabbani provides the spiritual and religious guidance by which the Taliban, the Pashtun mujahidin, is reorganizing Afghanistan's society.

See also Afghanistan; Lebanon; Palestine Liberation Organization; Taliban.
References Magnus, Ralph, and Eden Naby. *Afghanistan* (1998); Peters, Rudolph. *Jihad in Classical and Modern Islam* (1996).

Myanmar
See Burma

Nagaland

The Nagas of India, numbering about 500,000, live in the hill country borderlands between India and Burma. A tribal people, they are distinct from the general Indian population in race, religion, and language. They came under nominal British control in the early part of the nineteenth century but were administered separately from the rest of the province of Assam.

During the discussions over Indian independence, the Nagas argued that they should be granted the right to secede from the proposed Indian Union, but this idea was opposed by Jawaharlal Nehru, the leader of the Indian National Congress. On August 14, 1947 (the day before India became independent), the Naga National Council (NNC) declared the independence of the Nagas, but this declaration was ignored by the new Indian government. The NNC was invited to send representatives to the constituent assembly, which was drafting a new Indian constitution, but declined and again declared its desire for independence. In 1951, the NNC conducted a plebiscite in which the Nagas voted almost unanimously for independence, but in July 1952, Nehru dismissed the Naga demand as "completely unwise, impracticable and unacceptable."

The NNC then launched a civil disobedience campaign, to which the Indian government reacted by arresting the NNC leadership, abolishing the local tribal councils, and sending large numbers of police and soldiers into the region. Open warfare broke out in 1955, and on March 22, 1956, the NNC declared Nagaland to be a sovereign republic. The Indian army eventually crushed the rebels in a brutal campaign in which the Indian forces set fire to villages and engaged in widespread massacres and torture. Nehru also offered political concessions to the Nagas, and a Nagaland state was set up in 1963, with an area of 6,000 square miles and a population of 350,000. A cease-fire between the rebels and the Indian government was signed on May 24, 1964. The cease-fire was unilaterally terminated by the Indian government in September 1972, however,

following an assassination attempt on the chief minister of Nagaland.

See also India.
Reference Maxwell, Neville. *India, the Nagas, and the North-East* (1980).

Nagorno-Karabakh

Nagorno-Karabakh, a province largely inhabited by Armenians, was made a part of Azerbaijan in 1923 by the Soviet authorities. The province was physically separated from Armenia proper by a mountainous strip of land inhabited by Azerbaijanis. In 1988, Armenians in Nagorno-Karabakh revolted against Azeri rule, and by 1991, Armenia itself had joined the conflict. In 1994, Russia and the Organization for Security and Cooperation (OSCE) in Europe helped negotiate a cease-fire. At that time, Armenian forces held not only Nagorno-Karabakh but also the strip that separated it from Armenia as well as about 20 percent of Azerbaijan territory adjoining Nagorno-Karabakh.

Attempts by Russia and the OSCE to negotiate a return of Nagorno-Karabakh to Azerbaijan, but with the status of an autonomous republic, have been rebuffed by Armenia. In February 1998, Levon Ter-Petrosyan, the president of Armenia, was forced to resign after he advocated making concessions to Azerbaijan. He was succeeded by Robert Kocharian, a former president of the breakaway province and leader of Arakakh, the Nagorno-Karabakh independence party. He has pledged never to relinquish the territory and has also legalized the ultranationalist party, Dashnak—the Armenian all-national movement. Nagorno-Karabakh continues to function as the Republic of Nagorno-Karabakh with Arkady Gukasyan as its president.

See also Armenia; Azerbaijan.
References Carley, Patricia. *Nagorno-Karabakh: Searching for a Solution* (1998); Chorbaijian, Levon, Patrick Donabedian, and Claude Mutafian. *The Caucasian Knot: The History and Geopolitics of Nagorno-Karabagh* (1994); Croissant, Michael P. *The Armenian-Azerbaijan Conflict* (1998).

Narva and Petserimaa

Narva and Petserimaa are two small districts that were a part of Estonia until they were annexed by the Soviet Union in 1944. The original frontier between Estonia and the Soviet Union was determined by a war of 1918–1919 between the two countries, and it essentially followed the battle lines at the end of the war. The population of both districts had ethnic-Russian majorities, and after annexation, a large-scale immigration of Russian workers further reduced the proportion of ethnic Estonians.

When Estonia regained its independence in 1991, the border changes that had occurred under Soviet rule were declared to be invalid. Negotiations between Russia and Estonia were unsuccessful, and there have been several border incidents. In May 1993, hundreds of Estonian cyclists attempted to set up signposts at the old frontier but were stopped by Russian border guards. Polls show that the demand for the return of Narva and Petserimaa is supported by a majority of ethnic Estonians, as well as by all Estonian political parties.

See also Estonia.
Reference Forsberg, Tuomas. *Contested Territory: Border Disputes at the Edge of the Former Soviet Empire* (1995).

Native Americans of Canada

Approximately 1.4 million Native Americans reside in Canada, and they are divided into 235 tribes, or First Nations. From 1850 onward, following British practice, the Canadian government made treaties with the tribal nations and established reserves. Beginning in 1870, the Canadian government embarked on a policy of forcibly assimilating the native Indians. As a result, many Native Americans were divested of land rights and relocated. Many Indian children were separated from their parents and forced to attend government residential schools where they were forbidden to speak their native language. In January 1998, the Canadian government officially apologized for these policies.

Native American activism has been on the rise since the 1980s. The Assembly of First Nations, representing those Indians living on reservations, declared in 1981 that it did not accept the supremacy of the Canadian parliament nor the Canadian constitution. In 1986, the assembly claimed the right "to determine the nature of our on-going relationship with the federal and provincial governments within Canada." In 1990, armed Mohawk activists seized an important bridge in Oka, Quebec, to protest plans for a development project on sacred ancestral lands. The seizure was supported by Indian demonstrations across Canada. When the government forcibly retook the bridge, a policeman was killed.

The 1990s witnessed a number of lawsuits against the government. In 1998, the Supreme Court of Canada upheld claims of the Kipsiox Indians regarding 22,000 square miles of British Columbia. The other forty-nine tribes in that province are also laying claim to an additional 60,000 square miles of territory. Decisions favoring Native Americans have generated a backlash among nonnatives and businesses in the province, and the possible billion-dollar liability of the federal government if Indian claims are recognized has caused alarm throughout Canada.

In another major decision, the Nunavut political accord, the Canadian government granted autonomy in 1992 to Nunavut, formerly the eastern lands of the Northwest Territories inhabited primarily by Inuit (Eskimos). The future of the remainder of the Northwest Territories, home to several Native American tribes, is uncertain with several proposals for self-government being discussed. A movement for autonomy among the largest tribe of the territory, the Dene, has waned in recent years.

See also Native Americans of the United States; Nunavut.
References Dickason, Olive. *Canada's First Nations* (1997); Dyck, Noel. *Indigenous Peoples and the Nation State* (1985).

Native Americans of the United States

With a growing population of nearly 2 million, three-fourths of whom live on or near tribal lands, Native American tribes in the United States have been reasserting their sovereignty since the 1970s. In 1973, the American Indian Movement leader, Russell Means, and members of the Oglala Sioux tribe occupied Wounded Knee, South Dakota, to protest the treatment of Indians by the federal government. In an ensuing gun battle, several law officers and protesters were injured, and two Native Americans died. The siege lasted seventy days and ended after the government promised to examine Native American grievances.

Although Native Americans are citizens of the United States, the 554 tribes recognized by the federal government exist as semi-independent governing bodies. Legally, Indian tribes possess many of the powers granted to states—self governing and self-policing rights as well as sovereign immunity from civil suits—but they are subordinate to the federal government. The extent of Indian control on some 314 reservations is spelled out in a series of treaties enacted by the U.S. Congress between 1778 and 1871. In 1934, the Indian Reorganization Act, which allowed tribes to establish constitutions and to negotiate with local, state, and federal governments, revived Indian self-government.

Native American grievances that have been pressed in the courts since the 1970s include the return of sacred sites and relics; hunting, fishing, and water rights; the right to tax nonnatives living on reservations; claims for land beyond currently recognized tribal boundaries; and increased compensation and damages for previous injustices committed by the federal government. With the increase in the number of Native American lawyers and legal organizations, tribes have prevailed in several legal decisions at the state level. In Minnesota, for example, Native American tribes won the right to set state water standards at a far more strict level than the state legislature required.

Native Americans in the 1980s and 1990s have established a number of successful economic undertakings—the most well-known of which is the establishment of gambling casinos. Selling goods like cigarettes on reservations without state taxes has also provided income, as has making reservation land available for controversial projects like toxic waste disposal. By the 1990s, sovereignty battles were being fought against state governments and state congressional representatives. State governments have generally resisted new tribal land claims and have sought to control gambling within state borders or to increase their share of the gambling revenue.

Although federal courts have required states and tribes to reach a compact regarding tribal economic activities within state borders, much litigation is still pending, and the legal status of tribal nations remains unclear. Organizations like the American Indian Movement, which has been involved in armed conflict with government officers, insist that tribes are sovereign nations and not subject to regulation by state governments.

See also American Indian Movement; Lakota Nation; Native Americans of Canada.
References Bordewich, Fergus. *Killing the White Man's Indian: Reinventing Native Americans at the End of the Twentieth Century* (1997); Levin, Michael D., ed. *Ethnicity and Aboriginality* (1993).

Netherlands Antilles

Originally a Caribbean Dutch colony, in 1954 the Netherlands Antilles became an internally self-governing unit of the Kingdom of the Netherlands, with representation in the Dutch cabinet. At the time of independence, the islands included Curaçao, Bonaire, Aruba, St. Eustatius, Saba, and the Dutch part of Saint Martin. Complete independence is problematic because the smaller islands are afraid they would be dominated by Curaçao. By a large majority (82 percent), Aruba voted to separate from the Netherlands Antilles in 1977, and this became effective in 1985.

Reference Alexander, Robert J. *Political Parties of the Americas* (1982).

Nevis

Nevis, an island in the eastern Caribbean with under 9,000 inhabitants, is an ex-British colony that became independent in association with the larger island of St. Kitts (population 36,000) in 1983. Many of the inhabitants of Nevis complain that government spending is concentrated on St. Kitts and argue that their island, with its thriving tourist industry and offshore banking, would flourish as an independent country. In February 1997, the pro-independence Concerned Citizens Movement won three of the island's five seats, and in October 1997, the Nevis legislature voted unanimously to end the federation. The constitution of St. Kitts and Nevis, however, requires that any secession must be ratified by a two-thirds majority, and since only 62 percent of the voters were in favor of secession in a referendum held on August 10, 1998, the islands remained united.

New Caledonia

New Caledonia is an island in the South Pacific inhabited by indigenous Melanesians (44.8 percent), French settlers (33.6 percent), and other immigrant groups (21.6 percent). New Caledonia is an overseas territory of France and sends two deputies and one senator to the French parlia-

ment. At the end of World War II, a small number of wealthy settlers dominated the economy while most Melanesians and Europeans lived as subsistence farmers. In 1946, the islanders were granted French citizenship and representation in the French parliament. The Union Caledonienne (UC), a multiethnic reformist party, won majorities in the elections for both the French parliament and the territorial assembly throughout the 1950s and 1960s, and the party's leader, Maurice Lenormand, declared that the territory would remain French "by the irrevocable and perpetual consent of its inhabitants." A boom in nickel mining led to an influx of French immigrants, which was encouraged by France.

In the 1970s, a growth of Melanesian nationalism was inspired by the independence of other Pacific territories, and a series of militant pro-independence parties emerged. In 1977, the UC declared itself in favor of independence and contested the 1979 territorial assembly elections as part of an "independence front." The election results showed that most Melanesians favored independence but that a majority of the non-indigenous population was opposed. Subsequent elections have revealed a similar pattern, with the pro-independence parties receiving about a third of the vote in each election.

Deep-seated tension between separatists and loyalists has erupted into violence on several occasions. In 1984, an election boycott by militant nationalists led to armed clashes between settlers and Melanesians, and over fifty people died. The French government has made several initiatives to try and resolve the issue. In 1985, the Pisani plan proposed "independence in association" with France, after a referendum and elections. However, when the referendum was held in September 1987, the nationalists boycotted it, and 98 percent of those who voted opted for continued integration with France. (The nationalists argued that only those who had at least one parent born in the territory should be allowed to vote in the referendum, which would have disfranchised most of the whites and Asians.)

The provincial boundaries have been redrawn to allow each community control of its own area, and the economic situation of the Melanesians has been improved by increased financial aid from France. Another referendum was scheduled for 1998, but it was agreed by all parties to postpone it for another fifteen years.

References Henningham, Stephen. *France and the South Pacific* (1992); Kircher, Ingrid. *The Kanaks of New Caledonia* (1986).

Newfoundland

A province of Canada since 1949, the maritime territory of Newfoundland, consisting of Newfoundland Island and Labrador, became a British colony in 1583 and achieved self-government in 1855. Threatened by bankruptcy during the Great Depression of the 1930s, Newfoundland petitioned Britain for financial aid, and from 1934 to 1949, it was governed by a commission of six appointed members and a British governor. The British government had promised that "as soon as the Island's difficulties had been overcome and the country was again self-supporting, responsible government, on request from the people of Newfoundland, would be restored."

At the end of World War II, Newfoundland's financial situation had improved dramatically, and a prewar budgetary deficit of $18 million had been converted into a budgetary surplus of $32 million. The British government therefore announced, in December 1945, that a national convention would be elected to consider Newfoundland's future. The convention was elected in June 1946 and held its first meetings in September. The debates were broadcast and "Newfoundlanders in the most isolated outposts as well as the urban centres drank in every word." Delegations went to London and Ottawa, and in October 1947, Canada offered a set of "Proposed Arrangements for the entry of Newfoundland into Confederation." The convention decided that a referendum should be held in which Newfoundlanders would choose between three options: the retention of the present commission of government system for another five years, a return to responsible self-government, or confederation with Canada. Although the possibility of political union with the United States was discussed, it was not included on the ballot.

A bitter campaign followed, splitting clubs, families, and friends apart. St. John's, the capital city, was a stronghold of responsible government supporters while elsewhere, supporters of confederation were in the majority. Ethnic and sectarian factors played a major role. The Catholic Church, and people of Irish Catholic ancestry, opposed confederation while the Protestant Orange Order lobbied in favor. With 88 percent voting in the referendum on June 3, 1948, responsible government was favored by 69,400 voters, confederation by 64,066, and commission of government by only 23,311. In a second referendum held on July 22, in which voters were offered a straight choice between confederation and responsible government, confederation won by 78,323 to 71,334.

Despite this relatively small majority (52.3 percent), negotiations between Canada and Newfoundland on the details of union were successfully concluded, and on March 31, 1949, Newfoundland became Canada's tenth province. Opponents of confederation held mass rallies in St. John's, a petition signed by over 50,000 people was presented to the British House of Commons, and there were even fears of riots. The Responsible Government League, in a last defiant gesture, sent a message to the Canadian House of Commons declaring that it reserved the right to secede from Canada and restore Newfoundland's lost sovereignty.

Reference Eggleston, Wilfrid. *Newfoundland: The Road to Confederation* (1974).

Nigeria

With a population of 107 million, Nigeria is the most populous nation in Africa. Located in West Africa, it has more than 250 ethnic groups, many speaking their own language. The three dominant ethnic groups are the Muslim Hausa-Fulani of the northern region, with a population of 28 million; the Muslim-Anglican Yoruba of the western region, with a population of 20 million; and the heavily Catholic Ibo, or Igbo, of the eastern region, with a population of 17 million. The cultural, religious, and economic differences among these groups remain a major source of antagonism within the Nigerian state.

In addition, nine other ethnic groups, some larger than the population of other African states, have populations exceeding 1 million: the Kanuri, 4 million; the Ibibo, 3.6 million; the Tiv, 2.5 million; the Ijaw, 2 million; the Edo, 1.7 million; the Anana, the Nupe, and the Urhollo, each 1.2 million; and the Igala, 1 million. Although lacking the military resources to seek independence, many of these larger minorities have successfully pressed the federal government for special financial considerations in return for their loyalty to the regime. Additionally, they have been granted their own states, free from the rule of one of the three dominant ethnic groups. In the early 1960s, the Middle Belt Movement in the southern part of the northern region, largely non-Muslim and Tiv led, was one of the first successful efforts by smaller minorities to gain increased autonomy.

Relations among ethnic groups in Nigeria since independence in 1960 have been strained. Intertribal conflict has been common, particularly when economic development brought previously geographically segregated groups in contact with each other, often in the larger cities. In 1967, Nigerian society was torn apart when Iboland, the eastern region, seceded from Nigeria following an anti-Ibo military coup in the federal government and the subsequent massacre of thousands of Ibo in the northern region. In the ensuing civil war, ultimately won by the Hausa-Fulani dominated federal forces, the Ibo nation of Biafra was subjugated at a cost of millions killed, wounded, starved, or displaced. In the 1990s, the Ogoni, a small tribe in southeastern Nigeria, pressed demands for control over their oil-rich region, saying that only northerners were profit-

ing from oil operations that were despoiling the natural environment of the Ogoni. The federal government reacted by arresting outspoken Ogoni leaders and executing several of them.

Although the federal government has managed to contain secessionist movements through repression and the employment of superior military power, Nigeria, forty years after independence, has not developed as a cohesive nation. Although now in its Fourth Republic, much of independent Nigeria's history has been one of Hausa-Fulani dominance, often exercised through military dictatorship. Democratic periods have done little to break the northerners' hold over the federal government and control of the nation's wealth and resources. The alienation of the populous Yoruba and Ibo peoples remains high.

In 1993, a Yoruba, Moshood K. O. Abiola, was elected president of the republic. The military annulled the election, arrested Abiola, and suspended the constitution. The northern general Sani Abacha assumed the presidency, ruling as dictator. Sentiment for secession among the Yoruba grew although no effective mass movement was able to develop in the police state atmosphere of the Abacha regime. In 1998, following the sudden death of Abacha and the restoration of democracy, another Yoruba, retired general and former president Olusegun Obasanjo, was elected president. But many Yoruba distrusted Obasanjo, who had close ties with the northern generals, and he failed to carry any of the six Yoruba states. Whether Obasanjo's presidency will restore Yoruba confidence in the federal government remains to be seen. Frederick Fasheen, chairman of the nationalist Yoruba Odudua People's Congress, has vowed to fight against the continuing marginalization of the Yoruba in national affairs.

At the 1998 World Igbo Congress, while paying lip service to Nigerian unity, Chairman J. O. S. Okeke invoked a long list of grievances against the central government, including lack of federal investment in Ibo areas, discrimination against Ibos in the civil service, and the lack of Ibos in high government offices. He also berated the Yoruba for siding with the Hausas against the Ibos, which again points to the interethnic hostility existing between two of the major Nigerian ethnic groups.

In its democratic periods, Nigeria has attempted to defuse ethnic solidarity and hostility by proscribing purely ethnic parties and requiring that the national president win election in a plurality of states. A dampening of ethnic separatist aspirations has also been achieved by creating more states. From the original three regions in 1960, Nigeria now has thirty-six states, and lobbying continues for the creation of at least six additional states. The creation of new states, while appealing to the smaller ethnic groups, has been viewed by both Yoruba and Ibos as gerrymandering aimed at diluting their regional and national political power.

See also Biafra; Fernando Póo; Ogoni; Ojukwu, Odumegwu.
Reference Udogu, Emmanuel Ike. *Nigeria and the Politics of National Survival as a Nation State* (1997).

Nogays

Nogays are found in the southwestern part of the Russian Federation and are dispersed among a number of political jurisdictions: the republics of Kabardino-Balkaria, Karachay-Cherkessia, Chechnya, and Dagestan and the districts of Stavropol and Astrakhan. In no area do they constitute more than 12 percent of the population. The Nogays, who are descended from the Mongolian chieftain Nogay, grandson of Genghis Khan, are Sunni Muslims and speak a Turkic language. In earlier times, Russian texts referred to them as North Caucasus Tatars. Nogays today number about 100,000.

The major grievance of the Nogays is that, unlike many other ethnic groups of the Caucasus, they possess no administrative territory of their own. The Nogays are represented by Birlik (the unity society), which has pressed for the creation of an autonomous district in the Achikulak and Kayulin areas of Dagestan and additional territory in Karachai-Cherkessia and Stavropol. Ultimately, Birlik would like to establish a Nogay state that would encompass all Nogay territories.

See also Dagestan; Russian Federation.
References Kolga, Margus, et al., eds. *Red Book of the Peoples of the Russian Empire* (1993); Wesselink, Egbert. *The Russian Federation: Dagestan* (1995).

Nordic Council

Established in 1952 to facilitate cooperation among the nations of Denmark, Norway, Sweden, Iceland, and Finland, the Nordic Council is made up of delegates chosen by the respective national parliaments on the basis of proportional representation. The council meets annually to vote on proposals affecting the Nordic countries (the site rotates among the different capitals). The degree of legal and social integration among these five countries is greater than among any others in the world, creating what is virtually a common citizenship. Passport controls between them were abolished in 1952, work permits in 1954, and in 1956, any citizen of any of the five countries became entitled to draw social benefits if living anywhere within the Nordic bloc. In 1976, the franchise was extended to citizens of one country living in another.

This social and political integration reflects the countries' linked history and common culture. Norway was part of Denmark from 1397 until 1815, then ruled by Sweden until 1905, when it became independent under a Danish prince. Finland was a Swedish grand duchy until it was ceded to Russia in 1809. Iceland was under Norwegian rule (1262–1380) and then ruled by the Danes until becoming fully independent in 1944. All five countries have similar political systems and well-developed welfare policies. All are predominantly Lutheran. Their languages are mutually understandable, with the exception of Finnish, which belongs to a different language family.

References Derry, T. *A History of Scandinavia* (1979); Snyder, Louis L. *Macro-Nationalisms: A History of the Pan-Movements* (1984).

A site in Surdulica, Yugoslavia, which was hit by a NATO missile in April 1999, killing at least twenty people. (Reuters/Archive Photos)

Norfolk Island

A dependency of Australia in the South Pacific inhabited by descendants of the *Bounty* mutineers, Norfolk Island was discovered by Captain Cook in 1774 and remained a British colony until 1914 when it was transferred to Australian administration. The 2,000 islanders complain that the Australian administration has been autocratic and negligent. In 1996, they wrote a letter to the British prime minister, John Major, claiming that the island was never formally handed over to Australia and that they were therefore still British. The British government rejected the islanders' argument. One of the main concerns of the islanders, who are fervent monarchists, has presumably been relieved by the results of the November 6, 1999, Australian referendum on the monarchy. Despite the fact that all the major newspapers supported Australia's becoming a republic, the vote

was 55 percent to 45 percent to retain the monarchy, with every state and the Northern Territory rejecting the republican option.

Reference Lees, Caroline. "Bounty Islanders Stage a New Mutiny" (1997).

North Atlantic Treaty Organization

The North Atlantic Treaty Organization (NATO) was established in 1949 as a regional military alliance of Western European and North American countries. Its purpose was to provide security against the Soviet Union and its allies. The original members were Belgium, Canada, Denmark, France, the United Kingdom, Iceland, Italy, Luxembourg, the Netherlands, Norway, Portugal, and the United States. Greece and Turkey were added in 1952, West Germany in 1955, and Spain in 1982. With the collapse of the Soviet Union in 1991 and

Catholic children in Belfast stone British Army patrol vehicles, 1972. (Corbis/Leif Skoogfors)

the establishment of non-Communist governments in Eastern Europe, the original rationale for NATO became inoperative. Since that time, NATO has been evolving into a broader security alliance encompassing all European nations. Although resisted by Russia, which doubts the motives of the NATO nations, former Soviet allies and Warsaw Pact members Hungary, Poland, and the Czech Republic were admitted to membership in NATO in 1999. Other former Communist states have also expressed a desire to join.

In attempting to redefine itself as a keeper of order throughout Europe, NATO, in coordination with the United Nations, become involved militarily in 1995 in securing peace in war-torn Bosnia. In 1999, following the failure of negotiations with Yugoslavia over the treatment of ethnic Albanians in the Serbian province of Kosovo, NATO carried out an aerial bombardment of Yugoslavia.

See also Bosnia and Herzegovina; Kosovo.

Reference Yost, David. *NATO Transformed: The Alliance's New Roles in International Security* (1999).

North Borneo
See Sabah

Northern Ireland
Politically, Northern Ireland is part of the United Kingdom of Great Britain and Northern Ireland; geographically, it is part of the island of Ireland. In the seventeenth century, Scots and English settled in the north of Ireland, dispossessing the Gaelic population. The current division between Protestants and Catholics results from that time, with the Protestants being descended from the settlers and the Catholics the descendants of the native Irish. Religion has historically provided the basis for communal identity, and both communities have distinctive traditions, play different sports, and belong to different organizations.

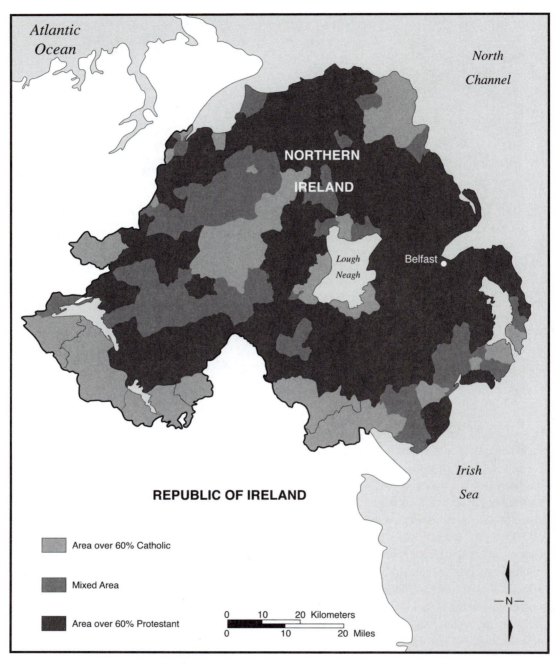

Atlantic
Ocean

North
Channel

NORTHERN

IRELAND

Lough
Neagh

Belfast

REPUBLIC OF IRELAND

Irish
Sea

Area over 60% Catholic

Mixed Area

Area over 60% Protestant

0   10   20 Kilometers
0   10   20 Miles

— N —

Even prior to the present conflict, there was a high degree of social and residential segregation between the two communities.

The communal identities are significant politically. When Irish nationalism emerged as a serious force in the nineteenth century, it drew mass support from only the Catholic population. The Protestants, in contrast, were unionists, in favor of remaining part of the United Kingdom and opposed to home rule. In 1916, militant Irish nationalists rose up against the British in what is called "the Easter rebellion." Although the rebellion was crushed, it inspired a guerrilla war throughout Ireland. The campaign was successful in the twenty-six southern Irish counties but made little headway in the six northern counties where Protestants predominated. In 1921, Ireland was "partitioned," and the counties of Armagh, Antrim, Down, Tyrone, Fermanagh, and London-derry remained in the United Kingdom while the rest of the island became the Irish Free State (later the Republic of Ireland). Northern Ireland was granted a devolved regional parliament, called Stormont, which had responsibility for in-ternal affairs, and also elected twelve representa-tives to the parliament in London.

Politics in Northern Ireland have traditionally revolved around "the national question," with Protestants overwhelmingly supporting the British link, and a plurality of Catholics favoring a united Ireland. Since Protestants constituted al-most two-thirds of the population, Stormont was dominated by the Unionist Party and the nation-alists were a permanent minority. The Catholic minority suffered from various forms of political and economic discrimination, and in the 1960s, the Northern Irish Civil Rights Association orga-nized a series of protest demonstrations. Their campaign provoked a violent backlash from Protestants, and widespread clashes took place in Belfast and Londonderry. As the disturbances es-calated, the British government intervened, send-ing in troops in July 1969 and taking over the ad-ministration of the province in March 1972.

In February 1971, the Irish Republican Army began a campaign to force Britain to relinquish Northern Ireland, which in turn led to counter-terrorism by Protestant "loyalists." Over 3,200 persons have been killed since 1968 in "the trou-bles," as the conflict is generally referred to in Northern Ireland. A variety of reforms and con-stitutional initiatives have been attempted, but there has as yet been no permanent resolution of the conflict, which is rooted in the clash of na-tional identities and allegiances.

See also Adams, Gerry; Anglo-Irish Agreement; Irish Re-publican Army; Northern Irish Peace Agreement; Provi-sional Sinn Fein; Social Democratic and Labour Party.
References Roche, Patrick J., and Brian Barton, eds. *The Northern Ireland Question: Myth and Reality* (1991); Rose,

Richard. *Governing without Consensus: An Irish Perspective* (1971).

Northern Irish Peace Agreement

After almost two years of talks, an agreement was finally reached on April 10, 1998, between North-ern Irish political leaders and the governments of the Republic of Ireland and the United Kingdom. The accord, signed on Good Friday, was widely seen as bringing to an end the sectarian conflict in which more than 3,200 people had died. The agreement was approved on May 22 by referen-dums held concurrently in the Republic of Ire-land and Northern Ireland. In the republic, 94 percent were in favor, and in Northern Ireland, 71 percent. Polls suggested that a majority of both Northern Irish Catholics and Protestants sup-ported the agreement, although support was higher among Catholics than among Protestants.

The agreement had three strands: One, it set up a 108-member assembly for Northern Ireland to be elected by proportional representation, using a single transferable vote system. Executive powers would be exercised by a cabinet account-able to the assembly, and ministerial and com-mittee positions would be allocated in propor-tion to party strength, which would ensure a sharing of power between Catholics and Protes-tants. Two, a North/South Ministerial Council would be established to promote joint policy-making in such areas of mutual concern as agri-culture, transport, and tourism. Three, a Council of the Isles would also be established "to promote the harmonious and mutually beneficial develop-ment of the totality of relationships among the peoples of these islands." In addition, the Irish Republic would amend its constitution, which currently claims the six counties of Northern Ire-land as part of its national territory. The decom-missioning of weapons held by the Irish Republi-can Army (IRA) and the Loyalist (Protestant) groups was declared to be an "indispensable part of the process of negotiation," but it was unclear how the decommissioning was to be achieved.

The assembly elections of June 1998 resulted

British Prime Minister Tony Blair (right) with Senator George Mitchell (center) and Irish Prime Minister Bertie Ahern (left) after they signed the agreement for peace in Northern Ireland, April 10, 1998. (Reuters/Dan Chung/Archive Photos)

in a clear victory for parties backing the peace plan, with supporters of the agreement winning eighty seats and opponents only twenty-eight. Protestant unionist parties won fifty-eight seats; Catholic nationalist parties, forty-two seats; and nonsectarian parties, the remaining eight. The two largest parties were the Ulster Unionist Party, led by David Trimble, which won twenty-eight seats, and the Social Democratic and Labour Party (SDLP), which won twenty-four. Trimble was elected first minister and Seamus Mallon of the SDLP deputy minister.

The agreement did not result in the immediate cessation of violence since extremists on both sides saw it as a sellout. Protestant extremists, an-

gered by a ban on an Orange Order march, engaged in sporadic rioting. On July 13, 1998, three small children were burned to death when a firebomb was thrown into a house in Ballymoney that was occupied by a Catholic woman, and on August 15, a breakaway faction of the IRA set off a bomb in the predominantly Catholic town of Omagh and killed twenty-eight people. The resulting public horror and revulsion produced by these two incidents brought an abrupt end first to Protestant loyalist violence and then to Catholic republican violence.

However, the agreement became deadlocked by a dispute over when the decommissioning of weapons should begin. The unionists insisted that the IRA should disarm before being allowed to participate in the executive while the IRA demanded that the new cabinet be appointed first. At the end of November 1999, George Mitchell, a former U.S. senator, was able to broker a compromise. The Ulster Unionist party agreed to participate in a power-sharing local government that would include two members of Sinn Fein. In return the IRA will be expected to name a representative to the disarmament commission "soon thereafter." So far the IRA has not given up a single item of its arsenal of weapons, and Pat Doherty, a Sinn Fein vice president, said in an interview with the *Boston Herald* that the IRA had no intention of disarming.

See also Irish Republican Army; Northern Ireland; Provisional Sinn Fein.

Nunavut

Nunavut (meaning "our land" in Inuit) is the name given to the new territory of Canada that was created in April 1999 out of what had been the eastern part of the Northwest Territories (NWT). In the whole of the sparsely populated NWT, whites made up about 38 percent of the total population, the Inuit (previously known as Eskimos) 34 percent, and Indians the rest. In the eastern portion, however, the Inuit constituted a clear majority (85 percent).

Partitioning the NWT was first proposed by the Diefenbaker government in 1960, and in 1977, the national Inuit organization, the Tapirisat, began to advocate partition. A few years later, the Indians called for the creation of Denendeh in the western portion of the territories, and a constitutional forum was established to plan the details of the government structures. The boundary between Nunavut and Denendeh was the subject of dispute since the traditional hunting grounds of the Inuit and the Dene overlapped. Another problem was the lack of economic development in the east. It was estimated that the Nunavut government would be dependent on the federal government for 95 percent of its budget, and after negotiations, the federal government in Ottawa agreed to transfer $1.5 billion to Nunavut; in return, the Inuit would give up their land claims.

In a referendum held in November 1992, 69 percent of those voting approved of the proposal to set up an autonomous Inuit territory in the eastern part of the NWT. The area comprises over 700,000 square miles and has only 25,000 inhabitants. The official languages are English and Inuit, and a three-year residency requirement for voting has been established in order to prevent newcomers from overwhelming the native population.

See also Native Americans of Canada.
Reference Fleras, Augie, and Elliott, Jean L. *The Nations Within: Aboriginal- State Relations in Canada, the United States, and New Zealand* (1992).

Ocalan, Abdullah (1948–)

Abdullah Ocalan is the leader of the separatist Kurdish Workers Party (PKK) of Turkey, which was founded in 1974 by a small group of left-wing Kurdish students. Ocalan, whose nickname "Apo" means both "uncle" and "holy man" in Kurdish, dominated the new group, which was also known as Apocus, or "followers of Apo." A former political science student at the University of Ankara, Ocalan had previously been a member of Dev Genc, a revolutionary Turkish organization. The new group, however, was against any alliance with the Turkish left.

The PKK's program declared that Kurdistan was a colony of Iran, Iraq, and Turkey; called for a national and democratic revolution; and declared that "the fundamental force of the revolution will be the worker-peasant alliance." The PKK's ideology was Marxist-Leninist, and close relations were established with the Soviet Union.

The PKK began to organize in the Kurdish region of eastern Turkey in the late 1970s and initiated a terrorist campaign of assassination directed against landlords, collaborators, and members of competing political groups. By 1980,

Turkish guards flank Kurdish rebel leader Abdullah Ocalan aboard a plane as he is flown to Turkey, February 17, 1999. (Reuters/Archive Photos)

the PKK, whose recruits came from the most marginal elements of Kurdish society, had killed at least 243 people. In September 1980, the Turkish military took power in a successful attempt to stop widespread political violence by the extreme right and the extreme left. More than 20,000 subversives were arrested, including 3,177 accused of separatist activities. PKK members, most of whom were poor workers, shepherds, or farmers, made up a majority (56 percent) of the separatists who were arrested.

Military repression proved only a temporary setback to the PKK, and by early 1983, an estimated 12,000 guerrillas had infiltrated the eastern border region. By 1987, the campaign had escalated, and the PKK was on the verge of setting up liberated zones. The PKK clearly enjoys significant popular support in Kurdish areas. In 1990, teenagers stoned Turkish soldiers, and thousands of demonstrators took to the streets for a "free Kurdistan."

Ocalan fled to Syria in 1980, but after Turkey threatened military action, the Syrian government deported him in October 1998. Failing to find sanctuary in Russia, Ocalan flew to Italy where he was arrested. Driven out of Italy after three months, he ended up in Kenya, and while being driven to Nairobi airport, he was kidnapped by Turkish agents in February 1999. After a trial in June, he was convicted of treason and sentenced to death by hanging. The death penalty requires the approval of the Turkish legislature, and there is considerable international pressure for Turkey to commute Ocalan's sentence to imprisonment. On the other hand, many Turks support the verdict against Ocalan, whose organization is blamed for the deaths of more than 30,000 people. Ocalan himself issued a call to the PKK to end the armed struggle and withdraw its forces from Turkey, and the PKK endorsed a cease-fire in August 1999.

See also Turkish Kurds.
Reference Gunter, Michael. *The Kurds in Turkey* (1990).

Occitania

Occitania is the name given to the region in France in which the Occitan dialect is spoken.

Traditionally, French dialects were divided into the "Pays d'Oil" in the north and the "Pays d'Oc" in the south, according to the word used for "yes." As Paris extended its control over the south, northern French, the dialect of Paris and the north, became the preferred version. Occitania, where the southern dialect is spoken, includes about one-third of France.

A cultural revival began after World War II with the founding of the Institut d'Etudes Occitanes. One of its leaders, Robert Lafont, argued that the region was an internal colony, and his group organized resistance to several unpopular policies of the central government, in particular a proposal to extend a military base at Larzac. Later, the group merged with other left-wing elements to form Lutte Occitane. Other Occitan groups have appeared, including the right-wing Parti Nationaliste Occitan and Volem Viure al Pais, which at first advocated decentralization and then called for political independence. Since these groups have never run in any national or local elections, it is difficult to assess their support. The Occitan Movement peaked in the mid-1970s, then declined as the national parties began to respond to regional issues.

See also France.

Oder-Neisse Line

At the end of World War II, Poland's western frontier was extended to the line formed by the Oder and Neisse Rivers, land that had been a part of Germany. Germany also lost territory to the Soviet Union in the east. As the legal successor to the Third Reich, the Federal Republic of Germany (West Germany, which included only half the territory occupied by the old Reich) took the position that a final settlement of Germany's borders could not be reached until German unification had been achieved.

However, the people who had been expelled or had fled from these territories maintained a strong attachment to their old homelands. The Bund der Vertrieben (League of Expellees) claimed 2 million members, and there were constituent organizations representing refugees from the Sudetenland, Silesia, Pomerania, and East Prussia. Their rallies, at which speakers denounced the current borders and called for the return of the "stolen territories," drew crowds numbering well over 200,000. Chancellor Konrad Adenauer and other high-ranking politicians often addressed the crowds and assured them that their cause had not been forgotten. One cabinet minister, Theodor Oberlander, even called for the reconquest of the lost territories.

The All-German Bloc of Expellees, later the All-German Party, obtained 1,617,000 votes (5.9 percent of the national vote) and twenty-seven seats in 1953 but failed to win any seats in the West German Parliament after that date. In treaties signed with Poland (1970) and Czechoslovakia (1973), the Federal Republic of Germany stated that it had no territorial claims against them, and in 1990, a reunified Germany formally accepted the Oder-Neisse line as its eastern frontier.

Reference Stoess, Richard. "Irredentism in Germany since 1945" (1991).

Ogaden

Ogaden is the Somali-inhabited region of Ethiopia. In 1887, Menelik II of Ethiopia (1889–1913) occupied the region, although the frontiers between Ethiopia and British and Italian Somaliland were never demarcated. Ethiopian administration of the Ogaden was erratic, involving no more than sporadic raids to gather taxes from the nomadic herdsmen. When the Italians invaded and occupied Ethiopia in 1936, they administered the Ogaden region as part of Italian Somaliland. After the British defeated the Italians in 1940, virtually all of the Somali-inhabited areas, including the Ogaden, were administered by Britain until 1948. This experience encouraged the development of Pan-Somali nationalism, and in 1947, when Ethiopia granted a fifty-year concession to Sinclair Petroleum in the Ogaden, the oil workers were physically attacked by the local Somalis.

When the Ogaden reverted to Ethiopia in

1948, the Somalis were enraged, and violent demonstrations broke out. Police opened fire, killing twenty-five members of the Somali Youth League, a nationalist organization. A correspondent for the *London Times* reported in 1956 that the Somalis were brutally treated and sometimes tortured by the Ethiopian police. Growing resistance to Ethiopian rule culminated in the formation of the Western Somalia Liberation Front (WSLF) in 1975. In 1977, Somalia's armed forces seized control of the Ogaden but were driven out by the Ethiopians in 1978. After that, the WSLF waged a guerrilla campaign for several years from bases in Somalia. In 1981, the WSLF announced that it was seeking an independent state of Western Somalia rather than unification with Somalia. Guerrilla attacks by the WSLF declined in the late 1980s, but a new organization, the Ogaden National Liberation Front emerged in 1986 and was still active in 1996.

See also Somalis.
Reference Woodward, Peter, ed. *Conflict and Peace in the Horn of Africa* (1994).

Ogoni

The Ogoni people, numbering about 500,000, live in the Niger River delta in oil-rich southeast Nigeria. The delta region's oil accounts for over 90 percent of Nigeria's exports, but the area has received little benefit from its natural resources, and most villages lack either clean water or electricity. Instead, oil spills have destroyed farmlands and fishing grounds in the area.

In 1990, Ken Saro-Wiwa founded the Movement for the Survival of the Ogoni People (MOSOP), which called for a share of the oil revenues and compensation for the damage to the environment caused by the activities of the Royal Dutch Shell Oil Company. Under his leadership, Ogoni demands for self-determination were transformed into a call for secession, threatening the central government's main source of revenue. The protests of the Ogoni, Nembe, Ijaw, and other delta peoples became more violent, and there were attacks on oil facilities and oil workers. A riot in May 1998 by members of MOSOP's youth wing resulted in the murder of four Ogoni chiefs who opposed the movement. Saro-Wiwa was accused of being responsible for their deaths and hanged on November 10, 1995, along with eight other activists. The executions brought widespread condemnation of Nigeria's military government from the international community. Nigeria was suspended from membership in the Commonwealth; the country's request for a $100-million loan from the World Bank was denied; and the sale of military weapons to the Nigerian army was banned by the United States.

See also Nigeria.
Reference Maier, Karl. *Into the House of the Ancestors: Inside the New Africa* (1998).

Ojukwu, Odumegwu (1933–)

A 1955 Oxford graduate, Odumegwu Ojukwu pursued a military career in Nigeria. He was appointed military governor of the eastern region (Iboland) in 1966, and following a coup by anti-Ibo northern officers, who installed Yakubu Gowon as head of state in July 1966, Ojukwu became the spokesperson for Ibo interests. After a massacre of Ibos in the northern region in the fall of 1966 and Gowon's refusal to grant the eastern region greater autonomy, secessionist sentiment increased among the Ibos.

In May 1967, with the consent of the regional assembly, Ojukwu declared independence, renaming the Ibo territory Biafra, and he was proclaimed head of the new state. The federal government refused to recognize the secession, and a devastating civil war broke out; lasting from 1967–1970, it resulted in the defeat of the Biafran nation. Ojukwu fled to the Ivory Coast where he remained until 1982 when he returned to Nigeria. Although he remains active in politics, Ojukwu's role is now marginal, and he has had little electoral success. Now referred to as Chief Ojukwu, he is viewed more as an elder statesman than as the leader of the Ibo.

See also Biafra; Nigeria.
Reference Ekwe-Ekwe, Herbert. *The Biafra War* (1990).

Okinawa

The Ryukyu Islands in the East China Sea, south of Japan, consist of four groups of islands, the largest of which is Okinawa with 700,000 inhabitants in 1960. The early Okinawan rulers were essentially independent, although they entered into a tributary relationship with the Chinese emperor. In 1609, the lord of Satsuma conquered Okinawa and held it as a feudal dependency. In 1879, Okinawa and the other southern Ryukyus became a Japanese prefecture. Staffed by Japanese teachers, the educational system became a vehicle of assimilation. Standard Japanese replaced the Ryukyu dialects, and by the 1900s, the Okinawans felt themselves to be Japanese.

After World War II, Okinawa was occupied by the United States, and under the 1951 peace treaty, the United States was granted "the right to exercise all and any powers of administration, legislation, and jurisdiction over the territory and inhabitants of these islands." During the Korean War, the strategic value of Okinawa as a supply base became apparent. Although Japan retained "residual sovereignty" over Okinawa, President Dwight D. Eisenhower declared, as late as 1957, that the United States would hold onto its military bases "indefinitely."

A strong "reversion movement" emerged in early 1951. The Association for the Promotion of Reversion to Japan sponsored a petition calling for reunification and collected almost 200,000 signatures (72 percent of the eligible voters). The Okinawa Teachers Association played a major role in the campaign, organizing hundreds of marches and demonstrations; all classes were taught in Japanese using Japanese texts. When the U.S. governor threatened to cut funds to school buildings and harassed the leader of the teachers' association by withdrawing his passport, these actions generated more support for the movement.

Most political parties on the island supported reversion. The People's Party demanded "immediate and unconditional reversion to the Fatherland, Japan," and the Socialist Party opposed U.S.

colonialism and military bases on Okinawa. The Ryukyu Nationalist Party, founded by Ogimi Chotoku, called for independence but received only negligible support. In the 1950 gubernatorial elections, the pro-U.S. candidate, who favored independence, was defeated by the candidate who advocated reversion by a margin of almost three to one. Two separate polls, taken in April 1951 and in December 1967, both found that 85 percent of the Okinawans favored reversion.

Hostility to the U.S. bases arose for several reasons. The bases occupied about 40,000 acres, or 12.7 percent of the total area of the island, and 40,000 farmers were dispossessed without adequate compensation. Armed troops had to be used to drive some farmers from their land. Constant jet flights disrupted classroom lessons, and accidents involving military vehicles—even plane crashes—led to over 180,000 death and injury claims being filed during 1945–1952. The island became a dumping ground for army misfits, and a series of vicious murders and rapes were perpetrated by U.S. soldiers upon the local civilians. The U.S. military presence led to the growth of a commercial sex industry, and traditional peasant families were appalled when their daughters became prostitutes.

The United States finally bowed to mounting pressure in both Okinawa and Japan. On November 21, 1969, President Richard Nixon and Prime Minister Eisaku Sato signed an agreement under which Okinawa was returned to Japan in 1972.

References Henderson, Gregory. *Public Diplomacy and Political Change* (1973); Higa, Mikio. *Politics and Parties in Postwar Okinawa* (1963).

Organization for Security and Cooperation in Europe

The Organization for Security and Cooperation in Europe (OSCE), sponsored by fifty-five North American and European states, was established in the early 1970s to promote dialogue between the East-West antagonists in the Cold War. In the 1990s, OSCE redefined its primary role as fostering security through cooperation in Europe. Its major activities include chairing arms-control negotiations, monitoring human rights, and overseeing elections. In recent years, OSCE has taken an active role in trying to bring peaceful resolution to ethnic conflicts in Europe. In 1999, OSCE had long-term missions in Croatia, Estonia, Georgia, Latvia, Macedonia, Moldova, Tajikistan, and Ukraine. Missions in Kosovo, Sanjak, and Voivodina in Serbia were withdrawn in 1993 following a break with Yugoslavia.

Since the signing of the Dayton peace accord in 1995, OSCE has been extensively involved in Bosnia, mostly to ensure that the electoral provisions of the treaty are carried out. Backed by the economic clout of the European Union, OSCE has banned from the ballot candidates accused of human rights violations by the United Nations, has intervened to ensure fair campaign practices, and has officially supervised the elections themselves.

See also Bosnia and Herzegovina.
Reference Organization for Security and Cooperation in Europe. Homepage

Orkney Islands

The Orkney Islands, located in the North Atlantic, have been part of Scotland since 1468. The population, like that of the Shetland Islands, is of Norse descent. The isolation of the Orkneys has produced a strong sense of local identity, and Orcadians still talk of "going away to Scotland." When it was proposed in 1997 that Scotland be granted its own legislative assembly and tax-raising powers, the Orkneys and the Shetlands were the only districts to vote against the devolution. The Orkney Movement, which was founded in the 1970s, advocates autonomy for the 20,000 islanders.

See also Scotland; Shetland Islands.
Reference McLean, Duncan. "Getting on the Map" (1998).

Oromia

Oromia is the name given to the Oromo-inhabited region of Ethiopia by the Oromo Liberation

Front. The Oromo, although divided into numerous subgroups, all claim descent from a common ancestor. The Oromo expanded in the 1500s and became the dominant power in what is now southern Ethiopia. They were organized according to a system of age groups, known as *gada,* which were highly democratic and had a system of checks and balances that prevented despotism and the development of excessive inequality. The *gada* system also allowed the Oromo to absorb the people they overran.

In the late 1800s, the Oromo were conquered by the ruler of Ethiopia, Menelik II. After that the Amhara, the dominant group in the Ethiopian empire, referred to the Oromo as Galla, a derogatory name not used by the Oromo themselves. Addis Ababa, the Ethiopian capital, was established in the heart of the Oromo lands on the site of the Oromo town of Finfine.

Ethiopian rule has been referred to as settler or tributary colonialism, analogous to that in South Africa. Menelik established garrison towns in strategic places, and the land surrounding the towns was expropriated and given to Amhara settlers. Many Oromo were enslaved, and estimates of the number of slaves exported from Ethiopia in the 1800s range from 500,000 to 2.5 million. The soldier-settlers looted the grain and cattle of those Oromo they did not enslave. Under the *nafxanya-gabbar* system, Oromo peasants were forced to work for their overlords without pay and to give them a share of the crops. The growth of coffee production in the 1920s and 1930s resulted in an increasing exploitation of the local population.

The Italian invasion and occupation of Ethiopia in 1936 was welcomed by many Oromo as a liberation from Amhara oppression. After British forces routed the Italians in 1940, one British official asked, "When we are fighting for freedom in Europe how can we restore the Gallas to Amharic tyranny?" In the end, however, Haile Selassie regained his throne in Ethiopia and continued settling more Amharas on Oromo lands. Millions of acres were confiscated and given to Ethiopian soldiers, civil servants, and the unemployed.

Several revolts by the Oromo took place during Ethiopian rule. An Oromo cultural renaissance began in the early 1960s, with the emergence of musical groups and the publication of Oromo-language magazines, and the first modern Oromo nationalist movement, the Macha-Tulama Self-Help Association, was formed in 1964. The new group attempted to improve living conditions by building schools, clinics, and roads, and it soon had a membership of over 2 million. The Ethiopian government responded by harassing its members; finally arrested its leader, Taddasa Biru; and dissolved the organization in 1967. There was then an emergence of guerrilla resistance in the Bale district. The guerrillas obtained guns from Somalia and initially were successful in driving out the government troops. However, military aid, including helicopters from the United States, enabled the Ethiopians to crush the revolt by 1970, and as many as 500,000 Oromo lost their lives.

The founding of the Oromo Liberation Front (OLF) in 1974 represented the culmination of Oromo resistance to Ethiopian rule. The OLF sought "national self-determination for the Oromo people . . . and the establishment of the people's democratic republic of Oromia." The founders of the OLF had been involved in the Macha-Tulama Self-Help Association, and ideologically, the movement was inspired by both Marxism and the traditional *gada* principles of social organization. The OLF gradually expanded its operations and by 1985 was active throughout most of the southern provinces. With the collapse of the military regime in 1991, the OLF became part of the new ruling coalition, which was dominated by the Ethiopian People's Revolutionary Democratic Front. Growing hostility between the OLF and the EPRDF led to the OLF's withdrawal from the governing council in June 1992. In December 1994, the newly ratified constitution provided for a federal system and the division of the country into nine states, one of which was Oromia. Each state was to have considerable autonomy and the right to secede.

The extent to which the Oromo are united in desiring an independent Oromia is uncertain. They are geographically scattered throughout southern Ethiopia, and there is considerable diversity among the Oromo-inhabited regions in the extent to which they have retained their traditional culture. Many of the Oromo have assimilated to the Amhara, some are Muslim, and some are Protestant.

The OLF has also been active in northeastern Kenya, where about 200,000 Oromo live. In October 1998, the OLF was blamed for a massacre in which 200 people were killed in the village of Bagala, but the organization denied any role in the attack.

See also Ethiopia.

References Jalata, Asafa. *Oromia and Ethiopia: State Formation and Ethnonational Conflict 1868–1992* (1993); Lewis, I. M. *Nationalism and Self Determination in the Horn of Africa* (1983); Woodward, Peter, ed. *Conflict and Peace in the Horn of Africa* (1994).

Padania

Since Italian unification in 1861, substantial differences have always existed between the prosperous north and the impoverished south. In 1984, the Lombard League was formed by Umberto Bossi to represent the interests of northern Italians, who argued that they were heavily taxed to support the south. In 1990, the Lombard League joined five other regional groups to become the Northern League. The league's ideology was a mixture of regionalism, populism, and hostility to southerners and Third World immigrants. "We want autonomy so that we can look after ourselves with our own resources without having to forgo them in favor of the South," said the leader of the parliamentary party. The party's core support came from the small-town self-employed. Its electoral fortunes improved steadily until in the elections of 1992, it took 8.7 percent of the national vote and 20.5 percent in Lombardy itself. It was briefly a member of the ruling national coalition from 1994 to early 1995, but political differences within the league led to its leaving the coalition. The league then split into two factions, with the anti-Bossi dissidents forming the Italian Federalist League.

The Northern League, which proposed that the northern provinces should secede to form Padania, obtained over 10 percent of the vote and eighty-six representatives in the Chamber of Deputies in the 1996 national elections. Bossi took an increasingly militant and secessionist line, and in May 1996, he convened a northern parliament and announced that the party's deputies would not cooperate with the national government. In May 1997, armed separatist rebels seized a historic tower in Venice, but government troops recaptured the tower and arrested the rebels without bloodshed. Bossi denounced the occupation and charged that it was carried out by agent provocateurs to embarrass the separatist movement. In October 1997, the league organized an election for a Padanian assembly to draw up a constitution for the proposed new state. Although the vote was dis-

missed as a meaningless joke by most Italians, it revealed the resentment of many northerners toward the central government and the way their taxes are used to subsidize the south.

See also Italy.
Reference Farrell, Joseph, and Carl Levy. "The Northern League: Conservative Revolution?" (1996).

Pakistan

Legally and constitutionally, India and Pakistan are both successor states of the British Raj, and they achieved independence simultaneously. However, historically and politically, Pakistan split from India as a result of a separatist movement among Indian Muslims. This is shown by the fact that India took over the name and legal personality of the former British colony while Pakistan was given a new name.

In the early 1900s, some Muslims, fearing domination by the Hindu majority, had begun to call for separation from India, and the Muslim League was founded in 1906. Its leader, Mohammad Ali Jinnah, withdrew from the Indian National Congress in 1920 after being shouted down during an acrimonious meeting. In a speech given in 1930, the president of the Muslim League, Mohammed Iqbal, called for a Muslim state to include the provinces of Sind, Baluchistan, the North-West Frontier, Jammu and Kashmir, and

In September 1947 Muslim refugees crowd into an overflowing train leaving New Delhi for Pakistan following independence and the division of former British India into India (predominantly Hindu) and Pakistan (predominantly Muslim). (AP Photo)

most of the Punjab. (Significantly, he did not include the Muslim province of East Bengal in his plan.) However, this was very much a minority position, and in the provincial elections of 1937, with separate Muslim and Hindu electorates, the Muslim League won only 108 of the 484 Muslim seats. However, relations between the two communities worsened, and in the 1945 elections, the league won an overwhelming majority among the Muslim electorate. In a desperate attempt to maintain a united country, a cabinet mission sent to India by the newly elected Labour government in Britain proposed that an independent India should consist of (1) a central union government with control over foreign affairs, defense, and communications; (2) two groups of provinces—one consisting of the predominantly Hindu provinces and the other of the predominantly Muslim provinces—which would make policy collectively on such issues as they desired; and (3) the provinces themselves, which would each deal separately with all other matters.

Jinnah, the leader of the Muslim League, ac-

cepted this proposal on the express condition that it be implemented without any modifications while Jawaharlal Nehru reluctantly accepted it on behalf of the Indian National Congress. However, almost immediately, Nehru gave a speech in which he claimed that the National Congress had accepted the proposal merely as a basis for further discussion.

Although historians differ as to who was to blame for the breach between the two parties, Penderel Moon, a high-ranking British official intimately involved in the negotiations, argued that "the reason for the failure to agree on some form of united India lay deeper. The truth is that the aims and aspirations of the two communities, as expressed by those whom they acclaimed their leaders, were irreconcilable. . . . The Congress leaders wanted a strong and united India, the League a divided or divisible one." The rift between the Muslim League and the National Congress provoked bloody communal rioting, and at least 10,000 were killed in Calcutta alone. By the time that Viscount Mountbatten became the viceroy of India in February 1947, partition seemed preferable to civil war, and on June 3, 1947, the division of British India into two nations was announced. Against Jinnah's wishes, the Punjab and Bengal provinces were partitioned by the Radcliffe Boundary Commission. Millions of people living on the "wrong" side of the lines became refugees, and by conservative estimates, 500,000 were massacred.

The Pakistan state that was created by the partition was in many respects an artificial entity, and in 1971, East Pakistan broke away to become Bangladesh. In West Pakistan, separatist movements have emerged among the Baluchis and the Pathans.

See also Baluchistan; Bangladesh; India; Jinnah, Mohammad Ali; Pashtunistan.
Reference Ziring, Lawrence. *Pakistan in the Twentieth Century* (1980).

Palestine Liberation Organization

The Palestine Liberation Organization (PLO) was founded in 1964 in order to unite Palestinian civic and political organizations and to coordinate efforts to achieve a Palestinian state. At the instigation of Ahmad al Shuquyri, a Palestinian National Council was convened, and it became the governing body of the PLO. An umbrella group, the PLO included student groups, trade unions, and professional associations as well as medical and educational organizations. It also included the militias of the Palestinian resistance movement—Fatah, the Popular Front for the Liberation of Palestine (PFLP), and the Democratic Front for the Liberation of Palestine (DFLP) being the most prominent.

The PLO was secular in its orientation, and it called for a democratic state in Palestine in which Muslims, Christians, and Jews would all have citizenship rights. In its first years of existence, the PLO was dominated by Pan-Arabists, followers of the Egyptian president Gamal Nasser who believed a Palestinian state would be created through the military victories of the united Arab armies. From this perspective, the PLO was

viewed as an instrument of the frontline Arab states. Defeat of the Arab armies by Israel in the 1967 war and the impressive showing of Palestinian militias shifted the balance of power in the PLO away from the Pan-Arabist bureaucratic elite toward the Palestinian militias. In 1968, Yasir Arafat's militia, Fatah, succeeded in forcing Israeli troops to withdraw from their attack on the Al Karameh refugee camp in Jordan, and by 1969, Fatah and the other militias had been able to take control of the PLO, and Arafat was elected chairman of the organization. Since then, Fatah has become the dominant power within the PLO.

Under the new leadership, the emphasis of the organization shifted from dependence on other Arab states toward a more autonomous stance. The PLO argued that Palestinian fighters would

Supporters of Palestine Liberation Organization leader Yasir Arafat march through city streets. (Express Newspapers/Archive Photos)

free Palestine, with the support of the Arab states. The organization refused to recognize the state of Israel, and Fatah continued to carry out terrorist actions against Israel. In addition to bombings and assassinations within Israel and the occupied territories, PLO guerrillas conducted raids against Israel from bases in neighboring Arab states.

After the 1967 war, the PLO militias operated primarily from Jordan, and PLO administrative structures were housed there as well. In 1970, alarmed by PLO attacks on Israel, which Jordan feared would lead it into another war, King Hussein I and his army drove the PLO militias out of Jordan. They relocated in Lebanon where they continued their assaults on Israel. In 1985, under pressure from Israeli and Syrian forces that had occupied parts of Lebanon, the PLO militias were again forced to relocate, this time to Tunis.

By 1973, all Arab states except Jordan had acknowledged the PLO as the legitimate representative of the Palestine people. In 1974, the UN General Assembly recognized the PLO and granted it permanent member status, allowing it to participate in most UN agencies. In the 1980s, the PLO increased its activities among Palestinian refugees, establishing businesses and social service agencies and providing educational and vocational training programs. In 1988, Arafat declared the PLO and its governing bodies the legitimate government of Palestine, and King Hussein I yielded his territorial claims over the West Bank to the PLO.

In 1993, the PLO and Israel signed the Oslo peace accord, in which the PLO accepted the existence of the state of Israel and renounced violence as the means of achieving a Palestinian state. In return, Israel agreed to withdraw from specified territories in the West Bank and the Gaza Strip. The PFLP refused to accept the terms and withdrew from the PLO. Hamas, the Islamic fundamentalist group, which was not part of the PLO, also denounced the treaty and continued its terrorist campaign against Israel.

The treaty facilitated the creation of a new Palestinian government, the Palestinian Author-ity. Although retaining their autonomy, PLO administrative bodies were largely merged into the PA, and Arafat appointed many Fatah members to government posts. The 1995 elections in Palestine overwhelmingly elected Fatah-PLO candidates to the Palestinian Legislative Council, the legislative body of the new Palestinian government, and Arafat was elected first president of the liberated areas. In December 1998, the PLO formally amended its charter to recognize the state of Israel. Arafat also announced his intention to declare Palestine a sovereign state in the near future.

See also Arafat, Yasir; Democratic Front for the Liberation of Palestine; Fatah; Hamas; Islamic Jihad; Israel; Palestinian Authority; Palestinians; Popular Front for the Liberation of Palestine.
Reference Nassar, Jamal Raji. *The Palestine Liberation Organization: From Armed Struggle to the Declaration of Independence* (1991).

Palestinian Authority

The Palestinian Authority (PA) is the autonomous self-governing body of those areas of the Gaza Strip and the West Bank that are not under Israeli occupation. The PA at the beginning of 1999 exercised full control over only 3 percent of the West Bank and 60 percent of Gaza. It is headed by an elected president, Yasir Arafat, and an eighty-eight-seat parliament, the Palestinian Legislative Council. The PA officially began functioning in September 1995. As spelled out in treaties with Israel, the PA's authority is currently limited to matters of civil administration although President Arafat envisages full statehood in the near future. The PA has established a judiciary, a security force, and ministries to deal with the economy, education, housing, and transportation.

See also Israel; Palestine Liberation Organization; Palestinians.
Reference Robinson, Glenn. *Building a Palestinian State* (1997).

Palestinians

The term *Palestinians*, as employed by Palestinian nationalists, refers to the Arabic-speaking inhabitants who resided in the British-ruled territory of Palestine prior to 1948 and their descendants. In 1947, the population of the area included 1.3 million Palestinians and 640,000 Jewish settlers. In 1991, after the Arab-Israeli wars, it was estimated that the Palestinian diaspora, which was scattered throughout the Middle East and other parts of the world, numbered at least 6 million. Of these, roughly 1 million lived in the West Bank and East Jerusalem; 600,000 in Gaza; 1,825,000 in Jordan; 730,000 in Israel (excluding East Jerusalem); 330,000 in Lebanon; 300,000 in Syria; 450,000 in other Arab countries; and 450,000 in other countries of the world. Given a high rate of population growth, Palestinians may today number 7 million. Palestinians are predominantly Sunni Muslims; Druze and Christian Arabs, as in neighboring Lebanon and Syria, constitute a small but significant minority. In Israel, Druze and Christian Arabs make up 25 percent of the population.

The region of historic Palestine is located on the eastern Mediterranean shore and is bordered by Lebanon, Syria, Jordan, and Egypt. Although Jewish kingdoms existed in Palestine before the Christian era, by the time of Byzantine rule in the fourth century, few Jews remained in the territory, having been exiled by the Romans. Most of the remaining indigenous inhabitants converted to Christianity. After A.D. 636, the Arab conquest brought about mass conversions to Islam and the adoption of the Arab language. Muslim rule continued until the defeat of the Ottoman Empire in World War I when the territory was conquered by the British. Under Muslim rule, Christians and Jews were free to practice their religion, and Muslim, Jewish, and Christian tourists all made pilgrimages to the holy sites in Jerusalem.

Significant immigration by European Jews began in the 1880s, at which time Arabs composed 95 percent of the population of 325,000. Jewish immigration was inspired by Zionism, the belief that a Jewish state should be created in Palestine. As Jewish immigration increased, it created pressure on Palestinian land ownership and led to the growth of a large class of landless peasants. The Palestinians originally welcomed Britain's takeover from the Ottoman Empire because the British held out the promise of an independent Palestinian state. In a 1915 letter written by Sir Henry McMahon, the British high commissioner in Cairo, to Sharif Hussein of Mecca, the commissioner stated that Britain would accept an independent Arab state within the region. However, in 1917, the Balfour Declaration, issued by the British foreign secretary, promised the Zionist Federation of Britain that Britain favored "the establishment in Palestine of a national home for the Jewish people."

Despite British attempts to control Jewish immigration, by 1936, 385,000 Jews lived in Palestine, up from 24,000 in 1880. They now constituted 28 percent of the population. In 1936, an Arab insurrection broke out demanding an end to Jewish immigration and the creation of the promised Palestinian state. Arabs feared Jews would become a majority of the population of Palestine if immigration were not checked, and bloody clashes between Arabs and Jews were frequent. The economic situation of the average Palestinian worsened while the largely autonomous Jewish economy continued to build a powerful infrastructure. An Arab high committee was created to coordinate Palestinian strikes and protests. Arab guerrilla bands formed in the countryside. As the insurrection grew, the British retaliated and managed through the use of military force to regain control of the country. Many Palestinian leaders were exiled, imprisoned, or killed in the fighting. A 1939 British white paper analyzing the revolt called for a partition of Palestine into Jewish and Arab sectors, but Palestinian leaders rejected the proposal.

Following World War II, the British turned the Palestine question over to the newly formed United Nations, and in 1947, that body voted to partition Palestine. The mufti (Muslim religious leader) of Jerusalem rejected the decision, and war broke out between Palestinians and Jews. The Jewish forces defeated the Palestinian fighters and the allied Arab armies that had joined them, and after the war, Israel held considerably more territory, including West Jerusalem, than had been allotted it by the United Nations. The Jewish state came into being on May 14, 1948, and nearly 800,000 Arabs fled Israeli-held territory, creating the Palestinian diaspora. Many Palestinians settled in the West Bank (controlled by Jordan), the Gaza Strip (controlled by Egypt), and the states of Lebanon and Syria.

After the creation of Israel, both the neighboring Arab governments and Palestinian activists encouraged the Pan-Arabism of Egyptian president Gamal Nasser. According to the tenets of Pan-Arabism, Palestine was to be taken back by the forces of the united Arab states, the Israeli state would be dismantled and a secular democratic state established in its place, and the land of the Palestinian refugees would be returned. Three major Arab-Israeli wars took place in 1956, 1967, and 1973. Israel won all three and, in 1967, occupied Gaza and the West Bank, the Sinai peninsula, East Jerusalem, and the Golan Heights in Syria. The latter two territories were annexed to Israel. In 1978, Egypt signed a peace treaty with Israel whereby Israel returned the Sinai to Egypt. Effectively, this treaty marked the end of the Pan-Arabic attempt to create an Arab Palestine through collective state warfare against Israel. Instead, the Palestine Liberation Organization (PLO) came to the forefront as the accepted vehicle for the goal of creating a Palestinian state.

The PLO is an umbrella organization. In addition to political parties, it also includes student groups, trade unions, and civic organizations like the Red Crescent (the Islamic version of the Red Cross). The PLO also has a militia, the Palestine Liberation Army (PLA). Some more militant factions among the Palestinians continued to operate independent of the PLO, carrying out guerrilla operations against Israel, and Fatah also engaged in guerrilla activities. Fatah, which had become the dominant faction in the PLO, emphasized the need for Palestinians to operate independently, liberating Palestine through the actions of its own military forces. In contrast, the Popular Front for the Liberation of Palestine

(PFLP) continued to stress a Pan-Arabic and socialist approach to the Palestinian question. Nevertheless, the PLO depended on surrounding Arab states for material support and territorial bases for its military and administrative operations. Frequently, PLO actions launched against Israel from neighboring Arab states resulted in massive Israeli retaliation against the host countries. In 1970, King Hussein expelled PLO forces from Jordan, and in 1982, after Israel's invasion of Lebanon in response to constant PLO attacks on northern Israel, Lebanon, aided by Syrian forces, also expelled the PLO.

In 1987, a spontaneous uprising, the Intifada, began in Gaza and spread to the West Bank. Including strikes, boycotts of Israeli products, and attacks against Israeli occupation forces, it proved costly to Israel both economically and militarily. In 1988, the PLO declared the existence of a state of Palestine in the West Bank and Gaza, with Jerusalem as its capital, and the PLO's governing body, the Palestine National Council, was declared the Palestine government in exile. King Hussein I of Jordan turned his claim to the occupied West Bank over to the PLO. Under prodding from the United States, the PLO accepted UN resolutions 242 and 338, which officially recognized Israel's right to exist. The PLO also renounced the use of violence against Israel. The fundamentalist Islamic groups Hamas and Islamic Jihad, which were not formally allied with the PLO, refused to accept these decisions and continued terrorist activity against Israel.

By supporting Iraq in the 1990–1991 Gulf War, the PLO lost financial support from the oil-producing Gulf states, and Kuwait expelled 300,000 Palestinians from that country after the war. Nevertheless, negotiations continued clandestinely under U.S. auspices, and in 1993, in an agreement signed in Oslo, Israel recognized the PLO. The Declaration of Principles on Interim Government was signed by both parties, the Palestinian National Council began to assume limited government responsibilities over specified West Bank and Gaza territories, and government functions were carried out by the newly established Palestinian Authority. In 1994, Israeli forces began to withdraw from some areas of Gaza and the West Bank, and in 1996, Yasir Arafat was elected president of the Palestinian-controlled territories. In 1998, further negotiations resulted in the Wye River accords, which spelled out the next stages of the Israeli withdrawal from the occupied territories.

Although Palestine now has limited self-government, the arrangements negotiated by the PLO have many critics. The Islamist groups Hamas and Islamic Jihad reject the agreements outright, saying all historic Palestine must be freed from Israeli control, and efforts by the Palestinian Authority to control terrorist attacks by these two groups have had only limited success. Other critics of the agreements argue that they grant too many concessions to Israel: they permit Israeli settlements in the West Bank and Gaza, they severely limit Palestinian sovereignty as a state, and they allow a large Israeli military presence in the West Bank and Gaza. One commentator referred to the liberated zones as being similar to the South African Bantustans. Issues not addressed in PLO-Israeli talks to date include the future status of Jerusalem, the claims of Palestinians to land expropriated by Israel after 1948, and the issue of a Palestinian "law of return" covering the Palestinian diaspora.

Other Palestinian objections concern the PLO, the Palestinian Authority, and Arafat himself. Some argue that Arafat has, in effect, sold out the legitimate demands of the majority of Palestinians for the opportunity of aggrandizing his own power. They charge that the Palestinian National Council is no longer run democratically and that the Palestinian Authority has turned the liberated areas into police states. Other complaints cite the inefficiency, cronyism, and corruption that pervade the Palestinian Authority.

See also Arafat, Yasir; Democratic Front for the Liberation of Palestine; Fatah; Hamas; Islamic Jihad; Israel; Palestine Liberation Organization; Palestinian Authority; Popular Front for the Liberation of Palestine.
Reference Farsoun, Samih. *Palestine and the Palestinians* (1997).

Pan-Africanism

Pan-Africanism is the ideology that advocates the political unification of Africa. In its earliest manifestation, Pan-Africanism was dominated by blacks in the West Indies and United States who called for a return of the black diaspora to its African homeland. One of the most important leaders was Marcus Garvey, a Jamaican, who founded the Universal Negro Improvement Association in 1919. After moving to Harlem in the United States in 1916, he attracted a large following and proclaimed himself "provisional president of Africa." Garvey designed a flag for the movement—with three stripes, black, green, and red—that is still used by black nationalist groups. Garvey called on his followers to create an independent black economy and himself set up the Black Star Line shipping company. He was indicted by federal prosecutors for mail fraud in connection with the Black Star Line and sentenced to five years in prison. After being pardoned by President Calvin Coolidge, he was deported and died in London in 1940.

The second influential Pan-Africanist was William DuBois. Unlike Garvey, DuBois was an intellectual and a scholar who wrote about the past glories of African civilizations. A founding member of the National Association for the Advancement of Colored People in the United States, he organized four Pan-African Congresses in Europe and the United States in 1919, 1921, 1923, and 1927. DuBois became increasingly alienated from the United States, joined the Communist Party, renounced his citizenship, and emigrated to Ghana where he died in 1963.

Modern Pan-Africanism emerged after World War II when educated Africans who had studied at Western universities returned home determined to liberate their homelands from colonial rule. One of the leading figures was Kwame Nkrumah, leader of Ghana, the first colony to win its freedom. Julius Nyerere of Tanganyika (now Tanzania) was also a passionate advocate of African unity, saying: "Our goal must be a United States of Africa. Only this can really give Africa the future her people deserve after centuries of economic uncertainty and social oppression." In 1958, Nkrumah organized the first Conference of Independent African States in Accra, the capital of Ghana. However, by the time the second conference met at Addis Ababa in 1960, the African states had split into two opposed factions, the radical Casablanca bloc and the more moderate Monrovia bloc.

The first group, made up of Morocco, the United Arab Republic, Mali, Guinea, and Ghana, called for political and economic unity and a joint military command. The second group, including most of the former French colonies, Liberia, Nigeria, Sierra Leone, Somalia, and Ethiopia, favored an African "community" rather than a political union. There were also disagreements among African leaders as to the best way to achieve unity. Nyerere believed that Pan-Africanism should be implemented gradually through regional unions while Nkrumah argued that regional unions would make continental unity more difficult to establish. Several attempts at union between independent black African states quickly ended in failure or existed only on paper. These included a federation between Mali and Senegal, from June to August 1960, and a union between Ghana, Guinea, and Mali, which was announced on December 24, 1960, but never implemented.

In 1963, the Organization of African Unity (OAU) was founded in an attempt to promote African unity and eradicate colonialism. The OAU resolved that the national boundaries inherited from the colonial era must be retained, since otherwise there would be chronic conflict. The Charter of African Unity pledged the members of the OAU to respect "the territorial integrity of every state and its inalienable right to an independent existence." Although the organization was able to resolve some disputes between its members and provided aid to liberation movements in southern Africa, it failed to become the basis for a unified Africa. The newly independent states were unwilling to surrender their sovereignty, and divisions between radical and moderate states frequently prevented them from agreeing on a common policy. In 1982, the Western Sahara issue led to such a bitter dispute among OAU members that almost half of them boycotted the annual meeting.

See also East African Federation; French West Africa; Western Sahara.

References Amate, O. C. C. *Inside the OAU: Pan-Africanism in Practice* (1986); Hazlewood, Arthur, ed. *African Integration and Disintegration: Case Studies in Political and Economic Union* (1967); Snyder, Louis L. *Macro-Nationalisms: A History of the Pan-Movements* (1984).

Pan-Americanism

After winning independence from Spain, Simón Bolívar attempted to unite South America politically and organized the first Pan-American Congress, which met in Panama in 1826. Attended by delegates from Peru, Colombia, Mexico, and Central America, there were calls for common citizenship and a unified military command to resist Spanish aggression. A second congress was held in Peru in 1847 and another in 1856 in Chile. Although these meetings were marked by pro-unification speeches, they had little practical impact. Indeed, the period was marked by increasing political fragmentation, with Venezuela and Ecuador breaking away from Colombia in 1830 and the Central American Federation splitting apart in 1838.

In 1889, the United States, seeking access to the resources and markets of Latin America, convened a Pan-American Congress in Washington, D.C. This was the first of several inter-American conferences, which were held every five to ten years and were devoted primarily to economic and commercial matters. In 1948, the conferences were replaced by the Organization of American States (OAS), with a permanent secretariat, the Pan-American Union. Although the OAS has played a useful role in resolving conflicts between member nations, Pan-American solidarity has been held back by Latin American resentment of what is believed to be intervention

231

by the United States in the internal affairs of the Latin American countries.

Reference Whitaker, Arthur P. *Nationalism in Latin America: Past and Present* (1962).

Pan-Turkism

Pan-Turkism is an ideology that emphasizes the links among Turkic-speaking peoples and seeks their political unification. The beginnings of this movement were in czarist Russia among the Tatars, who became increasingly aware of their historic and linguistic ties with other Turkic groups. The Tatars had been under Russian rule for centuries, and consequently, they had been exposed to the official policy of Russification. In response, a cultural revival was started in the 1880s under the leadership of Ismail Gaprinsky (or Gaspirali in Turkish). Gaprinsky, the mayor of a Crimean town, devised a revised Turkish vocabulary, reformed the local school curriculum so that it provided Turkish-language instruction, and published a newspaper, *Tercuman.* The paper, which had a circulation of 6,000 by the early 1900s, advocated the union of all Turkish groups within Russia. Another Tatar, Yusuf Akcura, published a pamphlet titled *Uc Terz-i Siyaset* (Three kinds of policies) in which he disparaged Pan-Ottomanism and Pan-Islamism and argued instead for a political union of all Turks.

Pan-Turkism was carried to Ottoman Turkey by Tatar intellectuals who immigrated from Russia. Such writers as Zia Gokalp and Tekin Alp developed the idea of "Turan," a Turkish homeland stretching throughout central Russia and western China. Gokalp was one of the founders of Turk Ocagi (Turkish Hearth), a society founded to better the Turkish race and language. Pan-Turkism was influential among "the young Turks," and when the Ottoman Empire declared war in 1914, one of the group's stated goals was the destruction of Russia and "a national frontier for our empire, which should include and unite all the branches of our race." In Azerbaijan, which remained under occupation by Ottoman troops for

several years, Pan-Turkish ideology was propagated in the newspaper *Azarabadegan,* but the Azerbaijanis remained hostile. The Russian Revolution of 1917 inspired many Pan-Turkists with the belief that their time had come, but the Bolsheviks showed themselves determined to hold on to the territories of the czarist empire. Under Ataturk, the newly formed Turkish Republic was hostile to the Pan-Turkish ideology, since its implicit irredentism endangered relations with the Soviet Union. The movement survived only on the political fringe, as émigré Turkish groups from the Soviet Union agitated on behalf of their compatriots.

Pan-Turkism emphasized the importance of blood and race, which meant that "the outside Turks" were part of the Turkish nation while Greeks and Armenians living in Turkey were not. During World War II, Turkey remained neutral, but many Pan-Turks called for war against the Soviet Union. When the activists organized mass demonstrations in 1944, the government cracked down, arrested the ringleaders, and banned Pan-Turkish organizations. The Nazis attempted to exploit Pan-Turkish sentiments by organizing captured Soviet prisoners of war who were of Turkish ethnicity into fighting units. As many as 200,000 may have fought alongside the Germans in order to "liberate" their homelands.

In the post–World War II period, Pan-Turkism has been represented by the Nationalist Action Party (NAP) under the leadership of Asparslan Turkes. In the 1977 Turkish elections, the party won sixteen seats and received 6.2 percent of the vote. The NAP was part of the government coalition from 1975 to 1980, but its youth wing was accused of provoking political violence in which over 200 people were killed, and after the military takeover of 1980, Turkes and other NAP leaders were tried and convicted of subversion. Pan-Turkish ideology failed to achieve any of its irredentism goals and had little influence on Turkish foreign policy except during the Cyprus crisis. However, the NAP received nearly 20 percent of the vote in the elections of April 1999, which may

Parti Québécois supporters at an election rally in Quebec, November 30, 1998. (AP Photo/Fred Chartrand)

indicate a revival of Turkish nationalism. During the election campaign, NAP posters showed a "greater Turkey" that included Kazakhstan and other areas of central Asia. The NAP also resists any concessions toward the Kurdish separatists who have been waging a guerrilla war in eastern Turkey.

See also Turkish Kurds.
Reference Landau, Jacob. "The Ups and Downs of Irredentism: The Case of Turkey" (1991).

Parti Québécois

The Parti Québécois (PQ) is the Quebec separatist party formed by René Levesque after he split from the Liberal Party of Canada in 1967. He first set up the Mouvement Souveraineté Association, which aimed to unite all separatist groups. After discussions with the leftist Rassemblement

pour l'Independence National (RIN) and the rightist Ralliement National (RN), the three groups merged and became the Parti Québécois. At its first convention in October 1968, the new party called for a sovereign French-language state that would be economically linked with Canada in a monetary and customs union. In 1970, in the first election contested by the PQ, the "Pequistes" received 23 percent of the Quebec vote, coming in second to the Liberals who called for a continuation of "profitable federalism." This represented a significant increase in the separatist vote since the 1966 elections in which RIN and RN together had received less than 9 percent of the vote. The election returns revealed that English speakers had voted overwhelmingly for the Liberal candidates, which led to angry charges that an ethnic minority had been able to thwart the will of the French-speaking majority.

The polarization between federalists and separatists was exacerbated by "the October crisis" of 1970 when the terrorist Front de Libération du Quebec kidnapped a British diplomat and the Quebec minister of labor. The federal government responded by invoking the War Measures Act and sending troops to Montreal. Levesque protested this "military occupation" and claimed that the Quebec government was "a puppet in the hands of federal leaders." The PQ increased its share of the vote in subsequent elections, and in 1976, it won control of the provincial legislature with 41.4 percent of the vote. The vote for the PQ should not be interpreted as necessarily measuring support for independence, since the party campaigned on good government issues rather than on sovereignty and promised that independence would come about only after a referendum was held on the issue. In May 1980, Quebec voters were asked to give the government of Quebec a mandate to negotiate a sovereignty association with Canada, but the referendum lost with only 40 percent approving negotiations. Support was concentrated among French speakers, but even in this group, only 48 percent approved.

The PQ increased its share of the vote to 49.2 percent in the 1981 provincial elections, but by the end of that year, the party had split over the party platform. Hard-liners argued that the party should reaffirm its commitment to independence while Levesque announced that sovereignty should not be an issue, "at least for the next election." Six ministers resigned from his cabinet, and several assembly members resigned from the party. Weakened by this split, the PQ suffered a crushing defeat in the 1985 election when its share of the vote declined to 38.7 percent whereas the Liberals received 56 percent. Under the leadership of Jaques Parizeau, the PQ returned to power in 1994 and promised to hold another referendum. In the referendum held on October 31, 1995, the vote for independence was 49.4 percent and lost by a mere 54,301 votes. PQ voters are drawn from all classes, but the party does particularly well among professionals and technicians, especially those working in the public sector. In every provincial election since 1976, except for 1985, a majority of French-speaking Québécois have voted for the PQ.

See also Front de Libération du Quebec; Levesque, René; Quebec.
References Newman, Saul. *Ethnoregional Conflicts in Democracies: Mostly Ballots, Rarely Bullets* (1996); Saywell, John. *The Rise of the Parti Québécois 1967–76* (1977).

Partido Nacionalista Vasco

Partido Nacionalista Vasco (PNV), the Basque Nationalist Party, was founded by Sabino de Arana in 1895, and historically, it has been the main vehicle of Basque nationalism. After the death of Francisco Franco in 1975 and the rebirth of Spanish democracy, the party emerged as the dominant political force in the Basque region. In the 1977, 1979, and 1982 national elections, the PNV received about a quarter of the vote in the four Basque provinces as a whole (Alava, Guipuzcoa, Vizcaya, and Navarra). In the regional assembly elections (from which Navarra was excluded), the party's best showing was in 1984 when it got 42 percent of the vote and thirty-two of the seventy-five seats.

However, cooperation between the Spanish Socialist Party and the PNV led to a split in the party in 1986, with the more nationalist faction, led by Carlos Garaikoetxea, taking the name Eusko Alkartasuna (Basque Solidarity). In the 1986 elections to the Basque parliament, the two wings each got seventeen seats. In the most recent elections, held in October 1998, the PNV received 28 percent of the vote and won twenty-one seats, compared to sixteen for the conservative Popular Party, fourteen for the Socialists, and fourteen for a more radical nationalist party.

See also Basques; Euzkadi ta Askatasuna; Spain.

Pashtunistan

The North-West Frontier Province of Pakistan is inhabited by the Pashtuns, who are the dominant ethnic group in neighboring Afghanistan. The

Pashtuns share a common Pashtu language and an intense devotion to the Islamic religion but are otherwise divided into feuding tribal groups. The international boundary between Pakistan and Afghanistan, the Durand Line, was demarcated in 1893 by the British, but the boundary was never accepted by Afghanistan, which has persistently called for the region to be united with Afghanistan or to become an independent state. The Pashtunistan (or Pushtunistan or Pakhtunistan) Movement was espoused by Abdul Ghaffar Khan and other Pashtun leaders in the 1940s, but the Muslim League's appeal to Islamic solidarity led many Pashtuns to support the new state of Pakistan.

In 1949, after the Pakistan air force accidentally bombed a village on the Afghan side of the frontier, Pakistan's offer of compensation was rejected, and the Afghan ruler, Zahir Shah, referred to the "freedom-loving aspirations of the trans-Durand Afghans." Kabul radio broadcast propaganda in favor of Pashtunistan and in support of Afghan claims, and diplomatic relations between the two countries were broken off from 1955 to 1957 and again from 1961 to 1963. Armed clashes took place between Pakistani forces and Pashtun tribesmen in 1960 and 1961, with the Pakistan government alleging that the Pashtuns were supported by Afghanistan.

In 1975, after the assassination of a local politician, H. M. K. Sherpao, the Pakistan government accused Afghanistan of training guerrillas and mounting a campaign of sabotage and assassination in support of its "aggressive and irredentist aims." In the same year, the National Awami Party government of the North-West Frontier Province was dissolved, and its leader, Wali Khan, was arrested on the grounds that the party was encouraging secession.

See also Afghanistan; Pakistan.
Reference Griffiths, John. *Afghanistan* (1981).

Pattani Malays

The three southern provinces of Thailand are inhabited by almost 1 million Muslim Pattani Malays. Beginning in the late-sixteenth century, the Thai kingdom gradually annexed the sultanate of Pattani, and in 1909, an Anglo-Siamese treaty delineated the border between the British Malay states and Siam (now Thailand), leaving Pattani under Siamese control. The Kingdom of Siam pursued a vigorous policy of centralization and assimilation. The sultanate was abolished in 1909, and Thai officials replaced local Malay rulers. The Primary Education Act of 1921 compelled attendance at state schools, where education was conducted in the Thai language, and the Thai Custom Decree of 1938 banned the use of the Malay language and even the wearing of sarongs. The Sharia courts and Islamic law were abolished.

Following the Japanese surrender in 1945, the Pattani Malay leaders petitioned the British to incorporate the region into Malaya. When the petition was denied, the Islamic Council of Pattani called for a self-governing Malay province to be established, with Islamic law courts and Malay as an official language. The Thai government responded by arresting the leader of the council, Haji Sulong. His arrest led to a revolt in 1948, which escalated after Haji Sulong disappeared—presumably murdered by the Thai police. Intermittent guerrilla activity has continued since then but had not posed any serious threat to Thai control.

The traditional leaders favor reestablishing the sultanate while the younger student leaders advocate an independent republic linked to Malaysia. (The Pan-Malayan Islamic Party of Malaysia has voiced support for the Pattani Malays.) Pattani Malay grievances include their economic situation. The per capita income of the region is below that of the rest of Thailand and neighboring Malaysia. Also, within the region, there are noticeable differences between the poor Malay peasants and the Thai and Thai-Chinese minorities, which own most of the large plantations and businesses.

See also Malaysia.
References Brown, David. "From Peripheral Communities to Ethnic Nations: Separatism in Southeast Asia"

(1988–1989); Christie, Clive J. *A Modern History of Southeast Asia* (1996); Lim, Jock, and S. Vani, eds. *Armed Separatism in Southeast Asia* (1984).

Penang Secessionist Movement

Penang was one of the three Straits Settlements in colonial Malaya; the other two were Singapore and Malacca. The majority (55 percent) of the population of about half a million were ethnic Chinese, most of whom were recent immigrants from China and their descendants. However, the commercial and business elite (the so-called Straits Chinese) were long-established in the region, English speaking, and loyal subjects of the British Empire. This cohesive group, whose members had been educated together at local private schools such as St. Xavier's and the Penang Free School, dominated local politics.

When the British proposed to create a Malayan Federation after the end of World War II, the Straits Chinese feared that the new state would be dominated by the ethnic Malays and that their historic links with Singapore and Britain would be destroyed. Their anxieties were increased by the decision in January 1946—later rescinded—to abolish Penang's status as a free port. The Straits Chinese thought that action was an indication that the prosperous commercial economy of Penang would be forced to subsidize the more-backward Malay states. More important, they saw themselves as becoming second-class citizens in a Malay-dominated society.

In late 1946, the Penang Chinese Constitutional Consultative Committee was formed, and it sent a petition to the British government arguing that it would be a violation of the principles of the United Nations if the political status of Penang were changed without the consent of its inhabitants. In December 1948, at a meeting of members of the business and professional organizations of Penang, it was resolved, by a vote of 200 to 12, "to adopt all constitutional means to obtain the secession of Penang from the Federation of Malaya." The Penang Secession Committee made no attempt to create a mass base of support but instead petitioned and negotiated with British officials. In the face of British determination to maintain the federation, the Penang separatist movement gradually died out. However, the Straits Chinese played a major role in creating the Malayan Chinese Association, which became part of the governing coalition in the new federation.

See also Malaysia.
Reference Christie, Clive J. *A Modern History of Southeast Asia* (1996).

Pishevari, Mir Ja'far (1892–1947)

Mir Ja'far Pishevari was born in 1892 in eastern Azerbaijan, in Iran. Of a working-class background and with only a high school education, he supported himself as a journalist, writing articles for left-wing newspapers. In 1920, Pishevari was involved in a revolt in the province of Gilan, and when it resulted in the formation of a Communist republic, he held office in the short-lived government. He was a delegate to the Congress of the Toilers of the East held in Baku and to the Third Congress of the Communist International held in Moscow. Arrested in 1930, he spent ten years in prison and was then exiled to Kashan.

In the debate among revolutionary intellectuals that took place after World War II, Pishevari advocated a "national" rather than a class strategy, since class consciousness was so poorly developed in Iran. When the Democrat Party of Azerbaijan was founded in 1945, he became its leader and was later the head of the Soviet-backed National Government of Azerbaijan. Along with other leading Democrats, Pishevari fled to the Soviet Union in 1946, where he was reportedly killed in a car accident in 1947. Other accounts claim that he was executed by Joseph Stalin.

See also Iranian Azerbaijan.
Reference Atabaki, Touraj. *Azerbaijan: Ethnicity and Autonomy in Twentieth-Century Iran* (1993).

Plaid Cymru

Plaid Cymru (literally, Party of Wales) is a Welsh nationalist party that was a rather insignificant force in the immediate post--World War II period. Of the eight Plaid Cymru candidates who ran in the 1945 British elections, seven failed to get even 12.5 percent of the votes cast. In subsequent elections from 1950 through 1964, they did equally poorly. The party was predominantly rural and Welsh speaking. Although most of its candidates were university educated, it was a party of amateurs and had only the most rudimentary organization in the English-speaking areas.

The party's electoral fortunes improved dramatically in July 1966 when the leader of the party, Gwynfor Evans, won a by-election to become Plaid Cymru's first-ever member of parliament. Evans proved to be an effective spokesman for Welsh grievances, and the party became an appealing alternative to the entrenched Labour Party. In several by-elections in Labour's working-class Welsh strongholds, large numbers voted for the Plaid Cymru candidates as a protest vote against a stagnant economy and the closing of many local mines. The language issue and devolution appear to have played little part. In the 1970 election, Plaid Cymru candidates polled 175,016 votes, or 11.5 percent of the total Welsh vote. This marked the high point of the party's electoral fortunes, and in subsequent elections, the party has received only about 7–8 percent of the Welsh vote, although it usually elects two or three members of parliament.

The party became increasingly left wing after 1970, and in 1981, its main goal was to establish "a democratic Welsh socialist state." The party's core support remains within the Welsh-speaking areas, and all the Plaid Cymru members of parliament have been elected from constituencies in which Welsh speakers are in a clear majority. There are signs that the increased use of the Welsh language in administration, education, and broadcasting has led to tension, with English speakers resenting what they see as employment preferences for the Welsh-speaking minority. In the May 1997 elections, Plaid Cymru won 9.7 percent of the Welsh vote and four seats in the UK Parliament.

See also United Kingdom; Wales.
Reference Davis, Charlotte. *Welsh Nationalism in the Twentieth Century* (1989).

Plavsic, Biljana (1930–)

The president of Srpska, the Bosnian Serb republic, Biljana Plavsic was born near Sarajevo in 1930. A biologist by training, she worked as a professor and university administrator in Sarajevo. Never a member of the Communist Party, she was one of the founders of Radovan Karadzic's Serbian Democratic Party (SDS). She served as vice-president of Srpska from 1992 though 1996, and when Karadzic was forced by international pressure to resign the presidency in 1996, Plavsic succeeded him. Later that year, she received 59 percent of the vote in the presidential elections.

Although a Serbian nationalist and an Orthodox Christian, her relationship with the Yugoslav president and fellow Serb, Slobodan Milosevic, is strained. She has accused him of being a political opportunist who can not be relied upon to defend the interests of Bosnian Serbs. In Bosnia, Plavsic's support of the Dayton peace accord, because it guaranteed international recognition of the Republic of Srpska, led to a break with former president Karadzic and his followers. Subsequently, Plavsic was expelled from the SDS.

In August 1997, she formed a new party, the Serbian National Alliance, to compete with the majority SDS party in parliamentary elections. In January 1998, Plavsic's party took only fifteen of eighty-three seats in the parliamentary elections. However, in coalition with the Socialist Party, she succeeded in having her candidate, Milorod Dodik, installed as prime minister. In presidential elections held later that same year, Plavsic was defeated by the ultranationalist Nikola Poplasen of the pro-Karadzic Serbian Radical Party. However, Plavsic's party continues to play an important role in the parliament.

See also Bosnia and Herzegovina; Dayton Peace Accord; Ethnic Cleansing; Greater Serbia; Karadzic, Radovan; Milosevic, Slobodan; Srpska; Yugoslavia.
Reference Holbrooke, Richard. *To End a War* (1998).

Popular Front for the Liberation of Palestine

The Popular Front for the Liberation of Palestine (PFLP) was established in 1967 by its current leader, George Habash. The PFLP, which initially joined the PLO at its formation in the 1960s, advocates socialism and Pan-Arabic unity. Its militia branch has engaged in numerous attacks against Israel. The PFLP denounced the PLO-Israeli peace accords signed in 1993 (the Oslo Peace accords) and suspended its cooperation with the PLO. Along with Hamas and the Democratic Front for the Liberation of Palestine, the PFLP boycotted the 1996 elections for the newly established Palestinian Authority. In 1998, the PFLP announced it was forming an alliance with the Islamic fundamentalist group Hamas to oppose the peace treaty. However, in 1999, the organization reached an accommodation with Yasir Arafat that allowed radical leader Mustafa Zubari to return to the West Bank. The PFLP still has neither endorsed Arafat's peace agreements nor renounced violence.

See also Palestine Liberation Organization; Palestinians.
Reference Farsoun, Samih. *Palestine and the Palestinians* (1997).

Postapartheid South Africa

Two of the most important issues in the negotiations between the South African government and the African National Congress (ANC) as to the constitution of a postapartheid South Africa concerned the relative powers of the central government and the regions and the boundaries of those regions. The ANC wanted a unitary state while the Nationalist Party (representing the white minority) favored a federal state. The final outcome granted extensive powers to the regions, although not as great as those desired by the Nationalist Party.

The development regions, already in existence, were the basis for the federal regions, but they were modified in response to lobbying by interested parties. The most important change was

the creation of a North-West Province, which includes most of what had been the "homeland" of Bophuthatswana and is also inhabited by large numbers of Afrikaans-speaking farmers. The nine federal provinces correspond in general to the distribution of ethnic groups within South Africa. The Western and Northern Cape Provinces have "Coloured" majorities, and Western Cape Province also has a significant number of whites. KwaZulu-Natal Province is predominantly Zulu, Eastern Cape includes most of the Xhosa areas, and the North-West Province is predominantly Tswana.

The potential for secessionist movements in what is an exceptionally volatile multiethnic state remains high. The two most likely areas where separatist agitation is likely to occur are the provinces of Western Cape and KwaZulu-Natal. Two academics, Adam and Moodley, predict that Natal and the Western Cape "could emerge as the Croatia and Slovenia of South Africa." The Cape region is the historic homeland of "the Coloureds," the mixed race created by Dutch settlers, Malay slaves, and the indigenous Khoisan people. The Coloureds, who are often referred to as "brown Afrikaners," generally speak Afrikaans, and many of them fear and resent the black majority. Under apartheid, the Cape was defined as a "Coloured labor preference area," and there were strict controls against blacks living or working there. When these controls were lifted in the 1980s, several hundred thousand blacks from the impoverished homelands of Ciskei and Transkei migrated to Capetown. In the first nonracial democratic elections of April 1994, two-thirds of the Coloured vote went to the Nationalist Party. Western Cape Province, with a population 59.7 percent Coloured and 22.1 percent white, was the only province won by the New Nationalist Party (with 54 percent of the vote).

KwaZulu-Natal Province is the homeland of the Zulu, a group with a distinctive language and pride in its history of military conquest. Inkatha, led by Mangosuthu Buthelezi, dominated the KwaZulu homeland government and deliberately

Provisional Sinn Fein leaders Martin McGuiness (third from left), Danny Morrison (center), and Gerry Adams (third from right) lead a protest march in Londonderry marking the twentieth anniversary of British troops' arrival in Northern Ireland, August 15, 1989. (Reuters/Rob Taggert/Archive Photos)

fostered Zulu nationalism. Violence between Inkatha and ANC supporters took thousands of lives in the 1980s, and Buthelezi has several times threatened to secede from South Africa if the region is not granted autonomy. The vote in the 1994 elections was reportedly 52.1 percent for Inkatha and 33.4 percent for the ANC (the results were challenged by the ANC). The election showed that Inkatha's greatest strength lay in the traditional rural areas while the urban centers of Durban and Pietermaritzburg were strongholds of the ANC.

In the South African elections of June 1999, the New Nationalist Party lost control of the Western Cape Province, although the Inkatha Freedom Party remained the largest party in KwaZulu-Natal.

See also Afrikaners; Apartheid; South Africa.
References Adam, H., and K. Moodley. "Political Violence, Tribalism, and Inkatha" (1992); Lemon, Anthony, ed. *The Geography of Change in South Africa* (1995).

Provisional Sinn Fein

Provisional Sinn Fein (PSF), which is the political wing of the Irish Republican Army (IRA), did not contest elections in Northern Ireland until 1982 when it adopted "the bullet and ballot" strategy of combining guerrilla warfare with political agitation. In the 1982 elections for the Northern Irish Assembly, the party called for "the immediate withdrawal of the British Army from our land, the disbanding of the sectarian UDR and RUC [Ulster Defence Regiment and Royal Ulster Constabulary, the local security forces] and self-determination for the Irish people." PSF won 10.1 percent of the vote in the 1982 assembly elections and slightly increased its share of the vote in subsequent elections. In the 1997 elections for the United Kingdom parliament, the party won 16.1 percent of the Northern Irish vote and two seats.

Refusing to recognize British rule, PSF is "abstentionist," and when elected, its candidates refuse to take their seats in the United Kingdom parliament. PSF poses an increasing challenge to the other nationalist party, the Social Democratic and Labour Party (SDLP), and currently receives about 40 percent of the Catholic vote. Compared to SDLP voters, PSF voters are more likely to be working class, young, and male. Not surprisingly, PSF voters had a highly favorable view of the IRA, and in a 1982 survey, 77 percent thought IRA members were "patriots and idealists." The leader of PSF, Gerry Adams, was involved in negotiations among the various political factions in Northern Ireland that resulted in the ending of conflict in 1998.

See also Adams, Gerry; Irish Republican Army; Northern Ireland; Northern Irish Peace Agreement; Social Democratic and Labour Party.

Puerto Rican Independence Party

The Puerto Rican Independence Party (PIP) was formed in 1946 when the *independista* wing of the Popular Democratic Party broke away and joined forces with the remnants of the Nationalist Party. Unlike the Nationalist Party, PIP rejected violence and sought to win independence through elections. In 1948, the party received 10.4 percent of the vote cast, and in 1952, 19 percent. Thereafter, the party's vote total declined, and in more recent elections, it has obtained only 3–5 percent.

Within months of the Cuban Revolution of 1958, the radical wing of the PIP broke away to form the Pro-Independence Movement, which later became the Puerto Rican Socialist Party (PSP). While the PIP is a moderate social democratic movement, the PSP is Marxist and pro-Cuban, and some of its members have been involved in terrorism. The PSP contested the elections of 1976 and 1980 but won only a few thousand votes. In a plebiscite held in 1967, less than 1 percent favored the independence option, and in a second plebiscite held in 1993, the proportion was still only 4.4 percent.

See also Puerto Rico.

Puerto Rico

The Caribbean island of Puerto Rico was a Spanish colony until it was annexed by the United States in 1898. The pro-independence Nationalist Party was founded in 1922, but in the elections of 1932, despite the charismatic leadership of Pedro Albizu Campos, the party obtained only 11,000 votes, less than 3 percent of the total. In 1936, a series of confrontations between the U.S. authorities and nationalists culminated in the assassination of Colonel Francis Riggs, the chief of police, and the arrest of Albizu on a charge of conspiracy to overthrow the government. This was followed by "the massacre of Ponce" on March 21, 1937, when police fired upon a Nationalist Party meeting, killing 18 and wounding almost 200. During World War II, the island became an important naval and military base, and the island's economy boomed.

In 1946, the Puerto Rican legislature passed a bill calling for a plebiscite to be held to ascertain the wishes of the people as to their political future. The appointed U.S. governor vetoed the bill, the legislature overruled his veto, and President Harry Truman, who had the final authority, vetoed the bill on the grounds that approval of the plebiscite "might erroneously be construed by the people of Puerto Rico as a commitment that the United States would accept any plan that might be selected at the proposed plebiscite." Since the U.S. Congress was unwilling either to allow the island to become independent or to become a state, the ambiguous constitutional status of the island in an era of decolonization was a potential diplomatic embarrassment.

The 1948 elections, in which the islanders were allowed to elect their governor for the first time, resulted in a landslide victory for the Popular Democratic Party led by Luis Muñoz Marin, with the Puerto Rican Independence Party coming in a poor third behind the statehood party. Munoz proposed that the island should become an *estado libre sociado* (literally, "free associated state"). In English, the term *commonwealth* was used to describe the relationship under which

Puerto Ricans would carry U.S. passports and be liable for the military draft but not pay federal taxes or be able to vote in U.S. elections.

After lengthy negotiations, Congress passed and President Truman signed into law on October 30, 1950, the Puerto Rican Federal Relations Act, which defined the island's new status. On the very same day, the nationalists declared independence and staged a revolt that left more than 20 dead and 100 wounded. More than 3,000 people were arrested on charges of sedition. In a related incident in Washington, D.C., two nationalists opened fire on Blair House, the temporary residence of President Truman. After the revolt was suppressed and with virtually the entire nationalist leadership in prison, a referendum was held in 1951. Although a large proportion of the electorate abstained, 76 percent of those voting approved the new constitutional status.

Since that date, the status question has dominated Puerto Rican politics, with the Popular Democratic Party supporting the current arrangements and the Statehood Republican Party (later renamed the New Progressive Party) wanting Puerto Rico to become the fifty-first state. Two *independista* parties exist, the moderate Puerto Rican Independence Party and the Marxist Puerto Rican Socialist Party. Although election results and plebiscites suggest that only a small minority of Puerto Ricans want independence, numerous terrorist attacks have taken place both on the island and in the United States. The main terrorist groups are the Fuerzas Armadas de Liberacion Nacional and Los Macheteros.

In March 1998, the U.S. Congress considered a bill to hold a plebiscite to determine Puerto Rico's constitutional future. The issue of whether English should become the official language of Puerto Rico proved contentious, and although the bill passed in the House of Representatives, it became stalled in the Senate. The governor of Puerto Rico then announced that a nonbinding referendum would be held in December 1998. However, the result was ambiguous, with 46.5 percent voting for statehood, 2.5 percent for independence, and less than 1 percent for "free association." A slight majority (50.3 percent) voted for "none of the above."

See also Albizu, Pedro; Fuerzas Armadas de Liberacion Nacional; Macheteros; Puerto Rican Independence Party.
References Fernandez, Ronald. *Prisoners of Colonialism* (1994); Nelson, Ann. *Murder under Two Flags* (1986).

Quebec

In 1608, the first permanent French settlement in Canada was established on the site of what was to become Quebec City. The colony remained in French hands until 1763 when it was ceded to Britain. The Quebec Act passed by the British Parliament in 1774 guaranteed the use of the French civil code in the colony and the position of the Roman Catholic Church. In 1867, the British North America Act established Canada as a dominion, with Quebec being one of the four founding provinces.

At the time of confederation, most of Quebec's population consisted of poor subsistence farmers, and the society was dominated by the church, which controlled the educational system and extolled the virtues of rural life. Industry and commerce were largely controlled by English speakers. Political relations between the French Canadian minority and the English-speaking majority were generally amicable, although there were occasional crises over such issues as conscription during the two world wars. By informal agreement, the position of governor general alternated between English and French Canadians. A similar norm prevailed within the Liberal Party, with the leadership rotating between the two groups. Within the Canadian House of Commons and in the cabinet, the French presence has usually been proportional to the French share of the Canadian population (this proportion remained at about 30 percent for a long while but has declined to about 25 percent).

The primary source of conflict between French and English has revolved around federal-provincial relations. The Quebec provincial government has consistently regarded itself as the guardian of French Canadian rights, and for this reason, it has sought to keep the federal government from acting in ways that would reduce provincial autonomy. This tendency is strengthened by the facts that the great majority of French Canadians have always lived in Quebec (86 percent in 1871 and 85 percent in 1991) and that the great majority of the Quebec population

is French speaking. Within Quebec, economic disparities were very noticeable with the average income of French speakers being 40 percent lower than that of English speakers in 1961. However, only with the social and economic modernization of Quebec, "the quiet revolution," did a significant separatist movement emerge.

The quiet revolution, a period of intellectual, social, and political ferment, began in 1959 with the death of Maurice Duplessis, provincial premier and leader of the Union Nationale. Pierre Trudeau and Gerard Pelletier founded the journal *Cite Libre*, which denounced the backwardness and corruption of the old regime. An acid criticism of the educational system, *Les insolences du Frere Untel*, by Jean-Paul Desbiens sold over 100,000 copies. The year 1961 saw the publication of Marcel Chaput's *Pourquoi je suis separatiste* (Why I am a separatist), which argued that the French Canadians formed a nation and that Quebec was its territory. A number of separatist parties emerged, including the Rassemblement pour l'Independence National and the Parti Québécois.

The Parti Québécois, which draws support from both middle- and working-class Québécois, quickly became a major political force. Support for independence grew from a trivial 8 percent in 1966 to 24 percent in 1976, and in the referendum of 1980, 40 percent supported negotiations with Canada over "sovereignty association." After the

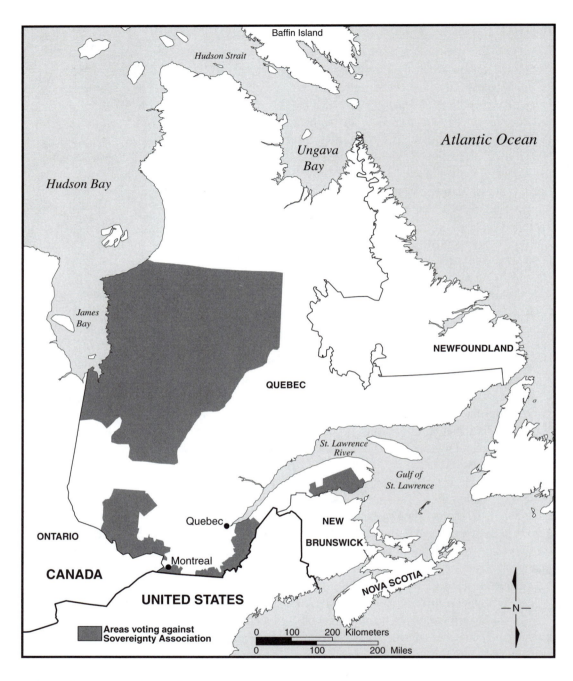

Areas voting against Sovereignty Association

defeat of the referendum, Pierre Trudeau, the Canadian prime minister, announced that he would repatriate the constitution from Britain. However, the issue of constitutional reform increased tensions between the federal government and Quebec and led to an increase in nationalist sentiment within Quebec. According to polls, support for sovereignty association surpassed 60 percent in the 1990s, and in 1995, the separatist option was only narrowly defeated in a second referendum. Since then, however, support for an independent Quebec has declined dramatically.

See also Front de Libération du Quebec; Levesque, René; Parti Québécois.

Reference Coleman, William. *The Independence Movement in Quebec 1945–80* (1984).

Quebec Partition

If Quebec were to become independent, several antiseparatists argue that the province itself would have to be partitioned, an idea that is advocated by the Special Committee for Canadian Unity, the Quebec Committee for Canada, and more than a dozen other groups. The Canadian prime minister, Jean Chrétien, also raised the issue in February 1996, saying that "if Canada is divisible, Quebec is divisible. It's the same logic, the logic of separatism." Partitionists point out that the borders of Quebec have changed several times and that much of the province's present territory was ceded to it by the federal government in 1898 and 1912. In the October 1995 referendum on sovereignty, the English-speaking areas of western Quebec and Montreal voted no by margins of ten to one, as did the Cree Indians of northern Quebec.

See also Quebec.
Reference Jenish, D'Arcy. *Battle over Borders* (1996).

Qwa Qwa

The smallest South African black homeland, Qwa Qwa was only 144 square miles in area and had a population of under 25,000 when it was created in 1971. Adjacent to the independent country of Lesotho, Qwa Qwa contained less than 2 percent of the southern Sotho, whose homeland it was supposed to be. It became self-governing in 1975. The South African government had hoped that Qwa Qwa would be annexed by Lesotho, but Lesotho was more intent on regaining the Sotho-inhabited territories it had lost in the 1860s than in acquiring the impoverished homeland of Qwa Qwa. In 1987, the Botshabelo district, with over 300,000 inhabitants, was incorporated into Qwa Qwa, but after the Qwa Qwa government objected, Botshabelo was returned to the Orange Free State. With all the other homelands Qwa Qwa was reintegrated into South Africa in 1994.

See also Black Homelands; South Africa.

Republic of Texas

The Republic of Texas Movement claims that Texas was illegally annexed by the United States in 1845. Its leader, Richard McLaren, issued passports, began filing bogus liens against property owners, and even laid claim to the state capitol building. In December 1996, he failed to appear in federal court in connection with a hearing into the bogus liens, and a warrant was issued for his arrest. In April 1997, an armed standoff between McLaren and sheriffs' deputies developed at the group's mountain headquarters near Fort Davies, Texas, after McLaren took two hostages and demanded that two of his arrested followers be released. The week-long standoff ended when McLaren and three other secessionists surrendered to a force of over 300 police officers. Two other men fled the scene, and one of them, Mike Matson, was killed in a subsequent shootout with state police. In November 1997, McLaren was sentenced to ninety-nine years for kidnapping, and his top lieutenant got fifty years.

R

State troopers gather during a shift change at sunset during the fourth day of the armed standoff between the Republic of Texas and law enforcement officials, May 1, 1997. (Reuters/J. David Ake/Archive Photos)

Hungary's Premier Victor Orban (right) with Marko Bela (left), leader of Romania's Hungarian Democratic Union, during an unofficial visit to Bucharest, July 1998. (AP Photo/Robert Ghement)

Réunion

An island in the Indian Ocean, Réunion has been a French possession since 1642 and became an overseas department in 1946. Its population of 600,000 is composed of East Indians, blacks, Vietnamese, and Chinese. The Socialist and Communist Parties favor self-determination, and a small Marxist group, the Movement for the Independence of Réunion, advocates independence.

Romania

Romania, a republic in the Balkan peninsula, has 23 million people, of which 89 percent is Romanian; 7.1 percent, Hungarian; and 0.5 percent, German. Ukrainians, Serbs, Croats, Russians, Turks, and gypsies make up the rest of the population.

The major ethnic conflict in Romania pits the majority Romanians against Hungarians. The Hungarians who reside in the Transylvania region of Romania (which belonged to Hungary until 1920) have called for the reunification of Transylvania with Hungary and, failing that, have argued, since 1989 and the collapse of communism, for the restoration of an autonomous Hungarian region (one existed briefly during the early period of Communist rule). They have also pressed the Romanian government for specific guarantees of civil rights and state aid for the Hungarian community. The German minority in Romania, also largely found in Transylvania, greatly decreased in the 1990s, largely because of voluntary migration to Germany, and the Germans have not mounted any significant demands for autonomy or community privileges. Romania has been criticized by the UN Human Rights

Commission for its long-standing and pervasive discrimination against gypsies (Roma), a small but widespread ethnic minority.

In the later years of the Communist government, Romania attempted to extinguish the influence of minority communities and force their assimilation into the Romanian socialist culture and language. Post-Communist governments, under pressure from both the United Nations and the European Union, have allowed ethnic minorities more latitude, resulting in the emergence of ethnic-based political parties and the end of proscriptions on the use of minority languages in schools and publications. Since 1997, the Hungarian coalition party, the Hungarian Democratic Union, has been part of the ruling coalition in the national parliament.

Since Moldova declared its independence from the USSR, the Romanian government and Romanian nationalist parties have called for that country to be reunited with Romania. Moldova, which is 65 percent Romanian speaking and was part of Romania between World War I and World War II, has shown waning interest in reunification in recent years.

See also Hungarians; Moldova; Transylvania.
Reference Sandborne, Mark. *Romania (Nations in Transition)* (1996).

Rugova, Ibrahim (1944–)

Ibrahim Rugova is the president of the self-proclaimed Kosovo Republic. A Muslim, Rugova comes from a family of wealthy traders and intellectuals. His father and grandfather were both Kosovar nationalists and were executed by Yugoslav partisans when he was a child. An academic, Rugova earned a doctorate in literature from the University of Pristina in 1971 and is the author of several books. In 1988, he was elected president of the Kosovo Writers' Union.

Rugova founded the Democratic League of Kosovo and was elected president of the Kosovo Republic in the unofficial elections of 1992. With Kosovo under martial law, Rugova's government

organized schools and health clinics and aided unemployed Albanians fired from their state jobs on orders from Belgrade. These programs were financed by a voluntary tax on working Kosovars and donations from the Albanian community abroad.

By the mid-1990s, Rugova's effectiveness as a leader was being questioned, as his actions had brought no improvement in the Kosovo situation. Petitions to President Slobodan Milosevic had gone unheeded, and the failure to secure a provision concerning Kosovo in the Dayton peace accord, signed by Milosevic, was interpreted by many in Kosovo as proof that Rugova's nonviolent path to independence was fruitless.

He was soon challenged politically by the incipient Kosovo Liberation Army (KLA), which advocated guerrilla warfare against the Serb occupiers. A believer in pacifism, Rugova argued that armed resistance against Serbia would be futile, but the early success of the KLA in capturing territory from the Serbs undermined his position. Even though the massive Serbian invasion routed the KLA in 1998, the popularity of the KLA was such that NATO officially recognized it and seated its representatives at the Rambouillet peace conference in February 1999. At that conference, Rugova was overshadowed by KLA leader Hashim Thaci. The KLA subsequently announced the creation of a provisional government for Kosovo with Thaci as the prime minister designate. This was a direct challenge to Rugova's shadow government.

Rugova remains popular among the people if not among the politicians and pundits of Kosovo. In 1998, during wartime conditions in the province, he was reelected president of the Kosovo Republic. His appearance with Milosevic on Serbian television at the height of the NATO attacks raised questions about Rugova's integrity. Rugova claims he was under duress, but he has still not explained fully his role in the event. Following the UN-NATO occupation of Kosovo in June 1999, it is unclear what Rugova's place will be in the future of the territory. Some say his time has passed, and Rugova continues to resist forming a coalition with the KLA.

See also Kosovo; Kosovo Liberation Army.
Reference Malcolm, Noel. *Kosovo: A Short History* (1998).

Rukh

Rukh, the Ukrainian People's Movement for Reconstruction, was one of the first organizations in Soviet Ukraine to call for independence for the Ukraine. Rukh also pressed for guarantees of human and civil rights during the Mikhail Gorbachev period. Rukh favors Western market reforms and opposes the postindependence parties of the socialist left. It is also strongly Ukrainian nationalist. Although it holds more than thirty parliamentary seats, Rukh is not organized primarily as a political party. It sponsors clubs, holds rallies, and disseminates literature on its positions. Rukh backed the losing candidate, Leonid Kravchuk, in the 1994 presidential elections. In the 1998 legislative elections, Rukh finished second to the Communist Party. The major strength of Rukh, which is chaired by Vyachislav Chornovil, lies in the western part of Ukraine.

See also Ukraine.
Reference Magocsi, Paul. *History of Ukraine* (1996).

Russian Federation

The Russian Federation was formed in 1991 following the collapse of the Soviet Union. The first Russian state dates from the ninth century, and in 1682, with the elevation of Peter the Great, Russia became an expansionary empire absorbing, through treaty and military conquest, many of the non-Russian ethnic groups found within the Russian Federation today. From 1918 to 1991, Russia was one of the ethnic republics of the Soviet Union, a federation largely controlled by Russians in the Communist Party of the Soviet Union. During the Soviet period, most of the federation's ethnic republics and regions were established and given special status. When Russia declared its independence in 1991, it inherited the ethnic autonomies within its borders, but at the same time, some republics like Tatarstan passed resolutions either declaring their independence or enlarging the scope of their sovereignty.

The Russian Federation consists of twenty-one ethnic republics and several ethnic-based autonomous territories. The population of the federation is estimated at 150 million, of which 120 million are Russian. Of the some 100 other nationalities within the federation, only 6 have a population exceeding 1 million: Tatars, Bashkirs, Chuvash, Mordovians, Ukrainians, and Belarusians. In many of the ethnic republics, Russians also make up the largest ethnic group. In the Mordovia Republic, Russians compose 60 percent of the population, and in Komi, 58 percent. Because of the Russian bias of the Soviet Union, even in ethnic republics where Russians are a minority, Russians continue to hold important government positions disproportionate to their numbers in the population. In some republics, ethnic nationals in leading positions rose to power under the Soviet system and resist nationalist demands in their republics for more independence from Moscow.

Language is a source of strain in the federation. Most non-Russians are bilingual, as Russian was compulsory in all Soviet schools. Additionally, fluency in Russian was a necessity for advancing in a professional or governmental career. In the multiethnic republics, Russian also provided the only means of communication between disparate ethnic groups. But few Russians in the ethnic republics prior to the breakup of the Soviet Union had learned to speak the native language of the ethnic republics in which they lived. Although some ethnic groups have largely ceased to use their native language—80 percent of Mari parents, for example, converse with their children only in Russian—others have tenaciously maintained their native language. One survey estimates that 92 percent of the Chuvash, 86 percent of the Tatars, and 67 percent of the Bashkirs use their own languages in their daily lives.

Since 1991, many ethnic republics have been undergoing a cultural renaissance, reviving their language and incorporating it in the school curriculum. In some republics, nationalist political organizations are demanding that all high government officials speak the native language. At the moment, the republics of Buryatia, Ingushetia, Sakha, North Ossetia (Alania), Tuva, and Adygea have passed laws stipulating that presidential candidates must speak the native language of the republic. In Komi, the Biarmiya Party would like to restrict Komi citizenship to Komi speakers. Such nationalist tendencies cause anxiety among the Russians of these republics and have led them to protest to Moscow and seek to nullify the language measures through the federal courts. Anti-Russian initiatives in the ethnic republics have also resulted in a growing support by Russian voters in federal elections for ultranationalist parties like Vladimir Zhirinovsky's Liberal Democratic Party.

Within the ethnic republics, language can heighten group antagonisms. The Turkic-speaking Kumyks have demonstrated against the political dominance of the Caucasian-language-speaking Avars in Dagestan. The Iranian-language-speaking Ossetians have gone to war against the Caucasian-speaking Ingush, and the Turkic-speaking Tatars have protested the linguistic policies of the Finno-Ugric-language Udmurts in the Udmurt Republic. To be sure, many of these disputes involve more than linguistic issues, but language differences heighten the animosity between the groups.

Religion also plays a role in ethnic disputes within the federation. Although no in-depth survey is readily available that studies the saliency and depth of commitment to religious denominations in the ethnic republics, it can be inferred, based on pre-Soviet religious practices, that up to 8 percent of the federation's population is Muslim. The greatest concentration of Muslims is found in the Volga region (Tatars and Bashkirs) and the Caucasus (Chechens, Ingush, and Avars, to cite three). It is probably not a coincidence that Chechnya and Tatarstan have been the strongest advocates of ethnic republic autonomy and that this position has been strongly supported by the citizens of the two republics.

The end of communism has led to a revival of religious sentiment throughout the federation. Although some radical Islamist groups have formed, in Chechnya and Dagestan, for example, for the most part Islamic movements and parties have avoided espousing anti-Russian sentiments and have advocated the retention of a secular, religiously tolerant state. President Mintimer Shaimiev of Tatarstan, while extracting unprecedented economic and political concessions from the federal government, has kept in check the radical Islamist groups within Tatarstan. He has also proved helpful in negotiating a compromise between the neo-Communist government of Tajikistan and the Islamic and democratic opposition.

In Chechnya, by contrast, the late president Dzhokar Dudayev (who was killed by a Russian rocket and is now a national hero and martyr) called Chechnya's battle for independence a jihad. During the actual fighting between Russia and Chechnya, Dudayev received the support of other Muslim republics of the Caucasus, and Muslim volunteers from the Caucasus republics also joined Chechen forces in resisting the Russians. In late 1999, after Islamic radicals from Chechnya invaded the neighboring republic of Dagestan, Russian troops launched a second invasion of Chechnya.

The Russians are inordinately fearful of Islamic fundamentalism and, as in Tajikistan, have used force to prevent its taking root. Since the end of communism, several national conferences of Muslims have taken place in the federation. Their proposals, for the most part, have been of a pragmatic and limited nature, aimed at improving the status of Islamic citizens of the Russian Republic and calling for an end to the conflict in Chechnya.

Calls for regional separatism in the federation have originated primarily in the northern Caucasus. With Chechnya leading the initiative, a Confederation of the Caucasian People's was established in 1989. Although some organizations in the group saw the confederation as a first step toward creating an independent Caucasian nation, the confederation to date has mostly concerned itself with trying to resolve disputes between its own members and assisting in resolving conflicts beyond the federation's borders, like the Georgian–southern Abkhazian war. Turkic- and Finno-Ugric-speaking peoples have also held national conferences and discussed the creation of language-based confederations, but no realistic separatist actions have been implemented.

Ethnic unrest in the Russian Federation in recent years cannot be divorced from the deteriorating post-Soviet economy. The collapse of communism has been followed by a decline in the standard of living of most citizens of the federation, and inflation, combined with rising unemployment and the cutback of Soviet-era housing and medical and educational benefits, has worsened the situation of many citizens. Moscow's halting moves toward a free market economy coupled with widespread convictions that a privileged few insiders are enriching themselves at the expense of the average citizen provide fertile ground for activists in the non-Russian republics to call for more political autonomy from Moscow. Compounding these problems is the inability of state enterprises to meet their payrolls because of the disorganization that exists in the central government. A coal miners' strike in Komi in 1998 is representative of the widespread dissatisfaction with economic and political conditions in the federation.

An additional strain affecting the federation republics results from the dismantling of the centrally planned economy. Under the Soviet system, all enterprises were linked, and privatization broke many of these bonds, which augmented problems of supply and eliminated buyers of the enterprises' products. Privatization, which redirects economic activity toward the world market, has also rendered many Soviet-era industries obsolete, resulting in plant closings and layoffs. The cutoff of government funding for military and armament industries has further exacerbated employment problems.

Although economic misery plagues the entire federation, in the non-Russian ethnic republics it is easy to blame the Russian-dominated central government for local problems. The ideology of the free market economy also provides republic politicians an opportunity to call for local control of the economy, which is frequently coupled with proposals for further political autonomy from the central government. Ironically, in the poorer republics like Mari El where Soviet-era politicians still dominate, nationalism can be invoked as a pretext for avoiding Moscow's free market directives for closing inefficient enterprises and dismantling state and collective farms. In the resource-rich republics like Tatarstan and Sakha (or Yakutia), the nationalist card is played in order to secure more favorable economic concessions from the central government.

Constitutional problems are another source of tension between the federal government and the constituent republics. The largest ethnic republic, Russia, has the least-developed administrative structure of any of the federation republics. Most decision making in the former Soviet Union was carried out by the Russian-dominated Communist Party, and although Russia became independent in 1991, it had few legal norms or institutions in place to govern the new federation. In 1991 and 1992, it drew up three treaties defining the role of the central government and the twenty-one constituent republics. It was not until 1993 that a federation constitution was approved through the referendum process. However, at the time of the Soviet Union's disintegration, several of the republics of the current Russian Federation revised their own constitutions, in effect greatly increasing the scope of their sovereignty. Two republics, Chechnya and Tatarstan, declared themselves independent nations and refused either to sign the federative treaties or to accept the new constitution.

The constitution itself contains an ambiguity that engenders conflicts between the federal government and the member republics. Although the national constitution declares the federation indivisible and allows no right of members to secede, it also declares that the constitutions of the member republics are legally binding. Thus, Tatarstan and Chechnya could claim the right to secede as their republic constitutions define them as sovereign nations. Although an issue of this nature in Western European nations is something that would be resolved by the highest judicial body of the state, in Russia, the Constitutional Court is rarely employed to adjudicate major issues involving the state, and to date, the court has remained relatively ineffective. Conflicts between the federation and the republics are usually handled in bilateral negotiations. The Chechen cease-fire, for example, was negotiated in 1966 by the former Russian general Alexander Lebed and Chechen representatives.

Confronted with the threat of two resource-rich regions, Chechnya and Tatarstan, seceding from the federation, the Yeltsin government reacted in two contradictory ways. It went to war with Chechnya, and it negotiated a special treaty with Tatarstan. The first war with Chechnya proved disastrous as Russia received worldwide condemnation. In the case of Tatarstan, the Yeltsin government, mindful of the republic's significant oil reserves, its strategic Volga location, and its symbolic role as the leading voice of the Turkic and Muslim citizens of the federation, chose negotiation and ultimately granted Tatarstan extraordinary political and economic concessions not available to the other federation republics. This asymmetric relationship is not unlike the special status granted to Quebec by Canada. Even though the treaty has brought Tatarstan back into the federation fold, it also encourages other republics to cut special deals with Moscow. From a legal perspective, the use of special treaties to resolve disputes between the federal government and the constituent republics undermines the efficacy and the legitimacy of the federation's constitution.

As has been noted, the complexity of ethnic

relations in the Russian Federation arises in part from the involuntary manner in which non-Russians were added to the Russian Empire in the eighteenth and nineteenth centuries. Though Russification and upward mobility in the developing economy of the Soviet Union attenuated particularistic attachments among many of the ethnic groups of Soviet Russia, others, like the Tatars, Bashkirs, and Chechens, maintained their ethnic solidarity and now draw on this resource to improve the status of their republics.

A second factor affecting ethnic relations in the Russian Federation also derives from the manner in which non-Russians were added to the empire. Unlike the United States, another multi-ethnic nation, where newly entering immigrants were dispersed territorially, in Russia, each ethnic nationality has a distinct territorial homeland, and early Soviet policy called for each of these significant Kremlin-defined ethnic groups to have its own administrative territory. Under Soviet rule, these autonomous republics and regions in Russia had little power, and with the demise of the Soviet Union, they came, by default, under the jurisdiction of the new Russian Federation. During this period of uncertainty, the ethnic subnations of Russia maneuvered through parliamentary measures to increase their autonomy.

Because each of the twenty-one republics had its own legislature and media, each had the institutional means to press its ethnonationalistic demands. Except for Chechnya, Tatarstan, and to a lesser degree Sakha and Bashkortostan, these demands for autonomy were held in check by Moscow's insistence that the federation was indivisible. The presence of large numbers of Russians and other ethnic groups in the republics also acted as a brake on excessive nationalist claims by the ethnic groups for which the republics were named, which were often in the minority. Poorer republics, like Mari El and Chuvashia, however enthusiastically they proclaimed their right to autonomy, were too dependent on state subsidies to wage any meaningful separatist adventures. In Chechnya, where neither state aid

Soldiers atop a Russian armored personnel carrier patrol the mountains of southern Chechnya, July 1996. Chechnya's separatist movement is but one of many threats to the unity of the multiethnic Russian Federation. (Reuters/Vladimir Svartsevich/Archive Photos)

nor the prospect of a negotiated political compromise worked, the Moscow-labeled outlaw republic was invaded by the Russian-dominated armed forces of the former USSR in 1996. The inability of the Russian military to bring the first Chechen campaign to a successful conclusion further vitiated the legitimacy of the federation. In 1999 the Russians again attempted to impose their authority over Chechnya by military force.

The Chechnya issue also reinforces the convictions of non-Russians in the federation that the Russians who dominate the political institutions of the federation have no wish to share power with former subjects of the Russian Empire. The fact that several ethnic republics accede to the policies of the Yeltsin government is perceived by demo-

cratic opposition groups as an indication that the pro-Russian bureaucracy of Soviet times remains firmly in control in these ethnic republics. In 1992, serious unrest swept the Kabardino-Balkar Republic. The grievance did not concern hostility between the two antagonistic ethnic groups but, rather, the obstinacy of the Soviet-era political elite to accommodate popular demands for change in the republic.

Muslim nationals of the federation are particularly wary of Russians. Not only are they aware of the popular disdain shown by Russians for Muslims and citizens of the Caucasus republics, they also do not forget or forgive Joseph Stalin's forcible exile of hundreds of thousands of Caucasian and Crimean Muslims from their historic homelands. The growing power of the Russian Orthodox Church in restricting proselytizing activities of other religious denominations is also perceived as a hostile to Islam. Ethnic animosities such as this have made situations like the Chechnya dispute extremely difficult to resolve.

Many of the so-called ethnic republics also seethe with hostilities. Dagestan, the most multiethnic of the non-Russian republics and the state that might serve as a model for the new Russian Federation, is awash with internal conflict and constantly trying to balance the contradictory political, linguistic, economic, and territorial demands of its ethnic communities. Wars that originate beyond its borders but still affect groups living in the republic make Dagestan a powder keg. Antagonisms involving Russians, Chechens, Ingush, Ossetians, Lezgins, Cossacks, and Abkhazians quickly spill over into Dagestan to produce feuds, kidnappings, and assassinations.

But Dagestan is but one of the federation's republics in which residents cannot accommodate themselves to their fellow citizens. In two of the republics established under the Soviet Union, Karachai-Cherkessia and Kabardino-Balkaria, a Caucasian-language people has been coupled with a Turkic group. In neither case has this centrally decreed marriage worked, and each of the four ethnic communities has pressed for its own republic since 1991. Previously, another dual nationality republic, the Chechen-Ingushetia Republic, was dissolved. In contrast to the cases just cited, the Chechens and the Ingush are both Caucasian peoples who speak a similar language and are both Sunni Muslims. Still, they opted for separation, the Chechens feeling that the Ingush were too friendly toward czarist Russia. A further problem afflicting some of the republics of the Caucasus is the return of ethnic groups exiled by Stalin. In Dagestan, Chechen-Akkins are laying claim to land now settled by Kumyks and Lakhs. In the Karbardino-Balkar Republic, the exiled Balkars are pressing for a return of the land they held in 1944.

Conflict between Federation republics is another source of instability. Ingushetia and North Ossetia have gone to war over disputed territory, and Chechnya claims territory that is now part of Dagestan.

As in postcolonial Africa, the borders of the federation's republics offend many groups. Drawn up in the Soviet era for several reasons— some strategic, some compensatory, some punitive, and some obscure—Russian Federation borders today leave many newly energized ethnic groups spread across several administrative jurisdictions. This situation allows a host of national groups to demand the creation of new republics or regions that would unite all their peoples. Tatar, Chuvash, Bashkir, and Adygean organizations have all pressed such claims, insisting that their fellow ethnics now in other republics be reassigned to the home republic bearing their name. Some smaller ethnic groups, like the Nogays, the Kumyks, and the Shapsugs, that have no territory allotted to their group have requested they be granted their own autonomous jurisdictions. Not surprisingly, the Federation government has resisted such demands, arguing the need for the Russian Federation to remain a unified nation-state.

The Cossacks, who are widely dispersed throughout Russia in both Europe and Asia, form another noteworthy group. Cossacks, since being resurrected from their Soviet nonexistence, have revived their traditional self-governing communities and become very active politically. They seek, not autonomy from the Russian Federation, but detachment from the non-Russian, non-Orthodox republics where Soviet history consigned them. Cossacks in Dagestan, Adygea, Chechnya, and Karachay-Cherkessia wish to be associated either with the Russian Republic or granted autonomy. Their fierce pro-Russian stance and their desire to serve as soldiers defending the borders of Russia and the former Soviet republics of central Asia, such as Tajikistan, have made them increasingly invaluable to the beleaguered government of Boris Yeltsin.

Ethnic problems in the federation are not limited to its borders. The Abkhazians of Dagestan wish to be united with the Abkhazians of the breakaway Georgian republic of Abkhazia, the North Ossetians have aided the separatist revolt in the Georgian republic of South Ossetia, and the Lezgins of Dagestan envisage a Lezgin republic carved out of Dagestan and Azerbaijan.

The Russian Federation, with its expanded post-Communist freedoms, is also the setting for more all-embracing if unrealizable desires calling for the union of all Turkic-speaking peoples, including the Uyghurs of China, for a Caucasian Muslim nation, for a Finno-Ugric based nation, and for the reconstitution of a Slavic neo-Soviet Empire.

See also Abkhazia; Adygea; Bashkortosan; Buryatia; Chechnya; Chuvashia; Confederation of the Caucasian Peoples; Cossacks; Dagestan; Ingushetia; Karbardino-Balkharia; Kalmykia; Karachay-Cherkessia; Komi; Krasnodar; Lezgins; Mari El; Mordovian Republic; Nogays; Sakha; South Ossetia; Tatarstan; Udmurtia.
References Mastyugina, Tatiana, and Lev Perelkin. *An Ethnic History of Russia* (1996); Remnick, David. *Resurrection: The Struggle for a New Russia* (1998); Sakwa, Richard. *Russian Politics and Society* (1996).

Russians in the Former Soviet Republics

The collapse of the Soviet Union in 1991 left some 25 million Russians in the newly independent former Soviet republics that are outside the Russian Federation. Traditionally, the Russians held managerial posts in government and industrial organizations, with many positions being linked to related political, military, and defense functions. The end of the Soviet Union brought about a rapid decline in the military-industrial complex and its array of prestigious, well-paying professions in the former Soviet republics.

Independence also resulted in the replacement of Russians by ethnic personnel in cultural and political institutions and a conscious effort to promote native economic managers. In many republics, non-Russian languages are replacing Russian as the first language of the country, and funding for Russian instruction in the public schools is being curtailed. Although most native political and economic leaders were bilingual under the Soviet system, Russians working in these countries frequently do not know the native language of the republic. Consequently, the career prospects for many of the Russian Soviet elite in the former Soviet republics remain dim.

Cultural factors affect the climate of relations in the new republics. Whereas Russians are warmly treated in Belarus, in Latvia and Estonia anti-Russian sentiment has resulted in measures that make it extremely difficult for Russians to obtain citizenship. In countries like Kazakhstan and Uzbekistan, where the governments tolerate Russians and grant them citizenship, the growing cultural divide between Muslim natives and Orthodox Russians has led many Russians to opt for migration to Russia. On the other hand, even where Russians have not been particularly welcome, as in the Baltic nations, the wretched performance of the Russian economy has convinced many Russians that they are better off staying where they are, citizenship or not.

Russian separatists in Transdniester and the Crimea have revolted against the governments of Moldova and Ukraine. The Transdniester region still retains its autonomy today while Ukraine has reached a temporary accommodation with the Russian regions of Crimea and the Donbas region of eastern Ukraine. Cossack Russians demand separation from non-Russian Muslim jurisdictions in the Caucasus so they might rejoin the Russian Republic. Cossacks also agitate for the annexation of parts of Kazakhstan to Russia. Nationalist politicians in Russia fan support for the expatriates' causes, calling in some instances for a reestablishment of the Soviet empire. The Russian government also threatened severe economic sanctions against Latvia if that country did not liberalize its citizenship laws, which it has recently done.

See also Belarus; Cossacks; Crimea; Donbas Russians; Estonia; Kazakhstan; Latvia; Russian Federation; Transdniester; Ukraine.
References Chinn, Jeff, and Robert John Kaiser. *Russians as the New Minority: Ethnicity and Nationalism in Soviet Successor States* (1996); Melvin, Neil. *Russians beyond Russia: The Politics of National Identity* (1995).

Rusyns

The Rusyns, also known as the Ruthenians, speak an eastern Slavic language, use the Cyrillic alphabet, and are either members of the Orthodox or the Uniate (Eastern rite Roman Catholic) Church. Rusyns are found in the Carpathian mountain region of central Europe, and like the Kurds, the Rusyns are citizens of several countries. There are approximately 1 million Rusyns in Ukraine, 120,000 in Slovakia, and 60,000 in Poland. Other Rusyns live in the Serbian province of Voivodina in Hungary and in Romania.

For most of their modern history, Rusyns were a part of the Austro-Hungarian Empire, but after World War I, Rusyns were divided between Poland, Hungary, Romania, Yugoslavia, and subsequently, the Soviet Union. However, the majority of the Rusyns were assigned to the newly created Czechoslovakia where they were granted considerable autonomy in their province, Sub-Carpathian Rus. Following the Munich agreement of 1938, the province was granted autonomy. In 1939, the province declared its independence, and it was almost immediately occupied and annexed by Axis Hungary. Following World War II, the territory was ceded to the Ukraine Soviet Socialist Republic and was renamed the Zakarpats'ka province.

In the 1990s, Rusyns pushed for greater self-determination, for despite attempts by the governments of both Slovakia and Ukraine to have Rusyns labeled as Ukrainians, Rusyns have insisted on their own identity. In the 1991 referendum that declared Ukraine an independent nation, 78 percent of the Rusyns voted for greater autonomy from Ukraine. Kiev ignored their vote. In 1993, a provisional government of the autonomous republic of Sub-Carpathian Rus was declared in the capital of the region, Uzhgorod. Since 1994, a fifty-one-member Transcarpathian National Council has been sitting. Ivan Turyanitsa is currently prime minister of the self-declared government and continues to push for Rusyn autonomy.

In Slovakia, under the authoritarian government of Prime Minister Vladimir Meciar, Ruthenians fought with little success to have their nationality recognized. At the Fourth World Congress of Rusyns held in Budapest in 1997, it was reported that Yugoslavia, Hungary, Poland, and post-Meciar Slovakia had acknowledged Rusyns as national minorities. Ukraine still refuses to grant Rusyns official recognition.

See also Slovakia; Ukraine.
References Bonkalo, Sandor. *The Rusyns* (1990); Shandor, Vikentii. *Carpatho-Ukraine in the Twentieth Century* (1997).

Rwanda

In 1994, Rwanda gained the attention of the world when the numerically dominant Hutus attempted the most extreme form of ethnic separatism: the extermination of the minority Tutsis within the country's borders. More than 800,000 Tutsis died in the genocide.

Rwanda, with a population of 8 million, is a landlocked country in the lakes region of central East Africa. The Twa, a pygmy group believed to have been the first settlers of the region, currently make up 1 percent of the population. The Hutus, who constitute 85 percent of the population, probably migrated to the region from the Congo basin and were primarily agriculturalists. These short, dark-skinned people were largely settled in Rwanda by the fifteenth century when the Tutsis, a tall, light-skinned group from the Horn of Africa migrated into the country. The Tutsis, traditionally pastoralists, soon established themselves as rulers of the region through the office of king, or *mwami,* and a feudal hierarchy. Europeans began to filter into the region in the nineteenth century, and in 1899, Rwanda was incorporated into German East Africa. In 1915, the Belgians took control from the Germans. After World War I, the League of Nations created the Belgian Mandate in Rwanda and neighboring Burundi. Following World War II, Rwanda became a UN trust territory under Belgian administration.

The Belgians worked mostly with the Tutsi elite, partly justifying this by reference to popular racial theories which argued that the Nilotic Tutsis were superior to the more Negroid Hutus. Although by the twentieth century both Hutus and Tutsis spoke the same language, Kinyarwanda, and both were predominantly Christian (80 percent), the two groups were visually distinguishable despite some intermarriage. After independence in 1962, mandatory national identity cards listed the ethnicity of each Rwandan, and during the period of the genocide, the identity cards facilitated the labeling of physically ambiguous individuals. The postindependence Hutu government also enforced racial quotas in education, government, and private employment, limiting the Tutsis to an artificially low 9 percent in each category. Consequently, both colonial and postcolonial governments pursued policies that kept alive the popular belief in the fundamental differences between Hutus and Tutsis.

Toward the end of Belgian rule, the Belgians, aided by church officials, encouraged the development of democratic institutions and attempted to redress some of the inequalities maintained by Tutsi dominance. When the Tutsis resisted, the Hutus revolted in 1959 and abolished the Tutsi monarchy. More than 180,000 Tutsis fled into neighboring Burundi. In 1961, the Hutu-dominated Parmethu Party won the national elections, and in July 1962, Rwanda became independent. Parmethu leader Gregoire Kayibanda became the first president, and he renamed the Parmethu Party the Democratic Republican Movement. An attempted invasion by a Burundi-based Tutsi army was repelled, and in Rwanda, Hutus responded by massacring 10,000 Tutsis. A Tutsi campaign against Hutus in neighboring Burundi caused thousands of Hutus to seek refuge in Rwanda.

In 1973, the Hutu general Juvenal Habyarimana staged a coup, dissolved the National Assembly, and banned political parties except for the newly created National Revolutionary Movement for Development (MRND). Habyarimana was reconfirmed as president in elections in 1978, 1983, and 1988. In 1987, a Tutsi army based in Uganda, the Rwandan Patriotic Front (RPF),

aided by Ugandan president Yoweri Museveni, vowed to retake Rwanda by force. In 1990, the RPF invaded Rwanda, blaming Habyarimana for failing to address the situation of the 500,000 Tutsis of the diaspora.

Although the invasion stalled within Rwandan territory, Habyarimana, under international prodding, agreed to move toward a multiparty state with Tutsis included in future governments. Hutu radicals were opposed to any concessions to the Tutsis, and their strength grew. Radicals in the MRND gained control over the Interahamwe, the party youth militia, and Zero Network, Hutu death squads, were organized. A new racist Hutu party, the Coalition for the Defense of the Republic (CDR) came into being. Headed by Jean Barahinyuru, the CDR also established its own newspaper and radio station. The latter played an important role in orchestrating and directing the subsequent genocide.

On April 6, 1964, the airplane carrying President Habyarimana and the president of Burundi was shot down near the Rwandan capital of Kigali, killing both leaders. The presidential guard, the military, the Interahamwe, MRND extremists, and regional government officials immediately began killing Tutsis and moderate Hutus throughout the country. Between April 6 and July 4, nearly 1 million people were killed. The Tutsi RPF intensified its military campaign, and by July 4, it had taken Kigali. It is estimated that 2 million Hutus fled Rwanda after the RPF takeover. Since that time, all but 100,000 are believed to have returned to Rwanda. The remainder, mostly in Congo (Kinshasa) are largely Interahamwe militia and former Hutu military personnel now reorganized as the Rwandan Patriotic Army (RPA). Supported by Congo president Laurent Kabila, these Hutu forces continue to wage armed struggle against the RPF in Congo and Rwanda.

In Rwanda, the Tutsi Pasteur Bizimungu is president, and former RPF military commander Paul Kagame is vice-president. The RPF governs through the Broad Based Government of National

Unity, which includes some Hutus. The government has arrested and jailed more than 100,000 Hutus believed to have been involved in the massacres, and 20 or so have already been executed. Hutu guerrillas, who returned to Rwanda with the refugee influx, remain active in several parts of the country. Whether national reconciliation can be achieved in the near future is questionable. No workable formula for a democratic government that is acceptable to both Tutsis and Hutus has emerged, and extremists on both sides continue to call for the extermination of the other.

References Gourevitch, Philip. *We Wish to Inform You That Tomorrow We Will Be Killed with Our Families* (1998); Prunier, Gerard. *The Rwanda Crisis: History of a Genocide* (1995).

Rwenzururu

Rwenzururu (Ruwenzori), the mountainous region of western Uganda, is inhabited by the Bakonzo and Baamba peoples and is part of the traditional kingdom of Toro. The dominant group in Toro, the Batoro, constitute a majority (55 percent) of the population while the Bakonzo and Baamba make up about a third. In 1954, the Bakonzo Life History Research Society was set up by Isaya Mukirane in an attempt to revive that people's traditions and culture. Its activities heightened Bakonzo grievances against the Batoro and their sense of lost independence. In 1962, the Rwenzururu Movement was formed and called for a separate district to be set up.

Prior to Ugandan independence in 1962, the Bakonzo and Baamba leaders insisted that the constitution of Toro recognize their tribes as having parity with the Batoro. When this condition was refused, Mukirane set up the secessionist Kingdom of Rwenzururu with its own army, taxes, and schools. The rebels raided Batoro villages and received wide support from the Bakonzo. Given the inaccessible terrain, the secessionist regime was able to maintain a de facto independence until the 1970s. However, when the Ugandan central government took over the administration of the Bakonzo and Baamba areas from the Toro government, many moderate Bakonzo withdrew their support from the rebels. Yet even in the 1980s, Rwenzururu guerrillas were still active in the area.

Reference Doornbos, Martin R. "Kumanyana and Rwenzururu: Two Responses to Ethnic Inequality" (1970).

Saami

The Saami people (formerly known as the Lapps) number about 60,000 and live above the Arctic Circle in northern Norway, Sweden, Finland, and Russia. Their homeland covers some 29,000 square miles, but they constitute a majority in only six Norwegian communes and one Finnish district. Originally, the Saami were nomadic reindeer herders, hunters, and trappers who spoke a language akin to Finnish. The Saami gradually came under the control of the expanding Nordic kingdoms in the twelfth century, but their traditional lifestyle was little affected, and treaties recognized their right to travel freely across international frontiers with their reindeer herds.

Norway, where more than half the Saami live, attempted to assimilate them by discouraging the use of their language. However, that policy was abandoned in 1947, and the right of children to be educated in their mother tongue was recognized by a royal commission on the Saami in 1959. Subsequently, several advisory bodies have been set up, including a Norwegian Saami Council, to make recommendations on government policy; a Saami Educational Council; and a Saami Cultural Committee. In 1980, a Saami Rights Committee was established, and it issued its first report in 1984. Although recognizing that the Saami were "a people in a political and sociological sense," the report concluded that the UN Charter did not establish the right to self-determination for them. However, the report proposed that a national Saami parliament (Sameting) be created, and the first elections for this were held in 1989. In 1984, a draft "Saami convention" proposed that an autonomous transnational territory should be created in those areas of Finland, Norway, and Sweden in which there is a majority Saami population.

Reference Hannum, Hurst. *Autonomy, Sovereignty, and Self-Determination* (1990).

Saar

The Saar in Germany is a coal-mining region with an important iron and steel industry. After World War I, the Saar was administered by France as a League of Nations mandate, but after a 1935 plebiscite, in which 90 percent voted in favor, it was reunited with Germany. At the end of World War II, it became part of the French occupation zone. France took steps to integrate the region with the French economy by creating a customs barrier with the rest of Germany and making the franc the legal currency.

Germany protested those moves, and in 1954, the two countries concluded an agreement whereby the Saar would become an autonomous territory within a western European union, subject to a referendum to be held in 1955. The agreement was supported by the Saar Socialist Party and its leader, Johannes Hoffman, but the anti-agreement parties formed the Heimatbund (Homeland League) and campaigned vigorously for the reunification of the Saar with Germany. At rallies held by the Heimatbund, the audience sang the German national anthem, *Deutschland über alles,* while meetings held by Hoffman were attacked by hostile demonstrators. The Saarlanders rejected the agreement by a majority of more than two to one, and the Saar was returned to Germany in 1956.

Reference Freymond, Jacques. *The Saar Conflict* (1960).

Sabah

One of the Malaysian states, located on the island of Borneo, Sabah was formerly known as North Borneo. The region was claimed by both the sultan of Sulu and the sultan of Brunei in the nineteenth century. The British North Borneo Company, established in 1881, administered—in casual fashion—a population of Malays, Chinese, and animist tribes. After World War II, North Borneo became a British colony, and in 1963, it joined the Federation of Malaysia as Sabah.

The population, of about 1 million in 1980, is divided into three main groups: Muslim Malays (51 percent), ethnic Chinese (16 percent), and the indigenous peoples (33 percent), the most important being the Kadazan and the Muruts. The indigenous peoples have largely converted to Christianity. Since 1980, the number of Malays has increased, largely as a result of Muslim refugees fleeing from the conflict in the southern Philippines. Estimates of the number of refugees range between 100,000 and 200,000.

The Philippines claimed Sabah, on the grounds that Sabah had once been part of the sultanate of Sulu, but officially relinquished the claim in 1977. Tensions also existed because the state government of Tun Mustapha allegedly provided the Moro insurgents with training and weapons. Mustapha claims descent from the sultan of Sulu, and his party, the United Sabah National Organization (USNO), was dominated by Sulu Muslims. USNO was defeated in 1976 by Berjaya (the Sabah People's Union), a victory that was attributed to Kadazan resentment of what they saw as Mustapha's attempt to transform Sabah into a Muslim-majority state by encouraging Filipino immigration.

There has been a growing rift between Sabah and the central government since Malaysia was created. The federation was established despite the misgivings of many in Sabah—the Kadazans in particular feared they would be swamped by the power of the Muslim Malay majority in the federation as a whole. Although promised that their special identity would be safeguarded by

"iron-clad guarantees," these guarantees were whittled down to a list of twenty points that were not incorporated in the constitution. Donald Stephens, the Kadazan leader, resigned from the federal cabinet, and his party campaigned in the 1967 elections as the defenders of Sabah against federal encroachment.

The victorious Tun Mustapha and his USNO vigorously promoted Islamization and the Malay language but fell out with the federation's government in Kuala Lumpur over the issue of oil revenues. Most recently, the Sabah Unity Party (PBS), drawing its support from the Kadazan and Chinese communities, has advocated renegotiating federal-state relations. The PBS won the Sabah state elections of 1985 and increased its share of the vote in subsequent elections. In 1990, it won sixteen of Sabah's twenty seats in the federation parliament. The PBS demanded restrictions on Muslim Filipino immigration, a greater role for Sabahans in the civil service (the staff of which is currently more than 65 percent nonlocal), a major increase in the state's 5 percent share of oil revenues, and revived constitutional guarantees. The National Front government in Kuala Lumpur responded by accusing the PBS of being part of a secessionist plot to take Sabah out of Malaysia and arresting its leaders on a variety of charges.

See also Kalimantan Utara; Malaysia; Moros.
References Ariff, Mohd. *The Philippines Claim to Sabah* (1970); Bedlington, Stanley S. *Malaysia and Singapore: The Building of New States* (1978); Kahin, Audrey R. "Crisis on the Periphery: The Rift between Kuala Lumpur and Sabah" (1992); Lim, Jock, and S. Vani, eds. *Armed Separatism in Southeast Asia* (1984); Roff, Margaret. *The Politics of Belonging: Political Change in Sabah and Sarawak* (1974); Tarling, Nicholas. *Sulu and Sabah* (1978).

Sakha

The Republic of Sakha, also known as Yakutia, is located in northeastern Siberia. In area, Sakha is the largest of the constituent republics of the Russian Federation, but its population numbers only about 1 million. The Sakha people, who number about 400,000, were originally nomadic herders and speak a Turkic language. The strength of Sakha national consciousness rests in the language. In 1994, Sakha was used as the primary language by 97 percent of Sakha households; in contrast, among the Evenk, another indigenous group in the territory, only 5 percent of households used Evenk as their primary language. After the Buryats, the Sakha are the largest indigenous group in Siberia. Historically, the Sakha tribes were bound together by their animistic religion, Tengi, but after Russian penetration in the seventeenth century, many Sakhas converted to the Orthodox religion. In the 1930s, Joseph Stalin repressed the animists and executed many of the shamans.

Russians began entering Sakha territory in 1632 and established a fortress at Yakutsk, which is now the capital. Russian traders, fur hunters, and gold prospectors were drawn to the region through the early twentieth century, but as late as 1917, Sakhas constituted a majority of the population. In 1922, Sakha became an autonomous republic of the Soviet Union. Stalin's ambitious economic development plans brought an influx of Russians, and by 1950, Russians outnumbered Sakhas. Soviet development, geared heavily to gold and diamond mining, bypassed most Sakhas who were forced onto collective farms. In 1979 and 1986, anti-Russian riots broke out, and an underground Sakha nationalist movement, Sakha Omut, which had been founded in 1921, became active again. In 1990, with the collapse of the Soviet Union, Sakha declared its sovereignty. In 1992, Sakha joined the Russian Federation as a constituent republic. Former Communist Party boss and a Sakha, Mikhail Nikolayev, was elected president of the republic and reelected to a five-year term in 1996.

Like Tatarstan, Sakha has used its nationalism and its extraordinary natural resources as a wedge to extract special concessions from Moscow. Nikolayev forced Moscow to grant the republic significant control over the diamond industry and to be allowed to retain a greater share of taxes. A bilateral treaty between the Russian Federation and Sakha granted Sakha enhanced political sovereignty, including the right to make international treaties but not the right to secede. Since then, Sakha has demonstrated its independence by suspending gold shipments to Moscow in 1998 over delinquent payments for previous deliveries. It has also begun making treaties with Asian Pacific nations. The Sakha parliament has proposed legislation that would make it difficult for non-Sakha speakers to hold political positions, a measure that would discriminate against Russian citizens in the republic. With the continued weakness of the federation and Sakha's natural wealth, some analysts think Sakha may someday demand full independence.

See also Russian Federation.
References Khazanov, Anatoly. *After the USSR: Ethnicity, Nationalism, and Politics in the Commonwealth of Independent States* (1995); Okladinov, Aleksi, and Henry Michael, eds. *Yakutia: Before Its Incorporation into the Russian State* (1970).

Salmond, Alex (1954–)

The Scottish National Party leader Alex Salmond was born December 31, 1954. His father, Robert, was a fervent Scottish nationalist, but his mother voted Conservative for many years. In 1987, Salmond was elected member of parliament for the Banff constituency and has been reelected ever since. Before being elected, he worked as an economist in the Department of Agriculture and Fisheries and subsequently for the Royal Bank of Scotland.

See also Scottish National Party.

Sanjak

Sanjak is a former Turkish administrative district located in the Yugoslavian republics of Serbia and Montenegro between Bosnia and Kosovo. The area has a population of 530,000 and is 67 percent Muslim. Like the Muslim population of Bosnia, the Sanjak Muslims are Slavs who converted to Islam during the years of Ottoman domination. In the nineteenth century, Sanjak was controlled by the Ottoman Empire and later the Austro-Hungarian Empire as a buffer state between the two Slavic states of Serbia and Montenegro, thus preventing their unification. Following the Balkan Wars (1912–1913), Sanjak was occupied and then divided by Serbia and Montenegro; some 27,000 Muslims were displaced to Bosnia. With the creation of the Kingdom of Serbs, Croats, and Slovenes in 1918 (renamed Yugoslavia in 1929), the administrative district of Sanjak was abolished. From 1943 to 1945, Josip Broz Tito's partisans treated Sanjak as an autonomous province. After World War II, Sanjak was again divided and lost its autonomy.

The disintegration of Yugoslavia and the abandonment of communism enabled Sanjak Muslims to organize politically. In 1991, the Party of Democratic Action (SDA) was formed, and it called for reunification and autonomy for Sanjak. In October 1991, the Muslim National Council, now renamed the Bosniak National Council (BNC), a coalition of Muslim parties and organizations, held a referendum on independence in Sanjak. Ninety-five percent of those voting approved complete political and territorial autonomy. In the summer of 1992, the BNC submitted a document known as "the memorandum" to the Serb and Montenegrin governments proposing a special status for Sanjak. The document was ignored by both republic governments of the rump Yugoslavia. In 1993, a Serbian court banned the publication of the memorandum on the grounds it incited religious hatred and threatened the integrity of the state. Several Muslim activists were subsequently arrested, and forty-five people were convicted of crimes against the state and given prison sentences. Serbian police and military were increased in the territory.

After boycotting elections from 1993 to 1995, the SDA participated in the November 1996 local and federal elections, winning two seats in the federal parliament and control over three cities. Shortly afterward, Serbia suspended the elected Muslim government of Novi Pazar, the capital of the region. Serbia then proclaimed emergency rule, declaring that Bosniak-Muslim parties were composed of Islamic fundamentalists seeking to undermine the state. Further prosecutions were threatened.

During the Bosnian war (1991–1995), Serbian paramilitary forces operated out of Sanjak, terrorizing Muslim residents and forcing one-fourth of the population to flee. In those years, the Helsinki Committee for Human Rights documented 34 killings, 131 kidnappings, and 18 armed attacks by Serb forces operating in Sanjak.

In recent years, the increasingly nationalist and repressive regime of Slobodan Milosevic, along with the splintering of Muslim political parties into factions, has dampened Sanjak attempts to achieve autonomy. The NATO bombing campaign against Yugoslavia that begun in early 1999 raised tensions in the Sanjak region. Fearing that Serbia might use the conflict as an opportunity to conduct further "ethnic cleansing," many Muslims fled the region and resettled in Bosnia.

In the more-liberal Montenegrin republic led by Milo Djukanovic, Sanjak politicians have supported the government. However, rumors of an impending coup in Montenegro by pro-Milosevic politicians and Serbian army units stationed in Montenegro make the future of Sanjak Muslims in that republic uncertain.

See also Montenegro; Yugoslavia.
Reference Judah, Tim. *History, Myth, and the Destruction of Yugoslavia* (1997).

Sanwi Liberation Front

The Sanwi Liberation Front was a movement organized among the Agni people of the southeastern Ivory Coast that sought independence for the region. The secession was encouraged by Ghana's Kwame Nkrumah and led to violence in 1959. In 1969, another rebellion broke out, but it was quickly suppressed by the Ivory Coast army.

See also Ghana.
Reference Morrison, Donald G. *Black Africa: A Comparative Handbook* (1989).

Sardinia

On Sardinia, a Mediterranean island that was politically united with mainland Italy in 1847, the islanders speak Sard, a distinctive Italian dialect that is not permitted in the schools. In 1948, Sardinia became an autonomous region against the wishes of most of its political leaders and "in the total absence of any nationalist agitation." Sardinian politicians relied upon the generous subsidies provided by the central government, although economic aid generated few jobs. In the late 1960s, a nationalist movement began to emerge as intellectuals rediscovered their local culture and called for the use of Sard in schools.

The PSd'Azione (Sardinian Party of Action), originally a federalist party in the immediate post–World War II period, proclaimed independence as a goal in 1979, and new members flocked into the party—its percentage of the vote increased from 1.9 percent in 1979 to 13.1 percent in 1987. In the regional elections of 1994, parties running on regionalist platforms received 11.5 percent of the vote and eight out of sixty-four seats. Support for Sardinian independence and for the PSd'Azione is highest among professionals and blue-collar workers and lowest among peasants. A 1984 survey found that 40 percent of Sardinians favored independence and 55 percent wanted more autonomy.

See also Italy.
Reference Clark, Martin. "Cheese and Modernization" (1996).

Schleswig

The Duchy of Schleswig was ceded to Germany by Denmark after the war of 1864. After a referendum in 1920, the northern part of Schleswig was returned to Denmark while the south voted to remain German. After World War II, the 50,000 Danes in South Schleswig agitated for a border revision or, failing that, for cultural autonomy. However, the share of the regional vote won by the South Schleswig Voters League, which represents the 50,000 Danes, fell from 9.3 percent (99,500 votes)

in 1947 to 1.3 percent (21,000 votes) in 1983. (The 1947 vote included large numbers of ethnic Germans who apparently regarded being part of Denmark as preferable for economic reasons.)

Scotland

Until 1707, Scotland was an independent country with its own parliament and its own king, although it had shared its monarch with England since 1603. In 1707, by the Act of Union, the two countries became the United Kingdom. Under the act, Scotland retained its own legal system and the established Presbyterian Church. The Scots have always been conscious of their own distinctive identity and their national history, the dominant theme of which is Scottish resistance to English domination. Language, however, plays almost no role in Scottish nationalism. Gaelic is spoken by a small number of people in the Highlands and western islands, but the majority of the Lowland Scots have always spoken English. There was an attempt by the poet Christopher Grieve to create a Scottish language, Lallans, out of the Lowland dialect, but this was a total failure.

In the nineteenth century, Scotland was one of the first parts of Britain to be industrialized, with Glasgow and the Clyde River becoming a center of shipbuilding and heavy engineering. Economic decline, deindustrialization, and high rates of unemployment characterized the region after the 1940s. The discovery of North Sea oil in 1971 boosted nationalist sentiments since it seemed to show that an independent Scotland would be economically viable. Several groups calling for home rule for Scotland had formed in the early part of the twentieth century, and the Nationalist Party of Scotland, the forerunner of the Scottish National Party (SNP), was founded in 1928. In the 1940s and 1950s, the SNP was a marginal electoral force obtaining only a handful of votes and winning no seats in parliament. In the 1960s, there was an upsurge in support for the party, and in October 1974, it polled 837,000 votes (30.4 percent of the total vote in Scotland).

The British Labour government responded to the growth of Scottish (and Welsh) nationalism by proposing a degree of devolution. The act required that a referendum be held but that 40 percent of the registered Scottish electors would have to approve the idea of a Scottish assembly. In a referendum held on March 1, 1979, a narrow majority of those voting (51.6 percent) were in favor of a Scottish assembly, but they made up only 32.8 percent of the eligible voters. Following the referendum, support for devolution and the SNP declined. The Labour government elected in 1997 promised another devolution referendum, and in September 1997, 74.3 percent of those casting a vote supported the creation of a Scottish assembly. A second proposal, to give the new assembly the power to raise and lower income tax rates by 3 percent, was also approved but by only 63.6 percent of the voters. The referendum was held on the seven-hundredth anniversary of the Battle of Stirling Bridge, in which William Wallace defeated an invading English army. The movie *Braveheart,* which starred Mel Gibson as the thirteenth-century Scottish hero, played to packed houses in the months before the campaign. Despite this nationalistic fervor, it should be noted that almost 40 percent of the electorate did not vote.

The first Scottish Assembly elections were held on May 6, 1999. The SNP won 29 percent of the vote, and thirty-five of the seats in the assembly, coming second to Labour, which garnered 39 percent of the vote and fifty-six seats. Alex Salmond, the SNP leader, claimed that the party had achieved its best result ever, but he conceded that his goal of an independent Scotland had been set back in the short run. It is uncertain whether devolution will strengthen or weaken the drive for full independence.

See also Salmond, Alex; Scottish National Party; United Kingdom.

Reference Brand, Jack. *The National Movement in Scotland* (1978).

Scottish National Party

The Scottish Home Rule Association was founded in 1918; in 1928, many of its members defected from the organization and joined with the Scots National League, which emphasized Gaelic culture, to form the Nationalist Party of Scotland. The dominant figure in the merger was John MacCormick, a law student and charismatic speaker. Disputes within the movement between those who wanted immediate independence and those who favored a gradual transition led to a split in 1942. MacCormick and his followers formed the Covenant Association, which campaigned for Scottish home rule. The campaign obtained over 1 million signatures for its covenant, but the organization disintegrated after the death of MacCormick.

In 1948, the Scottish National Party declared its goal to be "the restoration of Scottish national sovereignty by the establishment of a democratic Scottish government whose authority will be limited only by such agreements as will be freely entered into with other nations in order to further international cooperation and world peace." Despite some creditable showings in by-elections, the SNP vote as a percentage of the total Scottish general election vote was only 2.4 percent in 1964 and 3.0 percent in 1966. However, in 1967, Winifred Ewing won a by-election in Hamilton for the SNP, and support for the party surged. In October 1974, the SNP received 30.4 percent of the Scottish vote, but its share of the vote fell in the next two elections. Thereafter, it recovered slightly, and in the 1997 United Kingdom election, the party won 21.9 percent of the Scottish vote and six seats in Parliament.

It is difficult to classify the SNP as either left wing or right wing, and the party has attempted to appeal to all classes of Scottish society. SNP voters tend to be upwardly mobile and to be employed in newer industries such as electronics and chemicals. In the October 1974 election, the SNP argued that Scotland would be better off economically without England, campaigning with the slogans, It's Scotland's oil! and Rich Scots or poor Britons?

Leader of the Scottish National Party Alex Salmond addresses members of the Scottish Parliament at its official opening on July 1, 1999—the first Scottish Parliament in over three hundred years. (Corbis/AFP)

After the defeat of a 1979 devolution referendum, the party downplayed the independence issue and emphasized its opposition to the European Common Market and other economic issues. The party's poor showing in the 1979 election also led to bitter internal disputes. The party chairman argued that the SNP should adopt a social democratic ideology and a moderate stance on devolution while the largest faction was in favor of an uncompromising "independence or nothing" position. The most extreme group called for a Scottish socialist republic and advocated civil disobedience. Public opinion polls taken over a series of years show that although a majority of Scots support devolution, only about 20–25 percent are in favor of complete indepen-

dence. Furthermore, the rise of the SNP was not linked to an increase in pro-independence opinions, which suggests that for many Scots, a vote for the SNP served as a protest vote rather than as an endorsement of the party's agenda.

See also Scotland.
Reference Newman, Saul. *Ethnoregional Conflicts in Democracies* (1996).

Shan

The Shan inhabit the northeastern plateau of Burma (also known as Myanmar), and they are ethnically and linguistically akin to the Thai of Thailand. A Shan state was set up in 1947, with administration in the hands of the hereditary chieftains, or *sawbwas,* and the right to secede from the Union of Burma after ten years. However, the military government of Ne Win took away the powers of the *sawbwas* and revoked the right of secession. This action, coupled with the brutal behavior of the government troops in the area, led to the formation of several insurgent groups in the late 1950s and early 1960s, the most important being the Shan State Independence Army, the Shan National United Front, and the Tai National Army. The Shan insurgents lack unity, and many have degenerated into being mere bandits primarily concerned with taxing the lucrative opium trade.

See also Burma.
Reference Fredholm, Michael. *Burma: Ethnicity and Insurgency* (1993).

Shetland Islands

The Shetland Islands were part of Norway until 1649 when they came under Scottish rule. The islands were given to Scotland—in lieu of a dowry that was never paid—on the occasion of the marriage of James III to Margaret of Norway. Culturally, the islanders maintain their Norse heritage, but English had largely displaced the Norse language by the early 1800s.

The Shetlands sense of a separate, non-Scottish identity is caused by the fact that they are closer to the Norwegian port of Bergen than to Edinburgh. Politically, the Shetlands were one of only two districts to vote against membership in the European Economic Community in 1975. In 1997, when a referendum was held on whether Scotland should have its own legislative assembly, the Shetlands along with the Orkneys, voted against the devolution.

See also Orkney Islands; Scotland.

Sicily

After the end of World War II, there was agitation for an independent (or at least an autonomous) Sicily. The supporters of the independence movement were conservatives who feared the strength of the Communist Party and what appeared to be an imminent revolution in the industrial northern cities. In the 1946 national elections, the Sicilian Independence Movement received 171,201 votes, and its strong showing was a factor in the decision to grant Sicily a special status. In the first Sicilian regional elections held in 1947, the separatist list received 8.7 percent of the votes and eight seats out of ninety on the regional council. The separatist vote declined slightly in the 1953 regional elections, and the separatists won only five seats. In subsequent elections, the separatists failed to win any seats and disappeared from the political scene.

See also Italy.

Sikkim

Located in the eastern Himalayas bordering Tibet, Nepal, and Bhutan, the Indian state of Sikkim was an Indian protectorate until 1975. Heavy immigration by Nepalese Hindus after 1890 had made the Buddhist Bhutanese a minority in their own country. In 1974, the ruling monarch, the chogyal, claimed that since he had never signed an instrument of accession (unlike the other Indian princes), Sikkim was not a part of India. In March 1975, clashes occurred between demonstrators belonging to the Sikkim

Congress Party and the palace guard. On April 9, Indian troops disarmed the palace guard, and the following day, the Sikkim Assembly passed a resolution abolishing the office of chogyal and declaring that Sikkim was a constituent unit of India. In a subsequent referendum, 97 percent of those voting endorsed these actions. The incorporation of Sikkim into the Indian Union as the twenty-second state was approved by the Indian parliament on April 26. The Chinese government, however, declared that it did not recognize the annexation and would support the people of Sikkim in their struggle for national independence.

Singapore

Situated at the tip of the Malay peninsula, Singapore was founded by Thomas Raffles in 1819 and was governed as part of the British Straits Settlements for most of its history. Its fine natural harbor led to its becoming Southeast Asia's major port and commercial center. When the Malayan Federation was created in 1957, Singapore was excluded because its large Chinese population would have made the Malays a minority in the new country (when Malaya became independent in 1957, its population was 49.8 percent Malay and 37.2 percent Chinese, but if Singapore had been included, the Chinese would have made up 44 percent and the Malays only 43 percent).

In 1963, after talks between the Malayan prime minister, Abdul Rahman, and the leader of Singapore, Lee Kuan Yew, Singapore, Sabah, and Sarawak joined Malaya to form the Federation of Malaysia. Singapore, despite having a population of 1.5 million, was given only fifteen seats in the enlarged House of Representatives while Sabah (450,000) and Sarawak (750,000) were granted sixteen and twenty-four seats, respectively. Furthermore, since each state retained control over immigration, Singapore's crowded population would not be allowed to settle freely in the other territories. On the other hand, the proposed common market and consequent reduction in tariffs offered considerable economic benefits to Singapore. In a referendum held

National Day celebration in Singapore marking the thirty-fourth anniversary of independence, August 9, 1999. (Corbis/Larry Lee)

on September 1, 1962, 70 percent of the Singapore voters approved the merger.

Lee Kuan Yew then proceeded to challenge the Malayan Chinese Association (MCA) for leadership of the Chinese community. In the Malaysian federal elections of April 1964, Lee's People's Action Party (PAP) ran nine candidates for MCA-held seats. Although PAP won only one seat on the mainland, the party campaigned for the Chinese vote with the slogan, Malaysian Malaya. This represented a direct attack on the dominant political role of the Malays and threatened the deli-

cately balanced understanding between the two communities. Riots, in which 33 people were killed and over 600 injured, broke out between Malays and Chinese following the elections.

The crisis was resolved when Singapore was, in effect, expelled from the Malaysian Federation. Abdul Rahman, the Malayan leader explained his decision by reference to the "communal issue. . . . Irresponsible utterances are made by both sides, which reading between the lines is tantamount to challenges, and if trouble were to break out the innocent will be sacrificed." Despite predictions that Singapore would not be able to survive outside the federation, it has become a flourishing city state and has one of the highest per capita standards of living in the world.

See also Malaysia.
References Franck, Thomas M. *Why Federations Fail* (1968); Lau, Albert. *A Moment of Anguish: Singapore in Malaysia and the Politics of Disengagement* (1998).

Slavonia

Slavonia is an area of northeastern Croatia bordering Serbia. When Croatia seceded from Yugoslavia in 1991, the Serbs in western Slavonia revolted and established a Serbian autonomous republic (SAR). At the same time, Yugoslavian troops crossed the Danube River and helped local Serbs take over eastern Slavonia, an area with a Serb majority. In the battle, Serb artillery attacks leveled the city of Vukovar. In both parts of Slavonia, Croats were driven from the area. In 1992, a Serb-Croat truce was arranged, and UN peacekeepers were dispatched to the region.

In 1995, in a major offensive, Croatian troops recaptured western Slavonia and Krajina in central Croatia. Thousands of Serbs from these regions fled to eastern Slavonia. Just as the Dayton peace accord of 1995 agreed upon the disposition of Bosnia, a parallel set of agreements stipulated the gradual return of eastern Slavonia to Croatia. UN peacekeepers, later replaced by UN and Organization for Security and Cooperation in Europe monitors, were charged with seeing that the 60,000 Serbs native to the region were treated equitably. At present, it is estimated that at least 20,000 Serbs have departed the region. On January 15, 1999, the United Nations turned control of eastern Slavonia back to Croatia.

See also Croatia.
Reference "Eastern Slavonia: The Croats Are Coming." (1999).

Slovakia

Slovakia, the eastern territory of the former Republic of Czechoslovakia, was settled by Slavic tribes in the fifth and sixth centuries A.D. In the ninth century, Czechs and Slovaks were united in the Kingdom of Moravia. From the eleventh century until 1918, Slovakia was largely controlled by Hungary while the Czechs fell under Austrian domination. Even after its incorporation into the Austro-Hungarian Empire in the eighteenth century, Slovakia was ruled from Budapest, and its peasantry was dominated by Hungarian nobles. The nineteenth century saw a rise of Slovak nationalism, partly as a reaction against continuing campaigns to "Magyarize" Slovakia (the Magyars are the dominant people of Hungary). Although linguistically similar to Czech, a Slovakian literary language was promulgated during this period.

In 1918, modern Czechoslovakia was established, and it included Slovakia and the Czech lands of Bohemia and Moravia. Although Czechs and Slovaks are ethnically and linguistically related, they have had separate histories for more than a thousand years. Social and political life took different paths in the two areas. The Czechs became part of the cosmopolitan Viennese culture of the Hapsburg Empire and had a flourishing commercial economy. In contrast, Slovakia remained a traditional agrarian semifeudal society.

Wary of an association with the more populous and developed Czech lands, Slovakian discontent began to manifest itself in the 1920s. The Slovak Populist Party, headed by Andrej Hlinko, denounced the Prague-based centralization of the republic and called for autonomy. Hlinko's collaborator, Josef Tiso, ruled Slovakia as an independent state allied with Germany after Nazi Germany's annexation of Bohemia and Moravia in 1939.

In 1948, Slovakia became a constituent state in the reconstituted Republic of Czechoslovakia. However, the advent of communism brought about an increased centralization of power in Prague, and communism was resisted by the largely Catholic Slovaks. Even after Soviet troops occupied Czechoslovakia in 1968, ousting the Slovak Communist reformer, Alexander Dubcek, plans to grant more autonomy to Slovakia went

Vladimir Meciar, prime minister of Slovakia. Meciar is revered by many Slovaks as the father of Slovak independence. (AP Photo/TASR, Pavel Neubauer)

forward. In 1969, a new constitution established Czechoslovakia as a federal republic with both Czech and Slovak states granted considerable autonomy, albeit within the constraints permitted socialist governments during the Leonid Brezhnev era.

The fall of communism in 1989 again opened the way for the expression of Slovak nationalist sentiments, and the former Communist Slovak prime minister Vladimir Meciar became the leading spokesperson for Slovak independence. Beyond the Slovak conviction that Czechs looked down upon them as backward, Slovak nationalism stressed the unique cultural characteristics of the Slovak people. Additionally, Meciar and his party, the Movement for a Democratic Slovakia, argued that in any Czechoslovak state, Slovaks, who composed only a third of the population,

would always be a minority, unable to control their destiny through the democratic process. Equally distasteful to Slovaks were the market reforms that were enthusiastically endorsed in Prague. Saddled with large, inefficient Soviet-era armament industries atop a farming base, the poorer Slovak economy was less able and its leaders less willing to absorb the shocks of a rapid transition to a free market economy. In late November 1992, the Czechoslovakian National Assembly agreed to dissolve the republic, and Slovakia became independent on January 1, 1993.

Internally, the major ethnic minority in Slovakia is the Hungarians, numbering 600,000 and making up 11 percent of the population of the new state. Hungarians live in the southern part of Slovakia, the region bordering on Hungary. Because of Hungary's long domination of Slovakia, animosity toward Hungarians has deep roots among the Slovaks. Since independence in 1993, Meciar's nationalist government has implemented measures considered inimical to the Hungarians. Slovakian has been declared the national language, and all road signs, public notices, and government documents may be only in Slovakian. Recent measures that require some Slovakian to be used even in all-Hungarian schools are seen by many Hungarians as the beginning of a campaign to eliminate Hungarian-language schools.

Hungarians also fear a wider campaign to force their assimilation into the Slovak culture. In 1992 and 1994, large-scale protests by Hungarians were staged, demanding cultural autonomy. The internal situation is exacerbated by the glacial relations between the Hungarian and Slovak governments. The Hungarian government on more than one occasion has proclaimed itself the defender of Hungarian rights in Slovakia. It also proposed that the Slovak government create an autonomous Hungarian region within Slovakia, a suggestion that was flatly rejected by the Meciar government.

Hungarian Slovakians are represented in the Slovak parliament by the Hungarian Coalition, a union of three parties—the Hungarian Civic Party, the Hungarian Christian Party, and the Co-existence Party. The coalition polled 10.2 percent of the vote in the parliamentary elections of 1994, but its influence on the policies of the extreme nationalist government of Prime Minister Meciar has been negligible.

See also Czech Republic; Hungarians.
References Goldman, Minton F. *Slovakia since Independence: A Struggle for Democracy* (1999); Kirschbaum, Stanislav. *A History of Slovakia: The Struggle for Survival* (1995).

Slovenia

Slovenes, a southern Slavic people, migrated into present-day Slovenia in the sixth century A.D. Slovenes speak a southern Slavic language related to but distinguishable from Slovak and Serbian. In the thirteenth century, Slovenia came under Austrian Hapsburg rule and remained under its control into the early twentieth century. Following World War I, Slovenia, despite objections from Slovenian nationalists, became part of the newly created Kingdom of Serbs, Croats, and Slovenes. In 1929, the country was renamed Yugoslavia. Serbian influence over the kingdom's policies, however, was pronounced. In 1945, Slovenia became one of six federal republics of Communist-ruled Yugoslavia. In 1991, as the central control of the Yugoslavian state deteriorated, Slovenia seceded from the federation and declared independence.

Slovenians, because of their long association with Austria, view themselves as Western. Their alphabet is Roman, their religion is Catholic, and their cultural affinities lie with Western Europe. In the twentieth century, Slovenes resented the power exercised by Serbs in Yugoslavian affairs and felt estranged from the Serbs' Orthodox religion, their Cyrillic alphabet, and a culture that had been shaped by centuries of Turkish control. Further fueling separatist desires in Slovenia during the later Communist period in Yugoslavia was the advanced state of the Slovenian economy when contrasted with the economy of the other poorer republics. Slovenes often felt they were being required to carry the burden of these less developed regions.

A Slovenian independence movement gained strength and legitimacy in the 1980s. The establishment of independent trade unions, political parties, open elections, and a relatively free press, combined with the deterioration of the central government of the Yugoslav federation in Belgrade, gave Slovenians the means to vote themselves out of Yugoslavia in 1991. In 1992, Slovenia was recognized as a sovereign nation by the European Community.

See also Yugoslavia.
Reference Fink-Hafner, Danica, and John Robbins, eds. *Making a New Nation: The Formation of Slovenia* (1997).

Social Democratic and Labour Party

The Social Democratic and Labour Party (SDLP) is the moderate Irish nationalist party in Northern Ireland. Historically, there have been two strands of Irish nationalism: constitutional nationalism, which has sought Irish unity through peaceful democratic means, and republicanism, which has advocated armed struggle. In Northern Ireland, the Nationalist Party embodied the first approach and was the main political party representing the Catholic minority in Stormont, the Northern Irish legislature. The SDLP grew out of the Catholic civil rights movement of the 1960s. In the 1969 election, three civil rights activists defeated the sitting Nationalist members of parliament, and this served as a catalyst for the creation of a new party. After discussions, the SDLP was founded in 1970 as a coalition between six members of parliament (three civil rights independents, one Nationalist, one Republican Labour, and one Northern Ireland Labour Party).

The new party quickly displaced the disorganized and ineffective Nationalist Party and remained the dominant force among Catholics until Provisional Sinn Fein began to contest elections in the 1980s. The SDLP seeks the reunification of Ireland by consent and condemns violence. As its name suggests, the party claims to be social democratic in ideology, but this has very little relevance to its electoral appeal. Gerry Fitt, the first leader of the party, represented the social democratic faction, but he resigned in 1979.

After two Catholic rioters were shot by British troops in July 1971, the SDLP withdrew from Stormont and set up a symbolic Assembly of the Northern Irish People. Following the abolition of Stormont, the party took part in the short-lived power-sharing experiment of 1974, and after the collapse of the power-sharing executive, the SDLP advocated an enhanced role for the Republic of Ireland. John Hume, the leader of the party since 1979, argued that since an internal settlement could not be achieved, London and Dublin would have to take the initiative, a position that was implicitly adopted in the Anglo-Irish agreement of 1985.

In 1983, the SDLP established the New Ireland Forum, which attempted to redefine Irish nationalism in a contemporary context. Its report, issued in 1984, stressed that unity could be achieved only by agreement and discussed possible forms of Irish unity, including federalism and joint rule by Britain and Ireland. In the late 1980s, Hume initiated a series of discussions with Sinn Fein leader Gerry Adams with a view to weaning the Irish Republican Army away from violence and thereby launching what became known as the peace process. This inadvertently helped to raise the profile of Adams and Sinn Fein, but the SDLP still has the support of a majority of Northern Ireland's Catholic population.

See also Adams, Gerry; Hume, John; Northern Ireland; Provisional Sinn Fein.
Reference McAllister, Ian. *The Northern Ireland Labour Party: Political Opposition in a Divided Society* (1977).

Somalia

Somalia is located on the Horn of Africa and is bordered by Kenya, Ethiopia, and Djibouti. The Somalis claim to be descended from a common ancestor, Somal. In turn, the members of each individual clan claim to be descended from one of

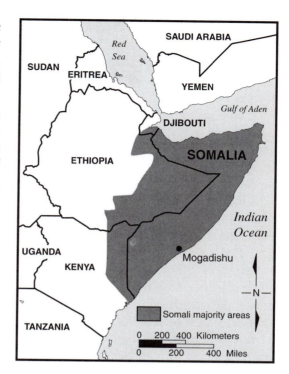

Somal's sons and grandsons. These clan groupings—Darod, Dir, Isaq—form the basis for political allegiance in Somali society. Despite clan rivalries, the Somalis are one of the most homogeneous people in Africa, sharing a common culture, a Cushitic language, and the Islamic religion.

Italian Somalia and British Somaliland became independent and united to form the Democratic Republic of Somalia on July 1, 1960. Somalia was a democracy until 1969 when a military coup brought General Mohammed Siad Barre to power, and the result was a one-party state based on the principles of "scientific socialism." After invading the Ogaden region of Ethiopia in 1977, Somalia was defeated by Ethiopia. Opposition to the military regime broke out in the north, and after a lengthy civil war, Siad Barre fled the country in 1991. Fighting between the three rebel factions devastated Somalia and led to intervention by the United Nations. U.S. Marines were sent to the country's capital, Mogadishu, to escort food convoys to famine zones. However, it proved impossible to arrange a cease-fire, and skirmishes between UN troops and rebel militia escalated. After eighteen U.S. soldiers were killed, President Clinton ordered the withdrawal of U.S. forces, and all UN forces had left Somalia by the end of March 1995.

The old colonial division between north and south has been reflected in demands for autonomy in the northern province. Northerners quickly became disenchanted with the union, and a popular song compared their situation to a man who marries a woman and then finds her to be less beautiful than expected. A majority of northern voters rejected the provisional constitution in June 1961, and this was followed by an abortive military revolt in December. In 1963, a secessionist rebellion broke out in Hargeysa, the provincial capital, and it resulted in several deaths before order was finally restored in early 1965.

After the downfall of Siad Barre, the northern region declared itself independent. The Somaliland Republic, led by Mohamed Ibrahim Egal, has its own courts and police force and has been able to maintain peace within its territory. Schools have reopened, and the economy is booming. However, the secessionist republic has not been recognized by any other country, nor is it recognized by any of the warring factions in the south. Independence was initially opposed by the smaller clans in the north, who feared domination by Egal's Isaq clan, which accounts for about 70 percent of Somaliland's population.

See also Somalis.
References Lewis, I. M. *The Modern History of Somaliland: From Nation to State* (1965); Prunier, Gerard. "Somaliland Goes It Alone" (1998).

Somalis

The Somalis of the Horn of Africa share a common language, culture, and religion, but during the colonial period, they were divided among French, British, and Italian Somaliland, the Ogaden region of Ethiopia, and the Northern Frontier District of Kenya. In 1960, British and Italian Somaliland became independent and were united as the Democratic Republic of Somalia. The new government was committed to a policy of uniting all ethnic Somalis into a greater Somalia, and its irredentist aspirations were symbolized by the design of the flag, whose five-pointed star represents the five segments of the Somali people. Somalia encouraged and supported Somali rebels in both the Ogaden and the Northern Frontier District. After a series of border clashes between Somali and Ethiopian troops, war broke out between the two countries in 1964, and the Somalis were decisively defeated in a matter of days.

After a 1969 coup brought General Mohammed Siad Barre to power, he declared Somalia to be a Marxist state, and military aid from the Soviet Union allowed the Somalis to build up a modern army of over 22,000 men. The Soviets also entered into an alliance with the revolutionary government of Ethiopia in February 1977 and thus found themselves in the strange position of arming both sides in the conflict over the Ogaden. After the Somalis invaded the Ogaden in July 1977, the Soviets were forced to choose between their two allies. The Somali army captured most of the region but were checked by the Ethiopians outside the city of Harar. When the Soviets refused to provide more weapons, the Somalis broke off the alliance and expelled all Soviet personnel. At this point, the Soviets supplied the Ethiopians with massive amounts of aircraft, tanks, and other military equipment. Aided by Cuban troops, the Ethiopian army counterattacked in February 1978 and drove the Somalis out of the Ogaden.

Although Somalia seeks to unite all ethnic Somalis under one flag, there have been signs of division within Somalia itself reflecting both clan rivalries and a north-versus-south regionalism resulting from the colonial division between British and Italian Somaliland.

See also Djibouti; Irredentism; Ogaden; Somalia; Somalis in Kenya.
References Cahill, K., ed. *Somalia: A Perspective* (1980); Castagno, M. *Historical Dictionary of Somalia* (1976).

Somalis in Kenya

The Northern Frontier District of Kenya includes nearly one-fifth of the country and is inhabited by about 200,000 Somali and Oromo nomadic pastoralists. The boundary between what was once Italian Somaliland and Kenya was demarcated in 1920 without regard to ethnic factors, and the Somalis moved freely across the international border. They were not, however, allowed to migrate into other parts of Kenya, and the region was administered separately from the rest of the colony. When independence talks began in 1961, the Somalis of the Northern Frontier District called for the area to be joined to Somalia, and the British government sent a commission to determine local attitudes. The commission reported that the Somalis were almost unanimous in desiring to secede and that large majorities in five of the six districts were in favor of joining Somalia.

That idea was adamantly opposed by the Kenyan nationalists, and when Britain announced that the area would remain part of Kenya, Somalia broke off diplomatic relations. Somali insurgents, known as *shifta* ("bandits") by the Kenyans, carried on a guerrilla campaign that lasted for over four years and was encouraged by Somali radio propaganda. The Kenyans declared a state of emergency beginning in December 1963 and claim to have killed 3,000 *shifta* during the period from 1963 to 1967. In 1967, the Somali government agreed to end its support of the insurgency.

Although various diplomatic initiatives have reduced tensions between the two countries, guerrilla activity by the United Liberation Front of Western Somalia was reported in 1974 and 1978. *Shifta* violence broke out again in the early 1980s, and the Kenyan police responded by massive sweeps of the region in which scores of ethnic Somalis were killed.

See also Kenya; Ogaden.
References Castagno, A. "The Somalia-Kenya Controversy" (1964); Meredith, Martin. *The First Dance of Freedom: Black Africa in the Post-War Era* (1984).

South Africa

South Africa is unique in that ethnic separatism was imposed by the government under the apartheid system introduced by the Nationalist Party after its election victory in 1960. South Africa's population includes whites, "coloureds," Asians, and Bantu-speaking blacks. This racial and ethnic diversity is the result of a complex history. The original inhabitants were the Khoisan peoples (previously known as Bushmen and Hottentots) with their distinctive click speech. The Khoisan are racially distinct from the Bantu-speaking blacks who gradually moved into southern Africa in the first millennium A.D. In 1652, the Dutch established a settlement in Capetown. The mixed-race Coloureds are descended from the Dutch settlers, the Khoisan, and slaves from the East Indies.

In 1806, the British took over Cape Colony, and three decades later, the Boers, as the descendants of the Dutch were now known, migrated inland in the Great Trek and set up the independent Boer republics of the Orange Free State and the Transvaal. When gold was discovered in the Transvaal, thousands of miners flocked into the area. Tensions between the predominantly British miners and the Boers led to the Boer War (1899–1902), which ended with the defeat of the Boers. The experiences of the Great Trek and the Boer War created the historical mythology of the Afrikaners (as the Boers came to be known). They saw themselves in Old Testament terms as God's "chosen people," who had been led to victory over the Zulu, Xhosa, and other tribes. During the war, the Boer women and children were put into concentration camps (the first time the term was used), and memories of this and other ill treatment at the hands of the British strengthened the Afrikaners' sense of national identity.

In 1910, the Union of South Africa was formed out of the four British colonies of the Cape, Natal, the Orange Free State, and the Transvaal. The franchise was largely restricted to whites, except for a few blacks and Coloureds in the Cape. As a majority of the voting population, the Afrikaners

Voters line up for hours at a polling station in Soweto, a black township outside Johannesburg, to vote in the country's first all-race elections, April 27, 1994. (AP Photo/Denis Farrell)

eventually obtained political dominance. The Nationalist Party, which came to power in 1960, established the apartheid system, which was intended to ensure white rule over the black majority. Increasing black resistance and the pressure of world opinion eventually led to negotiations between the South African government and the African National Congress. The first multiracial elections were held in April 1994 and resulted in the end of the apartheid system.

In 1994, it was estimated that the South African population numbered 40.4 million, with the following racial breakdown: blacks, 76.4 percent; whites, 12.6 percent; coloureds, 8.5 percent; and Asians, 2.5 percent. These categories can be further subdivided. Afrikaners make up over 60 percent of the whites, with most of the remainder being En-

glish speakers. Blacks are divided into several ethnic groups, of which the most important are the Zulu, Xhosa, Tswana, and Sotho. The racial inequality resulting from apartheid and racial discrimination can be seen by the fact that in 1987, per capita income (in Rands, the currency of South Africa) was 14,880 for whites, 4,560 for Asians, 3,000 for coloureds, and only 1,246 for blacks.

See also Apartheid; Black Homelands; Postapartheid South Africa.

South Moluccas

The South Moluccas (also called the Ambonese Islands) consist of some 150 small islands in eastern Indonesia. Under Dutch rule, two-thirds of the population was converted to Christianity by Protestant missionaries, and the region supplied most of the recruits for the Dutch colonial army (the KNIL). When Indonesia proclaimed its independence at the end of World War II, many Ambonese sought to retain their autonomy within a federal state of East Indonesia. However, the Dutch-backed federal system disintegrated, and a large contingent of KNIL troops based in Ambon (Amboina) proclaimed the Republic of the South Moluccas. (It should be noted that Ambonese troops were notorious for the atrocities they had committed during the Dutch attempt to reimpose colonial rule.) The republic lasted from April 1950 until November 1950 when Indonesian army troops finally overcame the last organized resistance, but even in 1955, separatist sentiments remained strong. Although the rebels were encouraged by their Dutch officers, they genuinely feared domination by the Muslim Javanese in an independent Indonesia.

About 40,000 soldiers and their families were transferred to the Netherlands, where a South Moluccan government in exile was set up. Some of the exiles engaged in acts of terrorism in a desperate attempt to obtain an independent South Moluccan homeland. In December 1975, seven Moluccans seized a train, and another group occupied the Indonesian consulate. Two years later, in May 1977, Moluccan terrorists took over an express train and a primary school, holding hostage the 51 passengers and 105 schoolchildren. The schoolchildren were released unharmed after four days, but Dutch commandos stormed the train and rescued the hostages, with six terrorists and two hostages being killed in the assault.

Since Indonesia's president Suharto's fall from power in May 1998, hundreds of people have been killed in clashes between Christians and Muslims in the Moluccas. Christians resent Muslim immigration and government favoritism toward the Muslims while Muslims allege that the Christians still harbor separatist sentiments.

See also Indonesia.
References Kahin, Audrey, ed. *Regional Dynamics of the Indonesian Revolution* (1985); Woodman, Dorothy. *The Republic of Indonesia* (1956).

South Ossetia

South Ossetia is a self-declared independent republic in north-central Georgia with a population of 150,000. Alania (formerly North Ossetia), which is an autonomous republic of the Russian Federation and adjoins South Ossetia, has a population of 400,000 Ossetes. Anti-Georgian sentiment combined with a desire to unite with their Ossetian neighbors has characterized the politics of South Ossetia in recent years.

Ossetians, unlike Georgians, speak an Iranian dialect and use the Cyrillic alphabet. Like Georgians, they are primarily Orthodox. The Ossetians are descendants of the Alans who gained control over the region in the first century A.D. In the eighteenth century, North Ossetia came under Russian domination; by 1801, South Ossetia, along with eastern Georgia, had also been absorbed into the Russian Empire. The nineteenth century witnessed several Ossetian revolts against Russian domination.

During the Russian Civil War (1918–1920), South Ossetians revolted against the short-lived Georgian republic. By 1922, Russian control over Georgia had been reestablished, and Ossetia was partitioned, with the larger northern territory ultimately becoming a republic within Russia and the southern part becoming an autonomous republic of the Georgian Soviet Socialist Republic.

In the 1980s, as Georgian separatists pushed for independence from the Soviet Union, South Ossetians began a campaign to secede from Georgia and form a state with North Ossetia. In 1990, the South Ossetian parliament declared the region independent. Georgia responded by abrogating South Ossetia's autonomous status. In subsequent fighting, the Ossetians succeeded in driving Georgian forces from the territory. Ethnic Georgians fled the region, and Russian troops and negotiators from the Organization for Security and Cooperation in Europe have brought about a cease-fire in recent years. However, South Ossetia's president, Lyudwig Chibirov, refuses to accept any return to Georgian rule.

See also Georgia.

References Denber, Rachel. *Bloodshed in the Caucasus* (1992); Suny, Ronald Grigor. *Making of the Georgian Nation* (1994).

South Tirol

In 1919, the South Tirol, which for centuries had been part of Austria, was annexed by Italy. The population was almost entirely German speaking, largely rural, and devoutly Catholic. Under the fascist regime, an industrial zone was created in the city of Bolzano (Bozen), and a massive in-migration of Italian workers was encouraged. Under an agreement with Nazi Germany, the southern Tirolese were given the option of renouncing their German ethnic identity or emigrating to Germany, and about a third were forced to leave their homes. At the same time, Italian policy attempted to de-Germanize the region. German-language schools were closed, and German-language publications were suppressed. Italian became the only language used in administration, the law courts, and education, and the fascists changed geographical and family names from German to Italian, even going so far as to alter the names on tombstones.

After the end of World War II, the De Gasperi-Gruber accord, signed by Italy and Austria, promised the region a substantial degree of autonomy. However, the Italians delineated the boundaries of the autonomous region of Trentino–Alto Adige so that it also included the province of Trento, thus creating an Italian majority. Furthermore, the southern Tirolese were largely excluded from jobs in the state bureaucracy and the public sector. For example, of the 2,500 railway jobs in the province in 1966, less than 10 percent were held by German speakers. These grievances led the southern Tirolese to agitate for a revision of the autonomy agreement, and they appealed to Austria and the United Nations. Separatist tendencies became stronger, and mass demonstrations took place, with demands for reunification with Austria.

In 1957, 35,000 southern Tiroleans rallied with shouts of *Los von Trient* ("quit Trento"). The party representing the German minority, the Sudtiroler Volkspartei (SVP), became more militant and withdrew from the regional council. Tensions rose, and a terrorist campaign, waged by the Befreiungs Ausschuss Sudtirol, began in 1957. Finally, after lengthy negotiations between the SVP and the Austrian and Italian governments, a new autonomy statute was enacted in 1969. It involved a massive transfer of legislative and administrative powers to the province from the region, a degree of autonomy for the school system, ethnic ratios for government jobs, and bilingualism within the province. The German share of the population has remained constant since 1953, about 63 percent.

See also Befreiungs Ausschuss Sudtirol; Italy; Sudtiroler Volkspartei.

References Alcock, Antony E. *The History of the South Tyrol Question* (1970); Czikann-Zichy, M. *Turmoil in the South Tyrol* (1978); Toscano, Mario. *Alto Adige, South Tyrol* (1975).

Southern Kuril Islands

Sovereignty over four small southern Kuril Islands, which lie to the north of the Japanese island of Hokkaido, is disputed between Japan and Russia. The islands (Habomai, Shikotan, Kunashiri, and Etorofu) came under Japanese rule in the late 1700s while the rest of the Kuril Islands were claimed by Russia. In 1855, the Treaty of Shimoda defined the boundary between Russia and Japan as passing between the islands of Etorufu and Uruppu. In 1875, Japan exchanged the island of Sakhalin for the Kuriles, and the islands remained under Japanese sovereignty until 1945.

At the end of World War II, the Soviet Union occupied the Kuriles, including the four southern islands. In 1946, the Kuriles were annexed, and all the Japanese inhabitants were deported. About 17,000 Japanese civilians lived on the four southern islands. Currently, the inhabitants, predominantly ethnic Russians and Ukrainians, number about 23,000. In addition, large numbers of Russian troops are stationed on the islands. The Japanese refer to the islands as "the northern territories" and believe them to be an integral part of Japanese territory. The Russians argue that the

Basque independence supporters outside a pro-independence assembly in Pamplona, February 6, 1999, a gathering of town mayors and councilors from France and Spain to promote an independent Basque homeland. (AP Photo/Jon Dimis)

islands are part of the Kuril Islands (which were returned to Russia under the postwar peace agreement) and, hence, Russian territory. However, Russian president Boris Yeltsin has indicated that Russia would be prepared to return the islands in exchange for financial aid, and Japan has offered $2.5 billion. Public opinion polls indicate that the islanders feel neglected by Russia, and many favor a return to Japanese sovereignty.

Reference Forsberg, Tuomas. *Contested Territory: Border Disputes at the Edge of the Former Soviet Empire* (1995).

Spain

Contemporary Spain consists of several nationalities, each with its own distinctive language and culture. Although the national language is Castilian Spanish, Catalan, Basque, and Galician are spoken in their respective regions. Spain was united by the marriage of Ferdinand of Aragon and Isabella of Castile in 1469, and its subsequent history is marked by chronic conflict between the centralizing monarchy and the rebellious regions. Under the constitution of the short-lived second republic (1931–1938), regional autonomy was offered subject to a plebiscite and approval by the Cortes, the Spanish legislature. However, although statutes were proposed for Galicia and the Basque provinces, only Catalonia achieved regional autonomy for a brief period, from July 1936 until May 1937.

The Spanish Civil War ended with the victory of General Francisco Franco in 1939, and during his long reign, all separatist movements were suppressed as threats to the unity of Spain. Basque and Catalan were banned outside the home, and the teaching of either language was prohibited. The Basque provinces and Catalonia were the industrial centers of Spain, and under Franco, they attracted large numbers of workers from the less developed areas. Throughout the period, Catalans and Basques remained hostile to the Franco regime, and there were widespread disturbances and mass defiance. Terrorism by the Basque group Euzkadi ta Askatasuna provoked government repression and further support for Basque independence.

With the death of Franco in 1975 and Spain's swift transition to democracy, the question of regional autonomy reemerged once again. The new democratic constitution of 1978 envisaged a system of autonomous regions throughout the whole country, although autonomy was initially offered only to the four historic communities (the Basque country, Catalonia, Galicia, and Andalusia). By 1983, however, autonomy statutes had been adopted in the other thirteen regions as well.

Under the constitution, each region may designate its own language and flag. The Cortes adopted the Ley Organica de Armonizacion del Proceso Autonomica in 1982, which laid down the process whereby autonomy could be achieved and defined the jurisdiction of the regional governments. Both the Basque provinces and Catalonia have control of their own police forces, and special financial arrangements were negotiated whereby the three Basque provinces and Navarra collect taxes and then remit a proportion to the central government. Surveys indicate that although the new decentralized structures are popular, a substantial proportion of Catalans (23 percent) and Basques (42 percent) would prefer independence or still more autonomy.

See also Andalusia; Basques; Canary Islands; Catalonia; Ceuta and Melilla: Galicia; Gibraltar.
References Gunther, Richard, Giacomo Sani, and Goldie Shabad. *Spain after Franco* (1986); Medhurst, Kenneth. *The Basques and Catalans* (1982).

Srpska

Formally known as the Republic of Srpska, Srpska is the Serbian-controlled portion of the Bosnian federation that proclaimed its independence from the Bosnian republic in 1992. Banja Luka is the capital, and Pale is a major city in the east. At one point following military victories, Srpska claimed 70 percent of the territory of Bosnia and Herzegovina. The Dayton peace accord, signed in 1995, reduced Srpska's territory to 49 percent of the land and compelled Srpska to join with Muslims and Croats in governing a reconstituted Bosnia and Herzegovina.

Radovan Karadzic, Srpska's first president and head of its major political party, the Serbian Democratic Party (SDS), was forced to relinquish both positions after his indictment in 1995 by the United Nations for war crimes. He was succeeded as president by Biljana Plavsic, a Serbian nationalist and a former follower of Karadzic. Plavsic's acceptance of the Dayton peace accord led to a break with Karadzic's supporters, and she was ousted from the SDS. Subsequently, Plavsic formed a new party, the Serb National Alliance. Confronted with an eighty-three-seat parliament dominated by the SDS and the ultranationalist Serbian Radical Party, Plavsic, with Western encouragement, called for new parliamentary elections in November 1997. In the election, the Karadzic forces, although still the largest bloc, lost their majority, and Plavsic's candidate for prime minister, pro-Western Milorod Dodik, succeeded in ousting the Karadzic supported former prime minister, Gorjo Klickovic.

In the presidential elections of 1998, Plavsic was defeated by the ultrarightist Nikola Poplasen of the Serbian Radical Party, although after a dispute with the UN high representative, Poplasen was removed from office. Srpska still consists of two separate territories divided by the Muslim-Croat Federation territory in the Brcko area. In the eastern section, where Karadzic has great influence, the sentiment to secede has increased because of what is perceived as a loss of power at the republic level.

See also Bosnia and Herzegovina; Dayton Peace Accord; Greater Serbia; Karadzic, Radovan; Plavsic, Biljana.

Stern Gang

The Stern Gang or Lehi, Fighters for the Freedom of Israel, was founded in 1940 by Avraham Stern after splitting from Irgun. Right wing, nationalist, and fiercely anti-British, the Stern Gang waged war on British personnel and, in 1944, assassinated a British government minister. Denounced by other Jewish groups as terrorists and gangsters, Stern and his followers were hunted by British and Jewish forces. In 1942, Stern was captured and shot by British police, and the strength of the movement waned and was ultimately suppressed after Israeli independence in 1948.

See also Irgun; Israel.
References Heller, Joseph. *The Stern Gang* (1995); Sachar, Howard. *History of Israel* (1996).

Sudan

The Sudan, the largest country in Africa, is divided into two distinct regions. The northern part is inhabited by Arabic-speaking Muslims, and the southern part is inhabited by black Africans who are generally Christians or followers of traditional African religions. The main southern groups are the Dinka and the Nuer, who constitute about 40 percent and 10 percent of the population of the area, respectively. Northerners display a racial and cultural contempt for southerners, who are often referred to as *abid* ("slaves"). Regional and cultural differences led to a civil war in the south that began before independence and has lasted until the present, except for one peaceful period between 1972 and 1983.

From 1899 to 1956, the country was officially an Anglo-Egyptian condominium but a de facto British colony. The British administered the south as a separate entity, and at one time considered linking it to British East Africa. Northern Sudanese were not allowed to enter the south, and the spread of Islam and Arab customs was discouraged. Partly as a result of its isolation, the southern region remained underdeveloped in comparison to the north. In 1956, when the Sudan became independent, northerners dominated the government, and only 6 of the more than 800 top administrative positions were occupied by southerners.

In 1958, southern troops mutinied when they were transferred to garrisons commanded by northern officers and killed hundreds of northerners, including government officials and merchants. The revolt was brutally suppressed, and seventy mutineers were executed. A military coup by General Ibrahim Abbud in 1958 was followed by an attempt to Arabize the southerners, which provoked armed resistance by the Anya-Nya guerrillas. However, the southern rebellion was hampered by tribal divisions and rivalries among different leaders and organizations. The most important separatist groups were the Sudan African National Union, the Azania Liberation Front, the Southern Sudan Provisional Government, and the Nile Provisional Government. Not until Joseph Lagu established the Southern Sudan Liberation Movement in 1970 were the rebels able to achieve a significant degree of unity and mount an effective military campaign.

Lagu obtained military aid from the Israelis, who were anxious to weaken a hostile Arab regime, and from Uganda (the Ugandans were generally sympathetic to the southerners since many tribes, such as the Langos, Kakwes, and Madi, lived in both countries). Ethiopia also gave sanctuary to the Anya-Nya guerrillas after 1965, primarily in retaliation for aid given by the Sudan to Eritrean separatists. However, in 1972, the Sudan and Ethiopia each agreed to stop supporting separatist guerrillas in the other's country. The Ethiopians then played the role of mediator between the Sudanese government and the southern rebels. The outcome was the Addis Ababa agreement of 1972, which gave autonomy to the three southern provinces of Equatoria, Upper Nile, and Bahr al Ghazal and brought about a cessation of the conflict for ten years. A regional president and an elected Southern Regional Assembly controlled local affairs, while fiscal planning, defense, and foreign affairs were the responsibility of the central government. Arabic was recognized as the Sudan's official language, but in the south, English was to be used in the schools and government administration.

Unfortunately, the accord fell apart in the early 1980s. General Jaafar al-Nimeiri suspended the Southern Regional Assembly in 1981, redivided the region into three provinces, and in 1983 established the Sharia, or Islamic law. Religious courts imposed such penalties as amputating the hands of thieves, and these measures provoked renewed southern resistance by the Sudanese People's Liberation Movement (SPLM) and its military wing, the Sudanese People's Liberation Army (SPLA). A cease-fire and negotiations between the government and the SPLM leader, John Garang, resulted in the 1986 Koka Dam Declaration, which called for the repeal of the Sharia and a Sudan free from racism, tribalism, and sectarianism. However, the civilian government was overthrown by the military in 1989, and the new military leader, General Omar al-Bashir, vowed to maintain the Sharia and win a military victory over the south.

The military fortunes of the SPLA have waxed and waned. By the beginning of 1991, it controlled most of the countryside and all but a few of the towns in the three southern provinces, and it was also active in Al Awsat province. Ethnic divisions among the southerners have proved to be significant. The SPLA originally was dominated by the two main tribes, the Dinka and the Nuer, and the government succeeded in setting up militias in areas inhabited by other tribes. In addition, in northern Bahr al Ghazal, Arab militias raided Dinka villages and were responsible for the killing of thousands of civilians, the massacre of women and children, and widespread destruction. The Sudanese air force has deliberately bombed hospitals, churches, and refugee camps; millions of villagers have become refugees; and famine is widespread. It is reported that large numbers of southerners have been taken as slaves to the north, although this claim has been denied by the Sudanese government.

In August 1991, the SPLA split into two factions. One group, led by Riek Machar, is based on the Nuer while the Dinka remained loyal to Garang. Taking advantage of the split, the government supplied arms to the Riek faction, and heavy fighting took place between the two SPLA armies. Substantial military aid from Iran enabled the government to launch a campaign in early 1992 that resulted in the recapture of many towns from the divided SPLA, but in 1994, the tide of battle turned again. The Garang-led SPLA not only regained control of most of the south but was able to form an alliance with opposition groups in the north. No end to the conflict, which has claimed well over 2 million lives, is in sight.

References Collins, Robert. *Shadows in the Grass: Britain in the Southern Sudan* (1983); Finnegan, William. "The Invisible War" (1999); Wai, Dunstan M. *The African-Arab Conflict in the Sudan* (1981); Woodward, Peter. *Sudan, 1898–1989: The Unstable State* (1990).

Sudtiroler Volkspartei

The Sudtiroler Volkspartei (SVP) is the dominant political party in the South Tirol. It functions as a catch-all party that tries with a high degree of success to represent all elements of the German-speaking population regardless of class or occupation. Its membership includes over a quarter of the voting-age population, and the party has an effective hierarchical chain of command. It is estimated that over 90 percent of the German speakers have consistently voted for the party in both national and local elections. Splinter parties to the right and left of the SVP have emerged, but they have never won more than a handful of votes. On socioeconomic issues, the SVP is conservative and strongly anti-Communist. The role of the Catholic Church in local affairs is considerable, and consequently the church exercises an influence in the political councils of the SVP and the local trade union.

After World War II, the party adopted a moderate strategy that called for cultural autonomy for the province while rejecting any but legal and peaceful means to achieve that goal. In 1957, a new and more nationalist group, led by Sylvius Mangano, who had served with the German army on the Russian front, took over the party's leadership. The SVP thereupon ended its alliance with the Christian Democrats, the major Italian party, and adopted an increasingly radical posture regarding autonomy. The nationalist rhetoric of the SVP encouraged some younger activists to engage in terrorism, but the violence led to a reaction within the party. After some internal dissension, the SVP leadership decided that increased autonomy within Italy was acceptable and resumed negotiations with the Italian government.

See also South Tirol.
References Katzenstein, Peter J. "Ethnic Political Conflict in South Tyrol" (1977); Toscano, Mario. *Alto Adige, South Tyrol* (1975).

Swazi

The Swazi of southern Africa number over 1 million, with about half living in the independent Kingdom of Swaziland and half in the Republic of South Africa. The Swazi never recognized the colonial border established in the 1880s, and many of those living in South Africa still think of themselves as loyal subjects of the Swazi king. In 1982, Swaziland proposed that KaNgwane, the Swazi homeland in South Africa, be annexed by Swaziland. However, despite support from the South African government, the idea was rejected by a judicial commission in 1983. In 1992, the prime minister of Swaziland again called for the "return" of KaNgwane to Swaziland, but the chief minister of KaNgwane, Enos Mabuza, responded by calling on Swaziland to join South Africa. Mabuza frequently expressed his support for the African National Congress and was the first homeland leader to allow trade unions to organize freely within his territory. Like the other homelands, KaNgwane was reincorporated into South Africa in 1994.

See also Black Homelands; South Africa.
Reference Macmillan, H. "A Nation Divided? The Swazi in Swaziland and Transvaal 1865–1986" (1989).

Taiwan

An island 100 miles off the south coast of China, Taiwan has a population of about 20 million. Several small islands, including the Pescadores and the offshore islands of Quemoy and Matsu, are also controlled by Taiwan. The aboriginal inhabitants of the island, who make up less than 1 percent of the population, belong to two groups: the earliest arrivals are related to the Ainu of Japan, and those who arrived later are of Malay-Polynesian origin. Chinese settlement began in the twelfth century, but their number was less than 25,000 in the early 1600s. The Japanese, Portuguese, Dutch, and Spanish established forts and trading posts on the island at various times, and it was not until 1662 that the island came under Chinese rule.

Taiwan remained a backward and lawless region until the late 1800s and was only raised to the status of a Chinese province in 1887. A few years later, in 1895, Taiwan was annexed by the Japanese. The Japanese ruled with an iron hand but embarked on a policy of economic modernization, building roads and railways throughout the island. After the Japanese surrender in 1945, the island was restored to China, and the Kuomintang forces took possession in October of that year.

After being defeated by the Communists, the Kuomintang (Nationalist) government headed by Chiang Kai-shek took refuge on Taiwan in 1949 and maintained that it was the legitimate ruler of all of China. The national assembly elected in 1947 was declared to be the legislature for all of China, with the legislators "temporarily" holding their seats until the mainland was liberated and new elections could be held (some of those legislators are still alive and still occupying their seats).

The Kuomintang regime was essentially a one-party dictatorship dominated by exile mainlanders, and Taiwanese nationalists were viewed as subversives and ruthlessly suppressed by the secret police. Taiwan continues to be controlled by the mainlanders and their descendants, who compose no more than 15 percent of the population. This cleavage is reinforced by the fact that the two

groups speak different dialects of Chinese, Mandarin versus Taiwanese. Until the late 1960s, the Taiwanese were largely excluded from top government and political positions; a 1967 survey found that mainlanders held 82 percent of the military and police positions and 34 percent of those in public administration. A constitutional amendment of 1966 allowed the holding of supplementary elections to the National Assembly, and the proportion of Taiwanese representatives increased slightly just after that date to about 5 percent.

After the death of Chiang Kai-shek in 1975, a Taiwanese cultural revival began, and magazines espousing dissident views were published. The Formosa group included several individuals who later became active in the pro-independence faction of the Democratic Progressive Party (DPP). After the Formosa group organized a mass rally in December 1979, which ended in a riot, many of its leaders were jailed or fled abroad. In an indication of Taiwanese sentiment, opposition candidates won over a quarter of the vote in elections held in 1980 and 1983.

In 1986, President Chiang Ching-kuo began a series of political reforms that were continued under his successor, Lee Teng-hui, a native Taiwanese. Martial law was lifted, press censorship was relaxed, and new political parties were allowed to organize. The DPP, founded in September 1986, won 24 percent of the vote in the December

1986 elections. The DPP is regarded as being antimainlander and pro-Taiwanese, and it includes a faction that favors independence. In 1989, the party increased its share of the vote to 35 percent and won several local government offices. It was noticeable that those DPP candidates who openly advocated independence got the highest votes and drew the most enthusiastic crowds. Some DPP candidates gave their campaign speeches in Taiwanese rather than in Mandarin. In 1997, the DPP defeated the Nationalist Party in local elections and is favored to win the presidential elections scheduled for 2000.

Both the Communists and the Nationalists resisted the idea that there were "two Chinas," so other countries had to choose whether to recognize the People's Republic of China (PRC) or the Republic of China (ROC). Over time, more and more countries recognized the PRC, and by the end of the 1980s, only a small handful of countries still accepted Taiwan as the rightful government of China. Even the United States moved to recognize the PRC, a process that began when President Richard Nixon visited Beijing in 1972 and concluded when President Jimmy Carter switched U.S. recognition from the ROC to the PRC in 1978. In the Shanghai communiqué issued at the end of Nixon's visit, the United States acknowledged that "all Chinese on either side of the Taiwan Strait maintain that there is but one China and that Taiwan is part of China. The United States government does not challenge that position." In 1978, the United States terminated diplomatic relations and its defense pact with Taiwan, but the two countries maintain close economic and unofficial ties.

Immediately after victory on the mainland, the People's Liberation Army forces were poised to invade Taiwan. However, after North Korea attacked South Korea in 1950, President Harry Truman ordered the U.S. Seventh Fleet into Taiwan Strait to deter a Communist invasion. (In return, the Nationalists agreed to cease provocative raids against the mainland.) In 1954, the Communists shelled the offshore islands of Quemoy and Matsu and forced the Nationalists to evacuate the nearby Ta Chen islands in the same year. The Beijing government called for the liberation of Taiwan and warned the United States of "grave consequences" if U.S. troops were not withdrawn from the island. Quemoy and Matsu were again bombarded in July 1958. The last military clashes took place in 1969 and were replaced with diplomatic overtures.

In 1971, China's foreign minister, Zhou Enlai, suggested that after peaceful reunification, there would be a long transitional period in which Taiwan would be able to maintain its own political and economic system. Since the opening of diplomatic relations between the PRC and the United States, the PRC has put forward several proposals about how reunification with Taiwan could be achieved. These proposals can be summed up by the slogan, One country, two systems. Taiwan would become a special administrative region, and its economic system and way of life would be preserved. Beijing has pledged noninterference in local affairs, and Taiwan would maintain its own armed forces. No mainland troops or administrators would be stationed in Taiwan, nor would the central government levy any taxes on the island.

Taiwan has begun to allow its citizens to visit the mainland, and Taiwanese investment in Chinese industry is substantial, as is trade between the two countries. However, despite these trends, a peaceful resolution of Taiwan's status is improbable. As Taiwan becomes more democratic, the independence movement is likely to grow in strength. A public opinion poll conducted just after China's takeover of Hong Kong in 1997 showed that a majority favored independence over reunification. On the other hand, Beijing has warned repeatedly that it would use force should Taiwan declare itself independent. In 1996, when Taiwan's President Lee Teng-hui made what was regarded as steps toward independence, China carried out military exercises in the Taiwan Strait. Thus, the conflict between separatist sentiments on Taiwan and China's irredentist claim to its lost territories appears irreconcilable.

See also Hong Kong; Macau.
References Gregor, A. James. *The Taiwan Independence Movement* (1985); Long, Simon. *Taiwan: China's Last Frontier* (1991); Martin, Joseph. *Terrorism and the Taiwan Independence Movement* (1985).

Tajikistan

Prior to the Soviet era, Tajikistan, with a current population exceeding 5 million, was never a state. The Tajiks are descendants of Iranian peoples and speak a Persian dialect. They are largely Sunni Muslims, although the separatist-minded inhabitants of the Gorno-Badakshan district in the southeast are Shiites belonging to the Ismaili sect. As many Tajiks live in Afghanistan and Uzbekistan as are found in Tajikistan, which has compounded tension in the area for much of recent history.

Tajiks have lived in central Asia since the first century B.C. Until their absorption into the Russian Empire in 1968, they were ruled by Persians, Macedonians, Arabs, Turks, and Mongols. They were converted to Islam by the Arabs in the seventh and eighth centuries. Following the Russian Revolution of 1917, many Tajiks, even though they were not Turkic speakers, were made citizens of the Turkistan Autonomous Soviet Socialist Republic. In 1920, the former Russian protectorate of the Bukharan khanate, which had a substantial Tajik population, was added to the republic. In 1924, a Tajik Autonomous Soviet Socialist Republic was established, and in 1929, it was elevated to the status of a constituent Soviet republic. The new state did not include the considerable number of Tajiks living in Bukhara and Samarkand, who were assigned to the new Uzbekistan Soviet Republic. Tajikistan was, however, given a large Uzbek population, which now numbers close to 1 million in the western region. Strains between Tajiks and Uzbeks underlie the politics of both Uzbekistan and Tajikistan today.

Following the disintegration of the Soviet Union in 1991, Tajikistan declared its independence. The government of the new state remained under the control of pro-Russian former Communist officials led by President Rakhman Nabiyev. In 1992, riots broke out in Dushanbe, and soon the government was faced with an armed rebellion. The opposition included Gorno-Badakshan separatists (Lali Badakshan); Rastokhez, a Tajik nationalist party; the Islamic Renaissance Party, a Muslim fundamentalist group; and the Democratic Party of Tajikistan (DPT), a liberal, democratic anti-Communist umbrella group. Opposition forces succeeded in taking Dushanbe but were driven back by Russian and Uzbek forces assisting the government. Imomali Rakhmonov, a former Communist and Uzbek-supported politician, was installed as interim president, all opposition parties were banned, and the activities of Muslim clerics were circumscribed. Guerilla attacks, aided by Tajik forces and Islamic radicals in Afghanistan, continued.

In 1994, facing little legal opposition, Rakhmonov was reelected president. Hostilities, now largely engineered by Islamic fighters, brought continued instability to the republic. With deaths estimated at between 30,000 and 60,000 people and an estimated 500,000 Tajiks displaced, Tajikistan also saw the flight of thousands to Afghanistan. In 1996, the Rakhmonov government acquiesced to UN and Russian pressure and signed an agreement with the United Tajik Opposition (UTO) headed by Said Abdullo Nuri. Under the agreement, the UTO was to be allowed to operate legally, and it was also to be included in a coalition government.

The idea of legitimizing Islamic fundamentalists was anathema to Islam Karimov, the former Communist and anti-Islamist president of Uzbekistan. Furthermore, the new compromise Tajikistan government largely excluded the pro-Communist Uzbeks ("the third power").

In July 1997, Abdumalik Abdullajanov, an Uzbek and a former Tajikistan prime minister whose center of power was in the Kurgan-Tyube region, called for an annulment of the 1996 agreement. He was particularly opposed to integrating Islamic militiamen into the Tajikistan army. When rebuffed, he declared the southwestern region of

Tajikistan an autonomous republic and then marched on Dushanbe. His forces, rumored to have been supported by Uzbekistan, were defeated and fled into Uzbekistan.

In January 1998, Uzbek President Karimov and Tajik President Rakhmonov signed a treaty of reconciliation. Both leaders feared worsening conditions if peace were not reached with the Islamic opposition, particularly as the Taliban continued to strengthen its control over Afghanistan. President Rakhmonov claims that Afghanistan continues to infiltrate radical Islamic terrorists into the country. As of 1999, a shaky peace was holding in the country although the Tajik parliament had passed a law banning religious organizations from associating directly with political parties. This law works to the detriment of the UTO, which depends heavily for support on the Islamic Renaissance Party, a banned religious and military organization, and other Islamist groups. Despite the truce, renegade militias and criminal gangs operate throughout the country.

See also Afghanistan; Taliban; Union of Soviet Socialist Republics; Uzbekistan.
Reference Djalili, Mohammed Reza, Frederick Grace, and Shirin J. Akiner, eds. *Tajikistan: Trials of Independence* (1997).

Taliban

The Taliban—Persian for "students"—is a radical Pashtun Sunni Muslim faction that had gained control over two-thirds of Afghanistan by 1996. Its leadership is provided by a ulema (religious council) headed by Mullah Muhammed Rabbani. The Taliban was formed in the 1980s by students in the madrasas (religious schools) set up in Pakistan for Afghan refugees during the war against the Soviet occupiers of Afghanistan. The Taliban has stressed strict adherence to its interpretation of Muslim law. It has banned alcohol, Western movies, and even children's games like marbles. Women are not permitted outside the home without permission, and even then, they must be covered from head to foot; they may not hold jobs or attend school. Punishment for break-

ing Taliban rules is meted out through public floggings, the amputation of limbs, and execution by stoning. Ayatollah Khomeini of Iran, a country that has supported the Afghanistan Shi'ite communities, called the Taliban a disgrace to Islam.

The Taliban mujahidin rapidly took over the Pashtun areas of the country, captured Kabul in 1996, and declared themselves the government of the Islamic Republic of Afghanistan. Former president Burhanudin Rabbani, a Tajik, fled north and joined forces with the Uzbek general Abdul Dostum to resist the Taliban militarily. With few exceptions, the Taliban was received openly by the war-weary Pashtun communities. In areas secured by the Taliban, other militias were required to surrender their arms and disband. Former Communists were imprisoned or hanged. The chief obstacle to Taliban control of the entire country is the armed resistance of the Tajik, Uzbek, and Hazzara minority communities. These groups, using military ordnance from the former Afghan armed forces and supported by Iran, Russia, and Uzbekistan, have joined with other anti-Taliban forces to form the Northern Alliance. By fall 1998, the Taliban had seized much of the territory formerly held by the Northern Alliance.

Although Pakistan provided much of the original funding for the Taliban, it is unclear how much control it is able to exercise over the Taliban today. Fighting continues between Taliban forces and the Northern Alliance while the United Nations seeks to convince the two sides to negotiate a settlement. The Taliban has given sanctuary to Osama bin Laden, who has been accused of masterminding the bombing of the U.S. embassies in Kenya and Tanzania.

See also Afghanistan.
References Magnus, Ralph, and Eden Naby. *Afghanistan* (1998); Maley, William, ed. *Fundamentalism Reborn: Afghanistan and the Taliban* (1998); Matinuddin, Kamal. *The Taliban Phenomenon* (1999).

Talysh

The Talysh live along the Caspian seaboard and are found in both Azerbaijan and Iran. It is estimated that there are 130,000 Talysh in the former and 112,000 in the latter. The Talysh speak an Indo-Iranian language and are Shi'ite Muslims. A Talysh khanate existed early in the nineteenth century, but it was annexed to the Russian Empire in 1828.

The Talysh language is related to Farsi, the major language of Iran, and since Turkic-speaking Azerbaijan received its independence from the USSR, Talysh activists have called for the Azerbaijan Talysh to be reunited with the Iranian Talysh. In 1993, Alikram Gumbatov led a mutiny in southern Azerbaijan and declared a Talysh republic. The mutiny was suppressed by the government of Azerbaijan, and in 1996, Gumbatov was arrested and sentenced to death. Azerbaijan has accused Iran of aiding the insurrection.

See also Azerbaijan.
Reference Banuazizi, Ali, and Myron Weiner, eds. *The State, Religion, and Ethnic Politics* (1988).

Tamil Eelam

The island of Sri Lanka (previously known as Ceylon) is inhabited by two main ethnic groups, the Sinhalese and the Tamils. The two groups differ in terms of race, religion, culture, and language. The Sinhalese are of Aryan origin and Buddhist while the Tamils are Dravidians and mostly Hindu. The Sinhalese claim to have arrived on the island in the fifth century B.C. while the Tamils migrated from southern India from A.D. 700 to 1300 and set up a Tamil kingdom in the north. A later migration of Tamils occurred in the latter part of the nineteenth century when the so-called Indian, or estate, Tamils were brought in as indentured laborers to work on the tea plantations. The two groups of Tamils form separate communities and live in different areas: the estate Tamils are in the central highlands, and the longer-established Tamils live along the northern and eastern coasts.

Ethnic animosities between Sinhalese and Tamils are historically rooted in the chronic warfare between the Sinhala and Tamil kingdoms.

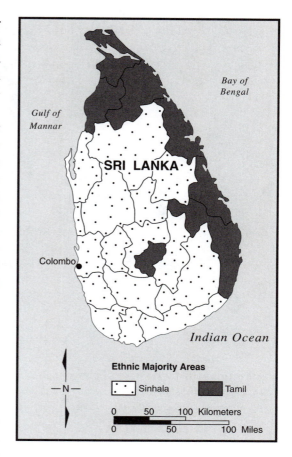

Under British colonial rule, the Tamils enjoyed access to Christian missionary schools, and consequently, when Ceylon became independent in 1948, Tamils held a disproportionately high proportion of the civil service and professional jobs. After independence, the Sinhalese majority adopted an affirmative action policy whereby racial and residential quotas were established for university admission. Sinhala was made the official language, and the estate Tamils were disenfranchised on the grounds that they were really citizens of India, not Ceylon. Although a 1956 pact promised that Tamil would be used in the Tamil areas and that regional councils would be established, the pact was never implemented.

Tamil separatism developed largely in reaction to the actions of the Sinhalese majority. The moderate Sinhalese government of the United National Party was ousted in the 1970 elections

Neelam Tiruchelvam, a lawmaker belonging to the Tamil United Liberation Front, was killed here in July 1999 by a suicide bomber suspected of belonging to the Liberation Tigers for Tamil Ealam, which opposes the more moderate group. (AP Photo/Gemunu Amarasinghe)

by the strongly nationalist Sri Lankan Freedom Party, and the new government adopted a new constitution in 1972. Under the previous constitution drawn up by the British, discrimination on the grounds of community or religion was prohibited. The new constitution enshrined the Sinhala-only language policy and "the duty of the state to protect and foster Buddhism." The name of the country was changed to Sri Lanka. Tamil youths found it increasingly difficult to get government jobs, and separatist sentiments grew strong. Another Tamil grievance was the government policy of encouraging Sinhalese settlement in Tamil areas. The Tamil Federal Party emerged in the 1960s, calling for a devolved federal structure, but it was replaced by the Tamil United Liberal Front (TULF), which advocated an independent Tamil Eelam (Eelam means literally "precious land"). In the 1977 elections, the TULF won majorities in the Tamil areas.

Communal rioting between Sinhalese and Tamils occurred in May 1958, August 1977, August 1981, and July 1983. The main victims in all the riots were the Tamils; hundreds were killed in 1958, and over 1,000 died in 1977. In 1981 and 1983, the violence took the form of organized pogroms. Tamils were beaten, hacked, or burned to death in the streets, on buses, and on trains. The rioters used voter lists to find the addresses of Tamil houses and businesses. A separatist insurgency by the Liberation Tigers of Tamil Eelam (LTTE) and other guerrilla groups began in the early 1970s. The guerrillas at first targeted police and soldiers, but since late 1984, they have massacred hundreds of Sinhalese civilians and bombed public places in Colombo, the capital city. The Sri Lankan security forces have responded with heavy-handed repression, detaining thousands of young Tamils without trial and killing many Tamil civilians.

India became involved for a number of reasons, including political pressure from Tamil leaders in southern India and the cost of supporting the more than 125,000 refugees who fled the conflict. After violence erupted in 1983, the Indian government sponsored talks between the TULF and the Sri Lankan government, which resulted in a devolution proposal. When this was rejected by Sinhalese politicians, the Tamil guerrillas increased their attacks. Another round of talks between the Sri Lankan government and a Tamil delegation made up of TULF and the five main Tamil guerrilla groups was held in July and August 1985. The Sri Lankan government refused to accept any of the Tamil demands for self-determination and a Tamil homeland, and this refusal and the massacre of 200 Tamils by the Sri Lankan military led to a new round of fighting.

By the end of 1986, the LTTE controlled the Jaffna peninsula, and after pressure from India, President Julius R. Jayawardene announced a new set of devolution proposals, which were widely perceived as the most generous yet offered. Under this plan, the northern and eastern provinces, where the Tamils were concentrated, would be granted control over internal law and order, education, and culture. However the LTTE rejected the proposals and set up a system of civil administration on the Jaffna peninsula. This provoked the Sri Lankan military into launching a major offensive against the Tigers. After heavy fighting, the area under Tamil control was reduced to the area around Jaffna city, whereupon India intervened. The Indo–Sri Lanka agreement of July 1987 provided for a cease-fire, enforced by the Indian army. However, the Tamil Tigers refused to surrender their arms, and a costly guerrilla war between them and the Indian army ensued, which only ended with the withdrawal of Indian troops in 1990.

Despite the continuing violence, the northern and eastern provinces were merged, and elections for a provincial council were held in late 1988. In the elections, which were boycotted by the LTTE, two Tamil nationalist parties won fifty-three of the seventy-one seats. In 1994, newly elected President Chandrika Kumaratunga initiated a two-pronged policy of making political concessions while attempting to defeat the Tamil Tigers militarily. As of December 1997, the president's People's Alliance government had succeeded in regaining control over most of the Tamil areas and was seeking parliamentary approval of a devolution of power to an autonomous Tamil region. The chronic violence between Tamils and Sinhalese has lasted for over fourteen years and claimed more than 70,000 lives. Militarily, the LTTE remains a force to be reckoned with, and in October 1999 it overran a string of government garrisons in the northeast. More than 100,000 civilians fled after the Tamil rebels warned the residents that they were about to attack the important town of Vavuniya.

See also Liberation Tigers of Tamil Eelam.

References Bose, Sumantra. *States, Nations, Sovereignty: Sri Lanka, India, and the Tamil Eelam Movement* (1994); Bullion, Alan. *India, Sri Lanka, and the Tamil Crisis 1976–1994: An International Perspective* (1995); Chadda, Maya. *Ethnicity, Security, and Separatism in India* (1997); Hannum, Hurst. *Autonomy, Sovereignty, and Self-Determination* (1990); Tambiah, Stanley. *Ethnic Fratricide and the Disuniting of a Democracy* (1986).

Tamil Nadu

Regional political parties advocating independence or autonomy have been strongest in the Indian state of Tamil Nadu and have dominated state politics there since the 1960s. The Tamil movement emerged in the early-nineteenth century as a reaction to the social domination of the Brahmins. Tamil scholars argued that the Dravidian peoples of southern India, who had been conquered by the Aryans, had a religion and culture that predated the Sanskrit civilization spread by the Brahmins. The Justice Party, founded in 1917, appealed to the racial pride of the lower-caste Dravidians against their Brahmin oppressors, and this "two-race" theory has remained a potent force. In 1944, E. V. Ramaswami Naicker renamed the party the Dravidian Federation and called for an independent Dravidian nation (Dravidasthan) that would include the speakers of Kannada, Telugu, Tamil, and Malayalam. The Linguistic States Reorganization program can be interpreted as an attempt to undermine the appeal of Dravidian separatism by splitting the movement along linguistic lines. The Dravida Munnetra Kazagham (DMK) split off from the federation and began contesting elections in the 1950s, winning control of Tamil Nadu in the 1967 state elections.

In 1962, the Indian government passed an amendment to the constitution that required political candidates to take a loyalty oath to the Indian Republic, and the DMK officially abandoned the demand for a separate nation. The party still emphasizes Tamil political autonomy and led the campaign against Hindi becoming the official national language. The party also wants the oppressive caste system replaced by an egalitarian society based on the ancient Dravidian social order. In 1972, another split led to the emergence of the All-India Anna Dravida Munnetra Kazagham (AIADMK), led by the film star, M. G. Ramachandran. AIADMK dominated state politics from 1977 through 1989, when the DMK returned to power.

Although the extreme separatist position is espoused by only a minority of the Tamils, the sense of a distinctive Tamil culture is strong and has been intensified by the conflict in Sri Lanka between the Tamil minority there and the Sinhalese majority. By the late 1980s, thousands of Sri Lankan Tamils had fled to Tamil Nadu, and Tamil politicians were calling for India's military intervention and the creation of a "greater Tamil nation." Training camps for the Tamil guerrillas were set up in Tamil Nadu, and when Indian Prime Minister Rajiv Gandhi ordered the expulsion of three militant Sri Lankan Tamil leaders, the DMK mobilized huge rallies in protest.

See also India; Tamil Eelam.
References Brass, Paul. *Politics of India since Independence* (1992);Chadda, Maya. *Ethnicity, Security, and Separatism in India* (1997).

Tangier

Tangier, a city in Morocco, is located on the southern shore of the Strait of Gibraltar, and the city's strategic position at the gateway to the Mediterranean meant that France, England, and Spain were all afraid it would fall under the control of one of their rivals. Hence, when Morocco was partitioned into Spanish and French protectorates in the early 1900s, Tangier and a 140-square-mile area surrounding the city became an international zone, neutral and demilitarized.

From 1923 until 1956, Tangier was governed by the International Control Commission, a body composed of representatives of France, Spain, Britain, the United States, Italy, Belgium, the Netherlands, and Portugal. (For a brief period from 1944 to 1946, Spain occupied the city in order to prevent a German attack.) An assembly composed of nine Moroccans and seventeen Europeans legislated on internal affairs while a mixed court of European judges administered justice. After World War II, Tangier prospered as a free port and an international financial center.

Politically, the city provided a safe haven for Moroccan nationalists in their struggle against French rule. At the end of March 1952, serious rioting broke out following a Moroccan nationalist demonstration, and nine were killed and eighty wounded when police fired into the crowd. The population numbered 172,000 at the time, and 30 percent of the residents were Europeans. In October 1956, it was agreed that the city would revert to Moroccan rule on January 1, 1957. After a two-year transition period, Tangier was fully integrated with Morocco.

References Spencer, William. *Historical Dictionary of Morocco* (1980); Stuart, Graham. *The International City of Tangier* (1955).

Tatarstan

Tatars arrived in the Volga region of Russia with the Mongol conquerors in the thirteenth century. A Tatar khanate was established at Kazan in the fifteenth century; in 1552, Ivan the Terrible captured the region, and it was absorbed into the Russian Empire. In 1920, following the Communist revolution, Tatarstan became an autonomous Soviet socialist republic within the Russian state. With the breakup of the USSR, separatist agitation grew in this Muslim state, and in 1991, it declared its independence, wrote its own constitution, designed its own flag, and adopted a national anthem. In 1992, 61 percent of the population, which is 50 percent Tatar and 43 percent Russian, approved sovereignty.

In Tatarstan, unlike Chechnya, Russia chose negotiation, not armed confrontation. It granted political and economic concessions to oil-rich Tatarstan without recognizing its independence from the Russian Federation. Mintimer Shaimiev, Tatarstan's popular president, seems satisfied with the degree of autonomy and economic control Tatarstan has negotiated. Russian is recognized as an official language, and Moscow retains control over fiscal and defense policies. Shaimiev has resisted making Islam the state religion. Tatars have actively participated in Russian parliamentary elections and still hold Russian passports.

A more radical movement that arose in the early 1990s, Ittifak, is chaired by Fauzia Bairamova. He has called for complete independence from Russia, made territorial claims on land inhabited by Tatars in other regions of Russia, and called for a union with Islamic Kazakhstan. Another nationalist organization, the All-Tatar Social Center, supports a Tatarstan for the Tatars movement. Such radical anti-Russian groups lost support when Shaimiev was able to work out an accommodation with Russia that is bringing economic benefits to Tatarstan.

Reference Rorlich, Azadeayse. *Volga Tatars* (1986).

Telangana

The Telangana movement was one of the earliest manifestations of regionalism in the Indian Union. Telangana, the Telegu-speaking area of Hyderabad, in southern India, was merged with Andhra in 1956 to form Andhra Pradesh, the first state established along linguistic principles. However, Telanganans complained that the arrangement disadvantaged them economically, as many non-Telanganans were receiving jobs in the educational system that were supposed to be reserved for Telanganans. Although the state government offered to replace non-Telanganan civil servants with local people, and to return surplus revenues to the region, widespread violent protests broke out in 1969, and at least twenty-three rioters were shot by the police. When the local Congress Party resisted calls for a separate Telangana state, defectors set up the Telangana People's Association. Although the defectors later rejoined the Congress Party, the Telegu National Party, which was founded in 1982, won a majority in the state elections of 1983.

See also India.

Tibet

The peoples of the Tibetan plateau region were unified under a Tibetan empire (680–842) and developed a distinctive cultural and political identity. Later, Tibet fell under the domination of first, the Mongols (1260–1368) and later, the Manchus (1368–1644). However, the vassal relationship between the Tibetans and their Mongol and Manchu rulers had little effect on Tibetan culture and society. Indeed, after the Mongols were converted to Buddhism, the Tibetan lamas established a Cho-Yon, or priest-patron, relationship with their Mongol rulers.

During the late 1900s, imperial rivalries between Britain, Russia, and China led to British involvement in Tibet. Lord Curzon, the viceroy of British India, characterized Chinese suzerainty over Tibet as a "constitutional fiction" and concluded an agreement, the Lhasa convention, with the Tibetans in 1904. This, in turn, provoked the Chinese into asserting their authority by sending a military force into eastern Tibet. However, the 1911 revolution, which overthrew the Manchu dynasty and established the Chinese Republic,

Supporters of Tibetan independence lie in front of the Chinese Mission in New York on the thirty-eighth anniversary of the Tibetan uprising against the Chinese that forced the Dalai Lama into exile. (AP Photo/ Richard Drew)

provided an opportunity for the thirteenth Dalai Lama to declare Tibetan independence in 1912. Under his rule, the groundwork for a modern system of government was created.

At the end of World War II, the Chinese Nationalist government still maintained its claim to sovereignty over Tibet while the Tibetans, although acknowledging a special relationship with China, considered themselves to be independent. On October 7, 1950, Chinese Communist troops invaded Tibet and easily overcame Tibetan resistance. On May 23, 1951, a seventeen-point agreement was signed between the Tibetans and the Chinese. "The Agreement on Measures for the Peaceful Liberation of Tibet" promised that Tibet would be governed under a system of "national regional autonomy" and that there would be no alteration in the country's religious and political system. However, the agreement placed Tibet under a military and administrative committee, thereby ensuring political control by China. The

Chinese set up the Tibet Autonomous Region but excluded most of eastern Tibet from it and incorporated those ethnic Tibetan areas into the Chinese provinces of Tsinghai (Qinghai), Kansu (Gansu), Szechuan (Sichuan), and Yunnan. The Chinese rapidly constructed a system of roads that allowed them to consolidate their hold over Tibet.

In 1955, the process of a "socialist transformation" in China was extended to ethnic minority areas, including Tibet. This involved the setting up of agricultural cooperatives and collectives and the destruction of "reactionary" aspects of each national minority culture, such as religion. The Tibetan population was divided into three classes, and the lower classes were encouraged to "struggle" against their exploiters. According to one account: "These struggles were diabolically cruel criticism meetings where children were made to accuse their parents of imaginary crimes; where farmers were made to denounce and beat up landlords; where pupils were made to degrade their teachers. Old lamas were made to have sex with prostitutes in public. And often the accused was beaten, spat and urinated upon." High lamas were publicly humiliated, beaten, and tortured as a demonstration of the powerlessness of their gods and the falsity of their religion.

Revolts broke out in eastern Tibet in 1956, with thousands taking to the hills and fighting a guerrilla campaign. In 1958, the revolt spread to central Tibet, including the Tibet Autonomous Region, and in March 1959, a series of anti-Chinese demonstrations in Lhasa led to an uprising. Although the Tibetan guerrillas were able to inflict numerous casualties, the overwhelming Chinese superiority in numbers and weaponry enabled them to crush the revolt. The Dalai Lama fled into exile in India, crossing the border on March 31, 1959. Before he did so, he formally repudiated the seventeen-point agreement and established a government in exile.

After the revolt was over, Tibetan culture was repressed. The great majority of the monasteries were closed and looted of their treasure. Between 1958 and 1960, the number of monks dropped from 114,100 (9.5 percent of the total population) to fewer than 20,000 (1.5 percent). Thousands of monks and other "counterrevolutionaries" were deported to forced-labor camps. The Chinese confiscated food and sent it to China, causing widespread famine. In 1984, the Tibetan government estimated that over 1.2 million Tibetans had perished as a result of the Chinese invasion and occupation—by starvation, forced labor, or execution and in battle. In the late 1980s, Tibetan demonstrations against Chinese rule turned into violent confrontations, and scores of demonstrators were killed and hundreds arrested.

The Tibetan government in exile has campaigned for international political support. The issue was raised at the UN General Assembly in 1961, and a resolution condemning China's human rights violations passed by fifty-six to eleven. In an address to the European Parliament at Strasbourg in 1988, the Dalai Lama called for Tibetan autonomy. The U.S. Congress passed two resolutions in 1987 and 1991 condemning China's occupation of Tibet, its mistreatment of the Tibetan people, and Tibet's right to self-determination. The increasing degree of international support for Tibet was symbolized by the awarding of the Nobel Peace Prize to the Dalai Lama in 1989. However, despite international condemnation and evidence that the desire for freedom remains strong among the Tibetan people, China appears determined to maintain control over Tibet. Indeed, mass Chinese immigration is transforming the Tibetans into a minority in their traditional homeland. Estimates suggest that there were at least 7.5 million Chinese compared to less than 6 million Tibetans in 1990 and that even in the Tibet Autonomous Region, Chinese outnumbered Tibetans.

See also China's Nationality Policy.
References Dalai Lama. *Freedom in Exile* (1990); Patterson, George. *Tibet in Revolt* (1960); Smith, Warren W. *Tibetan Nation: A History of Tibetan Nationalism and Sino-Tibetan Relations* (1996).

Tigray

Tigray, a state in Ethiopia, is occupied by the Tigrayans whose language, Tigrinya, is also spoken in northern Eritrea. Despite the close cultural similarities and historic ties between the Tigrayans and the Amhara, the area has often displayed separatist tendencies. In the late 1800s, the local ruler attempted, with the help of the French, to establish a Catholic kingdom. When the Italians invaded Ethiopia in 1935, Tigray was attached to Eritrea, and Italian rule was seen by many Tigrayans as preferable to being a province of the Ethiopian empire. The Italians abolished slavery; built roads, hospitals, and factories; and made Tigrinya the language of education.

After Tigray was returned to Ethiopian rule, a rebellion broke out in 1943 led by the Tigrayan nobility. The rebels seized the provincial capital and most of the eastern part of the country. Although the rebellion was brutally crushed, Emperor Haile Selassie was careful to grant Tigray a degree of autonomy, and prior to the Ethiopian revolution of 1974, the provincial administrators were members of the local nobility. A famine in 1972 led to widespread suffering and revealed the incompetence and lack of concern of the central government for the Tigrayan people.

In 1975, the Tigray People's Liberation Front (TPLF) called for an "independent democratic republic" and began an insurgency against the Mengistu regime. Peasant support for the TPLF was the result of several factors. Peasants were angered by agricultural reforms such as the formation of state farms, the prohibition against hiring wage labor, and the purchase of agricultural products at below market prices. The Mengistu regime, like that of Haile Selassie, meant domination by the Amhara ethnic group, and Amharic, rather than Tigrinya, remained the language of government administration. The TPLF presented itself as a defender of religion against the atheistic Communist central government. By 1988, the TPLF controlled most of the province.

Originally Marxist-Leninist in ideology, the TPLF became more moderate as it broadened its aims to include the overthrow of the central government. In alliance with the Eritrean People's Liberation Front, the TPLF became the core of an antigovernment coalition, the Ethiopian People's Revolutionary Democratic Front. After their troops marched into Addis Ababa on May 28, 1991, the leader of the TPLF, Meles Zenawi, became president of Ethiopia.

See also Ethiopia.
References Prouty, Chris, and Eugene Rosenfeld. *Historical Dictionary of Ethiopia* (1994); Young, John. *Peasant Revolution in Ethiopia: The Tigray People's Liberation Front 1975–1991* (1997).

Togoland

Togoland was a German colony in West Africa from 1884 until World War I when it was invaded by the British and French. After the war, Togoland became a League of Nations mandate and was divided into an eastern part administered by France and a western part administered by Britain. In a 1956 plebiscite, British Togoland voted to merge with the Gold Coast (now Ghana), and in 1960, French Togoland became the independent Republic of Togo. The Ewe, the largest ethnic group in Togo, have several times called for the unification of the Ewe regions of Ghana and Togo.

See also Ewe; Ghana.

Transdniester

The Transdniester region of Moldova, also known as Transnistria, is located on the eastern bank of the Dniester River and borders Ukraine. Unlike the rest of the country, which is largely Romanian, the majority of Transdniester's 700,000 people are Slavs—primarily Russian and Ukrainian. Local government, as was the case when Moldova was part of the USSR, is Slav dominated. After independence, the government continued to be dominated by former Communist officials. When Moldova declared independence from the Soviet Union in 1991, Transdniester seceded from Moldova and declared itself the Transdniester Republic. A five-month war erupted in which more than 200 were killed before a cease-fire was negotiated after Russian troops entered the region as peacekeepers.

When Moldova declared its independence, Slavic residents of the Transdniester region feared that the Moldovan parliament would vote to unite with Romania. They felt that would abridge the rights and power of the Slav minority in Moldova. The Moldovan parliament had voted to switch from the Cyrillic to the Roman alphabet as early as 1989, and pro-unification demonstrations increased after independence. Although Moldova's heavily Romanian-populated territory west of the Dniester had been part of Romania between World War I and World War II, Transdniester had been Soviet territory at the time. Even in the Soviet period following World War II, Russians in Transdniester Moldova had no worries about having their rights and privileges curtailed. Moldovan independence changed that.

The government of the so-called Transdniester Republic is located in Tiraspol. Its president, Igor Smirnov, is a Russian and a former Communist Party leader. The government is generally hostile to market reforms, preferring to retain the old centralized economy of the Soviet era. In December 1995 elections (which were not recognized by Moldova), voters approved by 81 percent a new constitution for the republic.

Russia, Ukraine, and Moldova, along with representatives of the Organization for Security and Cooperation in Europe, have been working to hammer out an agreement acceptable to both the government in Chisinau, the capital of Moldova, and Tiraspol. In the latest proposal, Transdniester would have the right to its own constitution, parliament, flag, state symbols, and anthem, and Romanian, Russian, and Ukrainian would all be official languages. Although Transdniester would determine the structure of its own local government and operate its own budget, it would remain part of the Moldovan state, which would be responsible for defense, foreign relations, and national budgetary matters.

The Transdniester government is still insisting on its independence. In summer 1998, the Tiraspol parliament revoked the license of the last Romanian-language school in the breakaway region, and more than 8,000 Russian troops remain stationed in Transdniester, despite the objections of the Moldovan government.

See also Moldova; Russians in the Former Soviet Republics.
Reference Dailey, Erika, Jeri Laber, and Lois Whitman. *Human Rights in Moldova: The Turbulent Dniester* (1993).

Transkei

One of the black homelands of South Africa, the Transkei declared itself independent on October 25, 1976. According to its constitution, the citizens of Transkei included not only those resident within the Transkei, and migrant workers temporarily absent, but also Xhosa-speaking Africans permanently living in the "white areas" of South Africa. This latter group is estimated to have numbered well over 1 million, or about a third of those legally defined as citizens of the new republic. The separation of the Transkei from the Republic of South Africa was denounced by most liberal scholars as a sham, intended only to legitimate the system of apartheid by reducing the number of blacks who were entitled to South African citizenship.

Unlike most of the other fragmented homelands, the Transkei was a compact region of about 16,600 square miles that corresponded to the traditional region occupied by the Cape Nguni tribes. With a primarily agricultural economy, the Transkei was overpopulated, and in 1968, it was estimated that 85 percent of the people were living in poverty. After becoming self-governing in 1963, Transkei was dominated by the Transkei National Independence Party (TNIP) led by Kaiser Matanzima and, later, his brother George. In the 1976 elections, held a month before independence, the TNIP won seventy-one of seventy-five the seats in the Transkei legislature. However, it is argued that those election results did not show support for independence, since less than a third of those eligible actually voted and opposition parties were harassed. (Just before the elections, the leader of the Democratic Party and several of that party's candidates were arrested.)

The extent to which the Transkei enjoyed genuine political autonomy is doubtful. The racial segregation that characterized apartheid was abolished, and there was a large increase in the number of black civil servants. On the other hand, there was little sign of the emergence of black businesses. The budget of the new state remained heavily dependent on South Africa, with 58 percent of the Transkei's revenue coming from that source in 1977–1978. The independence of Transkei was never recognized diplomatically by any country apart from South Africa. In September 1987, Matanzima was overthrown by his own army, led by Major General Bantu Holomisa. In early 1992, Holomisa wanted to call a referendum and negotiate the terms under which the Transkei would be reincorporated into the Republic. Following the first South African multiracial elections of 1994, the Transkei rejoined South Africa and became part of the Eastern Cape Province.

See also Black Homelands; Matanzima, Kaiser.
References Laurence, Patrick. *The Transkei: South Africa's Politics of Partition* (1976); Stultz, Newell M. *Transkei's Half Loaf* (1979).

Transylvania

The majority of Hungarians in Romania live in the northwestern region of the country known as Transylvania. Historically, Transylvania has been linked to Hungary since the ninth century, although it came under Turkish control in the sixteenth and seventeenth centuries only to come again under the Hungarian crown in 1699. In 1920, the Treaty of Trianon awarded Transylvania to Romania. In 1940, Hungary, as an Axis partner, got back two-thirds of Transylvania. In 1945, the region was occupied by Soviet troops, and in 1947, Transylvania was formally ceded back to Romania.

Although now a minority of the population of Transylvania, the Hungarians of Romania, also known as Szekelers or Magyars, number nearly 2 million. Migration to Hungary in recent years has kept the population from expanding significantly. Under the Communist government established after World War II, a Magyar Autonomous Region was established, but this was subsequently dissolved into separate counties without special privileges. Although proclaiming equal rights for all minorities, in later years the government of Nicolae Ceausescu became increasingly chauvinistic, curtailing and proscribing Hungarian schools and publications in a society in which freedom of speech, assembly, and the press had been effectively abolished. Ceausescu's massive "systematization" program, which destroyed traditional villages and forced peasants to resettle in new urban centers, may have displaced upward of 50,000 Hungarian peasants.

The Hungarian minority's response to Romanian dominance has consisted of demands to have Transylvania returned to Hungary, of efforts to establish an autonomous region within Romania, and, since 1989, of generating proposals seeking, through legislation, special concessions and guarantees of rights to the Hungarians in Romania.

The roots of Hungarian antipathy to Romanians run deep. There is the historical belief that Transylvania, "the cradle of Magyar civilization," is legitimately a part of Hungary. Culturally, the rift between the two ethnic groups, the Hungarians and the Romanians, is manifest in their disparate and mutually incomprehensible languages (Finno-Ugric Hungarian and the Slavicized Romance language of Romanian), in their religious differences (Hungarians are Catholic and Protestant; Romanians are Orthodox), and in their intellectual heritages (Hungarians are heavily influenced by Western, Austro-Hungarian traditions; the Romanians carry with them the Eastern influences of Turkic and Slavic civilizations). The fact that the traditional Transylvanian nobility was largely Hungarian while the poorest peasants were primarily Romanian serves to ground the Hungarian belief that Romanians are a backward, less-civilized people.

The fall of Ceausescu and the end of the Communist regime provided more opportunities for the expression and organization of Hungarian interests in Romania, but tensions between Romanians and Hungarians remain. In 1990, in Tirgu Mures in north-central Romania, 6 people were killed and 200 injured in clashes between Romanian nationalists and ethnic Hungarians demanding more cultural autonomy. In July 1997, bilingual signs in the same city were painted over in the colors of the Romanian flag. In the city of Cluj, the ultranationalist Romanian mayor, Gheorghe Funar, has resisted reforms favorable to Hungarians, particularly a proposal to create a Hungarian-language university. He, along with another anti-Hungarian group, the Romanian Cradle, advocated protests against the visit to Romania of Arpad Goncz, the president of Hungary.

Although the desire for union with Hungary may remain strong, most Hungarians in Romania realize that this hope is now unattainable. Under pressure from the United States and the European Union, the Romanians and Hungarians signed a treaty in 1996 guaranteeing the permanence of the borders between the two countries. Furthermore, in signing the treaty, the Hungarian government abandoned a clause that would have established "collective rights" under the Romanian constitution for the Hungarian community. Laslo Tokes, president of the Democratic Alliance of Hungarians in Romania, has accused the Hungarian government of being more interested in joining NATO than in securing the rights of Hungarians in Romania. In the Romanian parliament, Hungarians are represented by the Hungarian Democratic Union, led by Georgy Frunda, and the Hungarian Democratic Federation of Romania, chaired by Bela Markov. The Hungarian parties are currently part of Prime Minister Radu Vasile's ruling coalition and hold cabinet positions. In 1996 they received about 7 percent of the total parliamentary vote and 26 out of 143 seats.

In December 1997, the Hungarian Democratic Union Party chief, Csaba Takacs, threatened to bolt the government coalition unless Hungarians were granted the right to education exclusively in the Hungarian language. Hungarian nationalists also support the idea of granting dual Hungarian and Romanian citizenship status to Transylvanian Hungarians. Both proposals have met strong resistance in parliament.

See also Hungarians; Romania.
References Barta, Gabor, et al. *The History of Transylvania* (1994); *Witnesses to Cultural Genocide: First-Hand Reports on Rumania's Minority Policies Today* (1979).

Trieste

An important port on the Adriatic Sea, Trieste was ruled by the Hapsburgs until 1918. In the Treaty of Rapallo, Trieste and the Istrian peninsula were awarded to Italy, for which the city was part of *Italia irridenta* ("unredeemed Italy"). At the end of World War II, the area was claimed by both Italy and Yugoslavia and divided into two zones. Zone A (including Trieste) was under

British/U.S. military occupation, and Zone B was under Yugoslav control. The population of Zone A included 239,000 Italians, concentrated in the city of Trieste, and 63,000 Slovenes and Croats, who constituted a majority in the surrounding hinterland. In 1946, it was proposed to internationalize the area as the Free Territory of Trieste under the UN Security Council. However, the onset of the Cold War and the rift between the Soviet Union and Yugoslavia prevented agreement on how the scheme would be implemented.

Municipal elections held in May 1952 produced a clear majority (60 percent) for those parties supporting reunification with Italy while only 6 percent favored incorporation into Yugoslavia (the remaining vote went to parties that advocated retaining the current status of the territory). Serious rioting, in which six persons were killed, broke out in Trieste in November 1953 after the Allied military commander prohibited the flying of the Italian flag on public buildings. This unrest was followed by riots and demonstrations throughout Italy. In 1954, after years of fruitless negotiations, Zone A was annexed by Italy, and Zone B became part of Yugoslavia. A minor adjustment of the zonal borders ceded three small villages to Yugoslavia.

See also Irredentism.
References Campbell, John C. *Successful Negotiation: Trieste 1954* (1976); Novak, Bogdan. *Trieste 1941–54: The Ethnic, Political, and Ideological Struggle* (1970).

Tshombe, Moise (1919–1969)

The Katangan separatist leader Moise Kapenda Tshombe was born in November 1919, the eldest son of a wealthy merchant who was related to the paramount chief of the Lunda people. Educated by American Methodist missionaries, he was sent by his father to manage the family businesses in Elisabethville (now Lubumbashi), the provincial capital of Katanga (now Shaba). Tshombe displayed little aptitude for business—he went bankrupt three times—but he proved to be a gifted politician and was elected to the city and provincial councils. In 1959, Tshombe organized

Katanga's first political party, the Confederation des Associations du Katanga, or Conakat. Although the Lunda tribe formed the base of Conakat, it was also supported by most of the other Katangan tribes, and Tshombe's second in command was Godefroid Munongo, the brother of the paramount chief of the Bayeke. Tshombe and Conakat sought a weak federal government for the Congo, but the independence constitution instead established a strong centralized system.

In the chaos that followed the independence of the Belgian Congo in 1960, Tshombe declared Katanga's independence and became its first president, but Katanga's secession lasted only until Tshombe's regime was overthrown by UN forces in January 1963. Many African nationalists saw Tshombe as a Belgian puppet and a front for the powerful mining conglomerate, the Union Minière du Haut-Katanga. Tshombe, however, in an interview published in the *New York Times* on March 19, 1961, defended his use of white advisers and mercenaries saying: "I have the only disciplined army in the Congo today and the only effective administration . . . because I have foreign experts. Without foreigners Katanga would collapse into chaos." He was widely regarded as having been implicated in the murder of Patrice Lumumba, the first premier of the Congo, who died while in Katangan custody.

After the downfall of Katanga, Tshombe went into exile and then returned to become premier of the Congo from 1964 to 1965. After a coup by General Joseph Mobutu, Tshombe again went into exile. Condemned to death in absentia by the Zaire courts, he was kidnapped in July 1967 and flown to Algeria. He remained under house arrest in a comfortable villa until he died in June 1969.

See also Katanga; Zaire.
References Colvin, Ian G.. *The Rise and Fall of Moise Tshombe* (1968); Hempstone, Smith. *Rebels, Mercenaries, and Dividends: The Katanga Story* (1962).

Tuaregs

A nomadic people, the Tuaregs are fair-skinned Berbers who dominated the Sahara in the 1500s.

Tuaregs today can be found in Mali and Niger, where they make up 6 percent and 3 percent of the population, respectively, of what are predominantly black societies. They have rebelled on two occasions in Mali, seeking greater autonomy.

The first insurgency lasted for almost two years and was finally suppressed in July 1964 after the Malians poisoned the wells on which the Tuareg depended and bombed their camps. Droughts in 1970–1974 and 1984–1985 led to widespread starvation and reduced the number of Tuaregs to less than 50,000. The second rebellion began in 1990 and, according to the Malian government, was supported by Libya. Thousands of Tuaregs fled into neighboring Algeria and Mauritania amid reports of brutality by the Malian army. The rebels demanded a federal state with local autonomy for the northern region as well as more economic aid.

A rebellion by the Tuareg of Niger lasted from 1991 until April 1995 when the Organization of Armed Resistance and the Niger government signed a peace agreement. Under the agreement, new administrative boundaries would be drawn up, the Tuareg region would receive more development aid, and the rebels would be integrated into the national army.

Reference Press, Robert. "Africa's 'Blue Men' Flee Desert" (1992).

Tudjman, Franjo (1922–1999)

Franjo Tudjman, president of Croatia since 1990 and leader of the ruling party, the Croatian Democratic Union (HDZ), served as an army general in World War II and in Josip Broz Tito's Yugoslavia. Tudjman received a doctorate in political science from the University of Zagreb in 1972 and has published extensively in the field of military affairs.

Although a former partisan, Communist activist, and government official in postwar Yugoslavia, Tudjman's emerging Croatian nationalism led him into conflict with the unitary state philosophy of the Tito government. Tudjman promoted the notion that each Yugoslavian republic should have its own armed forces. He also rejected the idea that Croatians collectively were to blame for the atrocities committed in World War II by the pro-Nazi Ustashist regime. In 1967, Tudjman was expelled from the Communist Party. Suspected of forging ties with Croatian émigré groups, he was jailed in 1972 and again in 1981. Prior to Croatian independence in 1991, Tudjman professed to Western journalists that he was an advocate of a pluralistic democratic form of government.

In power, the Tudjman government, although democratically elected, has functioned as a one-party authoritarian regime with the state controlling the media. Tudjman's government also contains ultranationalists sympathetic to Ustashist ideals of national purity. Although constrained by the need for U.S. and West European support from endorsing a greater Croatia, which would incorporate the Croatian areas of Bosnia and Herzegovina into the Croat state, Tudjman, many analysts argue, had this as a long-term political goal. At present, under NATO pressure, the Croatian government endorses the Muslim-Croat entity in the post–Dayton peace accord Bosnian state. Tudjman died of stomach cancer on December 10, 1999.

See also Bosnia and Herzegovina; Croatia; Dayton Peace Accord; Ethnic Cleansing; Yugoslavia.
Reference Tanner, Marcus. *Croatia: A Nation Forged in War* (1997).

Turkish Kurds

Eastern Turkey is home to about 12 million Kurds, the largest concentration of this stateless people in the world. Known officially as Mountain Turks, the Turkish Kurds make up 20 percent of the country's population. Following Ataturk's revolution, which created modern Turkey from what remained of the Ottoman Empire, any manifestation of Kurdish identity was repressed. To this day, the publication of books and newspapers in Kurdish is forbidden, as is the publication of any books dealing with Kurdish history or cul-

ture. Use of the Kurdish language is not permitted in schools, in the courts, or for any official government business. The Kurds revolted in 1925 and again in 1930. After the latter revolt, the Turkish minister of justice declared: "The Turk must be the only lord, the only master of this country. Those who are not of pure Turkish stock can have only one right in this country, the right to be servants and slaves." Large numbers of Kurds were then deported from their homes and relocated throughout Turkey.

Taking advantage of the increased freedom of expression and association permitted under the liberal 1961 constitution, the separatist Kurdish Democratic Party was founded in 1965. However, following the military coups of 1971 and 1980, Kurdish political parties and organizations were banned, and thousands of Kurdish activists were arrested. It is alleged that many were tortured.

Since 1984, an insurrection led by the Kurdish Workers Party (PKK) has claimed some 30,000 lives. The PKK receives support from Syria and from the Kurdish diaspora in Europe. Half of Turkey's armed forces, about 250,000 men, are stationed in the Kurdish region, and brutal military repression has resulted in the destruction of thousands of villages and alienated the local population. Turkey and Iraq established a six-mile-wide security zone along their border, and on several occasions, Turkish troops have crossed into Iraq to attack Kurdish guerrilla bases. Making use of the rivalries between different Kurdish factions, the Turkish army has sometimes conducted its attacks on the PKK in alliance with the Kurdistan Democratic Party of Iraq. In 1996, Turkey announced the creation of a ten-mile-wide security zone in northern Iraq patrolled by Turkish troops. Abdullah Ocalan, the leader of the PKK, was captured by Turkish commandos, tried, and sentenced to death in 1999. He then issued a call to the PKK to end its campaign, and the PKK has observed a cease-fire since August 1999.

See also Kurdistan; Ocalan, Abdullah.
References Hannum, Hurst. *Autonomy, Sovereignty, and Self-Determination* (1990); McDowall, David. *A Modern History of the Kurds* (1996).

Turkish Republic of Northern Cyprus

The Turkish Republic of Northern Cyprus is the name given to the Turkish-controlled zone on Cyprus. After Cyprus became independent in 1960, constitutional disagreements between the Greek majority and the Turkish minority led to widespread violence. By the late 1960s, the Turkish Cypriots were being besieged in a number of enclaves scattered throughout the island. A coup overthrew the government of Archbishop Makarios and provoked a Turkish invasion in July 1974. After the invasion, the Turks controlled 37 percent of the island. Continued violence led to a mass exodus of Turks to the north and Greeks to the south (over 140,000 Greeks and at least 50,000 Turks became refugees). In February 1975, the Turkish Cypriots set up a Turkish Federated State of Cyprus under Rauf Denktash; in 1985, a constitution for the Turkish Republic of Northern Cyprus was approved by 70 percent of those voting.

Denktash has been elected president in every election. However, his National Unity Party split after Denktash was criticized for making too many concessions to the Greek Cypriots. The Turkish zone is much poorer than the Greek zone, has a sizable trade deficit, and must be subsidized by Turkey (in 1980, the subsidy was over $10 million). Forty thousand immigrants from mainland Turkey boosted the population to an estimated 186,000 in 1997. Despite lengthy negotiations between Greek and Turkish Cypriots, during which both sides made concessions, no agreement could be reached. Although the Greeks now accept the idea of a bizonal federation, the Turks resist demands that Greek refugees be allowed to return to their former homes.

See also Cyprus.
Reference Oberling, Pierre. *The Road to Bellapais* (1982).

Turkmenistan

Turkmenistan is the southernmost and least-populated of the former Soviet central Asian republics. It has a population slightly exceeding 4 million, of which 75 percent are Turkmen; Russians and Uzbeks each account for about 10 percent. The Russian population is almost entirely urban, having constituted the managerial and technical class under Soviet rule. Since independence in 1991, the high birthrate of the heavily rural Turkmen population, combined with a gradual out-migration of Russians in a country whose educational and cultural institutions are converting from Russian to Turkmen, is creating a more ethnically homogeneous population. Although the country continues to be ruled dictatorially by the former Communist boss Separmurad Niyazov, the Turkmenistan government, unlike that of former Soviet republics such as Estonia and Latvia, has granted citizenship rights to all ethnic citizens. There has been no significant ethnic conflict within the republic.

The Turkmen are a Turkic-speaking people and are Sunni Muslims. The Turkmen, who probably settled the area in the tenth and eleventh centuries, were subjugated by Seljuk Turks and Mongols. A largely nomadic people organized around clans and tribes, the Turkmen as a people achieved little unity before their unsuccessful resistance to the advancing Russian Empire in the nineteenth century. By 1881, the Turkmen had become part of the Transcaspia subdivision of Russian Turkistan. After the Russian Revolution of 1917, Turkmenistan emerged briefly as an independent state before being overcome by Bolshevik power. It first was designated a province of the Turkistan Autonomous Soviet Socialist Republic, but in 1924 it was designated a constituent republic, the Turkmenistan Soviet Socialist Republic. With the dissolution of the USSR in 1991, Turkmenistan declared its independence.

See also Union of Soviet Socialist Republics.
References Curtis, Glenn E. *Kazakstan, Kyrgyzstan, Tajikistan, Turkmenistan, and Uzbekistan* (1997); Nedvetsky, Alexander. "Turkmenistan" (1994).

Tuva

Tuva, a republic within the Russian Federation, is located in south-central Siberia to the north of Mongolia. The Tuvans speak a Turkic language with Mongolian influences. Unlike many minorities in the Russian Federation, Tuvans have retained their native language and resisted assimilation to Russian culture. Although nearly all Tuvans speak their own native language, only 60 percent are fluent in Russian. The Tuvan religion combines Tibetan Buddhism and shamanism. Tuvans comprise two-thirds of the republic's population of 300,000, with most of the rest being Russians.

Located in a geographically strategic location, throughout its history Tuva has been occupied by Turks, Chinese, Uyghurs, Kyrgyz, and Mongols. From 1757 until 1911, Tuva was part of China. Toward the end of Chinese rule, czarist Russia encouraged separatist movements in Tuva, and in 1914, Tuva became a Russian protectorate. Just after the Russian Civil War, Tuva declared itself the Tannu Tuva People's Republic and aligned with the Communists. In 1944, Tuva was formally incorporated into the Soviet Union as an autonomous province of the Russian Soviet Socialist Republic. Tuva had its status raised to that of an autonomous republic in 1961. When the USSR collapsed in 1991 and Russia became independent, Tuva entered the Russian Federation as one of its twenty-one constituent republics.

During the 1990s, several clashes pitted Tuvans against Russians. In 1990, an ethnic riot broke out at a youth dance, and later that year, Tuvans battled Russians in Kyzyl, the capital of Tuva. A Russian refusing to answer a question in Tuvan was murdered, and leaflets calling on Russians to leave Tuva were widely circulated. In 1992, the Free Tuva Party, a secessionist organization, called for a referendum on Tuva's complete independence from Russia. A new constitution, approved by the Tuvan parliament in 1993, includes a provision allowing for the secession of Tuva from the Russian Federation, a right not granted by the federation's constitution. The Tuvan government placed itself at odds with Moscow in 1994 by supporting Tibet's independence from China and, in 1995, by objecting to the use of Tuvan soldiers in the Chechnya war. Tuvan separatist sentiments have been held in check up to the present, primarily by Tuva's economic dependence on Moscow, but the continuing feebleness of Russia's economy serves to heighten Tuvan antagonism toward Russians in the republic. Because of the ethnic hostilities, many Russians have left Tuva.

See also Russian Federation.
Reference Wixman, Ronald. *The Peoples of the USSR: An Ethnographic Handbook* (1984).

Udmurtia

Udmurtia is a republic in the eastern part of the Russian Federation bordering on Tatarstan and Bashkortosan. It has a population of 1.7 million, of which Russians constitute 60 percent; Udmurts, 30 percent; and Tatars, 7 percent. Udmurts are the fourth-largest Finno-Ugric group in the world. Some 300,000 Udmurts live outside the Udmurt Republic—in the Yekaterinburg and Perm regions and in the republics of Tatarstan and Bashkortosan. Within Udmurtia, two dialects of Udmurt are spoken, the northern and the southern.

In 1920, the Votyak Autonomous Oblast was established in the Soviet Union; in 1934, it became the Udmurt Autonomous Republic. In 1991, following the collapse of the Soviet Union, Udmurtia became a republic in the Russian Federation.

A nationalist group, Udmurt-Kenesh, has been advocating the creation of an Udmurt shadow government to parallel the official state organs. In 1991, Udmurt Kalyk, the Udmurt People's Party, was formed, and it advocates complete economic and political sovereignty for the republic.

Also active in the republic is the Tatar Civic Center (TCC), which is opposed to Udmurt nationalist goals. The Society of Russian Culture was set up in 1991 to promote Russian patriotism, and politically, it sides with neo-Communist factions in Russia proper. The Bessermanians, a small rural minority who trace their origins to the Volga Bulgars, have organized a Bessermanian Society with the aim of restoring their cultural and national identity. This society is anti-Udmurtian in tone.

See also Russian Federation.
References Kolga, Margus, et al., eds. *Red Book of the Peoples of the Russian Empire* (1993); Mastyugina, Tatiana, and Lev Perelkin, *An Ethnic History of Russia* (1996).

Ukraine

Ukraine, with a population of 51 million is 73 percent Ukrainian and 22 percent Russian. Romanians, Hungarians, Poles, Tatars, and Roma

(gypsies) are among other ethnic groups found in the republic. The Ukrainian language, along with Russian and Belarusian, belongs to the eastern Slavic family of languages. The three languages are distinct but mutually intelligible. Because of Ukraine's long association with Russia, 40 percent of Ukrainians, including President Leonid Kuchma, use Russian as their first language.

In addition to Ukraine's linguistic dualism, there is an east-west division that reflects different patterns of historical development. In general, eastern Ukraine is the more Russianized of the two areas. The Crimea and Donbas regions contain significant populations of ethnic Russians and are a source of strain as the country attempts to reconstruct itself as a Ukrainian nation.

The first major Slavic state in Ukrainian territory was Kiev Rus, founded in the ninth century. At that time, the people were converted to the Orthodox faith and adopted the Cyrillic alphabet. The Mongol invasion of the thirteenth century subjected much of Ukraine to the control of the Asiatic conquerors, but the weakening of Mongol and Tatar rule in the fifteenth and sixteenth centuries eventually left much of eastern Ukraine, the part east of the Dniester River, under the control of the Russian Empire. In the eighteenth century, these Ukrainian lands were formally incorporated into the empire. In the nineteenth century, as Ukrainian nationalism stirred, Russia attempted to repress it, denying the actuality of a Ukrainian nationality. Ukrainians were referred to as "little Russians," and the use of the Ukrainian language was officially proscribed.

In western Ukraine, the Kievan Rus was succeeded by the independent principality of Galicia-Volhynia. In the fourteenth, fifteenth, and sixteenth centuries, the Ukrainian lands west of the Dniester came under Lithuanian and Polish rule, and in attempting to control the Ukrainians, Poland forced the Orthodox churches to unite with Rome, and thus the Uniate Church was established. Although continuing to use the Eastern rite, the churches were now subject to the Vatican.

The harsh rule of Poland and the Polish landlord class led in 1648 to a revolt of the Zaporozhian Cossacks, a Ukrainian warrior class whose forces were concentrated in the lower Dniester River region. An independent state came into being under Ukrainian national hero Bohdan Khmelnytsky, but it was short-lived. In 1654, the state submitted to Moscow. In the late-eighteenth century, the lands west of the Dniester, except for Galicia and Ruthenia, were also absorbed by the Russian Empire. Galicia, Ruthenia, and Bukovina in the south became part of the Austro-Hungarian Empire, and their subsequent developments were influenced by central European rather than Russian affairs. A united Ukrainian state emerged briefly after the collapse of the Austro-Hungarian and Russian Empires following World War I. In western Ukraine, Ruthenia was incorporated into the newly formed Czechoslovak Republic in 1919. In 1921, Galicia and Volhynia were occupied by Poland and became part of that state. Bukovina was annexed to Romania.

In eastern Ukraine, a Soviet socialist republic was established following World War I, and soon, under Joseph Stalin, it came to be dominated by Russian rather than Ukrainian Communists. Forced collectivization in the 1930s led to the death of millions of Ukrainians and generated great hostility to Soviet policies. Ukrainian attempts to develop a more Ukrainian Communist

leadership were aborted by Stalin, and many Ukrainian Communists fell victim to the great purges of the 1930s. The Ukrainian Orthodox Church was placed under the control of the Russian patriarch, the Ukrainian cultural elite was persecuted, and a policy of Russification was undertaken.

Following World War II, western and eastern Ukraine were reunited, and Ruthenia, Galicia, Volhynia, and Bukovina were incorporated into the Ukrainian Soviet Socialist Republic. Armed resistance to the Soviets continued in western Ukraine until the 1950s. In 1946, Stalin forced the Uniate Church to merge with the Orthodox Church and sever its ties with Rome. Nevertheless, the Catholic Church continued as an underground religion. In 1954, to commemorate the three-hundredth anniversary of the Ukrainian-Russian association, the Russian Soviet Socialist Republic ceded the Crimea and its largely Russian population to Ukraine, thus completing the territory occupied by the contemporary Ukraine state.

The 1970s saw the reemergence of a Ukrainian cultural elite. The Communist Party also took on a more Ukrainian composition, and Ukrainian journals and literature were published more frequently. As in Russia, a strong dissident movement arose. The Leonid Brezhnev era, however, was characterized by a clampdown on "bourgeois nationalism" and another purge of Ukrainian intellectuals. Economic stagnation and the possibilities created by Mikhail Gorbachev's glasnost (openness) policies resulted in another surge of Ukrainian nationalism. A new mass organization, The People's Movement of Ukraine, pushed for Ukrainian autonomy, and in 1989, Ukrainian was declared the state language. The Uniate Church was reestablished, and an independent Ukrainian patriarchate was proclaimed in Kiev. With the monopoly of the Communist Party broken, the People's Movement for Reconstruction (Rukh) openly advocated democratic reform and guarantees of civil and human rights. In 1989, Communist Party Secretary Leonid Kravchuk declared the sovereignty of the Ukrainian people.

Rukh called for complete separation from the Soviet Union, and in 1991, after the failed coup against Gorbachev, the Ukrainian parliament declared its independence. In a subsequent referendum, 90 percent of the voters approved.

The religious and cultural division between western Catholic and eastern Orthodox Ukraine continues to this day and is reflected in political attitudes. Voting patterns show that westerners are more receptive to market reforms and private enterprise while easterners remain more committed to Soviet institutions—centralized management of the economy, for example. In the 1994 presidential elections, westerners supported incumbent president Leonid Kravchuk while easterners favored the winning candidate, Leonid Kuchma.

Internally, Ukraine's greatest challenge to its integrity comes from the Russian populated areas of the Donbas and Crimean regions. Also in the Crimea, a Tatar community is being reconstituted by returning exiles from former Soviet central Asian republics. The Tatars are asking for political representation, recognition of Tatar as an official language, and restitution of lands and properties forcibly seized by the Soviet government. A mitigating factor, from Kiev's perspective, is that the Tatars blame the Crimean Russians for their plight. Although desirous of some autonomy, Crimean Tatars, in contrast to nationalist Russian Crimeans, support membership in the Ukraine state. In western Ukraine, Ruthenians (or Rusyns) who were part of the Czechoslovak Republic between World War I and World War II have agitated for more autonomy.

Ukrainian government policy toward separatist movements is to grant concessions regarding language and local government, but any attempts at a full-fledged regional breakaway are met with stern measures. In 1994, Kiev dismissed the government of the Crimean Autonomous Republic, suspended its constitution, and instituted direct rule from Kiev. Another measure that seeks to discourage ethnic and regional separatism is a ban on purely local parties. Exacerbating Ukraine-Russian relations within Ukraine has

been the deterioration of living standards in Donbas and Crimea since independence. This situation feeds support for reunification of these regions with Russia and for a resumption of the trade links that existed within the Soviet economy.

See also Cossacks; Crimea; Crimean Russians; Crimean Tatars; Donbas Russians; Rukh; Russians in the Former Soviet Republics; Rusyns; Union of Soviet Socialist Republics.
Reference Magocsi, Paul. *History of Ukraine* (1996).

Ukrainian People's Movement for Reconstruction
See Rukh

Union Démocratique Bretonne

Union Démocratique Bretonne (UDB), the main Breton separatist party, was founded in 1962 by left-wing members of the Mouvement pour l'Organization de la Bretagne (MOB, Movement for Breton Organization). The goal of the party was regional autonomy for Brittany and a revival of the Breton language. The party's charter also declared that true democracy required the overthrow of capitalism and its replacement by planned economic and social democracy.

The new party championed a variety of local causes, marching with unemployed stevedores and joining peasant protests against French agricultural policies. The UDB also opposed defense installations and military bases in Brittany. Party membership increased after 1968, and by 1980, it had reached 1,000 while the party's newspaper had a circulation of over 4,000. Students make up the great majority of the UDB's membership. The party has little electoral support, and in fifteen constituencies in 1978, its candidates obtained less than 2 percent of the vote. The more conservative wing of the MOB became the Breton National and European Federalist Movement and did equally poorly in the 1973 elections.

See also Brittany.
Reference Beer, William R. *The Unexpected Rebellion: Ethnic Activism in Contemporary France* (1980).

Union of Soviet Socialist Republics

Founded in 1922, the Union of Soviet Socialists Republics (USSR) in 1956 consisted of the Russian Soviet Socialist Republic and fourteen other ethnic socialist republics. In area, it was the largest country in the world. Although Slavs (Russians, Ukrainians, and Belarusians) accounted for 70 percent of the country's 289 million citizens, the USSR contained over 100 ethnic minorities, 22 of which had a population exceeding 1 million. Muslim Turkic-language groups (Kazakhs, Azeris, Uzbeks, Kyrgyz, Turkmen, Tatars, and Bashkirs) accounted for over 17 percent of the population. Other large minorities included Armenians, Tajiks, and Caucasian- and Finnish-language groups. In addition to the socialist republics, the USSR also included thirty-eight ethnic autonomous republics and regions located in the individual republics. By far the greatest ethnic diversity was in the Russian Republic, which had thirty-two ethnic subdivisions.

Although the fifteen republics were equal in theory, the nation was dominated by Russians who governed through the Communist Party of the Soviet Union, itself Russian dominated. Periodic Russification campaigns combined with efforts to eliminate traditional religions like Islam created resentment in the non-Russian areas of the country.

As the hold of communism weakened under Mikhail Gorbachev and central power deteriorated, demands for republic autonomy grew. Anti-Soviet demonstrations wracked the Baltic nations, and by 1990, the parliaments of several republics had asserted their sovereignty. Following an unsuccessful coup by hard-line Communists in Moscow in 1991, Russia, Ukraine, and Belarus declared the Soviet Union defunct. By late 1991, all the former Soviet republics had declared themselves independent nations, and on December 31, 1991, the Soviet Union was formally dissolved.

See also Armenia; Azerbaijan; Belarus; Estonia; Georgia; Kazakhstan; Kyrgyzstan; Latvia; Lithuania; Moldova; Russian Federation; Tajikistan; Turkmenistan; Ukraine; Uzbekistan.

References McCauley, Martin. *The Soviet Union 1917–1991* (1994); Remnick, David. *Lenin's Tomb: The Last Days of the Soviet Empire* (1994).

United Kingdom

The United Kingdom of Great Britain and Northern Ireland is a multinational state created by conquest and dynastic alliances. Although England is the dominant entity, with 90 percent of the population and 55 percent of the land area, the United Kingdom also includes Scotland, Wales, and Northern Ireland.

Wales was conquered by England in 1282, and in 1485, a Welshman became Henry VII, founder of the Tudor dynasty. Wales was formally annexed in 1536. The union of the English and Scottish crowns in 1603 was followed by the Act of Union of 1707, which united the two parliaments while preserving Scotland's separate legal system and the established Presbyterian Church. The union was favored by the Scottish merchant class, which obtained access to the English colonial markets as a result. The union also encouraged the development of local industry under Scottish entrepreneurs, and Scots played a prominent role in the British Empire as soldiers and administrators. Ireland was nominally under English rule as early as the twelfth century, but effective control was not achieved until the seventeenth century. The Irish parliament was subordinate to that of England, and since Catholics were excluded from political participation, it represented only "the ascendancy," the Anglo-Irish landowners. In 1801, the Irish parliament was dissolved, and Ireland was given representation in the British Parliament at Westminster.

Separatist movements emerged in the nineteenth century throughout the periphery. Catholic emancipation in 1829 allowed Daniel O'Connell to organize the Irish peasants into a political force, and later the Irish Party was organized under Charles Stewart Parnell. Frustrated by an inability to achieve home rule within the United Kingdom, Irish nationalism became increasingly radical, and the Easter rebellion of

1916 was followed by the victory of Sinn Fein in the 1918 elections. After a guerrilla war throughout Ireland, the country was partitioned in 1922 with the predominantly Protestant north remaining part of the United Kingdom and the Catholic south becoming independent.

In Scotland and Wales, nationalist sentiments were less intense and were assuaged by decentralization measures that recognized their distinctive cultural identities. The office of Secretary of State for Scotland was established in 1885 to articulate Scottish concerns and interests. A Scottish Home Rule Association was founded in 1886, and a second wave of agitation developed with the electoral success of the Labour Party in Scotland in 1922. Scottish Socialists argued that under home rule, Scotland would have a Labour government. In Wales, religious issues played an important role in reviving national feeling. Although a majority of the Welsh were nonconformists, they had to pay tithes to the established Anglican Church, and Anglican schools were supported by local tax rates. The movement for disestablishmentarianism thus went hand in hand with demands for home rule. The first recognition of Wales as a distinct legislative entity, the Welsh Sunday Closing Act of 1881, was a concession to two nonconformist concerns, Sabbath observance and temperance.

Although radicals and socialists were originally in favor of home rule, with the growing strength of the Labour Party throughout Britain many working-class leaders began to see the advantages of political centralization. Not only did it allow for government planning of the national economy, but national politics offered individuals greater career opportunities than local politics did.

In the post–World War II era, administrative devolution was expanded. The office of Secretary of State for Scotland not only administered Scotland's distinctive educational and legal system but also lobbied for regional development funds. Scottish Office pressure was instrumental in bringing major investments, including the Ravenscraig steel complex and the Linwood automobile plant, to the region. By the mid-1970s, government spending on a per capita basis was 20 percent higher in Scotland than in the rest of the Britain. The Welsh Office, set up in 1964, served a similar regional planning function.

There is little population movement among the different regions that make up the United Kingdom. When asked how they see themselves, most Scots describe themselves as Scots, and most Welsh people describe themselves as Welsh (rather than British). The polls also find that most Scots, Welsh, and English say that they are proud to be "British." In the past, party competition between class-based parties served to integrate the United Kingdom by linking together people of the same class living in different regions. However, since the 1980s, the growing regional imbalance in the vote for the two major British political parties has produced a looming political crisis. The Conservative Party vote has drastically declined in Scotland and Wales but increased in England, with the result that partisan and regional cleavages are increasingly correlated.

See also Mebyon Kernow; Northern Ireland; Scotland; Shetland Islands; Wales.
References Keating, Michael. *State and Regional Nationalism: Territorial Politics and the European State* (1988); Rose, Richard. *The Territorial Dimension in Government: Understanding the United Kingdom* (1982).

United Nations

Through its many agencies, the United Nations (UN) has become increasingly involved in peacekeeping missions necessitated by ethnic and national conflicts. Originally, the UN supplied personnel whose chief function was to monitor the maintenance of agreed upon cease-fire zones and to provide humanitarian assistance in war zones. In recent years, under Secretary General Boutros Boutros-Ghali, the UN has employed its forces more actively to compel belligerents to adhere to provisions of peace agreements. By the late 1990s, UN forces were involved in seventeen nations.

UN operations aimed at controlling ethnic hostilities have been mounted in Lebanon, through the UN Interim Force in Lebanon, and in Cyprus, Bosnia, and Kosovo. In Bosnia, the UN, acting through the UN Protection Force, became embroiled in the civil war with its "ethnic cleansing" without effectively curtailing it. Only after armed intervention by NATO forces in 1995 was peace obtained. The UN continues to provide 33,000 peacekeeping forces in Bosnia in an attempt to secure compliance with the Dayton peace accord. In 1998, UN peacekeepers were assigned to Kosovo, Yugoslavia, to monitor Serb-Albanian relations. In 1999, with the onset of a massive NATO aerial attack on Yugoslavia, the UN Kosovo mission was withdrawn. A UN contingent remains in neighboring Macedonia, however.

In addition to peacekeeping missions, the UN also supplies food and assistance to persons displaced by ethnic conflicts throughout the world. The High Commission on Refugees oversees these activities, and the UN Commission on Human Rights investigates and publicizes human rights violations affecting ethnic minorities. The commission has established two international criminal tribunals to try to prosecute human rights violators in the former Yugoslavia and Rwanda.

See also Bosnia and Herzegovina; Dayton Peace Accord.
References Durch, William, ed. *UN Peacekeeping, American Politics, and the Uncivil Wars of the 1990s* (1997); Ratner, Steven. *The New UN Peacekeeping: Building Peace in Lands of Conflict after the Cold War* (1997).

United States
See Black Separatism in the United States; White Separatism in the United States

Unrepresented Nations and Peoples Organization
The Unrepresented Nations and Peoples Organization (UNPO) is an organization of fifty ethnic communities not represented in international bodies like the United Nations. It was founded in 1991 and is headquartered in the Hague. It represents a range of groups from indigenous peoples, like Australian aborigines and the North American Lakota Nation, to semiautonomous states, like Sakha and Buryatia in the Russian Federation. UNPO conducts research and fact-finding missions and presents grievances to national and international bodies.

Reference UNPO. http://www.Unpo.org (1999).

Uyghurs
The Uyghurs are a Turkic people who live in the northwestern part of China and were only brought under the control of the Manchu dynasty in the 1700s when the region was renamed Xinjiang (or New Dominion). After Manchu rule was ended by Yakub Beg's rebellion (1864–1877), political turbulence lasted for several decades as China and Russia competed for control, and two independent republics were proclaimed: the East Turkestan Republic of 1933 and the Yining Republic of 1944. When the Chinese Communists moved into Xinjiang in 1949, they executed Muslim religious leaders and destroyed mosques in an attempt to crush Uyghur nationalism.

Under the Chinese Communists, the Uyghurs are recognized as a minority nationality, and the Xinjiang Uyghur Autonomous Region was established in 1955. The Sunni Islamic religion is an important aspect of the Uyghurs' identity. The Uyghurs form the largest nationality group (44 percent in 1985) in Xinjiang Province, but the region's ethnic composition is being changed by a flood of Chinese immigration. During the so-called Hundred Flowers period, when the central government relaxed its control over intellectual life and culture, Uyghur students called for the creation of an autonomous republic and protested the domination of ethnic Chinese in the local party organizations. The independence of the former Soviet central Asian republics appears to have encouraged Uyghur separatist sentiments, and scores of attacks have been attributed to Uyghur separatists since 1996. These include a series of bombings in Beijing and Urumqi (the capital of the autonomous region), in which twelve people were reported killed. Hundreds of Uyghurs have been arrested for separatist activities, and several have been publicly executed.

See also China's Nationality Policy.
References Gladney, Dru C. "Rumblings from the Uyghur" (1997); Rudelson, Justin Jon. *Oasis Identities: Uyghur Nationalism along China's Silk Road* (1997).

Uzbekistan

Uzbeks are descendants of Turkic-Mongol tribes from northwestern Siberia, and the name is probably derived from Oz Beg, a khan of the Empire of the Golden Horde from 1312 to 1341. The Uzbeks speak a Turkic language and are Sunni Muslims. The current population of Uzbekistan, 20 million, makes that country the largest Muslim nation of the former Soviet republics. About 8 percent of the population is Russian, a percentage that has been declining yearly since independence in 1991. Another 5 percent of the population is made up of Persian-speaking Tajiks, largely located in Bukhara and Samarkand.

Although several Uzbek local dynasties became powerful between the fifteenth and eighteenth centuries, by 1875, all of today's Uzbekistan was under Russian control and had become part of the Russian province of Turkistan. In 1916, Uzbeks and other central Asians participated in an unsuccessful uprising against czarist rule, and in the turmoil of the Russian Revolution of 1917 and the Russian Civil War (1918–1920), an independent Uzbek state emerged for a brief period. By 1924, the Soviets had consolidated their power and created the Uzbek Soviet Socialist Republic. In 1929, Tajikistan was separated from Uzbekistan and raised to the status of a soviet republic. Twenty percent of the people in the new Tajik Republic were Uzbeks. That caused no problems during the period of Soviet rule, but after the collapse of the USSR, it became a source of conflict between Uzbekistan and Tajikistan. Historically, the two ethnic groups have not gotten along

well and today confront each other not only in Uzbekistan and Tajikistan but also in Afghanistan where, in 1997, the two groups made peace in order to combat the Taliban government forces.

Staunchly hard-line Communist, Uzbekistan supported the 1991 attempted coup against Mikhail Gorbachev, and when the Soviet Union collapsed shortly after that, Uzbekistan reluctantly declared independence. The country has been led since independence by President Islam Karimov, a former Communist.

In his attempts to control the new state, President Karimov has banned the main liberal opposition parties, the Bulik and the Erk, and all Muslim religious parties. The government has cracked down on growing Muslim sentiment in the Fergana Valley, persecuting members of the puritanical Wahabi sect and the Islamic Renaissance Party, two groups that advocated the establishment of an Islamic state. The Islamic Renaissance Party has sprung up in several Muslim areas of the former Soviet Union and has as its aim, however impractical, the emergence of a greater Islamic state encompassing all the Muslim nations of Russia and the former Soviet Union. Additionally, to ward off any possible Tajik separatist movements, whether religious or nationalist, Karimov has banned all Tajik social and political organizations.

To forestall the ascendance to power in neighboring Tajikistan of pro-Islamic factions (which Uzbekistan alleges have ties to both Iran and Afghanistan), the Karimov government aided an Uzbek militia operating in the 1-million-strong Uzbek community in Tajikistan. Karimov also used all his influence to prevent the creation of a coalition government in Tajikistan that included members of religious parties. Ultimately, he was unsuccessful, as Russia brokered a cease-fire that sanctioned the creation of a neo-Communist and Islamist government there.

See also Tajikistan.
References Allworth, Edward A. *The Modern Uzbeks: From the 14th Century to the Present: A Cultural History* (1990); Curtis, Glenn E. *Kazakstan, Kyrgyzstan, Tajikistan, Turkmenistan, and Uzbekistan* (1997).

Valle d'Aosta

An Italian region bordering France and Switzerland, Valle d'Aosta has a population of about 110,000, the majority of whom are French speakers. The Union Valdotaine seeks increased autonomy for the region and received 29.0 percent of the votes (but no seats) when it first contested regional council elections in 1954. Since then, it has usually campaigned in alliance with other parties and is one of the strongest parties in the regional council.

See also Italy.

Vallieres, Pierre (1938–)

The leading theorist of Quebec's revolutionary separatists, Pierre Vallieres grew up in a Montreal slum. After working at a series of menial jobs, he became a journalist on *La Presse* and an editor of *Cité Libre.* He joined the Front de Libération du Quebec and with Charles Gagnon coauthored the underground journal *La Cognée,* which contained information on how to make bombs and carry out other terrorist acts. When other members of the terrorist cell were arrested, Vallieres fled to New York City where he was arrested after a hunger strike outside the United Nations. He was deported to Canada, and sentenced to life imprisonment in 1967 for having inspired bombing attacks.

While in jail, he wrote *Negres blancs d'Amerique,* which became the bible of the socialist wing of the separatist movement. The book is an autobiographical account of growing up in a poor French Canadian family and, at the same time, a polemic against the oppression of the Quebec working class by the Anglo-Saxon capitalists and their French Canadian lackeys. After being released from jail in 1971, Vallieres renounced violence and endorsed the Parti Québécois as the best means to independence.

See also Front de Libération du Quebec; Parti Québécois.
Reference Vallieres, Pierre. *White Niggers of America: The Precocious Autobiography of a Quebec "Terrorist"* (1971).

Vemerana

In 1980, the New Hebrides in the South Pacific was to become independent as the Republic of Vanuatu, but two months before independence day, a revolt on the island of Santo resulted in the formation of the Provisional Government of the Independent State of Vemerana. The revolt was carried out by the members of a movement called Nagriamel and was supported by local French settlers who were afraid that the new government would be dominated by the English-educated, Protestant majority. Eventually, the uprising was put down by troops from the neighboring state of Papua New Guinea. The secessionist movement was brutally suppressed, hundreds of rebels were imprisoned, and over 2,000 people were reportedly living in exile, including all the opposition members of parliament.

Reference Henningham, Stephen. *France and the South Pacific* (1992).

Venda

The smallest of South Africa's independent black homelands, Venda, located near the Zimbabwe border, was set up in 1971, became self-governing in 1973, and achieved independence on September 12, 1979. Unlike most of the homelands, a majority (68 percent) of the legal citizens lived within Venda. The ruler was Patrick Mphephu, a semiliterate clan chieftain who was made paramount chief by the South Africans. In the 1973 elections, Mphephu's Venda National Party won only four of the eighteen elective seats, and in the 1978 elections, only twelve of the forty-two elective seats. However, the nominated chieftains who made up a majority of the legislature supported Mphephu, and he was elected prime minister.

The opposition Venda Independence Party favored union with Zimbabwe, but most of its leaders were detained without trial after the 1978 elections. In October 1981, guerrillas belonging to the African National Congress attacked a police station, one of the first such attacks in the black homelands. In 1990, the Venda military seized power and petitioned to rejoin South Africa. Venda was reintegrated into South Africa in 1994, along with the other homelands.

See also Black Homelands.
Reference Sparks, Allister. "South African Tribal Homeland Venda Tense after Guerrilla Attack" (1982).

Vietnamese Reunification

Bordered by China, Laos, and Cambodia (or Kampuchea), Vietnam is 1,000 miles long from north to south. The Red River delta in the north, the Mekong River delta in the south, and the coastal strip linking them are inhabited by ethnic Vietnamese while the mountainous interior is home to the Montagnards. In the late 1800s, Vietnam fell under French control and was administered as part of French Indochina along with Laos and Cambodia. After World War II, Ho Chi Minh, the Vietnamese Communist leader, declared Vietnam to be an independent republic, and after almost a decade of fighting, the French were defeated at Dien Bien Phu in 1954.

At the Geneva Conference of 1954, Vietnam was divided into two parts: Communist North Vietnam and U.S.-backed South Vietnam. Although the Geneva agreement had declared that nationwide elections would be held within two years, the South Vietnamese government of Ngo Dinh Diem refused to allow them. It was generally assumed that free elections would result in a Communist victory, since Ho Chi Minh was regarded as a national hero who had liberated Vietnam from French colonial rule. Fearing such an outcome, the United States backed the South Vietnamese regime even thought the regime was corrupt, incompetent, and lacked popular legitimacy.

A war ensued between the Viet Cong guerrillas, supported by North Vietnam, and the South Vietnamese army, aided by U.S. advisers. More and more U.S. troops were sent to Vietnam until they totaled over half a million in 1968. Despite the use of napalm, free-fire zones, and massive bombing of North Vietnam, the Viet Cong remained undefeated. U.S. public opinion increasingly turned against the war, and in 1973, all U.S. troops were withdrawn. South Vietnam survived for less than two years more, and Saigon fell to Communist forces in May 1975. A year later, the Socialist Republic of Vietnam was proclaimed, uniting North and South Vietnam after a twenty-year-long conflict.

See also Montagnards.
References FitzGerald, Frances. *Fire in the Lake: The Vietnamese and the Americans in Vietnam* (1972); Hosmer, Stephen T., Konrad Kellen, and Brian M. Jenkins. *The Fall of South Vietnam* (1980).

Voivodina

Voivodina is a northern province of Serbia that enjoyed autonomous status until October 1988 when it was abolished by President Slobodan Milosevic. The region historically had been under Hapsburg and not Ottoman control, unlike the rest of Serbia. The region contains a large Hungarian minority as well as sizeable Czech, Slovak, and Ruthenian populations. The president of the Voivodina Coalition of opposition parties, Dragan Veselinov, requested the same autonomy promised Kosovo under the aborted 1998 Milosevic-Holbrooke pact.

See also Hungarians; Yugoslavia.
Reference Radio Free Europe. *Newsline,* October 19, 1998.

Volksunie

Founded in 1954, Volksunie, a Flemish nationalist party, stood for a federal Belgium in which Flanders and Wallonia would have a high degree of autonomy while Brussels would be a bilingual and neutral capital under the control of the central government. The party's vote increased rapidly, and in 1971, the Volksunie was the fourth-largest party in Belgium, with 11.1 percent of the vote. It drew support from all classes in Flanders and in its election campaigns argued that Flemish tax revenues should not be used to subsidize the declining economy of Wallonia. After 1978, the party faced increasing electoral pressure from the Vlaams Blok, a right-wing militant Flemish group. The Vlaams Blok advocated that Flanders secede from Belgium and form a confederation with the Netherlands. That group's share of the vote increased from 1.1 percent in 1981 to 6.6 percent in 1991, when it surpassed the Volksunie's 5.9 percent.

See also Belgium.

Vologda

Vologda, a region to the northeast of Moscow, is inhabited by 1.5 million ethnic Russians. Vologda proclaimed itself an independent republic in 1993, after 80 percent of its citizens voted for more autonomy, and the chairman of the Vologda regional council refused to sign Russia's newly drafted constitution. The grievances underlying the autonomy movement were primarily economic, since 60 percent of the region's taxes went to the central government. Russian president Boris Yeltsin called the autonomy demand "dangerous and unacceptable" and refused to make any concessions.

See also Russian Federation
Reference Brandus, Paul. "Fed Up with Moscow" (1993).

Wales

Wales is a principality within the United Kingdom. Despite having been united with England since 1536, the Welsh have a distinctive culture and a strong sense of separate national identity. They are the descendants of Celtic Britons who were driven into the western mountains by the invading Anglo-Saxons after the fall of the Roman Empire. Welsh identity and nationalism are closely linked to language, although only a minority of the population (20 percent) can speak Welsh, a Celtic language similar to Irish and Scottish Gaelic.

At the end of World War II, according to one historian, Welsh nationalism "seemed to be as dead as the druids," and in the 1945 election, the eight Plaid Cymru candidates all suffered humiliating defeats. Plaid Cymru, the separatist party, continued to make a poor showing throughout the 1950s, and demands for greater self-government were ignored by both Labour and Conservative governments. The Labour Party was, in fact, strongly opposed to devolution, both because it interfered with a centrally planned socialist economy and because Labour's strength lay in the southern, English-speaking mining region.

However, a number of issues helped to keep nationalist sentiments alive, such as the decision to flood the Welsh valley of Tryweryn to create a reservoir that would supply the English city of Liverpool with water. More important were fears that the Welsh language was dying out. In 1962, the veteran nationalist hero, Saunders Lewis, appealed for a militant campaign in defense of the language and for the use of Welsh in government and official business on an equal footing with English. The result was the emergence of the Welsh Language Society, which engaged in mass demonstrations and angry protests.

In 1966, Plaid Cymru won a by-election in Carmarthen and elected its first member of parliament. In the 1970 election, when Plaid Cymru contested all thirty-six Welsh seats for the first time, it won 11.5 percent of the vote. Faced with this rising tide of nationalism, the government

responded by passing the Welsh Language Act in 1967, which gave Welsh "equal validity" with English for governmental and legal purposes. In 1976, the Devolution Bill offered Wales and Scotland elected assemblies if a majority of the electorate voted for devolution, but in a referendum held on March 1, 1979, only 11.8 percent of the Welsh electorate voted in favor of the bill.

In 1997, however, the Labour government set up the Welsh Assembly, the first elections for which were held in May 1999. The Labour Party failed to win an overall majority in the sixty-seat assembly, and Plaid Cymru had some unexpected victories in what were traditionally Labour strongholds. The final result was Labour, twenty-eight; Plaid Cymru, seventeen; Conservatives, nine; and Liberal Democrats, six. During the campaign, Plaid Cymru announced that it did not seek independence.

See also Lewis, Saunders; Plaid Cymru; United Kingdom; Welsh Language Society; Wigley, Dafydd.
Reference Morgan, Kenneth. *Rebirth of a Nation* (1981).

Walloon Rally

The Belgian political party Walloon Rally was formed in 1968 to counter the growing strength of the Flemish nationalists, and it drew members and votes from the three traditional parties. By 1971, it had become the second-largest party in

Wallonia. The party frequently entered into an electoral alliance with the Democratic Front of Francophones, which represented the interests of the French-speaking majority in metropolitan Brussels. Both parties advocated full regional status for Brussels. In addition, the Walloon Rally protested the central government's economic policy, which it considered biased in favor of Flanders, and demanded additional aid to reverse Wallonia's economic decline and job losses. The Democratic Front claimed that the central government's employment policy favored Flemings in Brussels and called for changes that would redistribute government jobs to French speakers.

Linguistic policy within the Brussels region and the issue of the boundaries of the city proved to be the most sensitive and difficult problems in Belgian politics. French speakers pressed for a redrawing of the boundaries to include eleven residential suburbs, but there was adamant resistance to this proposal from the Flemish speakers as they feared a gradual extension of the French-speaking area into Flanders. An elaborate compromise was worked out whereby six municipalities were given limited bilingual facilities. However, French speakers in the six municipalities were not allowed to send their children to French-language schools. Furthermore, a procedure was institutionalized throughout Brussels for a language inspection of households when it was suspected that parents had falsely declared their children's mother tongue. After lengthy negotiations, the complicated linguistic frontier was frozen by imposing a permanent unilingual Flemish "collar" around Brussels.

See also Belgium; Volksunie.

Walvis Bay

Walvis Bay, a port in South-West Africa (Namibia), was a South African possession claimed by the South-West African People's Organization (SWAPO). Walvis Bay is the only deepwater harbor on the South-West African coast and an important air and sea base. Occupied by the British in 1878,

the enclave came under the administration of the Cape Colony in 1884, and title passed to South Africa in 1910 when the Cape became one of the four provinces of the new country. South-West Africa, a German colony, was conquered during World War I and transferred to South Africa under a League of Nations mandate. SWAPO fought a long guerrilla war to liberate the territory, which became independent as Namibia in 1990. SWAPO won the first democratic elections.

For purposes of administrative convenience, Walvis Bay was governed as part of South-West Africa until 1977. SWAPO claimed that because of this fact, as well as the economic and geographic links between the two, Walvis Bay was an integral part of Namibia. As part of the agreement between the South African government and the African National Congress, Walvis Bay was handed over to Namibia on March 1, 1994.

See also South Africa.
Reference Berat, Lynn. *Walvis Bay: Decolonization and International Law* (1990).

Welsh Language Society

The Welsh Language Society, formed by young members of Plaid Cymru in 1962, was dedicated to the militant promotion of the Welsh language. The group's first action was a 1963 blockade of traffic to protest the refusal of the Aberystwyth Post Office to use Welsh-language documents and notices. Thereafter, the group led a series of angry demonstrations in government offices, libraries, and universities to force the authorities to grant equal status for the Welsh language.

The campaign against English-language road signs generated considerable publicity and a large numbers of arrests. The society also protested the increasing number of holiday homes owned by English families in Welsh areas, and several properties were set on fire. A fanatical fringe formed the Free Wales Army and engaged in sporadic terrorist acts. The secretary of state for Wales was threatened, and a small child had his hands blown off by a bomb. The Free

Wales Army was condemned by the society, and when its leading saboteurs were imprisoned, the group disappeared.

See also Plaid Cymru; Wales.

West Irian

The island of New Guinea is divided into two parts: the independent nation of Papua New Guinea and West Irian, which has been a province of Indonesia (Irian Jaya) since 1963. When Indonesia became independent in 1949, West Irian, which had been part of the Dutch East Indies, remained under Dutch rule. The Dutch justified this on the grounds that the Melanesian inhabitants were racially and culturally distinct from the Indonesians. After years of diplomatic pressure by Indonesia, the Dutch handed West Irian over to the United Nations, and that body, in turn, gave it to Indonesia on May 1, 1963, with the understanding that a plebiscite would be held in 1969. However, the Act of Free Choice was a sham rather than a genuine test of the wishes of the population.

The territory consists of dense coastal swamps and forests, and the inaccessible highland valleys are home to tribal populations speaking more than 1,000 distinct languages. The new Indonesian rulers attempted to "civilize" the natives, encouraging them to speak the official national language (Bahasa Indonesian) and to change their customs and diet. The racist attitudes of Indonesians and their selfish exploitation of West Irian's natural resources provoked a rebellion by the Free Papua Movement. Beginning in 1968, the rebels carried out guerrilla attacks on Indonesian forces and development projects and claimed to have killed 3,513 soldiers prior to April 1978. However in 1978, the rebel leader, Jacob Prai, was captured, and Papua New Guinea agreed to take measures to prevent its territory being used as a base by the rebels.

In 1998, following the downfall of President Suharto, separatist activity increased, and in July, pro-independence demonstrators waving Free Papua flags were fired on by Indonesian troops. Unconfirmed reports claimed that seven demonstrators were killed.

See also Indonesia.
Reference Suter, Keith. *East Timor and West Irian* (1982).

Western Canadian Separatism

In response to what was seen as neglect by the federal government in Ottawa, some western Canadians have flirted with separatism. Protest groups such as West Fed and Western Canada Concept (WCC) talked of independence while Saskatchewan's Unionist Party advocated union with the United States. The WCC, with its main strength in the province of Alberta, had 12,000 members in 1982, but the number had declined to 1,000 by 1987. The movement began with a letter to the editor of the *Victoria Colonist* in 1975 by Douglas Christie. The widespread perception that western Canada's natural resources were being exploited by the eastern portion of the country led to a mushrooming of support. In 1981, the WCC was registered as a political party in Alberta, and currently, the party is also active in British Columbia, Manitoba, and Saskatchewan. Christie argues that western Canada, "with a regionally representative elected Senate, one language and one government . . . would be the richest and most freedom-loving nation of the world."

See also Quebec.
Reference Brimelow, Peter. "Four Canadas?" (1995).

Western Sahara

In October 1975, a United Nations mission reported that the majority of the inhabitants of the Spanish colony of Spanish Sahara (later Western Sahara) favored political independence. However, in November of that year, 350,000 Moroccan civilians crossed the frontier in a "green march" as a "demonstration of the popular will in Morocco to reclaim the Sahara." At the same time, Moroccan troops invaded the territory, which was then divided between Morocco and Mauritania.

The Polisario Front began a guerrilla war to obtain independence for the 200,000 inhabitants. After the rebels attacked rail and road links in Mauritania, the Mauritanians withdrew, and Morocco occupied the whole territory. The Polisario Front is recognized as the legitimate government in exile by more than half the members of the Organization of African Unity, and in 1984, the front joined that organization as the Saharan Arab Democratic Republic. Algeria provides the rebels with sanctuary and supplies. Although Moroccan forces were able to occupy the large towns and the so-called useful triangle in the northwest (which contains valuable phosphate mines), they came under increasing pressure from the Polisario guerrillas. Their response was to build a series of defensive walls, consisting of sandbanks, protected by barbed wire and minefields and equipped with electronic ground sensors and radar capable of detecting movement for several miles.

The conflict became a classic example of a war of attrition. The Polisario guerrillas, although unable to break through the Moroccan defenses, were able to tie down 100,000 troops. In 1991, the United Nations brokered a cease-fire between Morocco and the Polisario Front, and it was agreed that a referendum should be held to decide between independence or integration with Morocco. However, since the two sides cannot agree on who should be eligible to vote, the referendum has not yet been held.

Reference Lawless, Richard, and Laila Monahan. *War and Refugees; The Western Sahara Conflict* (1984).

White Separatism in the United States

In the United States, a number of white racist groups have proposed a territorial separation of the races. The Church of Israel believes that disaster awaits America, and the "small remnant of Germanic nordic peoples, the Israel of God,"

should organize themselves into "self-sufficient groups upon the land and away from the cities." The Christian-Patriots Defense League called, more ambitiously, for the creation of a secure "Golden Triangle . . . that may be defended and remain free when the present governmental systems of Mexico, Canada, and the United States collapse or precipitate into a ruthless Communist dictatorship." The triangle would include the southern, lower midwestern, and some of the upper midwestern United States.

There have also been proposals for the relocation of "non-Aryans" into separate enclaves, and in December 1984, the National Association of White People published a map showing America divided into New Africa, West Israel, Francia, Alta California, New Cuba, and Minoria. Richard Butler, the founder of Aryan Nations, advocated that a new Aryan state be created in the Pacific Northwest comprising Oregon, Washington, Idaho, Montana, and Wyoming. Although unrealistic, such racist fantasies have inspired several white separatists to move to the area. In 1988, the federal government went so far as to prosecute thirteen leaders of the white racist movement, including Richard Butler, Louis Beam, and Robert Miles, for seditious conspiracy, alleging that they had plotted to overthrow the government and set up an Aryan state. Although the defendants were all acquitted, the white separatist movement was severely weakened by the trial.

Some white separatists are followers of sovereignty, the idea that individuals can remove themselves from the authority of the federal government by renouncing their U.S. citizenship and getting rid of their social security numbers, drivers' licenses, etc. This idea has led to the formation of "sovereign townships," each with its own militia and courts, whose members do not recognize the laws of the United States. Two of the best-known examples are the Justus Township in Montana and the Republic of Texas. The Montana Freemen were involved in an eighty-one-day standoff with federal authorities in 1996, while in a 1997 showdown at the Republic of Texas com-

A member of the Freemen group (left) with Montana State Representative Karl Ohs, who hoped to bring an end to the standoff between the Freemen and the FBI, at the Freemen complex in Montana, May 16, 1996. (Reuters/Lee Celano/Archive Photos)

pound, a man was shot and killed after he refused to surrender to police.

See also Republic of Texas.
References Barkun, Michael. *Religion and the Racist Right* (1994); Dyer, Joel. *Harvest of Rage* (1997).

Wigley, Dafydd (1943–)

The leader of Plaid Cymru, the Welsh nationalist party, Dafydd Wigley was born April 1, 1943, ed-

ucated at the local grammar school in Caernarvon, and earned a degree from Manchester University. First elected member of parliament for Caernarvon in 1970, he has been reelected ever since. Before being elected, he worked as an industrial economist and academic. He has been very active on behalf of the disabled and sponsored the Disabled Persons Act in 1981.

Yakutia
See Sakha

Yeltsin, Boris (1931–)

More than any other individual, Boris Yeltsin helped bring about the dissolution of the Soviet Union, which led to the independence of Russia and the other fourteen ethnic republics that composed it. Originally a protégé of Mikhail Gorbachev, Yeltsin became an adversary after 1986 and, in 1991, helped force Gorbachev's resignation, which left Yeltsin as president of the Russian Federation, the most powerful political figure in the former countries of the Soviet Union.

Yeltsin was born in the Sverdlovsk region of Russia in 1931. He was trained as a civil engineer and worked for many years as a manager in the building industry. He joined the Communist Party in 1961, and by 1981, his accomplishments

Boris Yeltsin puts his hand on the constitution as he takes the oath as Russian president during a ceremony in the Kremlin, August 9, 1996. (Reuters/Alexander Natruskin/Archive Photos)

had earned him a seat on the central committee. In 1985, his longtime colleague, Gorbachev, selected Yeltsin to head the Moscow Communist Party organization and charged him with rooting out corruption. Subsequently, Yeltsin was made a member of the Soviet Politburo. Yeltsin's outspoken criticism of Party leaders and policies for their resistance to reform led to his losing his prestigious Party positions.

But Yeltsin was to stage a comeback. In 1989, with Gorbachev's electoral reforms in place and with Russians growing disenchanted with Gorbachev's rule, Yeltsin, running in the Moscow district, captured nearly 90 percent of the vote to gain a seat in the new Soviet parliament. In 1990, sensing the fatal weakness of the Soviet state, Yeltsin ran for the Russian parliament, this time from the Sverdlovsk district. He won handily. The parliament voted him their chairman, which, in effect, made him president of the Russian Republic. In that same year, Yeltsin resigned from the Communist Party, became an advocate of social and economic reform, and called for Russian sovereignty. In March 1991, in the first Russian elections for president, Yeltsin again proved victorious.

Utilizing his new power and popularity, Yeltsin helped suppress a coup against Gorbachev by hard-line Communists in August 1991. At the same time, he did all in his power to weaken Gorbachev and undermine the Soviet state. In December

1991, Yeltsin met with the presidents of Ukraine and Belarus, and a declaration was signed withdrawing the three countries from the Soviet Union. In its place, the three leaders proposed that a new voluntary, transnational organization be created, the Commonwealth of Independent States (CIS). By the end of December, Gorbachev had resigned, and the Soviet Union had been dissolved.

Although Yeltsin won a referendum on his presidency in 1992, successfully suppressed a parliamentary revolt in 1993, secured the passage of a new constitution enlarging the powers of the presidency, and made a surprising comeback to be reelected president in 1996, it is uncertain whether in the long run he accomplished much as president. The year 1998 witnessed a general collapse of the economic system, which cast doubt on the value of Yeltsin's economic and political reforms. The Commonwealth of Independent States has proved largely ineffective, although the organization has supplied peacekeeping troops in the former Soviet republics of Moldova, Georgia, and Tajikistan. Within the Russian Federation, Yeltsin managed to bring a halt to the war between North Ossetia and Ingushetia over disputed territory. He also engineered a treaty with the separatist-minded government of Tatarstan, keeping the Muslim republic within the federation. He refused to grant similar demands made by Chechnya and launched a disastrous war that lasted nearly two years and killed thousands. At the end of the conflict, Russian troops withdrew but without any concession from Chechnya on its demands for sovereignty. After Islamic radicals from Chechnya invaded the neighboring republic of Dagestan, and a series of bombings in Moscow were blamed on Chechen terrorists, Russian troops launched a second invasion of Chechnya in October 1999.

Relations between the central government and the ethnic republics of the Russian Federation remain legally unclear, and the court system has not evolved sufficiently to adjudicate issues of conflict. Myriad demands for increased sovereignty from ethnic groups within the federation continue unabated, and Islamist groups have become more active in ethnically fragile Dagestan. At the end of 1999 Yeltsin, whose health had long been precarious, resigned and was succeeded by his protégé Vladimir Putin.

See also Russian Federation; Union of Soviet Socialist Republics.

Reference Otfinoski, Steven. *Boris Yeltsin and the Rebirth of Russia* (1995).

Yemen

North and South Yemen, two very different societies, were united in May 1990. South Yemen, after achieving independence from Britain in 1967, was a secular Marxist regime allied with the Soviet Union; North Yemen was a traditional society dominated by tribal and Islamic values. North Yemen had a population of 9 million compared to 2.4 million in South Yemen. The withdrawal of Soviet patronage and the evacuation of Soviet and East German advisers forced the South Yemen government to redefine its foreign relations, and both governments saw unity as helping to reduce internal unrest and facilitate economic development.

Border clashes between the two states in 1971, 1978–1979, and 1982 had been followed by declarations of unity, and in 1988, the formation of a joint committee for a unified political system was announced. In May 1990, a draft constitution was ratified by both countries. Ali Abdullah Salih of North Yemen became president, and Ali Salim al-Bayd, the leader of South Yemen, became deputy president. President Salih announced that "the new state has removed forever the imaginary borderlines created during partition and is now embarking on a new era." However, the two dominant parties, the northern General People's Congress (GPC) and the southern Yemeni Socialist Party (YSP), immediately began to compete for administrative positions and public funds. In the elections of April 1993, the GPC won 123 seats and the YSP 56 while the Yemeni Reform Grouping, campaigning on an Islamic platform, won 62. The remaining seats went to smaller parties and independents.

Rivalries continued between the YSP and the two northern parties, and there were significant disagreements over constitutional changes and the merger of the two armies. Southern grievances included the lack of financial aid to that region, the fact that Aden had not become a free port, and the assassination of over 150 YSP officials—the YSP claimed that northern leaders had connived at, or even instigated, the killings. Southern demands for a federal system were rejected by Salih, and fighting broke out between northern and southern military units in May 1994. The conflict ended with a victory for the more numerous northerners, but thousands had lost their lives in the three months of fighting, and damage was estimated at around $200 million. Since the end of the conflict, southerners complain that northerners occupy most of the senior government positions and that alcohol has been banned by the Islamic-dominated regime.

References Al Suwaid, Jamal, ed. *The Yemeni War of 1994: Causes and Consequences* (1995); Kostiner, Joseph. *Yemen: The Tortuous Quest for Unity 1990–1994* (1996).

Yugoslavia

Now in its third political form, Yugoslavia was formed after World War I as the Kingdom of Serbs, Croats, and Slovenes and renamed Yugoslavia in 1929. In 1945, essentially the same territory became a Communist federation under former Partisan leader Josip Broz Tito. It consisted of six republics—Bosnia and Herzegovina, Croatia, Macedonia, Montenegro, Serbia, and Slovenia—and two autonomous federal regions—Kosovo and Voivodina.

Following Tito's death in 1980 and with economic problems increasing, demands for independence from the federation arose in four of the republics and Kosovo. In part, this was a reassertion of traditional ethnic nationalism, as in Slovenia and Croatia, and in part it was a growing resentment of the increasingly dominant role being played by Serbia in the Yugoslav government. By 1992, Slovenia, Croatia, Bosnia, and Macedonia had obtained independence, though not without a bloody civil war that lasted until 1995 when a U.S.-brokered cease-fire was established involving NATO occupation troops in Bosnia and Croatia. Also in 1992, the remaining two republics of Tito's nation, Serbia and Montenegro, created what is now commonly referred to as the third Yugoslavia. Responding to ethnic unrest in both Kosovo and Voivodina, Serbia effectively annexed those two regions.

The third Yugoslavia is dominated by Serbia, which has 94 percent of the population and controls the federal army. In 1997, the Serb nationalist and former president of the Serbian Republic, Slobodan Milosevic, was elected president of the Yugoslav federation. In the same year, the Montenegrins elected the anti-Milosevic candidate Milo Djukanovic as president of Montenegro.

With the breakup of Communist Yugoslavia, Milosevic, as Serbian leader, became the banker and arsenal behind the Greater Serbia movement, which used military force to wrest Serbian-populated territories in Croatia and Bosnia away from their former states. His actions brought a UN embargo upon Yugoslavia, creating severe hardship in both Serbia and Montenegro. In 1995, in exchange for a lifting of the embargo, Milosevic signed the Dayton peace accord, which guaranteed an independent Bosnian state. That accord has put a damper on Yugoslavia's goal of creating a greater Serbia.

Stability in the third Yugoslavia is challenged from three ethnic sources: Hungarians, Montenegrins, and Albanians. In the Voivodina region, which is contiguous with Hungary, the Hungarian minority, backed by Hungary, has been pressing for more rights. Relations between Serbia and Montenegro have become strained as the Montenegrin president, Milo Djukanovic, attempts to pursue a more independent path. Milosevic has countered by replacing the Montenegrin prime minister of the federation, Radoje Kontic, with Djukanovic's rival, Momir Bulatovic. Montenegro refuses to recognize the new prime minister.

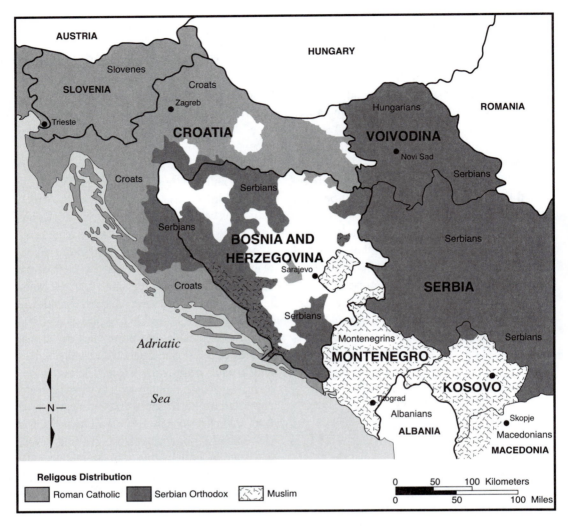

The Albanian-dominated province of Kosovo has posed the greatest problem for Yugoslavia. As president of Serbia, Milosevic stripped the province of its autonomy in 1989 after years of separatist agitation. After 1995, Yugoslav forces had to battle guerrillas belonging to the Kosovo Liberation Army, and they launched a massive invasion of the province in 1998, inducing nearly 1 million Kosovars to flee to Albania and Macedonia. In June 1999, NATO demanded an end to the Serb "ethnic cleansing" and human rights violations. When Milosevic refused to yield, NATO planes bombarded Serb forces in Kosovo and attacked military targets in Serbia. In June, Milosevic capitulated and withdrew his troops from Kosovo. The province came under UN-NATO control, and Yugoslavia was further diminished.

See also Bosnia and Herzegovina; Croatia; Greater Albania; Greater Serbia; Hungarians; Kosovo; Kosovo Liberation Army; Krajina; Macedonia; Milosevic, Slobodan; Montenegro; Sanjak; Slovenia; Voivodina.

Reference Judah, Tim. *History, Myth, and the Destruction of Yugoslavia* (1997).

Zaire

The Belgian Congo gained its independence as the Democratic Republic of the Congo on June 30, 1960. The country was ill-prepared for independence and had never had elections before 1957. Its population was divided into more than 150 ethnic groups, and most of the political parties that existed were regionally based.

In the chaos that followed independence, the authority of the central government was challenged in several areas. The province of Katanga seceded days after independence and was itself threatened by an uprising led by Jason Sendwe, the leader of the Balubakat. Sendwe's followers established a Baluba Republic of North Katanga. In neighboring Kasai Province, Albert Kalonji, whose faction of the Congolese National Movement won twenty-one of the provincial assembly seats, declared the formation of the state of South Kasai. His state included most of the diamond mines and half the province's population. The Alliance of the Bakongo (ABAKO), led by Joseph Kasavubu, was supported by the Bakongo of Léopoldville Province. ABAKO originally planned to link the Bakongo of Congo with those of Angola and Congo-Brazzaville and to reconstitute the ancient Bakongo empire that had flourished in the 1500s. In 1965, following ethnic unrest and political anarchy, the military, led by Joseph Mobutu (later known as Mobutu Sese Seko), seized power. In 1971 Mobutu changed the name of the country to Zaire. His autocratic and corrupt rule lasted until he was overthrown in 1997 by a coalition of forces under Laurent Kabila. The country was then renamed the Democratic Republic of the Congo.

After the downfall of Mobutu, regional and ethnic rivalries reemerged. The eastern region remained under the control of the Tutsi, supported by the government of Rwanda, while separatist aspirations reemerged in Katanga. At the beginning of the 1996–1997 rebellion, Rwandan officials displayed maps of a greater Rwanda that included large portions of the east.

See also Katanga.

References Hempstone, Smith. *Rebels, Mercenaries, and Dividends: The Katanga Story* (1962); Lemarchand, Rene. "The Fire in the Great Lakes" (1999); Reyntjens, Filip. "The Second Congo War" (1999).

Zanzibar

An island off the coast of East Africa, Zanzibar united with Tanganyika to form Tanzania in 1964, the only lasting union between two independent African states. Throughout recorded history, the coastal region had had important trading relations with Persia and Arabia. With an economy based on a lucrative trade in slaves and ivory and clove plantations, Zanzibar was the center of Arab influence in East Africa. The sultan of Oman became the dominant power in the late 1700s, and he moved his capital from Oman to Zanzibar in 1832. Zanzibar, along with the nearby island of Pemba, became a British protectorate in 1890. The coastal strip, running from Mozambique through Kenya, remained nominally under the sovereignty of the sultanate but was administered as part of Kenya. Tanganyika, a German colony since 1866, became a League of Nations mandate administered by Britain at the end of World War I. Tanganyika became independent in 1961; Zanzibar, in 1963.

The population of Zanzibar and Pemba numbered about 319,000 in 1963. The Shirazis, descended from Persian immigrants and local

Africans, made up the majority (59 percent), but the Arabs (16 percent) formed the ruling class and were the largest landowners. Mainland African immigrants and their descendants (20 percent) were usually landless laborers or poor squatters on the clove plantations. Politically, the first legislative elections were held in 1957, and politics quickly polarized along ethnic lines. In 1961, at least sixty-eight people were killed in anti-Arab rioting.

The Zanzibar Nationalist Party (ZNP) was based on the Arab community, although with some Shirazi support, while the Afro-Shirazi Party (ASP) appealed to the mainland Africans and the Shirazis. The Zanzibar and Pemba People's Party (ZPPP) represented the Shirazis of Pemba. Although the ASP won an increasing proportion of the vote and a majority (54 percent) in the last election, which was held in July 1963, the party did not win a majority of the legislative seats. Instead, the ZNP and the ZPPP formed a coalition government. This undemocratic outcome led to increasing tensions, and on January 12, 1964, there was a revolt by several hundred Africans in town of Zanzibar. The revolt, which overthrew the sultan's government in a few hours, was led by John Okello, a Ugandan. Thousands of Arabs were massacred, and a revolutionary government headed by Abeid Abdul Karume, the leader of the ASP, was set up.

The People's Republic of Zanzibar quickly established good relations with the Communist states, which provided economic and military aid. On the other hand, diplomats from Britain, France, and the United States were expelled. Tanganyika, which had supported the ASP and been hostile to the ZNP/ZPPP government, was concerned that the island might become "Africa's Cuba." Tanganyika's foreign minister, Oscar Kambona, declared, "Our first concern was the growing Communist presence, and second the danger of the Cold War coming in." President Julius Nyerere met with the revolutionary leaders the day after the revolution and in response to their request, sent a large contingent of Tanganyikan police to help restore law and order.

Just three months after the revolution, on April 23, 1964, the two countries announced their intention to unite. Several motives have been suggested for the union, the most important being Nyerere's belief in Pan-Africanism and fears as to Zanzibar's political stability. The union allowed Zanzibar a considerable degree of autonomy, with control over agriculture, education, and health and housing policies as well as its own legal system. The two ruling parties, the ASP and the Tanganyika African National Union (TANU) remained separate. Nyerere became president of the united country (renamed Tanzania in October), and Karume became first vice-president and head of the Zanzibar government. At first, the degree of integration between the mainland and Zanzibar was minimal, and Zanzibar's Revolutionary Council continued to follow radical left-wing policies. After the assassination of Karume in April 1972, and his replacement by Aboud Jumbe, however, the regime became more moderate, and in 1977, the ASP and TANU merged to become the Revolutionary Party of Tanzania.

Secessionist activities increased in Zanzibar, and in early 1984, after several Zanzibaris had been arrested and charged with anti-union activity, Jumbe resigned as vice-president. He was replaced by Ali Hassan Mwinyi. After Nyerere resigned and Mwinyi was elected president in October 1985, his becoming head of state temporarily reduced separatist sentiments in Zanzibar. However, opposition to the union persisted, and in 1989, members of an Islamic separatist group, Bismallah, based on the island of Pemba were arrested. Continuing tension between mainlanders and Zanzibaris became more apparent following the introduction of multiparty democracy in June 1992.

Although the ruling Revolutionary Party of Tanzania won the first multiparty elections held in 1995, the polling results in Zanzibar were widely denounced as fraudulent. The Zanzibar Democratic Alliance calls for a UN-supervised referendum to determine the future relationship between Zanzibar and the mainland while the

Zanzibar Organization supports full independence. At the same time, Christopher Mtikila, a mainland politician, made a number of anti-Arab and anti-Zanzibari speeches, for which he was arrested and accused of fomenting violence and sedition.

References Bailey, Martin. *The Union of Tanganyika and Zanzibar* (1973); Lofchie, Michael. *Zanzibar: Background to Revolution* (1965); Middleton, John. *Zanzibar: Its Society and Its Politics* (1965).

Zapatista National Liberation Army

The Zapatista National Liberation Army (EZLN), a clandestine militia drawn from Mayan peasants in the state of Chiapas in southern Mexico, emerged in January 1994 when it seized several towns and engaged in a battle with the Mexican army. Over 100 deaths were reported. Under the reputed leadership of subcommander Marcos, the Zapatistas, named after the early-twentieth-century peasant leader Emiliano Zapata, have called for a more equitable distribution of land, a more democratic political system, increased local autonomy, and a greater role for Indians in the political and economic life of the nation. The Zapatista revolt was launched on January 1 1994, the date the North American Free Trade Agreement took effect. The Zapatistas argued that duty free imports of U.S. and Canadian agricultural products, particularly corn, would further impoverish the native farmers. The Zapatistas have also complained that the hegemony of the Mexican ruling party, the PRI (Institutional Revolutionary Party), prevents the emergence of representative government in Mexico.

Since 1994, Mexican troops have reoccupied many of the towns seized by the Zapatistas, but other villages and some jungle territory remain under rebel control. Negotiations between the government and the guerrillas have taken place sporadically, but there has been only minimal progress toward any lasting resolution, with the Zapatistas claiming that the Ernesto Zedillo government has not fulfilled its promises. The Za-patistas have now espoused nonviolence and say they are not a political party but an alternative form of community organization.

In March 1999, the Zapatistas organized an unofficial referendum throughout Mexico asking voters whether indigenous peoples, 10 percent of the Mexican population, should enjoy broader civil rights and a greater voice in government. The referendum also asked if territories in rebellion should be demilitarized. Among those voting, the measures passed easily. The Zedillo government ignored the plebiscite and blamed the Zapatistas for the breakdown of negotiations.

See also Maya of Guatemala.
Reference Holloway, John, and Eloina Pelaez. *Zapatista! Reinventing Revolution in Mexico* (1998).

Zimbabwe

Zimbabwe was formerly the British colony of Rhodesia. The ruling white minority declared themselves independent from Britain in 1965, and two African guerrilla movements emerged to fight for majority rule: the Zimbabwe African People's Union (ZAPU), led by Joshua Nkomo, and the Zimbabwe African National Union (ZANU), led by Robert Mugabe. The division between the two groups was based on ethnicity, with ZAPU being drawn from the Ndebele tribe and ZANU based on the Shona.

After a lengthy guerrilla war, the Rhodesians finally agreed to elections in 1980. Out of the 100 seats, 20 were reserved for the white minority, ZANU won 57, and ZAPU won 20. The remaining 3 seats were won by the United African National Council. Voting was largely along ethnic lines, which accounts for ZAPU's victory since the Shona make up 68 percent of the country's population, compared to 20 percent for the Ndebele. After the election, ZAPU and ZANU formed a coalition government, and Zimbabwe became formally independent on April 18, 1980.

Dissident members of the ZAPU guerrilla army began a campaign against the Shona-dominated government in 1983. The rebellion in

Matabeleland, the region occupied by the Nde-bele, was brutally suppressed by Mugabe's security forces. According to a report by the Catholic Commission for Justice and Peace, at least 20,000 civilians were killed by the Fifth Brigade (trained by the North Koreans) from 1983 to 1988. Atroci-ties included burning people alive and torture. Since then, Zimbabwe has become a de facto one-party state, and no further separatist activity has been reported.

Reference Glickman, Harvey, ed. *Ethnic Conflict and Democratization in Africa* (1995).

1945	Arab League established
1945–1946	Separatist republic set up in Azerbaijan region of Iran with Soviet backing.
1945–1948	Jewish activists in Palestine wage guerrilla war against British authorities.
1946	Republic of Mahabad set up in Kurdish region of Iran with Soviet backing.
1946–1947	Movement for Sicily to become independent from Italy.
1946–1960	Calls for the political unification of the Ewe people, split between Ghana and Togoland.
1947	Partition of British India into the Indian Union and Pakistan.
1948	Israel becomes independent; Arab states declare war; Israel defeats Arab forces; hundreds of thousands of Palestinians flee Israel.
1948	Division of Korea into Communist North Korea and pro-Western South Korea.
1948	Newfoundland votes to join Canada.
1948	In Thailand, Pattani Malays revolt and call for autonomy.
1948	Islamic republic set up in Arakan region of Burma (also known as Myanmar).
1948	Faeroe Islands become self-governing but islanders remain Danish citizens.
1948–1950	Penang resists joining Malaya Federation.
1948–1958	Mon rebellion in Burma.
1949	Division of Germany into (Communist) German Democratic Republic in the east and Federal Republic in the west.
1949	Karen rebellion begins in Burma.

Chronology

1949	Party advocating independence from Germany wins 21 percent of Bavarian vote.
1949	Chinese Nationalists take refuge on Taiwan.
1949	Treaty of Friendship between India and Bhutan.
1950	Chinese Communists invade Tibet.
1950–1953	North Korea invades South Korea.
1950	Legislation creates new commonwealth status for Puerto Rico.
1950	Nationalist uprising on Puerto Rico; shots fired at President Truman's residence in Washington, D.C.
1950	French set up an autonomous Montagnard region, which is abolished when South Vietnam becomes independent.
1950	Republic of the South Moluccas proclaimed but is crushed by Indonesian troops.
1952	Egypt gives up its claim to the Sudan.
1952	Eritrea federates with Ethiopia.
1952	Kashmir granted internal autonomy within the Indian Union.

1952–1954	Dispute over the status of Trieste is settled by dividing territory between Italy and Yugoslavia.
1953	Federation of Rhodesia and Nyasaland created.
1954	Puerto Rican nationalists open fire in U.S. House of Representatives.
1954–1957	Ashanti people of Ghana agitate for autonomy.
1955	After a referendum, the Saar region is reunited with Germany.
1955–1959	Guerrilla insurgency on Cyprus, with the goal of uniting Cyprus with Greece.
1955–1964	Naga rebellion in India.
1955	Maltese Labour Party proposes integration with Britain; in 1956 referendum, 74 percent vote in favor.
1956	Israel and Egypt at war; Israel forced to relinquish captured territory.
1956	State boundaries within India redrawn to correspond to linguistic regions.
1956–1958	In Mauritania, rebels seeking to unite country with Morocco carry out attacks.
1956–1959	Tibetans revolt against Chinese rule.
1956–1962	The Irish Republican Army launches attacks in Northern Ireland.
1957	Formation of European Economic Community.
1957	International city of Tangier reverts to Morocco.
1957–1969	Terrorist campaign by South Tirol separatists against Italian rule.
1957–1960	Ghana bans regional and tribal parties and abolishes regional assemblies.
1958	Southern Sudanese troops mutiny, beginning the conflict between the Arab/Muslim north and the black south.
1958	Kurdish revolt breaks out in Iraq.
1958	Egypt and Syria unite to form United Arab Republic.
1958	Federation of the West Indies set up.
1958–1970	Bretons demand autonomy.
1958–1966	Separatist movement in Buganda.
1959	Zurich agreements on Cyprus between Britain, Greece, and Turkey.
1959	Separatist rebellion by the Agni people of the Ivory Coast.
1960	British and Italian Somaliland unite to form Somalia; new nation calls for all Somalis to be united under one flag.
1960–1961	Clashes between Pakistani army and Pashtun tribesmen calling for an independent Pashtunistan.
1960–1963	Katanga secedes.
1960–1968	Barotseland agitates for separation from Zambia.
1960–1968	Kurds revolt in Iran.
1961	Kachin rebellion begins in Burma.
1961	United Arab Republic breaks up.
1961	After referendum, unification of southern Cameroons with Cameroon Republic; northern Cameroons remain linked with Nigeria.

1961 India invades and annexes Portuguese colony of Goa.

1961– East African Federation between Kenya,
1964 Uganda, and Tanganyika discussed; negotiations fail.

1962 Breakup of the Federation of the West Indies.

1962 Chinese troops seize disputed area in Himalayas from India.

1962 Eritrea absorbed by Ethiopia; loss of autonomy leads to guerrilla resistance by Eritrean Liberation Front.

1962 France withdraws from Algeria.

1962– Tuaregs rebel in Mali and call for autonomy.
1964

1963 Spain raises issue of Gibraltar at United Nations.

1963 Fighting between Greek and Turkish Cypriots.

1963 Federation of Rhodesia and Nyasaland dissolved.

1963 Malaya, Singapore, Sabah, and Sarawak unite to form Malaysia.

1963– Somalis of Kenya's Northern Frontier
1967 District fight guerrilla war seeking to be united with Somalia.

1963– Intermittent terrorism by Quebec
1972 separatists.

1963– Kingdom of Rwenzururu secedes from
1972 Uganda.

1964 Zanzibar revolution is followed by unification with Tanganyika to form Tanzania.

1964 Montagnards revolt in South Vietnam and call for autonomy.

1965 Singapore expelled from Malaysia.

1965– Revolt in Chad by northern Muslims
1978 against rule by black southerners.

1966 Mizo National Front calls for independent Mizoram in northeastern India.

1966 First Welsh nationalist elected to British Parliament.

1966– Breton separatists set off bombs.
1978

1967 After negotiations between Britain and Spain break down, 99 percent of Gibraltarians vote to remain under British rule.

1967 In Puerto Rican plebiscite, fewer than 1 percent of the voters favor independence.

1967 In Six Day War, Israel defeats Arab armies and occupies the West Bank, the Gaza Strip, the Golan Heights, and East Jerusalem; United Nations passes Resolution 242, which calls for Israel to return captured territories in exchange for Arab recognition.

1967 In response to demonstrations by Welsh Language Society, United Kingdom government passes Welsh Language Act.

1967 Growing separatist movement in Malaysian state of Sabah.

1967 Tamil nationalist party wins elections in the Indian state of Tamil Nadu.

1967– Biafra secedes from Nigeria; civil war ends
1970 with surrender of Biafra.

1968 Free Papua Movement begins revolt against Indonesian rule.

1968 Basque separatists begin terrorist campaign.

1968– Rebellion by Oromo against Ethiopian rule.
1970

1969	After referendum, Anguilla secedes from St. Kitts.
1969	Members of American Indian Movement occupy Alcatraz.
1969	New autonomy statute enacted for South Tirol.
1969	Rebellion in southwestern Guyana backed by Venezuela, which claims large portions of Guyanese territory.
1970	Morocco relinquishes its claim to Mauritania.
1970	Cornish nationalist party, Mebyon Kernow, begins to contest British elections.
1970	Autonomy granted to Kurds in Iraq, ending twelve-year conflict; fighting resumes in 1974–1975.
1971	East Pakistan separates from West Pakistan to become Bangladesh.
1971	The Irish Republican Army begins terrorist campaign that will claim almost 2,000 lives.
1972	Autonomy granted to the southern Sudan; agreement results in twelve years of peace.
1972	Okinawa reunited with Japan after two decades of agitation.
1972	Moro National Liberation Front begins rebellion in southern Philippines.
1973	American Indian Movement occupies historic Wounded Knee battle site for seventy days.
1973	Yom Kippur War between Israel and Arab states; Israel occupies Sinai peninsula.
1973–1975	Azad Baluchistan rebellion in Pakistan.
1974	Arab nations recognize the Palestine Liberation Organization as the sole representative of the Palestinians.
1974	UN General Assembly grants official recognition to the Palestine Liberation Organization.
1974	Oromo Liberation Front begins guerrilla war against Ethiopian rule.
1974	After two decades of agitation, the French-speaking districts of Berne in Switzerland are separated to form the new canton of Jura.
1974	After fighting between Greek and Turkish Cypriots, Turkey invades Cyprus and establishes a Turkish-controlled zone in the north.
1974–1998	Republic of North Solomons set up on island of Bougainville in Papua New Guinea.
1975	Sikkim becomes India's twenty-second state.
1975	The Afar rebel against Ethiopian rule.
1975	Puerto Rican terrorists bomb Fraunces Tavern in New York City, killing five.
1975	Spanish (Western) Sahara annexed by Morocco and Mauritania.
1975	Kurdish insurgency begins in eastern Turkey.
1975	Guerrilla resistance by Somalis to Ethiopian rule begins in the Ogaden region.
1975	Tigray People's Liberation Front calls for independence from Ethiopia and begins insurgency.
1975	Morocco invades and annexes Western Sahara, but Moroccan rule is resisted by Polisario guerrillas.
1975	Indonesia invades and annexes East Timor; there is guerrilla resistance by FRETILIN.
1975–1989	Lebanese civil war.

1975–1979	Renewed demands for the political unification of the Ewe people, split between Ghana and Togoland.
1976	Black homeland of Transkei becomes nominally independent from South Africa.
1976	Civil War in Angola between the Marxist government and rebels belonging to the Ovimbundu tribe.
1976	Free Aceh Movement begins guerrilla war in Sumatra.
1976	Quebec separatists win provincial elections; enact French Language Charter in 1977.
1976–1980	Terrorist campaign by the Movement for the Self-Determination and Independence of the Canary Archipelago in an attempt to gain independence for Canary Islands.
1977	Philippines officially relinquish their claim to the Malaysian state of Sabah.
1977	Andalusians demonstrate for autonomy.
1977	Somalia invades Ogaden region of Ethiopia, inhabited by ethnic Somalis; driven out in 1978.
1977	Party advocating an independent Tamil state wins majority of seats in Tamil areas of Sri Lanka.
1977	Black homeland of Bophuthatswana becomes nominally independent from South Africa.
1978	Greenland granted home rule by Denmark.
1978	Communist coup in Afghanistan; civil war begins.
1978	Israel invades Lebanon in response to Palestinian raids.
1979	Referenda to establish devolved legislatures in Scotland and Wales fail to achieve necessary majorities.

1979	Camp David Accord; Israel and Egypt conclude peace treaty.
1979	Soviet troops invade Afghanistan.
1979	Black homeland of Venda becomes nominally independent from South Africa.
1979	Growing support on Taiwan for independence from China.
1979	In Catalonia referendum, 88 percent favor regional devolution.
1980	Island of Banaba calls for independence from Kiribati.
1980	Black homeland of Ciskei becomes nominally independent from South Africa.
1980	Political links between Cape Verde and Guinea-Bissau dissolved after a coup in Guinea-Bissau.
1980	Island of Santo declares itself independent from Vanuatu.
1980	In referendum on independence, 40 percent of Quebec voters are in favor.
1980	First elections for an autonomous Basque government in Spain.
1980	Constitutional amendment in Belgium devolves power to Flanders and Wallonia.
1980	Regional autonomy statute approved in Galicia, Spain.
1980s	Agitation for autonomy for the Cordillera region in the Philippines.
1980s	Widespread violence between Zulu nationalists and African National Congress in South Africa.
1980s	Growing separatist movement in western Canada.
1980–1984	Growing violence in Punjab by Sikh separatists culminates in Indian army assault on the Sikh Golden Temple.

1980–1985	Terrorist attacks by Guadeloupean separatists.	1987	In Italian elections, separatist party wins 13 percent of vote in Sardinia.
1982	Israel invades Lebanon; Palestine Liberation Organization militias forced out of the country.	1987	Meech Lake accord recognizes Quebec as a "distinct society" within Canada.
1982	Separatist rebellion begins in Casamance region of Senegal.	1987	After guerrilla insurgency by Miskito Indians, Nicaragua sets up two autonomous regions.
1982	Corsica granted increased autonomy by France.	1988	U.S. government prosecutes white racists for conspiring to set up an Aryan state in the Pacific Northwest.
1982	Argentine invasion of Falkland Islands defeated by British counterattack.	1988	Armenian populated province of Nagorno-Karabakh revolts against Azerbaijan rule.
1982	Provisional Sinn Fein, the political wing of the Irish Republican Army, contests election for the first time; wins 10 percent of the vote in Northern Ireland.	1988	In accepting UN Resolution 242, the Palestine Liberation Organization recognizes the state of Israel.
1983	Sudan suspends southern autonomy and imposes Islamic law; renewed rebellion in the south.	1989	State of emergency declared in Kashmir after increasing separatist violence against Indian rule.
1983–1984	Separatist bombings in Martinique.	1989	East Germans permitted to travel to West Germany; demolition of the Berlin Wall begins.
1984	Revolt led by Kurdish Workers Party begins in eastern Turkey.	1989	Soviet forces withdraw from Afghanistan.
1985	Anglo-Irish agreement provokes demonstrations by Protestants who fear it is the first step to a United Ireland.	1989	Taif agreement ends Lebanese civil war; Hezbollah continues war with Israel.
1986–1994	Terrorist attacks by Sikh separatists met with harsh repression on the part of Indian forces; thousands reported killed.	1989	Yugoslavia eliminates autonomous status of the Kosovo and Voivodina regions of Serbia.
1986	Black homeland of KwaNdebele decides against independence from South Africa.	1989	Separatist party wins elections in Barbuda.
1986–	Kurdish revolt in Iraq; fighting continues intermittently.	1990	North and South Yemen united.
1986	Autonomy agreement for Tamil region of Sri Lanka; Tamil nationalist parties win majority of new provincial council seats in 1988.	1990	Mohawk Indian activists seize bridge in Canada.
		1990	East and West Germany vote to reunify.
1987	Hawaiian sovereignty movement established.	1990	South Ossetia declares independence from Georgia.
		1990	Formation of pro-autonomy Northern League in Italy.

1990   Iraq invades and annexes Kuwait; driven out by a U.S.-led alliance the following year.

1990s   Demands for the return of Karelia to Finland from Russia.

1991   Guatemala renounces claim to Belize, which leads to a coup by Guatemalan military.

1991   North and South Korea sign nonaggression and cooperation pact.

1991   Chechen-Ingush Republic of the Russian Federation splits into two states.

1991   Chechnya declares independence from Russia.

1991   Slovenia, Croatia, and Macedonia declare independence from Yugoslavia; Yugoslavia responds militarily; Serbian populated areas of Croatia push for autonomy; Croatia and Yugoslavia go to war.

1991   Transdniester secedes from Moldova; Russians negotiate cease-fire.

1991   USSR is dissolved; fifteen former Soviet republics become independent nations; Commonwealth of Independent States formed by Belarus, Russia, and Ukraine.

1991   Afars seeking autonomy rebel in Eritrea.

1991   Eritrean People's Liberation Front defeats Ethiopian forces.

1991   Negotiations begin over new South African constitution; Zulu leader, Buthelezi, calls for self-determination for Zulu nation.

1991–   Tuareg rebels sign peace agreement with
1995   government of Niger.

1992   Latvia calls for return of Abrene district annexed by Russia in 1944.

1992   Abkhazia declares independence from Georgia.

1992   Bosnia and Herzegovina declares independence from Yugoslavia; civil war erupts between Croats, Serbs, and Bosnian Muslims; widespread "ethnic cleansing."

1992–   Tatarstan declares sovereignty; works out
1993   special bilateral arrangement with Russia.

1993   Eritreans vote to become independent from Ethiopia.

1993   Czechoslovakia divides into the Czech Republic and Slovakia.

1993   Oslo agreement between Palestine Liberation Organization and Israel allows for limited Palestinian autonomy.

1993   In Puerto Rican plebiscite, only 4.4 percent favor independence.

1994   Crimean Russians advocate secession from Ukraine; Kiev asserts control over the region.

1994   Zapatistas seize several villages in Mexican state of Chiapas.

1994   After overthrow of military regime in Ethiopia, the new constitution establishes a federal system with considerable autonomy for the country's ethnic regions.

1994   Walvis Bay ceded to Namibia by South Africa.

1994   Black homelands reunited with South Africa.

1994   Civil war in Yemen; victory for northern forces.

1994–   Russia-Chechnya war; cease-fire and
1996   withdrawal of Russian troops result in no resolution of Chechnya's status.

1994–   Pashtun Taliban militia emerges in
1999   Afghanistan and captures 90 percent of the country; war continues in the north.

1995   Dayton peace accord ends Yugoslavian war; new Bosnian state created with Muslim-Croat and Serb areas of governance.

1995	In second referendum on the issue, 49.4 percent of Quebec voters are in favor of independence.	1998	Nonbinding referendum on Puerto Rico's constitutional future produces ambiguous result.
1995	Leaders of separatist Ogoni movement hanged by Nigerian military government.	1998	Wye River accords between Israel and Palestine Liberation Organization.
1996	Yasir Arafat elected first president of Palestine Authority.	1999	Inuit homeland of Nunavut set up in Canada.
1996	Autonomy agreement between Philippine government and Moros ends twenty-four-year-long insurgency.	1999	Boundary dispute between Ethiopia and Eritrea leads to heavy fighting.
1996	Separatist activity by Uyghurs in Chinese-controlled Xinjiang.	1999	NATO launches air war against Yugoslavia to force withdrawal of troops from Kosovo and put a stop to "ethnic cleansing"; Milosevic yields; NATO/UN forces begin occupation of province.
1997	Hong Kong reverts to China but retains considerable autonomy.		
1997	Island of Nevis attempts to secede from St. Kitts.	1999	In May, Indonesia promises referendum in East Timor on future political status.
1997	Autonomy granted to Chakma people of Bangladesh following two decades of guerrilla warfare.	1999	Kurdish leader, Abdullah Ocalan, is captured by Turks and sentenced to death in June.
1997	Island of Anjouan attempts to secede from Comoros.	1999	In first Scottish Assembly elections, Scottish nationalists win only 29 percent of the vote.
1997	In referendum, 74 percent vote in favor of a Scottish assembly.	1999	In Kashmir, fighting escalates between Muslim guerrillas and Indian forces.
1997	Armed standoff between police and Republic of Texas group.	1999	In East Timor referendum in August, independence favored by large majority. Widespread violence by pro-Indonesian militia leads to intervention by international force to restore order.
1997	In Italy, Northern League holds mock elections for a Padanian assembly.		
1998	Northern Irish peace agreement ends thirty-year-long conflict between Irish nationalists and British loyalists.	1999	Macau reverts to China in December.
1998	Serbia battles Albanian separatists in Kosovo; refugees flee to Albania and Macedonia.	1999	In October, after Islamic radicals from Chechnya attacked Dagestan, Russia invades Chechnya for a second time.

Adam, H., and K. Moodley. "Political Violence, Tribalism, and Inkatha." *Journal of Modern African Studies* 30 (1992): 495–510.

Akinyemi, Bolaji. "Nigeria and Fernando Poo: The Politics of Irredentism." *African Affairs* 69 (July 1970): 236–49.

Alcock, Antony E. *The History of the South Tyrol Question.* London: Michael Joseph, 1970.

Alexander, Robert J. *Political Parties of the Americas.* London: Greenwood Press, 1982.

Allman, Jean Marie. "The Young Men and the Porcupine: Class, Nationalism, and Asante's Struggle for Self-Determination." *Journal of African History* 31 (1990): 263–79.

Allworth, Edward. *The Modern Uzbeks: From the 14th Century to the Present: A Cultural History.* Stanford, CA: Hoover Institution Press, 1990.

———. *The Tatars of the Crimea: Return to the Homeland: Studies and Documents.* Durham, NC: Duke University Press, 1998.

Al Suwaid, Jamal, ed. *The Yemeni War of 1994: Causes and Consequences.* London: Saqi Books, 1995.

Amate, O. C. C. *Inside the OAU: Pan-Africanism in Practice.* New York: St. Martin's Press, 1986.

Anaya, Rudolfo A., and Francisco A. Lomeli. *Aztlan: Essays on the Chicano Homeland.* Albuquerque: Academia/El Norte Publications, 1989.

Anthony, Andrew. "Passport to Padstow." *Observer,* January 3, 1999.

Antonius, George. *The Arab Awakening: The Story of the Arab National Movement.* New York: Capricorn, 1969.

Apter, David. *The Gold Coast in Transition.* Princeton, NJ: Princeton University Press, 1955.

———. *The Political Kingdom in Uganda.* Princeton, NJ: Princeton University Press, 1961.

Ariff, Mohd. *The Philippines Claim to Sabah.* Singapore: Oxford University Press, 1970.

Armstrong, Hamilton Fish. "The Troubled Birth of Malaysia." *Foreign Affairs* 41 (July 1963).

Arthur, Paul. *Government and Politics of Northern Ireland.* New York: Longmans, 1984.

Asia Watch Report. *Crackdown in Inner Mongolia.* Washington, DC: Human Rights Watch, 1991.

Atabaki, Touraj. *Azerbaijan: Ethnicity and Autonomy in Twentieth-Century Iran.* London: British Academic Press, 1993.

Austin, Dennis. *Malta and the End of Empire.* London: Frank Cass, 1971.

Bailey, Martin. *The Union of Tanganyika and Zanzibar.* Syracuse, NY: Syracuse University Press, 1973.

Bibliography

Ball, Margaret. *The Open Commonwealth.* Durham, NC: Duke University Press, 1971.

Banuazizi, Ali, and Myron Weiner, eds. *The State, Religion, and Ethnic Politics: Afghanistan, Iran, and Pakistan.* Syracuse, NY: Syracuse University Press, 1988.

Barkey, Henri J. "Kurdish Geopolitics." *Current History* 96 (January 1997): 1–5.

Barkun, Michael. *Religion and the Racist Right.* Chapel Hill: University of North Carolina Press, 1994.

Barrera, Mario. *Beyond Aztlan: Ethnic Autonomy in Comparative Perspective.* New York: Praeger, 1988.

Barta, Gabor, et al. *The History of Transylvania.* Budapest: Akademiai Kiado, 1994.

Bedlington, Stanley S. *Malaysia and Singapore: The Building of New States.* Ithaca, NY: Cornell University Press, 1978.

Beer, William R. "The Social Class of Ethnic Activists in Contemporary France." In Milton J. Esman, ed., *Ethnic Conflict in the Western World.* Ithaca, NY: Cornell University Press, 1977.

———. *The Unexpected Rebellion: Ethnic Activism in Contemporary France.* New York: New York University Press, 1980.

Bell, Andrew. *Ethnic Cleansing.* New York: St. Martin's Press, 1996.

Ben-Israel, Hevda. "Irredentism: Nationalism Reexamined." In Naomi Chazan, ed., *Irredentism and International Politics.* London: Adamantine Press, 1991.

Berat, Lynn. *Walvis Bay: Decolonization and International Law.* New Haven, CT: Yale University Press, 1990.

Bibliography

Bickerton, Ian J., and Carla L. Klausner. *A Concise History of the Arab-Israeli Conflict.* 3d ed. Upper Saddle River, NJ: Prentice-Hall, 1998.

Boehm, Christopher. *Montenegrin Social Organization and Values.* New York: AMS Press, 1983.

Bonkalo, Sandor. *The Rusyns.* Fairview, NJ, and New York: Carpatho-Rusyn Research Center and Columbia University Press, 1990.

Bordewich, Fergus. *Killing the White Man's Indian: Reinventing Native Americans at the End of the Twentieth Century.* New York: Doubleday, 1997.

Bose, Sumantra. *States, Nations, Sovereignty: Sri Lanka, India, and the Tamil Eelam Movement.* New Delhi: Book Review Literary Trust, 1994.

Brand, Jack. *The National Movement in Scotland.* London: Routledge, 1978.

Brandus, Paul. "Fed Up with Moscow." *US News and World Report,* July 26, 1993.

Brass, Paul. *Politics of India since Independence.* New York: Cambridge University Press, 1992.

Braveboy-Wagner, Jaqueline A. *The Venezuelan-Guyana Border Dispute.* Boulder, CO: Westview Press, 1984.

Brennan, Frank. *One Land, One Nation.* St. Lucia, Austral.: University of Queensland Press, 1995.

Brimelow, Peter. "Four Canadas?" *Forbes,* December 4, 1995.

Brorufs, Marie. "The 'Internal' Muslim Factor in the Politics of Russia." In Mohiaddin Mesbahi, ed., *Central Asia and the Caucasus after the Soviet Union.* Gainesville: University Press of Florida, 1994.

Brown, David. "From Peripheral Communities to Ethnic Nations: Separatism in Southeast Asia." *Pacific Affairs* 61 (1988–1989).

Bruchis, Michael. *Republic of Moldavia.* New York: Columbia, 1996.

Brzezinski, Zbigniew, and Paige Sullivan, eds. *Russia and the Commonwealth of Independent States: Document, Data, and Analysis.* Armonk, NY: M. E. Sharpe, 1997.

Bulag, Uradyn. *Nationalism and Hybridity in Mongolia.* New York: Oxford University Press, 1998.

Bullion, Alan J. *India, Sri Lanka, and the Tamil Crisis 1976–1994: An International Perspective.* London: Pinter, 1995.

Burton, Richard D., and Fred Reno, eds. *French and West Indian.* Charlottesville: University Press of Virginia, 1995.

Butler, Jeffrey, Robert Rotberg, and John Adams. *The*

Black Homelands of South Africa. Berkeley: University of California Press, 1977.

Cady, John. A *History of Modern Burma.* Ithaca, NY: Cornell University Press, 1960.

Cahill, K., ed. *Somalia: A Perspective. A*lbany: State University of New York, 1980.

Calvert, Peter. *The Falklands Crisis.* New York: St. Martin's Press, 1982.

Campbell, Greg. *The Road to Kosovo: A Balkan Diary.* Boulder, CO: Westview Press, 1999.

Campbell, John C. *Successful Negotiation: Trieste 1954.* Princeton, NJ: Princeton University Press, 1976.

Caplan, Gerald L. *The Elites of Barotseland 1878–1969.* Berkeley: University of California Press 1970.

Carley, Patricia. *Nagorno-Karabakh: Searching for a Solution.* Roundtable Report. Washington, DC: U.S. Institute of Peace, 1998.

Carmack, Robert, ed. *Harvest of Violence: The Maya Indians and the Guatemalan Crisis.* Norman: University of Oklahoma Press, 1992.

Carter, Gwendolyn, Thomas Karis, and Newell M. Stultz. *South Africa's Transkei: The Politics of Domestic Colonialism.* Evanston: University of Illinois Press, 1967.

Castagno, A. "The Somalia-Kenya Controversy." *Journal of Modern African Studies* 2 (1964): 165–88.

Castagno, M. *Historical Dictionary of Somalia.* Metuchen, NJ: Scarecrow Press, 1976.

Cayrol, Pierre. *Hong Kong in the Mouth of the Dragon.* Rutland, VT: C. E. Tuttle, 1998.

Chadda, Maya. *Ethnicity, Security, and Separatism in India.* New York: Columbia University Press, 1997.

Chaliand, Gerard. *People without a Country.* London: Zed Press, 1980.

Charton, Nancy, ed. *Ciskei: Economics and Politics of Dependence in a South African Homeland.* London: Croom Helm, 1980.

Chazan, Naomi, ed. *Irredentism and International Politics.* London: Adamantine Press, 1991.

Chenciner, Robert. *Daghestan: Tradition and Survival.* New York: St. Martin's Press, 1997.

Chilcote, Ronald H. *Portuguese Africa.* Englewood Cliffs, NJ: Prentice-Hall, 1967.

Chinn, Jeff, and Robert John Kaiser. *Russians as the New Minority: Ethnicity and Nationalism in Soviet Successor States.* Boulder, CO: Westview Press, 1996.

Chipperfield, Mark. "Safe Haven for Aussie Royalists." *Daily Telegraph,* January 3, 1999.

Chorbaijian, Levon, Patrick Donabedian, and Claude Mutafian. *The Caucasian Knot: The History and Geopolitics of Nagorno-Karabagh*. Atlantic Highlands, NJ: Zed Books, 1994.

Choudhury, G. *The Last Days of United Pakistan*. London: Hurst and Company, 1974.

Christie, Clive J. *A Modern History of Southeast Asia*. London: Tauris Academic Studies, 1996.

Clark, Martin. "Cheese and Modernization." In Carl Levy, ed., *Italian Regionalism*. Washington, DC: Berg, 1996.

Clark, Robert P. *The Basque Insurgents*. Madison: University of Wisconsin Press, 1984.

Clegg, Claude. *An Original Man: The Life and Times of Elijah Muhammed*. New York: St. Martin's Press, 1997.

Clough, Ralph. *Embattled Korea: The Rivalry for International Support*. Boulder, CO: Westview Press, 1987.

Cohen, Michael J. *Palestine to Israel: From Mandate to Independence*. London and Totowa, NJ: F. Cass, 1989.

Coleman, William. *The Independence Movement in Quebec 1945–80*. Toronto: University of Toronto Press, 1984.

Collins, Robert. *Shadows in the Grass: Britain in the Southern Sudan*. New Haven, CT: Yale University Press, 1983.

Colvin, Ian G. *The Rise and Fall of Moise Tshombe*. London: Frewin, 1968.

Connor, Walker. "Ethnonationalism in the First World: The Present in Historical Perspective." In Milton J. Esman, ed., *Ethnic Conflict in the Western World*. Ithaca, NY: Cornell University Press, 1977.

Conversi, Daniel. *The Basques, the Catalans, and Spain: Alternative Routes to Nationalist Mobilization*. Reno: University of Nevada Press, 1997.

Coogan, Tim Pat. *The IRA*. London: Fontana, 1972.

Coombs, H. C. *Aboriginal Autonomy*. New York: Cambridge University Press, 1994.

Crawshaw, Nancy. *The Cyprus Revolt*. London: George Allen and Unwin, 1978.

Creason, William. *Cossacks: Their History and Country*. New York: AMS Press, 1982.

Croissant, Michael P. *The Armenia-Azerbaijan Conflict: Causes and Implications*. Westport, CT: Praeger, 1998.

Cronin, Sean. *Irish Nationalism: A History of Its Roots and Ideology*. Dublin: Academy Press, 1980.

Crouch, Harold. *Government and Society in Malaysia*. Ithaca, NY: Cornell University Press, 1996.

Curtis, Glenn E. *Kazakstan, Kyrgyzstan, Tajikistan, Turkmenistan, and Uzbekistan: Country Studies*. Washington, DC: Federal Research Headquarters, Department of the Army, 1997.

Czikann-Zichy, M. *Turmoil in the South Tyrol*. New York: Macmillan, 1978.

Dabat, Alejandro. *Argentina, the Malvinas, and the End of Military Rule*. London: Verso, 1984.

Dailey, Erika, Jeri Laber, and Lois Whitman. *Human Rights in Moldova: The Turbulent Dniester*. New York: Helsinki Watch, 1993.

Dalai Lama. *Freedom in Exile*. New York: Harper Collins, 1990.

Davidson, Basil. *No Fist Is Big Enough to Hide the Sky: The Liberation of Guine and Cape Verde*. London: Zed, 1981.

Davis, Charlotte. *Welsh Nationalism in the Twentieth Century*. New York: Praeger, 1989.

Decalo, Samuel. *Historical Dictionary of Togo*. Metuchen, NJ: Scarecrow Press, 1976.

Denber, Rachel. *Bloodshed in the Caucasus: Violations of Humanitarian Law and Human Rights in the Georgia–South Ossetia Conflict*. New York: Helsinki Watch, 1992.

Derry, T. *A History of Scandinavia*. Minneapolis: University of Minnesota Press, 1979.

Dickason, Olive. *Canada's First Nations*. Norman: University of Oklahoma Press, 1992.

Djalili, Mohammed Reza, Frederick Grace, and Shirin J. Akiner, eds. *Tajikistan: Trials of Independence*. New York: St. Martin's Press, 1997.

Doornbos, Martin R. "Kumanyana and Rwenzururu: Two Responses to Ethnic Inequality." In Robert Rotberg and Ali Mazrui, eds., *Protest and Power in Black Africa*. Oxford: Oxford University Press, 1970.

Dorondo, D. R. *Bavaria and German Federalism*. New York: St. Martin's Press, 1992.

Drake, Christine. *National Integration in Indonesia*. Honolulu: University of Hawaii Press, 1989.

Dreifelds, Juris. *Latvia in Transition*. New York: Cambridge University Press, 1996.

Dreyer, June. *China's Forty Millions: Minority Nationalities and National Integration in the People's Republic of China*. Cambridge, MA: Harvard University Press, 1976.

Drohobycky, Maria, ed. *Crimea: Dynamics, Challenges, and Prospects*. Lanham, MD: Rowman and Littlefield, 1996.

Dunlop, John B. *Russia Confronts Chechnya: Roots of a Separatist Conflict*. New York: Cambridge University Press, 1998.

Dupont, Pierre. *How Levesque Won.* Toronto: Lorimer, 1977.

Dupree, Louis. *Afghanistan.* Princeton, NJ: Princeton University Press, 1997.

Durch, William, ed. *UN Peacekeeping American Politics and the Uncivil Wars of the 1990s.* New York: St. Martin's Press, 1996.

Dyck, Noel. *Indigenous People and the Nation State.* St. Johns, Nfld.: Institute of Social and Economic Research, 1985.

Dyer, Joel. *Harvest of Rage.* Boulder, CO: Westview Press, 1997.

Eagleton, W. J. R. *The Kurdish Republic of 1945.* London: Oxford University Press, 1963.

"Eastern Slavonia: The Croats Are Coming." *Economist* 346, January 10, 1999.

Eder, James. *On the Road to Extinction.* Berkeley: University of California Press, 1982.

Eggleston, Wilfrid. *Newfoundland: The Road to Confederation.* Ottawa: Information Canada, 1974.

Ekure-Ekure, Herbert. *The Biafra War.* Lewiston, NY: Mellen Press, 1990.

Evans, Grant, and Kevin Rowley. *Red Brotherhood at War: Indochina since the Fall of Saigon.* London: Verso, 1984.

Faron, Louis. *Mapuche Indians of Chile.* Prospect Heights, IL: Waveland Press, 1986.

Farrell, Joseph, and Carl Levy. "The Northern League: Conservative Revolution?" In Carl Levy, ed., *Italian Regionalism.* Washington, DC: Berg, 1996.

Farsoun, Samih. *Palestine and the Palestinians.* Boulder, CO: Westview Press, 1997.

Fedor, Helen, ed. *Belarus and Moldova: Country Studies.* Washington, DC: Library of Congress, 1996.

Femenia, Nora. *National Identity in Times of Crisis: The Scripts of the Falklands-Malvinas War.* Commack, NY: Nova Science Publishers, 1996.

Fernandez, Ronald. *Los Macheteros.* New York: Prentice-Hall, 1987.

———. *Prisoners of Colonialism.* Monroe, ME: Common Courage Press, 1994.

Filonyk, Alexander. "Kyrgyzstan." In Mohiaddin Mesbahi, ed., *Central Asia and the Caucasus after the Soviet Union.* Gainesville: University of Florida, 1994.

Fink-Hafner, Danica, and John Robbins, eds. *Making a New Nation: The Formation of Slovenia.* Brookfield, VT: Dartmouth, 1997.

Finnegan, William. "The Invisible War." *New Yorker,* January 25, 1999, 50–73.

Fisher, Alan. *Crimean Tatars.* Stanford, CA: Hoover Institution Press, 1978.

FitzGerald, Frances. *Fire in the Lake: The Vietnamese and the Americans in Vietnam.* Boston: Little, Brown, 1972.

Fitzmaurice, John. *Politics of Belgium: A Unique Federalism.* Boulder, CO: Westview Press, 1996.

Fleras, Augie, and Jean L. Elliott. *The Nations Within: Aboriginal-State Relations in Canada, the United States, and New Zealand.* Toronto: Oxford University Press, 1992.

Forsberg, Tuomas. *Contested Territory: Border Disputes at the Edge of the Former Soviet Empire.* Brookfield, VT: Edward Elgar, 1995.

Foster, Charles D. *Nations without States: Ethnic Minorities in Western Europe.* New York: Praeger, 1980.

Fournier, Paul. *A Meech Lake Post-Mortem.* Montreal: McGill-Queens University Press, 1991.

Franck, Thomas M. *Why Federations Fail.* New York: New York University Press, 1968.

Fredholm, Michael. *Burma: Ethnicity and Insurgency.* Westport, CT: Praeger, 1993.

Freymond, Jacques. *The Saar Conflict.* Westport, CT: Greenwood Press, 1960.

Friedman, Francine. *The Bosnian Muslims: Denial of a Nation.* Boulder, CO: Westview Press, 1996.

Fuller, Liz. *Georgian: Meskhetians Remain Homeless.* http://search.rferl.org/nca/features/1998/09/F.RU.9809231.html.

Gaitonde, P. D. *The Liberation of Goa.* New York: St. Martin's Press, 1987.

Gall, Carlotta, and Thomas DeWaal. *Chechnya: Calamity in the Caucasus.* New York: New York University Press, 1998.

Gallagher, Tom. "Portugal's Atlantic Territories: The Separatist Challenge." *World Today* (September 1979).

Garcia, Ignacio. *Chicanismo: The Forging of a Militant Ethos.* Tucson: University of Arizona Press, 1997.

Gardinier, David. *Cameroon: United Nations Challenge to French Policy.* London: Oxford University Press, 1963.

Gellner, Ernest. *Thought and Change.* London: Weidenfeld and Nicolson, 1964.

George, Sudhir. "The Bodo Movement in Assam." *Asian Survey* (October 1994): 878–92.

George, T. J. S. *Revolt in Mindanao.* Kuala Lumpur: Oxford University Press, 1980.

Georgieva, Valentina, and Sasha Konechni. *Historical*

Dictionary of the Republic of Macedonia. Lanham, MD: Scarecrow Press, 1998.

Gerard-Libois, Jules. *Katanga Secession.* Madison: University of Wisconsin Press, 1966.

Gerteiny, Alfred G. *Mauritania.* New York: Praeger, 1967.

Gertzel, Cherry. *The Politics of Independent Kenya, 1963–8.* Evanston, IL: Northwestern University Press, 1970.

Gilkes, Patrick. *The Dying Lion: Feudalism and Modernization in Ethiopia.* New York: St. Martin's Press, 1975.

Gladney, Dru C. "Rumblings from the Uyghur." *Current History* 96 (September 1997): 287–92.

Glickman, Harvey, ed. *Ethnic Conflict and Democratization in Africa.* Atlanta, GA: African Studies Association Press, 1995.

Goldman, Minton F. *Slovakia since Independence: A Struggle for Democracy.* Westport, CT: Praeger, 1999.

Gras, Solange. "Regionalism and Autonomy in Alsace since 1918." In Stein Rokkan and Derek W. Urwin, eds., *The Politics of Territorial Identity.* London: Sage, 1982.

Gregor, A. James. *The Taiwan Independence Movement.* New York: Crane, Russak, 1985.

Griffiths, John. *Afghanistan.* Boulder, CO: Westview Press, 1981.

Grivas, George. *Memoirs of General Grivas.* New York: Praeger, 1965.

Guill, James. *A History of the Azores.* Tulare, CA: Golden Shield, 1993.

Gunasekara, S. L. *Tigers, Moderates, and Pandora's Package.* Sri Lanka: S. N., 1996.

Gunter, Michael. *The Kurds in Turkey.* Boulder, CO: Westview Press, 1990.

———. *Pursuing the Just Cause of Their People: A Study of Contemporary Armenian Terrorism.* New York: Greenwood Press, 1986.

Gunther, Richard, Giacomo Sani, and Goldie Shabad. *Spain after Franco.* Berkeley: University of California Press, 1986.

Gurr, Ted Robert. *Minorities at Risk: A Global View of Ethno-Political Conflicts.* Washington, DC: U.S. Institute of Peace, 1993.

Hadawi, Sami. *Bitter Harvest: A Modern History of Palestine.* 4th ed. New York: Olive Branch Press, 1991.

Hall, Raymond L. *Black Separatism in the United States.* Hanover, NH: University Press of New England, 1978.

Hall, Raymond, ed. *Ethnic Autonomy: Comparative Dynamics.* New York: Pergamon, 1979.

Hancock, I. R. "Patriotism and Neo-Traditionalism in Buganda: The Kabaka Yekka Movement, 1961–1962." *Journal of African History* 11 (1970): 419–34.

Hannum, Hurst. *Autonomy, Sovereignty, and Self-Determination.* Philadelphia: University of Pennsylvania Press, 1990.

Harrison, Selig. "Nightmare in Baluchistan." *Foreign Policy* (fall 1978).

Hazlewood, Arthur, ed. *African Integration and Disintegration: Case Studies in Political and Economic Union.* London: Oxford University Press, 1967.

Hechter, Michael. *Internal Colonialism: The Celtic Fringe in British National Development.* New York: Routledge and Kegan Paul, 1975.

Heller, Joseph. *The Stern Gang: Ideology, Politics, and Terror, 1940–1949.* London and Portland, OR: Frank Cass, 1995.

Hempstone, Smith. *Rebels, Mercenaries, and Dividends: The Katanga Story.* New York: Praeger, 1962.

Henderson, Gregory. *Public Diplomacy and Political Change.* New York: Praeger, 1973.

Henningham, Stephen. *France and the South Pacific.* Honolulu: University of Hawaii Press, 1992.

Heraclides, Alexis. *The Self-Determination of Minorities in International Politics.* London: Frank Cass, 1991.

Higa, Mikio. *Politics and Parties in Postwar Okinawa.* Vancouver: University of British Columbia Press, 1963.

Hill, Christopher. *Bantustans: The Fragmentation of South Africa.* London: Oxford University Press, 1964.

Hills, George. *Rock of Contention.* London: Robert Hale and Company, 1974.

Hindley, Donald. "Indonesia's Confrontation with Malaysia: A Search for Motives." *Asian Survey* 4 (June 1964): 904–13.

Hoensch, Jorg, and Kim Traynor. *A History of Modern Hungary (1867–1994).* New York: Longman, 1996.

Holbrooke, Richard. *To End a War.* New York: Random House, 1998.

Holloway, John, and Eloina Palaey, eds. *Zapatista! Reinventing Revolution in Mexico.* Sterling, VA: Pluto Press, 1998.

Hooghe, Liesbet. *A Leap in the Dark: Nationalist Conflict and Federal Reform in Belgium.* Ithaca, NY: Cornell University Press, 1991.

Bibliography

Horowitz, Donald. "Irredentas and Secessions: Adjacent Phenomena, Neglected Connections." In Naomi Chazan, ed., *Irredentism and International Politics.* London: Adamantine Press, 1991.

Horrell, Muriel. *The African Homelands of South Africa.* Johannesburg: South African Institute of Race Relations, 1973.

Hosmer, Stephen T., Konrad Kellen, and Brian M. Jenkins. *The Fall of South Vietnam: Statements by Vietnamese Military and Civilian Leaders.* New York: Crane, Russak. 1980.

Hughes, Anthony. *East Africa: The Search for Unity.* Baltimore: Penguin Books, 1963.

Hyland, Francis P. *Armenian Terrorism: The Past, the Present, the Future.* Boulder, CO: Westview Press, 1991.

Ibingira, Grace Stuart. *The Forging of an African Nation.* New York: Viking Press, 1973.

Ignatieff, Michael. "Balkan Physics: Behind the Lines of Europe's Worst Conflict since 1945." *New Yorker,* May 10, 1999, 68–79.

Irving, Ronald. *The Flemings and Walloons of Belgium.* London: Minority Rights Group, 1980.

Jacques, Edwin E. *The Albanians: An Ethnic History from Prehistoric Times to the Present.* Jefferson, NC: Mcfarland and Company, 1995.

Jalata, Asafa. *Oromia and Ethiopia: State Formation and Ethnonational Conflict 1868–1992.* Boulder, CO: Lynne Rienner Publishers, 1993.

Jenish, D'Arcy. "Battle over Borders." *Macleans,* February 12, 1996.

Judah, Tim. *History, Myth, and the Destruction of Yugoslavia.* New Haven, CT: Yale University Press. 1997.

Julienne, Roland. "The Experience of Integration in French-Speaking Africa." In Arthur Hazlewood, ed., *African Integration and Disintegration.* London: Oxford University Press, 1967.

Kadian, Radesh. *The Kashmir Triangle: Issues and Options.* Boulder, CO: Westview Press, 1993.

Kagda, Sakina. *Lithuania.* New York: Marshall Cavendish, 1997.

Kahin, Audrey R. "Crisis on the Periphery: The Rift between Kuala Lumpur and Sabah." *Pacific Affairs* 65 (1992): 30–49.

Kahin, Audrey R., ed. *Regional Dynamics of the Indonesian Revolution.* Honolulu: University of Hawaii Press, 1985.

Kapur, Rajiv. *Sikh Separatism: The Politics of Faith.* London: Allen and Unwin, 1986.

Kasaev, Alan. "Ossetia-Ingushetia." In J. Azrael and E. Payin, eds., *U.S. and Russian Policy Making with*

Respect to the Use of Force. Santa Monica, CA: Rand, 1996.

Katzenstein, Peter J. "Ethnic Political Conflict in South Tyrol." In Milton J. Esman, ed., *Ethnic Conflict in the Western World.* Ithaca, NY: Cornell University Press, 1977.

Kearney, Robert N. "Ethnic Conflict and the Tamil Separatist Movement in Sri Lanka." *Asian Survey* 25 (September 1985): 883–97.

Keating, Michael. *State and Regional Nationalism: Territorial Politics and the European State.* New York: Harvester Wheatsheaf, 1988.

Keena, Colm. *A Biography of Gerry Adams.* Dublin: Mercier Press, 1990.

Khazanov, Anatoly. *After the USSR: Ethnicity, Nationalism, and Politics in the Commonwealth of Independent States.* Madison: University of Wisconsin Press, 1995.

Kihl, Young Whan. *Politics and Policies in Divided Korea: Regimes in Contest.* Boulder, CO: Westview Press, 1984.

Kimble, David. *A Political History of Ghana.* Oxford: Oxford University Press, 1963.

Kircher, Ingrid. *The Kanaks of New Caledonia.* London: Minority Rights Group, 1986.

Kirschbaum, Stanislav. *A History of Slovakia: The Struggle for Survival.* New York: St. Martin's Press, 1995.

Kolga, Margus, et al., eds. *Red Book of the Peoples of the Russian Empire.* http://www.Eki.Ee/Books/ Redbook, 1993.

Kostiner, Joseph. *Yemen: The Tortuous Quest for Unity 1990–1994.* London: Royal Institute of International Affairs, 1996.

Krickus, Richard J. *Showdown: The Lithuanian Rebellion and the Breakup of the Soviet Empire.* Washington, DC: Brassey's, 1997.

Kuromiya, Hiroaki. *Freedom and Terror in the Donbas: A Ukrainian-Russian Borderland, 1870s–1990s.* Cambridge and New York: Cambridge University Press, 1998.

Kusmer, Kenneth. *A Ghetto Takes Shape.* Urbana: University of Illinois, 1978.

Lai, David. *Land of Genghis Khan: The Rise and Fall of Nation-States in China's Northern Frontier.* Victoria, BC: University of Victoria, 1995.

Landau, Jacob. "The Ups and Downs of Irredentism: The Case of Turkey." In Naomi Chazan, ed., *Irredentism and International Politics.* London: Adamantine, 1991.

Lapidoth, Ruth. *Autonomy: Flexible Solutions to Ethnic Conflict.* Washington, DC: U.S. Institute of Peace, 1997.

Lapping, Brian. *Apartheid: A History.* New York: Braziller, 1987.

Larres, Klaus, ed. *Germany since Reunification.* New York: St. Martin's Press, 1998.

Latin American Studies Association. *Peace and Autonomy on the Atlantic Coast of Nicaragua.* 1986.

Lau, Albert. *A Moment of Anguish: Singapore in Malaysia and the Politics of Disengagement.* Singapore: Times Academic Press, 1998.

Laurence, Patrick. *The Transkei: South Africa's Politics of Partition.* Johannesburg: Ravan Press, 1976.

Lawless, Richard, and Laila Monahan. *War and Refugees: The Western Sahara Conflict.* New York: Pinter, 1984.

Lees, Caroline. "Bounty Islanders Stage a New Mutiny." *Telegraph,* November 30, 1997.

Leff, Carol. *Czech and Slovak Republics.* Boulder, CO: Westview Press, 1996.

Legum, Colin. *Ethiopia: The Fall of Haile Selassie's Empire.* New York: Africana, 1975.

Legum, Colin, and James Fairbrace. *Eritrea and Tigray.* London: Minority Rights Group, 1983.

Leiby, Richard. *The Unification of Germany, 1989–1990.* Westport, CT: Greenwood Press, 1999.

Lemarchand, Rene. "The Fire in the Great Lakes." *Current History* 98 (May 1999): 195–201.

Lemon, Anthony. *Apartheid in Transition.* Boulder, CO: Westview Press, 1987.

Lemon, Anthony, ed. *The Geography of Change in South Africa.* New York: John Wiley and Sons, 1995.

Levin, Michael D., ed. *Ethnicity and Aboriginality.* Toronto: University of Toronto Press, 1993.

Levine, Victor T. *The Cameroons: From Mandate to Independence.* Berkeley: University of California Press, 1964.

Lewis, I. M. *The Modern History of Somaliland: From Nation to State.* New York: Praeger, 1965.

———. *Nationalism and Self Determination in the Horn of Africa.* London: Ithaca Press, 1983.

Lieven, Anatol. *Chechnya: Tombstone of Russian Power.* New Haven, CT: Yale University Press, 1998.

Lim, Jock, and S. Vani, eds. *Armed Separatism in Southeast Asia.* Singapore: Institute of Southeast Asian Studies, 1984.

Lofchie, Michael. *Zanzibar: Background to Revolution.* Princeton, NJ: Princeton University Press, 1965.

Long, Simon. *Taiwan: China's Last Frontier.* New York: St. Martin's Press, 1991.

McAllister, Ian. *The Northern Ireland Labour Party: Political Opposition in a Divided Society.* London: Macmillan, 1977.

McCauley, Martin. *The Soviet Union 1917–1991.* New York: Longman, 1994.

McDowall, David. *The Kurds.* London: Minority Rights Group, 1985.

———. *A Modern History of the Kurds.* London: I. B. Tauris, 1996.

McKenna, Thomas M. *Muslim Rulers and Rebels: Everyday Politics and Armed Separatism in the Southern Philippines.* Berkeley: University of California Press, 1998.

McLean, Duncan. "Getting on the Map." *Independent,* September 20, 1998.

Macmillan, H. "A Nation Divided? The Swazi in Swaziland and Transvaal 1865–1986." In L. Vail, ed., *The Creation of Tribalism in Southern Africa.* Berkeley: University of California Press, 1989.

Magnus, Ralph, and Eden Naby. *Afghanistan: Mullah, Marx, and Mujahid.* Boulder, CO: Westview Press, 1998.

Magocsi, Paul. *History of Ukraine.* Buffalo, NY: University of Toronto Press, 1996.

Mahmood, Cynthia Keppley. *Fighting for Faith and Nation: Dialogues with Sikh Militants.* Philadelphia: University of Pennsylvania Press, 1996.

———. *Frisian and Free.* Prospect Heights, IL: Waveland Press, 1989.

Maier, Charles. *Dissolution: The Crisis of Communism and the End of East Germany.* Princeton, NJ: Princeton University Press, 1997.

Maier, Karl. *Into the House of the Ancestors: Inside the New Africa.* New York: John Wiley and Sons, 1998.

Malcolm, Noel. *Bosnia: A Short History.* New York: New York University Press, 1996.

———. *Kosovo: A Short History.* New York: New York University Press, 1998.

Maley, William, ed. *Fundamentalism Reborn: Afghanistan and the Taliban.* New York: New York University Press, 1998.

Markides, Kyriacos. *The Rise and Fall of the Cyprus Republic.* New Haven, CT: Yale University Press, 1977.

Marples, David R. *Belarus: A Denationalized Nation.* Amsterdam: Harwood Academic, 1999.

Martin, Joseph. *Terrorism and the Taiwan Independence Movement.* Taipei: Institute on Contemporary China, 1985.

Bibliography

Martin, Phyllis. *Historical Dictionary of Angola.* Metuchen, NJ: Scarecrow Press, 1980.

Mastyugina, Tatiana, and Lev Perelkin. *An Ethnic History of Russia.* Westport, CT: Greenwood Press, 1996.

Matinuddin, Kamal. *The Taliban Phenomenon: Afghanistan 1994–1997.* Karachi: Oxford University Press, 1999.

Maxwell, Neville. *India, the Nagas, and the North-East.* London: Minority Rights Group, 1980.

May, J. R., and Mathew Spriggs, eds. *The Bougainville Crisis.* Bathurst, New South Wales: Crawford House Press, 1990.

Mayer, Kurt. "The Jura Conflict." In Charles R. Foster, ed., *Nations without a State.* New York: Praeger, 1980.

Mayes, Stanley. *Cyprus and Makarios.* London: Putnam Press, 1960.

Medhurst, Kenneth. *The Basques and Catalans.* London: Minority Rights Group, 1982.

Meisalas, Susan. *Kurdistan: In the Shadow of History.* New York: Random House, 1998.

Melvin, Neil. *Russians beyond Russia: The Politics of National Identity.* London: Royal Institute of International Affairs, 1995.

Meredith, Martin. *The First Dance of Freedom: Black Africa in the Post-War Era.* New York: Harper and Row, 1984.

Middleton, John. *Zanzibar: Its Society and Its Politics.* London: Oxford University Press, 1965.

Miles, William S. *Elections and Ethnicity in French Martinique.* New York: Praeger, 1986.

Milne, R. S., and K. J. Ratnam. *Malaysia: New States in a New Nation.* London: Frank Cass, 1974.

Morf, Gustav. *Terror in Quebec: Case Studies of the FLQ.* Toronto: Clarke-Irwin, 1970.

Morgan, Kenneth. *Rebirth of a Nation.* New York: Oxford University Press, 1981.

Morris, D. *The Washing of the Spears: The Rise and Fall of the Great Zulu Nation.* London: Abacus, 1985.

Morrison, Donald G. *Black Africa: A Comparative Handbook.* New York: Irvington Publishers, 1989.

Morrison, Minion. *Ethnicity and Political Integration: The Case of Ashanti, Ghana.* Syracuse, NY: Syracuse University Press, 1982.

Moxon-Brown, Edward. *Political Change in Spain.* New York: Routledge, 1989.

Mozaffari, Mehdi, ed. *Security Politics in the Commonwealth of Independent States: The Southern Belt.* New York: Macmillan and St. Martin's Press, 1997.

Mughan, Anthony. "Modernization and Regional Relative Deprivation: Towards a Theory of Ethnic Conflict." In L. J. Sharpe, ed., *Decentralist Trends in Western Democracies.* London: Sage, 1979, 279–314.

Murray, Colin. "Displaced Urbanization: South Africa's Rural Slums." In William Beinart and Saul Dubow, eds., *Segregation and Apartheid in Twentieth-Century South Africa.* London: Routledge, 1995.

Mutibwa, Phares. *Uganda since Independence.* Trenton, NJ: Africa World Press, 1992.

Nairn, Tom. *The Breakup of Britain: Crisis and Neo-Nationalism.* Thetford, UK: Brydone Printers, 1977.

Nassar, Jamal Raji. *The Palestine Liberation Organization: From Armed Struggle to the Declaration of Independence.* New York: Praeger, 1991.

Navaratna-Bandara, Abeysinghe. *The Management of Ethnic Secessionist Conflict.* Aldershot, UK: Dartmouth Publishing, 1995.

Nedvetsky, Alexander. "Turkmenistan." In Mohiaddin Mesbahi, ed., *Central Asia and the Caucasus after the Soviet Union.* Gainesville: University Press of Florida, 1994.

Nelson, Ann. *Murder under Two Flags.* New York: Ticknor and Fields, 1986.

Newman, Saul. *Ethnoregional Conflicts in Democracies: Mostly Ballots, Rarely Bullets.* Westport, CT: Greenwood Press, 1996.

Nichols, Joanna. *Ingush.* http://Ingush.Berkeley.edu:7012/Ingush_People.Html, 1997.

Novak, Bogdan. *Trieste 1941–54: The Ethnic, Political, and Ideological Struggle.* Chicago: University of Chicago Press, 1970.

NUPI. *Adygey.* http://www.nupi.no/cgi-win/Russland, 1998.

———. *Karachay-Cherkessia.* http://www.nupi.no/cgi-win/Russland, 1998.

Nusseibeh, Hazem. *The Idea of Pan-Arabism.* Ithaca, NY: Cornell University Press, 1956.

O'Ballance, Edgar. "Sri Lanka and Its Tamil Problem." *Armed Forces,* December 5, 1986.

Oberling, Pierre. *The Road to Bellapais.* New York: Columbia University Press, 1982.

O'Brien, Conor Cruise. *To Katanga and Back: A UN Case History.* London: Hutchinson, 1962.

O'Clery, Conor. *Phrases Make History Here.* Dublin: O'Brien Press, 1986.

Okladinov, Aleksi, and Henry Michael, eds. *Yakutia: Before Its Incorporation into the Russian State.* Montreal: McGill-Queens University Press, 1970.

Olcott, Martha Brill. *Kazakhstan: A Faint-Hearted Democracy.* New York: Carnegie Endownment for International Peace, 1999.

OSCE. http://www.Osce.org, 1999.

Otfinoski, Steven. *Boris Yeltsin and the Rebirth of Russia.* Brookfield, CT: Millbrook Press, 1995.

Patterson, George. *Tibet in Revolt.* London: Faber and Faber, 1960.

Peires, Jeffrey. "Ethnicity and Pseudo-Ethnicity in the Ciskei." In William Beinart and Saul Dubow, eds., *Segregation and Apartheid in Twentieth-Century South Africa.* London: Routledge, 1995.

Peters, Rudolph. *Jihad in Classical and Modern Islam.* Princeton, NJ: Markus Wiener, 1996.

Pettman, Jan. *Zambia: Security and Conflict.* New York: St. Martin's Press, 1974.

Phillips, Lucy Colvin. *Historical Dictionary of Senegal.* Metuchen, NJ: Scarecrow Press, 1981.

Picard, Elizabeth. *Lebanon: A Shattered Country.* New York: Holmes and Meier, 1996.

Political Declarations of the Kosovo Liberation Army. http://www.Zik.Com/English/Kla8/Htm, 1998.

Pool, David. *Eritrea: Towards Unity in Diversity.* London: Minority Rights Group, 1997.

———. "Eritrean Nationalism." In I. M. Lewis, ed., *Nationalism and Self determination in the Horn of Africa.* London: Ithaca Press, 1983.

Porter, Jonathan. "Macau 1999." *Current History* 96 (September 1997): 282–86.

Poulton, Hugh. *Who Are the Macedonians?* Bloomington: Indiana University Press, 1995.

Press, Robert. "Africa's 'Blue Men' Flee Desert." *Christian Science Monitor,* February 11, 1992.

Prouty, Chris, and Eugene Rosenfeld. *Historical Dictionary of Ethiopia.* Metuchen, NJ: Scarecrow Press, 1994.

Prunier, Gerard. "Somaliland Goes It Alone." *Current History* 97 (May 1998): 225–28.

Ra'anan, Uri. *The Frontiers of a Nation: A Re-Examination of the Forces Which Created the Palestine Mandate and Determined Its Territorial Shape.* Westport, CT: Hyperion Press, 1976.

Radio Free Europe. *Newsline,* September 16, 1998; October 19, 1998.

Ramsey, Robert. *The Corsican Time Bomb.* Manchester: Manchester University Press, 1983.

Ratner, Steven. *The New UN Peacekeeping: Building Peace in Lands of Conflict after the Cold War.* New York: St. Martin's Press, 1995.

Reece, Jack E. *The Bretons against France.* Chapel Hill: University of North Carolina Press, 1977.

Reed, D. "South Africa's Champion of Nonviolence." *Readers Digest* 122 (January 1983).

Remnick, David. *Lenin's Tomb: The Last Days of the Soviet Empire.* New York: Vintage, 1994.

———. *Resurrection: The Struggle for a New Russia.* New York: Vintage, 1998.

Reyntjens, Filip. "The Second Congo War." *African Affairs* 98 (1990): 241–50.

Richler, Mordecai. *Oh Canada! Oh Quebec!* New York: Knopf, 1992.

Rieff, David. *Slaughterhouse: Bosnia and the Failure of the West.* New York: Touchstone, 1996.

Roberts, Diane. "The American South and the Rise of the New Right." *Southern Exposure* (Spring/Summer 1997).

Robinson, Glenn. *Building a Palestinian State.* Bloomington: Indiana University, 1997.

Robson, Peter. "The Problem of Senegambia." *Journal of Modern African Studies* 3 (October 1965): 393–408.

Roche, Patrick J., and Brian Barton, eds. *The Northern Ireland Question: Myth and Reality.* Brookfield, VT: Avebury, 1991.

Roff, Margaret. *The Politics of Belonging: Political Change in Sabah and Sarawak.* Kuala Lumpur: Oxford University Press, 1974.

Rogel, Carole. *The Breakup of Yugoslavia and the War in Bosnia.* Westport, CT: Greenwood Press, 1998.

Rorlich, Azadeayse. *Volga Tatars.* Stanford, CA: Hoover Institution Press, 1986.

Rose, Leo E. *The Politics of Bhutan.* Ithaca, NY: Cornell University Press, 1977.

Rose, Richard. *Governing without Consensus: An Irish Perspective.* London: Faber and Faber, 1971.

———. *The Territorial Dimension in Government: Understanding the United Kingdom.* Chatham NJ: Chatham House, 1982.

Rubin, Barnett. *The Fragmentation of Afghanistan.* New Haven, CT: Yale University Press, 1995.

Rubinoff, Arthur. *India's Use of Force in Goa.* Bombay: Popular Prakashan, 1971.

Rudelson, Justin Jon. *Oasis Identities: Uyghur Nationalism along China's Silk Road.* New York: Columbia University Press, 1997.

Rumer, Boris. *Central Asia in Transition: Dilemmas of Political and Economic Development.* Armonk, NY: M. E. Sharpe, 1996.

Bibliography

Sachar, Howard. *History of Israel.* New York: Knopf, 1996.

Sakina,Dillawala. *Armenia.* 2d. ed. New York: Marshall Cavendish, 1997.

Sakwa, Richard. *Russian Politics and Society.* 2d. ed. New York: Routledge, 1996.

Sancton, Andrew. *Governing the Island of Montreal: Language Differences and Metropolitan Politics.* Berkeley: University of California Press, 1985.

Sandborne, Mark. *Romania (Nations in Transition).* New York: Facts on File, 1996.

Sayeed, Khalid. *Politics in Pakistan.* New York: Praeger, 1980.

Saywell, John. *The Rise of the Parti Québécois 1967–76.* Toronto: University of Toronto Press, 1977.

Seidman, Hillel, and Mordecai Schreiber. *Menachem Begin: His Life and Legacy.* New York: Shengold, 1990.

Sells, Michael Anthony. *The Bridge Betrayed: Religion and Genocide in Bosnia.* Berkeley: University of California Press, 1996.

Shandor, Vikentii. *Carpatho-Ukraine in the Twentieth Century.* Cambridge, MA: Harvard University Press, 1997.

Sharp, Andrew. *Justice and the Maori: Maori Claims in New Zealand Political Argument in the 1980s.* Auckland: Oxford University Press, 1990.

Shea, John. *Macedonia and Greece: The Struggle to Define a New Balkan Nation.* Jefferson, NC: McFarland, 1997.

Sheehy, Ann, and Bondan Nahaylo. *The Crimean Tatars, Volga Germans, and Meskhetians.* London: Minority Rights Group, 1980.

Shipp, Steve. *Macau, China: A Political History of the Portugese Colony's Transition to Chinese Rule.* Jefferson, NC: McFarland, 1997.

Smith, Anthony D. *Nations and Nationalism in a Global Era.* Oxford: Blackwell, 1995.

Smith, Graham, ed. *The Baltic States: The National Self-Determination of Estonia, Latvia, and Lithuania.* New York: St. Martin's Press, 1994.

Smith, Martin. *Burma Insurgency and the Politics of Ethnicity.* London: Zed Books, 1991.

Smith, Paul, and Robert Warrior. *Like a Hurricane: The Indian Movement from Alcatraz to Wounded Knee.* New York: New Press, 1996.

Smith, Sebastian. *Allah's Mountains.* New York: I. B. Taurus, 1998.

Smith, Warren W. *Tibetan Nation: A History of Tibetan Nationalism and Sino-Tibetan Relations.* Boulder, CO: Westview Press, 1996.

Smock, David, and Audrey Smock. *The Politics of Cultural Pluralism.* New York: Elsevier, 1975.

Snyder, Louis L. *Global Mini-Nationalisms: Autonomy or Independence.* Westport, CT: Greenwood Press, 1982.

———. *Macro-Nationalisms: A History of the Pan-Movements.* Westport, CT: Greenwood Press, 1984.

South African Institute of Race Relations. *Race Relations Survey 1992/1993.* Johannesburg, 1993.

Southall, Roger. *South Africa's Transkei: The Political Economy of an 'Independent' Bantustan.* New York: Monthly Review Press, 1983.

Sparks, Allister. "South African Tribal Homeland Venda Tense after Guerrilla Attack." *Washington Post,* February 3, 1982.

———. *Tomorrow Is Another Country: The Inside Story of South Africa's Road to Change.* New York: Hill and Wang, 1995.

Spencer, William. *Historical Dictionary of Morocco.* Metuchen, NJ: Scarecrow Press, 1980.

Spiro, Herbert. "The Federation of Rhodesia and Nyasaland." In Thomas M. Franck, ed., *Why Federations Fail.* New York: New York University Press, 1968.

Srivastava, M. P. *The Korean Conflict: Search for Unification.* New Delhi: Prentice-Hall, 1982.

Stein, Eric. *Czecho/Slovakia: Ethnic Conflict, Constitutional Fissure, Negotiated Breakup.* Ann Arbor: University of Michigan Press, 1997.

Stoess, Richard. "Irredentism in Germany since 1945." In Naomi Chazan, ed., *Irredentism and International Politics.* London: Adamantine, 1991.

Stuart, Graham. *The International City of Tangier.* Stanford, CA: Stanford University Press, 1955.

Stultz, Newell M. *Transkei's Half Loaf.* New Haven, CT: Yale University Press, 1979.

Suhrke, Astri, and Leela Garner Noble, eds. *Ethnic Conflict in International Relations.* New York: Praeger, 1977.

Suljak, N. Dinko. *Croatia's Struggle for Independence: A Documentary History.* Arcadia, CA: Croatian Information Service, 1977.

Sullivan, John. *ETA and Basque Nationalism: The Fight for Euskadi.* London: Routledge, 1988.

Suny, Ronald Grigor. *Making of the Georgian Nation.* 2d. ed. Bloomington: Indiana University Press, 1994.

Suter, Keith. *East Timor and West Irian.* London: Minority Rights Group, 1982.

Swietochowski, Tadeus. *Russia and Azerbaijan.* New York: Columbia University Press, 1995.

Taagepara, Rein. *Estonia: Return to Independence.* Boulder, CO: Westview Press, 1993.

Tambiah, Stanley. *Ethnic Fratricide and the Disuniting of a Democracy.* Chicago: University of Chicago Press, 1986.

Tanner, Marcus. *Croatia: A Nation Forged in War.* New Haven, CT: Yale University Press, 1997.

Tarling, Nicholas. *Sulu and Sabah.* Kuala Lumpur: Oxford University Press, 1978.

Taylor, John. *Indonesia's Forgotten War: The Hidden History of East Timor.* London: Zed Books, 1991.

Taylor, Peter. *Behind the Mask: The IRA and Sinn Fein.* New York: TV Books, 1997.

Thayer, George. *The British Political Fringe.* London: Anthony Blond, 1965.

Thomas, Raju G. C. *Perspectives on Kashmir.* Boulder, CO: Westview Press, 1992.

Thompson, Virginia, and Richard Adloff. *Conflict in Chad.* Berkeley: University of California Press, 1982.

Tiryakian, Edward, and Ronald Rogowski. *New Nationalisms of the Developed West.* Boston: Allen and Unwin, 1985.

Tonkinson, Robert, and Michael Howard. *Going It Alone? Prospects for Aboriginal Autonomy.* Canberra, Austral.: Aboriginal Studies Press, 1990.

Toolis, Kevin. *Rebel Hearts: Journeys within the IRA's Soul.* New York: St. Martin's Press, 1996.

Toscano, Mario. *Alto Adige, South Tyrol: Italy's Frontier with the German World.* Baltimore: Johns Hopkins University Press, 1975.

Trask, Haunani-Kay. *From a Native Daughter: Colonialism and Sovereignty in Hawaii.* Monroe, ME: Common Courage Press, 1993.

Udogu, Emmanuel Ike. *Nigeria and the Politics of National Survival.* Lewiston, NY: Mellen Press, 1997.

UNPO. http://www.Unpo.org, 1999.

Vallieres, Pierre. *White Niggers of America: The Precocious Autobiography of a Quebec "Terrorist."* New York: Monthly Press, 1971.

Van der Vliet, Leo, ed. *Voices of the Earth: Indigenous Peoples, New Partners, and the Right to Self-Determination.* Amsterdam: International Books, 1994.

Vanezis, P. *Makarios: Faith and Power.* London: Abelard-Schuman, 1971.

Vickers, Miranda. *Between Serb and Albanian: A History of Kosovo.* New York: Columbia University Press, 1998.

Vickers, Miranda, and James Pettifer. *Albania: From Anarchy to Balkan Identity.* New York: New York University Press, 1997.

Wai, Dunstan M. *The African-Arab Conflict in the Sudan.* New York: Africana, 1981.

Wallace, Elizabeth M. *The British Caribbean: From the Decline of Colonialism to the End of Federation.* Toronto: University of Toronto Press, 1977.

Wallach, Janet, and John Wallach. *Arafat: In the Eye of the Beholder.* Secaucus, NJ: Carol Publishers Group, 1997.

Watson, J. H. "Mauritania: Problems and Prospects." *Africa Report* 8 (February, 1963): 3–6.

Welch, James, and Paul Stekler. *Killing Custer: The Battle of Big Horn and the Fate of the Plains Indians.* New York: W. W. Norton, 1994.

Wesselink, Egbert. *The Russian Federation: Dagestan.* http://www.Turkiye.net/Sota/Dagestan.html, 1995.

Wexler, Rex. *Blood of the Land: The Government and Corporate War against the American Indian Movement.* New York: Everest House, 1982.

Whitaker, Arthur P. *Nationalism in Latin America, Past and Present.* Gainesville: University of Florida Press, 1962.

White, Barry. *John Hume: Statesman of the Troubles.* Belfast: Blackstaff, 1984.

Witnesses to Cultural Genocide: First-Hand Reports on Rumania's Minority Policies Today. New York: Committee for Human Rights in Rumania, 1979.

Wixman, Ronald. *The Peoples of the USSR: An Ethnographic Handbook.* Armonk, NY: M. E. Sharpe, 1984.

Woodard, Komozi. *A Nation within a Nation: Amiri Baraka and Black Power Politics.* Chapel Hill: University of North Carolina Press, 1999.

Woodman, Dorothy. *The Republic of Indonesia.* London: Cresset Press, 1956.

Woodward, Peter. *Sudan, 1898–1989: The Unstable State.* Boulder, CO: Lynne Rienner Publishers, 1990.

Woodward, Peter, ed. *Conflict and Peace in the Horn of Africa.* Brookfield, VT: Dartmouth Publishing Company, 1994.

Yost, David. *NATO Transformed: The Alliance's New Roles in International Security.* Washington, DC: U.S. Institute of Peace Press, 1999.

Young, John. *Peasant Revolution in Ethiopia: The Tigray People's Liberation Front 1975–1991.* New York: Cambridge University Press, 1997.

Zammit, J. Ann. *The Belize Issue.* London: Latin America Bureau, 1978.

Ziring, Lawrence. *Pakistan in the Twentieth Century.* New York: Oxford University Press, 1997.

Zweig, Ronald, ed. *David Ben-Gurion: Politics and Leadership in Israel.* Portland, OR: F. Cass, 1991.

Index

Page numbers in boldface refer to main entries.

Bobar, Mate, 123
Bophuthatswana, 47, **48–49**, 183, 238
Bophuthatswana National Party, 48
Borneo, 148, 181–182, 262
Bosnia and Herzegovina, xv, **49–50,**
    77, 81, 116, 140, 150, 161, 178,
    190–191, 219, 280–281, 310, 325
Bosniak National Council, 264
Bosnian Muslims, 49–50
Bossi, Umberto, 223
Bougainville, **50–51**
Bougainville Revolutionary Army, 51
Boutros-Ghali, Boutros, 309
Braveheart, 266
Brazil, xiii, 129
Brazzaville group, 104
Breton. *See* Brittany
Brezhnev, Leonid, 271, 306
Britain, 274–275, 292, 293, 296, 318, 324
    and Canada, 189, 243
    Falklands/Islas Malvinas, **97–98,**
        135
    former colonies, 99, 110, 113, 119,
        151, 154, 262, 275, 281, 289, 329
    Gibraltar, **114**
    Hong Kong, **123–124**
    in India and Pakistan, 143, 223–225
    League of Empire Loyalists,
        169–170
    Malta, **182–183**
    in Palestine, 136–137, 228
    South Africa, **275–276**
    Zanzibar, **327–328**
    See also United Kingdom
British Honduras. *See* Belize
Brittany, **51–52**, 104–105, 307
    language revival, 51–52
Brown Berets, 66
Brunei, 148, 262
Brussels, 318
Buganda, **52–53,** 175
Bukhara, 311
Bukovina, 306
Bulatovic, Momir, 191, 195, 325
Bulgaria, 177–179
Bund der Vertrieben, 216
Bunyoro, 52, 53
Burma, **53–55**
    Arakan, **27**
    Kachin, **148**
    Karen, **150–151**, 192
    Mon, **192**
    Nagaland, **201**
    Shan, **267**

Buryatia, **55**, 193, 251
Buthelezi, Mangosuthu, **56–57**, 165, 238
Butler, Richard, 320
Byzantine Empire, 77, 177

Cabinda, 24
Cameroon, **59–60**
Campos, Pedro Albizu, 240
Canada, 320
    armed conflict with Mohawks, 202
    constitutional disputes, 202–203
    French Language Charter, **102–103**
    Front de Libération du Quebec,
        105, 234
    Levesque, René, **173**
    Meech Lake Accord, **189–190**
    Native Americans, **202–203**
    Newfoundland, **205**
    Nunavut, 202–203, **213**
    Parti Québécois, 173, **233–234**
    Quebec, 105, **243–245**
    Quebec partition, **245**
    Vallieres, Pierre, **313**
    Western Canadian separatism, **319**
Canary Islands, **60**
Cape Verde, **60–61**
Capeland, 18
Capricornia, 18
Caribbean Revolutionary Army, 118,
    187
Casablanca group, 104
Casamance, **61**
Casamance Movement of Democratic
    Forces, 61
Casley, Leonard, 125
Catalonia, **61**, 279
Caucasian Mountain Republic, 71–72
Ceausescu, Nicolae, 298
Césaire, Aimé, **61–62**
Ceuta and Melilla, **62**
Chad, **62–63**
Chakma, 68
Chameria, **63**
Chamoun, Camille, 171
Chang, John, 156
Charlestown accord, 190
Chavez, Cesar, 66
Chechen-Ingush Autonomous
    Republic, 130
Chechnya, xiii, xv, **63–65**, 71, 74, 81,
    130, 251–254, 293, 324
    declaration of independence, 64
    Dudayev, Dzhokhar, 64, **83–84**
    wars with Russia, 64–65, 253–254,

    303
Chesterton, Arthur, 169
Chiang, Ching-kuo, 285
Chiang, Kai-shek, 67, 285
Chiapas, xiii, 188–189
Chibirov, Lyudwig, 277
Chicano Liberation Conference, 34
Chicano Movement, 34, **65–66**
Chicano Student Movement of Aztlan
    (MECHA), 66
Chile, Mapuche, **185**
Chin, 53-54
China, 232, 268, 303
    ethnic groups in, 66–68
    Hong Kong, **123–124**
    Macau, **177**
    Mongolians, 68, **193**
    nationality policy, **66–68**
    Taiwan, **285–287**
    Tibet, 68, **293–295**
    Uyghurs, 68, **310–311**
Chittagong Hills, **68–69**
Chornovil, Vyachislav, 250
Chretien, Jean, 245
Christie, Douglas, 319
Chuvash Party of National Rebirth
    (CPNR), 69
Chuvash Sociocultural Center, 69
Chuvashia, **69**, 250, 253
Circassians, 14
CIS (Commonwealth of Independent
    States), **71**, 324
Ciskei, 45–47, **69–70**
Ciskei National Independence Party, 69
Cleaver, Eldridge, 48
Clinton, William, 107, 122, 134, 274
Coalition of Mayan People's
    Organization, 189
Comité de l'Unité Togolaise, 96
Common Market. *See* European Union
Commonwealth, **70**, 87
Commonwealth Immigration Act of
    1962, 70
Commonwealth of Independent States
    (CIS), **71**, 324
Communism, 73, 79, 111, 124, 147,
    168, 178, 190, 192, 193, 236, 248,
    249, 250–252, 264, 268, 270, 271,
    285–286, 293, 294, 297, 298, 303,
    306, 308, 310, 311, 314, 320, 323,
    328
    fall of and independence
        movements, xiii
    Martinique, 186

Index

Index

Index

Index

Index

Index